The Smithsonian

The Smithsonian

A Guide to Its National Public Facilities in Washington, D.C.

by

Charlotte L. Sclar

McFarland & Company, Inc., Publishers
Jefferson, North Carolina, and London

From time to time, curators and exhibit staff at the Smithsonian make altera-
tions to exhibits or replace them entirely. For instance, changes are made to
the First Ladies' Hall with the advent of a new hostess in the White House.
Such changes will inevitably have occurred since the completion of this guide;
author and publisher regret any inconvenience this may cause.

Library of Congress Cataloguing-in-Publication Data

Sclar, Charlotte L., 1907–
  *The Smithsonian : a guide to its national public
facilities in Washington, D.C.*

  Includes index.
  1. Smithsonian Institution—Guide-books.
  2. Washington (D.C.)—Public buildings—Guide-books.
  3. Washington (D.C.)—Description—Guide-books.
  I. Title.
  Q11.S8S35 1985   069'.09753   84-43209

ISBN 0-89950-151-6 (sewn softcover; acid-free natural paper)

Printed in the United States of America

McFarland   Box 611   Jefferson, NC 28640

Each year, millions walk through the doors of the multiple facilities of the Smithsonian, most unaware of the vast and varied number of exhibits and programs offered therein. With the assistance of this guide, it is my hope that those planning a trip to Washington can discover what is available at the institution and select what might personally be of interest (it is rare one can take advantage of everything in a single visit).

More than a few people have left the Smithsonian feeling they have participated in some very rewarding experiences. It is to prospective visitors this book is dedicated.

Contents

Introduction

Many readers familiar with the delightful novels **Tom Sawyer** and **The Adventures of Huckleberry Finn** learn to their surprise that Mark Twain, on occasion, could use a barbed pen to write caustic, opinionated criticism with limited knowledge of his subject. In **Innocents Abroad** he speaks of the Smithsonian Institute (sic) as "a poor, useless, innocent, mildewed old fossil, the repository for an odd assortment of things including seeds and uncommon yams and extraordinary cabbages and peculiar bullfrogs." Even Mark Twain, who was one of our country's foremost writers, was sometimes capable of writing unmitigated nonsense. In truth, this world-renowned institution, by its charter the administrator of the national museums of the United States, attracts over twenty-five million people each year to its national public facilities in Washington, D.C. and is regarded everywhere as an outstanding educational, research, cultural, and service organization.

Because of their favorable geographical location, interested Washingtonians and those from the surrounding areas are indeed fortunate because they can visit the Smithsonian as often as they wish and become familiar with its splendid exhibits, national treasures often found nowhere else, and excellent services offered in each of these multiple national public facilities. They have an advantage over others who must travel long distances and therefore can visit Washington and the Smithsonian only occasionally. Of those who come from afar, a great many are only vaguely familiar or are totally unaware of much that exists there, which, if it were known would be of great interest. There have been no guides provided in hometown libraries or book stores, prior to this one, which people could consult before a visit to Washington, and which could inform them of specific Smithsonian facilities, halls, exhibits, and wonderful services (tours, lectures, films, demonstrations, etc.) which are discussed in this guide.

The prospective visitor, before leaving for Washington, may browse through this guide while relaxed at home, and make selections of exhibits and services of interest, noting where these can be found. This preparation will enable him to go directly to places of his choice rather than wander aimlessly through a maze of buildings and exhibits on the Mall and elsewhere in Washington, often missing things that would be of particular interest.

Emerging from the Metro's cavernous Smithsonian tunnel exit onto the Mall and into the sunshine one fine October day, we were stopped by a visitor with an unmistakeable English accent who asked most politely if we would point out the Smithsonian building. (Volunteers who man the Information Desks at all facilities tell us they have innumerable requests each day from visitors who, like the Englishman, believe the Smithsonian is housed in a single building and want to know in which one it is located.) We explained to our foreign visitor that the Smithsonian was not contained in a single building but had fifteen national public facilities in Washington, eight of them on this Mall and seven located elsewhere in the city. While talking to him we were facing south, looking towards the buildings on the north side of the Mall. Taking as a starting point the Museum of American History, home for the First Ladies' Gowns, which is at 14th Street on the north side of the Mall, we moved east towards the Capitol, pointing out and naming the next building, the Museum of Natural History, home for the Hope diamond, and then next the buildings of the National Gallery of Art, giving very briefly some highlights found in each of them. And then, in order to get a clearer view of the buildings on the south side that faced north, we crossed the Mall. Beginning with the immensely popular National Air and Space Museum (almost directly across the Mall from the National Gallery of Art), we briefly mentioned highlights he might expect to find in it. Then moving westward in the direction of the Washington Monument we pointed out in turn the Hirshhorn Museum and Sculpture Gardens, the Arts and Industries Building, the Castle (the original Smithsonian building), and the Freer Gallery of Art, briefly mentioning highlights found in each.

We further explained to our British visitor that away from the Mall were seven other Smithsonian facilities that include: the National Portrait Gallery at Eighth and F Streets N.W. and the National Museum of American Art at Eighth and G Streets N.W. (both of these facilities found in a single building, the Fine Arts and Portrait Gallery Building); the Renwick Gallery of Art at Pennsylvania and 17th Streets N.W.; the Museum of African Art at present located at 318 A. Street N.E., but which will be moved to Independence Avenue when its facility will be completed; the National Zoo with its main entrance at 3001 Connecticut Ave. N.W.; the Kennedy Center for the Performing Arts at 2700 F Street N.W.; and the Barney Studio House on Sheridan Circle. We briefly pointed out highlights found in each of them. All of these highlights and much more specific information about each facility of the Smithsonian are described in the chapters that follow.

Following this Introduction, the reader will find that the guide is divided into three sections. The first and largest section consists of eight chapters in each of which an individual national public facility of the Smithsonian in Washington is described (the exception in chapter six discusses all eight of its affiliated art museums.) The second section, the QuickGuide, is an appendix that gives concise information about locations, entrances, cafeterias, shops, and services (tours, demonstrations, lectures, films, etc.) generally provided in each facility. Finally, the third section, an Index, contains some of the "most-asked-for" or important or interesting artifacts, a very useful reference tool for locating items in the facility in which they are housed.

There is a twenty-two foot long, fiberglass model of a dinosaur on the Mall near the Museum of Natural History called Uncle Beasley, a charming triceratops, which had once appeared in a 1968 TV Children's Theater Production called "The Enormous Egg." Young children delight in climbing all over this dinosaur. The reassembled bones of real dinosaurs (which little ones cannot climb) and descriptions of their lifestyles are found in the Dinosaur Hall in the Museum of Natural History where young and old come in droves to marvel at the size and structure of the skeletons of these monstrous looking reptiles. In this same museum they also marvel at the abundant and varied kinds of live insects and some of their arthropod relatives displayed in an Insect Zoo, the only one of its kind in the country. In another live exhibit in this Museum of Natural History are animals and plants that inhabit a Coral Reef where both enjoy a symbiotic relationship in this fragile habitat.

The exhibit most visitors to the Museum of American History wish to see is the First Ladies' Gowns. Men are interested in this facility in the antique cars, railroads, bridges and tunnels. As women learn of the beautiful glass and ceramic displays on the third floor, they frequently spend a great many hours in those halls; and everyone loves the Star Spangled Banner displayed on the second floor and the hall of Underwater Explorations on the third floor.

The only authentic Leonardo da Vinci painting in the western hemisphere, "Ginevra d'Benci," can be seen at the National Gallery of Art, one of three outstanding art galleries on the Mall—the other two are the Hirshhorn Museum and Sculpture Gardens and the Freer Gallery of Art. Each of these art galleries is world-renowned and contains splendid art works in which both the knowledgeable art lover or the average citizen without any special art training can find much to admire. Off of the Mall are other fine art museums, among them the National Museum of American Art (formerly called the National Collection of Fine Arts), and the National Portrait Gallery, both housed in the Fine Arts and Portrait Gallery Building, but each operated as an independent facility. Two affiliates of the Museum of American Art are: the Renwick Gallery of Decorative Arts, Crafts, and Design located on Pennsylvania Avenue next door to Blair House; and the Barney Studio on Sheridan Circle. The Museum of African Art is, at present, located on A Street N.E. but will eventually find permanent quarters in the Quadrangle being built on Independence Ave. Further information about these art galleries affiliated with the Smithsonian is found in chapter six. Excellent art works are also found throughout the Museum of American History, the Museum of Natural History, the National Air and Space Museum, and in the Kennedy Center for the Performing Arts.

Many learn, much to their surprise, that two important facilities affiliated with the Smithsonian are the National Zoo and the Kennedy Center for the Performing Arts. Each has abundant exhibits and services that will delight the eyes and ears of visitors. Neither is on the Mall, but their locations and a little about their programs can be ascertained in chapters seven and eight as well as from the QuickGuide.

Everyone is welcome to come into the original Smithsonian Building, the towered Castle on the south side of the Mall. It is easily recognized because photographs of this sandstone, red-towered building, the first in the Smithsonian complex, have appeared innumerable times in newspapers and magazines. Once inside the Castle the visitors will find a Visitor Information Desk and an Associate Member's Reception Center. The latter is for members who are Smithsonian Associates paying annual dues and who receive **Smithsonian,** the monthly magazine. The Smithsonian Associates, if they ask, will receive in this Castle a kit that contains pertinent information about the Institution that includes a map of Washington. The Visitor Information Desk is for any visitor who drops in with questions. It is manned by a staff of helpful volunteers who will try to answer any questions about the "what, where, when, and how-do-I-get-there" that relate to the Smithsonian. They will also give visitors a small brochure about the Institute's facilities that includes a map of those on the Mall and several that are off the Mall. A few prototype exhibits describing special exhibits found in other facilities of the Smithsonian are displayed in the large entrance room of the Castle. Inside the Castle's north entrance (as one comes in from the Mall) is a little bit of England, a crypt brought from Italy in 1904 by Alexander Graham Bell that contains the remains of James Smithson, the founder of this Institution, and whose story is briefly told in chapter one.

Learning is a purposeful pursuit at the Smithsonian and to foster it the Institution serves not only the general public but scholars and students as well. The work areas of the Smithsonian, some in Washington, others on its outskirts or in other parts of the country, or even outside the United States are generally restricted to members of the staff, their associates, as well as scholars and students whose research, explorations, and publications in many fields are promoted by the Institution. To mention just a very few of these, there is the Fort Pierce facility in Florida where temperate and tropical plants and marine animals are studied; the National Anthropological Film Center which provides a means to develop, study, and preserve changing ways of life and cultures of the world; Academic Programs which award grants to undergraduate, graduate, and post-graduate students for research in a wide variety of disciplines; the Department of State's Bureau of Educational and Cultural Affairs that has given the Smithsonian a leading role in administering overseas archeological projects financed by excess foreign currencies available through agricultural surplus sales; and the Smithsonian Tropical Research Institute located on Barro Colorado Island in Panama and on other tropical areas where basic research about plants and animals including man is conducted. These projects (plus scores of others) do not come within the purview of this guide and are therefore not discussed here. The guide is limited to describing the Smithsonian's national public facilities in Washington, D.C.

The national museums, art galleries, Zoo, and the Kennedy Center, on the other hand, open to the public everyday (except Christmas) with no admission fees, is within the scope of this guide. Since the backgrounds and interests of its millions of visitors are so diverse, this guide can be of assistance in helping each discover particular areas of interest throughout the Smithsonian that can be of recreational, avocational, or vocational interest, inviting him to find through these pages what could provide the greatest satisfaction when one gets to its facilities. There may be areas that could prove to be fun, or capture one's imagination, or render intelligible concepts that could help better understand ideas never fully grasped before, or even learn new ones. Except in a few halls, too high a degree of scientific literacy is not required of visitors viewing the exhibits. A surprising amount of knowledge and understanding can accrue to one willing to carefully examine (and perhaps study) the thoughtfully planned exhibits. Some encounters with these can often contribute memorable experiences giving one a feeling of vicarious participation in our American heritage, widening horizons, or opening doors to new interests in a range of scientific, art, or other fields heretofore never seriously contemplated. It is our sanguine expectation that those unfamiliar with its multifaceted facilities will come to Washington better prepared to explore the Smithsonian if they first browse through this guide and make selections while quietly reviewing this guide in their own home.

It would be impossible to point out in this one volume all of the thousands upon thousands of artifacts on exhibit at the Smithsonian. There are items not mentioned because space in this text precludes it. The chapters which follow do describe each national public facility of the Smithsonian in Washington, in general, by providing the visitors with an introduction to its contents as a means of acquainting them with what exists there. It should be pointed out that although permanent exhibits frequently remain for ten or more years in the same location, exhibits do change, just as numbers in a telephone directory change, but we still find it enormously helpful to use that directory for information. New galleries are opened and older exhibits are eventually updated or replaced. Visitors are encouraged to inquire at Information Desks in each facility for whatever items or exhibits they wish to see and cannot find.

As exhibits change, so do visitor services. The Information Desks as well as Bulletin Boards should be consulted by everyone for current information about special exhibits (this guide is limited to permanent exhibits), tours, lectures, films, concerts, demonstrations, etc. in each facility. By doing this visitors can be brought up-to-date about things they can see and do during the time they spend at the Smithsonian facilities. These programs are well worth investigating for they can very often please the mind, the eyes, or ears, and not to be scorned, bring relief for the weary feet of museum goers.

One is humbled as he views throughout the Smithsonian evidence of man's genius. Some of the spectacular accomplishments he has achieved in medicine, science, and technology; his courage in explorations and discoveries; his research and explanations of the history of the earth and its habitants, and of the moon, solar system, and of the universe; and his creativity in the arts are among the marvels revealed here. Astronauts reached for the moon and got there six times and in the National Air and Space Museum we see evidence of some of the giant steps that were taken for this unbelievably difficult task. Will visitors to the Smithsonian in the twenty-first century see evidence of giant steps men took to arrive at solutions for equally difficult or even more difficult tasks? Will there be documented evidence displayed of the giant steps men took in their efforts to successfully overcome man's inhumanity to man in conventional and nuclear wars which only have as concomitant horrors starvation, disease, and result in the displacement of millions of innocent men, women, and children? Will exhibits show what men have done or are doing to create an ecologically sound and aesthetically pleasing world favorable to the survival and continued growth of civilization—among these to stop commercial emissions of pollutants, one of the causes of acid rain which is a potent threat to the environment, in some areas resulting in economic disaster! Will exhibits show evidence of a new source of energy, fusion, which unlike nuclear energy will have no waste material to cart away and dispose of in so-called safe unleakable places where they can lie buried for thousands of years? These are only a few of many, many other topics, but they indicate subjects of thought visitors in the twenty-first century would find of interest and value to examine.

Dr. Daniel J. Boorstin, a former Director of the Museum of History and Technology (now called the Museum of American History) and the present Librarian of Congress, once remarked that the opportunity to discover things one never knew were there is a part of the American experience. The statement could be a motto for the Smithsonian. The sights and sounds of the Institution quicken interest, impart knowledge, and bring enjoyment, entertainment, and a sense of pride to the more than twenty-five million visitors each year. It does not belong exclusively to the Washingtonians. It belongs to children and adults, students and hobbyists, curious passersby and the dedicated scholars from everywhere. It belongs, in fact, to anyone who walks through the many doors of its numerous facilities.

1

The Castle, the Institution and Its Secretaries

James Macie Smithson (1765-1829) bequeathed to the United States the original funds for the Smithsonian Institution, as well as its name and statement of purpose. An illegitimate son of Hugh Smithson, Duke of Northumberland, James Smithson was born in France, although he later returned to his father's homeland and became a naturalized British citizen. Smithson, a man of some means and a life-long bachelor, spent most of his time in study and in travel on the continent. He engaged in research in chemistry and mineralogy, subjects in which he had made a brilliant record at Oxford. He knew many of the prominent English and continental scientists of his day, and was a member of two of England's most distinguished societies, the Royal Society and the Royal Institution.

By the terms of Smithson's will the United States government became the recipient of an unexpected and unprecedented bequest. The letter containing notice of this gift came to our London representative—and through him to President Jackson in 1835. At that time our government was notified that funds held in escrow as residual legatee (Smithson's primary legatee, his nephew Henry James Hungerford had died without issue just six years after his uncle) and which, under the terms of the will, were to be used "to found at Washington under the name of the Smithsonian Institution an Establishment for the increase and diffusion of knowledge among men."

President Jackson, with the consent of a majority in Congress, dispatched Richard Rush to London to pursue the matter of this bequest, and after two years in the Court of Chancery the funds were released to the United States. Controversies arose in Congress, however, initially about the acceptance of such a gift from a foreigner who had never set foot in this country and later about the final disposition of the funds. Former President John Quincy Adams (who had by then returned to Congress as a representative of Massachusetts) offered keen support for acceptance of the gift. Adams later concerned himself closely with the disbursement of the Smithsonian funds (approximately $500,000), which almost immediately upon their receipt had been loaned by the U.S. Treasurer for state bonds. When several states defaulted on these bonds, Adams convinced the government to accept responsibility and replace the monies in the Smithsonian fund.

Richard Rush ushered the bequest through the English Chancery, and funds were delivered in 1838, but eight years and several sessions of Congress were to pass before final plans for the disposition of the bequest were formulated. The suggestions ranged from a university to a school for orphans, and included a botanical garden, an observatory, a zoological institute, an institution for the promotion of agriculture, and a school of astronomy. The Smithsonian Act, which formally established the institution, was finally passed by Congress in 1846. Among those responsible for its formulation and final passage were Joel R. Poinsett, John Quincy Adams, Richard Rush, William J. Hough, Rufus Choate, Robert and David Owen, George Marsh, and Alexander Dallas Bache. Joseph Henry was chosen as the Smithsonian's first Secretary. Henry, a dynamic leader and an eminent physicist, was also an able administrator. He set the course which in large measure the Smithsonian has followed ever since, and which ably interpreted the language of Smithson's will enjoining its trustees to make the Institution serve for "the increase and diffusion of knowledge among men."

On May 1, 1847 the cornerstone of the Smithsonian Institution was laid in Washington on the south side of the Mall in an unkempt open space which, in order to reach it, it was necessary to cross a then existing bridge spanning the Washington Canal (a rather smelly open sewer that was later filled in) on the Mall. Completed in 1855, the twelfth century Norman-style castle was designed by James Renwick, Jr., who by the time the Board of Regents chose him as the Smithsonian Building's architect had already designed Grace Church and St. Patrick's Cathedral in New York. Renwick's design called for unequally-sized turrets on the roof of the red sandstone building with rooms in the towers which in the early days housed young research scientists and with other tower rooms used as administrative offices for the Smithsonian staff, and as meeting rooms for the Board of Regents. Unfortunately, a fire in 1865 gutted the lecture hall and art gallery in the central section of the second floor and destroyed the large north and south towers as well. The fire also claimed many of James Smithson's personal effects, which Richard Rush had brought to this country in 1838 along with the Smithsonian funds. Smithson's irreplaceable manuscripts and a valuable collection of thousands of minerals and meteoric stones which he had carefully collected in Europe were all lost. Some two hundred Indian paintings deposited in the building by John Mix Stanley also went in the flames. Those surveying the extent of the damage to the building determined the building's original construction had been faulty, and the repair work that followed was enormously costly.

In 1861 the National Institute, a scientific organization begun some twenty years earlier as an organization of scholars and serious patrons of science with a history of encouraging explorations of distant and unknown regions, was dissolved. Its collections became the property of the United States and were turned over by our government to the Smithsonian. Among its specimens were objects collected by the 1838 United States Exploring Expedition under the command of Lieutenant Charles Wilkes; items donated by foreign governments, institutions, and societies; and some sent to the Institution by our ministers and consuls abroad. Army and Navy officers, surveying parties, and government bureaus such as the Corps of Topographic Engineers as well as the United States Patent Office donated material. Joseph

Henry, the institution's first Secretary, sifted out from this diverse assortment what he considered suitable for research or exhibit and sent duplicate items to other scientific institutions or to colleges, discarding artifacts he considered "freakish" or unsuitable for the Smithsonian.

This first Smithsonian building eventually became so over-crowded with collections that Congress agreed (after some prodding) to appropriate funds for the construction of another building. This new structure was completed in 1881. Originally called the Annex, it was later renamed the Arts and Industries Building. While it tem-porarily relieved the crowding of the Castle, both buildings were soon filled to capacity with additional collections. The only relief came in 1911 when the new Museum of Natural History took in the overflow of both the Castle and the Annex.

When a visitor comes to the Castle today he will see a limited number of exhibits shown in the Great Hall as an introduction to a few of the offerings in the various museums. The Smithsonian's Visitor Information and Reception Center is also in the Great Hall of the Castle, its volunteer staff happy to answer any questions about the Institution. In addition, visitors can obtain information about current Smithsonian special exhibits, events, and services.

The building also houses some Smithsonian offices and confer-ence rooms for higher echelon administrators. The Woodrow Wilson International Center for Scholars is located in this towered castle. The Center, a memorial to President Woodrow Wilson, was created by Congress for scholars from all over the world. They carry on work in historical and cultural fields as well as in Russian and Soviet studies, Latin American studies, and international securities studies.

In an alcove in the north hall rests the crypt of James Smithson. Brought to this country by Alexander Graham Bell in 1904 from a cemetery being demolished in Genoa, Italy, the crypt now has as its final home a place in the Institution that Smithson founded. Over three thousand miles separate Smithson's tomb from that of his father who lies buried in Westminster Abbey.

Eight men chosen by the Board of Regents have, thus far, served the Smithsonian as Secretary, the chief executive officer. Joseph Henry (1799-1879) was the first Secretary, and the only one to reside with his family in a Smithsonian building (they occupied the Castle's east wing) during his term in office. Henry already enjoyed an interna-tional reputation as a physicist when he came to Washington from what is today Princeton University. Secretary for thirty-two years, Henry laid the ground work for those who followed him and which helped shape the institution. His work in meteorology led to the even-tual establishment of the United States Weather Bureau; he set up the International Exchange Service, which aids foreign governments, scientific societies, and educational institutions in the exchange of scientific and other publications of potential benefit to the world community. He arranged as well for popular lecture programs, but perhaps his most significant contribution to the Smithsonian and the public was his encouragement of original research and its subsequent publication by the Institution. A large bronze statue of Joseph Henry stands on the south side of the Mall, in front of the Castle and shows him looking toward the other buildings on the Mall.

Henry's assistant, Spencer Baird (1823-1888), became the second Smithsonian Secretary in 1878. Baird was interested in the American West and in Alaska and supporting scientific research and explorations of these territories; in fact, information Baird collected about Alaska later was to prove a significant factor in the United States' decision to purchase that land from Russia. A biologist, a naturalist, a writer and a capable administrator, Baird contributed a great deal to the eventual establishment of the United States Bureau of Fisheries and the Marine Biological Station at Woods Hole, Massachusetts. His ornithological studies and his many publications also attest to his energy and his further accomplishments. As Assistant Secretary and later as Secretary he gave unstintingly of his time, enthusiastic about developing the Smithsonian's museum holdings and pursuing its scientific efforts in many directions. He was responsible for obtaining from various sources many collections for the institution, including many exhibited at the Centennial Exposition in Philadelphia, some of which are included in the "1876" exhibit in the Arts and Industries Building (the Annex), which originally opened in 1881 during Baird's term in office.

Samuel P. Langley (1834-1906), Baird's successor, was an eminent physicist known for his work in solar-radiation and flight mechanics. His pioneer work in aerodynamics is said to have inspired the Wright brothers. Langley was responsible for the establishment of the National Zoological Park, and saw, during his term in office, the first formal exhibit in the Smithsonian museums of the collected art works of the United States, a collection called in Langley's time the National Gallery of Art, but which then became known as the National Collection of Fine Arts and today is known as the National Museum of American Art. Langley served the Smithsonian well as its third Secretary from 1887 until 1906.

Charles D. Walcott (1850-1927) became the director of the United States Geological Survey in 1894 and remained at this post until 1907 when he was called by the Regents to become the fourth Secretary of the Smithsonian. A world-famous geologist, Walcott was known for his special studies of Cambrian rocks and the fauna of both the United States and Canada. In addition to his service with the Geological Survey (where he had been influential in efforts to reclaim some of our western land), Walcott had also worked in the Forest Service and the Bureau of Mines. In 1911, during Walcott's twenty year term as Secretary of the Smithsonian, the Natural History Museum was completed. This new museum almost at once began filling with the overflow collections kept in the Castle and the Arts and Industries Building.

Charles G. Abbot (1872-1973) began his career with the Smithsonian in 1896 as acting director and later director of the Astrophysical Observatory. At the Observatory he explored the nature of atmospheric transmission and absorption; he was also an instrument maker, and devised instruments for measuring solar heat and the use of solar energy. He established a division to study the effects of radiation on organisms and he also published books and papers on technical subjects among these five highly regarded volumes, **Annals of the Astrophysical Observatory.** During Abbot's term as Secretary, Andrew Mellon made the Smithsonian a magnificent gift, his art collection

and a building (completed in 1941) located on the Mall known as the
National Gallery of Art. Abbot returned to his research in 1944, after
sixteen years as Secretary.

The sixth Secretary of the Smithsonian was Alexander Wetmore
(1886-1978). An internationally noted ornithologist, Wetmore worked
for fourteen years with the Department of Agriculture's Bureau of
Biological Survey (now a part of the Fish and Wildlife Service).   At
the Bureau of Biological Survey he engaged in both ornithological
and mammalian research. He wrote prolifically on a range of topics
that included ornithological classification and distribution, as well
as fossil birds. Wetmore served at one time as President of the American Ornithologist's Union. He also engaged in scientific explorations
of islands in the Pacific. He first became associated with the Smithsonian in 1925 as Administrative Head of the National Zoological
Park and was later Assistant Secretary of the Smithsonian in charge
of the United States National Museum, a position he held for twenty
years. During Dr. Wetmore's term as Secretary of the Smithsonian
he encouraged the development of collections that eventually expanded
into the National Air and Space Museum. He encouraged, as well,
the increased scope of the Smithsonian's Tropical Research Institute
in Panama, a research and educational organization devoted to the
study and conservation of tropical flora and fauna. Dr. Wetmore became
the Smithsonian's Secretary in 1945 and resigned in 1952 to return
to his own research.

Leonard   Carmichael   (1898-1973)   became   the   Smithsonian's
seventh Secretary in 1953. A former president of Tufts College, he
had taught psychology at Princeton, Brown, and Rochester Universities
and had served at a number of other important institutions before
his appointment at the Smithsonian. During his term in office the
monumental Museum of American History (then known as the Museum
of History and Technology) rose from planning to completion, opening
its doors in 1964. In that same year Dr. Carmichael resigned to become
Vice President for Research and Exploration at the National Geographic
Society. His interest in the Smithsonian continued, however, and
he and J.C. Long wrote a book about the Institution, **James Smithson
and the Smithsonian Story,** that was published in 1965.

S. Dillon Ripley (1913-) came to the Smithsonian as its eighth
Secretary in 1964. He had been an assistant curator of birds at the
Smithsonian before joining the United States Office of Strategic
Services and subsequently served as commanding intelligence officer
in Southeast Asia during World War II. After his return from service
he became an associate curator at the Peabody Museum, a Professor
of Zoology at Yale, and Director of the Peabody Museum before he
accepted the appointment as the Smithsonian's eighth Secretary.
Dr. Ripley inaugurated a variety of public service programs, and
during his tenure the Anacostia Neighborhood Museum in Washington
opened (note: this is not a national public museum and is, therefore,
not discussed in this guide). The John F. Kennedy Center for the Performing Arts, the Renwick Gallery of Arts, the Museum of African
Arts, and the Barney Studio House have all become a part of the
Smithsonian during his time as Secretary. Dr. Ripley was instrumental
in obtaining for the institution the Joseph Hirshhorn's superb art collection, now installed in the Hirshhorn Museum and Sculpture Garden

on the Mall. Still other members of the Smithsonian family to be born or affiliated during Dr. Ripley's administration were the National Air and Space Museum (1976), the most popular museum in the world, and in New York the Cooper-Hewitt Museum, also the two buildings on Independence Avenue nearing completion in back of the Castle as independent facilities. One building will serve as the new Museum of African Arts, and the other, the Sackler Gallery of Oriental Art, as an adjunct museum to the Freer Gallery (but not a part of it).

In late January of 1984 an announcement appeared in the press of Dr. S. Dillon Ripley's approaching retirement. As the ninth Secretary of the Smithsonian the Board of Regents have selected Dr. Robert McCormick Adams, Jr., Provost of the University of Chicago, to succeed Dr. Ripley. Dr. Adams received all of his college education including his doctorate at the University of Chicago and has served there as an assistant professor, a professor (in anthropology and archeology) and then as Provost of the University of Chicago. He has done research in the Middle East and in Central America and has authored books and articles in the field of his competence. At the Smithsonian he will succeed a number of distinguished scientists, each of whom made significant contributions and left his indelible mark on the institution. We look forward to the programs Dr. Adams will initiate as he takes over the reins of this important, topmost scientific and cultural institution.

2

The National Museum of American History

General Remarks

In James Thomas Flexner's **An American Saga: The Story of Helen Thomas and Simon Flexner,** a biography of his parents, he writes that his father was considered subnormal by his teachers and dropped out of school before completing the eighth grade. Failure followed in whatever jobs he took and a bout of typhoid fever nearly cost him his life. Then, when he recovered from his illness, he apprenticed in a pharmacy for a kindly Dr. Davis while attending Louisville College of Pharmacy at night for two years.

His studies at Louisville College of Pharmacy won him a gold medal, his first major achievement. This and the salary he received at his brother Jacob's pharmacy, which helped in the support of the Flexner family, caused them to regard him in a new and favorable light. He considered that good luck came for him through the use of a microscope ordinarily used in the drugstore for urinalyses, but which gave him an opportunity to study tissues doctors brought him from autopsies. He taught himself with the help of books the subjects histology and pathology. Simon, with the assistance of doctors who frequented the drugstore and recommended him, applied to the University of Louisville Medical School and after two years of four winter months each supplemented by experience with a practising physician earned an M.D. degree from the university. However, he never practised medicine, confining his spheres of interest to pathology and bacteriology. A fellowship he won to Johns Hopkins in Baltimore made possible an opportunity for him to study under the great pathologist Dr. William Welch there. As the results of significant achievements in research in pathology and bacteriology Simon received appointments first as associate professor of pathology at Johns Hopkins, later as professor in pathology at the University of Pennsylvania, and eventually he was profferred the first directorship of the Rockefeller Institute of Science for Medical Research. In the History of Medicine Hall in the Museum of American History a reproduction of a bacteriological research laboratory of 1905 can be seen and in it instruments and equipment that once belonged to Simon Flexner.

While there are interspersed throughout the Museum of Ameri-

7

can History well-mounted exhibits and services that are just good fun and entertainment, there are far more that contribute to a wider understanding and appreciation of the political, scientific, cultural, military, technological, agricultural, transportation, and industrial developments that occurred in this country's history beginning in some cases with colonial times. This museum is a custodian of our cultural heritage and in it are preserved these tangible reminders for the American people which help give them a feeling for and understanding of their past.

The permanent as well as special exhibits are prepared with infinite care by departments in charge of them: graphic arts and photography; postal history; numismatics; textiles; cultural history that includes costumes and furnishings, ethnic and western cultural history, musical instruments, and preindustrial history; industries department that includes agriculture and mining, ceramics, glass manufacturing, and transportation; national and military history that includes political history, naval history, military history; science and technology that includes electricity and nuclear energy, mechanical and civil engineering, medical sciences; and physical sciences. These departments staffed by curators, script writers, label writers, preparators and others who collaborate will often plan a hall three or more years in advance, researching, preplanning, coordinating, and, at times, building full scale mock-ups of the exhibits before plans are finalized. These people attend to the minutest details and using original artifacts or exact replicas display them in an interesting manner so that the attracted viewers want to stop and examine them.

As the reader browses through this chapter at home, he will find that each hall on the several floors is introduced by a paragraph or two followed by brief examples of selected exhibits in it. The introductions are there to assist the browser quickly by-pass a hall that does not in the least interest him, or to discover from the introductions those halls which spark an interest. These are the halls he may wish to select as choice places to note and to visit.

There is no attempt to tell the entire story of everything to be seen in this extraordinarily large Museum of American History. We can only indicate part of the artifacts that are exhibited. Visitors coming into areas of interest frequently become so absorbed they spend a great deal of time in that one hall. Many who are delighted and stimulated by what they see displayed develop an abiding interest in the subject which they later pursue. Others have found outlets for their leisure in new hobbies (building model ships, railroad cars, automobiles; an interest in photography, philately, numismatics, etc.) that bring self-fulfillment. Many a young person has been influenced in the selection of a vocation by visits to this and other museums of the Smithsonian.

If one could sit at the Information Desk for an hour or two, he would soon learn that the most-asked-for hall in this museum is the First Ladies' Hall. Other halls, however, perhaps not as well-known, actually have material equally as interesting depending on its importance and appeal to the individual. We came upon a couple from Ohio who have an absorbing interest in mathematics and who were thoughtfully examining the exhibits in the Hall of Mathematics and Computers. Another individual concentrating on exhibits in the Hall of Atom

Smashers was a physicist from Berkeley. Others were engrossed in Hall of Photography. The quickening interest of both children and adults examining exciting exhibits in the Hall of Underwater Exploration is quite apparent. So is that of the philatelist pursuing an avocational interest in the Hall of Stamps and Postal History, or the numismatic buff, indifferent to others passing around him, as he studies specimens of gold coins from the Josiah K. Lilly, Jr. collection in the Hall of Money and Medals. There are literally scores of other equally absorbing exhibits in this museum that attract those with specialized avocations, vocations, or hobbies. A glance at the directory which follows gives one a clue as to what he may expect to find in the halls of the Museum of American History.

A variety of excellent visitor services (many of them free) includes additional special exhibits (not permanent exhibits such as those described in this guide), films, demonstrations, tours, concerts, and lectures. Notice of these are always posted on Bulletin Boards. The QuickGuide (an Appendix) provides one with concise information about location, phone number, entrances, and visitor services that are generally available in the Museum of American History. To supplement the QuickGuide for the most current information, one should consult the Bulletin Boards located at entrances to the building where current activities for the day, week, or month are announced, or inquire at the Information Desk. These visitor services are very much worth looking into for not only are they entertaining or informative, but the price is right (often free), and the change of pace for the weary feet of museum goers can indeed be welcome. Wheel chairs are available free at checkrooms. Ask for a free copy of **Smithsonian: A Guide for Disabled People** at Information Desks where provisions for the handicapped in this and other facilities of the Smithsonian are described. One can also write ahead for a copy to the Office of Public Affairs/Smithsonian Institution/Washington, D.C. 20560. In this building there is a regulation U.S. Post Office on the first floor Constitution Avenue side. On the ground floor there is a large bookstore, a cafeteria, and a quick food service. Museum shops are located on both the ground and second floors.

Exhibits do change in this museum as they do in the other museums of the Smithsonian. After five to ten years some of the permanent exhibits are removed and replaced with new ones. This cirumstance, regretfully, may occur after the guide has been published, as often happens with a telephone directory. However, the greater number of exhibits described in the pages that follow will probably still be there. In the event a visitor cannot find what he especially wishes to see, he should inquire about it at the Information Desk.

This museum always proves to be a fascinating place to visit for it contains incredibly interesting and diverse exhibits on all three floors which Roger Kennedy, its director, once described as a "can opener to American history." The wife of an English couple was overheard to remark to her husband that she thought this museum which revealed for her a new slant on American history was "simply smashing."

The building, faced with rose-white Tennessee marble, was planned in the 1950s, the first building of contemporary architecture constructed on the Mall, but it was not until 1964 that it was opened to the public. Before one enters its doors from the Mall visitors should take note of the quotations carved on the walls of the building for they are very impressive. They may also want to note the fluid line of the stainless steel sculpture "Infinity" standing on the plaza in the form of a Möbius curve beautifully executed by Jose de Rivera. There is no admission fee to this nor to any Smithsonian facility. A free brochure found at the Information Desks includes a map of the floors that shows the locations of the halls in the Museum of American History. Courteous guards are also very helpful.

As one enters the building through the Constitution Ave. doors, he will find he is on the first floor (through the Mall entrance he will be on the second floor of the building). If one enters through the Constitution Ave. doors, there is on the left of the entrance a country store brought from Headville, West Virginia, which had, at one time, served as a country post office and which today serves in this building as a regulation U.S. Post Office. Follow a corridor to the left or right and one will come to the Foucault Pendulum in the Central Area. The Star Spangled Banner is on the second floor just above the Foucault Pendulum.

Directory of Halls and More Popular Exhibits

For the reader's convenience page references have been provided for each hall listed below.

I. FIRST FLOOR, EAST SIDE

Farm Machinery Hall, p. 15
Historic farm implements
Jefferson's mold board for a plow
19th and 20th century implements
Historic farm combines
Mechanized farm equipment
Barbed-wire fencing
*Live honey bee hive

**Hall of American Maritime
Enterprise**, p. 18
*Models of a variety of 17th, 18th and early 20th century ships
A colonial warehouse
Towboat pilot house
Tatoo artist's parlor
Marine underwriter's insurance office
Lighthouse lens
Navigational equipmment
Ship's power plant

Land Vehicles Hall, p. 21
*Historic horsedrawn vehicles
Historic motor vehicles
*Historic bicycles
White Star Gas Station

Railroad Hall, p. 23
*Historic and newer locomotives
Historic railroad coaches
Early streetcars (models)
Seattle Cable Car
Railway equipment
Models of historic locomotive works
Safety devices

**Hall of Civil Engineering:
Bridges and Tunnels**, p. 25
Tunnel methods and models
Bridge models, historic and modern types
Subway models
Brooklyn Bridge (large model)
Drilling tools and mechanisms

*Of special interest to young children.

Hall of Electricity, p. 28
Pioneers in electricity; telephone;
    telegraph; and radio
Life and works of Edison; Bell
Voltaic and other kinds of cells;
    batteries; generators; and other
    equipment
Early electric appliances
Recent advances in generating
    power
Electricity and telephone Dis-
    covery Corner

Hall of Power (Heavy) Machinery,
    p. 32
Engines: steam, gas, electric,
    diesel, internal combustion
Generators; turbines; pumps;
    boilers and boiler auxiliaries
Original large scale power machin-
    ery
Development of refrigeration,
    showing examples

Hall of Hand and Machinery Tools,
    p. 35
18th & 19th C. hand tools of:
    coppersmiths; wheelwrights;
    blacksmiths; woodworkers
Originals and reproductions of
    machines (or scale models) that
    replaced hand tools for: boring;
    drilling; grinding; planing; cut-
    ting; turning; milling
Measurement instruments for
    making interchangeable parts
19th C. completely outfitted
    machine shop

Timekeeping and Light Machinery:
    clocks; watches; typewriters;
    phonographs; locks, p. 37
Sundials; clocks; watches; Chinese
    equatorial sundial; typewriters;
    phonographs; locks; De'Dondi
    astronomical clock; chronome-
    ters; atomic clocks

*Foucault Pendulum, p. 39
Demonstrates earth's rotation

Water-powered sawmill, p. 40
19th C.

I. FIRST FLOOR, WEST SIDE

Hall of Mathematics and Com-
    puter Devices, p. 40
Historic calculating devices
Harmonic analyzers, synthesizers
Historic mathematical instru-
    ments
Ferrell Tide Predictor
Hollerith Tabulating Machine
Computers: mechanical; electron-
    ic; digital; analog; Mark I;
    Eniac; Whirlwind; IAS
Guidance systems: Atlas; Mod I

Hall of Physical Sciences, p. 42
Astronomy; Geodesy; Hydro-
    graphy; Meteorology; Ocean-
    ography; Optics; Physics; Seis-
    mology; Surveying
Pioneers in above sciences
Scientific instruments
Benjamin Pike's instrument shop
Henry Fitz's telescope shop
Reproductions of Chemistry Labs:
    1790 and 1890

Hall of History of Medicine, Den-
    tistry, Pharmacology, and
    Health, p. 44
Medical history exhibits
Dental history exhibits
Some key figures in medicine and
    dentistry
History of pharmaceuticals; jars
    used for pharmaceuticals
Pharmacies: 18th C. and 1830
Microscopes and microscopists
Bacteriology: some leaders, a
    laboratory
Vision and its care
Research on the heart; some key
    figures
Resuscitation equipment; some
    pioneers
History of X-rays

*Of special interest to young children.

200 years of physical medicine in
    the U.S.
Medical superstitions

Hall of Iron and Steel, p. 49
Historic iron works in U.S.
Bessemer process
Bethlehem's Universal Mill
    (model)
Ford Motor's Steel Plant (model)
Shaping and use of metals
Porcelain-enameled steel

Hall of Textiles, p. 50
Techniques: inventions and their
    inventors
Jacquard looms
Looms: making plain and designed
    textiles
Art of: spinning, weaving, em-
    broidering, knitting and making
    coverlets; equipment used
Textile printing processes

Atom Smashers, p. 53
History of nuclear energy and
    atomic physics
Early pioneers and exhibits of
    their works
Pioneers of atom smashers:
    cyclotrons, synchrotrons, beta-
    trons, linear accelerators,
    circular accelerators
Fermi: copy of part of Stagg
    Field Reactor; section of radio-
    carbon dating equipment using
    Geiger-Muller counter tubes
Atomic beam apparatus
History of storage rings and col-
    liding beams
Slide show: How atom smashing is
    carried on by accelerators

II. SECOND FLOOR, EAST SIDE

**Hall of Everyday Life in the Ameri-
can Past,** p. 56
Domestic and farming life with
    artifacts of early colonists com-
    ing chiefly from Europe

Historic houses
18th & 19th C. period rooms
Federal silverware; pewterware;
    heating devices
Copp family artifacts
*Child's 1890 bedroom: toys, dolls,
    games
One-room New England school-
    room
19th C. confectioner's store
California history: Sutter's gold
    nugget; Western ranch kitchen

First Ladies' Hall, p. 60
First ladies' gowns
Chinaware of the presidents
Presidential memorabilia
White House furnishings

Hall of "We the People", p. 63
Our country and its evolving
    government
Artifacts of well-known people
The census; balloting; politicking;
    voting
Preamble to the Constitution:
    justice; defense; health; educa-
    tion; welfare--how each is fur-
    thered
Amendments to the Constitution:
    redress of grievances; women's
    rights; civil rights; Indians and
    the government

II. SECOND FLOOR, WEST SIDE

"A Nation of Nations" Hall, p. 69
A teaming nation of nations
    bringing a variety of skills:
    farmer; textile worker; tailor;
    cabinet maker; carpenter; etc.
Artifacts of ethnic groups
Artifacts of Indian tribes
Slavery artifacts
English settler's kitchen, 1695
Shared experiences: education;
    army service (posters, uni-
    forms), becoming a citizen; em-
    ployment; housing; politics; en-
    tertainment (sports, movies,

*Of special interest to young children.

movie stars)

Baseball uniforms; movie clips; Yankee Stadium seats; U.S. Army Barracks (Fort Belvoir)

Westward migration: transportation; defense; farming; sources of energy (windmills); tools

Cleveland classroom, 1883

Early 20th C. housing; factories; making autos; sewing machines; typewriters; photographic equipment; immigrants also employed as brewers, cabinet makers, bakers, watchmakers, fishermen, lumbermen, farmers

II. SECOND FLOOR
CENTRAL AREA

*Star Spangled Banner, p. 75

*Bradford Doll House, p. 76
Central Area East; by Hall Everyday Life in the American Past

Greenough's Statue of George Washington, p. 76
Central Area, West

III. THIRD FLOOR, EAST SIDE

*Hall of Underwater Exploration, p. 76
Historic diving gear and equipment
Artifacts retrieved from the sea; preservation methods of these artifacts
Finds of Teddy Tucker, a Bermuda diver
Diorama of a modern underwater exploration

Ordnance Hall and Gunboat "Philadelphia", p. 77
Historic large and small weapons and some ammunition
Swords, sabres, rapiers, daggers
Modern weaponry and equipment;

weapons assembled from interchangeable parts systems
Inventors and armorers
Gatling machine gun
Ship models
*Gunboat "Philadelphia"

Hall of Armed Forces History, p. 80
Leaders, equipment, and some memorabilia of army, navy, marines, and coast guard in wars in which they participated
Exhibits of: French & Indian War; Revolutionary War; War of 1812; Mexican War; Civil War
Contributions of armed forces in other areas of national interest
*General George Washington's tent and memorabilia
General Sheridan's horse "Winchester"
Ship models
Uniforms of all services
*Discovery Corner: "Spirit of '76"

Hall of Photography, p. 83
Historic & modern techniques for producing optical images
Cameras; lenses
Prominent men and their techniques in the history of photography
Additional uses for photography: many scientific areas; art work; war offices; banks; microfilming; mass production of designs; police work; etc.
Motion pictures: equipment; stars
Early types of projectors: phenahistiscope; mutoscope; stereoscope; Rosenfeld Illustrated Song Machine
Trans-Lux Newsreel Theater (1930 films shown free)

Hall of the History of Money, Medals, and the Medallic Arts; Orders and Decorations, p. 86
Worldwide history of money
Techniques in designing and cre-

*Of special interest to young children.

ating coins

Monetary history of the United States: gold standard for U.S.; Federal Reserve System

Specimens of checks of well-known people; U.S. paper currencies; counterfeit notes

U.S. medals and tokens

Foreign coins; paper currencies

Specimens from: Lilly Gold Coins Collection; Dupont Russian Collection of Coins & Medals; Chase Manhattan Bank Collection; Straub Collection of Gold & Silver Coins; President Grant's Collection of Ancient Japanese Coins; Neinken Collection of Paper Currencies & Documents

Orders, medals, and decorations: awarded for military, civil, & religious achievement

III. THIRD FLOOR, WEST SIDE

Henry Luce Hall of Newsreporting, p. 90

A multi-media history of news-reporting beginning with colonial times

Prominent figures in the history of journalism

Foreign language newspapers

Inventions that assisted the reporting, printing and delivery of news

Trans-Lux Movietone News of the 1930s (free)

Hall of Printing and Graphic Arts, p. 93

Historic typographic methods and graphic arts explained

Older and recent printing equipment

Patent model presses; printshops; postal relay station and print-shop

Franklin's printing press he used in London, 1726

Page from Gutenberg Bible

Gallery of graphic art works

Diorama of Japanese woodcarving

Hall of Philately and Postal History, p. 94

*Historic mail service, world wide

Mail service in America beginning with colonial times

Additional services given by post-office and some men responsible for these

Stamp printing methods & equipment

Stamp production methods & equipment

Commemorative stamps

Selections from the National Stamp Collection

*Owney, the Postal Dog

Information for philately buffs

Philatelic rarities

Hall of Musical Instruments, p. 98

Historic string, wind, brass, and keyboard instruments, restored

Folk instruments

Violin treasures: Gaspero de Sallo, Amati, Stradivari, Guanari

Hall of Ceramics, p. 100

European famous manufactories: Meissen, Hochst, Capo-di-Monte, St. Cloud, Sevres, Limoges, Chelsea Bow, Minton, Wedgewood, others

European famous ceramists: Bottger, Herold, Kaendler, Melchior, others

American famous manufactories: Rockingham, Weller, Grueby, Fenton, Bennington, Tiffany, others

Oriental ceramics: Imari, others

Hans Syz Collection of Porcelains

Larsen Collection of English Staffordshireware & Earthenware

Leon Collection of Yellow Glazed English Earthenware

*Of special interest to young children.

Wires Collection of Tiles
McCauley Collection of Liverpool
   Jugs

Hall of Glass, p. 104
History of Glassmaking
Glassmaking techniques
Islamic glass
European glassmaking beginning
   with Venice
Famous glass artists: Daum

brothers, Galle, Broccara,
Rousseau, Sala, Decorchemont,
Marinot, Lalique, Carder, Tif-
  fany
American glassmaking of 18th,
   19th and 20th C.
Glass manufactories in the U.S.:
  Wistar, Stiegel, Amelung,
  Gallatin, Tiffany, Stueben
Napoleon's banquet centerpiece

Descriptions of Halls and Exhibits

Farm Machinery Hall (First Floor, East Side)

While in 1776 nearly 90 percent of the people in this country were farmers, today there are fewer than 5 percent located on farms. A recent story that appeared in a newspaper told about a very young city boy who came across a pile of empty milk cartons and thought he had found a cow's nest. No youngster of colonial times would have been in doubt about where milk comes from, nor would he have had much leisure time to be out playing baseball or other games for he would have been needed on the farm to help with the numerous chores there.

The beginnings of colonial agriculture were fraught with difficulties. The earliest colonial settlers were very much indebted to the Indians for the help they gave these emigrants to keep them from starving and teaching them how to grow and cultivate the corn crops. The American colonists usually found only subsistence farming possible because they so often lacked proper tools for tilling and harvesting (most farming tools, at the time, came from abroad). Gradually, better tools became available, first hand-made versions and later manufactured ones made in this country. Displays show some original objects or accurate scale models of them and show over the years how the invention of labor saving farm machinery played a major role in the rapid expansion of American agriculture. At the same time that people were migrating west and farm holdings were becoming larger, inventors were developing better and better equipment, such as large horse-drawn combines. Eventually, power-driven machinery took the field. Some of these tools and machines, both historic and modern, are on exhibit in this hall.

The early colonists depended on their tillage implements to plow and prepare the soil for planting. Implements were so rare that in the seventeenth century Massachusetts plow owners were paid a bounty to keep their implements in good repair and available for plowing neighbors' fields. Seventeenth century English plows shown here include a: Lincolnshire disc, Coulter plow, Sussex single wheel plow, a plow made in 1769 by a German blacksmith in New York. While the earliest plows used in America were made entirely in Europe as a rule, soon only the iron parts were imported. With the development

of local iron works, about 1838, the entire plow was made in this
country to cut deep straight furrows into the rich soil of the land.
Among early plows shown here is one made at Ipswich, Massachusetts
in 1740; a wheeled plow of 1769; a Pennsylvania plow of 1807; a Carey
plow (early 19th century); a Nourse "Eagle" plow of 1850; a Side-Hill
plow of 1875; and a plow with an attached mold-board described by
Thomas Jefferson which he felt farmers of his time could duplicate
with simple tools and fit them to their plows minimizing the effort
of both plowman and animal pulling the plow. There is also a mowing
machine (1880) shown which when attached to the Hussey cutting
apparatus could be used by farmers with one horse.

There is other early American mowing equipment as well
as implements for raking, and forking hay. An exhibit describes many
of the early forks and a "flop over" hay rake patented in 1822. Some
other early farm implements include flails, winnowing pans, forks,
a grain drill and some other horse-drawn implements on display. Other
mowing machines, some dating from about 1800 are exhibited, as
well as more recent harvesting self-propelled machines that travelled
across the field and baled.

Among the reapers and mowers shown in scale models is the
earliest known reaper used by the Gauls in the first century A.D.
Then there are the Bell reaper, invented in Scotland in 1826; reapers
invented by Obed Hussey in 1833 and 1850; and a Cyrus McCormick
reaper of 1834 which revolutionized American agriculture. Among
the several mowers shown here is an 1822 model by Jeremiah Bailey
of Pennsylvania, and one invented in 1832 by William Manning of
New Jersey.

Nineteenth century cultivators used for row crops, such as
cotton, beans, corn, and potatoes are on display. There are also hand
cultivators, horse-drawn cultivators, grain drills, and harrows and
rollers which helped increase crop yields. Some of the horse-drawn
treadmills exhibited in this hall were used throughout the nineteenth
century to pull small threshers, planters, cultivators, and other farm
machinery. There are also shown examples of early steam propelled
farm equipment which could be attached to threshers, planters, and
cultivators and driven across the fields. The inventors of these implements made important strides that assisted farmers in producing
more and cheaper food as well as other types of crops to meet the
demands of an ever-increasing population in this country and abroad. The
great westward expansion of the American people in the nineteenth
century was aided, in part, by great technological advances in farm
equipment and mechanization to make farming much easier for the
farmer who needed to clear the fields of stumps and stones, and to
break up the soil. The mechanized farm equipment, particularly large
tractors for pulling and powering heavy farm implements, brought
great changes to rural America.

Some examples shown that introduced the "mechanized revolution" include an 1869 portable steam engine, the first steam engine
made by the J.L. Case Company that produced about eight horsepower
and supplied belted power for driving tractors, threshers, and saw
mills and an 1877 portable steam engine that could be attached to
a threshing machine and used in the fields. Also shown is the Huber
Steam Tractor (1901) made at Marion, Ohio that could burn either

wood or coal and develop nearly thirty horsepower and another Huber Steam Tractor (1924) which had eighteen horsepower made expressly to be used in the wheat fields. The Har-Par Tractor (1903) was powered by an internal combustion engine while the Waterloo Boy Tractor made by John Deere Company (1918) was driven by kerosene. Other tractors on exhibit include the Fordson (1918), a relatively cheap, easily operated machine; the crawler-type tractor (1929) built by Benjamin Holt that was called "Cat-10" and pulled a "Detroit Harvester" mower used for orchard work; and a gas turbine tractor of 1965 and other gasoline and diesel driven tractors on view here. These, along with increased knowledge of the use of fertilizers, brought about a great increase in the crop yields.

Another exhibit in this hall features the first horse-drawn combine. It was built by Benjamin Holt at Stockton, California in 1886 and was pulled by twenty horses or mules. It could harvest and thresh seeds at the same time, and, with the McCormick thresher, helped revolutionize American agriculture. Benjamin Holt later invented the caterpillar tractor, also shown here. The use of combustion tractors was of immense importance not only for cultivating, but for picking corn, cotton, and other farm crops. The red McCormick-Deering Cotton Picker called "Old Red" stands at the entrance to this hall. It was the first commercial spindle cotton picker built in 1943. It was of such great significance to American agriculture that it has been designated an historic landmark of agricultural engineering.

Barbed wire fencing and hybrid corn were two other innovations that helped speed the revolution in American agriculture and ranching. An exhibit shows the evolution of barbed wire fencing which made cheap, effective fencing a reality and a great help to Western settlers who had little or no other fencing materials available to them. From the 1870s on it confined animals, protected crops, and staked out farm and city holdings. Various types of barbed wire shown here includes among others: Brink Twist (1879), Four Point Wager (1879), Champion Zigzag (1879), Shinn's Four Point (1881), and Buckthorn (1881). Farmers of today have done things with corn the Indians never dreamed of doing. The hybrid corn developed by modern agronomists has resulted in greater corn yields for animal fodder (its chief use), as well as increasing the amount available for human consumption. There is talk of converting some part of these crops into ethyl alcohol, a product that can be used instead of gasoline to propel vehicles. The large scale business for the farmers who grow hybrid corn was facilitated by mechanization that speeded the revolution of agriculture in America that is described in this hall.

A live honey bee hive furnished by the Department of Agriculture has a niche in this hall. Its activities can only be observed for a part of the year, for it is removed to a farm in Beltsville, Maryland in the late fall. It is returned to the Farm Machinery Hall in the spring. In order to help the bees make honey the hive has an exit to the out-of-doors which allows the bees to come and go freely in their search for nectar and pollen (but visitors are off limits to them). The exhibit describes the lives and the work of this highly developed community of bees beginning with the queen who is responsible for laying the eggs (sometimes as many as 2000 eggs a day); the drones who mate with the queen (their sole function); and the workers who divide the labor of the colony between them. Another live bee hive can be observed in the Museum of Natural History in the Insect Zoo Hall on the second floor.

Hall of American Maritime Enterprise (First Floor, East Side)

At its entrance there are exhibited items that appeared on vessels sailing in and out of our American ports in the 17th, 18th, 19th, and early 20th centuries. Among those shown are a huge steering wheel and carved wooden figures of women carried on the prows of these ships to decorate them. There is also a huge beacon light that for many years warned ships approaching danger spots when nearing port. An accurately scaled model of the "Mayflower," a ship that carried more than one hundred men and women to Plymouth Rock in 1620, is also seen here.

Natural harbors along the eastern seaboard became busy ports in the early days of our country (as they still are today). Exhibits describe not only the business carried on at these ports, but show (in scale models) vessels that plied the seas nearby ferries, tug boats, great liners, lighters, pilot schooners, packets, dredges (utilized by the Corps of Engineers to help maintain the harbor and prevent it from silting up), fireboats, car floats, excursion boats, and others. There are also lighthouses and channel markers described and illustrated to help bring the vessels safely into berthage. To guide a large vessel safely into port required the services of a local pilot who intimately knew the conditions of the harbor. He utilized a pilot ship which might have been a tug boat, pilot schooner or other type of vessel. The men competing for the business of bringing ships safely into harbor developed sleek and fast vessels. Two model pilot schooners shown are the American "Anna Marie" (later captured by the British off Sandy Hook, N.J.) and "The Columbia" of 1894.

Models of other vessels displayed that could be found in or near harbors include a large model of the 1775 ship "Brilliant" built for commerce with Great Britain; a sloop "Mediator"; two schooners, "The St. Anne" built before 1736 and the "Chaleur" of 1764, a square top sail schooner; two steam tugs "The Brooklyn" of about 1910 and "The Rattler" designed for coastwise towing; a 1902 scow schooner "James F. McKenna"; a 1911 tannery tender "Bonita"; and a 1912 steam powered lighter "The Mauch Chunk."

America built vessels during and after the Revolution that were capable of evading the British privateers blockading our commerce. Shown are models of some agile privateers and schooners that were utilized as blockade runners: the schooner "Berbice," 1779; the privateers "Rhodes," 1780 and "Oliver Cromwell," 1777. One of the important industries of our new country was shipbuilding of vessels built in Philadelphia, New York, and on the Chesapeake Bay. There are models of some of these that include packets that carried passengers, mail and cargo across the Atlantic and the lean clipper ships built in the 1849s and 1850s for passage to China, California, and Australia. Among some models shown are the cargo ship "The London" built for English merchants; a brig "The Swift," 1778 and another brig "The Numa," 1801; the Royal Navy purchase of a three-masted schooner built in Baltimore; a square topsail schooner of 1811 "The Fly"; the square topped sail schooners "The Lynx," "The Experiment," and "The Isabella"; a brig "The Diligente," 1839 was used in the slave trade; the clipper ship "The Challenge," 1851; and "The Savannah," a packet ship whose sailing power was supplemented with an auxiliary steam engine (to be used only when the vessel encountered doldrums) and whose ship's log is shown.

A scene in this hall depicts a colonial warehouse in a small tidewater port in Virginia of about 1775 where merchants displayed and stored typical trade products for export and import utilizing many sizes of barrels as containers. America sent raw material such as timber, furs, pig iron, pitch, rice, tobacco, and indigo. From overseas came the manufactured goods, luxury items, and necessities displayed in this warehouse.

Even in the late 1800s and early 1900s bulk cargo schooners were used to move the coal, lumber, guano, and sugar for commerce because these ships were better adapted for sailing along the coast with their loads and could be handled by a relatively small crew. Of these bulk cargo schooners some models shown include: "The Emily F. Whitney," 1800 and "The Tillie E. Storbuch," 1883. There were even ships built called hermaphrodites of which a model shown is the brigatine "Kohale," 1901. There were four, five, six, and seven-masted schooners among which a few models shown include the four-masted "Priscilla W. Alden," and the "C.C. Mengel, Jr." built in 1916.

New Bedford, Massachusetts was the whaling capital of the world. Its subsidiary industries (tool works, copper shops and others) were geared to this one large industry. A sailing ship (not a model) from this city is on exhibit as are models and illustrations of other whaling ships.

Another important industry in this country was and is commercial fishing, utilizing, especially, the fishing grounds from Cape Cod to the Grand Banks for large catches obtained there. Among models of some fishing schooners are shown: "Mt. Vernon," 1830s; "Dauntless," 1855; "Etta G. Fogg," 1857; "Spencer F. Baird," 1882; "Grampus," 1836; and "Fredonia," 1889.

The Louisiana Purchase in 1803 nearly doubled the size of the United States. In this area the Great Lakes and the Rivers of the Mississippi Valley provided our country with a transportation system of unbelievable possibilities. However, it took the efforts of steam engines pioneered by John Fitch and James Rumsey in the 1780s and Robert Fulton and John Stevens in the 1800s to help make practical use of these waterways, river systems, as well as those along the Ohio River, the Hudson River, and the eastern coastal waters for commerce and other uses. Exhibits display Steven's screw propelled experimental engine of 1804; models of "The Rochester," 1836; "The Francis Sheddy," 1852; "Buckeye State," a packet ship; "Idlewild," a shoal draft stern wheeler; the "Mark Twain," and "The Showboat," 1918. Models of Great Lakes cargo vessels show the steam barge "Edward Smith," 1890; the scow schooner "Milton," 1867; the steamship "Frank Rockefeller," 1896; and an ore carrier "James R. Barker," 1971, among others. An actual towboat pilot's house of the 1970s is on display with its array of sophisticated equipment that includes a DE-760 Fathomater Depth Sounder; and Sperry M-K-12 Radar Controller Valves for steering levers instead of the big steering wheels of former days. The scenery observed along the Mississippi appears as real as in the days of Mark Twain, but is actually projected slides shown on a screen. A recorded talk by a pilot captain explains the operation of this towboat which pushes (not pulls) barges filled with merchandise along the river.

A huge power plant below floor level that was tended by an engineer shows a marine engine built by John W. Sullivan Co. of New York in 1921 and installed in the USCGC cutter called "The Oak" which tended buoys. At floor level is a typical radio room that may have been part of "The Oak."

In another section of this hall visitors will find themselves looking at the oak paneled lounge of the old German liner "Leviathan" that was captured by the U.S. in World War I. In this lounge one can see memorabilia from that liner.

A section in this hall discusses "The Seaman." His early life was not an easy one in colonial days and even up to the early 1900s when he began to take a stand for his rights through collective bargaining, there were difficulties. The exhibits in this section show a storefront tatoo artist's parlor of long ago that has been recreated here and with the help of a film shows a man (actually a mannequin) being tatooed. Nearby is displayed a collection of scrimshaw done by sailors that depict whale hunts, harbor scenes, and portraits.

A marine underwriters' insurance office of the late 1800s has been recreated in a part of this hall. There have been, since colonial days, efforts to reduce the risks to life and property by introducing more stringent safety rules, and in expediting rescue and salvage operations. First efforts to prevent disasters involved the establishment by Congress as early as 1790 of building and operating lighthouses. Responsibility then went to the Lighthouse Board in 1852 of which Joseph Henry, first Secretary of the Smithsonian, was a member. They ordered the installation of new types of modern lamps with prismatic lenses that were conceived by Augustine Fresnell in 1820. An operating Fresnell lighthouse lens from Table Bluffs, California flashes its lights across the ceiling in part of this hall. There are models of a lighthouse district ship "Joseph Henry" and of a lighthouse tender, "USSS Grenbriar." An actual bell buoy of the early 1930s is shown. Operated by batteries it served at the mouth of the Elk River near Chesapeake Bay.

An exhibit explains the differences in equipment used for navigation—what was once used and what is used today in plotting a course and maintaining it. As vessels of ocean-going size grew larger and larger it was difficult to "keep a course." Clever inventors began to devise methods for steering—first by steam and then by hydraulic motors. Beginning in the 1920s it began to be possible to steer simply by changing the compass heading. Exhibited are Sperry Gyrocompass of 1910 and a Sperry Single Unit Gyropilot of 1923 called "Metal Mike."

On the day Japan surrendered its forces in China, September 9, 1945, the ship "Empress of Russia" was destroyed by fire. It had served as a troop transport in World War I and World War II. A very large model of it is shown in this hall.

Land Vehicles Hall (First Floor, East Side)

You can hear the clippity clop of horses' hooves in one corner of this hall as one moves through the section that describes horse-drawn conveyances. In this area a goodly selection of authentic, restored vehicles stand where the viewer can note the changes in construction and maneuverability of these historic conveyances. Each is shown on the type of road material current for its day. The visitor interested in closely examining the different types of vehicles for each period can follow the changes wrought in overall construction, frame suspension systems, and wheel mountings, among other things about these authentic vehicles. By 1905 the number of horse-drawn vehicles reached a peak and after that began to decline. By the beginning of World War I the horse and buggy era came to an end with the advent of horseless carriages which at this time began to come into their own. However, before the automobiles arrived on the scene, foot powered vehicles (along with horse-drawn vehicles) played an important role in transporting people. As an aftermath of a cycle craze involving the demands for new and better roads by over four million individuals and bicycle club members from all parts of the country using the new safety bicycles in the 1880s and 1890s, new roads were built and were of significance for riders of all vehicles on the road and for the horseless carriages whose inventors were working feverishly to develop these cars in this and other countries. Some of the earliest as well as later models of historic bicycles and automobiles are displayed in this hall.

Among the most popular light-weight horse-drawn passenger vehicles in America prior to the Civil War were the chaise (from the French word meaning chair) and the gig. Shown in this hall is a 1770 chaise, a two wheeler with wooden wheels five inches in diameter with iron tires laid in sections, that is the oldest vehicle in the collection; and a gig (meaning anything that moves rapidly and easily) of 1800 which is also a two wheeler but which has iron tires all in one piece with its wheels canted for stability. The chaise is suspended by means of leather straps or braces which pass underneath the body from one end of the frame to the other and are attached to a wooden cantilever spring, while the gig has C springs with leather braces extending from them underneath the body of the coach. Models and restored specimens of other horse-drawn vehicles (some by famous makers) abound in the exhibit. One called the Conestoga Wagon and sometimes later called the Prairie Schooner originated in 1760 to carry heavy loads over the Pennsylvania terrain. Also shown are: a Concord Coach of 1848, an Albany Cutter, a Hack Passenger Wagon (frequently referred to as "mud wagon") of about 1880, a landau (used by the wealthy) built in 1879, a town coach built in 1851 (also used by the wealthy), and a Rockaway carriage of about 1860, a popular family type of carriage. Among other authentic early horse-drawn vehicles shown are a light-weight coachee of 1810; a piano box buggy (sometimes called the road wagon) which was a versatile, relatively inexpensive vehicle mass produced from about 1860 to 1920; a phaeton; surrey; cabriolet; brougham; sulky; dray; farm wagon; and other types of useful wagons. A Victoria of 1905 shown here was used by two presidents: Theodore Roosevelt and Woodrow Wilson.

An exhibit describes various types of harnesses put on the horses who pulled the vehicles. Among these are the coach harness of 1851; the wood harness; the double ox-yoke of the 19th century; and a single ox-yoke. Also shown in this exhibit is a tar bucket of 1836, a container used to carry lubrication for the axles of a wagon.

Horse-drawn conveyances were not alone in claiming the roads before the advent of the automobiles. Foot-powered vehicles preceded the motor driven ones. Among the cycles shown here are an 1818 Draisine; a Pierce Bicycle of 1900; a Columbia Bicycle of 1896; a Columbia Tandem of 1896; an Overman Bicycle of 1889; a Starley Bicycle of 1887; a Beeston Humber Racing Bicycle of 1886; a Smith Tricycle of 1880; a child's bicycle of 1885; and a vehicle with pedals called a coaster or hobbyhorse. There are also shown velocipedes of 1868 and 1869 one of which is an 1869 Roper Steam Velocipede that looks like a bicycle with a smoke stack. There are also a Long Steam Tricycle, monocycles, and high wheelers (called ordinaries, they had one large front wheel, one small rear wheel and were popular for only about two years). Also shown are tandems, quadricycles, and a lady's safety cycle. In the 1880s and 1890s the bicycle was as common a mode of transportation in this country as it still is in many countries of Europe and Asia today. Many well-known motor cycles are exhibited in this hall, among them a Reinhardt that was ridden 25,000 miles over Europe and Asia in 1935; a 1949 Raleigh ridden from Bogata, Columbia to New York; and two 1965 Schwinns (one with a ten speed control), and a Sting Ray.

Today's automobiles arrived on the scene through a combination of fortuitous circumstances. These included the invention of a small internal combustion engine, patented by a German engineer, N.A. Ott; the discovery in 1859 at Titusville, Pennsylvania that petroleum was not only a source of oil but useful for other fuels (heretofore the leftovers had been discarded, for at that time, petroleum's greatest use was for kerosene); and the inventions of horseless carriages by several men working independently. Early autos were handmade, and among those shown are restored vehicles: the first Duryea (1893), the first Haynes (1894), the Balzar (1894), the first Franklin ever sold (1920), the gasoline driven Oldsmobile of 1903, and the first Winton racing cars to travel across the country (1902 and 1903). Electric vehicles shown include a Riker (1900), a Columbia (1904), a Commercial electric truck (1913), and a Rauch and Lang (1914). Steam propelled vehicles shown include a 1900 Locomobile identical to an early Stanley Steamer, and a 1902 White.

Another early automobile on display is a 1913 Model T Ford (the famous Tin Lizzie, the car largely responsible for bringing about the change from the horse and buggy to the automobile age). It is parked at the lobby entrance on the Constitution Avenue side of the building.

Other early cars shown in this hall are: a 1903 Mercedes, a Winton of 1903, a 1912 Pierce Arrow Runabout (a real luxury car), a 1912 Simplex, a 1917 White Motor bus, a Mack Bulldog truck, a 1905 Cadillac, a Packard Phaeton of 1932, a Model A Ford of 1937, and a couple of racing cars that competed in the Indy "500," one of them the winner in 1969 that was driven by Mario Andretti.

At the entrance to this hall is a White Star Gasoline Station

with its outdoor Tokheim gasoline pump of 1910 that could be wheeled
into the station at night. Also shown here are: a Wayne gasoline pump
of 1918 and a Gilbert and Barker gasoline pump of 1922.

Shown at one time but now in the reserve collection is a stained
glass window incorporating a picture of a Rolls Royce. Millard Newman
loved his Rolls Royce so much that he had this stained glass window
designed for his mausoleum. Having second thoughts about the suitabili-
ty of such a window for a mausoleum, he shipped it to the Smithsonian
where, at one time, it was incorporated in the decor of this hall.

Railroad Hall (First Floor, East Side)

Many, as children, heard the story of **The Little Engine that
Could.** Even today little children enjoy hearing or reading it. In this
hall is the retired Olomana, a locomotive called by Walt Disney the
nearest thing to a Mickey Mouse engine. It worked for sixty-two seasons
on a Hawaiian sugar plantation. This efficient engine built by the
largest lomotive builder in the world, Baldwin of Philadelphia, could
probably qualify as "the little engine that could." Engines like the
Olomana were used for short hauls between 1870 and 1940 to do a
vast amount of work in steel mills, brick yards, saw mills, stone quarries
and on farms. Before its final retirement to the Railroad Hall in the
Smithsonian the Olomana had once appeared in a Hollywood movie.
Those who know the story of **The Little Engine that Could** will, undoubtedly, feel a genuine rapport with this little engine.

Railroads by providing cheap, quick, and efficient transportation between the east and west played a major role in the industrializa-
tion of our country. In addition to cutting freight hauling time and
tremendously reducing the cost of shipping goods, it helped shift
the country from a primarily agricultural land to a booming industrial
economy. Railroads provided a better means of transportation, relatively cheaper and more efficient to construct than the canals which
had been built (the Erie Canal, for example, which connected Albany
on the Hudson River with Buffalo on Lake Erie, took eight years to
build at a cost of seven million dollars, and though it did cut freight
costs and traveling time, was useful for only about seven months
of the year due to flooding, freezing, and sometimes even droughts).
Canals could not travel over steep mountains to get to some major
cities. Railroads were also better than horse-drawn vehicles which
could only carry a limited amount of goods or people. Trams used
in the coal and ore mines of Europe between the sixteenth and nineteenth centuries to haul loads to the surface, first by hand and later
by horses, were the beginnings of the railroad systems which first
ran on wooden rails and later on cast iron ones. Even in the United
States the horse-drawn trams carried coal and ores from mines to
surface.

In 1829 the Delaware and Hudson Canal Company opened
a railroad line to connect the company's coal mines and the canal
from Honesdale to Carbondale, Pennsylvania. The Stourbridge Lion
(a restored one with its brightly painted lion's face on its boiler) built
in England and shown in this hall was the first full-sized commercial
steam locomotive to run on this railway in all of North America.

Other early locomotives and coaches (most in scale models) are also on display here. Also shown are railway and safety equipment and models of early types of interurban, elevated, street cars, and a cable car.

Full sized locomotives and coaches stand on tracks that are in a brick paved area of this hall. Most are among the first of their kind ever used in this country. In addition to the restored Stourbridge Lion mentioned above, the hall features the original 12½ ton locomotive Pioneer, a bonnet-stacked, wood-burning, light passenger steam locomotive built by Seth Wilmarth of Boston in 1851 for the Cumberland Valley Railroad. The wooden American type passenger coach seating forty-eight was built for the Camden and Amboy Railroad in 1836 and is one of the earliest types of passenger coaches. It shows a single open compartment with a center aisle and rows of seats on either side, and a door, steps and a platform at each end of the car. The Puffing Billy (grasshopper type locomotive) was named Puffing Billy because it was steam powered and had an arrangement of connecting beams and rods. It is another locomotive that can be seen in this area, which also shows the restored John Bull, a steam locomotive built in England in 1831 that ran on the Camden and Amboy Railroad in New Jersey as a part of the line between New York and Philadelphia, a railroad line that was credited with starting mechanical railroad transportation in this country. The John Bull, believed to be the oldest operable locomotive in the world, celebrated its 150th anniversary on September 15, 1981 when it was moved out of this hall and made several three mile trips along the canal near Fletcher Boat House in Georgetown at fifteen miles an hour. It was returned to the Museum of American History and is now shown in the hallway on the approach to this hall. The Gowan and Marx is still another American type of locomotive shown which by 1870 carried about 85 percent of all United States traffic. A Pioneer Zephyr Diesel engine of 1934, also shown, was built for the Chicago, Burlington and Quincy Railroad and used for light and high speed service.

Perhaps visitors will be startled when they hear the locomotive 1401, a 208 ton Pacific type locomotive that was built in 1926 by the Southern Railway System, start up and a conductor shout (via taped broadcast), "all aboard!" They might well expect 1401 to take off on the railroad track on which it is mounted, but the only place for it to go would be through the wall of the hall, which, of course, it could never do.

Precisely executed scale models of locomotives and railway cars are provided in abundance in this hall. There is an 1803 steam locomotive built by Richard Trevithick; the 1857 Phantom; the Philadelphia of 1844-49; the 1851 Croton; the Rocket of 1829, a pioneer steam locomotive designed by George and Robert Stephenson of Great Britain that won a contest for locomotives and influenced the design of all subsequent steam locomotives, making the slow moving "grasshopper" locomotives obsolete; the Tom Thumb, a tiny steam locomotive which proved capable of negotiating the sharp curves on the Baltimore and Ohio lines and which was built in 1830 by Peter Cooper, a wealthy inventor; the Forney type of 1878; the Columbia of 1893; the Atlantic type of 1900; and the 1914 K-4 Pacific.

A cut-away scale model of a 1935 diesel-electric locomotive

shows a type that supplanted the steam locomotive. There is also a replica of an experimental electric locomotive built by Moses G. Farmer at Dover, New Hampshire in 1847. It is a copy of one he used for demonstration purposes when he lectured on electricity. Farmer devised an electric motor in 1846 that drove an electric train of two cars on an 18 inch gauge track. There is a large scale model of a diesel electric passenger locomotive of 1949 which was made for research purposes to study designs of the E-8 series prior to their being built and used between 1949-53.

The exhibits of scale models in this hall also feature early locomotive workshops, among them the first locomotive workshop founded in 1823 at Newcastle, England by George Stephenson and his son Robert. The Stephenson team won the contest for steam locomotive designs mentioned above. Another model is of the 1855 Norris Locomotive Works in Philadelphia. Still others are carefully executed scale models that show freight cars including boxcars, flat cars, hoppers (in early days called coal jimmies), gondolas, refrigerator cars, cabooses, and others which indicate mechanical advances and other contributions of famous designers.

The exhibits that discuss railway equipment and safety devices show 1905 semaphore signals and automatic railway signalling devices; an 1831 driving wheel used on one of the DeWitt-Clinton locomotives of the Mohawk and Hudson Railroad; couplers that began as primitive chain and draw bars of the 1840s, later replaced by the link and pin which in turn was replaced by automatic couplers. Among the braking equipment shown here are the first air brakes patented by George Westinghouse in 1869. Additional railroad equipment displayed includes: historic rails (cast iron plate used to cover wooden rails, wrought iron strap rails, roll rails, steel rails, and welded rails); rail fastenings, cross ties, gauges; and other railway equipment and safety devices.

Early types of street cars, used chiefly for city transportation, made an important contribution to the growth of the big city because they provided the first efficient means for public transportation. They are shown here in scale models. Among them are the horse-drawn car of the late 1850s and 1860s, the Burney Safety Car; and the Peter Dewitt car of 1915. An interurban electric car, a lightweight 1939 interurban, and the president's conference committee car are other models on display. A scale model shows the New York City 1880 elevated railway, which ran on Third Avenue until it was finally abandoned in 1955. A full-sized old 1898 electric street car which ran in the District of Columbia until 1912 is also on display. Perhaps more impressive is the full-sized cable car used from 1888 to 1910 in Seattle, Washington. One can see beneath the car the section of narrow gauge track on which it sits and the heavy underground construction required for its propulsion.

Hall of Civil Engineering: Bridges and Tunnels (First Floor, East Side)

Bridges have been used to span water and other obstacles from time immemorial, and in this hall is traced something about their history and development. Where it was not convenient or possible to go over, enterprising people sometimes went under. Two types of tunneling methods are described and illustrated in exhibits. Rock tunneling and soft ground tunneling are traced historically, showing how technology advanced from basic timber frame supports, used in the mining operations of early Europeans, to the methods employed by the skilled tunnel engineers of modern times.

Man's first bridges were trees over streams, but the story of bridges in this hall begins with the Romans whose bridges were usually of stone. Shown in extremely accurate scale models and illustrations are the Pont Dugard Aqueduct Bridge near Nimes, France built from 27 B.C. to 14 A.D., and a two thousand year old bridge over the Tagus River at Alcantara, Spain which, incredible as it seems, is still used today. A timber bridge built across the Rhine called Caesar's bridge (55 B.C.) took the Romans only ten days to complete; a model of it is on display, as are illustrations of medieval bridges: the London Bridge built and used between 1176 and 1209, a bridge at Entraygues, France built about 1270, and the marble Rialto Bridge of 1591 believed to have been designed by Michelangelo.

The display of other scale models explores the five major bridge types found in this and other countries: wood, stone, iron, steel, and concrete. Models of wooden truss bridges in Italy, built by Palladio about 1570 are shown, as is a wrought iron suspension foot bridge of about 1615. The models of bridges built in the eighteenth century include: a wooden bridge over the Rhine at Schaffhausen, Switzerland built in 1758 by a carpenter; a bridge built in 1785 at Bellow Falls, Vermont; the Neuilly Bridge over the Seine, designed by the great French bridge builder Jean Perronet in 1784. Cast iron bridges were first introduced in England by Darby and Wilkinson to span the Severn River and a model of this metal Coalbrookdale Bridge of 1779 is shown as is an illustration of the iron Sunderland Bridge of 1796 over the River Wear in England built by Rowland Burdon; and the Chestnut Street cast iron bridge in Philadelphia. Evidently the use of cast iron for bridges was abandoned after the collapse of Tay Bridge over the Firth of Forth in 1879. It is believed that wrought iron had been used for bridges in the Orient before the birth of Christ. We know that it was used to make suspension bridges in this country and elsewhere as models show: a suspension bridge built in Bhutan in the eighteenth century; Finley's Suspension Bridge over Jacob's Creek in Pennsylvania built in 1801 (Finley built forty similar suspension bridges); and Thomas Telford's wrought iron Menai Strait Bridge in Wales built in 1826 that shows details of connecting links, cables, and other features. Wrought iron was also used for railroad bridges by such well known bridge builders as Benjamin Latrobe, Wendel Bolman, and Albert Fink. Models show these and examples of the Bolman truss and the improved truss of Fink.

An exhibit describes the work of Whipple and Trumbull who in the nineteenth century carried on the mathematical study of structural stresses begun by Perronet of France. Models show Whipple's "bowstring" truss bridge across the Erie Canal, as well as a truss bridge of Trumbull's.

The growth of railroads in the nineteenth century created a need for the development of bridge engineering for the trains that had to cross rivers, gorges, and other obstacles. In 1840 William Howe using iron rods threaded to carry all tensile stress in the webbing system designed a truss bridge that became a model for American railroads until 1910. Other builders of truss bridges were Colonel Stephen H. Long of the U.S. Corps of Topographical Engineers, and Thomas and Caleb Pratt whose truss bridges made entirely of iron became the most popular kind used for all bridges of this type. A model of one of the Pratt bridges is shown. Bridge builders have, of course, used a variety of materials as well as techniques. Wrought iron was probably used for bridges in China and Japan as early as 200 B.C. Among the scale models of wrought iron bridges are a suspension foot bridge of 1615 and railroad bridges built by Benjamin Latrobe (a chief engineer of the Baltimore and Ohio Railroad) and his two assistants, Wendall Bolman and Albert Fink.

Models also illustrate steel bridges. Although steel had been known for centuries, it was the Bessemer, Kelly, and Muchet processes that resulted in strengthened steel that could be cheaply made in large enough quantities to make it feasible to use as structural material. The earliest known bridge containing steel was built in Vienna, Austria in 1828. Models of modern steel bridges shown here include the Mackinac Bridge, the Quebec Bridge, and the Henry Hudson Bridge. There is also a scale model of the Firth of Forth Bridge built in 1890 in Queensferry, Scotland that is considered by many to be the world's strongest bridge. The Brooklyn Bridge (1883) was the first great steel suspension bridge in the world. A large scale model of this bridge is on display. An exhibit and illustrations show how its steel wire cables were intertwined for strength. John Roebling was responsible for the design and began the work, which (because of John's illness) was completed under his son Washington Roebling's supervision. John Roebling also built the 1855 Niagara Falls suspension bridge shown in a model.

Models also illustrate the use of concrete as a structural material for bridges. Models of early bridges featuring structural concrete include the Alvord Lake Bridge (1889) in San Francisco's Golden Gate Park and the Prospect Park Bridge (1871) in Brooklyn. Bridges constructed with reinforced concrete include Cincinnati's Eden Park Bridge and the Walnut Lane Bridge in Philadelphia. There is also a scale model of the Liege Exposition Bridge (1905) designed by Francois Hennebique, a French bridge engineer who had worldwide influence in the structural use of reinforced concrete.

The Hall of Civil Engineering shows overhead exhibits of a series of wooden arches that illustrate the methods of tunnel timbering used in the Austrian, English, and American systems. Small scale models describe soft ground tunneling (about 1855) using the Austrian systems. Scale models also describe how the Hoosac Tunnel through Hoosac Mountain in Massachusetts was built (1851-1875). The Brunel Thames Tunnel shown here in scale model was the first tunnel ever constructed under water. Completed in 1843, the tunnel's builders employed jackscrews to propel forward a cast iron shield that provided continuous support of the soft clay of the riverbed. A second Thames tunnel shown in scale model is the Greathead Tower Subway, built in 1869. It was also constructed using the jackscrew principle and cast iron shield but this tunnel was completed in less than a year.

The Beach Broadway Subway Tunnel in New York was completed in 1870. Instead of the propelling screws used in the shield by Brunel and Greathead, Beach used eighteen hydraulic rams set around the circumference of the shield and activated by a hand-operated pump. The Beach Tunnel is shown here in scale model as is the Haskin's Hudson River Tunnel (begun in 1880 but not completed until 1904). Haskin developed pneumatic tunneling, an entirely new construction concept for underwater tunneling. Another model is the 1890 St. Clair Tunnel across the St. Clair River between Port Huron, Michigan, and Sarnia, Ontario. This was the world's first major subaqueous tunnel to accommodate full-scale railroad traffic. Three crucial factors distinguished its construction: compressed-air support of the work, a movable shield during construction, and a cast iron permanent lining.

There are displayed in this hall such important drilling tools and mechanisms as the 1861 Sommeiller drill, the 1871 Ingersoll tripod mounting that increased the flexibility of drilling operations, the 1865 Burleigh drill (a successful piston-type drill that operated simply and efficiently), and the Leyner hammer drill that replaced the piston drill. The latter is still used extensively today.

Hall of Electricity (First Floor, East Side)

As a result of the interest aroused when electrical science became popular in the nineteenth century, parlor games (much as electronic games so eagerly played today) were created. One of these games "The Electric Kiss" is illustrated in a diorama that stands at the entrance to the hall.

Electricity as a generator of power has enormously accelerated man's ability to produce and enjoy better physical and material well-being, demonstrated in improved industrial, communication, and transportation systems and the benefits of better health. Early pioneers in electricity like Ohm, Volta, and Ampere have been honored by having their names given to units of electricity. Their discoveries and that of other ingenious scientists and inventors who made enormous contributions to society through their perceptive analysis of the problems involved when working with great perseverance in the fields of electricity, telegraphy and the telephone are described in this hall along with some of the machines, instruments and other artifacts (or patent models, or replicas of them) that they devised.

Among some leaders stimulating and furthering the development of electricity, telegraphy, and the telephone along many avenues in the period between the 1800s and the 1900s and whose works are discussed in this hall are: David E. Hughes, a Kentucky school teacher, who invented an important printing telegraph and whose patent models of it and of a contact transmitter are shown; William Thompson (Lord Kelvin), a British physicist, who made important technical and scientific contributions to the Atlantic cable and devised a sensitive mirror galvonometer which is shown here; Sir Charles Wheatstone, an English physicist who with W.F. Cook began a telegraph system in Great Britain and whose model of a single needle telegraph instrument is shown, as is Wheatstone's early dynamo. It might be of interest to learn that aid in capturing a murderer in England through a telegraph message boosted the need for this invention as a necessary means of communication and was later used by England during the Crimean War. Samuel F.B. Morse, an artist interested in technology, built with his assistant Alfred Vail, a telegraph instrument in 1835 that is discussed and illustrated, and later devised a printing telegraph, illustrated also: Moses Farmer, whose patent model is shown here, a duplex telegraph instrument of 1875. Francis Blake, a skilled craftsman, whose invention of the carbon transmitter, very important to the telephone is discussed. A model is shown of a transmitter by Clement Ader, a Frenchman; other transmitters shown in models are those of a transmitter by Philip Reis, a German school teacher, and a variable resistance tin can transmitter by Emile Berliner. E.S. Ritchie, a Boston instrument maker, designed an induction coil shown here. Other artifacts exhibited include: some precision instruments used in laboratories and devised by C. Poillet of France; the machine built by H. Pixii to get current to flow in one direction (direct current); the dynamo of 1867 designed by W. Ladd of England; another dynamo designed by Zenobe Gramme, a Belgian who in 1870 demonstrated a motor he designed at the Centennial Exhibition in Philadelphia that created quite a stir in this country when it lighted an arc light. There is a reproduction of a Faraday motor that could set up a magnetic effect; a Vermont blacksmith, Charles Davenport, devised a commutator shown here; an Italian designer, Antonio Pacinotti, devised an efficient armature shown here that was later used in motors and generators; and Gustav Froment, a Frenchman, designed a commutator for which he was awarded a prize by Napoleon III.

An entire section in this hall describes the part Edison, "the Wizard of Menlo Park" played in the electrical age, giving by means of photographs, models, and artifacts all carefully labeled a description of his life, his times, and of his work. This is supplemented by a moving picture about this genius-inventor that chronicles further his life and his work. Edison had an incredible number of inventions to his credit, but perhaps his greatest was his light bulb, the incandescent lamp invented in 1879 just over one hundred years ago which led to a whole new system of electrical generation and the distribution of light. Among other of his inventions shown here is a phonograph of 1878 and a carbon-resistance telephone of 1878 shown here in a patent model. Edison was a business entrepreneur, building and selling small lighting systems to light homes and factories for which he developed generators, wires, switches, fuses and meters. He also built larger systems to supply light through a central station, one of which (at 257 Pearl Street in New York City) is shown here in a model.

Another great inventor was Alexander Graham Bell who was by no means the first to devise an instrument capable of transmitting sound, but wisely patented his invention with the U.S. Patent Office which could not be overturned in the courts by Daniel Branbaugh who claimed to have invented a telephone in the 1870s. Artifacts and illustrations are shown of Bell's original photophone (in which a speaker's voice vibrated a mirror that reflected light waves to a distant receiver and were picked up by the receiver cell containing a selenium photo cell). Bell and the man who assisted him, Tainter, obtained a patent in the 1880s. Other earlier telephone designers included: an Italian immigrant to New York, Meucci, who claimed to have invented a telephone in the 1850s; Philip Reis, a German school teacher, who claimed he made an instrument capable of transmitting sound in the 1860s; Francis Blake, who devised a carbon transmitter that was crucial; and Elisha Gray, an electrician, whose work in the 1870s paralleled Bell's but who did not patent it; and others whose models are shown in this hall. Messages were converted into electrical signals with transducers exhibited here. A transducer is a device by means of which energy can flow from one or more transmission systems to one or more other transmission systems. There is a brief moving picture shown of telephones used in old movies that had been made by such companies of early periods as Glen Telephone Co., Northern Electric Manufacturing Co., and Western Electric Co. Other companies are described in exhibits with information about the laboratories they established and training programs in electrical and electronic techniques they established in universities. A section in this hall shows equipment a telephone company used for carrying telephone messages. In the 1960s these companies used communication satellites (models are shown) which provided the means for relaying microwave signals over long distances. These communication satellites were also used by the President and his staff when he made trips outside of Washington in the United States or abroad. A switchboard called Presus, used by the White House staff, is shown in replica here.

Exhibits carefully explain the construction, operation, and utilization of batteries, generators, dynamos, electrostatic machines, motors, meters and other important features that are part of an electrical system; and carefully reading labels supplemented by examining graphs, photographs, models, instruments, and machines will help the layman better understand how they are used. Anyone not acquainted with the many facets of electricity and its language may find this material not easy to comprehend, but if he takes the time to study the labels and carefully examine the explanatory material he will be rewarded for his perseverance.

Theories about electricity did not spring full blown in the eighteenth and nineteenth centuries like the Greek myth of Athene from Zeus' head. Static electricity had been known since the time of Thales (600 B.C.), or perhaps even before, when an individual could by rubbing an amber rod with cloth attract feathers and other objects—an attraction Thales could not explain. Dr. William Gilbert, physician to Queen Elizabeth I, noted in 1600 that a number of materials have forces of attraction he called electricity. Early theories about electricity are discussed in this hall.

On display are several early electrostatic machines, machines that can generate electricity and measure a charge. These include an apparatus made by Charles Coulomb; a quadrant electrometer credited to William Henley; Nicholson's Doubler (1788); Marius von Marum's plate machine (1791); and Edward Nairne's 1794 machine. Later models show Holt's machine (1865); an 1860 Varley; Carre's (1868) machine; and Voss' machine of 1880.

There are several types of Leyden jars exhibited. They were named for the town where they were first invented in 1746 (however, they were independently discovered in 1745 in Camin in what is now Poland). A Leyden jar is essentially a modified plate condenser in the form of a glass jar coated inside and out with metal. Among those exhibited here is one of the one hundred that were used with a friction machine constructed by Marius von Marum in 1784, as well as one reputed to have been used by Benjamin Franklin. The hall also shows a reproduction of Franklin's electric wheel in which an electrostatic generator in the bottom of the case gives a positive or negative charge to the center rod of four Leyden jars and as positively charged thimbles on the wheel approach a negative post it is attracted, then as a spark passes charging the thimbles negatively the wheel is propelled on its way to the next post (positively charged).

Several exhibits explain the works of other early pioneers in the field of electricity and magnetism. In the eighteenth century French physicist Charles Coulomb established the universal law for magnetic attraction now known as Coulomb's law. Hans G. Oersted in experiments in Copenhagen about 1819 made an important discovery of a relationship between electric current and magnetic force that provided the means for detecting a current by its magnetic effect, and a model of some equipment Oersted used is shown. Andre Ampere, French physicist and mathematician, with whom current measurement is associated confirmed and enlarged upon Oersted's work. In this hall, also, is illustrated the work of Michael Faraday who in 1831 was one of the first to devise a simple generator or dyanmo, called a magneto-electric machine. Joseph Henry, the first Secretary of the Smithsonian, in 1830 independently demonstrated the theory of electromagnetic induction using many windings of insulated wire wrapped around an iron core, and with it lifted over 1000 pounds. One of his magnets is shown in this hall. The electromagnet, the basic element in many electrical inventions, was discovered by Henry and Faraday almost simultaneously and enabled men to begin to convert electrical energy into a mechanical force.

The invention of the battery in the beginning of the nineteenth century opened the doors for many new discoveries and inventions. Since a battery could produce a constant electric current it provided power for magnets that led to its use in telegraph, telephone, and machines in many industries. A Voltaic cell, named for its inventor, Alessandro Volta, is exhibited. It consists of two plates of dissimilar metals suspended without touching in a solution of acid or salt with the resulting chemical action producing an electromotive force which, when multiplied, the effect of several pairs of dissimilar metals in solution become a source of electric current such as used in a battery. On display, also, is a reproduction of a Voltaic pile, a Daniell cell, a Leclanache cell, a Gross cell, a Gravity cell, and others; all of these helped increase man's knowledge of electromotive force. The hall provides, too, a reproduction of the experimental apparatus used by analytical chemists A.P. von Troostwijk and J.B. Deiman of Holland in 1787 who were able with this equipment to pass an electric current through water and decompose it into hydrogen and oxygen. Other works shown are Leopoldo Nobili's 1825 precision instrument for measuring electric current, Foucault's of 1855, and Wilhelm Weber's 1840 electro-dynamometer that has a coil inside instead of a magnet. Exhibits follow the efforts of two other great pioneers in the field, Heinrich Hertz and Henry Rowland. The hall contains an illustration of James Clerk Maxwell's theory of the electromagnetic nature of light, as well as reproductions of some of the apparatus he used that provided confirming evidence of his predictions. Luigi Galvani of Bologna was the first to determine in 1791 that electricity was fundamental in certain biological processes. His experiments of the effects of chemicals on electric currents led to important discoveries about animal electricity discussed in this hall. This may have been partly responsible for the invention of several unsuccessful electric medical devices displayed in this hall that attempted to cure a variety of illnesses: an electric eel, a medical battery, and an electrical discharge machine for curing headaches, among others.

When electricity left the lab and was put to work, home appliances were among its earliest practical applications. Exhibits include early washing machines, fans, ironers, toasters, stoves, and heaters. The exhibits of historic and recent advances in generating power and electricity show the advances that scientists and inventors made. These include fuel cells, solar cells, and a display on the conversion of nuclear power to electricity.

In a Discovery Corner in this hall visitors can relax as they hear and see an illustrated lecture about some basic concepts of electricity, especially as it applies to the telephone. Inquire at the Information Desk about the days and time for the lecture in the Discovery Corner.

Hall of Power (Heavy) Machinery (First Floor, East Side)

From the eighteenth to the twentieth centuries steam power ran America and helped shift the economy of the country from a primarily agricultural one to one largely industrial. While steam powered factories and mills had their beginnings in the east, railroads powered by steam locomotives and vessels by steam engines accelerated the west's development of factories and mills, all of these eventually changing the character of the country and the life style of its people from an agrarian to an industrial nation. This hall features steam powered engines as well as some powered by diesel, internal combustion and gas that produced mechanical energy to power machinery. These were assisted by pumps, boilers, generators, and turbines which are also displayed in this hall. The development of refrigeration is still another area traced here.

In "The Period of Speculation" are exhibits which trace man's long fascination and history of experimentation with heat and pressure. One is a demonstration of Torricelli's well-known 1643 experiment, which proved the effect of atmospheric pressure simply by inverting a mercury-filled tube into a dish of mercury. Another, a working model of a device contrived by Heron of Alexandria that opened temple doors, seemingly by magic, but actually operated by priests on the floor below using water, steam and compressed air to manipulate the temple doors.

One of the earliest uses of pumping engines was to clear mines of accumulated water. Shown here are illustrations and some early pumps including: Newcomen Mine Pump of the mid-eighteenth century; the Worthington Pumps of 1840 and 1844; Ericsson's Hot-Air Pumping Engine patented in 1880; DeLaval Centrifugal Pump of 1900; and a model of a Compound Steam Pumping Engine that was designed by E.D. Leavitt, Jr. and used for the Louisville Municiple Water System.

A series of exhibits illustrates the development of steam engines which proved to be prime movers for factory machinery in the Industrial Revolution. It begins in this hall with the Newcomen, a 1712 reciprocating steam engine, the first of the many forerunners of the modern steam engine and one which played an important role in the Industrial Revolution. Other important steam engines shown in models include the Corliss automatic cut-off engine (1848), two Watt lap engines (1788 and 1830), Green's cut-off engine (1857) and Worthington pumps of 1840 and 1889.

Detailed exhibits explain the development of the reciprocating steam engine from 1780 to the present. Pictures and models describe steam engines of increasing efficiency, including Hornblower's (1781); Perkin's Unaflow (1827); Ericsson's Compound Engine (1849); Porter-Allen's 1862 engine; and Corliss' Demonstration Engine (1860). Other large exhibits show: a Westinghouse Compound Engine (1896); a Porter-Allen Engine of 1881 (which was the most successful high-speed steam engine up to that time); and a Shipman Self-Contained Automatic Steam Engine of 1886 which burned liquid fuel or gas.

Steam engines have come in a variety of forms; among those illustrated or shown here are the marine beam engine, the bottle frame engine, the triple expansion engine, and the vertical marine engine. There are illustrations of Shipman's Self-Contained Automatic Steam Engine (1886), Benson's Swash Plate Engine (1847); and models of Ericsson's marine engine (1858), Shlarbaum's Oscillating Engine (1863), and several steamboat engines including Rumsey's of 1789. Among large models of steam engines shown are the Watt's "Lap Engine" of 1788; Balswin's 6 HP Steam Engine of 1829; the Harlan & Hollingsworth's Mill Engine; Holloway's 10 HP Condensing Engine of 1819; Faber's Steam Engine of 1850; the efficient Naylor–Corliss Driving Engine of 1855; models of Trevithick HP Steam Engine of 1805; and Evan's "Columbian" Engine of the early nineteenth century.

Boilers capable of sustaining greater pressures were gradually developed, and these increased the capabilities of steam engines. Among the boilers described in illustrations, models, and specimens are plain and flue boilers, a wooden steam boiler, a riverboat boiler, a fire tube boiler, a locomotive boiler, a Scotch marine boiler, and a once-through boiler (for supercritical pressures). There are also boiler auxiliaries shown: an 1859 piston steam gauge, an injector, a percussion water gauge, a Seller self-acting injector, and a Bailey boiler meter, as well as governors and indicators.

By the early twentieth century turbines began to replace reciprocating engines for driving certain generators. The hall shows examples of three main kinds of turbines: water, steam, and gas. The early development of hydroelectric turbines is illustrated in a diorama. Water turbines are illustrated by models of the 1896 Niagara Falls Hydroelectric Station. Examples of steam turbines include: the Parsons' Turbogenerators of 1884-85 and 1905; DeLaval Steam Turbogenerator of 1893; the Curtis Steam Turbine of 1895; and the Terry Steam Turbine of 1910. Gas turbines are represented by a Boeing Gas Turbine Engine of 1948 that was part of an internal combustion engine.

The gas engines displayed in this hall are representative of those used in the engine rooms of some factories. Among these are the Otto and Langen Atmospheric Gas Engine (1872), the Otto Silent Gas Engine (1880), the Atkinson Cycle Gas Engine (1889), and the Otto Vertical Gas Engine (1895).

Diesel engines invented by Rudolf Diesel and patented in 1892 in Germany have played an important role in American industry. Some of them are illustrated in this hall with some on display that include: a M-A-N Diesel Engine (air injection) of 1903, one of the early engines built by Maschinenfabrik Augusbury of Germany, the firm which assisted Diesel in his basic experiments; part of a three cylinder 120 horsepower American Diesel Engine (air injection) of 1905 that had been connected to a generator and operated until 1958; an Atlas Imperial Marine Diesel Engine (common rail mechanical injection) of 1921; a Caterpillar Diesel Engine of 1930 mass produced by the company for track-type tractors; a Cummins Turbocharged Diesel, a 12 cylinder V-type still used today; and the GM 2-stroke Cycle Diesel, which is a current model used.

The technology necessary for the development of an internal combustion engine was not available until the early twentieth century when mechanics and metallurgists devised engines that were compact, portable, and lightweight. Models of LeBon's proposed gas engine of 1799, the first known design for an internal combustion engine powered by a hydrocarbon fuel, and a 1902 Buick gasoline engine, among others, help trace the development of the internal combustion engine.

A great many full scale power machinery units exhibited in this hall include a ten horsepower Hollaway Condensing Engine (1819), a six horsepower Baldwin Steam Engine (1829), a Boyden Turbine Runner (1844), a Harland and Hollingsworth Mill Engine (1851), a Hendy Rotary Engine (1870), a Backus Water Motor (1874), and an Ericsson Hot Air Pumping Engine (1880). There is a Pelton Impulse Engine (1880), a DeLaval Turbogenerator (1893), and a Porter-Allen high-speed steam engine (1881) that was used to drive an 1885 Edison bi-polar, direct-current generator for steam power for early electric generating plants. A Curtiss Steam Turbine (1895), a Westinghouse Compound Engine (1896) that was used to drive an alternating current generator, a Quimby Screw Pump (1899), and a Riedler Pumping Engine driven by a 1901 Pelton Turbine are also here. Others shown include a Parson Turbogenerator (1903), a Skinner Universal Unaflow Engine (1926), and a compound steam pumping engine built for the Louisville, Kentucky Water System and used from 1883 to 1961. An actual unit of one of nine 12,000 horsepower double compound engines installed for generators to power New York's first subway, the IRT, is shown in the hall. Two of four cylinders are cut away to show the action of the pistons and valves.

Finally, visitors to the hall can trace the development of refrigeration, beginning with natural refrigeration (ice, of course), its use by the Romans, and continuing through the technological advances of modern times. There are shown a Master's Refrigerator patented in 1844; a Monroe Iceless Refrigerator invented in 1871; a Frick Ammonia Compressor of 1898; a Fleus-Raplin Vacuum Machine of 1898; the first four-stage centrifugal compressor built by Willis Carrier in 1922; and a Brunswick-Kroeschall Refrigerator Compressor of about 1925.

Hall of Hand and Machinery Tools (First Floor, East Side)

Coppersmiths, wheelwrights, blacksmiths, and woodworkers in the eighteenth and nineteenth centuries laboriously performed tasks with hand tools that were later accomplished with greater speed and precision by machines. These hand tools and the machines that eventually replaced some of them are shown in this hall. Some machine processes began as early as 1775; a model of Wilkinson's 1775 boring mill illustrates how early inventors developed better methods for tooling. Other exhibits illustrate the development of grinding, cutting, planing, broaching, and milling machines which have greatly increased a host of important and useful products. Standards for measurement were very important especially in the making of interchangeable parts for products.

Among the many hand tools of the traditional trades of the eighteenth and nineteenth centuries displayed in this hall are cooper's tools (beetle, hoop-tightener, craw knife, croze, sun plane, splitting froe, cooper's adz); wheelwright's tools (spoke tenon-cutter, spoke pointer, wheel hub, marking gauge, and spoke shave); carpenter's woodworking tools (mitre, mallet, square, bevel, plumb bob, bob drill, gimlet, gauge, chisel, auger, plane, brace and bit, hammer, screw driver, pliers, and saw); and blacksmith's tools (swage box, hoof-parer, pincer, hot cutter, cold cutter, and cold chisel).

Original and reproductions of machines or scale models of them on view in this hall include Eli Whitney's power-fed milling machine (about 1818) that he once used in his gun factory. A reproduction of Blanchard's gunstock lathe (1821) that was used in the production of gunstocks was very important for it was one of the earliest machines to produce interchangeable parts and contributed to increased American productivity. Lincoln's milling machine (about 1860) was first used to make firearm parts and later parts for sewing machines and other light machinery parts. A multi-spindle drilling machine patented in 1905 drilled holes for cash registers, typewriters, and sewing machines. A centerless grinding machine shown here was invented by Louis Heim in 1918, and an operating model of Dr. John Ireland's automatic pin-making machine (1838) is the first such pin-maker we and probably most other visitors have ever seen.

Also on display are historic ornamental turning lathes driven by foot pedals, including one made by Matthew Lambert Xhourst, a Belgian artisan in the service of the Duke of Lorraine; a 1794 lathe by John Jacob Holtzapffel; an English lathe dated 1800-1850; and an 1809 English lathe used in the Smithsonian Experimental Shop during the development of Samuel Langley's heavier-than-air aircraft. Other historic machines shown here are a universal milling machine designed by Joseph R. Brown which was a landmark in milling machine development; Fellow's 1900 gear shaper; a universal grinding machine of 1885 designed by Abraham Landis; an automatic screw machine (1888) developed by Christopher Spencer; and several other early automatic screw machines.

Man has felt the need to arrive at methods for measuring a great many kind of things including weight, time, speed, electrical and mechanical force, and length. Measurements for length, for example, were reckoned differently in different countries: the cubit was used in Egypt, the foot rule in Rome, and the rod in Germany. In this country beginning in 1838 brass copies of the national standard yard were supplied to the states by the Treasury's Office of Weights and Measurements (a copy of which is shown here). Later when the meter was recognized as an alternative length unit, the Office of Weights and Measurements supplied the states with standard meters (also shown).

During the Civil War weapon manufacturers in the North began to make interchangeable parts. It was the beginning of that process that proved so important in this and other countries. Today interchangeable parts are used in the manufacturing of automobiles, bicycles, sewing machines, etc., making the parts for each unit much more economical to produce. It is necessary, however, for these manufacturers to have parts that are accurately sized. This has led to the use of precise shop measurement instruments like micrometers, calipers, bench micrometers, lightwave micrometers, snap gauges, screw and pipe thread gauges, toolmaker gauges, screw thread comperators and other types of precise measuring instruments which are shown in an exhibit.

Among the smaller-scale exhibits are items such as an 1859 automatic graduating machine invented by J.R. Brown which can correct its own inaccuracies; a Rogers-Bond universal comperator (1850); and several screw cutting lathes. There is an illustration of a screw cutting lathe made by Leonardo da Vinci about 1500, Ramsden's 1774 screw cutting lathe, and a model of Wilkinson's 1798 screw cutting lathe. There are also gear cutting devices, including a replica of a geared astrolabe (1221-1222), and an illustration of elliptical gears (1348). Visitors can also see such items as mill gears of the sixteenth century, Polheim's 1729 gear cutting engine, a 1775 Ramsden-Hobbs gear cutting machine, and Brown and Sharp's formed milling cutter of 1854.

The exhibit on metal cutting depicts a process first begun in England and Germany between 1870 and 1880. Various dynamometers are on display. A small diorama depicts the Bethlehem Metallurgical Laboratory of 1900. Another exhibit traces the evolution of the milling cutter. Historically, milling processes required both milling machines and file cutting machines, and illustrated is the earliest milling machines in this country built before 1840 by Gay and Silver of Massachusetts. A model of a Leonardo da Vinci file cutting machine of about 1500 reconstructed from his sketches, and a patent model of an 1873 file cutting machine are on display.

Wilkinson's 1775 boring machine was important to James Watts in the development of his steam engine. There is a model of Wilkinson's boring machine and also a model of an 1875 angle boring machine that could bore heavy timbers for the construction of bridges and other large structures shown in the hall.

The display of planing tools illustrates how they evolved from simple wooden planing tools to modern machinery. There are several different broaching tools, including a 1940 push broaching tool, and a model of an 1870 planing machine. A diorama shows the planing of printing press ribs in 1835. A Daniel's Wood Planer of 1860 was of a type used almost for a century in this country because it was so versatile and accurate. Other large machines displayed show an early Universal Grinding Machine of 1883, a Universal Milling Machine of 1865, and a Fellow's Gear Shaper of 1900.

The Philadelphia tool shop of John White has been recreated in a small diorama. Mr. White's 1816 invention, the press screw, was first used for pressing seeds for vegetable oil. It was later used for compressing tobacco and cotton bundles.

Visitors to this hall can view a completely outfitted mid-nineteenth century machine shop, restored to operating condition. The machine tools on display are labeled, and visitors are invited to pick up the telephone receivers on the ledge of the open side of the shop and hear the story of the shop and its equipment. Museum docents give demonstrations on the uses of these tools. Please consult the bulletin boards or inquire at Information Desk for dates and times of these demonstrations.

Hall of Timekeeping and Light Machinery (Including Clocks, Watches, Typewriters, Phonographs, and Locks) (First Floor, West Side)

Long before he invented clocks, man had devised other means for measuring and indicating time. Mechanical clocks were finally developed in Europe in the late thirteenth century; it was not until the eighteenth century, however, that watches came on the scene. Visitors who have the time can review the history of timekeeping devices in this hall, as well as the development of typewriters, phonographs, and locks.

The sundial was one of many predecessors of the clock. On display here is a large, rare, bronze Chinese sundial, the only one of its type known to exist in the Western hemisphere. There is a portable Saxon dial of the tenth century, an Egyptian dial (tenth to eighth centuries B.C.), a hemispherical dial (about 270 B.C.), Indo-Persian astrolabes of the seventeenth century, a universal ring dial (1710), and a diptych or folding dial (1613). American sundials (1760 and 1779), a nineteenth century Chinese folding dial, and a Japanese folding dial are also exhibited.

Since sundials were useful only on clear days, mankind created waterclocks in an attempt to offset the sundials's limitations. An Egyptian waterclock (about 330 B.C.) is on exhibit, together with a Roman waterclock, and a rewindable nineteenth century waterclock. Other predecessors of mechanical clocks are shown in this hall: graduated candles (said to have been used by King Alfred), burning rope, incense sticks, candlenuts strung on a reed, and an hourglass or sandglass that was unaffected by weather or temperature and could be used day or night, on land or at sea.

Mechanical clocks can be dated from 1286, when mechanical figures that struck a bell on the hour were first installed in St. Paul's cathedral in London. More precise mechanisms became available in 1656 with the invention and patent of a pendulum clock by Holland's Christian Huygens. Later devices, such as hair springs, balance wheels, and escapements further refined clockworks and improved their accuracy. There are displays of a Gothic clock (about 1500), a recoil anchor escapement clock (1671), a Russian calendar clock (about 1880), and some very interesting Japanese timekeeping devices. There is also a copy of the Riesler clock built in the 1890s and several electronic clocks, superior in accuracy to mechanical clocks.

Among the more unusual clocks is an astronomical clock (South Tyrol, 1764) designed by Father Borghesi and built by Antoine Bertolla, and a reconstruction of an earlier astronomical clock, devised by Giovanni De'Dondi in 1364. There is a wooden tower clock built about 1830, an orrery, an electrochronograph invented by John Locke in 1848, and several types of atomic clocks. One atomic clock, of quartz crystal, is an experimental atomic-beam tube clock (1955); another is an atomic frequency standard clock (1960).

When in 1759 Thomas Mudge of London devised the lever escapement, the development of pocketwatches took a long step forward. The hall shows examples and information about such features of watchmaking as compensation balance wheels, cylindrical, ball, and Dreguet hair springs, and the uses of oil and jewels. Pocket watches from Europe and America are on display in a wide variety.

John Harrison's chronometer won the prize Britain's parliament offered in 1769 for the development of such an instrument (a timepiece or timing device with a special mechanism for ensuring and adjusting its own accuracy—of some importance in determining longitude). Harrison's chronometers are on exhibit, and a chronometer shop exhibit contains the machinery and furnishings of William Bond of Boston. The first to make a chronometer in the United States, Bond and his sons became the leading American manufacturers of chronometers.

Typewriters are of a considerably more recent vintage than clocks. In 1714 a patent for a typewriter was issued in England to Henry Mills, and one to William Burt in the United States in 1829, but it was a typewriter patented by Sholes, Glidden and Soule in 1868 and put on the market by Remington in 1878 that proved to be the first practical model. Historic typewriters exhibited here include Burt's typographer (1829), Thurber's 1843 typewriter, Beech's 1856 typewriter, and Pratt's typewriter of 1868. Hansen's 1872 typewriter and Remington's of 1878 are shown among the historic models, along with an 1883 Caligraph, an 1893 Blickensderfer, an 1888 Columbia, an 1892 Williams, an 1894 Oliver, an 1897 Underwood, a 1908 Remington, and a Hammond of 1914. The historic exhibits of typewriters continue tracing their development through the electric typewriters of today.

Visitors to this hall can also discover the development of phonographs and other types of sound-recording equipment. The displays include the first machine of Edison's to reproduce recorded sound (1877) and Berliner's disk record player (1887), which he called a gramophone. There are Berliner hand-operated gramophones (about 1897 and 1899) and a Bell and Tainter Graphophone (1887). The Thomas MacDonald graphophone (1898) was compact and featured a spring drive motor; the Victor Talking Machine (1903), a five cent coin-operated machine (1898), an Edison phonograph (about 1903), and the Victor Orthophonic (1925) are all on display.

Another exhibit features some of the Volta Laboratory's experimental apparatus used between 1880 and 1886 for sound research. The Volta Laboratory for Sound Research was established by Alexander Graham Bell with the $10,000 Volta prize awarded by the French government for Bell's invention of the telephone. Among the experimental apparatus here is an experimental recorder with a metal diaphragm; a tool for turning a record blank before recording; a notebook kept by Charles F. Tainter describing his work at the Volta Laboratory; and an experimental disk-type machine. A wall mural portrays some famous recording artists including Heifitz, Kreisler, Elman, Scotti, Melba, and Ferrar.

Finally, the hall leads the visitor from the opening of the possibilities of sound to the shutting of doors, as exhibits trace the origins and development of locks. A bar fastened from the inside must have been among the first locking devices; the need to operate the inside bar from the outside presumably dictated the next advance. Displayed here are locks and bolts found at archeological sites including an Egyptian-type lock (about 2000 B.C.), a Grecian lock (about 700 B.C.), a door lockbolt (about 100 B.C.) found at Herculaneum, and a container lockbolt (about 100 A.D.) found in Austria. A mural shows a 1698 locksmith at his forge and filing and fitting together parts of a lock; and on exhibit are tools used by early locksmiths including a vise (about 1800), seventeenth century dividers and screw cutting tools.

An eighteenth-century French locksmith still advertises his wares, his sign on display in this hall. Locks entered their modern age in 1778 when Robert Barron introduced tumblers. Locks of this and other periods on display include a Bramah lock (1784), a Chubb lock of 1818 and a Savage lock (1847). New materials and new engineering led to more secure locking devices, as illustrated by Linus Yale's 1884 development of the cylinder lock, which had a radial pin tumbler. Among the Yale locks on display is a 1954 electric combination lock.

(This hall has been undergoing renovation. When it reopens the exhibits may not be the same as those described above, some will be missing. However, a sufficient number of them will probably be there for the interested visitor and with these there will be new ones which will, undoubtedly, also be worth investigating.)

Foucault Pendulum (First Floor, Central Area)

The Foucault pendulum, one of the most popular exhibits in the Museum of American History, demonstrates the earth's rotation on its axis. The device was first demonstrated in 1851 by Jean B.L. Foucault, a French physicist, who suspended a pendulum in the Pantheon in Paris and traced its path in sand on the floor. The suspended Smithsonian Foucault pendulum appears to swing clockwise as it moves. A pin at the end of the pendulum's bob knocks down, in turn, pegs set up around a marble ring on the floor. A label points out that while the direction of the plane of oscillation appears to change, it is actually the floor beneath the pendulum that has rotated.

Water-Powered Sawmill (First Floor, Central Area)

This display includes the carriage, saw, and gearing from a nineteenth-century sawmill, which was powered by a waterfall. It was originally located in eastern Pennsylvania.

Hall of Mathematics, Instruments, and Computer Devices (First Floor, West Side)

A piece of clay tablet shown in this hall was used by a Babylonian merchant to calculate interest. From earliest times the human mind had devised a variety of systems to represent and arrange quantities. These systems range from elementary arithmetic (the mathematics of numerical quantities), to algebra (the theory of whole numbers and properties), and geometry (spatial quantities), to calculus and its analytic methods. The exhibits in this hall emphasize the application of mathematics to other branches of knowledge, such as medicine, agriculture, meteorology, physics, space, and computer science.

Early on man developed devices to aid him in his calculations. Many of these devices are shown here, primarily in replicas or illustrations: Japanese and Chinese abacuses; an ancient Greek counting table; the counting rods or "bones" of John Napier (1550-1617); Gunter's 1620 slide rule (a forerunner of the modern slide rule); a section of Blaise Pascal's simple adding machine (1642); Leibnitz's improved mechanism (about 1672) for multiplication by repeated addition; and the Thomas (1820) and Tates (1895) arithmometers which could be used for adding, subtracting, multiplying, and dividing. Other early calculating machines shown are Odner (1875) and Marchant (1925). Later came the cranked, key-set adding machine patented by W.S. Burroughs in 1890, the Dalton adding machine (1909), the Monroe (1915), Bolles (1889), and the Mercedes-Euclid (1923) calculating machines displayed here. The brilliant English mathematician, Charles Babbage, a contemporary of Sir John Herschel, designed a Difference Engine #1 in 1823 (a portion of which is shown in reproduction) which was a calculating machine. It was a forerunner of present-day calculating machines, but was never completed because materials and skills essential to its construction were not available until the next century. Also shown is Scheutz's Difference Engine #1 (a machine in transit to the modern computers) which was built in 1853. Scheutz had been inspired by an account of Babbage's Difference Engine.

The Hollerith Tabulating Machine was developed by Herman Hollerith who developed in the 1880s this electro-mechanical machine shown here for data processing. It handled punched cards and was first used by the census departments in the United States and abroad. With the use of this machine it was possible to publish the results of a census in one year instead of taking up to ten. It was later able to perform many other statistical recording tasks.

Also displayed here are several harmonic analyzers and synthesizers, integrating machines that determine the components of a curve; the Michelson-Straten Harmonic Analyzer (about 1898); the Henrici-Coradi (also about 1898); the Kelvin Harmonic Synthesizer (1872); the Kelvin Harmonic Analyzer (1876); and the Mader-Ott

Harmonic Analyzer (1931) can be seen here. The Tide Predictor built in 1882 by William Ferrell, an employee of the United States Coast Guard and Geodetic Survey, was used to prepare tide tables the agency published between 1883 and 1910 and is also shown in this hall.

Computers are today electronic machines capable of handling information in its memory banks that make it possible to do certain tasks beyond the capacity of man to do easily, and that can retrieve information with lightning speed. It accomplishes, for example, cost effective systems in a plant that might take men two weeks or more to do which the computer can do in one day or less.

Analog computers solve problems that can be represented by differential equations. A mechanical analog computer (important parts of which are shown here) was developed in 1930 by Vannevar Bush and his associates at the Massachusetts Institute of Technology. It was called the Bush Mechanical Differential Analyzer to solve mathematical problems that are represented by differential equations. Mechanical analog computers have now been replaced by electronic analog computers, whose operations aid in the design of motor vehicles, hydraulic devices, gas turbines, electronic circuits, and other machinery.

Digital computers help in obtaining numerical solutions to scientific problems, and in data processing in general. The first digital computer, Mark I (shown here) built at Harvard University in 1944 had a controlled sequence of mathematical operations. Mark I was called Preceptron, a preceptron, as explained here, "is composed of a neural network with sensory association and response signals, generating units for receiving and transmitting signals and for connecting with other units in the network." The Eniac was the first electronic digital computer. It was built in 1946 at the University of Pennsylvania for the military to calculate ballistic machines. It is exhibited here along with parts of another electronic digital computer, the Whirlwind. The Whirlwind was built at Massachusetts Institute of Technology and has an unbelievably long string of "firsts" to its credit described in the exhibit.

The IAS computer was designed and built at the Institute for Advanced Studies. In the early 1950s, John von Neumann and other scientists and engineers worked on an electrostatic memory machine. Parts of their IAS computer are on exhibit here. In the mid-1950s and later, companies like IBM started getting into solid state computers instead of using vacuum tubes because they were cheaper to operate. In 1965 prices for solid state transistor components dropped and companies began to build mini-computers. Later when complete systems could be packaged in $1\frac{1}{2}$ inch square chips, the prices went down still further. The exhibit traces these changes.

The hall also displays material on the computers used by space scientists for such tasks as determining flight paths, processing information from space, performing astronomical calculations, and analyzing the bodily reactions and health of humans or animals on a space project. Exhibited is the Atlas guidance computer Mod-I, a computer that tracks space vehicles. It provided ground guidance for many satellite launchings and several Atlas ICBM tests, including the first successful full-range Atlas missile flight. Among the satellites launched with the help of the Atlas guidance computer Mod-I was the SCORE communication satellite, the first to transmit a human voice from outer space.

There have now been devised robots controlled by mechanisms on computers attached to them that are capable of doing simple, automatic tasks such as men have been doing in factories on assembly lines. In the medical field micrometers control prosthesis, and in industry computers are bringing startling new achievements such as computers that can talk to each other, or double check on each other for accuracy and security.

Hall of Physical Sciences (First Floor, West Side)

Thomas Jefferson, our third President and the author of the Declaration of Independence, was a versatile man. In addition to being a political thinker he was a diplomat, an architect, a scientific farmer, an inventor, a lover of music who played the violin, and had, among other things, a profound interest in the sciences. For example, his interest in meteorology led him to make and record daily observations of temperature, rainfall and winds that has provided some notable scientific data of his times. Also, as an amateur astronomer, he made precise observations of the heavens with telescopes and clocks he kept in his study for this purpose. Note is taken of some of these scientific pursuits of Jefferson in this hall.

Photography is critical to the recording of astronomical observations and on exhibit in this hall are early astronomical photographs made in the United States. There are several star photographs taken by Lewis Rutherfurd in 1868, and a daguerreotype of the sun and the moon made in 1860 by John Draper who was also successful in taking the first daguerreotype of the diffraction spectrum of the sun, all shown in this hall. Henry Draper, John's son, photographed the moon, the sun and distant stars. The work these men did is explained in an exhibit.

In this hall visitors can explore the history and accounts of some of the discoveries made in the physical sciences: astronomy, meteorology, seismology, geodesy, oceanography, hydrography, surveying, and physics (including optics). Each discipline is illustrated with scientific instruments, many of which were built by the scientists themselves, but more often were crafted by skillful instrument makers. There are also shown some scientific apparatus that had once been used in teaching the sciences in American colleges and universities. The collection that is on display includes a whirling table used to explain the motion of planets around the sun that came from the United States Military Academy; a refracting telescope which scanned the skies for comets and other celestial curiosities that came from Georgetown University; a wave demonstrator which showed how a to-and-fro motion could produce a forward traveling wave that came from the University of Georgia; an electroscope which could detect the presence of an electric charge that came from Columbia University; and other instruments that came from other institutions.

Early documented scientific instruments dating back to medieval times show the art and the progress of the instrument makers. Tycho Brahe (1541-1601) designed the equatorial armillary reproduced here that could determine the equatorial coordinates of a star. An exhibit "The Art of the Instrument Maker 1150-1850" displays and describes astrolabes used by the Persians in the twelfth century, some used by the Moors in the thirteenth century, the English in the fifteenth century, as well as other early astrolabes. Other instruments shown include a level used by the Germans in the sixteenth century and other early levels; an armillary sphere of Italian origin in the sixteenth century; early quadrants, dials, astronomical compendiums, sectors, sun dials, compasses, orreries, a Dutch perpetual calendar of the seventeenth century, and other instruments. The meridian circle invented in the late seventeenth century shows the relative positions of stars by accurately measuring their passage across the meridian. A copy of Ramsden's dividing engine for which he applied for a patent in 1775 is shown. Two of Henry A. Rowland's inventions are exhibited: the ruling or dividing engine which is a precision instrument operated by a long micrometer screw whose diamond point makes parallel lines on a curved surface; and an invention setting rules on a spherical surface making it possible to obtain a real spectrum without a lens. Rowland was a physicist at Johns Hopkins University and was responsible for beginning the technique of precision ruling.

Newton's reflecting telescope, which used a curved mirror instead of a lens, is shown in replica. Telescopes made between 1850 and 1890 are shown, some of them still used today. There is an equatorial telescope and a reflecting telescope moved by clockwork that keeps a fix on the astronomical object it is following, that is displayed. A full-scale reconstruction of the interior of Henry Fitz's late nineteenth century telescope-making shop is shown in this hall.

Exhibits illustrate how meteorology developed in the nineteenth and twentieth centuries. These include descriptions of work done by Joseph Henry, first Secretary of the Smithsonian. Among the many instruments displayed are barometers, thermometers, and hygrometers that James Green made for the United States Naval Observatory, the United States Weather Bureau, and the United States Military Academy. There are also reproductions of an early wind vane and a rain gauge. There is a French barograph; Daniel Draper's balance barograph for recording temperature, humidity, rain and snow fall; an electrical barograph (about 1865) by G.W. Hough; a mechanical barograph by C.F. Marvin of the United States Weather Bureau (1904); and the aneroid barograph developed by Maltheus Hipp of Switzerland (about 1871). A meteorograph developed about 1890 by the United States Weather Bureau recorded on a revolving drum information about sunshine, rainfall, and wind direction and velocity. Also exhibited are several balloon meteorographs, a kite meteorograph, and radiosondes, which take meteorological measurements at high altitudes and radio the information to recording stations on earth.

Geodesy is the branch of applied mathematics which determines the exact position of various points, as well as the shape and size of large portions of the earth's surface. The displays on geodesy include discussions of geomagnetism, and of the important work of the United Coast Guard Geodesy Survey. Oceanography and hydrography are represented in exhibits by such artifacts as an ocean bottom core sampler, apparatus for sounding the depths of water, tide and river gauges, and current meters described by Henry, Ott, and Price.

Surveying exhibits contain British and colonial American surveying instruments, including theodolites of many kinds including transit compasses and transit mounted telescopes. A diorama depicts Andrew Ellicott and Benjamin Banneker surveying the northwest boundary of the District of Columbia. The actual instruments they used are on display in this diorama.

Nineteenth century optical instruments include goniometers for measuring the angle that one crystal face makes with another; polariscopes which are devices for producing and measuring the effects of polarized light which help one better understand crystalline structures; and spectroscopes which can focus light on a prism or grating to produce a color spectrum, all of these are shown in an exhibit and their uses are explained. The front of Benjamin Pike's nineteenth-century optical instrument shop is reproduced here. Nearby is a display of some instruments used and produced in this shop.

An exhibit describes some of the work of Albert Michelson, the first American Nobel Prize winner. It was Michelson who developed an interferometer to measure minute differences in the speed of light along different paths. Michelson worked to perfect machinery for diffraction gratings in order to produce spectrums for accurate optical work. One of his interferometers is exhibited.

Large dioramas contain reproductions of two chemical laboratories typical of their periods. A very simple 1790 laboratory contains glassware that had been owned by Joseph Priestly after he came to America in 1794. It was Priestly who isolated and described the gases oxygen, ammonia, chlorine, sulfur dioxide, and hydrochlorine, contributing a great deal to the reformation of chemistry through his research on these gases. The 1876 chemical laboratory across the hall was modeled after one used by Ira Remsen, first chemistry professor and later president of Johns Hopkins University which was one of the first American institutions devoted to research. The equipment shown in this diorama did not actually belong to Remsen, but is authentic for the period of 1876.

Hall of the History of Medicine, Dentistry, Pharmacology, and Health (First Floor, West Side)

A series of displays and period rooms illuminate the history of medicine and several attendant healing arts dating from Greek and Roman times to the present. In addition to medicine, dentistry, bacteriology, and pharmacology are discussed in this hall. The exhibits profile many key figures in the medical arts, along with their observations, instruments, and working environments.

Before the practice of medicine was established, there was only magic and superstition—although these last exist even today for a few people around the world. Displayed in this hall are exhibits of various superstitious practices and the magical devices people created to ward off "the evil eye" in order to protect themselves against ills that might befall them. Since there is no scientific basis for the use of amulets, talismans, fetishes, and charms they are shown here to expose them as valueless. Primitive peoples all over the world have relied on magic for preventing or curing diseases. Other people use "touch pieces" or copies of "hurt" areas for healing. Superstitions like the effect of madstones, cramp rings (made from nails taken from a coffin), or sacred writings have also been used. Phrenology and other quackery have also been employed as a means of helping the sick. All are fakes and never have been known to help anyone. The hall also exhibits apparatus used by unscrupulous or naive inventors in an attempt to treat physical, muscular, and nervous disorders. One of these demonstrates an 1895 electrotherapeutic static machine, which administered a static "spray" or "breeze" (an electric charge) that was supposed to have curative powers.

Even following medical advice, one man's treatment is not another's, however. Visitors might be hesitant to follow the 2100 B.C. prescription found here, in replica, impressed on a Sumerian clay tablet. The exhibit also includes some of the earliest known medical writings which show reproductions of two works by the Greek physician Galen (second century A.D.), whose writings remained in standard medical texts until the eighteenth century.

Physicians have always had need for a variety of instruments. There are some displayed that were used in past ages and others now in current usage for physical examinations. Among the replicas of antique instruments are several types of speculums found in Pompeii, replicas of an ear speculum (about 1610), and a sixteenth-century mouth speculum. Modern mechanical and electrical speculums such as the ottoscope are on display, as are the perforated concave mirrors, devised by Frederick Hoffman of Germany, that concentrate light into a body cavity. There are endoscopes and bronchoscopes, laryngo-scopes and stethoscopes, opthalmoscopes and sphygmomanometers (blood pressure instruments). As instruments became more precise and sophisticated, they became increasingly useful for diagnosis and treatment.

Modern surgery advanced greatly with the advent of anes-thetics. The pioneers of anesthesia are profiled here: Horace Wells, William Morton, and Crawford Long. There are displays of modern anesthesia machines which anesthetists are specially trained to use. Patients have also benefitted from the development of antiseptic techniques, here illustrated by a replica of Lister's spray apparatus (1870) for carbolic acid, used to prevent septic infection. Displays discuss methods devised to control bleeding during surgery, and recent improvements in equipment such as surgical knives (some newer types are plastic and disposable), and surgical drills, shown here, invented in the 1960s by Dr. Robert V. Hall. A small diorama recreates the 1805 operating amphitheater at the University of Pennsylvania where Dr. Philip S. Physick, the "Father of American Surgery," operated on a patient, removing a parotid-glandular tumor without anesthetics while other prominent physicians looked on. A surgical milestone was made when artificial heart valves were implanted for damaged ones. A discussion and illustration of this procedure is shown in an exhibit along with the instruments used for doing the surgery. There is also a discussion with illustrations of deep brain surgery done in the 1950s.

America's first trained nurse, Linda Richards, is the subject of a diorama. She is shown caring for a patient at the Massachusetts General Hospital in Boston in 1875. Massachusetts General Hospital was the third hospital in the United States to give nurses' training.

Pharmaceuticals are still used by physicians as one of the most common treatments for illness. The display of an eighteenth-century, old-world apothecary shop is filled with rows of elegant, highly decorated drug jars, many of them used in pharmacies of the sixteenth to the eighteenth centuries. Many of these have been donated or carefully collected by curators in this department of the Smithsonian. Also in the shop are balances, mortars and pestles, and other pharmaceutical equipment. In the back laboratory visitors get a glimpse of a tortoise, a fish, a stuffed crocodile, and other curiosities reputedly used as part of some antique remedies. An 1830 drugstore, once located in Washington, D.C. on Eighth and I Streets, is now restored in this hall. The view from the front reveals patent medicines, cosmetics, hygenic supplies, and other merchandise generally carried in nineteenth-century apothecary shops. Visitors can also catch a glimpse of the pharmacist's laboratory at the back of the store.

On display is apparatus used in the manufacture of pharmaceuticals. A copper percolator is shown (c. 1890) that was used to extract soluble ingredients from powdered medicinal plants, as is a Lloyd's Cold Still (1904), a still percolator to extract plant products which could not take the heat of ordinary distillation; and a drug mill machine (second half of the nineteenth century) for making powdered drugs. Other displays show the machines that first made medicinal dosage forms, thus revolutionizing drug manufacture. Included here are tablet presses, a suppository mold, and a capsulating machine. Another exhibit discusses the development of such antibiotics as penicillin, aureomycin, achromycin, streptomycin, and chloromycetin. A 1945 submerged fermentation device is shown that is similar to ones used in the original manufacture of penicillin. There is also an agitation device, used in antibiotic production. A display explains and illustrates the origins of drugs while a nearby exhibit gives a list of drugs from A (for ambergris) to Z (for zinc acetate). There are some beautiful drug jars displayed. They begin with Egyptian-Grecian jars dated from 300 B.C. to 500 B.C.; Phoenician (200 B.C.) and Roman (from 100 B.C. to 100 A.D.); the Near East drug jars developed in the Middle Ages in Syria and Persia; examples of Hispano-Moresque drug jars from the sixteenth century; Italian Majolica jars of the sixteenth century; French Faience jars of the eighteenth and nineteenth centuries; German faience and glass jars of the seventeenth and eighteenth; Dutch delft jars of the eighteenth century; English Lambeth Delft of the seventeenth and eighteenth centuries; and American glass jars of the nineteenth and twentieth centuries. There are also some porcelain drug jars from France of the nineteenth century; England of the nineteenth century; and Vienna of the eighteenth and nineteenth centuries.

The reproduction of a 1905 bacteriological research laboratory in this hall contains items that once belonged to Simon Flexner, the first director of the Rockefeller Institute of Medicine. In this bacteriological laboratory are also some tools and research apparatus that belonged to Frederick Novy, a University of Michigan microbiologist who had worked with Louis Pasteur and Robert Koch and who had brought back equipment from their laboratories in Europe. Many of the artifacts in this exhibit were donated by the University of Michigan.

A section of this hall is devoted to the development of the microscope that begins with replicas of early models. Among these are instruments made by the seventeenth-century Italian Giuseppe Compagni, Anton von Leeuwenhoek (1632-1690) of Holland, and Robert Hooke (1635-1703) of England. Among the microscopes on display are a Culpepper-type (1740), a Nuremberg microscope (about 1750), a screw-barrel microscope (about 1760), a compass microscope (about 1800), an aquatic microscope (about 1820), a binocular microscope (about 1875), a Bausch and Lomb (about 1880), and a Zeiss (about 1925).

The work of several scientists who made important contributions to medical knowledge through microscopic studies is discussed. A number of these men lived in Germany: Johannes Muller (1801-1858) the founder of scientific medicine in Germany; Theodore Schwann (1801-1882) who propounded the theory that all living animals are composed of cells; Rudolph Virchow (1821-1902) who traced the pathology of several diseases to altered conditions within the cell; Robert Koch (1843-1910) whose contributions to bacteriology earned him a Nobel Prize; and Paul Ehrlich (1854-1915) who developed a chemotherapeutic cure for syphillis. Theobald Smith (1859-1934) an American bacteriologist who pioneered in the study of allergies, and Louis Pasteur (1820-1895) of France who laid the foundations of modern bacteriology have their work also discussed here.

The history of X-rays, so important a tool in modern medicine is traced here. The German physicist Wilhelm Roentgen discovered X-ray in 1895, a discovery for which he won a Nobel Prize. An X-ray tube used by Roentgen during some of his later experiments is displayed here. X-ray was first used by physicians to detect fractures and foreign objects; with improvements it later could reveal most of the internal organs, and later became a tool for destroying certain malignant growths. An exhibit discusses the work of Dr. Edmund Kells who began to use X-rays for dental examinations in 1898. He was unaware of the need to shield himself from the rays and died from excessive exposure. The development of modern X-ray tubes and equipment that is improved in safety and quality is shown with the new equipment and illustrations that discuss them.

A section in this hall illustrates and exhibits resuscitation equipment and techniques that have been used to aid and restore breathing. Creating perhaps the first mechanical breathing aid was Paracelsus of Switzerland in 1530 who used ordinary fireplace bellows to help restore breathing. Bellows were also used by John Hunter in Britain about 1775. James Currie in 1815 developed one of the first tubes for insertion into the windpipe. Illustrations of resuscitators include cabinets made in 1840, 1876, and 1906. A full-sized iron lung of 1931 was a modification of the Drinkwater respirator of 1928.

Electrocardiography's contribution to healing lies in the detection of disease. Exhibits recount the work of such leaders in this field as Carlo Matteucci of Italy, Albert von Kalliker of Switzerland, Sir John Samuelson and August Waller of England, and Willem Einthover of Holland who received a Nobel Prize for devising a string galvanometer to record the electrical activity of the heart. The work of Frank Wilson in electrocardiography of the United States, and others are also discussed. Instruments on exhibit include the Williams-Hindel

galvanometer (1914), a Beck-Lee electrocardiograph (1937), and a
direct writing electrocardiograph (1954). Visitors will find on display
a book called **Daniel Hale Williams, Negro Surgeon** that was written
by Helen Buckler and profiles a great American surgeon and pioneer
in open heart surgery. The informative exhibit "Pain and Its Relief"
will be on display for a long time.

The assistance given patients by mechanical heart pumps
is described in several exhibits. Displayed is the Lindbergh-Carrel
pump which greatly added to the knowledge of organ functions and
of the conditions necessary for the maintenance of life. Lindbergh
worked with Dr. Alexis Carrel of the Rockefeller Institute in the
1930s to develop this perfusion pump, the first step in the creation
of a heart-lung machine designed to keep isolated organs alive outside
the body. Part of the experimental mechanical heart pump built by
Dr. William Sewell, Jr. in 1950 is shown. Also on display is the machine
built in 1952 by Dr. Forest Dodrill and his team of medical investigators
and engineers at the General Motors Research Laboratories. This
machine was the first to successfully bypass one side of the heart
during surgery.

"Rehabilitation: Triumph Over Disability" is an exhibit that
follows the development of rehabilitative medicine for patients who
have been the victims of disabling illnesses from blindness to heart
disease. The exhibit attempts to provide information about the kinds
of treatment and training for these people that is available in an
effort to restore as much normalcy to their conditions as is physically
possible. Among the exhibits are gymnastic apparatus, prosthetics,
pacemakers, mechanical hearts, and other aids. Exhibits highlight
famous Americans, among them Franklin D. Roosevelt and Helen
Keller, who overcame physical disabilities. At one time there was
on display the rocking chair used by John F. Kennedy. A Discovery
Corner in this hall gives visitors an opportunity to examine and operate
limbs and other devices made for the handicapped and to recognize
their use as important tools which handicapped people can use as
tools for living. Seeing these should help dispel fears and psychological
barriers against physically handicapped people.

The exhibit on eye care and the conservation of vision contains
a collection of eyeglasses and describes their probable invention about
1300 in Italy. The collection includes Chinese spectacles and others
from many countries around the world: lorngettes, spectacle frames
from the 1720s to the present, and modern bifocals. Various optometric
refracting instruments are also displayed.

At one time George Washington's false teeth made of gold
and ivory (not wood) were displayed in a section of this hall. The
teeth were made in 1795 during Washington's second term in office.
Incised on the inside of the teeth are the words: "This was the Great
Washington's teeth." Unfortunately in June 1981 someone stole George's
false teeth, and so those who might like to see them will have to
wait a long while until they are returned. There are displays in this
hall on the history of dentistry that include exhibits of extraction
instruments (keys, pelicans, and forceps, among others); filling implements, and drilling instruments. Also exhibited are vulcanite dentures
and instruments for cleaning teeth. Another exhibit missing in this
hall is the work of Dr. Charles H. Land, a maternal grandfather of

Charles Lindbergh, who invented and had patented vacuum dentures (nineteenth century). The works of several important early American dentists are discussed. Reconstructed here is the 1885 dental office of Dr. G.V. Black who invented the dental foot engine and was later Dean of Northwestern University's Dental School. Also shown is the 1912-20 laboratory and study of Dr. Edward Angle who established orthodontics as a dental specialty.

Hall of Iron and Steel (First Floor, West Side)

Iron and steel production did not originate in the United States, as some people might easily be led to believe, but our country is today the world's largest producer and consumer of these commodities. Man's discovery of iron is ancient and unrecorded, but it is known that steel was made in small quantities before the birth of Christ. Iron and, later, steel were produced in increasing quantities for commercial purposes beginning with the Industrial Revolution in Europe in the 1700s. The exhibits in this hall, limited to the United States, trace the manufacture of iron and steel in this country from colonial times to the present. Several processes are illustrated, and exhibits show the steps in the manufacture of certain industrial and consumer goods made with iron, steel, or both.

"Hammersmith," the first American iron works, was established in 1847 on the Saugus River in Massachusetts. A recreation of "Hammersmith" in a small-scale diorama shows three settings: the blast furnace, the forge, and the rolling and slitting mill with labels that explain each process.

A model of the Norris Locomotive Works in Philadelphia, which in 1855 was the largest locomotive plant of its time, is shown in this hall. The exhibit shows shops in the plant used for erecting and steam hammering purposes.

An early converter of the Bessemer type, on loan from Bethlehem Steel Company, is exhibited in the hall. It was used commercially about 1862 in the conversion of pig iron into steel. It was first used experimentally by William Kelley who independently arrived at the idea of burning out the impurities in iron to make it malleable. In 1907 Charles M. Schwab, president of Bethlehem Steel, was so impressed by the accomplishments of Henry T. Grey's universal mill in Germany (it could produce wide flange beams and columns and roll them deeper and wider than standard I beams), that he established a similar plant in Bethlehem, Pennsylvania. The product that this plant was soon able to turn out proved a boon to the construction industry. An exhibit explains the processing of the steel ingots by heating, soaking, rolling, pressing, and hydraulic shearing to crop off the blanks.

In making pig iron for the production of steel, a blast furnace is necessary. A scale model of blast furnace "J" at Bethlehem Steel Corporation's Sparrow Point plant near Baltimore is shown and its operation is explained. Models are also shown of open hearth furnaces at Bethlehem Steel Corporation's Sparrow Point plant with explanations of their operations in the production of steel.

A basic oxygen furnace, shown in a model, was first developed about 1949 in Austria, and later adapted for American use in 1954 by Kaiser Industries engineers. It is used today in over forty percent of raw steel production in the United States. The model shown here was a gift from the engineering department of Kaiser Industries.

There is also a model of the Ford Motor Company's steel plant in River Rouge, Michigan. The plant has an integrated series of operations, beginning with the unloading of ships full of raw material (iron ore, coal, and limestone), continuing with the manufacture of iron and its conversion into steel which is then cast and forged into various shapes or rolled into sheets. The exhibit was a gift from the Ford Motor Car Company Fund. A scale model of a modern steel plant, a gift of the United States Steel Company, also shows an integrated series of operations from raw material to rolling mills.

The hall presents, as well, material explaining and illustrating the magnetic forming or shaping of metals and their subsequent uses. The shaping of various light to medium gauge metals is often done by a special type of machine, exhibited here, where metal is shaped by applying magnetic pressure of up to 50,000 pounds per square inch in pulses lasting only ten to twenty millionths of a second.

One of the modern uses of steel for porcelain enamel is a special glass that is fused to metals at high temperatures. The production of this porcelain-enameled steel is described in an exhibit. The finished product is used for such items as household appliances, bathtubs, silos, and jet engine parts, among other uses. Because porcelain enamel has such a wide range of uses, its manufacture in this country has become a large industry.

Hall of Textiles (First Floor, West Side)

In early colonial days the wealthier settlers in this country imported almost all of their fabrics from England. However, when communications with England became strained and threatened to disintegrate the colonists were thrown on their own resources for the production of textiles. What is more, as the American population grew, cottage industries making woven cloth were unable to produce sufficient fabrics to supply their needs. To meet the demand for more and better textiles, and to relieve the drain of money for imports from England, manufacturers organized new factory systems to deliver the much needed goods. First confined to areas where water falls could produce power for the machinery, the industry spread to other locations as other energy sources became available.

The textile industry was most dramatically advanced during the middle years of the eighteenth century by the development of new techniques for spinning and weaving. Milestone makers in the history of textile manufacturing included Englishmen, Americans, and a very brilliant Frenchman. Richard Arkwright invented the water frame, a spinning machine operated by water power which he had patented in 1769 (he is credited with starting the factory system). James Hargreaves invented the spinning jenny which doubled the production in the carding process. Samuel Crompton invented the "mule" which in one operation (drawing, twisting, and winding the cotton) produced a very fine yarn. Samuel Slater was a textile worker trained in England who escaped with his knowledge of cotton manufacturing machinery to this country, which he felt offered him greater opportunities, and was able to construct Arkwright machines here, later establishing factories throughout New England. Slater established the first successful cotton mill in America located in Rhode Island, and became known as "the Father of the American cotton industry." Eli Whitney's cotton gin separated the seeds from the fibers, a laborious task which was successfully speeded up by his invention. Joseph Jacquard was a brilliant Frenchman whose mechanism revolutionized looming techniques. A variety of artifacts connected with these inventors are featured in this hall with others displayed in the halls "We the People," "A Nation of Nations," and "Everyday Life in the American Past." The Textile Hall contains selections from almost 40,000 textiles, implements, and machines in the National Textile Collection.

Spinning and weaving techniques are demonstrated in this hall on certain days (consult the Information Desks or Bulletin Boards for schedules). The wool is cleaned, carded, and spun on a spinning wheel, and skeins of wool are made. The demonstrator also prepares flax for weaving: rippling the flax to remove the seed pods (saving some for next years crop, and some for medicinal purposes), retting the flax (soaking it in water), beating it to remove the tough outer fibers, combing it through hackles, wrapping it on the distaff, and finally spinning it on a spinning wheel.

When Joseph Jacquard invented the Jacquard mechanism in 1804 it radically changed the textile weaving industry. Thousands of silk workers in France were thrown out of work by Jacquard's machine and irate workers threatened Jacquard's life. Fortunately for all, the French government recognized the value of the mechanism, purchased the patent, and made the loom public property. This hastened the lowering of silk prices—and French silk workers were then rehired. A small schematic model loom demonstrates the operation of a Jacquard loom. A large eighteenth-century operating loom in the hall has an 1840 Jacquard mechanism attachment: visitors can see how a single craftsman using the Jacquard mechanism could, by himself, weave complex, patterned fabrics for which he would have required at least one helper.

Ingrain design carpet weaving was also aided by a Jacquard mechanism attached to carpet looms, which before this mechanism was used could only weave simple geometric patterns. Examples of ingrain carpet weaving are on display. The hall also contains drawloom woven patterns, richly figured silk damask and brocade, in a variety of weights and textures that were used in the nineteenth century for clothing, upholstery, and coverlets. The weaving of these materials, too, was aided by Jacquard's invention.

In this hall is a reproduction of a nineteenth-century four-harness loom with four treadles. An itinerant weaver using it could completely and rather swiftly dismantle the loom and take it to homes where he was engaged to weave for the family. Depending on its width, a piece of cloth between ten and fifteen yards long would take the weaver ten to twelve hours.

Textile manufacturing was by no means confined to weaving, however. The process of printing on fabric was greatly speeded when the design was placed on a roller printer, instead of the original copper plates. There are examples here of various roller-printed fabrics made in the United States, and rollers used to do this kind of printing on fabrics.

An eighteenth-century French knitting machine in the hall was used for making linen, wool, silk, and cotton stockings. By 1775 there were about one hundred such machines in use in Germantown, Pennsylvania and the surrounding area. Other knitting machines here include a Scott and Williams circular knitting machine used for making silk (and later nylon) stockings; home knitting machines; lace-knitting machines; and several kinds of straight knitting machines.

The collection has a variety of coverlets shown on a rotating basis. One specimen is a painted cotton coverlet in a "Tree of Life" design; made in India, it has an inked inscription indicating it was purchased in 1737 from an English smuggler of East Indian goods. There is also a double bow-knot pattern coverlet of indigo wool and white cotton, made in Jackson County, Ohio about 1867; a Jacquard double weave coverlet in a stylized floral pattern with patriotic border emblems, and an appliqued and embroidered bed cover of the mid-nineteenth century that was made by Dr. Josiah Hasbrouck and his wife showing his entire family in rowboats near the bottom center.

Also on exhibit are some interesting and unusual works that show the further artistic possibilities of textiles. A stone-like sculpture of sisal and hemp, one in a series produced by Barbara Showcroft, which she calls "small habitats" that give the viewer the experience of feeling spatial concepts, is shown. Then there is a screen called "The Elements," designed and woven by Ted Hallman in 1969. It is made of hand-colored linen, cotton, and rayon yarns and has affixed to it acrylic plastic cut-outs.

Embroidery has sometimes been called needle painting; it is an art that has been practised by primitive and civilized peoples for thousands of years, and in eighteenth and early nineteenth-century America it was a popular creative art among women. This hall provides examples of embroidery equipment including embroidery frames, and shows such works as an embroidered man's waistcoat, white-on-white embroidery, a canvas pocketbook embroidered in silk, a silk apron embroidered with silk and metallic threads, also an apron of cotton with linen embroidery, a crewel embroidery valance, and embroidered pictures and samplers, among many other embroidered articles displayed here.

Examples of embroidery work by Indians can be seen in the hall "A Nation of Nations," and those of early American settlers can also be seen in this same hall. In the hall "We the People" are embroidered pictures made for our Centennial Celebration of 1876, and in that hall are handmade quilts with interesting designs. In the "First Ladies' Hall" look at the purse Martha Washington holds on her lap; it was made by her from parts of an old dress she owned and an old uniform of George Washington's. Other gowns in the "First Ladies' Hall" are also of interest because of the textiles used and some beautiful embroidery work on some of the dresses. Not to be outdone by women, but more probably to pass the lonely hours, parts of a few uniforms in the hall "Armed Forces" were embroidered by men in the services.

Atom Smashers (First Floor, West Side)

As he concluded his broadcast on April 14, 1981 after the space shuttle "Columbia" landed safely at Edwards Air Force Base in California, John Chancellor said, "We make most of our miracles routine and the space shuttle is just the latest." Working in quite a different discipline, the question arises, "Will our nuclear energy scientists be able to devise new sources of energy that will be a safe, affordable boon to mankind and prove to be still another miracle which becomes routine?" These scientists are devoting much time and effort to this problem because our future energy needs are of grave concern to our government and to industry. The exhibits in this hall might not be easy at first glance for the average layman to understand. A knowledge of physics would be helpful. However, there are some individuals who will understand some if not all of it, and by carefully reading the labels describing the exhibits garner enough information about atomic energy and its history to open new vistas. It might lead some future scientists to delve further into this difficult subject, reading books, taking courses, or (as has been known to happen) making a lifetime career of it.

A cyclotron, whose basic design of a tool scientists use to study the nuclei or cores of atoms, was introduced in 1930 by E.O. Lawrence, an imaginative and creative genius. It is the oldest form of atom smasher and is one used to study the properties of matter so tiny their trails can only be detected on film by using a microscope. When electric voltage is used repetitiously to excite the speed of sub-atomic particles, later further increased by the use of a magnet to bend the particles back again for increased speed, they can be accelerated to near the speed of light. These fast-moving particles directed at target nuclei are able to smash the nuclei releasing neutrons and protons which collide leaving trails that scientists are able to detect and study on film with the aid of a microscope. There were many physicists beginning in the 1920s who began devising schemes for accelerating neutrons. At first, not altogether successful because of the limitations of the equipment of the period, they were not stopped but kept experimenting with other avenues to solve the problem. Among the physicists whose historic work in high energy physics are discussed and illustrated are Gustav Ising, Leo Szilard, and E.T.S. Walton who with John Cockcroft in Rutherford's Laboratory at Cambridge University in 1932 built the first successful atom smasher which was able to disintegrate lithium and other light nuclei. An illustration of the voltage multiplying arrangement of rectifiers and capacitors constructed by Cockcroft and Walton at Cambridge University is presented in this hall.

Another researcher working on the problem was Robert J. Van de Graaff of M.I.T. who designed the linear accelerator constructed in 1932 by M.A. Tuve at the Carnegie Institute of Washington. This accelerator, used to measure the powerful forces that bind nuclei, was the first machine to produce 1,000,000 electron volts. Both a model of the accelerator built by Van de Graaff and the large one constructed by Tuve are on exhibit.

The 1938 Dunning cyclotron, also on display, the principles for which were formulated by E.O. Lawrence of the University of

California at Berkeley, was built by J.R. Dunning of Columbia University and used to split the nuclei of atoms of natural uranium in order to obtain the rare isotope uranium 235. The procedure was first performed with this cyclotron and as a result scientists achieved an understanding of how to control nuclear fission.

Ernest O. Lawrence, a Nobel prize winner who had conceived the basic idea for a cyclotron, was a scientific genius who contributed an enormous body of knowledge to the study of high energy physics. At the University of California at Berkeley, Lawrence and his team had collaborated in the 1930s in the development of circular accelerators, which can be found today in the Fermilab and the Super Proton Synchrotron. His death at age 58 was a tremendous loss to science. Artifacts in an exhibit about Lawrence's life show a picture of him that appeared on the cover of **Time** (11/37), information about his early, very small cyclotrons (4 inch, 11 inch, and 27 inch) made of borrowed or surplus equipment, and of his 60 inch cyclotron and his ideas for a betatron. Also discussed was his interest and promotion of the bio-medical application of radiation.

The betatron is used in industry and medicine in this country and abroad. Lawrence had done work on it. The first successful magnetic induction accelerator (betatron) was designed and constructed by Donald W. Kerst in 1939. Exhibited here, it could generate two million volts, more powerful than any previous accelerator. Also on exhibit is a German betatron (1944) that could generate six million volts.

A cut-away of a proton linac accelerator is shown. An original was constructed in 1947 by a team of scientists led by Louis W. Alverez. It was a next step in the development of accelerators.

Macmillan and Vekster devised the electron synchrotron that made possible the further development of circular accelerators used today. The first proton synchrotron made at Brookhaven National Laboratories, called COSMOTRON, could produce three billion volts. It was designed and constructed by Ernest Koraunt, M. Stanley Livingston, H.S. Snyder, and John Biewett. A large exhibit, a mock-up section, shows and describes an electron linac synchrotron made at Stanford University; a two mile accelerator that could produce twenty billion volts.

Other exhibited artifacts include a quartz fiber electroscope of 1934 used as a particle detector to investigate gamma rays and radio active isotopes; an ionization chamber used in investigating carbon 14 in the first transuranium element, neptunium 239; an anti-coincident "screen wall" Geiger-Muller counter system constructed by Willard F. Libbey in 1947 for the first radio carbon dating; and the Geiger-Muller counter tubes (1947) used with uranium graphite piles in the first self-sustaining chain reaction.

In still other exhibits are shown and described parts of Donald Glaser's experimental bubble chamber (1952) for which he was awarded a Nobel prize; a Cerenkov Counter of 1955, the first important counter to measure the velocity of particles and with it to discover anti-protons; a linear amplifier developed in 1946 at the Manhattan Project Clinton Laboratory and later at Oak Ridge National Laboratory; and a section of Fermilab's synchrotron huge tunnel which museum visitors can enter. The great contributions of nuclear scientists not previously mentioned (the Varian brothers, Hansen, Geiger, Mueller, and Gell-Mann, another Nobel prize winner for his contributions and discoveries of the classification of elementary particles and their interactions) are also discussed in this hall.

There is a replica of one-half of the world's first nuclear reactor. The original was built by Enrico Fermi and his associates at Stagg Field, the University of Chicago, and put into operation on December 2, 1942. Fermi, Harold Urey and other scientists with this type of equipment conducted experiments in controlled nuclear fission using fuel rods, stationary metal rods that contain the uranium fuel. Each rod is several feet long and no more than a few inches thick. There are in each rod, of which there are hundreds or thousands in a typical reactor core, small pellets of uranium surrounded by a relatively thin metal shield. Knowledge gained in the Fermi reactor eventually led to the creation of the atomic bomb. The counters Fermi devised to detect neutron and gamma radiation are explained.

A full-scale reproduction of a Figure 8 Stellerator for fusion of nuclei rather than for fission is exhibited. Built in 1951 by Dr. Lyman Spitzer of Princeton University, the original could raise the temperature of deuterium (heavy hydrogen) to 1,000,000 degrees C., thus fusing nuclei and resulting in a release of heat. It was believed this machine represented a potential new source of energy, one that would not contaminate the atmosphere with radioactive material.

An exhibit shows an atomic beam apparatus that was used to study the structure and internal energy of isolated, electrically neutral atoms. Otto Stern worked on this type of apparatus in Germany in 1920; I.I. Rabi and his students worked on it at Columbia University in the mid-1930s and greatly increased the sensitivity and the versatility of the apparatus by introducing the "magnetic resonance method." The apparatus shown here was constructed in 1953 at the Brookhaven National Laboratory under the direction of V.W. Cohen, and was used to investigate the structure of the radioactive nuclei.

An exhibit discusses and illustrates the history of storage rings and colliding beams beginning with a replica of the first storage ring built near Rome, Italy in 1960 and finishing with a beam collision section from the Intersecting Storage Rings at Geneva, the world's largest such installation. There is also a cut-away shown of the vacuum chamber of the Stanford University electron-position storage ring called SPEAR.

There are demonstration models explaining the basic principles of accelerator physics which are operational by visitors. In each case by pressing a button one can activate small dioramas that explain nuclear fission by showing an atomic reaction in which a uranium atom is struck by a sub-atomic particle called a neutron, splitting it and creating two smaller atoms plus released energy in the form of radioactive waves and particles. A slide show also explains how atom smashing is carried on by acclerators. Other artifacts displayed are documents, notebooks, and letters of atomic scientists.

The Palm Court

In this area one can relax on some white wicker furniture

and take note of exhibits that include a counter that once belonged
to an old Washington, D.C. confectionery store called Stohlman's
and automatic equipment once part of a Horn and Hardart's Automatic
Cafeteria. In the nineteenth-century ice-cream parlor, a part of the
Palm Court, one can enjoy an ice-cream soda or sundae, a cup of
tea or coffee, or a soft drink. For these, of course, there is a charge.

Hall of Everyday Life in the American Past (Second Floor, East Side)

The exhibits in this hall describe the everyday lives of early
Americans who came mostly from European countries, beginning
during the different decades of the seventeenth and eighteenth centuries, each bringing or making their furniture, household goods, and
utensils illustrated here. Colonists began arriving in America before
the mid-seventeenth century. While the number who came over was
small at first, over time it steadily increased when those seeking their
fortunes and freedom in the new land were lured to these shores.
The immigrants brought with them a richness of cultural heritages,
traditions, beliefs, and styles which often remained intact, and just
as often to them were added new forms—changing, in turn, the culture
of the new land. Their traditions are reflected in the settlers' domestic,
religious, and cultural artifacts shown in this hall. The full-scale
reconstructions or reproductions of houses they and their children
built and furnished, the period rooms, as well as the displays of objects
they brought or made and used in everyday living portray the history
of early domestic life of these hardy settlers and their heirs in this
country.

English, Scottish, and Irish settlers formed the mainstream
of immigrants, and many of their artifacts are shown. Included are
some rarely found outside of museums today: a Scotch door latch,
snuff mill, and "quaich" or spirit cup, an English earthenware pot,
and an Irish earthenware bottle, a silver basting spoon and tankard,
a wooden doll, a stumpwork embroidery box (stumpwork embroidery
was a type of elaborate colored embroidery in high relief and employing
a variety of materials), a coattail or turn-chair, and a medieval triangular chair.

The hall's collection also contains artifacts of Spanish settlers
and Franciscan missionaries that feature oil lamps, brass bowls,
castanets, a guitar, majolica plates, lusterware, a vargueno (a small
chest or desk made to sit on top of a table or chest), a stone metate
(a mortar and pestle for grinding grain), a wooden cross with straw
decorations, a wooden candle sconce, a scourge of agave fibers, and
a silver crown for a religious statue.

The display of French settlers' relics includes brass oil lamps
and a brass Hannukah lamp, candle snuffers, wrought-iron door keys
and scissors, a lace-maker's lamp, a pounce box (a small box with
a perforated top, used to sprinkle sand or pounce on writing paper
to dry ink), an adjustable chamber candlestick, and a tobacco jar.
Among the French furniture are pieces in the style of Louis XIII and
Louis XIV, a pine utilitarian cupboard, and a rocking chair. There
is also a sugar mold, a tin weathercock, and a carved domino board.

Articles belonging to Dutch and Flemish settlers include

a diamond-engraved decanter, slip-decorated wall tiles and porringer, a Flemish forged-iron rotary grill and a double cruse, Dutch oil lamps, a foot-warmer, a silver drinking bowl, a kas (a huge wardrobe), and a child's rocking chair. The Scandinavian settlers are represented here by such items as a Finnish wooden plate, an axe, a hand-forged key from Sweden, a carved corner cabinet and chest from Norway, carved wooden tankards from Denmark and Norway, and a Danish silver dish.

By 1776 America's German and Swiss settlers numbered about 200,000. Their lives in the new country had such old-country touches as the Tyrolean forged iron door knocker, an enameled toasting glass, silver cups and spoons, pewter plates, a hunting knife, a "Martin Luther" candlestick, slip-decorated earthenware, pipkin jugs, a salt-glazed stoneware beer mug, and a Swiss pewter flagon.

A variety of artifacts represent Americans of African backgrounds and of the early years of slavery. We are shown a large picture of the cruelty of the slave traders who stowed these slaves in an inhuman manner on an eighteenth-century English slave ship. Other African artifacts include carved elephant tusks from Gabon, a leather pouch from Liberia, a copper bracelet from the Congo, brass anklets and a breech cloth from Nigeria, an Arab slave chain, a dress or cloak used by members of the Wolof tribe in Senegal, West Africa, and wooden funerary figures.

Archeologists have recovered many items buried in the distant— and not so distant past. The hall contains findings from an early colonial settlement in seventeenth-century Virginia: a Dutch majolica platter and a gin bottle, bone curtain rings, a glass linen smoother, and a Spanish wine jug. Also from the seventeenth century is a collection of utensils and tools, among them plates, platters, iron pots, a felling axe, a broad axe and nails, an auger, a spade, and a kettle. A broadside printed in London in 1622 is posted in one of the exhibits. It gives advice to settlers preparing to go to Virginia.

Settlers going to Virginia or anywhere else on the new continent may very well have taken heed of this advice for their duties in colonial times and in the early days of the republic were varied and most often very arduous. In addition to farming his land, a farmer was responsible for fire protection, defense, carpentry, shoemaking, iron forging, keeping accounts, and other tasks. Artifacts are shown here that pertain to each of these duties. The duties of the farmer's wife in the same period were, if anything, even more onerous than those of her husband. In addition to helping him with the farm work, she was responsible for weaving and dyeing cloth, sewing, making soap, dipping candles, managing the kitchen (with limited equipment), raising and frequently educating the children, caring for the sick, washing and ironing, and a host of other duties. The hall presents a variety of articles she used at that time in performing each of her many duties.

Food preparation in colonial times was likely to be time consuming, and sometimes smoky. Food was boiled, roasted, or broiled upon an open hearth; baking was done in brick ovens built into the fireplaces. Food was served from pewter serving pieces into wooden bowls or trenchers, although some households were fortunate enough to have brought or have sent to them porcelain, earthenware, or stoneware. Jonathan Copp's household included pieces of English delftware and Chinese porcelains which are shown in an exhibit describing the Copp household. Whole or more often shards of some types of imported ceramics in the seventeenth century that have been recovered show a gravel-tempered earthenware pan, a Dutch red earthenware \cooking pot, an English sgrafitto-decorated earthenware dish, a salt-glazed "bearded man" jug from Germany, and a Dutch earthenware extinguisher jar for storing hot ashes at night. Other such artifacts came from Portugal and Spain.

The early settlers obviously required some comfort amid the hardships, and a number of them comforted themselves with alcoholic beverages. Among the beverages drunk during this period, and discussed in an exhibit, were hard cider, beer, Madeira, sack, aquvit, rum, and gin. Beers and ciders were homemade, the others were imported. Surprisingly, tobacco was first used as a medical cure-all, and only later as a source of comfort and pleasure by smokers. An exhibit reveals tobacco to have been an important export crop in the new country.

The services of skilled artisans in early America also helped make life more comfortable for the settlers. This was especially true for those who lived in the coastal ports, the cities, and even in some small villages. Handtools displayed indicate what tools carpenters, silversmiths, coopersmiths, and others used. Gathered from the towns of some of the northern colonists and displayed here are such handcrafted objects as furniture, pipes, bricks, iron, and silver. The exhibit of New England home furnishings from the first quarter of the eighteenth century shows some imported and locally made goods and examples of colored "feather-edge" pine wainscotting, boxed-in beams, plastered ceilings, lead glass casement windows (some with bull's eye glass), and a bofat or corner cupboard made by professional artisan specialists.

The colonists used pine splints, open lamps with yarn wicks fed by fish oil, and tallow candles, tin and glass lanterns, whale oil lamps, and even chandeliers to provide them with light. They also worked or read by the light from their great fireplaces. Between 1780 and 1830 artificial lighting was beginning to come into use, later considerably improved by the use of the Argand lamp named for a Swiss chemist who invented it. The Argand lamp operated on the principles of combustion, and while older forms of lighting were still used in many places, this lamp was successful in bringing artificial lighting forward a long way.

From colonial times through the mid-nineteenth century pewter was typical American tableware. An exhibit provides examples of colonial pewter, both cast and hammered in a variety of shapes, forms, and sizes. Artisans in the Connecticut Valley, New York, and Pennsylvania produced pieces of excellent quality and design. Another exhibit shows American silver of the Federal period (roughly 1789 to 1820), used by the wealthier classes. Silversmiths of this period adopted classical forms for their wares, discarding the heavy rococo designs of the late colonial period.

The iron industry was established in Pennsylvania after 1725 and among other products stoves and furnaces were made. The German settlers favored the stoves more than the fireplaces which the English preferred. Examples of stoves and furnaces are displayed that include a stove Benjamin Franklin invented whose popularity lasted for many years. Other domestic heating devices used in the seventeenth and eighteenth centuries are shown.

A section of this hall exhibits material on California, the Golden Quest. The original lump of gold found at Sutter's Mill in California in 1848 and a reconstruction of George Washington Arbaugh's 1862 frontier home are displayed. So eager were prospectors to get to California to make their fortunes that in addition to crossing the states from east to west, some even sailed around Cape Horn in their rush to get the gold in California. Examples of artifacts used to attempt to find the gold are displayed. Shown also is an exhibit of some advertisements that appeared of articles for sale like: a windmill, a stoneware churn, a homemade chair, and a Mexican cowhide trunk. The variety of people who came included Englishmen, Irishmen, Italians, Germans, Chinese, and others all interacting with one another and in this great melting pot producing a new kind of culture—Californian.

This hall is undergoing a renovation. Many of the exhibits will be replaced, but a sufficient number will be retained with others added so the visitor of American history will find much of interest to engage his attention.

This hall boasts a number of full-scale, well-described historic period rooms and houses:

The Seth Story House was built in 1680 at Essex, Massachusetts; the records of this family go back 275 years. Shown is a large second floor sleeping room. No modern conveniences (plumbing, electricity) were ever installed in this dwelling.

The Richard Dole House was built at Newbury, Massachusetts in 1670 but by 1725 the interiors were out of style and the Dole family installed new paneled and molded woodwork as well as plaster on the ceiling. A chamber of this house is reproduced here.

The Miller Log House was built at Mill Creek Hundred, Delaware about 1740.

The **front entrance** of a house once owned by John Hancock of Massachusetts, a signer of the Declaration of Independence, is shown. It was part of the house in Worcester, Massachusetts built in 1742.

*The Hart House was built first around 1752 in Ipswich, Massachusetts. Exhibited here in various stages of construction, it shows several features of colonial framed house construction used by New England builders, a construction technology traceable to medieval England.

*Roger Kennedy has made plans to expand the exhibit of the Hart House. From research done by his staff they all learned more about the chronology of the house, who lived in it and when, who stayed there during the years it served as an inn and what else it was used for (a stop on the Underground Railroad, Revival Meetings, etc.). It is Mr. Kennedy's wish to make the Hart House a "living experience" and for this purpose will have people taken through the house with docents who can explain things about it which they might not otherwise notice.

The **Reuben Bliss Home** was built in mid-eighteenth century at Springfield, Massachusetts. The paneled parlor of this home that is shown contains lovely Queen Anne furniture.

The **William Eley Home** was built about 1780 in Virginia. The parlor shown is elaborately paneled and pleasantly furnished.

A one-room **Adobe House** in the eighteenth century at Sante Fe, New Mexico shows a blending of Spanish and Indian styles of architecture and furnishings.

The **Edmond and Deliverance Crowell Home** at Martha's Vineyard was built about 1808. We are shown here a parlor of this home markedly different from the Sante Fe, New Mexico home.

The **Copp Home** of Stonington, Connecticut was used by them from 1750 to 1850 and features in this hall the family's eighteenth-century setting room complete with furnishings. Another nearby exhibit shows books from the Copp family library, and miniatures, a family tree, and utensils and eighteenth-century tableware the family used.

The **Harral-Wheeler Home** was built in 1846 at Bridgeport, Connecticut. The bedroom reproduced here was furnished in Gothic Revival style.

In the wealthy **Benjamin Comegy Home** in Philadelphia, the beautiful library contains nineteenth-century books and furnishings. Shown nearby is the front door of this 1850 home.

George Washington Arbaugh's Frontier House was built in California about 1862. The western ranch kitchen, part of the two-room house, is displayed in a section devoted to California history.

The one-room **New England Schoolhouse** was an institution throughout the New England states. The interior of one displayed here dates from about 1863.

A **Shaker Home** bedroom is in sharp contrast with the Harral-Wheeler Gothic Revival styled bedroom. The Shaker bedroom has beautifully handcrafted furniture of simple style.

The toys, dolls, and games exhibited in a child's bedroom of 1893 belonged to a wealthy home near Malden, Massachusetts.

A **Confectioner's Shop and Ice Cream Parlor** comes from the Georgetown section of Washington, D.C. and was built at the end of the 1800s.

A **Brooklyn, New York Home** shows the dining room and furnishings of about 1915.

First Ladies' Hall (Second Floor, East Side)

So popular is this First Ladies' Hall, one of the stellar attractions at the Smithsonian, that heavy foot traffic has worn through repeated installations of heavy carpeting. Entrance to this hall is made through a copy of a doorway in the White House, and in the dioramas in the hall are found four mantels that were originally part of the White House. The visitors come, of course, to see the nine glass-enclosed period settings (dioramas) and the mannequins wearing the gowns (not all inaugural ball gowns) that belonged to each first lady or hostess for the president. The faces of the mannequins are the same, but each mannequin is fashioned in the size, shape, and coloring of the first lady or hostess it represents, her hair dressed as she wore it and wearing a gown actually belonging to her. A special type of dim blue lighting is used throughout the hall, as harsh lights would damage the delicate fabrics. However, visitors should soon accustom themselves to this lighting and have no trouble reading the labels giving the information about each gown.

The first diorama represents George Washington's bedroom in the Philadelphia Executive Mansion at 190 High Street that was the United States' temporary capital from 1790-1800. It was furnished with objects that belonged to the Washingtons (as did most of the furniture in the drawing room of the next diorama). In this bedroom a Chippendale bed, wing and side chairs, a mirror, brass candlesticks, and other items were brought to the Philadelphia capital from Mt. Vernon.

The drawing room of the Philadelphia Executive Mansion contains three gowned figures. The figure representing Abigail Adams, the wife of one president and the mother of another, wears pinned on her lace collar a gold brooch with locks of hair from John Adams, Abigail Adams, and John Quincy Adams. Martha Jefferson Randolph, the daughter of Thomas Jefferson, is also here, as is the seated figure of Martha Washington dressed in a hand-painted salmon faille dress. Her dress is decorated with North American wildflowers and insects, her shawl of Mechlin lace, and on her head the white lace "mobcap" worn in her day.

The Music Room in the White House at Washington, D.C., 1809-29, was furnished in part by John Quincy Adams. In this diorama the first gowned figure represents Mrs. John Quincy Adams (Louisa), who was born in London while her father was American consul there; Maria Monroe Gouverneur, the daughter of President James Monroe and the first White House bride, is shown in her imported French gown; President Monroe's wife, Elizabeth, and Mrs. James Madison, the famous Dolley, who is credited with hurriedly packing and saving a number of White House paintings and furnishings before the British arrived in 1814, are shown in this Music Room.

In a reception room in the White House, 1829-45, several ladies are shown who served as White House hostesses. The gowned figures here represent Emily Donelson Jackson, niece of President Andrew Jackson; and the wife of his adopted son, Sarah York Jackson (who here wears her wedding dress); both acted as hostesses for Jackson. Angelica Van Buren, served her father-in-law, President Martin Van Buren, as hostess. President William Henry Harrison's daughter-in-law, Jane, and her mother, Jane Irwin Findley, both served as hostesses in place of his sick wife, Ann. President John Tyler's first wife, Letitia, died while he was in office; in this diorama we see the second Mrs. Tyler, Julia, whom Tyler married while still president.

In a large parlor in the White House, 1845-69, is the gowned figure representing Mary Todd Lincoln dressed in royal purple velvet, her favorite color. Martha Johnson Patterson, daughter of and hostess for President Andrew Johnson, who here wears a voluminous wool outdoor cloak, an Algerian burnoose, which was wide enough to cover the hoop-skirted gowns of her day. Also seen here are figures representing Sarah Polk, Abigail Fillmore, and Jane Pierce, the latter called by newspapers "the shadow in the White House" because she did not appear at public functions, and who always dressed in mourning for a son who died in a railway accident in 1853. Harriet Lane Johnston served her bachelor uncle, President James Buchanan, as hostess and Harriet is wearing her wedding dress, one of the most beautiful gowns in the entire collection. Mary Taylor Bliss, the daughter of President Zachary Taylor, is wearing one of the last dresses among those shown that was made entirely by hand.

The Blue Room of the White House, 1869-93, shows a gowned figure representing Julia Grant in silver brocade, the material a gift from the Emperor of China. Lucy Hayes, also here, was the first wife of a president to graduate from college, and opposed to the use of alcoholic beverages and serving none, she won the nickname of "Lemonade Lucy." Lucretia Garfield was the wife of President James A. Garfield who was assasinated a few months after taking office. Mary Arthur McElroy served as hostess for her brother, President Chester Arthur. Rose Elizabeth Cleveland, a well-known author and lecturer in her day, served as hostess for her brother for the first two years of his first term. Also shown here is President Benjamin Harrison's wife, Caroline, who was much interested in American history and the preservation of the White House as an historic mansion, and it was she who started the White House china collection.

In the Blue Room, 1893-1921, is a gowned figure representing Frances Cleveland, the young woman President Cleveland married during the latter part of his first term. Another figure represents Ida McKinley, an invalid for much of the time her husband was in office. Also shown are Edith Kermit Roosevelt, the second wife of President Theodore Roosevelt (his first wife died before Roosevelt became president). Helen Taft who was instrumental in getting the cherry trees planted along the Potomac River and was the first of the wives to give her inaugural gown to the Smithsonian. Ellen Louise Axson, the first Mrs. Woodrow Wilson, who died in the White House in 1914, and Edith Bolling Galt, the second Mrs. Woodrow Wilson, are both present in this diorama.

The East Room, 1921- , displays figures of Florence Harding, who always wore a black velvet neckband; lovely looking and graceful Grace Coolidge; Lou Henry Hoover, a Stanford University graduate in geology; Eleanor Roosevelt, that much loved, though controversial figure; Bess Truman, and Mamie Eisenhower.

The ninth diorama shows the thirteen by twenty foot Red Room, traditionally the first ladies' sitting room, called the Empire Parlor since the time of Dolley Madison. In this diorama it looks like it did during the Kennedy Administration when the red fabric wall covering was recreated by the firm that made the original material. The room is furnished with a rug and curtains used during the Kennedy Administration along with other furnishings of the period on loan from the White House or from the Smithsonian collections. In this Red Room are seen figures representing Jacqueline Kennedy Onassis, Claudia (Lady Bird) Johnson, Thelma Patricia Nixon, Betty Ford, Rosalynn Carter, and Nancy Reagan.

A number of exhibit cases in the hall hold examples of china patterns used during the administration of each president, beginning with George Washington. Other cases display articles that belonged to various presidents or members of their families.

Hall of "We the People" (Second Floor, East Side)

The evolving role of government in this country begins in this hall with colonial times (Mayflower Compact, etc.). Its functions are described in absorbing exhibits that show major developments in the political, social, and cultural institutions of the past two hundred years which had profound political, social, cultural, and economic impacts on the country. Questions arose of vital interest to the young nation, and we are given an insight of how the people and the officials grappled with the problems. The responses of our democratic government's three branches (whose purposes and responsibilities are spelled out in the Constitution and its amendments illustrated here) to gradually meet the challenging, changing needs for an ever-increasing and diverse population are described in this hall. The exhibits provide examples of many past and present functions of our government describing how these were handled. Among them were the responsibilities for national defense, the safeguarding of civil liberties, the promotion of education and the general welfare (among the latter housing, community development, social security, better mental and physical well-being of our citizens, and other programs including support of the arts, research in science, and conservation and national park programs).

As one walks through this hall he will note artifacts that belonged to some well-known people, among them a pair of glasses worn by Thomas Jefferson; a naturalist's microscope owned and used by John Quincy Adams; a 1751 Virginia land survey made by George Washington; a book by Benjamin Franklin describing his Philadelphia experiments and observations on electricity (Paris, 1752); the first telegraph key made by Samuel F.B. Morse which he used in 1844 to send a message from Washington, D.C. to Baltimore; Major John W. Powell's life preserver and journals that he kept while leading exploration and surveying parties on the Colorado River in 1869-75; Leonard Bernstein's draft notations for his **Mass** composed in honor of the Kennedy Center's opening; and the brief case used by Adlai Stevenson when he was United States ambassador to the United Nations (1961-65).

The phrases which appear prominently displayed in separate sections of the hall are taken from words uttered by Abraham Lincoln in his Gettysburg Address on November 19, 1863: "of the people," "by the people," and "for the people." These phrases succinctly describe what the exhibits delineate as the provisions which with great foresight the "Founding Fathers of Our Country" included in the Constitution and the Bill of Rights (the first ten amendments of the Constitution). Among some we might mention are the ballot, a most important influencing instrument in our democratic form of government; the equally important amending process that was provided for in Article V of the Constitution; and the very first amendment in the Bill of Rights, the right of the people to petition the government for redress of grievances. These and other important matters provided for in the Constitution and the Bill of Rights are discussed in this hall.

The section "of the people" offers displays of items of great symbolic importance chosen by the people as symbols of the people of the American nation that are recognized around the world: the American flag, the Liberty Bell, a poster of Uncle Sam, the Statue of Liberty, the American bald eagle, and the Great Seal of the United States with its eagle and shield. After we won our freedom from England, nations recognized America as an independent nation and our President and other high officials began to receive gifts and expressions of friendship and appreciation of which some are on exhibit in this hall. They include the guns given to President Jefferson by the Emperor of Morocco; a model of Mt. Vernon made entirely of cultured pearls by Mikimoto Cultural Pearl Industry in Japan and presented to the United States in 1933; the donkey cart presented to General George C. Marshall by the people of Sicily in 1953 in gratitude for World War II assistance under the Marshall Plan; a large carved teakwood elephant (the ancient emblem of Siam) given in friendship to President Eisenhower in 1960 by Siam; a pair of crackleware bowls made in 1736-96 given to President Grant in 1879 during his world tour, plus many other gifts that are exhibited here.

"Of the people" also shows exhibits about the national census, the first one taken in 1790, which since that time has been compiled by our government every ten years (Article I of the Constitution). The census contains statistical information accounting for the nation's population, income, industries, transportation systems, agriculture, housing, etc. which helps measure its growth and changes that occur every decade. Both government and private industries make use of this data in their planning and decision making. And, since the number of representatives that a state sends to Congress is based on the state's population, the census helps determine how many representatives from each state will sit in the House. A five minute film, "Census: Accounting for the Nation," shown in this hall, gives an explanation of the census and its accomplishments. The nineteenth-century Hollerith tabulating machine exhibited here helped speed the organization of information gathered in earlier census.

Americans come from all countries and are of all races. Busts displayed in this section "of the people" represent some of the many kinds of people who call themselves Americans. These include the Indians, who were the native Americans when the first colonists arrived, to the most recent citizens.

"By the people" discusses the American system of government. The political power of the people began with the arrival of the first colonists coming to a land which had no formal government. When it became evident that their situation, increasingly complex, called for a government that was best suited for the needs of the new Americans, people began to form political systems. The exhibits examine the roots of our American democracy and explain how various practices have gradually evolved over the years, in some cases, becoming more centralized and efficient. Since 1620 when the Pilgrims still aboard the Mayflower pledged to "convenant and combine ourselves togeather (sic) into a civill (sic) body politick (sic)," Americans have been shaping and reshaping our government. On display is an engraving of the Mayflower Compact. In colonial days citizens met, as some still do, in New England town meetings and voted by ballot for the laws by which they governed themselves. The ballot, still our basic instrument of government, assures rule by majority. Displays of convenants and artifacts of early-settling religious groups (the Pilgrims, Puritans, Shakers, Quaker, Mormons, and others) who worked for the common good, and of volunteer groups (fire-fighters, vigilance committees, and others) who labored for the safety and well-being of the people convey an impression of many informal types of government first established here. With the establishment of the republic, its Constitution set up a more formal type of government. Copies of the Constitution and the Bill of Rights, the first ten amendments of the Constitution, are displayed.

At first not everyone could claim the protection of the Bill of Rights. It took the Abolitionist movement, the Civil War, and the adoption of the Thirteenth (1865) and the Fourteenth (1868) Amendments before blacks were freed from slavery and guaranteed equal protection under the law. Photographs and other artifacts shown here of Abolitionist leaders include: Horace Greeley, President John Quincy Adams, Wendell Phillips, Henry Ward Beecher, Harriet Beecher Stowe, Sojourner Truth, John Brown, Harriet Tubman, Frederick Douglass, William Lloyd Garrison, and others. Also shown are Abolitionist broadsides, a cane and medal given to John Quincy Adams for his support of the movement, and an engraving of Henry Clay proposing the Compromise of 1850 to preserve the Union.

Abolition was only one great issue in the Civil War—secession was the other. Secessonists based their dispute with the North on political, social, and economic issues. Among artifacts shown here are broadsides from South Carolina, the first state to secede, and pictures of leaders of the Confederacy. When peace was at last restored at the end of the Civil War, the Confederate states remained in the Union, but it had all been at a great cost. Artifacts of General Lee's surrender shown here include a facsimile of his order to his troops to lay down their arms and to return home; a white towel used as a flag of truce at Appomattox; and the furniture of the McLean, Virginia courthouse where the surrender was signed in 1865.

Our country passed through a bloody Civil War, but the right to vote remained a limited one. In this section of "by the people" the struggle of the disenfranchised for the right to vote is discussed. Long after the Civil War and the passage of the Fourteenth Amendment, southern states still imposed poll taxes to keep blacks and poor whites from voting. This was prohibited in 1964 by the Twenty-fourth Amendment, a copy of which is shown.

The First Amendment in the Bill of Rights declares the "right of people peaceably to assemble, and to petition the government for a redress of grievances." Although not always observed for all people, it finally led to the expansion of suffrage (including women, after a hard struggle) and helped more voters to use the ballot to obtain redress of grievances. For a long time women had no voting rights. Through the strenuous efforts and leadership of Elizabeth Stanton, Susan B. Anthony, Lucretia Mott, Carrie Chapman-Catt, Alice Paul and many others working over a period of seventy years, they pushed for and finally saw passed in 1920 the Nineteenth Amendment which prohibited voting discrimination on the basis of sex. The Smithsonian has developed a women's history collection that traces the women's political struggle in this country. Exhibited in this section is the table on which the Declaration of Sentiments was written at the first Women's Rights Convention in 1848, and photographs of some of the women's voting rights leaders.

In some states Indians were declared ineligible to vote, even though in 1924 Congress had declared Indians citizens. As part of the Civil Rights Act and the Voting Rights Act (copies of which are shown here) the power of any state to curtail the right of any citizen to vote was prohibited. Posters urging Indians to register and photographs of Indians voting are displayed. There is also shown a ballot that had been used by the Oglala Sioux Indians before 1906. The hall also details the struggles for voting rights that occurred as increasing numbers of immigrants arrived from abroad, particularly from Ireland and Germany in the nineteenth century. There were groups of citizens who believed only native born Americans should govern. They formed anti-Catholic, anti-immigrant organizations urging a twenty-one year residency requirement for citizenship. Some of their leaders formed secret societies which took an oath not to divulge any information about the society and their members became known as the "Know-Nothings." For a while this society was influential in political affairs.

Dramatizing the right to petition for redress of grievances as guaranteed in the First Amendment is a huge exhibit. Figures and banners mounted in this enormous display show petitioning groups marching for various causes in front of the Capitol, a logical place to protest since Congress makes the laws. There are huge mock-ups of posters, banners, photographs, etc. of causes, past and present, with figures of people who are marching and holding large signs alerting everyone to the important causes for which they are so energetically striving. Some included in the display show marchers with signs for: the peace movement ("war is not healthy for children and other living things"), black civil rights, the draft movement, women's voting rights, better economic conditions for various groups (among those shown are Coxey's Army, Pullman Railroad workers, World War I veterans, and others), and improved neighborhood schools.

The hall also illustrates some of the methods candidates used in conducting early and later presidential campaigns, and as the causes and candidates changed, the American electorate changed. Changing styles and techniques of the candidates are seen illustrated in campaigns conducted over the years. In the early years of our nation the candidates met in private homes ("parlor politics") believing it was not dignified to seek office by campaigning openly. An exhibit displays such a parlor. In the early nineteenth century open campaigning begun by Andrew Jackson accelerated. The campaign conducted in 1840 by William Henry Harrison against Martin Van Buren is worth noting. His followers set up log cabins (to indicate Harrison, born in a log cabin, had humble beginnings) which they set up at election headquarters with other cabins that were pulled along on the campaign trails, giving out cider and staging huge parades with banners, torches, and music. In this campaign, too, which was one of the wildest and most exciting, colorful and nonsensical of all campaigns, Harrison (Tippicanoe and Tyler too) defeated Van Buren. Large balls bearing slogans were rolled across the country (thus the origin of the slogan "keep the ball rolling"). Large displays show banners, buttons, hats, torchlight parade, flyers, flags, bumper stickers, and other election momentos that were used in the campaign for presidential candidates. Recorded music, especially composed for each candidate's campaign,

and recorded excerpts of some of the candidates' speeches are broadcast in the hall. Huge mock-ups portray street parades, stump speechmaking, front porch speechmaking where people came to hear the
candidates, whistle-stop railroad speechmaking where the candidate
went to the people, as they did also from automobiles. There is on
display the completely outfitted cabin section of the airplane "The
Caroline" (the first aircraft to be used by a candidate as a campaign
vehicle) in which John F. Kennedy rode while campaigning for the
presidency. In it one can see Kennedy's bathrobe, beverages and
notepads. There are descriptions in a section called "The Media and
the Message" which discuss how the press, radio, and television aided
or hindered candidates seeking office.

The first debates between presidential candidates were those
between Lincoln and Douglas on the expansion of slavery, but debates
did not really get under way to any great extent as a campaign forum
until the Kennedy-Nixon debates. The televised debates between
Ford and Carter were federally funded but were sponsored by the
League of Women Voters. All of these are described here.

A large section in this hall describing "for the people" discusses
the territorial expansion and settlement of our young nation from
thirteen states to our present fifty. Because the Constitution became
the law of the land, "for the people" also examines how the nation
approached the goals of the Constitution's preamble to "establish
Justice, insure domestic Tranquility, provide for the Common Defense,
promote the General Welfare, and secure the Blessings of Liberty...."
It defines these areas of responsibility that the people wanted their
government to assume.

Illustrations with maps, paintings, documents, and other artifacts show the territorial expansion of our country westward from
the Atlantic coast. These were first unveiled by explorers and later
by settlers. The westward movement accelerated in 1803 when President Jefferson purchased the whole of the western watershed of the
Mississippi River from Napoleon. The Louisiana Purchase, as it was
called, immediately doubled the size of the country, and Jefferson
sent Lewis and Clark on an expedition with scientific equipment to
explore the newly acquired land, to make astronomical observations,
to take notes about the geology of the land, gather specimens of
plants and animals as well as information about the Indians. The Lewis
and Clark expedition brought back or sent back a great deal of this
scientific information and an exhibit shows some specimens that
were collected by them. This pattern of information-gathering was
repeated in territories acquired later: Florida (bought from Spain
in 1819); Texas (annexed in 1845); the Oregon Territory (acquired
from Great Britain in 1846); and as a result of the Mexican War in
1848 land that today includes California, Nevada, Utah, and parts
of New Mexico, Arizona, Colorado, and Wyoming; the $10,000,000
Gadsen Purchase in 1853 which the United States paid Mexico, added
another large strip of land; Alaska purchased from Russia in 1867
for $7,200,000 (at the time called "Seward's Folly"); the Philippine
Islands, Hawaii, Guam, Puerto Rico, the Panama Canal Zone, and
the American Samoas, all eventually entered the American sphere.
Among the artifacts on display in this hall is a large painting "Grand
Canyon of the Yellowstone," by Thomas Moran. Moran accompanied

the United States Geologic Survey party in 1871 and the painting
he made at this time was said to have inspired many people to go
west, for it suggested the vastness and beauty of the wilderness that
awaited nineteenth-century settlers. Also shown are journals kept
by Major W. Powell, the great one-armed ethnologist who conquered
the rapids of the Colorado River and kept records of his journey and
of the Indian populations he met and studied; photographs and specimens
of plants and animals; scientific data resulting from surveys by topographical engineers, as well as other data gathered by the United
States Geologic Survey.

The new territories attracted both settlers and business.
The Homestead Act of 1862 (a copy is displayed) granted one hundred
sixty acres to any settler who took up residence and cultivated the
land for five years. Land for settlement was also granted to war
veterans. Public land was given to railroad and canal companies for
rights of way, thereby encouraging their expansion and helping to
bring more people and business west. The Northwest Ordinance of
1787 (a copy is shown here) established the procedure to be followed
by a territory seeking statehood. A new star was added to the flag
on the Fourth of July following the admission of a new state; an 1861-63
flag in the hall shows thirty-four stars. Also exhibited is the front
page of a 1959 newspaper whose headline announces Alaska's statehood.

In another part of this hall is a copy of the Northwest Ordinance
of 1787 in which it was decreed that each township must set aside
a plot of land for educational facilities. A copy of the Morrill Act
of 1862 is also shown which gave public land to each state for the
promotion of higher education in agricultural and mechanical arts
(the land could be and frequently was sold to finance education).
Certificates of transfer of public land from federal to state government
under the terms of the Morrill Act of 1862 are exhibited, as are other
artifacts that suggest the variety of government programs designed
to meet educational needs.

The preamble of our Constitution lists the establishment
of justice as a goal second only to forming a more perfect union.
Exhibits in a section of this hall describe the establishment of the
Supreme Court which has jurisdiction in cases concerning the constitu-
tionality of laws, controversies arising from decisions rendered by
lower courts, and controversies between states. Exhibited is a gown
of a Supreme Court justice, the official seal of the Supreme Court,
a handpress used to affix the seal to decisions, a bench chair used
by Justice Felix Frankfurter from 1939 to 1962 while he was a member
of the Court, and pictures of former Supreme Court justices. Some
information about landmark decisions made by the Supreme Court
are exhibited, a few of which were "Marbury v. Madison" in 1803
which established the Constitution as the undisputed law of the land
and the Courts as its interpreters; "Dartmouth v. Woodward" in 1819
which established the validity of private contracts; "McCulloch v.
Maryland" in 1819 which established that, in addition to the powers
specifically granted by the Constitution, the federal government
possessed implied powers necessary to meet specific needs, and that
federal powers prevail over state powers; "Gibbon v. Ogden" in 1824
which defined commerce, restated Congress' authority to regulate
interstate commerce, and ruled that the federal powers are superior

to state powers in such cases; "Brown v. Board of Education of Topeka" in 1954 which established that racial segregation of public schools is unconstitutional, overturning the "Separate but equal doctrine."

Discussed in an area of this hall is Article I, Section VIII, Number 10 of our Constitution that instructs Congress to promote the progress of science. From earliest times explorations of our country have had scientists collecting natural material and doing surveys of its geology and mapmaking. Scientific work was done and still is in connection with warfare with science an important part of the education of students at West Point and Annapolis. The government has had a hand in encouraging the arts by federally funding many of its programs. Some of these include the theater, music, dance, and for those working in the arts of sculpture, painting, printmaking, etc.

The preamble of the Constitution which speaks of providing for the common defense is clarified with material in an area of this hall which discusses the responsibilities of the president (commander-in-chief of the armed forces) and of Congress (which is instructed to provide for the common defense). Both must work together to make preparations for the defense of this country (either in peace and at war). As exhibits discuss their joint efforts they explain that while the president may make treaties with other nations, he must obtain the advice and consent of a two-thirds majority of the Senate. Among artifacts exhibited in this area are a nameplate from the battle-ship "Maine" and the front page of a newspaper whose headline announces the United States' declaration of war on Japan in December of 1941.

In the course of promoting the general welfare of the people, the several branches of government have been faced with situations never anticipated by the Founding Fathers. Several of these situations and the government's response to these needs are discussed in this section of the hall. To protect employees in their jobs, for example, the National Labor Relations Board was established in 1935. The Fair Labor Standards Act of 1938 was promulgated to aid employees who work under conditions detrimental to their health and well-being. In 1964 food stamp programs were initiated to enable the poor to buy more and better food than they might otherwise be able to afford. The Food and Drug Administration was organized to help in the control of food quality and drug safety and effectiveness. Congress has enacted patent and copyright laws to protect the rights of authors and inventors for a limited time. More health care and adequate housing are now available to people who are otherwise unable to afford them. These and many other programs for the general welfare for citizens of the United States are described in exhibits in this section of the hall.

Hall of "A Nation of Nations" (Second Floor, West Side)

In the preface to the 1855 edition of **Leaves of Grass**, Walt Whitman said, "We were not merely a nation but a teeming nation of nations." This hall highlights the diversity of immigrant cultures and their contributions to their new land. They came, despite the hazards of sea voyages, to escape political or religious oppression or to improve their economic conditions. "Europe is the parent country of America," said Thomas Paine, "and America is an asylum for mankind." Prior to the 1920s when their numbers were greatly curtailed by immigration laws, newcomers arrived here from everywhere, settling in both urban and rural areas. This hall explores some of the common experiences the immigrants shared; to what extent their hopes were realized; what influences the American culture had on them; and in what ways they helped enrich their new country.

Before Columbus encountered the people he called Indians, an experience he wrote about in his journals, there were natives long established here. When the very earliest European settlers came to these shores, many would not have survived if the Indians they met had not helped them by teaching these newcomers how to grow crops (especially corn) and what methods to use to withstand the cold winters. Some artifacts of prehistoric Indians displayed are from New Mexico, Arizona, Florida, Georgia, and elsewhere. These include metato and mono stones for grinding grain into meal; grass sandals; chipped stone arrow heads; fragments of natural fiber baskets; objects made from earthenware (some are painted, others corrugated and fired); bones used to work leather for clothing; and stone axes.

The people who first journeyed here—mostly from England and western Europe, but also from other parts of the world—brought with them a rich variety of skills. Benjamin Franklin observed, "Here people do not inquire of a stranger what he is, but what he can do. If he has any useful art, he is welcome." The English, primarily, set the patterns for government, language, and law, and contributed many workable skills as well. Among the artifacts of English settlers displayed in this hall are a looking glass brought to Plymouth on the Mayflower (1620); a great chair made for Jonathon Copp (about 1700); an earthenware dish made at North Devonshire, England and used in Virginia; a lantern pot made in London (about 1680); a child's armchair (about 1785) from New England; a child's crewel-embroidered, hand-woven linen dress from New Hampshire (about 1750); an eighteenth-century hornbook of the alphabet; and an eighteenth-century hatchel or hackle for combing flax. There are also examples of English hardware: hinges, locks and keys, and other items. Also shown is a casting of a slate gravestone, and an English Bible printed at London in 1613.

A restored New England craftsman's kitchen exhibited here was originally built about 1695 in Malden, Massachusetts, by a weaver. It was a typical English settler's kitchen in which both living and cooking (everything from deer and squirrels to game birds, fish, and fruit) took place. All of the cooking was done in the large open fireplace; the oven at the back was used for baking. A stairway presumably leading to sleeping quarters upstairs can also be seen.

Artifacts of other ethnic groups who arrived during colonial times abound. Among the German colonial artifacts shown here are wrought iron hinges from New York and Virginia (about 1740); a cannon stove by Heinrich W. Stiegel of Elizabeth Furnace, Pennsylvania (about 1749); an eighteenth-century loom from Hanover, Pennsylvania; and salt-glazed stoneware (1660). Artifacts shown here from the Dutch colonial communities include an eighteenth-century New York forged iron weathervane with the initials of the owner; a carved oak foot-warmer, dated 1675; a Dutch Reform Bible printed at Amsterdam in 1643; a pewter deepdish by Peter Young of New York (1775); and a silver brandy bowl made by Benjamin Wynkoop for Nicholas Roosevelt in 1707. Among the articles representing the Spanish colonial communities displayed are an eighteenth-century "Our Lady of Sorrows" in gesso relief-modeling on wood paneling; a 1710 painting on hide of "St. Anthony of Padua" made for a mission church at Santo Domingo, New Mexico; and a wooden statue of "St. Michael" carved (about 1770) for a Franciscan mission church at a Zuni pueblo, also in Santo Domingo. Among the Chinese colonial artifacts shown in this hall is a Ming porcelain cup used at King's Mill plantation in Virginia in the early seventeenth century, and a ladder for carrying cheese and dairy products that came from the vicinity of Rumford in Maine (about 1800). There are also a number of representative colonial artifacts from other ethnic groups including Italians, Jews, Russians, Swedes, Scots, Irish, Swiss, Africans, and French.

The immigrants learned a great deal from native Americans they found already in the land, and they, in turn, influenced the Indians. Included in the displays of Indian artifacts of the colonial period are a Mohawk beaded pouch of tanned leather; an Iroquois box made of birch bark with a European design in quill work; a glass-beaded woven sash; a French-type iron felling axe; a Chippewa bark and moose hair box; and an Arapaho Spanish-type bridle. The Northwest Coast Indians are represented here by a carving of a man in a frock coat; and the Navajos by a silver necklace in a Hispanic-Moorish squash blossom pattern. The display of Indian crafts of the early nineteenth century includes Hopi sticks for working embroidery yarn; shake sticks for hunting rabbits; Navajo weaving combs that separated woolen warp threads; sticks that beat down weft threads; and a vertical loom which still shows the remains of some blue woolen fabric. There is a Cheyenne quiver containing bows and arrows; a deer call made of wood; a Ute rabbit snare woven from fibers; an Apache headdress with feathers used in a ghost dance; tongs of mesquite wood for picking cactus fruit; reed burden baskets with tan leather fringes; and a reed canteen sealed with pine resin. Zuni Indians are represented here by a digging stick of wood and a pot with matte black finish; and the Sioux by a magnificent bonnet of eagle feathers. From the Chilicat comes a blanket of dyed wool used as a ceremonial gift; and from the Great Plains Indians a war trophy made from human scalps, feathers, and quills. From the Iroquois there is a carved mask used by members of a secret society when trying to frighten illness away. The Tlinglit are represented by a dance mask of carved and painted wood, and a fishing hook and float. The Kiowa display shows a stone arrow straightener and a bone arrow smoother. There are many other Indian artifacts (not mentioned above) that are featured in displays. (For those interested in more material on the Indians, it is suggested that they visit the halls of Native Peoples of the Americas and Prehistoric Peoples of North America and North American Archaeology found on the first and second floors of the Museum of Natural History.)

Pictures and photographs show some unbelievable conditions that prevailed—particularly in the steerage sections—aboard the sailing vessels that brought the earliest immigrants to America. The sufferings these passengers had to endure were exceeded in horror only by those of the Africans in the holds of slave ships. The owners of these sailing vessels were interested only in a profit, and cared little for the health and welfare of the immigrants on the boats; the owners' indifference was matched by the indifference of the countries that failed to enact legislation regulating shipboard conditions. The abuses were not ameliorated until well into the early part of the twentieth century. In addition to pictures the display also includes artifacts like a German passport cover used by a Slovene; an 1854 logbook of the ship "Medallion," some ships' hour glasses, ships' barometers, octents, and other navigational instruments. There are also models of vessels that carried immigrants. They include the "Cohota," an 1840s packet ship that carried thousands of immigrants across the Atlantic; and a clipper ship built in 1872 that carried thousands more from Hamburg to New York (it accomodated 850 passengers, 620 in steerage).

Many of the newcomers and their children migrated westward across the country, hopeful of settling in areas that might offer a new and better life. Some of these became farmers, others trappers, traders, peddlers, and itinerant preachers. All of them pioneers who helped to open up the wilderness. Among the artifacts shown is a New England peddler's cart used before 1900 that contained tinware, notions, brooms, lanterns, dresses, and textiles; and a European-style painted backpack (about 1800) of a New England peddler. On exhibit are knives and weapons the pioneers carried with them for protection, for hunting, and for trading. Some of these were hunting knives, bowie knives, scabbards, trade knives, Kentucky flutelock, percussion, plains, and other rifles.

Also exhibited is an 1880 mud wagon (or hack coach) that served regions inaccessible by river or, later, by railroad. A model of the 1880 side-wheel steamer "Joseph Henry" is shown that transported thousands of immigrants and their belongings to the interior of the country. Some western railroads offered, in place of coaches, economy sleepers, in which the travelers had to provide their own bedding and food. There is a model of an 1885 sleeping car shown. A variety of trunks and chests used by immigrants during this period is displayed with artifacts people of many European countries brought in them. They include among other things: a gray dress and blue wool coat from Finland (1900); a German wood chest (1740) brought to South Carolina; a German flatiron carried to Wisconsin (about 1860); and a Russian furniture scarf or embroidered and crocheted linen damask brought to Colorado (1909).

Once the settlers arrived on their land, they had to provide energy for all of the farmwork that had to be done. This was furnished by the men and women with the assistance of animals and the windmills they built. Much needed doing—such as breaking up the soil, raising crops, building and furnishing houses, raising, clothing, and feeding families. Displayed is the original equipment of a grist mill called a molino from Trampas, New Mexico that was used to grind corn or wheat into flour. The mill is of a very old design; inside are volcanic millstones, hidden by a wooden drum. A total of more than six million windmills were in use in this country between 1880 and 1930. Most were used to pump water, run sawmills, or grind grain. Later windmills were also used to produce electrical power until superseded by rural electrification. An exhibit shows a huge, Great Plains windmill once used for grinding grain.

Another exhibit provides examples of the hand tools that helped farmers survive. Among these are a flail, a pitchfork, a grain-scoop, a winnowing basket, and a grain sickle. There are other tools and artifacts shown such as a reaper hook, a grain cradle, a threshing stone, a hoe, an ox-yoke, a feeding trough cut from a log, a double-shovel plow, a meat grinder, a wine press brought from Switzerland, a Utah blacksmith's worktable and tools, and a forge. A Spanish smooth-bore fowler with misquet lock (1813) is also shown.

Artisans often specialized in making artifacts that reflected their original homelands, or produced distinctive varieties of common objects. The Chinese artifacts displayed include bamboo baskets carried on a pole, and stoneware jars for preserving sweetmeats; an apothecary cabinet of painted wood from Philadelphia; and a gateleg table used in San Francisco's Chinatown restaurants. There are many glazed stoneware jars, and a Chinese laundry sprinkler. European equipment shows tools brought from Russia, Germany, and England that were used by craftsmen of many trades. A Singer Sewing Machine of very early vintage is also shown.

An exhibit of Afro-American artifacts includes fish-traps made of oak splints (Virginia), a sedge or grass basket (Louisiana), a basket made of grass and pine needles (Alabama), and a cornhusk basket made in Tennessee. In this same exhibit is an identification collar of a slave (about 1800) bearing the name of his Kentucky owner; an 1833 identification tag for a porter slave in South Carolina; an iron bell (about 1860) used to call slaves from the fields of Virginia; and an Alabama sales receipt for slaves.

In the early days skilled craftsmen gathered in certain towns where the making of cloth was still a cottage industry. Samuel Slater had been trained in England as a textile worker. When he emigrated to this country he was able from memory to create the water frame he had used there and designed the cotton-carding machine, as well, which he put to use in Pawtucket, Rhode Island. On exhibit is a water frame (1790) he had built, as well as accessories for other crafts including a cabinetmaker's workbench and tool chest (1880) used in Baltimore; a foot-powered lathe used to make mother-of-pearl buttons (New Jersey, about 1905); and an 1889 tool belonging to a Rochester, New York custom tailor. Many types of spinning wheels—German, English, Tyrolean, and Saxon are also shown.

Old ways in the New World would not be complete, of course, without material on the religious heritages of the settlers. Among the religious artifacts of many faiths, there is a Catholic chalice (1916) used in a Slovene-American church; a carved and painted wooden Decalogue used in a Philadelphia synagogue before 1900; and a Protestant revival-meeting oilcloth banner with biblical inscriptions, from Massachusetts. There is even a Romanian gypsy hanging covered with phrenology and palmistry charts, and a roadside sign found in Kentucky (1970) that says, "Get right with God."

An area in this hall sketches shared experiences such as becoming a citizen, educating the children, military service, employment, politics, entertainment, sports, and housing. There is a large photograph of Albert Einstein at the time he renounced his Swiss citizenship

74   National Museum of American History

for American citizenship, and in another exhibit a symbol of education in America. An entire nineteenth-century sixth grade classroom from the Dunham Elementary School in Cleveland, Ohio is set up showing children's desks, blackboard, teacher's desk, teacher's wardrobe, a case for holding the stereoptocin slides, a mapcase with the map of Africa showing, and on the blackboard the day's lesson is written. In a broadcast the children can be heard reciting the "Pledge of Allegiance to the Flag" which they recited in unison daily, then followed by singing the "Star Spangled Banner," "America the Beautiful," and "My Country 'Tis of Thee."

The section that describes military service contains a full-scale reconstruction of part of an army barracks (Fort Belvoir, early twentieth century), complete with a section showing the latrine, and another section showing the bunk beds and foot lockers all arranged in perfect, military order. A photograph memorializes the drawing of the first draft number picked during World War I, and recruiting posters urging young men to join the armed forces. The most famous of the posters is one by James Montgomery Flagg that shows Uncle Sam pointing a finger and saying, "I Want You For the U.S. Army." World War I and II uniforms are on display.

The entertainment and sports displays, of course, draw the largest crowds. Clips of old movies bring the likes of Charlie Chaplin, Greta Garbo, Al Jolson, Amos and Andy, Fred Astaire and Ginger Rogers, Judy Garland, and other famous actors and actresses to life once again on the silver screen. The clips are accompanied by the movie house music of earlier times. Pictures of early vaudeville entertainers like Sir Harry Lauder, and the stars of operettas and musical comedies are also shown on a screen. A display which shows Charlie McCarthy, Edith and Archie Bunker's chairs from "All in the Family," ruby slippers worn by Judy Garland as Dorothy in the "Wizard of Oz," the dress of Ginger Rogers worn when she danced with Fred Astaire, momentos from "Mash," "Dallas," and other television programs are exhibited. There are even some seats from the old Yankee stadium as well as an original 1923 Yankee Stadium ticket booth that can be seen. Baseball players, among them Babe Ruth, Hank Greenberg, Lou Gehrig, Willie Mays, and Phil Rizzuto can be seen on film executing spectacular hits or runs. Gloves and a robe that belonged to boxing champion Muhammad Ali are on display as are boxing gloves that belonged to Joe Louis. There is a bat used by Phil Garner in the 1979 World Series, the helmet and suit worn by Janet Guthrie, the first woman to compete in the Indianapolis 500, Chris Evert Lloyd's tennis racket, and a golf club that had belonged to Jack Nicklaus. Also shown here are Abraham Lincoln's hand ball and Woodrow Wilson's tennis racket.

"A Nation of Nations" takes visitors (by means of photographs, films, and artifacts) back into the factories where many immigrants worked producing the goods for which consumers clamored including the automobiles made at the Ford factory and the revolvers made by Colt. This section in the hall illustrates the variety of work newcomers engaged in when they came to America in the late nineteenth and early twentieth centuries, and where different ethnic groups tended to settle and to work. Depicted are "greenhorns" working in the garment industry sweatshops in New York and Philadelphia, and Italians working in the construction industry and on the country's railways, subways, and street car lines. Other exhibits trace the German workers who brought skills from the old country that qualified them to work in breweries and at cabinetmaking, bookbinding, baking, watchmaking, and farming. The Scandanavian immigrants and their descendants often became fishermen, mariners, lumbermen, or farmers. The new Slavic workers chronicled here tended to settle in large cities where they were frequently employed in iron and steel mills. Polish immigrants, too, settled in large cities like Pittsburgh, Milwaukee, Detroit, Buffalo, and Chicago. In Chicago many of them worked at the stockyards and meat-packing plants, in Detroit on the assembly lines of large automobile factories. The immigrants who came in the late nineteenth century came because they were poor and hungry for work. They worked twelve and more hours each day, many doing piece work. As a result of poor working conditions (cold factories, sometimes airless factories, and other poor treatment) there were times when strikes occurred. The men and women formed unions to protest these conditions and for a better wage.

Products that were mass produced by these immigrants in addition to automobiles and revolvers included typewriters, photographic equipment, and sewing machines. Examples of these and other manufactured goods in which they participated are shown in a large exhibit. An interesting sidelight on the sewing machines manufactured is the story of a patent which proved to be extremely important. Walter Hunt in 1832 invented a lock stitch sewing machine (this ingenious man also invented a fountain pen, a safety pin, and, of all things, suction shoes for walking on the ceiling). He did publish information about these things but, foolishly did not take out a patent. This left him without a leg to stand on when Elias Howe, in 1846, took out a patent for a sewing machine using a similar idea to Hunt's. Although Howe lived in England from 1846-1849, he sued anyone who dared infringe on his patent. He widely advertised the sewing machine (a first consumer product to be advertised), and collected royalties on every sewing machine made until 1867. There are over 1000 examples and models of sewing machines in the Smithsonian collection, but only a few of the early ones are on display. Among these are Howe (1846), Singer (1851), Wilson (1852), Gibbs (1857), Perry (1858), and Heyer (1863).

Housing for these immigrants of the late nineteenth and early twentieth century was usually extremely humble—and often wretched, improving only as wage earners were able to earn a little more in acquired savings. The living room, bathroom, bedroom, and kitchen of a typical workingman's home of the early twentieth century is reconstructed and exhibited in this hall.

The Star Spangled Banner (Central Area, Rotunda)

This is the original flag that flew over Fort McHenry in 1814 when it was under attack by the British, and that had inspired Francis Scott Key to write the words of our National Anthem (the tune comes from an old English ballad). The flag, 30 x 40 feet, parts of which are repaired or where missing painted on its mounted background, hangs in an atmosphere of filtered air that keeps it dust free; and where it is also carefully controlled for temperature and humidity. At regular intervals throughout the day drapes open to reveal the flag and a recorded talk by Archibald MacLeish gives the history of the flag that is broadcast in this area for the benefit of visitors. The Star Spangled Banner was given to the Smithsonian in 1912 by descendants of Major Armisted who was at the time of the bombardment its fort commander.

The Bradford Doll House (Central Area, East)

The Faith Bradford Doll House presents in miniature (on a scale of one inch to one foot) a turn-of-the-century home of a family of comfortable means. The open front doll house is complete from basement to attic in its room arrangements, furniture, and furnishings. While some of the articles were hand-made in this country, others had been ordered from all over the world. Children walk up two steps onto a platform to get a better view of the house and its contents and older visitors viewing it step back into memories of bygone days.

Greenough's Statue of George Washington (Central Area, West)

This classical statue of George Washington clad in a toga was completed in 1840 in Florence, Italy by Horatio Greenough, an important American sculptor. Shortly thereafter it was brought to this country and exhibited in the rotunda of the Capitol. Most members of Congress as well as other people considered the statue undignified because Washington was not, in their opinion, properly dressed. They were influential enough to have it moved out of the rotunda of the Capitol to the Capitol grounds where it remained for sixty-five years. It was then shunted into the original Smithsonian building (the Castle). In 1964 when the Museum of History and Technology (today called the Museum of American History) was completed the final move of Greenough's statue was made to its permanent location on the second floor of this building.

Hall of Underwater Exploration (Third Floor, East Side)

If you are a deep sea diver or interested in locating wrecks, the surveying, measuring and recovery techniques used by other divers, briefly described here, may be of some interest. Even if you are neither, many find this hall a fascinating place to visit because the carefully planned exhibits take one into areas with which most of us have little or no contact, except perhaps on television.

The historical record of underwater explorations begins in this hall in the sixteenth century and its exhibits recount the gear and equipment used over the years to locate and retrieve items. Also described in this hall are the old trade routes used by Europeans going to and from America and the underwater sites of some of their wrecked ships. Some of the objects recovered, many found by accident or by means of charts and official documents found in archives and libraries (a few of the sites reproduced on maps) are shown.

Trade routes ran from Mexico and the West Indies to Europe through the Florida Keys, as indicated on a large map. Strong currents and sharp coral reefs made the voyages hazardous, and ships sometimes foundered and sank; other ships were sunk by raiders or pirates. The exhibits of Spanish-American treasures retrieved after some grueling searches in the waters of this area include silver and gold coins, doubloons and half-doubloons, pieces of eight, silver bars, and emeralds and pearls. Among other items recovered and displayed here are a bronze bell (1751), an eighteenth-century iron ship's anchor, a fragment of a sixteenth-century wrought iron cannon barrel, and some solid iron shots.

The cumbersome Neufeldt-Kuhnke armored diving suit displayed here was developed in Germany before World War II and was worn by divers carrying bottles of oxygen and other equipment strapped to their backs. More recent advances in equipment for diving and underwater exploration, as detailed here, include the development of lightweight diving wear (rubber suits and flippers that give divers greater mobility) and electronic gear that indicates the presence of electrically conductive metals (for detecting shipwreck sites). There are also illustrations of submarines and diving bells that may possibly be constructed in the future.

Contrasted with the divers of old who depended on lung power alone, the underwater diver today has all the wonders of modern electronics, physics and chemistry to assist him in the search for underwater treasures. In this hall is a life-sized diorama of modern divers exploring a wreck site. The visitor can see two divers measure and excavate a site while a third is taking moving pictures.

The 1951 underwater find by Teddy Tucker, a Bermuda diver, includes the remains of a Spanish ship and its cargo. Part of this find on exhibit here shows iron bolts, a brass hand grenade, musket balls, a breech-lock for a swivel gun, a shark hook, and a pewter porringer among many other things.

A final exhibit explains the Smithsonian laboratories' methods for preserving underwater finds, which might otherwise disintegrate after being dried out.

Ordnance Hall and the Gunboat "Philadelphia" (Third Floor, East Side)

Colonel Bruce McDonough, a graduate of West Point and a veteran of both the European and Vietnam theaters of war, visited this Ordnance Hall on a bus man's holiday. He examined with considerable interest the naval and military arms from colonial times to the Korean War and weapons (many in replica) from the primitive ages through biblical times. He found early Roman weapons displayed and military weapons and supplies used in Europe, and some brought from Europe to the American colonies in the seventeenth and eighteenth centuries. Among these latter he found the wheel lock, the flintlock, swords, sabres, muskets, powder horns, and pistols. Land artillery equipment is also displayed and there are naval guns and models of tanks used in World War I. There is a four-pounder cannon cast during the American Revolution that was used during Paul Revere's campaign of 1799. What especially intrigued Colonel McDonough was the oldest existing American man-of-war, the gunboat "Philadelphia" built by the Americans during the Revolutionary War, and today displayed on a platform adjacent to this hall.

Artillery has been in use from earliest times, but, as chronicled here, it entered its modern age in the seventeenth century, when Gustavus Adolphus of Sweden discovered how to make field artillery more maneuverable. Frederick the Great later introduced horse drawn artillery, thereby greatly increasing the flexibility of military campaigns. Shown are models of a nine-pounder demiculverin, a wrought iron breechloader, a six-pounder field gun, an iron twelve-pounder, and other guns. Artillery weapons of the early eighteenth century are also on exhibit.

Displays trace the development of modern naval guns, and recount how Henry VIII cleverly deployed them to gain naval superiority over other European powers. Included are models of a fifteenth-century wrought iron breechloader, a sixteenth-century brass muzzleloader, a brass cannon of the early seventeenth century, and a late eighteenth century cast iron twenty-four pounder.

A special area of the hall displays large models of ships, among them the U.S.S. "Missouri" on which the formal surrender of Japan to the Allied Powers was signed at the close of World War II. Also featured here are the aircraft carrier "Yorktown," battleship "Maine" sunk at Havana in 1895, armored cruiser "New York," armored cruiser "Brooklyn," and the protected cruisers "Baltimore," "Olympia," and "St. Louis." The destroyer "Manly" is here, as is the submarine "S-48," the dreadnought battleship "North Carolina," the nuclear ballistic missile submarine "George Washington," and the nuclear-powered frigate "Bainbridge."

Visitors will find themselves comparing in this hall the arms used in colonial America between 1526 and 1688 with those used between 1689 and 1783. Among these arms are swords, sabres, rapiers, daggers, muskets, and other ordnance pieces.

Exhibits describing the early history of American military weapons and ammunition display for the period 1795-1840 the muskets, pistols, rifles, and other weapons that were used. Included in the display of weapons and ammunition used between 1841 and 1860 are small arms such as Elgin cutlass pistols, cavalry carbines, percussion breechloaders, and Colt revolvers. Other arms developed in this period (and shown here) include semi-automatic and automatic rifles, buffalo rifles, metallic cartridge handguns, single and multi-barreled handguns, and percussion breechloaders. All types of cartridges for these arms are featured, too.

The next war period in American history is, of course, the Civil War. Exhibits describe the Union's supply of weapons and ammunition. Flintlocks were converted at first to the percussion system by supplies purchased abroad. The North later began to manufacture modern muzzleloaders and a variety of breechloading and repeater weapons, as shown here. The artillery was primarily smoothbore iron thirteen-inch seacoast mortars and six and twelve-pounder field guns.

As described here, the Confederate Army was also forced by the shortage of firearms to convert obsolete arms to the percussion system. The South later manufactured weapons, but also used those captured from the North. The Confederacy was further handicapped by the Union's blockade of its ports, which prevented them from obtaining much-needed arms from abroad. Shown here are a Palmetto musket, a Cook carbine, a Cook rifle, a Sharp carbine, and other Confederate weapons.

The creation of the interchangeable parts system played a significant role in the history of firearms and hastened, as well, the development of many manufacturing industries which could use interchangeable parts. Patterns, templates, and precise measuring gauges of all types are shown here. Aided by the work of inventors and armorers like Eli Whitney, John Hall, Thomas Blanchard, Samuel Colt, Paul Mauser, Eliphalet Remington, and others, the United States was the first country to arm itself with a weapon completely assembled from standard interchangeable parts. In this hall are examples illustrating some of the ingenious inventions these men produced. There is also on display a Gatling gun, invented in 1862 by Dr. Richard Gatling. It was the first practical machine gun until 1910. After that date its appearance was not much, until it reappeared as the "Vulcan," an air force rapid firing cannon.

The swords of various periods in our country's history are shown in several large display cases. Among some military swords on exhibit are an 1807 cavalryman's sabre, a presentation sword of the War of 1812, a non-commissioned officer's sword, a musician's sword, and a medical staffer's sword. Also exhibited are swords of the Confederacy, the United States Navy, and highly ornamented presentation swords awarded for distinguished service.

Many rare ordnance items have been contributed to the Smithsonian by individuals who inherited them. When Chapman Grant of Escondido, California was eighty-six years old he donated a muzzle-loading derringer to the Smithsonian. What made this short-barreled pistol unique was that it had once been owned by his grandfather, Ulysses S. Grant. Chapman Grant was the son of Jess Root Grant, youngest of President Grant's three sons.

The gunboat "Philadelphia" shown at the entrance to this hall was designed by Benedict Arnold as part of a fleet of eight man-of-war gunboats built for the Revolutionary War's defense of the northern frontier against the British. The boat was sunk by the British at the Battle of Valcour Island on Lake Champlain in 1776 and it was not recovered until 1935. Even so, a period of twenty-five years elapsed before it found a permanent home with the Smithsonian in this museum.

The gunboat is flat-bottomed, constructed of oak timbers and plankings to a length of fifty-seven feet, with a seventeen-foot beam. The vessel carried forty-five men who were responsible for maneuvering the oars and square-rigged sails, and for handling the guns and other ordnance material on board. The only protection from the elements was a large overhead tarpaulin.

The "Philadelphia" had a midship gun deck with a three-quarter pounder swivel gun in a bracket and a nine-pounder broadside gun on a truck carriage at the starboard. At the bow was a cannon with a slide carriage and a twelve-pounder with side racks. A twenty-four pounder British shot can still be seen embedded in the side of the "Philadelphia's" planking, which was thought to be the probable cause

of its sinking. Although this gunboat had rested under ten feet of
water for a century and a half, the main mast was still standing upright
when the boat was discovered and retrieved from Lake Champlain.

Artifacts on the boat include a partially restored brick hearth
on which all of the crew's meals were prepared, a kettle, a frying
pan, towing bitts, lead-lined hawser pipes, catheads, anchors, a bar
shot, and a wrought iron shot gauge. Some other items recovered
and shown in a nearby glass case include knives, spoons, other cooking
equipment, and an hour glass. A nearby exhibit illustrates with the
use of model boats the Battle of Valcour Island in which the gunboat
"Philadelphia" participated on October 11, 1776.

Hall of Armed Forces History (Third Floor, East Side)

In the early seventeenth century, American fighting men
were equipped with heavy armor quite unsuitable for battle in this
land and carried swords made in Europe also not very suitable. Fighting
in the New World was different from combat in Europe and the American armed forces—the Army, Navy, Marine Corps, and the Coast
Guard—over the years gradually evolved more suitable equipment
for our climate and terrain for its needs. The exhibits in this hall
begin with the colonial era and continue through the final battles
of the Civil War, recounting the history of the armed forces through
displays of historic documents, scale model ships, equipment, gear,
uniforms, and other authentic artifacts. A presentation called "Spirit
of 1776" dramatizing the everyday life of the citizen-soldier during
the American Revolution, is given in a Discovery Corner in this hall
on Tuesdays and Thursdays at 12:30 and 2 p.m.; on weekends at 11
and 3 p.m.

The collection of uniforms is considerable; uniforms worn
by the Virginia Regiment of Volunteer Militia during the French and
Indian Wars, and of the first Regiment of Artillery worn by American
militia during the Revolutionary War. There are uniforms worn by
a revenue marine and a navy surgeon (both of 1834); there is also
the full dress uniform of a sergeant of the Dragoons (1833-50), and
an early nineteenth-century uniform that belonged to Brigadier General
Peter Gainsvoort. There are the Mexican War uniforms of an infantry
private, and of Marine Major Levy Twiggs; the uniform of a voluntary
militia sergeant in the Regiment of Mounted Riflemen (1851-54);
and a non-commissioned officer's summer service uniform for the
Seminole War. The Civil War uniforms include the uniforms worn
by Union and Confederate soldiers from privates to artillery captains,
and on up.

No exhibit on the armed forces would be complete without
a display of artifacts associated with some well-known people. Among
these are swords carried by Andrew Jackson (in the War of 1812)
and the Count de Rochambeau (in the Revolutionary War), epaulets
and a gold medal presented to Lieutenant Charles Wilkes, and a bronze
head of naval scientist Matthew F. Maury. Some silk cloth and a
lacquered box brought from Japan by the Perry expedition are on
exhibit, as are a medal and a sword awarded General Winfield Scott
for his services in the Mexican War, and the mounted figure of Civil

War General Philip Sheridan's horse, Winchester. Also shown, among many other items, is the service dress cap and dress coat worn by Rear Admiral David G. Farragut.

Between 1607 and 1688 the standard military equipment and gear used in America included heavy body armor, swords, match and wheel lock muskets, and pikes brought from Europe, as shown here. Many of these items, unsuitable for fighting in the New World, were later replaced by flintlock firearms, rapiers, plug bayonets, breast plates, and other lighter equipment exhibited here.

The colonists were involved in the French and Indian War (1754-63) which was fought between French and English settlers for the control of territory and trade in the New World. The war ended with the British victorious. They took control over the lands drained by the Ohio River, part of Canada, and all French possessions east of the Mississippi. Britain took Florida from Spain as well. Included in the exhibit of items of this period are a squaw axe, glass beads, powder horns, John Edwards' enlistment papers, a thirteen-inch bomb recovered from Lake George, New York, and the epaulets Washington wore as a colonel of the Virginia militia.

Prior to 1760 the colonies had not seriously considered independence from the mother country. Events which followed that date served to incite the majority of the people with a desire to make a far reaching change. The Revolutionary War (1775-83) led to the colonist's break with Britain. George Washington in a desperate attempt to rally his men and save the war, successfully struck at British forces at Trenton and then at Princeton. These victories reaffirmed the faith of his men and of the people. The Battle of Saratoga (1777) led by General Horatio Gates against General Burgoyne was an important victory for it succeeded in taking out of action a large part of the British army. Two paintings here show the surrender of General Burgoyne at Saratoga, and General Washington at the Battle of Trenton. The colonies required the assistance of France, who came in after the Battle of Saratoga, and victory came with the defeat of Cornwallis at Yorktown in 1781. The 1783 Treaty of Paris gave the thirteen colonies their independence and the territories lying east of the Mississippi River that Great Britain held. A wide variety of items of this period on display show swords, helmets, muskets, a militia knapsack, a canteen, and pictures of Hessian mercenaries the British had hired. There is also a medicine scale, a belt axe, entrenching tools, and paintings of the Battle of Lexington and Concord, and of the surrender of Cornwallis at Yorktown. Documents, letters, maps, broadsides, and cartoons are other items of this period displayed.

The hall displays such notable artifacts as General George Washington's eighteen by twenty-eight foot headquarter's tent of unbleached linen trimmed with a scalloped edge on top with its inside contents that show a camp bed, a folding camp stool, a bottle chest, woolen blankets, and brass traveling candlesticks. A reproduction of Washington's commission as general and commander-in-chief of the army, a portrait of him by Charles Peale Pope, and his camp chest are among other items of Washington's on display in this hall.

The army's activities between 1798 and 1815 included fighting a second war with Great Britain in 1812. The leadership of Winfield

Scott and Andrew Jackson was important, contributing to the eventual victory and peace. Artifacts such as the twelve-pounder carronade shown here that could be mounted on the upper works of warships and merchant ships were used mainly in close engagements with the enemy. Other items (some in replica) shown of this period of this country's second war with Great Britain trace our army's occupation at this time.

In 1803 President Jefferson after negotiating with France acquired an enormous piece of land known as the Louisiana Purchase that doubled the American territory. This land would eventually become twelve new states and part of another. President Jefferson sent Lewis and Clark on an expedition to survey that land and the western lands beyond. The army was of primary importance in the assistance it gave towards protecting the expedition and the aid it gave Lewis and Clark in innumerable ways at this time. Exhibits show documents, letters, and artifacts brought back for information.

The artifacts and displays in another exhibit tell of the army's participation in the war with Mexico (1846-48), and describe American leaders of that time: Zachary Taylor, Winfield Scott, Ulysses S. Grant, and Robert E. Lee. The war ended with Mexico's ceding to the United States all lands north of the Rio Grande—eventually this land became the states of Texas, California, New Mexico, Utah, Nevada, and part of Colorado. Artifacts on display include percussion rifles, flintlocks, pistols, swords, and sabres carried by soldiers in the American army (1846-48).

The Civil War (1861-1865) exhibits interpret the Union army's role and the Confederate army's role in it. Such Union and Confederate army leaders as Grant, Lee, Jefferson Davis, Stonewall Jackson, George Mead, William Sherman, Philip Sheridan, and others are discussed. Exhibits also sketch some important battles, including Vicksburg, Gettysburg, Richmond, Scottsylvania, and Mobile Bay. Equipment and gear used by both armies is displayed including a twelve-pounder field gun, a basic field piece called a Napoleon (some parts of it are reproduced). The diary of a Union soldier who participated in the Vicksburg campaign is a sad, nostalgic item.

The history of the Marines begins in 1775 when the Continental Congress authorized two battalions to serve on ships in support of the Continental Navy. Marines on board these warships helped maintain discipline and supported the navy men when boarding enemy ships. At the close of the Revolutionary War the Marine Corps was disbanded, but it was later reformed. Flintlock muskets, swords, canteens, and a grenade are among Marine Corps articles exhibited. Both graphic exhibits and scale model vessels here suggest marine activities in the naval war with France (1798), in Tripoli (1801), in the War of 1812, in the Seminole Wars, and in the Mexican and Civil Wars.

The sea-going police force originally known as the Revenue Marines was founded in 1789 by the First Congress. Its name was first changed to the United States Revenue Cutter Service, and later to its present name, the United States Coast Guard. As an armed force, the Coast Guard supervises the entire American coastline. Artifacts of the Coast Guard services are shown.

Many of the maritime artifacts on display in the exhibits of our navy's history date back to the colonial period, when ships brought supplies to the colonies and returned to Great Britain with native American products. The story of the participation of the navy in military activities begins with the Revolutionary War. A most intriguing audio-visual exhibit describes the 1781 Battle of the Capes of the Chesapeake, an important Revolutionary War encounter between the naval forces of Britain and our country. It was the colonists, with the help of France who bottled up Cornwallis there and forced him to surrender, thus assuring American independence. The navy's history continues with the descriptions of vital naval participation in the War of 1812, the Mexican War, and the Civil War in which the navy's successful blockade of supplies and equipment from abroad destined for the Confederate forces proved decisive to the war. One of the great Union admirals was David G. Farragut whose work is discussed in an exhibit.

Other material in this hall that depicts the navy's role in various explorations includes diplomatic services and scientific and engineering projects. Charles Wilkes' expeditions to the west coasts of North and South America are described, and the navy's role in diplomatic activities, including Commodore Matthew Perry's opening of trade relations with Japan is described. In a case is shown a Japanese Samurai armor of the Tokuguawa period (17th-19th centuries) that came from the Columbian Exposition collection. The navy has also contributed its energies and resources to scientific and engineering projects. Among those described here are Matthew F. Maury's study of ocean currents, the laying of the first transatlantic cable, and the development of steam power for transportation.

Detailed scale models of all types of navy vessels are on display, among them the British frigate "Boston" (1748), the American frigate "Constellation" (1797), the forty-two gun raider "Bonhomme Richard" (1779), and the privateer "Rattlesnake" (1780). The 1797 frigate "Constitution," the iron battleship "Old Ironsides," and the 1813 sloop-of-war "Niagara" are also recreated in models, as are the "Fulton," an 1813 steam battery, the 1842 frigate "Congress," and the famous ironclad "Monitor." Other models depict the seventy-four gun "Delaware," the Confederate dispatch boat "Planter," the Confederate blockade runner "Modern Greece," the gun battleship "Missouri," the "USS Hartford," a Civil War steam sloop-of-war and the "CSS Tennessee" which took part in the 1864 battle of Mobile Bay.

Hall of Photography (Third Floor, East Side)

There always seems to have been a desire to record images of people and the world about us, and exhibits in this hall display some of the historical devices men used to accomplish this goal. While experimental attempts were made long before the early nineteenth century, it was only then that independent efforts in France, England, and the United States resulted in significant advances in photographic techniques. Among the men who played important roles in the nineteenth-century development of photography were William H. Fox Talbot, Louis Daguerre, Joseph Niepce, R.L. Maddox, Robert Bingham, Sir John Herschel, Matthew Brady, Sir James Clerk Maxwell, and others. Their work and the work of others described in this hall made possible the sophisticated equipment and techniques used today by industrialists, engineers, people in the medical fields, scientists (including astronomers, biologists, botanists, microscopists, and others), police, educators, artists, the entertainment industry, and just plain folks.

An ancient device for observing optical images was the camera obscura (meaning dark chamber). It was known to Aristotle, and a diagram of it appeared in a manuscript of 1519 by Leonardo da Vinci. Other early scientists and non-scientists over the years continually improved it. A camera obscura is on exhibit here, along with an 1807 camera lucida (meaning light chamber) patented by William H. Wollastan and used as a drawing aid by artists who used it in reducing large drawings to smaller size and in transposing sketches.

Many of the early nineteenth-century photographic inventors mentioned in this hall have examples of their work displayed. The photographic work of Joseph Niepce of France is discussed and a copy of the earliest existing permanent photograph, his 1826 heliograph is shown. The camera exposure for this picture took an entire day. The important photographic techniques developed by William H. Fox Talbot of England in 1841 were those for the negative-positive photographic prints. They made possible shorter exposure time for photographs than those achieved by Niepce. In this hall we see examples of Talbot's earlier efforts made in 1834-35 of photogenic drawings produced from mechanically made negatives, the callotype process, and of the negative-positive photographic prints. A large diorama shows Talbot's botanical photographic laboratory in England and in it the photographic equipment, furniture, and some of the glassware he used.

In this hall are discussed the works of Sir John Herschel of England, the producer of the first glass-plate negative; Louis Daguerre of France, inventor in 1839 of the light-sensitive silver-coated copper plate called the daguerreotype; R.L. Maddox of England, who in 1871 used a gelatin emulsion for making glass prints; and Robert Bingham, who in 1850 devised the collodion wet-plate negative popular between the 1850s and the 1870s, but was superseded when commercially-prepared collodion wet plates took the place of emulsions the photographers prepared themselves.

A diorama shows a photographer of about 1860 coating a glass plate with a collodion emulsion in a dark room. Matthew Brady, the Civil War photographer and Lincoln portraitist, developed glass plate negatives in this country with which he made portraits of nearly every important American of the latter half of the nineteenth century, some shown here. George Eastman, also of the United States invented in 1880 a plate-coating apparatus for mass-producing gelatin dry plates and a diorama is shown of women working in the print room of the Eastman Dry Plate and Film Co. Other photographic pioneers whose works were innovative achievements are discussed including E. Howard Farmer, C. Wellborn Piper, Abel Niepce de Saint-Victor, J.W. Sloan, and others.

On display are many historic photographic lenses: one of the earliest is an 1812 Singlet; an 1839 F/15 achromatic landscape lens; a replica of Josef Petzval's 1840 F/3.5 portrait lens; an 1860

Duplet lens; several Zeiss lenses of different periods, and a 1935 nine-lens camera, in which the lens can simultaneously expose separate images on one strip of film.

Early photographers could produce only one print, so the invention of a means for obtaining multiple prints was important. William H.F. Talbot, Sir John Herschel, Louis D. Blanquart-Evrard, and others pioneered in this, and exhibits portray the results of their efforts.

Sir John Herschel was also concerned with making photographic enlargements which he first described in 1839. Among other pioneers in this endeavor were Alexander Wolcott, and O.J. Wallis, both of New York, and D. Van Monockhoven of Belgium; an exhibit describes their work (1840-1870). On display is an 1880 Woodward Solar Camera made by David A. Woodward of Baltimore, in which an external condenser lens focused sunlight for hours at a time on a negative, a lens inside the camera projected an enlarged image of the negative onto sensitive enlarging paper attached to the easel.

Another exhibit describes the color photography process first introduced in 1861 by James Clerk Maxwell. A continuous slide show also describes the processes and history of color photography; among those whose works are discussed are Louis Ducos du Hauron and Charles Gros.

Because of these and other advances, photography is now used in scientific work, where the camera can record phenomena the human eye is unable to detect. John Dancer of England reduced a twenty-inch document to one-eighth inch on a daguerreotype plate in 1839, opening a flood of uses for this kind of photography including: secret war-time messages, cancelled bank checks, miniaturization for mass production of designs, and microfilming done by libraries and other industries, among other uses. Modern cameras fitted with microscopes can magnify sights of the biological world: of blood, a drop of water, or a pollen grain. Aerial photography for mapping, and for reconnaissance work can help in explorations or in war work. High speed photography is demonstrated by a bullet cutting through a card, and in photographing the motions of a horse's legs when running. Time lapse photography can take single photographs over a period of time showing the process of transformation of flowers, of decaying fruit, or maggots attacking a dead animal. Medicine has been helped in many instances by photography. X-rays are a useful tool; a sensitive sound-emitting camera can record such things as a fetus in the mother's womb; and Kurlean photographs show a Kurlean aura which suggests biogenetic emenations that tell if something is wrong with a person. Photographs can assist in underwater research or in heavenly research. A colossal camera telescope photographs the sky at Tucson, Arizona and can detect objects more than six million times fainter than the eye alone can see. All of these can extend our knowledge of the world and provide us with a new way of looking at it; these and other more recent uses are illustrated in this hall.

Dioramas in this hall highlight both photographic advances and important photographers. Roger Fenton, an early American photojournalist is portrayed in a diorama photographing military life in a battle zone of the Crimean War. This kind of work had previously been done by artists. Fenton's photographic prints were published in newspapers and sold by subscription with wood engravings of them that appeared in the **London News.** Portrayed in a large open floor diorama is an American explorer–photographer (about 1870) shown with his assistant, his pack mule, and the tent he used as a dark room. Another diorama features members of an 1840s family who are shown gathered in a large living room of that period examining photos and photograph albums.

An alcove gallery provides temporary, changing displays of the works of some well-known photographers. Among the photographic artists whose works have appeared here are Charles Berger, Todd Walker, Jan Portner, Peggy Douglas, Len Gittleman (whose serigraphs were created from photographs taken on the Apollo 15 mission), Claus Mroczynski, Ilene Lake Jack, and Scott Hyde.

Photography has not been restricted to professionals, of course, and amateur photographers were aided by the development of flexible rollfilm, which made possible smaller and lighter cameras. Amateur photographers may be interested in one of the slide shows in this hall, which explains photographic processes especially for their benefit.

Moving pictures have held a fascination for many. On display are four old-fashioned, hand-cranked peep shows, in which the rapid cranking of the pictures produces an illusion of movement. Several exhibits record the history of the motion picture industry and the flexible rollfilms, special cameras, lenses, and other improvements that contributed to its growth. Photographs of early motion picture stars are featured.

An alcove in this hall shows free "movies" on a number of very early projectors. These include a phenahistiscope, a forerunner of the cinema, which was designed as a toy in 1832, and in which the observer can see images reflected in a mirror through cuts in a revolving disc; a zoetrope, another forerunner of the motion picture, invented in 1834 it had a rotating drum with slots in its side through which the viewer can see a number of drawings lining the wall of the drum and which gives an appearance of motion when the drum is revolved; also shown are mutoscopes, and stereoscopes. Displayed, too, is the historic 1902 Rosenfeld Illustrated Song Machine, whose sound reproduction system incorporated an Edison cylinder. It was among the first devices to combine sound and pictures, a forerunner of the "talkies."

In the hall is a Trans–Lux Theater that shows newsreels of the 1930s, many of them narrated by Lowell Thomas, and for which there is no admission charge.

The store front of a tin type photographic shop is shown. Tin types were introduced in 1852 and became popular for portraits because they were relatively inexpensive. This shop is not open for business, but the tin type photographic shop in the Arts and Industries Building across the Mall and located in the Museum shop is. The photographers will provide clothing of the period for the portrait.

Hall of the History of Money, Medals, and the Medallic Arts (also Orders and Decorations) (Third Floor, East Side)

Do you know which president's portrait appears on the $100,000 bill? If you visit this hall in the Museum of American History you will soon find out. The attractively displayed exhibits draw even the most casual visitors into the hall and security for these valuable collections are extra stringent, constantly monitered for all areas of the hall. The collections cover a wide number of cultures and the history of some of these cultures can be traced in their coinage.

As one enters the Hall of Money and Medals a reproduction of a huge coin stamper designed by Leonardo da Vinci can be seen. There is also a geometric lathe, an important mechanical device, which can prevent or help detect forgeries because its ornamentation of coins, bills, or valuable documents are difficult to reproduce. A foot-high model for the Kennedy half-dollar is shown here along with many real half-dollars on display.

The National Numismatic Collections are considered among the finest research collections of their kind in the world. The Smithsonian received some donated by private collectors, others were given by corporations, and several collections were purchased by government agencies and later turned over to the Smithsonian. Items on view from one of the largest collections in the country (24,000 specimens) came from the Chase Manhattan Bank Money Collection. Given to the Smithsonian it provides examples of currency from primitive times to the present that include examples of 2,500 year old Egyptian gold rings, Chinese tao from the fifth century B.C., a Carthagenian decadrachm struck between 241 and 1146 B.C., and other historical coins and currency up to modern American and European coins and paper currency including American colonial paper currencies. There are specimens of many interesting checks including a check written in the 1950s to Howard Hughes for $25,000,000 for 550 feature films; a check with a red and blue ink border designed by Benjamin Franklin; and checks signed by every U.S. president, and by Susan B. Anthony, Charles Dickens and Helen Keller. Specimens are shown from another collection that show U.S. paper currencies issued since 1861 which were transferred to the Smithsonian from the Treasury Department. Specimens from other world famous collections are on display in this hall. Among these are coins from the Josiah K. Lilly, Jr. Collection of United States and Foreign Gold Coins. This collection was acquired for the Smithsonian through an act of Congress in 1968 and consists of over six thousand gold coins, covering over twenty-six centuries. There are also coins from the Willis H. Dupont Collection of Russian Coins and Medals which include the famous Grand Duke Georgii Michailovich Collection; it is said that only Leningrad's Hermitage has a finer Russian collection. There are specimens exhibited from the Paul A. Straub Collection of more than 5,500 gold and silver coins from the Americas and Europe since about 1500; and there are specimens of the collection of ancient Japanese gold and silver coins given President Grant by the Japanese government. Still another collection from which specimens are exhibited is the Mortimer and Anna Neinken Collection of Paper Currencies of the World. More exhibits provide specimens from United States and Canadian coins, paper monies used during most periods of United States history, and coins used for propaganda purposes.

Among the oddities on display here are the works of counterfeiters and among them examples of the work of two American master

counterfeiters, William Brockway and Emanuel ("Jim the Penman")
Ninger. There are also Bank of England counterfeit notes made by
prisoners forced by the Nazis to do so in World War II German concentration camps. These notes were so cleverly executed they escaped
detection until the equivalent of almost half a billion dollars had
been circulated. A replica of the first lump of gold taken in 1848
from Sutter's Mill in California (the original can be seen in the Hall
of Everyday Life in the American Past) is also found in this hall.

An exhibit "From Mine to Mint" gives an overview of coinage
that begins with the ancient mining of metals as early as 4000 B.C.
The display continues down through the ages illustrating the use of
metal for coins by such methods of striking coins as intaglio-cuts
and drop-hammer, roller, screw, and toggle pressed. A nineteenth-
century screw coining press is on exhibit and a cast steel screw press
manufactured by Edward Stahler in 1847 for the Smithsonian can
also be seen. The display on minting operations in the United States
includes illustrations of the way in which an artist creates a design
for coins or medals. It was Thomas Jefferson who felt the need for
the establishment of a system of uniform coinage and precise weights
and measures. It was primarily his efforts that led to the creation
of the U.S. Mint in 1792.

The history of money as described in many exhibits begins
(appropriately enough) with "The Moneyless Economies," which tells
how early civilizations bartered surplus commodities of recognized
value as their means of exchange. Among these were tea bricks which
had legal tender status in Tibet, Mongolia, and Southern Siberia. As
tender in ancient Egypt there were grain banks while ancient Rome
used salt. On the Yap Islands the medium of exchange was a coin
made from a form of limestone called argonite. In the western hemisphere there were wide and varied artifacts used for barter ranging
from shells of all kinds (abolone, clam, dentalium, and others), teeth
of caribou or elk, cocoa beans, and fish hooks to woodpecker scalps,
axe blades, obsidian blades, and copper shields. On the African continent some unused tools and weapons, certain commodities, and
even copper crosses were bartered. These bartered surplus commodities
are all illustrated in the hall.

The first known coins date back to seventh century B.C. and
maps displayed here pinpoint the earliest civilizations to use coins.
On exhibit are coins from Lydia, Ionia, Persia, Sicily, Corinth, and
other ancient lands. One on the Hellenic world displays Greek city-state
coins. Among these on display are coins struck during the period of
Athenian supremacy; during the rise of Macedonia as a power; during
Alexander's empire; and during the period of the Hellenistic kingdoms.

"Ancient Rome" follows the course of Roman coinage during
the age of the Roman republics. There are also coins and medallions
of the Roman empires, with a series showing portraits of all of the
Roman emperors. The display on the Byzantine empire notes that
coins like the ones exhibited here circulated freely in Islamic countries
during the time of the Crusades. These coins significantly eased trading,
while the lack of such currency in other parts of the world handicapped
commerce.

The now humble penny was at one time silver, coined under
the money reforms instituted by Charlemagne and used until nearly

the end of the thirteenth century. The penny became the basis for the money economies of France, Germany, Italy, Scandinavia, Bohemia, and England. During the Middle Ages, crusaders returning from Islamic countries helped reestablish trade between East and West bringing back these coins. Exhibits point out how this trade revival necessitated coinage of suitable currency. Shown are some of the first gold coins struck in the West, among them the ducat, and the augustalis. The tiny groats (multiple pennies) exhibited here were used during the twelfth century as trade coins. Testons (coins with portraits) came into circulation in Vienna in the 1470s. An exhibit describes how, about 1486, the Archduke Sigismund of Tyrol initiated the use of the thaler (dollar) because there was a need for larger trade coins. The dollar quickly came into use in other countries and eventually became an important unit of world trade.

The dollar is now the basic unit of the United States, but this was not always so. A display on barter on the frontier, for example shows items exchanged between Indians and traders (among these items previously mentioned, but in addition, sea otter skins, horses, buffalo robes, deerskins, beaver skins, eagle feathers). In colonial America (1607-1765) various currencies circulated among the first settlers, French, English, and Dutch who brought coins with them. Specimens of these coins are shown as are coins struck in Massachusetts in 1652, and bills of credit issued there in 1690. Paper currency issues of the several states and the Continental Congress (1764-1787) are displayed as are state coins and items loaned by France, Holland, and Spain to the new and financially hard-pressed country.

Hamilton, Jefferson, and Robert Morris were of great assistance to the new country in organizing its finances and creating banks, and a national currency as the "Building a Nation" exhibit explains. The United States mint was established in 1791 at Philadelphia and an exhibit shows some of the copper, silver, and gold coins made there at that time and also later.

Between 1812 and 1860 the United States underwent a series of financial crises that eventually resulted in the establishment of a new banking system. An exhibit discusses both these crises and the gold discoveries in California, North Carolina, and Georgia that helped stabilize the country. Between 1860 and 1873, during the Civil War and the Reconstruction Period that followed, Congress issued paper money to help pay for the war. Specimens of these are on display as are "greenbacks" and Confederate dollars.

In the following years the country began an economic growth and with it the establishment of a gold standard. On display are copies of two legislative acts of this period that were of great financial importance, the Bland-Allison Act (1878) and the Sherman Silver Purchase Act (1890). Another exhibit describes the establishment of the Federal Reserve system in 1913 and how it reorganized the country's banking and paper currency system.

United States medals and tokens displayed in the hall include, among others: Smithsonian award medals (the Hodgkins, Langley, and the Smithsonian gold medals), the Washington medal, Indian peace medals, art medals, Civil War tokens, and "Hard Times" tokens awarded as substitutes for cash.

The practice of giving orders and decorations in reward for

civil, military, and religious achievements grew out of a medieval custom whereby knighthoods were conferred by religious orders created during the Crusades. One of the earliest of these religious orders dates back to the twelfth century and was known as the Knights Hospitaler, but better known as the Knights of Malta. These knights limited themselves at first to caring for pilgrims and the sick, but later fought in the Crusades. The Order of Knights Templar, the Order of Christ, and the Order of Teutonic Knights are other ancient orders of knighthood whose decorations, badges, and symbols have specimens on exhibit. Among the artifacts of more recent orders are those of England's second highest order, the Honorable Order of the Bath created in 1725 by King George I. A scarlet robe and badge, worn at investiture to this order, are on exhibit. The one shown was worn by Henry M. Stanley at the time of his being knighted.

The hall contains medals and badges of early secular orders of chivalry, including the Most Noble Order of the Garter founded in 1350 by the English King Edward III; the badges displayed show St. George, the patron saint of England, killing the fabled dragon. Among other specimens displayed are the Italian Order of Annuziata founded in 1362; the Order of the Golden Fleece of the Holy Roman Empire, founded in 1492 at Flanders, and conferred mainly on members of the House of Hapsburg and other ruling princes.

Many orders are named for a symbolic animal, and the hall exhibits a variety of medals struck for such orders: the Order of the Elephant (Denmark), the Order of the White Eagle (Poland), the Order of the Golden Lion (Hesse), the Order of the Golden Eagle (Wurtemberg), and the Orders of the Black Eagle and the Red Eagle (both from Prussia). There are also medals struck for orders named for saints: the Order of St. Andrew (Russia), and the Order of St. Hubert (Palatinate).

Other orders whose decorations are on display include the Most Illustrious Order of St. Patrick (Ireland), the Order of Merit (Prussia), the Order of Danneborg (Denmark), the Orders of the Polar Star and Seraphim (both of Sweden), the Order of St. Isabella and the Order of Elizabeth (Portuguese and Austrian orders of ladies), the Order of the Aztec Eagle (Mexico), the Order of the White Elephant (Siam), the Order of the Chrysanthemum (Japan), the Order of the Tuetzal (Guatemala), and the Order of the Kapiolani (Hawaii). The hall also has on exhibit an Imperial badge with the head of Napoleon and a Republic badge with the allegorical head of the French Republic, both, of course, from France. Most orders are graded into several classes for which stars, crosses, ribbons, and other insignia are awarded to designate the different classes.

Henry Luce Hall of Newsreporting (Third Floor, West Side)

If you were a member of Benjamin Franklin's family, what newspapers might you have been reading? The history of American newsreporting recounted in this hall begins with colonial times. There are copies of important broadsides, newspapers, and magazines that influenced public opinion, and that illustrate the journalistic styles of successive periods in American history. The artifacts on display show the impact of advancing technology in equipment that made possible quicker reporting of the news as well as speedier delivery—whether in print, on radio, or on television. Many people are discussed in this hall who made significant contributions helping to influence their profession by shaping the news of their times.

At the entrance to the hall is a replica of the 1910 Charles Ludwig newswagon, above which the first electric sign in Salt Lake City once suggested "Read the Salt Lake Tribune." Newspapers from all over the world were sold from this newswagon. When opened it revealed counters and benches along with the newspapers and periodicals it sold; when not in use the wagon could be closed up tighter than a drum.

Exhibits trace the American newspaper industry beginning about 1679. Among the artifacts shown is a copy of **The Newsletter** (Boston, 1704-76), a colonial newspaper issued weekly with about two-thirds of its news clipped from English newspapers and letters that came to the American shores. There is a newspacket exhibited from the first issue of the **Boston Gazette** (1719-98), a paper edited by five successive Boston postmasters; American reprints of the **London Gazette** (the copy shown is dated 1679); Franklin's **New England Courant** (1721-26); and the **American Weekly** of Philadelphia (1719-49). The **Philadelphia Gazette**, of which a copy is shown, was published by Benjamin Franklin from 1737 to 1776 and continued in print until 1815. There is a copy of the **New York Weekly Journal** which was published by John Peter Zenger, whose acquittal in a libel suit instigated by a British governor contributed to the establishment of a free press. The **Pittsburgh Gazette** (1786), of which a copy is shown, was the first newspaper in the west and is shown along with some other early newspapers.

The **Pennsylvania Journal** (1742) and the **Boston Gazette** (1719) have copies displayed here, both editorialized against the Stamp Act. The Act was passed by the British parliament in 1765 to help pay for the French and Indian War. The Act caused the price of newspapers to increase fifty percent, but was repealed in 1766.

In the 1830s the **New York Sun** advertised that the unemployed might earn money selling its newspapers. An open floor exhibit shows a boy of about ten hawking its newspapers from his wagon.

The **New York Times** (1851-) is considered by many one of the greatest American newspapers of all time. It was the first paper to use wireless services to report news from Europe and from the North Pole; and the index of its articles since 1851 is an invaluable research tool. Many artifacts connected with the **New York Times** are on display.

Among the names prominent in the annals of American journalism are Horace Greeley, E.W. Scripps, William Randolph Hearst, Joseph Pulitzer, Adolph Ochs, Francis P. Church, and Henry Luce. These men and some of their activities on their respective papers are portrayed in selected exhibits.

A manifestation of America's ethnic diversity was the appearance in the eighteenth century of foreign language newspapers. Although today their number is declining, such newspapers are still being published. An exhibit includes copies of German, French, Italian, Spanish, Swedish, Yiddish, and Chinese language newspapers. Black

Americans also began to publish their own papers to offset the racial bias of other newspapers, and to publicize black concerns and achievements. On exhibit are copies of black American publications, as well as material on the pioneers of black journalism.

The tradition of the American newsmagazine is as vital as that of the American newspaper. Exhibits on the development of newsmagazines include the **American Magazine** (about 1699). It was one of the first newsmagazines issued in the colonies that reported current events and political debates, and also carried legal notices. The **Royal American Magazine** (1774) carried engravings by Paul Revere and an "advice to lovers" column, while **The Portfolio** (1801) featured drama, poetry, music, art, travel, fashions, current events, and politics. Among the picture magazines patterned after the **Illustrated London News** were **Harper's Weekly** (1857) and **Frank Leslie's Illustrated Newspaper** (1855); among later illustrated magazines displayed here were **Life** (1936) and **Look** (1937). Other periodicals that gave digests of the news were **Scribner's** (1887), **Literary Digest** (1890), **Time** (1923), **U.S. News and World Report** (1933), and **Newsweek** (1937).

A variety of inventions helped meet the continual demand for more rapid gathering of news and its dissemination to the public. Because newsreporting is a product of the interaction of men, events, and machines, exhibits in this hall highlight the impact of the telephone and typewriter, steam presses, automatic typesetting machines, wireless telegraphy, teletype (working machines in this hall deliver line copy from the United Press International and the Associated Press), photo printing, phototransmittal, and other kinds of equipment including the radio and television.

International news first arrived on our shores via packet ship, later brought by clipper ship, and still later by steamer. The time required for such journeys gradually decreased from ten weeks to eighteen days. In 1858 a transatlantic cable began providing rapid newsreporting. This was supplanted by wireless telegraphy invented by Marconi, which provided even faster transmission of the news. Photo-transmission by both wire services and wireless was inaugurated in 1925 and has been improved continuously. Displays show radio-transmitted pictures of an earthquake in Japan, Lindbergh's arrival in Paris, a train disaster abroad, and other events.

The collection and dissemination of international news by radio and television was aided by earth-orbiting satellites, one of which was Syncom II, launched in 1963. In this hall we can see Syncom II's backup model. A display of television pictures and news dispatches from around the world shows (on tapes) the first live television broadcast from the moon, made in 1969.

Another exhibit focuses on the history of radio newscasting, beginning with station KDKA Pittsburgh's 1920 broadcast of the Harding–Cox election returns. This and others on tapes can still be heard here today. From a Crosley Pup radio comes a 1924 newscast from station WEAF, and on General Motors Midget radio we hear a 1934 newscast. Visitors can hear H.V. Kaltenborn on a 1939 RCA portable reporting from London, and Francis Church's famous letter "Dear Virginia...Yes there is a Santa Claus," among others available here on recordings taped for rebroadcasting.

Taped historic television broadcasts are replayed at regular intervals on television sets here. Among these are Walter Cronkite's half-hour broadcast in 1963 describing the assassination of President Kennedy; Edward R. Murrow's 1954 confrontation with Senator Joseph McCarthy, and the 1960 Kennedy-Nixon presidential campaign debates. Footweary tourists can relax in the Trans-Lux Newsreel Theater which offers free newsreels of the 1930s, many narrated by Lowell Thomas.

Hall of Printing and Graphic Arts (Third Floor, West Side)

The Gutenberg Bible was one of the first books printed by movable type. Visitors in this hall can view a page from an original Gutenberg Bible shown in a securely locked exhibit case. The invention of movable type in 1459 and subsequent improvements in printing methods and equipment hastened the dissemination of human knowledge, increasingly bringing ideas and information within the reach of every person who could read.

The hall exhibits of both historic and recent printing and typesetting are, for the most part, limited to those used in the United States. Tools, explanations, and illustrations provide a brief historical background of the relief, intaglio, planographic, and seriographic processes and with the explanations are presented outstanding examples of works created and produced by hand and by photochemical processes. An alcove gallery hosts changing exhibits of graphic arts, prints of old masters as well as modern artists.

At the entrance to the hall a handsomely mounted diorama depicts the traditional nineteenth-century Japanese method of making woodcuts and producing prints. The equipment and clothing in the diorama were given to the Smithsonian by the Japanese government.

There are four reconstructed eighteenth and nineteenth-century shops outfitted with operational printing equipment. The late eighteenth-century printshop and post office has, among other equipment, the English press at which Benjamin Franklin worked in the London printing office of John Watts in 1726. A figure representing Franklin stands at the doorway receiving a bag of mail delivered by the pony express. A mid-nineteenth-century typefoundry contains both hand and machine casting equipment: the hand molds are eighteenth and nineteenth-century European and American molds. A Bruce pivotal typecaster is also on exhibit there. The job printshop of about 1860 features four specialized handpresses: a Firefly ticket press, a Ruggles card press, a Gordon card and billhead press, and a large Washington press. The newspaper shop of about 1885 has a Hoe large-cylinder press and with it a Baxter steam engine. Also displayed in it are two smaller presses, a Baltimore press and a C & F galley-proof press.

An 1819 Wells press is among other full-scale presses on exhibit in this Hall of Printing and Graphic Arts. Invented by John Wells of Hartford, Connecticut, the 1819 Wells press was the first press to have a toggle joint for lowering the platen, an important new mechanical principle for handpresses. There is also an 1820 Ramage press made by a Scottish immigrant who came to this country and earned a well-deserved reputation for the presses he made. Another press is an 1861 R. Hoe and Company railway newspaper-press named for the two rails on which the roller of the press ran. Two Gordon-Franklin presses are on display, an old style of about 1863, and a new style of about 1872. Still another large-scale press shown is a Columbian handpress of about 1865. The first iron printing press in the United States shown here was invented in 1813 by George Clymer of Philadelphia, Pennsylvania. Other large-scale presses shown are an 1896 Harris E-1 envelope press; the 1905 Rubel offset press (made for the Union Lithograph Company of San Francisco); and the 1906 Harris offset press which was the first commercially successful offset press and marked the beginnings of the large industry of offset lithography.

The hall boasts some twenty patent model presses which illustrate the development of nineteenth-century presses in the United States. While some of these presses are operational, they are now displayed in enclosed glass cases to protect them from being handled.

Among the full-scale typecasting machines exhibited is an 1885 Ottmar Merganthaler Second Band Machine. In 1886 Ottmar Merganthaler invented a successful typesetting machine which by the action of a keyboard that resembled a typewriter assembled, not the type, but matrices which could cast one whole line at a time in one piece called a "slug" of type metal. This revolutionary typesetting machine called a linotype was important to all printing industries including newspapers. The 1890 Merganthaler Blower Linotype machine displayed here was the first successful American linotype machine. A monotype machine, invented by Tolbert Lanston, cast and set each character separately. The machine is programmed by a keyboard unit that punches holes in a roll of paper; the paper is then taken to a casting unit where the position of the holes determines the casting and assembling of type. Shown here is a monotype keyboard of about 1897 and a monotype series 1900 caster.

In a special section of this hall, exhibits illustrate the four printmaking processes: relief, intaglio, planography, and seriography showing the tools that are employed for each and giving a brief chronological history of each process. A small gallery that adjoins this section features changing exhibits of the works of modern graphic artists as well as some of the great masters of the past. Shown, for example, have been Currier and Ives lithographs of sporting events and western subjects; drawings and etchings by the German expressionist artists Paul Kleinschmidt and Ludwig Meidner; intaglio prints by Lois Fine; woodcuts by Isabelle Walker; and prints by Albrecht Durer.

Demonstrations on hand-set printing presses in the eighteenth and nineteenth-century print shops are given in this hall on certain days and at regular hours. Consult the Information Desks or Bulletin Boards for the exact time when these demonstrations are offered.

Hall of Postal History, Stamps, and the Mail (Third Floor, West Side)

If you collect stamps or have a child or grandchild that does, this hall is a wonderful place to visit. One sees as he enters the hall a large track-side mail crane used on the Baltimore and Ohio Railroad lines until 1968 for loading and unloading mail.

The history of mail services begins in this hall about 2500 B.C. with Sumerian letters that were written in cuneiform on clay tablets and delivered by relays of foot couriers. The exhibits chronicle postal services in early Assyria, Persia, Egypt, the Orient (which impressed Marco Polo), and the Holy Roman Empire, as well as postal services during the biblical times as described in the Old Testament's Book of Esther, and medieval European periods where communication took place between trade centers within the Teutonic Order of the Hanseatic League. Among exhibits of other European postal systems are those of the Venice post, which functioned from 1300 to 1797; the Thurn and Taxis private courier services of Italy (1290-1867); the Spanish and Portuguese postal services; Russian, Scandinavian, Prussian, and French postal services; and the British mail. The chief emphasis of exhibits in this hall, however, is to relate the history of postal services in this country, beginning about 1620 with the colonial period and continuing with postal services available after independence from England and followed up to relatively recent time (briefly discussing air, rocket, and missile mail). The exhibits generously describe and illustrate the services offered, in some cases, the rates offered, the equipment that printed and cancelled stamps, and models of the vehicles that transported the mail throughout our country's history. Changing loan exhibits have featured stamps and other philatelic artifacts from many nations such as Scandinavia, Malta, Israel, Great Britain, Mexico, as well as from many old German districts and from Imperial Germany and its colonies, and the old Kingdom of Hawaii. The hall also offers an interesting group of slides on postal history and philatelic curiosities.

As assistant postmaster and later postmaster, Benjamin Franklin instituted many reforms in American postal services. A figure representing Franklin stands in front of an eighteenth-century colonial print shop and post office greeting the postal relay rider delivering the mail. The building is a replica of a shop similar to one he may have operated that served as a relay post office station for the pony express.

The Dillsburg, Pennsylvania post office, reconstructed here, served as a railway post office in the early twentieth century. It is complete with posted pickup schedules and lockboxes.

Another display stars Owney, the Postal Dog, a stray who wandered into the Albany, New York post office in 1888 and became the mascot of the Railway Mail Service between 1888 and 1897. He is shown here, as he so often appeared, wearing on his special coat the many medals awarded him by the different countries he visited.

Another exhibit features a nineteenth-century store counter that served the storekeeper-postmaster as a general delivery window. The visitor can see behind the counter a letter case for separating incoming mail and a desk for postal business. There is a postmaster's office in another exhibit in which we see the boxes people could rent for the delivery of their mail; also a window for general delivery and stamp and money order purchases; and slots through which papers, packages, and letters could be dropped for mailing.

U.S. precancelled stamps are described. These stamps are used for bulk mailing for third class mail such as circulars, advertising matter, and parcels. Permits must be obtained to use these stamps.

From 1883 to 1894 there were postal notes purchased for sending small sums (under $5), as were domestic money orders and money order hand stamps from 1891 to 1905 and orders for under $10 from 1945 to 1951; and it was possible to save money in postal savings from 1911 to 1966. Descriptions of these can be found in an exhibit. Some complete sheets of U.S. Revenue stamps are also shown.

Other exhibits show basic items used for postal functions. Among them are mail pouches, both leather (nineteenth century) and canvas (twentieth century); exhibits that describe changes in letter mailboxes over the years, and changes in mailmen's uniforms. Large photographs are shown of big city post offices in New York, Chicago, Providence, and Cleveland. There are cancelling machines, and exhibits that show the gradual mechanization of commercial mail through the use of postage meters. From 1840 to 1865 the postal system underwent great changes as it became a government monopoly and, beginning in the latter part of the nineteenth century, additional services were added including special delivery, parcel post, free rural delivery, and expanded city services which are all described and illustrated in displays.

Before mail is delivered it often has to travel great distances. Exhibits in this hall describe past and present mail service delivery done first by pony express, later wagons, railways, automobiles, and overseas by boat, and by airmail. For these services it has been carried over the years in a variety of vehicles. Scale models depict these land, water, and air vehicles used by the United States Government Postal Service.

American post office records (such as dead-letter records) and Benjamin Franklin's records are among items highlighting postal history. An account describes censoring mail which took place in this country during periods of war. Shown here are a prisoner's letter of the Civil War, a World War I army officer's letter to his family, and a World War II soldier's letter mailed from Alaska. Items salvaged from disasters are other highlights shown: a charred postcard sent to the addressee when the Hindenburg Zepplin burned in 1937; a charred stamp from the Chicago Fire, and mail rescued by Admiral Byrd when his plane, the "America" was forced to land in 1927.

In addition to the hall's display on postal history there is discussed in a special area the designing of stamps with many excellent photographs that show how stamps are first created by an artist developing the stamp design. In modern stamp production an engraver then prepares a master die on which he copies the design in reverse on steel using tools shown in the exhibit. The production of stamps includes some of the following printing methods: intaglio, engraving, acid-etched die printing, and modern combined printing methods (shown) where some prints are made simultaneously in several colors as described. There is an analytical balance shown which the Bureau of Engraving and Printing uses to weigh accurately small amounts of the ink ingredients. There are examples of stamps produced by typography, lithography, photogravure, offset, type set, embossing, and other processes. A 1914 Stickney rotary stamp printing press that was used until 1960 (and then replaced by newer presses) is shown along with a modern perforating machine, a Stickney coiling machine of 1920, and a die transfer press used by the Bureau of Engraving and Printing for the preparation of printed plates in stamp production. The Leavitt Cancelling Machine shown here is credited with beginning the United States Postal mechanization program. It was first hand-cranked, but was later replaced by belt driven models. There is also a Pitney-Bowes Model A Metering Machine and other early equipment used by the U.S. Government Postal Services. Explanations for the operation of each machine is given.

The hall's display of philatelic rarities may intrigue collectors. Among the curiosities is a 1918 stamp with an inverted center; an 1865 Mexican bisected stamp; a five-cent designation on two-cent plates (1916-1917); and an unwatermarked sheet without perforations. The 1962 Canal Zone issue commemorating the Thatcher Ferry Bridge has the bridge missing; there is an inverted vignette on a 1901 Pan-American issue, and other errors in color and spelling are displayed.

Since 1890 stamp designs have been printed showing a wide variety of subjects. Series of American commemorative issues have been printed on many subjects, among them stamps honoring some very important people. Other subject series have included: airmail-carrying planes, children, fish, birds, flags, animals, flowers, maps, music, medicine, ships, sports, trains, waterfalls, and important historical events in this country. Selections from many of these series are exhibited. A section of this hall shows some remarkable design and proof sheets. The Bureau of Engraving and Printing transfers certified plate proofs of U.S. postage stamps to the Smithsonian's National Postage Stamp Collection. These form a complete record of the bureau's stamp production from 1894 to the present. In most other countries special events are commemorated with souvenir stamps, and a selection of some of these is on exhibit. At one time at least twenty-five countries issued Martin Luther King, Jr. stamps. In 1982 the U.S. Postal Service issued as part of the Great American Series a regular postage stamp honoring Crazy Horse, the revered leader of the Sioux Indians. The 250th birthday of George Washington was not only noted on stamps in this country, but by other countries around the world.

One of the busiest areas in this hall is found at the back where representative stamps from almost every stamp-producing country in the world can be found and where people are constantly pulling out frames to consult or to verify information about stamps. The comprehensive National Postage Collection has more than twelve million stamps, postal covers, and other philatelic artifacts. Selections from its collection are on exhibit here.

There are exhibits illustrating the terminology of philately. Philatelists use certain terms to accurately identify features of philatelic objects, such as: paper (its texture, thickness, ingredients of fibers, threads, coating, watermarks), multiple designs, overprints, continuous patterns, adhesives, and color. Stamped envelopes are also a part of this philatelic exhibit. For the philatelic buff there are philatelic journals displayed that would be of interest. Included are typical early periodicals of the period 1873-75; early catalogs of 1862-64; the American Journal of Philately 1868-86; journals of philatelic societies from 1878-91; stamp albums from 1872; and a price list of trade papers 1868 and 1900; and **The Stamp Collector's Handbook of 1894.**

This hall would not be complete without mentioning the innovations introduced by three postmasters-general: William T. Barry,
the first postmaster-general to have cabinet rank; John Wanamaker,
who in 1889 introduced free city delivery, rural free delivery, postal
savings, parcel post, and other services; and James A. Farley, who
furthered the efficiency of the post office department by authorizing
extended airmail, construction of hundreds of post offices, and the
mechanization of mail handling. These men were instrumental in
overhauling the postal system and making the post office a very important part of our government service.

A Headville, West Virginia, country store where everything
from bicarbonate of soda to ladies' corsets were for sale had also
served as a post office for over fifty years. Now reconstructed and
located on the first floor at the Constitution Avenue entrance of
this museum, it still functions as a regulation United States post
office. Here one can purchase stamps, postcards, and airmail sheets
and send out mail that is cancelled with a special Smithsonian postmark.

Hall of Musical Instruments (Third Floor, West Side)

Joan Wardell plays a harpsichord with a quintet in an art
museum of one of the largest American cities, performing
chiefly eighteenth-century baroque and classical music. Hearing a
concert on the harpsichord in this Hall of Musical Instruments was
for her, she told us, a most gratifying experience. A display of restored
string, wind, brass, and keyboard instruments of western European
and American origin grace this hall and musicians perform on these
instruments each week interpreting for the audiences the sounds
of various compositions when played on the instruments for which
they were originally written. These concerts are usually offered on
the small concert stage in the hall at 11 a.m. Monday through Friday
by various members of the Division of Musical Instruments, and
there is no charge. Music for a different instrument is offered for
each performance. The details can be obtained at Information Desks
or from Bulletin Boards. On the first and third Saturday of each month
concerts called "Saturday Live" are given free at 2 p.m. These concerts
may range from bluegrass, old-time and folk music to London sonatas
of Joseph Haydn played on a 1794 piano.

Among the restored string instruments on exhibit is a 1718
bass viola da gamba (Barak Norman, London), a 1759 violin (John
Marshall, London), a 1705 viola d'amore (George Aman, Augusburg),
a 1750 violin (Claude Francois Viullame, France), an eighteenth-century
violin from the workshop of Amati in Cremona, a violin by Ferdinando
Gagliano (Naples, c. 1780), a violoncello by J.B. Tononis (Bologna,
1740), a violin by Antonia Grangorani (Livorno, 1783), and a viola
by Gennaro Galgliano (Naples, 1762). In addition, special exhibits
on "Violin Treasures" explain the works of four of the greatest violin
makers the world has ever known who lived during the sixteenth,
seventeenth, and eighteenth centuries in Italian towns of either Brescia
or Cremona. There are examples of violins shown of Gaspero de
Sallo de Brescia (1540-1609), Niccolo Amati (1596-1684), Antonio
Stradivari (1644-1737), and Giuseppe Guarneri (1698-1744), all of whom

worked in Cremona. In the entire world there are ten surviving Stradivarius violins that, in addition to their fine sounds, are delicately decorated front, back, and sides. One of these known as the Hellier Strad (named for its eighteenth-century English owner) is a part of these collections; another, but not ornamented, is the Parera Violin. A violincello made by Stradivari in 1701 is also on exhibit.

The display of restored plucked string instruments includes guitars, lutes, mandolins, a pandurina, a colascione, and a chitarrone.

A host of wind instruments has been restored also. There are a 1411 clarion; a three-keyed, early nineteenth-century oboe from Paris; and a mid-eighteenth-century oboe de caccia (hunting oboe). A six-keyed bassoon (London, early nineteenth century); a descant recorder (mid-eighteenth century); and a tenor clarinet (Berlin, early nineteenth century) are exhibited, together with a five-keyed clarinet in C (Litchfield, Connecticut, about 1830); a three-keyed serpent bass cornetto (London, 1805); a natural trumpet in E flat (Nuremburg, late eighteenth century); an orchestral horn with case and crooks (Paris about 1825) which has no valves; and other wind instruments.

The Smithsonian's Department of Musical Instruments has over one hundred fifty restored pianos; square, upright, grand, combination square, and others, some of them on exhibit. Also on exhibit are instruments from the harpsichord collection, one of them from London of about 1743, and another the Dulcken built in Antwerp in 1745. There are other restored harpsichords with one and two manuals, as well as spinets, virginals, clavicytheriums, and clavichords: fretted double and triple strung, unfretted double strung, and miniature unfretted. Both pipe and reed organs (chamber organs, melodeons, harmoniums, and lap organs) are represented, and miscellaneous keyboard instruments: pianolas, player pianos, and a coin-operated barrel piano. Because space in the hall is limited, instruments mentioned above are shown on the floor for a while and then rotated for others in storage. Also in the collection, although not always on display, is the Steinway Concert Grand piano Paderewski played (and autographed) while on his 1892-93 American concert tour. The piano is a gift from the Steinway family, whose other contributions include a piano in the First Ladies' Hall and another in the Grand Salon of the Renwick Gallery. There is also in the collection Irving Berlin's scarred mahogany piano made especially for him by Weser Brothers which they fitted with a mechanism called a transposing keyboard to shift the keyboard right or left into a different musical key (Berlin could only play in the key of F sharp).

An exhibit case at the entrance to this hall shows the hammered dulcimer, long a part of America's musical heritage since it was first brought here in colonial times and used throughout the nineteenth century and even remained a popular folk instrument until the 1920s. Some of the other folk instruments exhibited in this hall were made to be played by their makers or their makers' friends at barn dances and other social gatherings. Here are banjos, dulcimers, fiddles, mouthbows, tunebows, and other instruments. There are folk instruments made especially for the Smithsonian by black musicians in the Delta Mississippi area. A slide show complete with sound track demonstrates these instruments.

Among the more unusual instruments exhibited here are a sarrusophone, a crwth, a Swiss Alp horn, American bones (clappers), and a theremin (an electronic instrument). Musical instruments of North American Indians, and instruments from Africa, China, Polynesia, and Thailand are on the first floor of the Museum of Natural History.

The Division of Performing Arts sells an album of Bach recordings for which original instruments in the Smithsonian collections were used. They also have recorded a full range of baroque masters' instrumental works that are performed on original instruments or some faithfully reconstructed copies. These are for sale in the museum shops or by mail from Smithsonian Customer Service, P.O. Box 10230, Des Moines, Iowa 50336.

Hall of Ceramics (Third Floor, West Side)

When President Nixon visited the People's Republic of China in February 1972, he presented Chairman Mao Tse-tung with a gift from the people of the United States, the magnificent "Mute Swans" made by the Edward Marshall Boehm Company in Trenton, New Jersey. It took nearly two years and 509 molds to manufacture these beautiful birds. The company made three sets of these "Mute Swans," for in addition to those given Mao Tse-tung, one set was given to the Smithsonian and a third set is now on display in the Boehm Museum in New Jersey. While at one time these swans were displayed in this Ceramics Hall, they are now shown on the Cafeteria level near the escalator. Other porcelain birds of North America made by the Boehm Company (ring-necked pheasant, woodcock, bob-white quail, Canadian goose, mourning dove, red-start, cedar waxwing, ptarmigan, ruffed grouse, blue jay, Carolina wren, yellow-throated warbler, black-throated warbler, song sparrow, and others) are displayed in exhibits in the Ceramics Hall as are beautiful botanical specimens of various flowers.

The Smithsonian has been most fortunate to have been the recipient of a number of valuable ceramic collections from which many selections are on display. One of the largest collections of porcelains "the aristocrat of ceramics" was generously donated by Hans Syz, who gave, among other things, extremely beautiful pieces of Vienna, Meissen and other German, as well as many other European and oriental porcelains. Shown in this hall, too, are specimens from the Stanley E. Wires Collection of Decorated Tiles, the Robert McCauley Collection of Liverpool Jugs, the Ellouise Baker Larson Collection of English Earthenware, and the Leon Collection of Yellow Glazed English Earthenware. There have been additional acquisitions through bequests, individual gifts of pieces, or funds with which to purchase them. The hall presents selections from the above named collections of soft and hard paste porcelains, earthenware, stoneware and tiles, some works of American potters and factories. Such familiar potteries as Meissen, Wedgwood, Sevres, Bueno Retiro, Bow, Minton, Limoges, Chelsea, Frankenthal, Hochst, Nymphenburg, Volkstedt, Oude, Berlin, Ludwigsburg, Vincennes, St. Cloud, Liverpool, and many, many other European factories are well represented in this hall.

The interested layman will find in this hall explanations for the differences between earthenware and porcelain. Also described are the differences between soft and hard paste porcelains. In one room of this hall, devoted exclusively to Meissen ware, there is a chart which shows the factory marks used as a signature (usually the crossed swords in blue) on Meissen porcelains during various periods. Some factories were known to have forged or imitated these markings.

Chinese and Japanese artisans developed the technique for making fine porcelains long before Europeans acquired the art. Exquisite examples of oriental bowls, plates, vases, and figures of the seventeenth and eighteenth centuries are on display. Wealthy Europeans traveling in the Orient brought back many fine porcelains, pieces like those shown here. Japan also made and exported to Europe Imari porcelains (made specifically for export) in the seventeenth and eighteenth centuries which are also shown. The artisans of the orient would never reveal their secrets for making their porcelains, so European artists had to discover these techniques for themselves. At first European artists copied oriental decorations like the ancient Chinese flowering plum tree design which were used by Meissen, Wedgwood, St. Cloud, and other factories. In one narrow area of this hall original Japanese and Chinese porcelain designs and their European counterparts stand side by side for comparison. Most of these pieces come from the Hans Syz Collection and are displayed by categories: chinoiseries, harbor scenes, birds, animals, and landscapes.

A German apothecary's apprentice, Johann Friedrich Bottger, an alchemist and the originator of Meissen porcelain, was in 1709 the first to discover the formula for hard paste porcelain in Europe. Bottger was employed by Augustus the Strong, the Elector of Saxony, who issued a patent authorizing a factory near the village of Meissen near Dresden to produce a red stoneware (shown in an exhibit dated 1710-20) which Bottger had first created. It became very popular and continued to be used even after Bottger succeeded in his efforts to produce a true hard paste porcelain. An exhibit shows early Meissen porcelain manufactured during the period 1713-1720, a period which ended with the death of Bottger in 1719. Some of these and other Meissen pieces from periods that followed Bottger's death are from the Hans Syz Collection. The work of John Gregor Herold, an enameler, who came from a Vienna factory, began the second important period at the Meissen factory. An exhibit of the period 1722-1740 of Meissen ware shows decorative changes Herold introduced using colored grounds and themes borrowed from oriental patterns. An exhibit of beautiful Meissen porcelain dated 1725-1770 shows ware decorated in blue underglaze. A third period in Meissen ware began in 1731 when Johannes Kaendler was employed by Augustus the Strong as a modeler in the factory. He became Model Master, creating many beautiful porcelain figures and dinner services in the baroque designs. So influential did Kaendler's work become, he was copied by many factories throughout Europe during the eighteenth century. Another exhibit dated 1735-1755 in the Meissen room reflects changes in porcelain style decorations from baroque to the rococo which are shown here. An exhibit shows the work of hausmalerai, independent home painters who were enamelers who took blank pieces of porcelain from manufacturers like Meissen to their homes or shops to decorate in a wide range of styles and subject matter.

An exhibit in the German room shows Hochst and Meissen

porcelains for the period 1745-1765. The set of dishes shown is from a tableware service made in the Meissen factory in 1745. However, only replacements or additions for Meissen ware were produced between 1760-65 at the Hochst factory. While the Meissen pieces were marked with crossed swords in blue underglaze the Hochst pieces were marked with crossed swords and, in addition, with the impressed initials I.S. Many technicians who learned their art at Meissen or Hochst were induced to go to other factories where they divulged secrets about kiln construction and other techniques, enabling the new manufacturers to also produce fine porcelains. An exhibit shows Hochst porcelains dated 1767-85. At this time their Master Modeler, Johann Peter Melchior, produced lovely figures and figure groups, some of them shown in this exhibit.

Two exhibits show Vienna porcelains. One is of the period 1719-1744, and the other of the period 1744-1810. Perhaps the most famous of the Vienna porcelains is of the DuPacquier period 1719-1744, first produced when in 1718 Charles VI, Emperor of the Holy Roman Empire and Archduke of Austria, granted DuPacquier a twenty-five year privilege for manufacturing porcelain. DuPacquier, unable to produce the hard paste porcelain he sought to make, lured two workers away from the Meissen factory and began in 1719 to produce the baroque patterns using iron red, green, black, purple, and gold colors that were stylistically his in hard paste porcelains. The DuPacquier wares carried no factory mark.

Other Hans Syz contributions in porcelain are found in the German room in this hall. Here one can see representations from many factories: Berlin; Anspach; Nymphenberg (which had lured a master technician, John Jacob Ringler, from Vienna and Hochst to help produce hard paste porcelains); Ludwigsburg which, in turn, had lured John Jacob Ringler from Nymphenberg to be its manager; Wurzburg; Frankenthal; Furstenburg which employed Johann Benckgraff, a technician who had learned his trade at Hochst (its factory mark shows variations of a cursive F in blue underglaze); Closter-Veilsdorf (its factory marks used prior to 1897 were variations of the monogram C.V.); Volkstedt (whose factory marks show crossed hayforks in blue underglaze); Fulda (which made very fine tableware and porcelain figures); and others.

A section in this Hall of Ceramics displays continental European ceramics. A soft paste porcelain factory established at the royal palace at Capo-di-Monte in 1743 in southern Italy was begun by Charles, King of Naples, and then moved to Buen Retiro in 1759 when Charles ascended the throne of Spain. When he went to Spain he took some of his workers to establish a fine soft paste porcelain factory. The factory declined after Charles' death in 1788 and closed in 1808. There are pieces shown in exhibits representing both Capo-di-Monte and Buen Retiro porcelains which show either no factory marks or variations of the fleur-de-lis impressed in blue or gold.

Exhibits show representations of eighteenth-century porcelains of the Low Countries: in Holland, Hague (which had a factory mark of a stork with a fish in its beak); Weesp (which had a factory mark in blue underglaze of crossed swords with blue dots interspersed); and Oude. In Belgium was the soft paste porcelain factory of Tournay which had factory marks of a tower or blue and gold swords.

Representatives of Swiss porcelain factories show: Zurich (which had factory marks used during the eighteenth century that show variations of the letter Z in blue underglaze); and Nyon (which had a factory mark prior to 1813 of variations of a fish in blue underglaze). Examples of porcelains from Denmark show fine examples of Copenhagen figures which are really very beautiful.

Large exhibits show examples of French porcelains: representative pieces of St. Cloud (which began about 1700 producing soft paste porcelains of beautiful cream ware); Vincennes; Sevres (which had factory marks prior to the French Revolution of intertwined Ls, since it was under the patronage of Louis XV); Mennecy; Bourdeaux; Limoges; Arras; Choicy; Le Roi; Chantilly; and Paris which had many factories, some named for the street on which they stood.

A room in this hall displays English wares. The earliest commercial manufacturers of English porcelains were believed to be Bow and Chelsea. Pieces of Bow soft paste porcelains of about 1744-1766 are shown. Chelsea factory also produced soft paste porcelains of very fine quality from about 1745-1784. Both the Bow and Chelsea businesses were bought by William Duesbury, a porcelain decorator, who moved first the Bow and later the Chelsea models, molds, and equipment to his successful factory in Derby. Representative pieces of Derby porcelain are also shown. Other English porcelains shown are: Longton Hall (exhibited are pieces from 1750-1760); Lowestoft (with exhibited pieces from 1751-1802); Worcester (with exhibited pieces from 1751-1783); and representative pieces from the factories of Liverpool, Bristol, Minton, and others. Some of the Minton pieces are pate-sur-pate porcelains decorated by Marc-Louis Emanuel Solon.

Other English ceramics show earthenware and stoneware from the seventeenth and eighteenth centuries, including representative pieces from Staffordshire potters. Among selections from these factories shown are those by Josiah Wedgwood who was influential in the industry during the eighteenth century; and the Delft ware (first known as galleyware, it was later called Delft because of its resemblance to Dutch tin glazed earthenware). Other potters in the Staffordshire area with representative pieces of "American Views" displayed here are Thomas Mayer, Thomas Godwin, Ralph Stevenson, John and William Ridgeway, Ralph and James Clews. Representative Liverpool Jugs from the Robert F. McCauley Collection show additional "American Views," as do some from the Ellouise Baker Larson Collection of English Earthenware. An entire corner in this part of the hall is devoted to Josiah Wedgwood's pieces of English ceramics dating from about 1770 to 1810. He was a master potter in Staffordshire who produced unique ceramics that influenced other potters of his time. There are pieces from the beautiful Leon Collection of Yellow Glazed English Earthenware, 1785-1835, displayed as if in an English ceramics shop waiting for a customer to select items for purchase.

An exhibit in this hall discusses the development of the American ceramic industry. Independent potters in colonial times worked to make articles needed for household use. Some potters in rural areas and even in some urban areas continued as individuals to make ceramics and examples of their wares are shown. However, the inevitable rise of factories for manufacturing pottery occurred in

1826 when William Tucker established the first porcelain factory in the United States at Philadelphia. This hall displays pieces of Tucker's ware and of Rockingham ware, a molded pottery covered with a mottled brown and cream glaze. This Rockingham ware was popular in the mid-nineteenth century and was produced by a number of American potteries. Among other American potteries represented in exhibits are pieces from Weller, Grueby, Bennington, Norton, Fenton, and Tiffany.

A ceramic fountain by Donald Raitz of Alfred University (1963), an example of contemporary American ceramic work, is displayed. There is a large free form vase by Henry Takimoto (1960) among other modern pieces shown. The exhibit of contemporary American studio pottery includes changing works of a number of influential artists. Among some who have been exhibited are Rudolph Staffel, Bernard Leach, Joan Pearson, Ernie Kim, Sojie Hamad, Paul Cox, Gertrude and Otto Natzler, Toshiko Takaezu, Marion Fosdick, and Adelaide A. Robineau.

The Stanley E. Wires Collection of Decorative Tiles have representative pieces on exhibit in this hall. There are examples of American and foreign tiles from many lands among them, ranging from antiques to the contemporary.

Hall of Glass (Third Floor, West Side)

We do not know when man first made glass; some have estimated that the technique may have originated as early as three to four thousand years before the birth of Christ possibly in Egypt or Syria, but the origins are not really known. The exhibits in this hall trace the art of glassmaking techniques and the improvements rendered over time in achieving its better quality and appearance. While the earliest glass was formed in molds to make beads or formed around sand cores to make small vessels, one of the greatest events in glassmaking came when the blowpipe was introduced, another historical event not recorded but believed to have occurred shortly before the birth of Christ. While the ingredients in making glass—sand (silica), an alkali; soda (either sodium carbonate or sodium oxide), a stabilizer; lime (calcium oxide), and waste glass to assist in the mixture—are the same ones always used from earliest time, their proportions have varied. From time to time other ingredients like lead, potash, boron, and others have been added to change the quality of the glass, or copper, cobalt, manganese, and other minerals have been added to change the color. Ancient glass has survived when much else has disintegrated and pieces of glass found in ancient tombs are helpful to archeologists in identifying past civilizations.

Shown in exhibits in this Glass Hall are pieces each of which is described and labeled for period and place of origin for glass from Egypt, Syria, Mesopotamia, Persia, Rome, Venice, England, France, and other European countries, as well as glass made in the United States. There are representative pieces made by each of three basic ancient glassmaking techniques: coreforming (sand core method), mold pressure, and cutting (abrasion). All three techniques were developed before the first century B.C. During the Roman domination of Egypt (100 B.C. - 400 A.D.) skilled Egyptian artisans in Alexandria improved upon the existing techniques for producing mosaics, color band millefiori, painted decorations, and cased cameos. Representative pieces are shown of small bottles, bowls, pendants, vessels, and small figures, as are pieces of Phoenician Sidonian glass in mold-blown design motifs, signed by the glassmakers who were extremely proud of their work.

It was possibly the accidental discovery of the glass-blowing tube at the beginning of the Christian era that made possible new types of glass and helped increase its productivity. Artisans using these new techniques and improved versions of older Roman processes could create cut, engraved, mold-blown, millefiori, cameo, threaded, gilded, and enameled glass and representative pieces of each type are on exhibit. Iridescent glass of this period is also shown with labels that explain the chemical and physical changes that caused the irides-cence. Roman and post-Roman glassmaking techniques (300-600 A.D.) resulted in new kinds of glass made available, and of these specimens are shown. After the decline of glassmaking in Rome, it was Persia, Mesopotamia, Syria, and Egypt that became centers for the art. The Islamic glass artifacts (600-1220 A.D.) on exhibit show the great skill of the artisans in glass cutting, enameling, and gilding. Representa-tive pieces of Islamic art shown are jars, bottles, flasks, beakers, and mosque lamps.

Following the Crusades, Venice became the center for the manufacture of fine glassware. Strict control of the secrets of the art was carried on for many years, particularly over the workers on the island of Murano who produced exquisite glass pieces. These Venetian craftsmen revived and improved upon ancient Roman tech-niques. Representative pieces of their works are shown here, including millefiori, latticino, and vitro-di-trina. The specimens shown include footed bowls, footed dishes, flasks, jugs, vases, both covered and uncovered goblets, plates and goblets of lacy glass all made by Venetian artisans during the sixteenth and seventeenth centuries. On display, also, is a nineteenth-century work of art, a beautiful Venetian enameled plate depicting the dome of St. Marks.

Representative pieces of Austrian, German, Bohemian, and Spanish glass that are either facet-cut, or engraved (some with scenic views and commemorative inscriptions), or enamel-decorated glass, are all of outstanding beauty.

It is thought glass may have been made in England as early as 1226, but the first known glassmaking house was established in the 1500s by Jean Carre, a Frenchman. However, glass manufacturing as an important industry in England began only after 1673 when George Ravenscroft, a businessman, began experimenting and perfecting the formula for lead glass. Pieces of his work are shown, as well as English glass of the eighteenth and nineteenth centuries that include cameo glass made when two layers of different colors are blown together. The outer layer is ground away and modeled to create a relief in one color with a contrasting color in the background. The origins of cameo glass probably spread from Alexandria by way of Italy to England.

French glass came into its own in the nineteenth century with the emergence of St. Louis, Baccarat, and Clichy wares. The display of French glass of the nineteenth and twentieth centuries show representative pieces of the fine millefiori and mosaic techniques practiced during these periods. Examples from the works of nineteenth and twentieth-century glassmakers include the works of the Daum brothers and Emil Galle, whose Art Nouveau wares were characterized by complex cameo techniques and subtle shadings; Joseph Broccara; Eugene Rousseau; Jean Sala; Francois Decorchemont; Maurice Marinot; and Rene Lalique, whose extraordinary pieces were made by the lost wax process. There is an enormous glass banquet centerpiece displayed that was made for Napoleon I by a court artisan in the early nineteenth century. Napoleon gave the piece to his stepson, Eugene Beauharnais, Viceroy of Italy.

The first glass factory in America was built in 1608 in the Jamestown colony in Virginia where there was a plentiful supply of good sand, but the first successful large-scale manufacturing of glass was made in the New Jersey factory of Caspar Wistar in 1739. Fine quality colonial glassware was also made by H.W. Stiegel's Elizabeth Furnace and Manneheim factories in Pennsylvania. Exhibits of American art glass from the early eighteenth through the late nineteenth century includes works by craftsmen like: Caspar Wistar; W.H. Stiegel; John F. Amelung (whose glass factory near Frederick, Maryland produced, for the short period it operated, superbly executed ware); Albert Gallatin (whose glass factory in western Pennsylvania, also of short duration, produced wares characterized by simple shapes, and pale green and yellow colors); Louis C. Tiffany (who produced the iridescent glass for which he earned a well-deserved reputation in the 1800s); and designers employed at Steuben (like Carder); and Libby factories. Also on display are products manufactured by other American glass-making factories. In about 1827 the invention of glass pressing equipment introduced yet a new kind of glass that was manufactured by several companies: South Jersey Glass, United States Lacy Press, Boston, and Sandwich Glass (which in its early days manufactured inexpensive glass, but later became a very large company and produced fine ware, too). Pieces in the exhibit of nineteenth and twentieth-century American cut glass show features as miter cuts (V-cuts), facets, diamonds, flutings, and butts' eye (punties). These basic cuts sometimes were combined to create a variety of motifs such as the hob star, pinwheel, hobnail, block, vesica, and fan star.

Some of the nineteenth and twentieth-century European and American paperweights displayed here are collector's items prized for such techniques or designs as millefiori, latticino, and cameo; while other types of paperweights shown in this hall include encrustations, flowers, and insects.

There are no exhibited pieces representative of Ireland's fine Waterford glass in this hall. However, examples of that country's fine Waterford crystal consisting of chandeliers with four matching sconces and glassware in exhibit cases are on view in the south lounge of the Concert Hall at the Kennedy Center for the Performing Arts. One can also see at the Kennedy Center: eighteen beautiful Orrefors chandeliers and matching sconces that hang in the main, red-carpeted foyer that were given to the Kennedy Center by Sweden; an exquisite chandelier and additional light fixtures that hang in the Opera House, a gift from Austria; and Norway's gift of eleven crystal chandeliers.

In the Renwick Gallery of Art (next door to Blair House) there are changing exhibits of designs, crafts, and decorations. Among these have been shown the art of glassmakers. At different times there were exhibited pieces of glass designed by Frederick Carder, a noted glass designer for Steuben; the works of Dale Chihuly, who also demonstrated his skills; and Venini glass from a Venetian firm on the island of Murano.

3

The National Museum of Natural History

"We want to see the mummies, where can we find them?" demanded a lively group of Falls Church, Virginia elementary school children visiting the Smithsonian for the first time.

"They are in several halls on the second floor of this museum," the smiling aid at the Information Desk told them, at the same time pointing out the locations of the halls on a map of the building. She and other volunteers are quite prepared to answer such questions and a battery of others for the large number of visitors who daily stream into this building of Natural History.

The National Museum of Natural History, situated on the north side of the Mall between the Museum of American History and the National Gallery of Art, is a house of treasures that contributes something valid and unique to a wide audience. The museum provides an introduction to the unfamiliar, sometimes strange mysteries of the natural history world chiefly on the non-academic level. These can form a basis for a science education which few other media can equal. People are born with a natural curiosity about their environment and their indulgence in satisfying this curiosity about the order and beauty of nature can frequently find answers in this building. Carefully organized exhibits stimulate an interest in the very foundations of civilization and in man's history. For children who come to this museum it can initiate an interest in certain areas which often results in helping them learn natural history material more readily and more meaningfully. Some youngsters visiting this museum develop an abiding interest in natural history, pursuing this interest in their leisure time when they are young and very often continuing as they get older. If these children are accompanied by a knowledgeable adult or are guided by trained docents who recognize the important differences between merely transmitting the facts of science and inspiring children with an awareness of their significance, they can develop habits of careful observation, lead the children to make logical deductions, and help them develop correct attitudes toward our environment's preservation as well as toward other people who inhabit this earth.

The dramatic exhibits created by skilled preparators, script writers, and label writers who work with scientists associated with this museum (cultural and physical anthropologists, vertebrate and invertebrate zoologists, entomologists, botanists, archaeologists, paleontologists, geologists, mineralogists, and others who spend years gathering, critically examining, and evaluating what they have collected, all of which they carefully record so that future scientists will have verifiable material as a basis for comparison) are useful for informing and interpreting scientific concepts to the public because they can contribute immediate, significant experiences often not as easily obtained from other sources. Through these exhibits along with tours, films, illustrated lectures, and tapings, these specialists can frequently help open windows on a world hitherto unknown to many.

As the reader browses through this chapter at home, he might note that the halls are introduced by a descriptive paragraph or two which are then followed by brief examples of selected exhibits in the hall. The introduction is there to assist the browser quickly bypass a hall that does not in the least interest him, or discover those halls which spark an interest. These latter are the halls he may wish to visit when he arrives at the Museum of Natural History. This chapter does not attempt to tell all that is contained in exhibits in every hall in this very large museum—it is possible only to indicate some of what is on display, hoping these can communicate ideas that hint at others not mentioned and in the process arouse the interest and imagination of the reader.

Greeting a visitor when he enters the museum's Rotunda from the Mall is the thirteen foot tall Fenykovi elephant. It was a former resident of the African bush. Another modern giant, a ninety-two foot model of a blue whale, can be seen mounted in a diving position in the Hall of Life in the Sea. The fossil remains of other colossal animals, now long extinct, are found in the paleontology halls on the first floor. Among them are dinosaurs, mastodons, sloths, a reconstruction of a woolly mammoth that once roamed the Alaskan tundra, as well as other gigantic creatures who once walked the earth. There are among the fossils some which were not giants, but rather small—and some of these, too, can be seen in the absorbing Halls of Paleontology.

Other specimens on display in this fascinating museum are gems (including the blue Hope diamond), minerals, butterflies, Indians (natives of North, Central, and South America), African tribes, peoples of the Mideast, the Far East (China, Japan), India, Tibet, Indonesia, Polynesia, Micronesia, Melanesia, Malay, and other areas; the history of the earth and of the moon, moon rocks, mummies, birds, fish, mammals, reptiles, snakes, shells, totem poles, as well as a live insect zoo, an attractive live coral reef; with many other colorful things that can be seen.

In one hall, "Western Civilizations: Origins and Traditions," on the second floor is a remarkable series of exhibits that trace western civilization's development from camp life in the distant past to village life, followed by the move from the village to the city, and finally the establishment of a number of cities which later formed states. In another hall "Dynamics of Evolution" on the first floor, the evolution of new species is demonstrated and one of them, the interesting evolution of the horse, is among many other illuminating examples describing evolution shown in this large hall.

There is a special Discovery Room on the first floor for youngsters twelve years and under where they may not only see natural specimens, but are encouraged to touch them (something not permitted elsewhere in the museum). They can read or have read to them about all kinds of natural history material in books provided for them here. They can also examine short film strips, discovery boxes, stumpers, and costumes.

Colorful banners at the entrances to halls around the Rotunda on both the first and second floors announce the names of their halls. Visitors inquiring at Information Desks will receive a free map indicating hall locations. A glance at the Directory which follows gives some clues of what one can expect to find in each of the halls of the Museum of Natural History.

The QuickGuide (an Appendix) gives basic information about location, entrances, and visitor services (programs) generally offered at the Museum of Natural History. For more specific information about these excellent services, they should be supplemented with specific current information from the Information Desks or from Bulletin Boards which announce current programs for the day, week, or month. Wheel chairs can be borrowed (free), and there are special toilets for the handicapped. The Information Desks will supply a special brochure for anyone handicapped called "A Guide for Disabled People," or one can send for this brochure in advance before coming to Washington by writing to the Office of Public Affairs, Smithsonian Institution, Washington D.C. 20560.

On the first floor is a large public cafeteria, a museum shop, and the Discovery Room, while on the ground floor is the Gallery Theater, and the Learning Center where there are classrooms. There is an Associates' Dining Room on the ground floor limited to card-carrying Smithsonian Associates and their guests.

A story appeared in the Sunday edition of the **New York Times Magazine** of November 20, 1983, describing some theories of evolution propounded by Stephen Jay Gould who is a paleontologist, popular teacher at Harvard University, and a writer of many excellent science books. In part it said, "The legend is (and he swears it is true) that he determined to become a paleontologist at the age of five when his father, a court stenographer, took him to see Tyrannosaurus Rex at the American Museum of Natural History." Our National Museum of Natural History in Washington also has a hall full of dinosaurs and other halls filled with natural history material that might touch the hearts and minds of other alert boys and girls just as they affected Stephen Gould. These halls are listed in the DIRECTORY OF HALLS AND POPULAR EXHIBITS that follows this introduction. Some of these could prove of great interest for adults as well as for children who come with an open mind to visit, to explore, and perhaps to discover new ideas in science.

The Museum of Natural History annually attracts a huge attendance. This is a tribute to a museum which provides so much that is gratifying to the interests, curiosity, and education of millions of children, students, and adults who come to explore and to learn about our strange, wonderful world and its inhabitants.

Aristotle once said, "The search for truth is in one way hard and in another way easy, for it is evident that no one can master it fully nor miss it fully. But each adds a little to our knowledge of nature, and from all the facts assembled there arises grandeur." There is much of grandeur to be discovered in this museum.

Directory of Halls and Popular Exhibits

The numbers given after each hall below refer only to the page numbers in this book, where a more detailed description of exhibits may be found.

I. FIRST FLOOR, ROTUNDA

Fenykovi Elephant
Information Desk
Rental Wands describing exhibits

I. FIRST FLOOR, EAST SIDE

Hall of Dinosaurs, p. 120
Specimens of Ornithischians
Specimens of Saurischians
Specimens of Ichthyosaur;
  Mosasaur, and Pleisosaur
Skull and trunk of armored fish,
  Dinichthys
Model of Quetzalcoatlus ("winged
  lizard" with a 40 foot span)
Time Column (27 feet tall)
Mural: Tracing Evolution of Dino-
  saurs

**Hall of Fossil Plants and Inver-
  tebrates,** p. 121
Specimens of microscopic plant
  fossils 3.1 billion years old
Specimens, models, and explanations of plant development
Specimens, models, and explanations of invertebrate development

**Hall of Fossil Fishes, Amphibians
  and Reptiles,** p. 124
Specimens, models, and explanations of fish development
Specimens, models, and explanations of amphibian development
Specimens, models, and explanations of reptilian development
  and of the amniotic egg

**Hall of Fossil Mammals of North
  America,** p. 126
Mammal evolutionary development
  during the Tertiary
Specimens and descriptions of

Paleocene mammals
Specimens, descriptions, and
  mural of Eocene mammals
Specimens, descriptions, and
  mural of Oligocene mammals
Specimens, descriptions, and
  mural of Miocene mammals
Specimens, descriptions, and
  mural of Pliocene mammals

**Hall of Ice Age Mammals and the
  Emergence of Man,** p. 128
Glaciers, their history and effect
Extinction of gigantic mammals
Recovered fossil mammal speci-
  mens from Tar Pits, Cumber-
  land Cave, Fairbanks Tundra
Early man's cultural development
  models of four archeological
  sites
Diorama of Neanderthal burial

**Cultures of Africa, the Mideast
  and Northern Asia,** p. 131
Arts, crafts, music, and religious
  beliefs of approximately 45
  countries or regions on the continent of Africa
Some African sculptures by Herbert Ward
Mideast countries: Israel-Judaic
  religion and culture; Iran-Moslem
  culture
Northern Asian arts, crafts, religious beliefs: China, Japan,
  Tibet, Korea, Ryuku Islands

**Cultures of Southern Asia, Ocean-
  ic Islands, and Other Pacific Is-
  lands,** p. 136
Southern Asian arts, crafts and
  religious beliefs: India, Pakistan,
  Indonesia, Cambodia, Laos,
  Thailand, Malaysia
Oceanic Islands arts, crafts, and
  religious beliefs: Melanesia
  Micronesia, Polynesia

Other Pacific Islands-Arts, crafts,
and religious beliefs: Australia,
New Zealand, Philippines

I. FIRST FLOOR, WEST SIDE

**Cultures of Native Peoples of the
Americas-Arts, Crafts, and Religious Beliefs,** p. 140
Eskimos
Indians of North America
Indians of Mexico
Indians of Central America
Indians of South America
Totem Poles; 14 skin bison tipi;
Sioux war bonnet; Hopi Snake
Dance

I. FIRST FLOOR, CENTRAL AREA

Hall of Dynamics of Evolution,
p. 144
Explanations and illustrations of
fundamental concepts: genetic
combinations, natural selection, genetic mutations,
Mendel's **Laws of Genetics,**
Darwin's **Origin of the Species**
Diversities brought about through
changes in environment, climate, geographic isolation,
hybridization, artificial selection
Evolution of horses
Descriptions and illustrations
identifying inherited characteristics of birds, insects

I. FIRST FLOOR, WEST SIDE

World of Mammals, p. 147
Illustrations, descriptions and explanations of habitats of
North American mammals,
African mammals, primates
Descriptions and explanations of
monotremes, marsupials, placentals
Descriptions and explanations of

mammal: classification, speciation, migration, concealment,
locomotion, offense, defense
Chart showing 18 orders of mammals and their families existing
today (Rodentia, Artiodactyl,
Carnivora, Chiroptera, etc.)

Birds of the World, p. 151
Specimens of continental, island,
and oceanic birds
Illustrations of habitats of world
birds
Illustrations and explanations of
bird: courtship, nests, eggs, incubation, parasitism, feeding
patterns, care of young, migratory habits, speciation, flight
capabilities, extinction

Life in the Sea, p. 154
Models of oceanic fishes
Models of invertebrates (Porifera,
Coelenterata, Echinodermata,
etc.)
Specimens of marine mammals:
sea otter, walrus
Model of 92 foot Blue Whale
Description and illustration of reproduction and parental care of
enlarged microscopic marine invertebrates
Live coral reef and monitoring research laboratory
Model of research submarine: "The
Alvin" and its work

I. FIRST FLOOR, NORTH SIDE

Splendors of Nature Hall, p. 157
To get there go through Dynamics
of Evolution Hall
Beautiful specimens of nature

Northwest Discovery Room, p. 158
For children and handicapped
Admittance by pre-arrangement
See Information Desk or call 381-
6135
(Go through Eskimo and Indian
Culture Halls)

First Floor Public Area
Public Cafeteria, Museum Shop,
Restrooms
(Go from Rotunda in a northwest
direction between Hall of Birds
and Hall of Eskimos)

II. SECOND FLOOR BALCONY

Herbert Ward sculptures of African natives

II. SECOND FLOOR, EAST SIDE

Hall of Minerals, p. 159
Large lighted exhibit cases with
specimens of all mineral
classes
Classification and illustrations of
minerals: their physical properties, chemical combinations,
crystalline structures, and locations where found
Donors of minerals to Smithsonian
collections; notable mineralogists
Diorama: Cave of the Swords
Fluorescent minerals

Hall of Gems and Chinese Jades,
p. 161
Diamonds: Hope, Victoria, Trans-
vaal, Marie Antoinette's ear-
rings, others
Sapphires: Star of Asia, Logan,
Bismarck, others
Rosser Reeves Star Ruby
Gerais blue topaz; Galach emerald,
and other famous gemstones
Abundant examples of other gem-
stones: opals, turquoise, chryso-
beryl cat's eye, garnets, lapis
lazulis, black pearl, others
"Jewelry Fit for a Queen"-all gifts
to the Smithsonian
World's largest, flawless crystal
sphere
Maude Monel Vetlesen Room:
Carved Chinese jade pieces

**Hall of Earth, Moon, and Meteor-
ites: Our Restless Planet,** p. 162
Theory of evolution of solar system, its central planets, and
the earth's origin
Description of basic geologic
structure of the Earth: core,
mantle, crust
Descriptions and specimens of
earth's crust: igneous, metamorphic, and sedimentary rocks
Effect of weathering
Illustrations of richest hill on
Earth in Butte, Montana
Underground water creating caves,
pseudomorphs, underground
springs, wells, and artesian
water systems
Descriptions and effects of volcanoes and earthquakes on our
planet
Evaporation as a mineral process
Exhibits of ores found in earth:
copper, iron, lead, zinc, others;
"noble" metals: gold, silver,
platinum, uranium
Descriptions and specimens of
meteorites, chrondites, tektites
Room of Moon Geology describes
moon's evolution and geology;
specimens of rocks brought back
from moon by astronauts

**Halls of Prehistoric Peoples and
North American Archeology,**
p. 168
Theory of Asiatic peoples who
came to North America about
12,000 to 20,000 years ago
Explanations and illustrations of
methods used by archeologists
to date past N.A. cultures: radio-
carbon, obsidian, varve, thermo-
luminescent, pollen, magnetic,
and dendrochronology
Descriptions of agricultural practices of prehistoric Indians of
N.A. and illustrations of crops
grown in different regions
Stone shaping, wood, ivory, and
bone, pottery, and textile arts
of N.A. Indians
Historic changes in hunting tools

of N.A. Indians
Mummy of prehistoric male
Aleut
Descriptions and artifacts of prehistoric Californian Indians:
northwest, semi-arid central
valleys, southern maritime
peoples
Description and artifacts of Anasazi Indians including a diorama
of Pueblo Bonita
Description and artifacts of Folsom man (Paleo-Indian)
Description and artifacts of prehistoric: Plains Indians, Middle
Atlantic, eastern cultures,
those in Ohio and nearby lands,
Woodland Indians, Upper Great
Lakes Indians (where a diorama
shows them mining copper), and
the league of Indians called
"Five Nations" that included
the Iroquoian speaking Cayuga,
Mohawk, Onondago, Oneida,
and Seneca tribes
Description of prehistoric Indian
religious cults
Description and artifacts of
archaic peoples of Southeast
N.A.

**South America...A Continent and
Its Cultures,** p. 174
Human adaptations in four major
environments: The Grasslands
(Pampas-Patagonia); The Tropical Forest (Amazonia); The
Mountain Valley (Central Andean Highlands); The Arid Coast
(Central Andean Coast)
Descriptions and artifacts of prehistoric Moche and Chimu civilizations; and the great Inca
civilization
Diorama of Tehuelche Indians capturing guanacos with bolas

II. SECOND FLOOR, WEST SIDE

**Hall of Human Origin and Varia-
tions,** p. 178
Descriptions and illustrations of

physical anthropology (human
biology, evolution, the range
and variety of populations)
Comparisons of humans with
other primates and descriptions
of forbearers of humans
Illustrations of evolutionary effect of upright postures and
tool uses on human brain and
speech development
Descriptions and specimens showing sex differences and racial
stock differences in skull, hip
bone, sacrum, and other joints
in humans
Human fetus specimens at different developmental stages reflecting normal skeletal changes
Human mummies each preserved
in a different way
Population explosion in this country, charted with human skulls
Replica of skull and lower jaw of
zinjanthropus (1,900,000 year-
old fossil found by Leakeys)
Specimens of human bones (skulls,
hips, shoulders, wrists, etc.) at
different ages, their development controlled by genes, hormones, environment, nutrition
Descriptions and models of worldwide body types (endomorph,
mesomorph, and ectomorph)
Models and descriptions of facial
features and body build of people from different geographic
areas (mongoloid, caucasoid,
and negroid)
Body modifications in various cultures (teeth, feet, head, and
tatooing), descriptions and illustrations
Descriptions and illustrations and
fossils of the art of skull surgery
practised by prehistoric Incas
(trephination)

II. SECOND FLOOR, WEST SIDE

**Halls of Western Civilization: Ori-
gins and Traditions,** p. 181
Artifacts of peoples who lived in

caves and made tools for hunting out of stone, bone, and wood

Photographic reproductions of Ice
Age cave paintings

Changes peoples made in life
styles necessitated by geography,
terrain, climate beginning approximately 12,000 years ago

Exhibits indicate changes made
from hunting (nomads) to a settled agrarian life

Exhibits of metal artifacts indicate advancing cultures, beginning about 5500 B.C.

Reproductions of graves and grave
goods, 3100 B.C.

Exhibits discuss the development
of Tigris-Eurphrates civilization and Indus River civilization
about 2500 B.C.

Reproduction of Sumerian inscriptions of reign of Rim-Sin in
Mesopotamia (1822-1763 B.C.)

Dioramas of ancient sites: Ali-
Kosh, an Iranian village of 7500
to 5000 B.C.; metalsmithing
outside city of Larsa; a section
of an area near Larsa in about
1800 B.C.; a Pakistani bazaar
(large diorama)

Knowledge of ancient Egyptian
religion and culture; benefits
derived from the Nile; illustrations of Egyptian monumental
architecture (pyramids, other
tombs, temples); Egyptian mummy cases

Exhibits show locations on maps
and artifacts of colonies established by Assyrians, Phoenicians,
Etruscans, Greeks, and Romans
and the trade networks for ex-
changing pottery, glassware,
ceramics, metalwork, textiles
and other goods (exhibited)
which ultimately helped spread
ideas and techniques into Europe;
also shown are metal coins that
aided easy trading

Bronze Age in Europe–exhibits of
Swiss Lake Dwellers

Exhibit discusses translation by
Henry Rawlinson of cuneiform

writing system

Hall of Cold-Blooded Vertebrates, p. 186

Descriptions of life cycles of amphibians (frogs, toads, salamanders) hatching as aquatic larvae
and metamorphosing to air
breathing adults

Descriptions of life cycles of reptiles (lizards, snakes, alligators,
crocodiles, turtles) which have
scales or horny plates; born on
land

Description of foods eaten by
various cold-blooded vertebrates
(some vegetarian, some carnivorous, some omnivorous)

Description of various forms of
offensive and defensive methods
employed by cold-blooded vertebrates

Specimens of cold-blooded vertebrates that are of benefit to
man, and those harmful to humans

Dioramas of a wide variety of
habitats of cold-blooded vertebrates in warmer climates;
some in deserts, others in tropical or subtropical lands; a scene
in the Florida Everglades

Hall of Osteology, p. 188

Descriptions with specimens of
skeletal characteristics of various classes of vertebrates (animals with a backbone) that include fishes, reptiles, amphibians, birds, mammals

Descriptions of the structure and
function of bone and cartilage
which together with tendons,
ligaments and connective tissues support the organs and
muscles of the body

Descriptions of the protective
functions as well as other important functions of bone in vertebrates; sources of production
for blood cells; control of specific gravity; transmission of
vibrations; support the weight

of the body; plus many other
functions
Exhibit traces the origin and development of skulls and jaws
Skeletal characteristics used by
ornithologists in classifying
birds

Insect Zoo, p. 191
Description and specimens of five
classes of arthropods:
Insecta—which has many orders;
among specimens in this hall:
bees, beetles, moths, ants, butterflies, cockroaches, dragon
flies, mosquitoes, waterstriders,
praying mantis, grasshoppers,
crickets, locust (plus many more)
Crustacea—which has many specimens in this hall, among them:
sowbugs, crabs, shrimps, crayfish, lobsters, barnacles, plus
many more
Arachnida—includes spiders,
scorpions, mites, ticks, and tarantulas among others exhibited
Chilopoda—includes the worm-
like centipedes with each segment of the body having a pair
of legs
Diplopoda—includes the millipedes shown here
A 50 foot long display case shows
the habitats (behind plexiglass
walls) of insects living in different environments and climatic conditions
Exhibit of arthropods of past ages

shows "Life in a Swamp 300 Million Years Ago"
"How Arthropods Grow," an exhibit describing three types of
metamorphosis: complete, incomplete, and gradual
"How Arthropods Eat," an exhibit
describing their feeding habits—
some very unusual
The useful role of camouflage in
the lives of some arthropods
Insect societies that cooperate
among their own kind: live bees,
and live leaf cutter ants

III. GROUND FLOOR

**North Entrance on Constitution
Avenue**
Ramp for the handicapped
Inside Constitution Ave. entrance
are: elevators to other floors;
Information Desk; Check Room
(free); Rest Rooms; entrance to
Naturalist Center for serious
amateurs only

South Side (in back of the escalator): Smithsonian Associates
Dining Room; Baird Auditorium
(lectures, films, etc.)
Glass exhibit cases: Birds of Washington, D.C.

Central Area
Evans Gallery for Special Exhibits
Special Theater

Descriptions of Halls and Exhibits

Geological Time Chart for the Halls of Paleontology

The reader wishing to become acquainted with the Paleontology
Halls which follow may find it helpful to refer to the very much sim-
plified time chart on the following page. It is so constructed to
show the oldest periods at the end and the youngest periods at the
beginning. There is much overlap, and one cannot precisely pin down
with accuracy the time when the occurrences mentioned below exactly
took place.

CENOZOIC ERA

QUATERNARY PERIOD
Began about 2,000,000
years ago

      Recent Epoch   Emergence of homo sapiens; all other homonids died out. Periodic glaciation

      Pleistocene Epoch   Uplifting of mountains; gradual cooling of tropical climate; shrinking of wide forest lands; growth of woodlands and savannas

LATE TERTIARY PERIOD
Began about 15,000,000
years ago

      Pliocene Epoch   Increase in number of mammals; mammals become dominant

      Miocene Epoch   Climate tropical; first grasses; advent of grazing mammals. Emergence of different, primitive homonid families. Cooling climate
      "Age of Apes"

EARLY TERTIARY PERIOD
Began about 69,000,000–
80,000,000 years ago

      Oligocene Epoch
      Eocene Epoch   Advent of first primates; birds; insectivores; growth of forests. Many
      Paleocene Epoch   archaic mammals became extinct

MESOZOIC ERA

CRETACEOUS PERIOD
Began about 135,000,000
years ago

                                 Climate mild, becoming cool; flowering plants (angiosperms) began to displace gymnosperms. Dinosaurs and ammonites died out at end of Cretaceous

JURASSIC PERIOD
Began about 135,000,000
years ago

                                 Climate warm; abundant numbers of ammonites, dinosaurs (marine, terrestrial, flying reptiles); cycads, conifers

TRIASSIC PERIOD
Began about 220,000,000
years ago

> Climate warm. "Age of Reptiles";
> first dinosaurs (plesiosaurs, ichthy-
> osaurs); true ammonites; modern
> coral; advent of first very small,
> primitive mammals; modern plants;
> trees that looked like pines

PALEOZOIC ERA

PERMIAN PERIOD
Began about 275,000,000
years ago

> Climate warm in northern hemi-
> sphere, glaciers in southern hemi-
> sphere. Rise of many reptile am-
> phibians, modern insects. Last of
> trilobites, blastoids, eurypterids

CARBONIFEROUS PERIOD
Began about 355,000,000
years ago

> Warm climate becoming glacial in
> some areas. First reptiles, sharks,
> lungfish. Brachiopods, blastoids
> abundant. Climax of crinoids. Coal
> forests flourish. Primitive ammo-
> nites. Advent of winged insects

DEVONIAN PERIOD
Began about 410,000,000
years ago

> Known as the "Age of Fishes." Cli-
> mate moderate becoming warm.
> Armored fish abundant; rise of lung-
> fish, ganoids, sharks; and fresh
> water mollusks. First forests; first
> amphibians and ammonites

SILURIAN PERIOD
Began about 430,000,000
years ago

> Climate warm. First land plants ap-
> peared. Great numbers of shelled
> animals; many coral reefs; euryp-
> terids and nautiloids abundant; first
> terrestrial air-breathing animals
> (scorpions) appeared

ORDOVICIAN PERIOD
Began about 490,000,000
years ago

> Climate moderate to warm. Sea-
> weeds, algae; advent of land plants.
> First corals, crinoids, starfish, bry-
> ozoa, pelecypods, and fish-like ani-
> mals first appear. Graptolites and
> trilobites abundant

CAMBRIAN PERIOD
Began about 580,000,000
years ago

> Climate cold becoming warm. First
> well-preserved fossils of marine in-
> vertebrates. Trilobites, brachiopods
> and gastropods abundant

PROTEROZOIC ERA

PROTEROZOIC ERA
Began about 2,500,000,000
years ago

> Climate alternating glacial and
> moderate. Time of primitive marine
> life. Very few fossils of primitive
> multi-cellular organisms: bacteria,
> algae, fungi

ARCHEOZOIC ERA

ARCHEOZOIC ERA
Began at least 3,980,000,000
years ago

> Earth's crust was formed. Time of
> larval life. Unicellular organisms.
> No known fossils

The halls of Paleontology which follow exhibit fossils, the remains of past life. According to scientists geologic records found in stratified rock formations indicate life began about four billion years ago in the seas. The oldest known fossil organisms, believed to be about three billion years old, are represented by bacteria and blue-green algae of the Proterozoic era. A specimen of blue-green algae that scientists have dated of this period can be seen in Hall 4. Numerous fossils are shown in the Halls of Paleontology: Plants and Invertebrates in Hall 4; Fishes and Amphibians in Hall 3; Dinosaurs and other Reptiles in Hall 2; Mammals of North America in Hall 5; and Ice Age Mammals and the Emergence of Man in Hall 6. The geologic record above can help the reader get a better perspective of events in the vast span of time referred to in each hall.

Hall of Dinosaurs (First Floor, East Side)

Almost as popular as the Hope diamond and "jewelry fit for a queen" in this building is the hall which shows skeletons primarily of dinosaurs which archaeologists retrieved and carefully restored. Exhibits tell us about the different kinds of dinosaurs and how they lived on earth millions and millions of years ago. Highlights in this hall feature a twenty-seven foot high illuminated Time Column illustrating a 700 million-year span of life on Earth from single-celled animals to modern man, and a spectacular mural painted by John Gurche which traces the evolution of dinosaurs from their initial appearance in time.

Scientists have identified about two hundred and fifty kinds of dinosaurs which were as diverse in their physical structures and life habits as are animals of today's world. While some were extremely large, others were no bigger than a pheasant. It was during the Mesozoic era (divided by scientists into the Triassic, Jurassic, and Cretaceous periods) and popularly referred to as the "Age of Reptiles" that dinosaurs became the dominant creatures on Earth, flourishing in geographical areas where they generally enjoyed tropical or semi-tropical climates. While some of these reptiles lived on the land, there were incredible creatures which flew through the air and others which swam in the seas.

The cotylosaurs, progenitors of all reptilian groups, are known as "stem reptiles" whose first traces appeared in the Carboniferous period and were flourishing in the Permian period. These were plant-eating reptiles with sprawling, generally weak limbs such as characterized Diadectes, Seymouria, and Hypsognathus whose skeletons are shown here. The fossil remains of pelycosaurs, another group of primitive dinosaurs of a very early period, show skeletons and teeth that scientists say may indicate the beginnings of mammalian characteristics. Dimetredon Grandis, a formidable predator exhibited here, was a pelycosaur whose reconstructed skeleton shows spines growing out from its back that scientists believe supported the sail-like fin whose function they do not clearly understand.

A third spectacular exhibit shows a model of a Quetzalcoatlus, a huge dragon-like pterosaur (sometimes called "wing lizards") which had a wingspan of forty feet and is suspended from the ceiling in this hall in a diving position. This largest flying animal on record was the only reptile capable of powered or true flight. Neither Quetzalcoatlus nor any other pterosaur shown here ever evolved into birds.

Scientists divide the dinosaurs into two major groups: Saurischia (meaning lizard-hipped) and Ornithischia (meaning bird-hipped). Among the skeletons of extinct dinosaurs exhibited here is the giant Diplodocus, a Saurischian that reached a length of ninety-seven feet with a slender S-shaped neck, a long tail, and fed on aquatic plants and some small plant-fed animals it found among the aquatic plants. Among other Saurischians shown here are Antrodemus, a ten-foot tall and twenty-foot long fierce and fleet dinosaur, and Tyrannosaurus, the largest and most ferocious dinosaur; both were flesh eaters. Some armored types shown here like Stegosaurus and Ankylosaurus were Ornithicians. Some sauropods like Apatosaurus (formerly called Brontosaurus) walked on all four feet. A few Ornithiscians (mostly vegetarians) like the Trachodons walked on two feet, but, generally, most walked on all fours.

Joining the above mentioned land dinosaurs on exhibit in this hall are Hadrosaurus (a duckbilled dinosaur); Dilophosaurus; Deinonychus; Coelophysus; Triceratops (with three sharp horns—one over each eye and a smaller one on its nose, and wearing a bony frill around its neck); Ceratosaurus (another Saurischian flesh eater); and Edaphosaurus, a herbivore (another dinosaur with a large fringed appendage of bony spines along its back). Other dinosaurs are arranged in groups that describe the periods in which they lived and the locations where each was found.

In the Mesozoic era there were some reptiles that had re-adapted to life in the sea. Some of their body parts were modified so that they were able to live and pursue their quarry in water. Among some whose skeletons are shown are the streamlined Icthyosaur, some-times called "fish lizard," which resembled modern porpoises; a Mosasaur, a marine dragon often twenty-five feet or more long and a swift swimmer with its paddle-like feet and a long tail; and a Plesio-saur, a large marine reptile that lived in the waters about seventy million years ago and killed its prey with sharp teeth eight inches long. Another specimen shown that lived in the waters about 300 million years ago is found inside the entrance to this hall. It is the skull and trunk of a huge, ferocious-looking, joint-necked, armored fish, Dinichthys, whose body may have reached a length of twenty-six feet with a headshield more than three feet long and was the largest predator in the waters of its time.

One can see displayed on the balcony of this hall huge twelve-foot slabs of limestone, phosphate-bearing rock, coal, and oil-bearing sandstone, and diatomaceous earth in each of which one can see embed-ded fossils that bear the imprints of ancient shellfish, including clams and oysters that lived during the early Cretaceous period. One can enter this balcony from the second floor or he can go upstairs in the Dinosaur Hall.

Informative exhibits in this hall attempt to answer questions such as: what is a dinosaur, what did they eat, why did some grow to be so gigantic, and what caused them to die out and become extinct? The dinosaurs are displayed in this hall with plants, invertebrates, and early mammals that lived among them in the same geographical areas and during the same periods.

Since no man ever saw a living dinosaur (they became extinct about sixty-three million years ago, millions of years before any man ever appeared on Earth), the movie clips shown in this hall taken from "One Million Years B.C.," "King Kong" and other science fiction movies must be understood to be just that—science fiction. This should be emphasized and explained to children who might otherwise believe such things actually happened.

Hall of Fossil Plants and Invertebrates (First Floor, East Side)

Nan, a delightful child of four, was already an "expert" in recognizing fossil trilobites, one of the earliest species of the phylum Arthropoda. She demonstrated this ability while we chatted in the

122   National Museum of Natural History

Hall of Fossil Plants and Invertebrates with her father, a physician, whose avocation was paleontology. Introducing Nan at an early age to natural history material will, undoubtedly, leave an indelible impression on her young mind. It may evoke a genuine interest that in later years may continue in studies of natural history subjects.

The fossil remains of plants and invertebrates have been found all over the world, and some shown in this hall represent the oldest known forms of life that have ever existed on earth. Exhibits trace the evolution of some of these plants and invertebrates. All forms of life have evolved from simple organisms which began in pre-Cambrian times billions of years ago. Through the discoveries of some of their fossil remains preserved in many forms, scientists have been able to collect, screen, and process them and by using sophisticated techniques (some described in this hall) have been able to determine their ages. In many cases a comparison has been made of modern species of the same phylum with those of some of their fossil forms indicating some of the changes that have taken place.

"Nature's History Book" illustrates how identical fossils found in separate rock layers around the world aid scientists attempting to date rock strata, the "pages" in nature's history book. A final determination of the age of these fossils is often made by a study of the radioactive minerals in the rocks. A piece of silicified rock on exhibit here contains microscopic plant fossils, probably related to blue-green algae, and estimated to be about 3.1 billion years old. A specimen sliced from this rock and placed on a slide to magnify it shows the cell structure of these ancient plants.

Fossil specimens and models of plants that lived during past geologic ages are on display with algae (green algae are thought to be ancestors of earliest land plants) with stomatolites and fungi as probably among the world's original plants. Psilophytes, a group of primitive vascular plants, now extinct, were among other early plants as were thallophytes (among them diatoms) simple aquatic plants that reproduced by spores. Bryophytes that include the mosses, liverworts, and club mosses were also among the first plants to live on land. These earliest plants were aquatic, but about 425,000,000 years ago a few began to find their way onto the mud flats and river banks and grow there. To really survive they needed to develop structures that differed from their requirements in the water. Among the new needs were water-resistant cuticles to protect them from drying out; outer layers of thick, water-filled cells to support them on land; a vascular system to push water and nutrients for nourishment; and, very important, provision for reproduction. The fundamental life processes of plants discussed in exhibits in this hall include descriptions of their evolutionary development, among these new reproductive methods and the growth of leaves that manufactured food by photosynthesis. Reproduction by vegetative propogation (which takes many forms) and by spores are still used by plants, but the development of seeds eventually became the chief method for plant reproduction and today dominates other methods. Gymnosperms producing seeds in cones or cone-like structures rather than in flowers originated in the tropics and sub-tropics. Examples of gymnosperms in our forests today include firs, pines, redwoods, and other conifers. Among the fossils of ancient gymnosperms shown in this hall are cordaites, cycads, cycadeoids, and conifers. Angiosperms, true flowering plants bearing their seeds within protective coverings, are of an evolutionary higher type than gymnosperms. Angiosperms first appeared nearly 130,000,000 years ago and are today the most widely distributed and advanced of all plant groups in the world. Fossils of angiosperms shown include specimens of grasses, palm, alder, oak, sassafrass and ancient sycamore trees. Exhibits describe the very slow steps that made possible the survival of plants on land.

There are exhibits of giant fossil trees like the scale tree, ancient fern and calamite that lived during past geologic ages; and stumps of trees uncovered by workmen in New York, the Gilboa trees, survivors of the oldest trees on Earth, their age estimated at about 360,000,000 years. An illustrated exhibit of coal swamp forests describes the trees which grew in the tropical primitive forests between 345,000,000 to 280,000,000 years ago and died as climates changed. The trees were gradually buried and compacted by the blown sand and clay that fell upon them and over the ages exerted great pressure on them. It is the remains of these trees that form the great coal beds of today. An exhibit describes the palm trees which today number more than 2500 species and are distributed throughout the tropics and subtropics. Their early development began about 80,000,000 years ago and specimens of fossilized palm leaves and trunks are shown.

A few microscopic investigating invertebrates that dwelt in the ancient waters (probably arthropods) began to explore the shore lines and for brief periods crawled out of the water and walked on the banks. A large chart illustrates the most basic requirements for the survival of invertebrate life on the land. Some of these include body support in the form of anatomical structures for assistance (the natural buoyancy of the water had supported them there); means for conservation of body fluids to prevent drying out in the air and sun; vital gas exchange (previously easily accomplished in the water); and a means of reproducing. The changeover from water to land for the invertebrates took millions of years in very slow steps to accomplish. Microscopic arthropods (animals with segmented bodies and jointed limbs) such as those related to Paleozoic eurypterids and scorpions shown in exhibits were among the first to try. An exhibit describes what made their venture possible.

There are fossil species of invertebrates on exhibit that thrived in ancient waters and died leaving no descendants. Still others left descendants, and some, though changed, flourish on land and in the waters today. Some are in the phylum Protozoa, those microscopic single-celled animals like the amoeba, euglena, paramecium, and foraminifera; in the phylum Porifera are the sponges; in the phylum Coelenterata are included the corals, sea anemones, Portuguese man-of-war, jellyfish, and hydras; in the phylum Platyhelminthes are the flat worm-like animals such as planaria, liver flukes, and tapeworms; in the phylum Nemathelminthes are the roundworms that include pinworms, hookworms, and trichinae (found in pork); in the phylum Annelida are segmented worms that include earthworms, sandworms, and leeches; in the phylum Echinodermata are those invertebrates with external spines such as the starfish, crinoids, sea urchins, sand dollars, sea cucumbers, and sea lillies; in marine and fresh waters are found thousands of fossil species belonging to the phylum Bryozoa "moss animals" in which the bugula, as an example, occur in colonies; in the phylum Brachiopoda are lamp shells and other articulate and inarticulate forms (the brachiopods nearly dominated the seas in the Paleozoic era, but are much less abundant today); in the phylum Mollusca (classes include Gastropods, Pelecypods, and Cephalopods) are soft-bodied animals, some with limy shells, that include snails, slugs, clams, oysters, scallops, mussels, limpets, albalones, nautilus, ammonites, octopus, and squid; in the phylum Arthropoda (the largest phylum in which are found classes of Crustaceans, Arachnoids, Myriapods and Insects) are the animals with jointed legs and an outer skeleton of chitin which they shed during periods of growth; among these animals are the crayfish, lobsters, shrimp, spiders, cockroaches, scorpions, mites, and all insects. It is believed that arthropods were among the first animals to venture onto the land.

The Paleozoic era (ancient life) was the age of invertebrate animals 380,000,000 years ago and fossils of these ancient invertebrates have been found in the clay, lime, and sand that formed the sedimentary rocks, especially those sediments deposited in or near the rivers, lakes, or other bodies of water. In this hall visitors can examine the fossil invertebrates of nearly every phyla mentioned above. The exhibits show records of their history including their life cycle, habitats and relative abundance during different geologic periods.

Hall of Fossil Fishes, Amphibians, and Reptiles (First Floor, East Side)

The earliest predecessors of today's fishes were jawless animals covered with hard bony plates instead of scales. Approximately forty million years after their appearance the first jawed fishes began to appear, and another ten million years passed before true fishes with bony skeletons appeared in the Devonian period. It was during the latter part of the Devonian that amphibians began to evolve. Amphibians are distant descendants of fishes, but developed what fishes do not possess, paired limbs with toes instead of fins; and while some lived in water throughout their lives and breathed through gills, others developed lungs for breathing and lived in water only during their larval stages. The exhibits in this hall trace the evolution of fishes, amphibians, and reptiles and follow the course of a few of the first animals to move from the water to the land. The first animals with backbones were fishes. Some of them rose to become amphibians and some of the amphibians on the basis of their structure and development gave rise to reptiles and to other new forms of life.

Scientists have called the Devonian the "Age of Fishes," for it was during that period fishes underwent great development and vertebrate fishes became dominant worldwide. Fossils of this period found in both the Arctic and Antarctic are similar, and indicate a uniformity of the world's climate. Among the fossils of fishes on exhibit are those of an ancestral group, the bottom-dwelling ostracoderms ("shell-skinned"—named for their bony armor), jawless fishes that appeared in the Ordovician period. Fishes of great evolutionary importance, all ostracoderms disappeared (except for lampreys and hagfish) during the Devonian period. Among other fossil specimens of fish exhibited is one of a fast-swimming giant shark-like fish called Cladoselache, a forerunner of certain cartilaginous fishes. Indeed it is from such primitive, shark-like fish as Cladoselache that all higher groups of fishes are believed descended.

The formation of jaws in fishes were another development of great evolutionary importance. An exhibit discusses its significance and provides models and several specimens of early and more advanced jawed fishes. Ancient jawed fishes were cartilaginous, that is, without true bones. Living representatives of this group are sharks, rays, and chimaeras. Displayed material includes fossil parts of several of these ancient fishes.

Ray-finned fishes underwent great anatomical changes about three hundred twenty-five million years ago. An exhibit shows fossils of chondresteans, holosteans, and teleostats, all early ray-finned fishes. The teleostats are now the most abundant of all backboned fishes, having replaced chondresteans and holosteans. An exhibit that attracts many people is the skeleton of a fish called Xiphactinus, a fourteen-foot long precursor of the modern herring, which lived in the Cretaceous period. This fossil was found in the chalk formations at Austin, Texas. Still lodged in its skeleton can be seen Xiphactinus' last meal, a fish called Ananogmius.

Those interested in evolutionary developments will find in this hall exhibits of fishes possessing transitional characteristics that appeared later in certain land vertebrates. Among these ancestors of land vertebrates were lung fish, Dipnoi, which had primitive lungs for breathing oxygen outside the water; and lobe-finned fish, Crossopterygians, within its fleshy-lobed fins were bony skeletal supports such as amphibians had. Lobe-finned fish also possessed air bladders that assisted respiration. While the water was still their natural environment, these fishes, in cases where their water pools dried out, could move over dry land in search of other pools of water.

Exhibits show specimens of fringe-finned fishes. Eusthenopteron, which possessed a passage for breathing, linking their nostrils with the roof of their mouths, also had lobes at the base of their fins strong enough to support them on land. Eusthenopterons are considered direct ancestors of amphibia.

The term "amphibian" comes from the Greek meaning "living a double life." This aptly describes the water and land living habits of our common amphibia, for during the first part of their existence they live in the water and breathe by means of gills as fish do, later they develop lungs, discard the gills and breathe air, much like reptiles do. Exhibits discuss the progressive developments in water animals which enabled them to perfect the ability to live on land. They did have to return to the water, however, to lay their eggs. For a long period of time these pioneers had the land to themselves. It was from among some of these that the reptiles very slowly evolved.

Exhibits display specimens of six fossil amphibia, each approximately 260,000,000 or more years old, and labels explain the differences in their life styles. Displayed are the reconstructed massively toothed skull and limb bones of the six-foot long amphibian Eryops, largest of ancient North American amphibia which spent much of its time 270,000,000 years ago in the swamps of what is now Texas; the flat skull of Trimerorhaus indicates it was completely aquatic; Lysorophus, whose fossil skeleton indicates a snake-like body, coped with drought by burying itself in a coiled position in the mud; Diplocaulus, another completely aquatic amphibian possessed a triangular head; Seymouria, a three-foot long land dweller had stout limbs, a short body and tail; and Neopteroplax, an aquatic amphibian close to fifteen feet long which swam in an eel-like fashion. None of these left descendants. An exhibit displays the fossil remains of Buttneria, completely aquatic amphibia which once visited a little pond some 200,000,000 years ago. A drought apparently drove scores of them to this pond which contained water entirely inadequate for all of them. Their massed bones reveal the tragic story of the demise of these Buttneria.

Set in an imaginative scene in what is today the central United States a diorama shows what might have taken place approximately two hundred seventy million years ago when two reptiles, Dimetrodon and Edaphosaurus, engaged in a battle for survival. Amphibia Cacops (with huge head, no neck, and short tail which had a carapace of bony plates down the middle of its back) and Diplocaulus (the odd-looking amphibian with the arrow-shaped head), and Seymouria (considered transitional from amphibian to reptile) are shown in this diorama observing the conflict.

A major evolutionary breakthrough for animals that began to live on land was the development of the amniotic egg which is typically protected by a shell. Reptiles were the first land vertebrates to reproduce by means of such eggs. This important breakthrough is discussed, but because of their fragility, no ancient fossil specimens are shown, except for some crocodile and dinosaur eggs which are about 90,000,000 years old.

The voice of amphibia were almost the first to be heard on the land. Equipped with a pair of vocal sacs (acting as resonators) their voices could be heard for some distance broadcasting their song.

Hall of Fossil Mammals of North America (First Floor, East Side)

The opossum is the only member of the marsupial family remaining in North America. Marsupials are mammals that lack a placenta, but have a pouch for their undeveloped newborn in which they are nurtured after birth until they are mature. Although marsupials reigned for forty million years long ago, they lost out in the evolutionary race on this continent in the struggle for existence to placental mammals which mature their young internally and show greater ability in brain development. There is fossil evidence in the Natural History Museum of marsupial life dating from the very dawn of the "Age of Mammals" but it is believed they were unable to compete successfully with placental animals and migrated south across then connecting land masses we now call North America, South America, Africa, Antarctica, as well as Australia, all once believed connected in a single land mass, Gondwanaland. During periods of continental drift these land masses eventually broke away from each other and drifted apart. Although mammal fossils have been found on Antarctica, few mammals exist there today; but the marsupials which got to Australia, free from competition by placentals, survived and left descendants.

During the Tertiary period of the Cenozoic era and following on the extinction of the dinosaurs, mammals began their major evolutionary climb. Geologists have divided the Tertiary period of our earth's history into five epochs: the Paleocene, Eocene, Oligocene, Miocene, and Pliocene. Separate alcoves in this hall are devoted to each epoch and each alcove contains fossils of North American mammals that lived during the epoch reviewed. Some of the fossils are of animals familiar in their modern forms (rhinoceros, whales, tapirs, horses, camels, llamas, deer, and antelopes) with changes that can be noted for these mammals from epoch to epoch. Other animals whose fossils are shown here (multituberculates, creodonts, patodonts, titanotheres, oreodonts, and chalicotheres) have completely disappeared. Huge murals for each epoch beginning with the Eocene depict these animals as they may have looked in life; the artist's conception is based on a study of the fossil remains.

The first epoch of the Cenozoic era, the Paleocene ("ancient-recent"), began about eighty million years ago. The exhibits of this epoch include fossils of archaic mammals from the Great Plains, Rocky Mountains, and other western regions. Few species survived to modern times, and the fossil remains are fragmentary. Shown in this hall are teeth of a multituberculate, the jaw of a primitive creodont, and a taeniodont's skull, as well as skull and jaws of other Paleocene mammals, including primates, insectivores (small primitive mammals that feed mainly on insects), and marsupials.

The Eocene epoch ("the dawn of the recent"), the second of the Cenozoic era, began about sixty million years ago. Many of the fossil remains of this epoch, exhibited in this hall, were found in regions of the Rocky Mountains, particularly in the Bridger Formation in southwest Wyoming; these fossils show the beginnings of modern mammalian orders. Among the Eocene mammalian fossils on exhibit (or depicted in the Eocene mural) are horses (orohippus), ancestral tapir-like animals, primitive titanotheres, rabbits, rhinoceros, various kinds of true rodents, sloths, and armadillos. Two gigantic species, an elephant-like Uintatherium robustum (a herbivorous land animal), and Basilosaurus cetoides (a marine whale-like animal whose skeleton appears to be about seventy-five feet long), are also featured. The displays show lower primates, especially primitive lemurs whose evolution began in earlier periods and who were increasingly in evidence in the Eocene. There are also on exhibit fossil reptiles of the Eocene such as crocodiles, turtles, snakes, and lizards.

The exhibits of the third epoch of the Cenozoic era, the Oligocene, which began about forty million years ago, show the beginnings of many recognizably modern mammalian features. Among the fossil skulls and skeletons exhibited here are some that were found in or around Nebraska. The fossils on exhibit (or shown in the Oligocene mural) are of ancestral forms of gophers, jumping mice, beavers, tapirs, peccaries, camels, and horses (mesohippus and orohippus), as well as cricetids, tragulids, oreodonts (an aquatic plant eater), titanotheres (left no descendant, but were somewhat related to rhinoceroses), merycoidodon (led an aquatic life with eyes placed forward and almost level with the top of their head), sabre-toothed cats, giant entelodonts, and many kinds of even-toed, hoofed animals. There is also evidence during the Oligocene of the evolution of carnivorous cats, dogs, and mustelids (a family which now includes badgers, minks, and otters).

The Miocene, the fourth Cenozoic epoch, began about twenty-five million years ago and lasted for fifteen million years. On exhibit are fossil mammalian skulls and skeletons of the Miocene recovered from several American sources, including the Agate Spring Quarry in Nebraska and the Calvert Formation in eastern Maryland and Virginia, as well as the world's seas. Some of the fossil mammalian skeletons and skulls on exhibit—and shown in the Miocene mural—take on increasingly modern appearances. Among the Miocene mammals featured here are larger horses (some odd-toed: parahippus and merichippus), camels, small hornless deer and deer antelope, bear-sized dogs, rhinoceros, giant pigs nearly six feet tall, and oreodonts, whales, porpoises, seals, and manatees. It was during the Miocene that horses changed from browsing to grazing.

The fifth Cenozoic epoch, the Pliocene, began about ten million years ago and lasted for nine million years. In the Pliocene the animals considered true forerunners of modern mammals first appeared. The exhibits show fossil mammalian skeletons of the Pliocene that were recovered in the western Plains states. Among the mammals whose fossils are exhibited here (and pictured in the Pliocene mural) are rhinoceros, sabre-toothed cats, rabbits, large long-faced peccaries, shovel-tusked mastodons, pony-sized horses, camels with elongated necks and legs, true cats, short-faced dogs, and rodents—some with horns on their snouts, as well as other horned animals, some of these horns positioned in most peculiar places. The fossils of several of these mammals are grouped in an early Pliocene diorama as they might have appeared in life, gathered around a swamp or water hole. The scene was created with fossil skeletal remains found in several western states, particularly the high Plains region with an artist's rendering of several of these animals in the background. Shown are: antelope-like animals with branched antlers on their skulls, a mastodon, a rhinoceros, a true cat, a sabre-toothed cat, a short-faced dog, a rodent with horns on its snout, rabbits, peccaries, horses (pliohippus), and camels.

Hall of Ice-Age Mammals and the Emergence of Man (First Floor, East Side)

A very large map in this hall charts the intermittent cycles of ice ages and melting periods that occurred during the earth's 4,500,000,000 year history. It appears that repeated glaciation was a critical factor in Pleistocene life. Exhibits describe several theories about why glaciations occurred. There is also material displayed on the data-gathering techniques geologists and other scientists have used to help determine more accurately the age of fossil remains; deep sea cores (which when analyzed by scientists provide records of great climate changes), pollen cores, ice cores, and carbon 14 and potassium-argon dating. A small, circular Glacier Theater near the center of the hall presents audio-visual material describing glaciation. The scouring effect of glaciers advancing from Canada in the past frequently benefitted the American Midwest by depositing rich soils to its plains. Large photographs illustrate glaciers and other geologic features.

A section of the hall is devoted to South American mammals of the Pleistocene epoch. An exhibit describes the arrival in South America of certain mammals from North America by way of a then existing land bridge. Among the fossil skeletons shown are of some mammals now extinct: an armadillo, a llama, two giant ground sloths (whose feet were the largest of any land animal), a glyptodont (a descendant is the present armadillo), a tree sloth, a porcupine, and an opossum.

A mammalian group described in this hall lived near what is today Hagerman, Idaho. Scientists found a wide variety of animal skeletons which had lived there over three million years ago during a period when the climate was mild (an interglacial period). Displayed are some fossil skeletons that include a horse (plessipus), New World wild pigs, skulls of a pond turtle, an otter, and the jaws of a muskrat. A mural by Jay Matternes recreates faunal groups that lived along the Snake River in Idaho three and a half million years ago, just as the Pleistocene was beginning. Depicted in the mural, with some skeletal specimens placed in front of the mural, are such animals as ground sloths, otters, turtles, a muskrat, a sabre-toothed cat, a pronghorn antelope, a weasel, a frog, a mastodon, a zebra-like horse, a rabbit, a short-faced bear, a llama, a stork, a cormorant, grebe, mallard, rail, pelican, and swan.

Following the interglacial period other exhibits describe how fossils of several North American faunal groups of the Ice Age were preserved. One of these describes a section of the Rancho La Brea Tarpits in California that shows how animals became victims when seeking food by unwittingly walking into the tar pools. Struggling to extricate themselves, they attracted predators which also became casualties mired in the tar. Included in the Rancho La Brea Tarpits exhibit are skeletal remains of a pronghorn antelope, bear, dire wolf, peccary, teratornis (a vulture-like bird), a sabre-toothed cat, and ground sloths. The exhibit of the fossil skeletons found in the Cumberland Cave of Maryland is interesting because it not only shows fossils of small mammals which probably lived and died in the cave, but of other animals carried in by predators which died there. Among those shown from the Cumberland Cave are fossil skeletons of a wolverine, woodchuck, meadow vole, a woodrat, brown bat, red squirrel, muskrat, white-foot mouse, bear, shrews, and other mammals.

The fossil skeletons of a woolly mammoth and a mastodon found in the tundra at Fairbanks, Alaska are also on display. The teeth of the mammoth and the mastodon (separately exhibited), which visitors are permitted to touch, indicate differences in structure because of the differences in food each animal chewed. Also shown in this tundra exhibit, well preserved in the cold climate of Alaska, are fossil skulls of giant beavers, short-faced bear, Alaskan brown bear, musk ox, yak, and a lion. There are also fossil skeletons of such animals as the wolf, wolverine, badger, and sheep. Mummified parts of a bison and an Arctic ground squirrel; parts of horses and mammoths found there are among others exhibited.

A large wall panel depicts some of the extinct mammals of the Pleistocene. The panel gives the probable dates and some of

the possible causes of their extinction. On a circular island nearby
are specimens of animals which reached gigantic sizes and then became
extinct. Among those shown are the Irish elk, the diprotodon, and
the New Zealand mao.

The distinctive development of humans from our hominid
ancestors began slowly in the early Pleistocene epoch when, as some
scientists theorize, "the genetic and cultural adaptations of these
hominids enabled them to develop tools, communicate with one
another, and use fire." Exhibits describe various stages in man's development in four different geographic regions. The small-scaled reconstructions of archaelogical sites shown in an area in this hall include
such physical and cultural remains as tools early humans made, their
art work, and show small models of their skulls, bones, and teeth.
Australopithecus (meaning "southern ape"), an extinct man-like primate,
lived in Africa about one and two-tenths to three million years ago.
Scientists working in the arid highlands of East Africa found leg and
skull fragments of Australopithecus Africanus which, when they
used dating techniques, they discovered to be at least three
million years old. From the leg fragments they were able to determine
that our ancestors had been bipedal.

In a small recreated excavation site at Olduvai Gorge, Tanzania,
one million nine hundred thousand years old, scientists Mary and Louis
Leakey discovered in their digs an original site with stone tools that
Australopithecus had made for hunting and for gathering. Displayed
above this recreated site are graphic renderings of Australopithecus
and Homo habilis who at different times occupied this same site.
A second small recreated site shows the remains of Homo erectus
(the first man to use fire). This site, some three hundred thousand
years old, was found at Torralba, Spain. In the cool climate that then
prevailed, men had formed groups using fire for large game hunting
drives and later for butchering animals. They also made the Acheulean
tools they required for these and other tasks that are shown in small
models here. The third small recreated site is of Homo sapiens neanderthalensis (a variety of modern man) who left his mark at Combe-Grenal,
Dordogne, France between 100,000 and 50,000 years ago. Small models
of numerous tools and a skull are on display in this small diorama,
as is the figure of an archaeologist seen excavating the many layers
of earth to find artifacts of Mousterian cultures and some earlier
cultures found in this cave. The fourth small recreated site is of Homo
sapiens sapiens who lived in what is today Dolne Vestonice, Czechoslovakia 25,600 years ago. Found there and shown recreated here
are small scale models of skulls, teeth, carved figures, shell necklaces,
clay beads, and tools of ivory, bone, horn, and stone belonging to
or made by Homo sapiens. The exhibit also has a small scale model
of a hearth homo sapiens used for firing tiny clay animals and human
figures.

A dramatic large open floor diorama in this hall portrays
Homo neanderthalensis in a cave burial that took place about
79,000 years ago. The original burial site was discovered on a farm
near Regourdon, France. A skillful rendering of what might have
taken place at this burial shows a shaman (priest), a boy of about
ten, a woman, and a dead man of about nineteen whose body was
placed in a bound position on a bearskin in a stone-lined pit at the

back of the cave. Wearing bear and deerskin clothing, the members of the burial party are seen with ritual offerings of bear meat, flowers, and stone tools all placed on a stone slab that eventually would be placed over the body.

Hall of Cultures of Africa, Asia, and the Mideast (First Floor, East Side)

The wide diversity of human cultures found in exhibits in this hall introduces us to the daily home life, religion, art, clothing, and crafts of some peoples in China, Japan, and Korea, as well as to the many native cultures of Africa which in this hall are divided into a number of broad ecological and cultural regions. Various peoples of the Mideast are also described. A visit to this hall will never replace a visit to these lands, but the hall is a good place to become acquainted with these peoples and some of their customs and cultures.

A very large wall map located before one entrance to the hall describes Asian contributions to Western civilization indicating the origin of certain religious concepts, inventions, techniques, and skills—even plants first domesticated in Asia that found their way to other parts of the world via early land and sea routes. It is well worth examining.

One of China's notable art forms is opera. A large diorama portrays a scene from the Chinese opera, "Second Return to the Palace." When we press a button which activates the music we can listen to the words and music of the moral dilemma facing a young woman whose father is attempting to wrest the throne from her young son, the rightful ruler. Music is not merely another art form to the Chinese; as with many other peoples, the Chinese find a relationship between their music and their philosophic and religious beliefs. An exhibit of Chinese musical instruments includes a short lute, a beggar's fiddle, a mouth organ, a reed pipe, a dulcimer, a long zither, gong, hammer, stone chime, and bronze cymbals.

Chinese writing, calligraphy, is considered an art form held in great esteem in Asia. An exhibit discusses how difficult a skill calligraphy is to master and displays many artifacts including scrolls, printing blocks, a writing set as well as examples of calligraphy. For those interested, other beautiful examples of Chinese calligraphy can be seen in the Freer Gallery.

On view is a shrine to Confucius, the greatest teacher of Old China, with illustrations of temples dedicated to his memory. Some religious artifacts shown here include an altar, ritual vessels, and written records of rites.

The religion Lamaism, as practised in Tibet ("the roof of the World"), is the subject of another exhibit. Displayed are such items of Tibetan life as a papier-mache ritual mask, a gilded copper aspergill (holy water sprinkler), scriptures, a wool pile rug, and a woolen blanket. Also shown is a Tantric apron, worn by Tibetan priests, partly made of human bones. The Tantric religion is based on the worship of the Divine Mother Shiva Shaki, the Godhead, who is also known by such names as Shakti, Devi, Kali, Durga, and Parvati.

Shintoism is the national religion of Japan, and it has had a profound influence on the character of the Japanese people. The religion is described in an exhibit with a model of a Shinto shrine and various ritual objects shown.

A basic part of any household is the kitchen. Japanese kitchen utensils, both traditional and modern, on exhibit include objects used in daily life such as an earthenware steamer, an earthenware jam jar, an earthenware pickling jar, an aluminum kettle, and a charcoal stove. Toys, games, and ritual objects shown in an exhibit are a few from a vast number the Japanese produce in factories, many of which still reflect early folk traditions often associated with magic and superstition. Others shown are dolls, skillfully made, twirling drums, poem playing cards, horsemen, and fertility charms.

The advent of modern farming equipment made great changes in Japan's rural economy. An exhibit shows the type of farming tools used in early times and those used more recently; many modern tools were borrowed from the west.

A colorful Japanese samurai armor is exhibited. This armor was presented to President Theodore Roosevelt by the Emperor of Japan after the Portsmouth Peace Conference, in appreciation of Roosevelt's efforts in ending the Russo-Japanese War, on September 5, 1905.

The exhibits on Asian countries also feature a diorama that depicts a Korean home furnished in a style that looks remarkably modern except the scale of furniture appears smaller than ours. The home's heating system is discussed in the exhibit. From Korea, too, comes a large sculpture shown here of Buddha holding a container of medicine in his left hand; it is said that Buddha, in his aspect of great physician, vowed to heal the physical and mental ills of all people. Buddhism is the principal religion of Korea.

Between Japan and Formosa lie the Ryukyu Islands where they manufacture wonderful textiles of many kinds including Kasuri silk (a stencil dyed fabric), other silks, banana fiber wrapping cloth, cottons, silk and cotton mixed fabrics, and other textiles. Examples of these are shown.

There is a wealth of Mideastern material on display in this hall. An exhibit shows Iranian textile printing from the communities of Isfahan, Hamadan, and Yezd which shows design techniques similar to techniques used in India. Among articles displayed are blocks, a dye pot, control and stamp cloths, a brush, and scales. Everyday objects for the workers in Isfahan show a teapot, a samovar, a tobacco water pipe, a brazier and a fire fan, and a straw-covered water jar.

A map pinpoints predominantly Moslem (or Islamic) countries. There is a display of objects pertaining to the religion, Islam: a mosque lamp, a ewer and basin, a Koran, an Islamic rosary, and other religious artifacts. There is also a display of Arabic weapons from the Near East and North Africa. Their owners used these weapons in situations ranging from blood feuds and banditry to religious wars. Often highly decorated, these weapons reflect the social status of their owners. The Berber culture of Morocco was enriched by both Islamic and southern European influences; artifacts of this culture, exhibited here, include musical instruments, jewelry, pottery, and clothing.

An exhibit on Israel features ritual ceremonial objects of Judaism. Among them are the sacred scriptures called the Torah, which includes the first five books of the Old Testament; these are shown with their cases. There are also menorahs, an ark light, torah mantles and pointers, a Passover ritual set, phyllacteries, a prayer shawl, a skull cap, and a santification cup, among other things.

Visitors quickly learn by examining maps and exhibits in this hall that the African continent is huge (three times the size of the U.S.) with extremely diverse environments. On the African continent is the world's largest desert, the Sahara; there are huge expanses of tropical rain forests thick with lichens, mosses, and other plants; and even wider expanses of savannah (grasslands) where large numbers of game animals live including the hippopotamus, giraffe, gorilla (all three found nowhere else on earth), plus others (see African part of Halls of World of Mammals). Climates on the African continent vary from very, very hot in the deserts and rain forests to very, very cold on the highest mountains. Over one thousand culturally diverse groups live in various environments, speak different languages or dialects and have distinctly different ways of life. The make-up and distribution of some of the African people include: Semites–Arabs and Jews who live in northern Africa; Hamites–Berbers and Juaregs in northern Africa; Copts in Egypt; Ethiopians and Somalis in northeast Africa; Sudanese (Negroes) in West Africa between Equator and Sahara; and Bantus (Negroes) who live mostly in the southern peninsula; Bushmen (Negroes) and Hottentots (Negroes) who live in southwest Africa; Pygmies (Negroes) who live in the forests of the Congo, Equatorial Africa, and Kenya; and the Europeans (Whites) who live mostly in far north or far south.

Many peoples of Africa believe that ancestral spirits maintain continuing contact with their tribes. Exhibits describe African art such as masks and other carvings (made of wood or other materials) created especially for religious purposes; or cloth woven for ceremonial robes, or necklaces made to help ward off an evil spirit. These creations always have functions other than decorative ones. Believers trust they embody the powerful spirits of ancestors and departed leaders. Worshippers offer food and perform masked dances with masks worn for special ceremonies asking for guidance by ancestors, and then go through rituals in an effort to appease the spirits, win their cooperation, and avoid bringing misfortune and sickness upon themselves and their families. Taboos have strong influence on the conduct of many tribes and their governments with many tribes relying on the power of medicine men and witchcraft to help avoid or overcome evil happenings.

In the past the governments of Africa ranged from loose groups of small wandering bands (of closely knit families) to highly organized countries with millions of people. In 1879 (ten years after Stanley and Livingstone) the race started for African lands among the European countries. Today Africa is rapidly undergoing changes. Complicated forms of political authority exist in many African countries, as described in exhibits in this hall. Almost every tribe is governed by a complex social system regulating marriage, inheritance, and ownership of land. There are also well-established and strictly enforced local rules governing hunting expeditions, and other communal activities. For many years the dominant political tribe of Ethiopia has been the Amhara, whose official language is Amharic. An exhibit contains artifacts pertaining to their Christian religion and the Amhara culture. Among the other Ethiopian tribes are the Tigreans, who are also Christian, the Gallas, who practise a mixture of Christianity and Islam, and the Ogadens and Issaos who are mostly Moslems. The Somali tribespeople are predominantly nomadic cattle herders. They are found in the horn of Africa east and south of Ethiopia. Some Somalis cultivate the land; their chief crops are corns and coffee. The language they speak, Cushitic, is related to that spoken by ancient Egyptians and to that spoken by modern Berbers of North Africa. Artifacts of their cultures are displayed.

Other exhibits highlight the history and culture of the people of Rwanda and Burundi (two independent nations formed in 1962 from the former territory Ruand-Urundi) and point out existing remnants of their feudal system. Another East African people, the Nuer of the Upper Nile in Sudan, are nomadic cattle herders who depend on their cattle for both food and clothing. Other Sudanese tribesmen are camel breeders. Perhaps because of their nomadic life, these peoples have no central government. An exhibit features Sudanese artifacts.

In Kenya the official language is Swahili. An exhibit features artifacts of the tall Masai people of eastern Africa. The Masai, a cattle-keeping people, live in the arid highlands of southern Kenya and northern Tanzania. They travel the land in search of grazing for their prized cattle, sheep, or goats. These herdsmen look upon their herds not only as a source of food, but also as wealth, social status, and sacred responsibility. They kill cattle only on very special occasions. The main foods are goat and sheep meat and cattle milk, and blood taken in small quantities from the neck of the cow, which does not hurt the cow. The Masai have an interesting social and political system which seems to fit in with their herder's way of life. All males are subject to a system of age sets. The members of a particular age set remain together all of their lives, first beginning with junior and then senior warriors and progress to junior and senior elders. Warriors have the responsibility for protecting the family and flocks. Males do not marry until they become junior elders, when they marry and have children. Later they become senior elders responsible for directing the affairs of the tribe through a tribal council. The Masais, among other herdsmen, are finding their grazing lands impinged upon by farmers and by the establishment of political boundaries which cut them off from their grazing lands. The life of the Masai is discussed in exhibits.

A one hundred year old door from an old house on Zanzibar Island (Tanzania) is shown in an exhibit. It was carved by artisans from jack fruitwood. In addition to symbols carved in the door, the inscription carved above it reads, "He who helps me in hardship truly is my friend."

The Mbuti are Pygmy hunters who live in the Ituri rain forest of the Congo. Working with the materials at hand, the Mbuti make clothing of bark or palm fiber. An exhibit displays their artifacts. The Fahng (or Fang, also known as the Pahouin) are a farming people who live in the tropical forests of central equatorial Africa. The Fahng clear the forest land they need for agriculture by burning it; when a field becomes depleted, the farmers abandon it and clear new fields. Artifacts of their culture are exhibited here.

For many centuries agriculture rather than hunting and gathering or herding has been the most important economic activity in Africa. Agricultural products and techniques vary greatly from area to area. In general, Africans have specialized in the cultivation of grain crops in the more temperate areas and the cultivation of root crops in the tropical zones. The Chagga who irrigate their fields with water from mountain streams are shown farming the fertile soil found on the steep slopes of Kilimanjaro, the volcanic mountain in northern Tanzania where they grow bananas, coffee, maize, and sugar cane. They also raise cattle, goats, and sheep to provide meat and milk.

Embroidered pile cloth displayed here comes from the Kasai area of the Congo. A diorama shows the cloth as it is first woven from raffia palm fibers by the men, and later embroidered by the women. Called Kasai velvet, the cloth's texture is produced by shaving the top of the embroidered patterns, so that small tufts are left; garments made from Kasai velvet are worn on ceremonial occasions. The Yoruba of southwestern Nigeria are also interested in fine cloth and spend a good share of their income on quality clothing, examples of which are shown. As a display here indicates, music also plays an important role in their lives. Music plays an important role in the lives of most African peoples for it is an important adjunct to their ritual functions, and seems to help unite the worshippers' religious feelings and the feelings of the community. Dancing and singing are accompanied by the music of instruments that are plucked, shaken, or struck. An exhibit features such African musical instruments as drums, lutes, musical bows, harps, marimbas, and thumb pianos; colored slides of these various instruments synchronized with sound recordings indicate how they are played, all activated by just pushing a button. In addition to musical instruments, Africans have devised many signaling instruments, one-toned and multi-toned, to relay important information across considerable distances. Examples of many kinds of signaling instruments are shown.

In northern Cameroon in west Africa live iron smelters who work in the Mandara Mountains. A small diorama shows the workers at their primitive furnaces fashioning iron tools. The Hottentots of southwest Africa are also iron smelters, and are knowledgeable potters as well. An exhibit describes the Hottentots, whose ancestors are said to include Bushmen, Negro, and Hamatic peoples. The Bushmen, a people small in stature, who occupy a section of the northern Kalahari Desert in southwestern Africa, are hunters and gatherers—the men hunt for antelope and other game, the women and children forage for tubers, roots and other edibles with specially shaped digging sticks. They practise no agriculture but possess some knowledge of medicinal plants. A diorama illustrates how the men make poisoned arrows for hunting, while the women make shell beads from broken ostrich egg shells and use them for barter.

Among the Bantu speaking peoples are the Shona, Thonga, and Venda tribes who are believed to have lived in Zimbabwe and Mozambique for centuries. Some of their artistry and craftsmanship on exhibit here show a water jar, drum, medicine man's bag, dancing ax, soapstone bowls, diving dice and other artifacts usually made with some specific function in mind. There are also masks for religious rituals, ceremonial robes, weapons, and other equipment. Other African tribes who speak forms of the Bantu language are the Nguhi, Zulu, Hottentot, Bushmen, Hosa, Thembu, Mpomodo, Swazi and the south-eastern Ndebele, whose women make exquisitely designed beadwork and elaborate mural paintings.

A life-sized diorama recreates a domestic scene of the pastoral, cattle-keeping Herero shown in a hut-shaped exhibit. They are of southwest Africa. The Luvale are of the southern Congo, now known as Zaire; their initiation ceremonies for young boys passing into adulthood are illustrated here.

Other exhibits feature the crafts of the western African countries of Ghana, Benin, and Guinea. The people of Benin are artists of great skill in bronze and ivory carving and examples of their work are shown. Another country discussed is Gambia in western Africa. It is the country in which author Alex Haley found his "roots."

Herbert Ward's beautiful and sympathetic sculptures of African natives can be found in this hall and around the balcony on the second floor. For those who enjoy African art, the Smithsonian's Museum of African Art (see chapter 6) has additional artifacts to show.

Halls of the Cultures of Oceania, Indonesia, Australia, India, and Other Parts of Southern and Southeastern Asia (First Floor, East Side)

Movies, periodicals, newspapers, and even books cannot do justice to the diverse peoples described here, and even exhibits in this hall can only hint at the complexities of societies and cultures found in these areas of the world. The displays are richly varied and feature such items as Hawaiian capes made with feathers of now extinct birds, the gold-masked Bali Monkey, and a monumental rough-hewn head from Easter Island. There are ritual and household objects; weapons and musical instruments from many lands. While the peoples whose artifacts are described all live in the same general area of the world, their lives and traditions are very different from one another. The general term Oceania refers to the numerous islands scattered across the vast expanse of the Pacific Ocean on which are found Polynesian, Micronesian, and Melanesian cultures and soci-eties. Also described are societies and cultures of India, Pakistan, Malaysia, Cambodia, Indonesia, the Philippines, and Australia. Visitors who examine the hall's exhibits will find themselves amply rewarded for their time.

Polynesia encompasses the easterly, mostly volcanic islands of the south Pacific included in a rough triangle whose three points are Hawaii, New Zealand, and the Easter Islands. Although the Poly-nesians are separated from one another by thousands of miles of ocean, they speak variants of a single language. Some other Polynesian islands include Tonga, Samoa, Society, Tahiti, Cook, Tuamoto, and Marquesas. The lives of the people living on these islands are intimately involved with the sea—in fact, they refer to themselves as "children of the sea." They are expert fishermen with great knowledge of the habits of different kinds of fish. Artifacts displayed that they use in fishing show a hook retriever, an octopus lure, a fish club, netting needles, a plummet sinker, a hand net, and fishhook box. The display of their cultural artifacts reflects this dominance of the sea in almost every aspect of their daily life. As expert boat builders and sailors, they made long voyages over vast stretches of the ocean. Many who migrated to other islands became the Polynesian predecessors of peoples found there today. Music and dance are very important in their daily lives and we see exhibits of musical artifacts like a ukelele, gourd whistle, drums, dance skirts, and dance wands. Important in their lives are the continuing roles of kinship ties, a sense of obligation to ancestors, and (in the past) warfare. Exhibits also reveal their great skill in crafts; this includes making tapa cloth from bark.

On exhibit is a monumental rough-hewn head, one of many similar memorial monuments found on Easter Island. The Polynesians once believed that its spirit, when invoked by priests, could enter the living. Religion and magic play an important role in their lives. We see exhibited amulet stones, temple images, and a stone carving of "Ku-ula," Hawaiian god of fishermen. Included in the display of Easter Island artifacts are ancestral figures, weapons, tools, dance wands, an elaborate feather headdress, and a tiki (a wood or stone image). The Polynesians thought being a warrior was the ultimate attainment of a man, and avenging an insult to a kinsman was a sacred trust.

A diorama recreates a scene from the ritual kava drinking ceremony of Polynesian chiefs on the Samoan Islands. A young woman of high rank and her attendants, by tradition, always prepare the beverage for the chiefs. The Samoans have developed social and political organizations that are beneficial to the populace.

Hawaii is believed to have been settled by Polynesians from Samoa. Exhibits show royal bowls made of wood (there was no clay for pottery), containers for preparing poi, musical instruments, weapons, religious objects, and ornaments. Two priceless feather capes, elaborate and beautiful, which were worn only by kings and chiefs, are shown. These capes took years to make and contain the plumages of a now extinct bird. The Maoris are also a Polynesian people. Their territory is now the northern island plus the northeastern half of the southern island of New Zealand. A diorama depicts a group of Maoris, highly skilled tatooists, practising their art.

The geographic area called Micronesia includes the small coral islands north of the equator, between Hawaii to the east and the Philippines to the west—principally the Mariana, Yap, Palau, Caroline, Marshall, and Gilbert Islands. The lives of the Micronesian peoples, like the Polynesians, are intimately tied to the sea, as reflected here in exhibits of the artifacts that show fishing tackle containers, fish traps, a fishing kite, canoes, weather charms, etc. Some of their artifacts shown are a bark garment, loom woven cloth, a tortoise shell bracelet, and a coconut shell vessel. Other objects used in their daily lives shown are gardening tools, household articles, ornaments, ceremonial objects and several kinds of money. The money includes a six-foot stone disk from Yap Island that was used primarily as a status symbol of wealth rather than as a medium of exchange.

The islands of Melanesia lie in the Pacific, west of Samoa and Tonga and on the side of the Coral Sea northeast of Australia. Among the Melanesian peoples are the natives of New Guinea, the Admiralties, Santa Cruz, New Britain, New Ireland, New Hebrides, New Caledonia, and the Solomon, Fiji, and Loyalty Islands. The natives of New Guinea are adept at wood carving and other crafts using obsidian and pearl shells. They have a strong belief in the powers of spirits and demons, ghosts and ancestors whom they attempt to appease through special ceremonies. Many of the art works shown here were made for use on these occasions. Although the Melanesians, like other Pacific peoples, had no metal before the coming of the Europeans, they developed special skills to do wood carving, shell working, and making feather ornaments, among other things, with tools of stone, bones, and shell. The Dems of western New Guinea, represented in a diorama are just now emerging from a Stone Age culture. They live in villages in the rain forests where the women cultivate the gardens of sweet potatoes, taro, sugar cane, and bananas. The Dems are shown in a diorama preparing a ritual meal of roast pig cooked in a shallow pit with tree fern and banana leaves which are drawn up and then weighted with hot rocks.

The more than two hundred islands comprising the Fiji group (some of whom were in the past cannabalistic) are inhabited by a people skillful in carving and weaving, basket and potterymaking. They also make tapa cloth for clothing which is made by pounding and felting together the inner bark of a tree. An exhibit of these items demonstrates the islanders' talents.

Another diorama in this hall shows the Ifuago of the Philippines (whose official language is Tagalog) in a scene harvesting rice. The Ifuago are a primitive tribe who cultivate rice and other crops on the steep mountainsides by constructing terraces with supporting walls of stone. These terraces took hundreds of years of hard labor to build. They were produced by a primitive people, but so skillfully were they accomplished that these terraces are considered a marvel of engineering.

There are also exhibits featuring the craft work of the original natives of Australia who lived there long before the English sent convicts to that continent and designated it a penal colony. The original natives were confined by the British to reservations in the torrid deserts of north central Australia called Arnhem Land where even today they eke out a precarious existence as hunters, fishermen, and gatherers of wild plants. These natives believe that mythological half-animal half-human ancestors created and shaped the world, and founded human society. They further believe that these ancestors are still present in nature and control fertility of nature and thus the continuity of the tribe. The songs and dances of the natives reenact the ancestors' adventures and wanderings. Each social group has special spiritual ties with certain plants or animals (totems) which spring from an ancestral Fertility Mother. These totems appear on many of the sacred objects exhibited in cases in this hall.

The hall also features a display of beautiful, skillfully made shadow puppets of Malaysia. They were used in plays in which the audience watched the shadows cast by the performing puppets on a cloth screen, or, sometimes, the beautiful puppets perform without a screen. These puppets and the Kathakali dance costumes, part of a large collection of ethnological objects, were given to the Smithsonian by the government of Malaysia. A colorful male Kathakali dance figure on exhibit portrays a wicked king in a Hindu epic. Eye movements and hand gestures are important features of this type of dancing.

A remnant of the ancient Khmer culture that dominated Cambodia still exists as an archeological site in the northwestern Cambodian ruin at Angkor Wat. It was once a vast religious center, a part of which is recreated here. An illustration of a modern conference hall in Pnompenh is shown. Artifacts from Cambodia on display show: a rice knife, some rice baskets, a clay stove for cooking, a silk wall hanging, a ceremonial drum, a presentation tray, and other items made by the people of Cambodia. Just as the Khmer culture once pervaded Cambodian life, so Buddhism, the national religion of Laos, played a dominant role in Laotian life. On display are many bronze and wooden Buddhas, a Buddhist scripture written on palm leaves, a text written on wood, both of these written in Pali script. The music of Thailand shows a musician sitting cross-legged before the gong chimes which are arranged in a semi-circular pattern in front of him. These gong chimes are used not only in Thailand but also in Burma and Cambodia. Thai craft work shown here includes a coverlet with gold stamped floral design, a lacquered box with mother-of-pearl inlay, a lacquered vessel with a pedestal base, silver containers, lacquered bowls, brass bowls and trays, etc.

The Republic of Indonesia includes a number of volcanic islands which lie between Asia and Australia in the Malay Archipelago. Formerly called the Dutch (or Netherland) East Indies, they include the islands of Sumatra, Celebes, Java, Madura, the Moluccas, and Bali as well as parts of Timor, Borneo, and New Guinea. There are also hundreds of smaller islands (many uninhabited) that form part of the republic. There are still Indonesian tribal people on these islands whose chief religious beliefs are based in a world of deities and that spiritual and magical forces control much of their daily lives. The need to appease ancestral ghosts is of deep concern to these people in order not to bring misfortune on them and their households. To do so they carve guardian images and masks to repel demons, images of ancestors, and magical charms—some of these shown here. Indonesians place in high regard those who are skilled in games like top-spinning, dice, and card playing, or those performing on a musical instrument, or in dances. On the island of Bali they do the Kathakali dances in which the actor is believed to merge into the character that he portrays, as a result of concentration. A colorful brilliantly-costumed sacred figure, the gold-masked Bali monkey, is shown here. It was used in one of the Kathakali dances, and when performed in Bali there was offstage a singer and a musician playing a large copper drum that accompanied the dancer.

There are many dialects of the two main language groups spoken in India. The Tamil-Telegu group is spoken in southern India. Indo-Persian, the larger group, is used everywhere but in the far south. Within the Indo-Persian group, which comes from the ancient Sanskrit, the following languages are spoken: Bengali, Gujerati, Marathi, Sindhi, Punjabi, Hindi, and Hindustani or Urdu. There is a sizable display of India's religious artifacts, architecture, and crafts shown. An exhibit of stringed instruments indicates the important role music plays in Indian life. Other exhibits feature such items as miniature figurines, armor, basketry, and metalcrafts especially the beautiful bowls, trays, vases, pitchers, and other items achieved by hammering designs on thin sheets of brass. Folk jewelry from India and Pakistan

shows rings, head ornaments, chokers, earrings, etc. The exhibit of
fine textiles from India and Pakistan (whose official language is Urdu)
includes a goathair shawl from Kashmir, a cotton quilt from East
Bengal, a cotton skirt from Pakistan, and a collection of beautiful
cotton and silk saris, among them some silk marriage saris from
Rajasthan, East Bengal, Orissa, and Uttar Prudeth, each of which
represents their geographical region which is quite different from
one another in the vast subcontinent.

The kitchen of a Sindhi family in West Pakistan is recreated
in a diorama. While a servant churns butter, the lady of the house
is shown nearby wearing her jewelry (which is the family's world wealth)
and which is at once a personal status symbol and a symbol of the
financial security of the family. Pakistani religious architecture and
crafts are also the subjects of exhibits.

Native Peoples of the Americas (First Floor, West Side)

Exhibits in adjoining halls present material about selected
native peoples of North, South, and Central America as well as Mexico
who had lived in the New World long before white settlers arrived.
The exhibits offer insights into the lives of these diverse peoples,
among them the Eskimos of the far north and the Indians of the sub-
Arctic. The California and Northwest Coast tribes are featured, as
are the Plains, Apache, Navaho, Seminole, and desert tribes, and
the Pueblo and Woodland Indians. The exhibits of the native peoples
of Mexico and Central and South America describe such tribes as
the Huichol and the San Blas Cuna, the Guatemalan, Araucanian,
Aymara, Jivaro, and Inca Indians, and the Tehuelche, Carib, Ona Foot-
man and Yahagan tribes. A large map in the hall pinpoints where
skills and imaginative creations of these peoples originated. Among
the many highlights of early North American ingenuity are dog sleds,
birch bark canoes, and pueblo architecture. Bolas (weighted ropes)
used for hunting, terrace agriculture and woven fiber armor are a
few examples of ingenuity from South America. The map also notes
the variety of foods, such as corn, beans, pumpkins and squash, wild
rice, maple sugar, and sweet potatoes that Indians introduced to white
settlers. Although exhibits do not particularly focus on the languages
of the American Indians, it is interesting to note that there are a
multiplicity of linguistic stocks from which were derived many of
the spoken languages of these peoples. A few of these are: Eskimoan,
Athabascan, Algonkian, Iroquoian, Salishan, Shoshonian, Siouan, and
Muskogean. Some Indians shared common cultures, but spoke totally
unrelated languages, while some spoke closely related languages but
possessed vastly different cultures.

Eskimos, despite their wide geographical distribution in North
America, share a common language spoken along the Arctic coast
from the Aleutian Islands to Labrador, and certain key elements in
their culture. They were dependent on hunting and on fishing for
which they used the kayaks when weather permitted. Since their harsh,
cold environment is poor in plant foods they obtain their food from
the resources of the ocean: seals, walruses, whales, fish, and water
fowl supply their needs. Their artifacts of useful objects like tools

and weapons displayed in this hall are frequently adorned with art work that reflect their daily pursuits. They have excelled in sculpture carved from bone, stone, and ivory. Among other useful objects displayed are eye shades which give protection from the glare of the sun reflected from the ice and snow, holders for seal or walrus oil which contain a wick for lighting and heating their houses (two or three of these oil lamps make it possible to heat houses comfortably), harpoons, sleds, snow knives, and many other objects used for daily living. Some present-day suits of Eskimo clothing are shown, accompanied by descriptions of how skillfully they were made by the women using different skins for decorative effects. In addition to sealskins, Eskimos used caribou hides, walrus skins, Arctic fox furs, and polar bear and bird skins for clothing. The snow block igloo is used only on hunting expeditions in an emergency. Other housing of stone or earth built up with frames of whale bones or drift wood are covered with sod.

The caribou-hunting Indians of the sub-Arctic are true Indians, although they share many customs with the neighboring Eskimos. As described in the exhibits these Indians, made up of bands (groups of people related by blood or marriage) move from resource to resource hunting caribou and moose, fishing, and gathering berries. In the winter, toboggans pulled by dogs are used for transportation. Their homes (wigwams) are sometimes domed, sometimes conical in shape and covered by caribou skins or sheets of birch bark. Birch bark, the plywood of the Indians, grows abundantly in this region and is used for many, many things including containers and canoes. They have no pottery.

For the Northwest Coast Indians artifacts are exhibited of the Haida, Tlinglit, Kwakiutl, Tshimshian, Chilkat, Salish, and Coola tribes who lived for centuries in permanent settlements along the Pacific coast. They had no agriculture or domesticated animals. As exhibits indicate their staple foods include such abundant products of the sea as mussels, clams, salmon, etc. While their everyday clothing is simple, their ceremonial dress is elaborate. The women are skilled weavers, the men skilled woodworkers, renowned for their realistic representations. In the past, the men constantly engaged in war with neighboring tribes, and between times occupied themselves by holding potlatches (great giveaways). These Indians are famous for sculpture in wood, and on exhibit are several huge cedar totem poles with family crests on which the creatures represented some non-human ancestors from which they believed they were descended or which had played some role in their past lives and are objects of worship as guardians of the village.

The Hupa Indians make their home in northern California. An exhibit notes that their traditional staple food was once the acorn. After the Hupa women extracted the harmful tannic acid from the acorns, they pounded the residue into a flour. The Pomo Indians also live in California. Pomo women are renowned for their fine coiled and twined basketry, the artistic quality of which is of such a remarkably high level in weaving and decorating that specimens possessed by museums are highly prized. Exhibits show Pomo women at their craft ornamenting finished baskets with feathers and mother-of-pearl. Some of these are on display along with other artifacts of the Pomos.

Other exhibits feature the Navaho Indians (whose headquarters for the ever-increasing Navaho population is in Windsor Rock, Arizona) and show them as sheep herders and silversmiths, skills they adopted from the Spaniards and Mexicans; and as they were in the past, great warriors and raiders. The Navahos are renowned as weavers of serapes and blankets. They adopted as their own many elements of neighboring cultures. Many aspects of Navaho culture are subjects of exhibits. The Apaches, like the Navahos, were once a skilled warrior and raiding tribe (two of their most famous leaders were Geronimo and Cochise). The Apaches (the term means "the enemy") were formerly nomadic bands, living in temporary shelters, shown here, called wickeyups. They were never farmers, but today are successful cattle raisers. The Apache women continue to be adept at basketry; several exhibits display these and other artifacts of their culture.

Also featured in exhibits are the Indians of the North American southwestern deserts, among them the Mohave, Pima and Seri tribes, perhaps among the most culturally deprived of all North American Indian tribes. In such extremely inhospitable lands these peoples were rarely able to rely on crops. They spent most of their waking hours scrounging for food, rounding out their meager diets with edible cactus, such wild seeds and berries as they could gather, and some poor hunting of rabbits, grasshoppers, lizards, and snakes.

The Woodland Indians also lived by hunting, and fishing, gathering wild nuts, fruits and berries, and growing such crops as the climate permitted. As exhibits describe, what these Indians did not eat fresh in season, they dried in the open air or over a fire, for winter use. Exhibits also feature their crafts, religious beliefs, and their daily lives at war and peace. The pottery of Woodland Indians was not painted. Vessels were shaped and before they became dry the designs were prepared into the surface of the clay by cordage and textiles. At first, the East Woodland Indians lived in circular houses, but changed to rectangular (long houses) covered with bark. Woodland Indian tribes include the Chippewas, the Ottawas, the Hurons, the Potawatamis, the Menominees, the Winnebagos, and the Iroquois. In exhibits are masks of the Iroquois False Face Society, still made and used today. Also shown are small dioramas showing their home life including the long houses in which they lived.

The Plains Indians including the Kiowas, Arapahos, Sioux, Cheyenne, Crow, Assiniboin, Shoshonis, Utes, and Blackfoot are described in several exhibits. They lived a migratory life mainly hunting bison (or "buffalo") which was their staff or life. It was their source of food, clothing, and shelter, and of such items as tools, toys, and rope. They also hunted other large game like elk and antelope. Exhibits detail their religious ceremonies (Sun Dance, Ghost Dance, and the use of peyote which gives hallucinations in color) and their decorated ceremonial clothing, as well as their traditional mode of warfare. A diorama shows a tipi covered with fourteen bison hides in which some Arapahos once lived year-round; pemmican, strips of surplus meat, can be seen drying on a rack which is later smoked then pounded and mixed with fat and berries, and which can be kept year round. Other artifacts of their daily lives are shown including the V-shaped frame of poles, known as travois on which the dismantled tipi was dragged from place to place by horses or dogs when moving to a new settlement. Women were responsible not only for making the tipi cover but when the group moved, for dismantling it and later reerecting it. Their crafts included embroidery, quill, and silver works which are illustrated. A magnificent, colorful Sioux (Dakota) war bonnet worn on special occasions shows 77 eagle feathers, each achieved for a daring or brave deed. The Plains Indians did not practice agriculture. They had no pottery, but used containers made of buffalo hides in which they prepared meals.

The Seminole Indians of the Florida Everglades are a branch of the Creek Indians who did not exist prior to the white man's coming to this country. Some Indians began to desert their tribal influences. They drifted down into Florida where they were joined by a great number of escaping negro slaves. These became known as the Seminoles—the refugees. The Seminoles' principal form of transportation was once the pirogue, or dugout canoe, from which they speared fish. Artifacts of the Seminole culture, past and present, are shown.

In a number of other dioramas the hall presents scenes of selected North American Indian life. One series recreates the life of the Hopi Indians, a Pueblo Indian tribe. In one scene we observe the interior of a Hopi apartment where we see not only its furnishings, the clothing worn by women, but the different hair styles worn by married and unmarried women. In another diorama, one phase of a nine-day religious ceremony, the Hopi Indian Snake Dance is performed in which snakes stored in four pottery vessels are taken out of the vessel and placed between the lips of men of the Snake Society to be used as messengers to the gods in a dance; the snakes eventually thrown over the cliff are sent to petition the gods for much-needed rain after a severe drought and to control the water supply for the crops when rain does come. There is also a scene in a Hopi kiva, a large ceremonial chamber used only by the men of the tribe. There is a diorama that shows a Blackfoot Indian buffalo drive. In a diorama, Navaho women are engaged in spinning and weaving blankets and serapes, and the men in making silver ornaments—accompanying case exhibits show many specimens of these crafts. In still another diorama Hupa Indian women of northern California are shown removing harmful tannic acid from acorns before pounding the acorns into flour. Captain John Smith is depicted in a diorama trading with the Powhatan Indians on the James River in 1607. A family of Kutchin Indians, a caribou hunting tribe of the sub-Arctic, is pictured in summer dress in a diorama. Another charming diorama depicts with delightful humor a small seal catch by a young Polar Eskimo boy which seems to amuse the entire group of onlookers.

Many distinctive Indian cultures also exist south of the North American continent. An exhibit describes the Huichols, a conservative mountain tribe of Mexico; there are illustrations of their temples and of items used in their religious rituals. Another exhibit focuses on the San Blas Indians of Panama showing their homes, dress, rituals, religious beliefs, and fishing gear. There is also an exhibit of the Indians of Guatemala; each town where these natives live has created a distinctive native costume. The Araucanian Indians of Chile live in the Andean highlands. As a display of their artifacts indicates, they are skilled weavers (of both llama and sheep wool) and are fine silversmiths. Another tribe of the Andean highlands shown here, the

Aymara, live on the high plateau above Peru and Bolivia. Their principal foods are potatoes and fish which they net in Lake Titicaca; they also raise llamas.

By contrast, the Jivaro Indians of eastern Ecuador are a warlike people who carry on prolonged blood feuds in the mountainous jungles of their homeland. Artifacts of their culture are on exhibit here, as is material describing the natives of Tierra del Fuego, the Ona Footmans and the Yahagans. These peoples are the world's southernmost inhabitants; their land is cold, forlorn, and barren, and as inhospitable as are its primitive inhabitants. The Ona Footmans and the Yahagans get most of their food from the sea, but they also hunt the guanaco, a native land animal.

Scenes of South American and British Guyanan Indian life are recreated in a series of dioramas. There are Peruvian Incas terrace farming in the highlands of their country; the nomadic Tehuelche of Patagonia in Argentina riding horseback as they hunt guanacos and capture them with bolas; and Carib women of British Guyana preparing cassava, the staple food of their tribe.

Hall of Dynamics of Evolution (First Floor, Central Area–behind Elephant)

Some of the fundamental concepts of evolution are described in illuminating exhibits in this hall. They show, among other things, how cumulatively over millions of years great differences slowly arose in living organisms with new ones developing and old ones dying out. Diversity of plant and animal life, extensive throughout the world, shows differences occurring within a species that are due in part to changing genetic combinations, some of these the result of sexuality that gave rise to amalgamated cells with new combinations of genes producing slightly different organisms with new characteristics. Great diversities are also accounted for by genetic mutations, by changes in environmental or climatic conditions, geographic isolation, hybridization, and artificial selection of species by people. The survival by natural selection of stronger organisms, and how those succeeding in hiding from predators through color concealment, camouflage, or mimicry are able to survive in the competition for food, space, and mates leaving more of their offspring in the genetic pool are explained in this hall's exhibits.

What is the potential for offspring survival? Many organisms under unhampered circumstances could conceivably produce enough offspring not only to assure the survival of the species, but, if not checked, could probably blanket a good part of the world. This shocking thought is brought home in a striking exhibit of a kitchen filled with cockroaches that is labeled "If All Offspring Survive." Somehow nature takes care that populations do not become too large for the resources (food and space) available to survive and reproduce. An absorbing exhibit, the life cycle of the sock–eye salmon, is illustrated and discussed. The female of this species can lay as many as 1,000 eggs, which even though fertilized by the male (both male and female salmon die after egg laying) will result in the loss of many of these eggs by silting, drying out, pollution, or to diseases or predation. Those which escape these disasters are still not free of danger, for many of the hatching fry or those even larger are eaten by fish, birds, bears, and man or are attacked by parasites or diseases. To maintain the population of sock-eye salmon only two offspring of the original fertilized eggs of each pair need survive.

The diorama of an eastern oak woodland scene in late spring appears so peaceful, but one is made aware of a struggle for survival if he carefully examines the individual organisms residing there. Most of the 5,000 acorns produced by the white oak are eaten by squirrels, chipmunks, deer, and other animals; some of the others are attacked by weevils and other insects, while most of those remaining which succeed in sprouting will not survive because they fell too close to the white oak tree and are overshadowed by its branches. The female green frog lays about 2,000 eggs fertilized by the male. The eggs may become exposed and die if the pond level goes down, which may also be true for the tadpoles hatched from the eggs and living in the pond from three to ten months; these tadpoles must also escape predators like fish, large aquatic insects, turtles, water birds, crayfish, and others. The tent caterpillar has stripped the cherry tree of leaves as shown here; and a skunk has found the snapping turtles nest and robbed it of its eggs.

Genes are units of chemical information tightly packed in DNA molecules that are located on paired chromosomes in the cell's nucleus. The genes of an offspring resulting from the union of a female sex cell with a male sex cell will carry inherited traits of each in the DNA molecules. The results of the recombination of inherited traits are organisms in a population different in many characteristics from the parents or siblings. Other differences may result from mutations of the DNA genetic molecules. Mutations may occur in a changing environment where organisms are subjected to cumulative effects of ionizing radiation in the earth's atmosphere or through other mutagens. These can cause gene mutations resulting in the development of new species or the death of others. A mutation may be beneficial or not for the species. Generally, only mutations that result in new inheritable characteristics are transmitted to future generations through the sex cells.

Much attention is devoted in exhibits to demonstrate how traits are inherited and with what results. Gregor Mendel, an Austrian monk who was also a botanist, worked out in the 1860s the important basic principles of genetics during his experiments in plant breeding. They are known today as Mendel's laws and are the foundation of "classical genetics." Two large, colorful exhibits show snapdragons (red and white to start) which effectively illustrate the principles of Mendel's laws of genetics. They are displayed with labels to clearly explain what changes occur when cross pollination between these flowers takes place. Human populations also show variations of physical traits they inherit as the result of combinations of male and female cells, each carrying the inherited characteristics of their parents. A large montage displays photographs of people from all over the world with characteristic facial features, each noticeably different from the other as a result of genes which each inherited in a given population.

Another area in this hall discusses natural selection of organ-

isms in the struggle for survival. The first to publish on this subject
was Charles Darwin who wrote in **The Origin of the Species,** "This
preservation of favorable variations and the rejection of injurious
variations, I call Natural Selection." He goes on to explain in his book
that those competitors that survive in the struggle for existence,
in general, pass these favorable traits on to succeeding generations.
Natural selection can also be achieved through selection by predators
(such as those which catch the conspicuous, tasty organisms, and
avoid animals with stingers, spines, or poisons); through concealing
coloration (the dark pepper moths on the bark of trees in an industrial
English city is an example); through camouflage (with examples of
color, pattern, shape, and sometimes behavior of katydids, walking
sticks, underwing moths, copperhead snakes, and others); through
warning coloration (with examples of animals that use the distinctive
warning colors of red, orange, yellow, white in combination with
black) as seen in skunks, monarch butterflies, yellow jackets, bees,
wasps, hornets, and others; through mimicry (with examples like the
Viceroy butterfly, a tasty morsel to birds that mimics the Monarch
butterfly which is not a bit tasty, and the longhorn beetle that mimics
the yellow jacket, or the robber fly that mimics the bumblebee).
There are also selections by parasites like the sickle cell and malaria
cell parasites shown on slides in microscopes which visitors can
examine. In all of these and other cases the survivors have passed
their survival traits on to the next generations.

There is always competiton for mates and in a large diorama
we see two battling elks using their antlers to attack each other in
order to win the females, and of male birds using their plumage to
attract the female. Even plants, in order to attract insects or birds
which can pollinate their flowering plants, have evolved showy parts,
odors, and nectars.

People have had a hand in the diversification of plants and
animals by artifical selection. The Indians in Mexico as early as 10,000
years ago collected the seeds of a wild ancestor of corn, an early
grass called teosinte. Much later in sorting the plants they collected
they saved the best seeds to plant and cultivate for better size and
yield. Much, much later agronomists began to hybridize corn which
would improve the quality and yield of the crops. People have also
had a hand in the artificial selection and evolution of dog breeds.
All are discussed in exhibits.

Differentiation may occur in the same species as the result
of geographic isolation brought about by separation from each other
by barriers such as mountain ranges, rivers, islands, or even oceans.
Exhibits show examples of how differentiation by geographic isolation
occurred in species of finches, snails, bears, and others.

An absorbing section in this hall is devoted to the evolution
of horses for which fossil evidence of their existence approximately
50,000,000 to 60,000,000 years ago is available. The ancestral horse
Eohippus ("dawn horse") that lived during the Eocene was not much
larger than a cat. It had four toes on its front feet and three on the
hind feet and was found in both the Old and New Worlds. Body structures of this animal changed as it grew in size and its environments
changed, particularly the shape of its feet and jaws. During ancient
times tropical forests grew in this region of the world and horses

were browsers eating the leaves of trees, but when there was an uplift of the Rocky Mountains with an accompanying cooler climate the tropical forests disappeared and grasslands grew on the plains. It was then that the horses became grazers chewing grasses that contained silica. These eating habits necessitated changes in the horse's jaw formation in order to accommodate the larger and stronger teeth necessary to grind this coarse, gritty grass. For millions of years grass grazers and tree browsers coexisted, but eventually the grazers won out because the open plains favored fleeter horses that could outrun their predators (for which purpose these grazers gradually also had to change the shape of their feet). Orohippus was an early ancestral horse somewhat later and more advanced than Eohippus. Orohippus evolved in North America from tiny, four-toed animals to full sized horses. It is interesting to note that the horse became extinct in North America and was later reintroduced on the North American continent by early Spanish explorers. As portrayed in a mural horses evolved so that in the Oligocene lived the Mesohippus; in the Miocene, Merychippus; in the Pliocene lived Pliohippus and Plesippus (one-toed horse); and in the Pleistocene and Recent period lived Equus. These changes are all discussed and illustrated in the mural.

Various species of birds, insects, and amphibia have a niche in this hall. The markings (particularly of male birds) and their songs (recorded and broadcast in the hall) help identify them to their own species, both of these are inherited characteristics important for the continuation of the species. Male fireflies while flying at night send a unique pattern of light flashes to the female of its species that is waiting on the ground and which will only respond to signals of its own kind and return the signal, a mechanism in courting that helps maintain the genetic integrity of a particular firefly species. Rare and exotic butterflies and moths from all over the world are displayed and described in an area of this hall with information about their life cycles, habitats, uses of coloration and reactions to environmental pressures.

Do you know how entomologists specializing in fleas (they are called pulicologists) identify the various species of fleas (of which there are over 2,000 species)? Primarily by examining the genetalia of male fleas!

Halls of the World of Mammals (First Floor, West Side)

After being rulers of the earth for approximately 140,000,000 years, at the end of the Mesozoic era dinosaurs became extinct. Inconspicuous mammals living at that time, small in size and numbers, but successful in evolving metabolic and anatomical modifications that helped prepare them for climatic and environmental changes began a push which eventually led to their dominance. Many orders of mammals (Phylum Chordata, Class Mammalia) have populated the earth, but of these only eighteen now remain, the others are extinct. Of the existing orders of mammals, the largest in the world today is Rodentia (which includes rats, mice, squirrels, beavers, rabbits, porcupines, woodchucks, marmots, prairie dogs, gophers, and others);

second comes Artiodactyl (camels, bison, llamas, giraffes, antelopes, deer, sheep, hogs, pigs, goats, hippopotamus, elk, moose, and others); third is Carnivora (wolves, dogs, cats, bears, raccoons, foxes, cougars, lions, weasels, minks, badgers, seals, otters, and others); with Chiroptera (bats) as fourth. The other living orders include Marsupials (kangaroos, opossums, koalas, and others); Monotremes (platyplus and echidnas); Primates (baboons, chimpanzees, orangutans, gorillas, monkeys, lemurs, man, and others); Tubulidents (aardvarks); Proboscids (elephants); Edentates (three-toed sloths, nine-banded armadillos, great anteaters, and others); Hyrax (hyraxes); Lagomorphs (rabbits, hares, and others); Sirens or Seacows (manatees, dugongs); Perissodactyls (zebras, horses, mules, asses, tapirs, rhinoceros); Cetaceans (whales, porpoises, dolphins); Pholidotes (pangolins); Dermopteras (flying lemurs); and Insectivores (shrews, moles, hedgehogs, and others). Many in each classification are described in this hall.

Mammals developed better brains than earlier vertebrates and they used them advantageously in coping with their environment. Generally characterized as animals with warm blood, they have a backbone and, among other things, the ability to suckle their young with milk and give them care after birth. Representative characteristics of three kinds of mammalian orders, monotremes, marsupials, and placentals, are described in exhibits. There are also exhibits that discuss how mammals make their way in the world protected by their coloration or speed, or using nature's weapons to prey on others and obtain food. Some of man's mammalian relations depicted here are good neighbors, such as pocket gophers which help improve the soil; free-tailed bats which destroy insect pests; and beavers which aid in soil and water conservation. Others are less benign. These include the Norway rat, woodchuck, mountain beaver, some squirrels, the duckbilled platypus, and the spiny anteater (echidna). In addition, some bats, the black rat, white-lipped peccary, and the black-tailed squirrel are carriers of disease, and therefore, very harmful to man.

Adjoining halls offer an opportunity to learn more about the familiar and unfamiliar mammals of the world. For sheer joy and wonder there are some rare, or unusual, or very popular mammals displayed in dioramas showing their natural habitats. One can observe in exhibit cases the pygmy hippopotamus, the koala, the giant fruit bat, the aardvark, the kangaroo, the Tasmanian devil, the giant armadillo, the capybara, the hyrax, the nutria, the giant panda, the coatimundi, the wombat, the pygmy opposum, the least armadillo, the naked mole rat, the Maryland shrew, and the nocturnal kinkajou, an unusually friendly and gentle mammal that lives in Central America and northern South America.

Of the three types of mammals described in the halls, the monotremes are the most primitive and retain certain reptilian characteristics like laying eggs. Monotremes include only the duckbilled platypus and the echidna (the spiny anteater), and are found primarily in New Zealand, Australia, and Tasmania. Their eggs which are passed from the body of the female shortly after fertilization are eventually hatched and the young find their way to the minute pores on the skin of the mother's abdomen which exude milk and which these newly hatched lick or suck up for nourishment. The marsupials, such as kangaroos, opossums, and koalas, by contrast are born alive at a very early stage in their development, find their way to the mother's pouch where they cling to teats inside it for nourishment until capable of a more independent existence. The placentals (including, among others, bears, elephants, whales, cats, dogs, rabbits, monkeys, and humans) are completely formed within the mother's womb before birth, although generally still dependent after birth for varying lengths of time for care and nourishment.

Other exhibits in these halls explore the biological principles of speciation and subspeciation, showing how these occur when genetic diversions (changes or mutations) arise in species that may be geographically isolated from their ancestral stock. Certain groups of cottontails, gray foxes, and squirrels that have been geographically isolated are used for illustration here. As the exhibits explain, they develop, over time, characteristics that differ from their ancestral stock and, therefore, can no longer interbreed with them.

A most absorbing exhibit explores the parallel developments in populations of placental and marsupial wolves, moles, flying phalangers, and wallabys that had been geographically isolated from their common stock. The marsupials of each are compared with their placental counterparts. Another very interesting exhibit shows members of four different mammalian families (dogs, cats, bears, and wild pigs) assembled from all over the world. There are marsupial and placental members in each family which are exhibited side by side in large glass cases. The differences in anatomy, color, and size among the geographically separated members of the same family are amazing!

A successful species is one in which the members survive and thrive in their particular environments. In some cases, they have had to make modifications in the structure of their extremities, necessary for new forms of locomotion so they can obtain food, mates, or to defend themselves against predators, or to secure territories. In this hall exhibits describe different methods of locomotion employed by such diverse animals as the two-toed sloth, the porpoise, raccoon, Chinese civet, chevrotain, antelope, jerboa, pocket gopher, leaf-nosed bat and other mammals. The exhibit labels explain the different and best forms of locomotion each has achieved and the anatomical changes that had to take place in order to provide for meeting their needs for locomotion in their environment.

An exhibit shows animals that have developed highly skilled gliding techniques. Included in the display of these gliders are the flying squirrel, flying phalanger, flying lemur, and flying opossum. The only mammal that can truly fly is the bat.

In a variety of ways mammals have adapted to the climatic conditions (temperate, tropical, sub-tropical, desert, and Arctic) in which they live. An exhibit describes many of these adaptations. For example, certain mammals, like the caribou, American elk, bison, and white-footed mouse cope with climate changes by migrating seasonally; the exhibit shows where they go and discusses why. Others like the woodchuck and the jumping mouse hibernate, while the ground squirrel estivates, spending cold periods asleep in burrows, although they may come out on warm days in the winter. Tropical and sub-tropical mammals like tapirs, agouti and rice rats, as a rule, have few offspring and are provided anatomically with features to help pass off body heat. Most desert mammals like Australian jumping rats, kangaroo rats, greater jerboas also have anatomical features to pass off body heat; during the day they stay in their burrows and are active only at night. Arctic mammals like the tundra vole, red-backed mouse, and the musk ox also have anatomical features along with dense fur to help them conserve body heat. An exhibit describes each of these animals.

Concealment coloration is yet another adaptive feature described in an exhibit. Certain mammals (especially their young) have evolved blending coloration that helps conceal them from predators. Among mammals which have evolved such concealing coloration are the least chipmunk, skunk, mongoose, raccoon, lesser panda, American badger, okapi, young wild pigs, deer fawn, and the young tapir all are shown here. Still another adaptive feature for some animals is keen hearing that alerts them to danger and aids them to escape and hide; such mammals include the pika, the snowshoe hare, the jack-rabbit, the brush rabbit, the cottontail rabbit, and the Rock Mountain cony all are shown in a display.

The hedgehog and certain types of porcupines have spines or quills that serve for protection against predators as well as for heat regulators. The echidna (spiny anteater) like some venomous snakes has poison glands and sharp pointed spur-like glands with which to inflict poison against predators in an attack. Another exhibit describes how the shrews and the platypus use poison for purposes of both protection and attack. An exhibit illustrates the defensive and offensive capabilities of the skunk, opossum, elk, deer, cougar, and other animals.

Bats and porpoises are able to use reflected sound waves (sonar) to avoid obstacles in locating food. Animals like the anteater, short-tail shrew, bear, badger, monkey, and the non-toothed whale use a variety of other rather uncommon means to obtain their food. Exhibits explore the lifestyles and habitats of these animals.

The lemmings (rodents) of Scandinavia provide a remarkable example of adaptive behavior. When overpopulation threatens their food supply of mosses and lichens, and shelters are no longer adequate, the lemmings in this stressful situation begin a mass migration from the mountains to cultivated valleys seeking food and new shelters that takes them from the highlands to the sea. They do not hesitate to go into large bodies of water, too wide to cross, where millions are drowned. Many others die of injury, diseases, or exhaustion. A chart, shown here, records the lemming migration from 1862 to 1939.

One large section in these halls is devoted to North American mammals. A series of large dioramas recreates the native habitats and briefly describes the lifestyles of the following animals: the black bear, wapitit (American elk), the grizzly bear, bison (American buffalo), puma (mountain lion), wolf, pronghorn antelope, big-horn sheep, mountain goat, white-tailed deer, moose, caribou, Virginia opossum (the only marsupial in the United States), the nine-banded armadillo, and the musk ox.

Another section shows dioramas of native habitats of many African mammals (among them some President Theodore Roosevelt brought back from East Africa and gave to the Smithsonian). The African mammals in these dioramas include the African hartebeet, Thomson's gazelle, square-lipped rhinoceros, African buffalo, African lion, dik-dik, and the hippopotamus.

One large section in these halls displays African game mammals of the Great Plains. Some of these are the impala, the klipspringer, sable, harnessed antelope, the eland, the springbuck, the white-eared kob, the gerenuk, the reticulated giraffe, the zebra, the Colobus monkey, and Thomson's and Grant's gazelles. Other exhibits in this section feature animals that coexist with the game animals on the Great Plains of Africa. Among these are the African migrant and monarch butterflies, thistle butterflies, darkling beetles, desert locusts, the striped grass rat, Egyptian cobra, the banded mongoose, boomsland (a snake), the Mamqua dove, the ulu francolin (a bird), the dormouse, the red-breasted shrike, the genet, and the harsh-furred mouse.

Primates which represent an order of highly intelligent mammals include monkeys, apes, lemurs, marmosets, and man. All except man are exhibited in a large section of these halls. Primates representative of an order of mammals found in tropical and sub-tropical regions are shown in dioramas with skillfully painted backgrounds and with descriptions of their lifestyles. Included are gibbons, chimpanzees, gorillas, and orangutans (the largest of the primates). Proboscis, rhesus, African, Asian, and capuchin monkeys are others shown. The primates known as great apes or anthropoid apes (manlike apes) most closely resemble man in some physical characteristics such as in their general structure, the shape of the spinal column, sternum, and pelvis. There are, of course, differences between man and anthropoid apes that are explained in exhibits. Gibbons live in southeast Asia, the orangutans in Borneo and Sumatra, the gorillas in west equatorial Africa, and the chimpanzees in west and central equatorial Africa. Specimens of the African and Asian monkeys, abundant and varied species on both continents, are shown in separate exhibits. There are also displays of such South American primates as the baboon, marmoset, and howler monkey. There are true lemurs (lemurs are nocturnal, large-eyed creatures) from Madagascar, and some relatives of the lemurs, the nocturnal, aboreal lorises are shown here. Other primates on exhibit are tarsiers from the southwest Pacific islands, and southeast Asian tree shrews.

Hall of Birds of the World (First Floor, West Side)

Joseph Smith of the Audubon Society found himself absorbed in the exhibits in this hall. Members of the Audubon Society are not the only ones interested in birds. People all over the world are interested and evidence of such interest has been found as far back as Neolithic times in paintings on the walls of caves or of engraved records on horn, bone, or stone of birds. Birds are by tradition symbolic of freedom and a host of other human aspirations, but man has not hesitated to use them for food and ornament. More prosaically, birds constitute a widely diffused, large, and diverse group of warm-blooded animals covered with feathers. Characteristic representatives of about twenty-seven orders and one hundred seventy families are shown in very large cases in this hall. One order, the song birds, makes up the largest number and is found everywhere except Antarctica and the wide expanses of the open seas. Of some birds the characteristics of their environments, courtship, reproduction, and life habits are examined in exhibits. There are also exhibits that discuss and illustrate bird evolution, ecology, migration, and the physical characteristics that permit birds to fly. The habitat exhibits offer a unique opportunity to study some species in their natural environments. In many ways birds are beneficial to mankind: insectivorous birds help in insect control, others as distributors of seeds, and as agents of nutrient recycling. On the other hand, birds can be the dispersal agents of insect pathogens, and in certain cases agents in tree damage.

A bird that seems to fascinate almost everyone is the penguin. Living chiefly south of the equator in the Antarctic regions, the twenty or more known species of penguins, varying in size from the four foot emperor to the sixteen inch little blue penguin have their own peculiar characteristic qualities. They do not fly, but move swiftly through water with the aid of modified wings somewhat similar to a seal's flippers, and their feet which are extended behind serve as a rudder. The penguins shown in a diorama in this hall were collected by Admiral Richard E. Byrd on his several trips to Antarctica and donated to the Smithsonian.

One of the main features of avian evolution was the modification of reptilian scales into feathers, but many other modifications in anatomy and bone structure had to take place before flight was possible. An explanation in this hall supplemented with a description in the Hall of Osteology on the second floor is helpful in understanding bird flight history. An exhibit discusses the speciation of birds, noting that evolutionary changes sometimes occur when genetic mutations (or diversions) arise in populations that are, over time, geographically isolated from the main stock. Other causes for speciation have been man-made when he crossed and selected birds for desired traits.

The illustrations in one exhibit explain how birds fly, exploring the physical principles of flight and noting the speeds of certain birds. Among those described are the duck hawk, which can achieve the incredible speed of one hundred eighty miles per hour; the homing pigeon, ninety-two miles per hour; the starling, thirty-five to forty-five miles per hour; and the bronzed grackle, twenty-eight miles per hour. The song sparrow attains only seventeen miles per hour.

Scientists are not yet certain what exactly determines the migration of birds. All sorts of explanations have been offered to account for it. Could it be availability of food, changes in seasonal temperature due to the amount of sunlight reaching the earth, or safer breeding grounds, or a combination of these and other factors? Few birds live the entire year in the range they occupy during the nesting periods. Larger birds generally migrate during the day, smaller species at night. The main flyways of certain New and Old World birds are illustrated in an exhibit.

We do know that the food and feeding habits of bird species are extremely varied. The food preferences of species can range from grass, flowers, nectar, seeds, and grain to insects, mollusks, crustaceans, fish, reptiles, and even carrion. The physical adaptations of their bills, beaks, tongue, feet, etc. of each species are important in securing and digesting desirable food. Exhibits describe some of these adaptations and the diet of certain birds and how they obtain their food.

There are birds characteristic of particular environments. Continental birds—the birds of North and South America, Europe, Africa, and Asia are each grouped in separate exhibits. Other birds are characteristic of large islands such as those found in Australia, New Zealand, and Madagascar, each shown in separate exhibits. Other exhibits feature ocean birds, upland game birds of Asia and Europe, and birds of paradise each separately displayed.

Just as food and feeding habits are idiosyncratic, so is courtship behavior. Courtship displays have several purposes, as discussed in an exhibit, and take several, sometimes spectacular forms. The male spends much time in courting the female by posturing, plumage display, and/or platform building exhibited in the courtship of the peacock, the crested bronze wing dove, the snowy egret, the wild turkey, the Argus pheasant, the sage grouse, the rockhopper penguin, and the mandarin duck.

All birds lay eggs, but as a display reveals there is a wide variety among the nests birds make for their eggs and young. Some birds that live along rocks build no nest, laying their eggs on the rocks, while others along the shores have a few pebbles with some bits of grass in which they lay their eggs. From such simple nesting places on the ground to some very strong, elaborate nests in trees there are descriptions and examples shown in exhibits. The eggs laid vary by species in size, shape, color, markings, and texture as well as in the number laid in each clutch. The period of incubation for eggs varies too. On exhibit are many specimens of nests and eggs of different species. The care of young hatchlings also differs among species. Exhibits point out that altricial birds, who are born helpless, often naked and blind, need more care than precocial birds, which are down-covered at birth and able to fend for themselves within a few hours or days.

Parasitism has been a successful evolutionary adaptation for several kinds of birds, and what takes place in these relationships is described here. Among parasitic birds described are the North American cowbird, European cuckoo, pintail weaver, greater honey guide, and black-headed duck. Cowbird eggs are frequently laid in the nest of yellow warblers whose young are victimized by the much larger cowbird hatchlings, grabbing the food and often pushing them out of the nest. Yellow warbler nests have been found with as many as three floors, indicating that the adult warblers, recognizing the cowbird eggs, have built new floors over the eggs and started afresh.

A series of dioramas in this hall depicts the environments of selected birds, among these the palm chat of the Dominican Republic and Haiti; the Carolina paroquet, an extinct bird that lived in the eastern United States; the Hoatzen, a pheasant-like bird of South America which feeds on leaves of plants (in this same diorama one can see a scarlet ibis, snow egret, spatulate billed roseate spoonbill, and boat-billed heron); the satin bower bird of Australia and New Guinea which is shown with the bower the male built to attract a mate; the rhinoceros hornbill of Borneo and Sumatra which shows the male feeding its mate through a slit in the tree home which he has enclosed so the female can safely lay her eggs and remain until the young are ready to fly; the Argus pheasant of Borneo, Malaysia, and Sumatra with wings outspread over his head in a courtship behavior;

and the African greater honey guide which leads the ratel (honey badger) to the bees' nests which the ratel tears open to feed on the honey, and leaves for the birds the wax of the honey comb (the bird has special bacteria in its stomach to help digest it), the bees and larvae. The honey guide lays its eggs in the nests of hole-nesting birds and the young, on hatching, kill the hatchlings of the other birds with needlesharp bill hooks and consume the food brought by their foster parents.

Many modern birds have become extinct. An exhibit discusses their disappearance and notes among the extinct species: the Guadeloupe flicker, cara-cara, huia, dodo, Norfolk Island parrot, Martha, great auk, heath hen, and the passenger pigeon. Other species like members of the rail family are imperiled and stand a chance of becoming extinct. An exhibit describes the California condor, Semper's warbler, akepa, whooping crane, trumpeter swan, ivory-billed woodpecker, St. Vincent parrot, Cuban snail kite, and the Hawaiian goose which are also endangered species.

Man has affected the environments of many birds, changing their habitats and challenging their adaptability. Man has preyed upon birds for both food and ornament, contributing to the decimation of many species. An exhibit illustrates how man's presence has sometimes proved a deadly one for birds.

Birds found in the Washington, D.C. area are shown in exhibit cases on the ground floor of this building near the Baird Auditorium.

Hall of Life in the Sea (First Floor, West Side)

In this hall visitors will gain new insights into the great riches and complexity of life in the sea if they pause to examine the exhibits which display some of the astounding number of species from microscopic invertebrates to huge vertebrates thriving in this marine environment. Not only do people depend on some of these for food, but also for tools, clothing, and ornament. The hall features everything from whelks to whales, and depicts a range of life as simple as sponges and to mammals as complex as the sea walrus. Two illuminating exhibits in the hall describe reproduction and parental care of microscopic marine invertebrates which should prove extremely interesting, especially to those unfamiliar with these creatures. There are several films about sea life communities screened almost continuously in the hall.

The brightly colored Coral Reef exhibited in a 3,000 gallon tank shows approximately 200 live species in this environment. The algae covered turf and other plants of a coral reef ordinarily collect energy from the sun which they convert for their needs in a process called photosynthesis. The coral reef in this hall is a self-supporting ecosystem warmed by strong metal halide lights (simulating tropical sunlight) with mechanically produced waves which help create a tropical setting as close as possible to that of a real-life situation for its inhabitants. These include starfish, sea fans, anemones, spiny spider crabs, spiny lobsters, long pinned urchins, queen conch, horned feather worms, snails, parrot fish, damsels, blennies, grunts, butterfly fish, corals, and others; and plants like blue, green, red, and blue-green algae, turtle grass, and others. This coral reef is constantly being monitored by a group of research scientists working in a marine laboratory nearby to study and keep records of its natural equilibrium. Visitors can observe them working behind a large plate glass window in the well-lighted laboratory. Accompanying this exhibit is an interesting film "Coral Reefs; Understanding Their Passage Through Time."

Suspended dramatically from the ceiling in this hall near its entrance is an eye-catching model of a diving blue whale, ninety-two feet long which grew to that enormous size from its birth length of about twenty-four feet. The blue whale, now an almost extinct species, when fully grown weighs as much as 150 tons and is probably the largest creature that has ever lived. Other species of whales which include sperm, narwhal, pilot, killer, and bowhead are drawn to scale and shown on the wall in a large mural. Although they are marine animals, all whales are true mammals with backbones, warm blood, and young who are suckled with milk.

Another interesting exhibit is "The Alvin," a scale model of the navy's deep diving research submarine which is famous for its part in the discovery and exploration of the deep-sea hydrothermal vents. On its deep sea dives it discovered new biological frontiers about communities of animals which cluster around geothermal springs at the Galapogas Rift in the East Pacific. On exhibit in a nearby case are specimens of tube worms, crabs (several kinds), limpets, mussels, spaghetti worms, and clams that had been gathered from these geothermal springs. Another major discovery "The Alvin" has made at sea floor level in the East Pacific are the spreading centers where plates that make up some of the earth's crust are moving apart. "The Alvin" is owned by the Office of Naval Research and is operated by the Woods Hole Oceanographic Institution in a program jointly sponsored by the Office of Naval Research, the National Science Foundation, and the National Oceanographic and Atmospheric Administration.

Among the large species featured in the hall, sharks have the most unfortunate reputation. There are models of mako, white, big-eyed thresher, and other sharks shown here. There are also models of such "kings of speed" as the Pacific sailfish, bluefin, tuna, black marlin, and bottlenose, grampus, white-sided, and spinner porpoises. The fourteen foot black marlin on display always attracts sports fishermen who stop to closely examine it.

Two unusually fine exhibits show greatly enlarged models depicting reproductions of microscopic or slightly larger marine invertebrates and the parental care or lack of it given by some to their young. Both sexual and asexual reproduction are illustrated, and the sexual reversals of isopods and silver limpets are described. Some invertebrates have evolved physical parts that protect their eggs and young, and one exhibit points out, among other things, the brood chambers of bryozoans, the barrel-shaped cases of pelagic amphipods, the large underside pouches of syllid worms, the pockets of sea stars, and the vase-shaped capsules of dog whelks used for this purpose.

Visitors to this hall can see in an exhibit many models of fishes that provide food for man and animals: herring, sardine, trout, cod, perch, red snapper, haddock, tuna, bonita, flounder, halibut, salmon, smelt, and skate, to name a few. This exhibit tells where each is found, and, in some cases, the yearly quantities fishermen catch. There is also an exhibit showing invertebrate sea animals that are caught and used for food such as jellyfish, sea anemone, shrimp, lobsters, crabs, octopus, queen conch, clams, limpets, squid, scallops, abalone, and oysters.

In addition to providing man with food, invertebrates also supply the stuff for tools and ornaments and on exhibit are specimens of some of these including pearly oyster, black coral, red abalone, money cowry, precious coral, dye murex, cat's eye, top shell cuttlefish, and sheepswool sponge. Exhibits feature other products that men obtain from vertebrate marine animals such as fur pelts from seals, sperm oil, and ambergris (for perfume) from whales, and ivory from walrus.

Marine life is sometimes so beautiful it is displayed to advantage in a darkened alcove in this hall as if in a jeweler's window. Among those exhibited are deep sea shells from the Indian and Pacific oceans, boxer crabs, rough keyhole limpets, purple-dye murex, Portuguese man-of-war, pinion cone shells, deep sea and reef (or lettuce) coral, and shallow water shells.

Marine animals range from the simple to the complex. Sponges (Phylum Porifera), for example, are primitive marine animals that spend their lives attached by a base or stem to a rock or other object on the sea bottom and feed by pumping water in and out of their openings. Sponges occur in many different forms. Some exhibited here include leaf, black Caribbean, horny, velvet, hardheaded, and loggerhead sponges.

Coelenterates are also primitive multicellular marine animals which are radically symmetrical with tentacles armed with stinging cells. Some coelenterate species reproduce sexually and asexually alternately. An exhibit of them shows a hydra, a Portuguese man-of-war, purple sails, jellyfish, sea fans, black and organ pipe corals, anemones, ostrich plume hydroid, and sea pens.

The many invertebrates called worms are not all closely related to each other—they actually belong to several phyla (Platyhelminthes, Nemathelminthes, Trochelminthes, and Annelida). Among some segmented and unsegmented marine worms on exhibit are planaria, flukes, leech, tapeworms, threadworms, hookworms, hairworms, palolo worms, polyclads and nemertean flatworms, bamboo worms, nematodes, trumpet worms, and acorn worms.

Mollusks belong to the Phylum Mollusca that includes several classes: gastropods, pelecypods, and cephalopods. They have soft unsegmented bodies, which are often protected by a calcareous shell. Among some mollusks exhibited here are clams, oysters, scallops, and mussels belonging to the pelecypod class; snails, slugs, whelks, limpets, abalones, conches, and purple dog winkles belonging to the gastropod class; and nautilus and octopus belonging to the cephalopod class. Mollusks obtained from the Pacific and Atlantic coasts are displayed in separate exhibit cases.

There are more than twenty thousand species of marine arthropods characterized by segmented bodies covered by a jointed external skeleton (exoskeleton) with paired jointed appendages on each segment. The exoskeleton must be shed periodically to prevent it from blocking the growth of the arthropod. One class of arthropods are the Crustacea (gill breathers with two pairs of antennae) which have the largest numbers that are aquatic. Specimens of crustaceans shown, among others, include spiny lobsters, isopods, shrimps (many kinds), crayfish, barnacles, water sow bugs, copepods, water fleas, amphiopods, crabs (many kinds), and ostracods.

Another class of arthropods is Insecta in which are found marine specimens such as water striders, back swimmers, water scorpions, water bugs, water boatmen, crawling water beetles (and other beetles) and caddis flies.

Still another class of arthropods that make their home in the water is in the class Arachnoidea. These include water spiders and horseshoe or king crab shown in an exhibit with others.

Echinoderms ("spiny skinned" animals) are other invertebrates radially symmetrical (usually five rayed) marine or brackfish water animals having no definite heads or brains. The exhibit of echinoderms features crinoids (sea lily, feather star), sea urchins, sand dollars, sea stars (star fish, asteroids), basket stars, and sea cucumbers.

Shown in other exhibits in this hall are marine mammals. One is a display of the sea otter, highly prized for its thick, smooth, and even-textured fur. Once considered an endangered species, sea otters are increasing in numbers because they are now protected by law. Their principal food is abalone, crab, and sea urchins.

Another marine mammal featured in this hall is the huge sea walrus. It is the largest of the fin-footed aquatic mammals. The adult reaches a length of about twelve feet and a weight of over three thousand pounds. Walruses live in large Arctic colonies, some of which include more than two thousand individuals. They courageously defend their territory and protect their young against predators like killer whales and polar bears. They eat clams, whelks, and other shell fish. Their ivory tusks are highly prized. A film on the walrus' life at work and at play is screened continuously in the hall.

Splendors of Nature Hall (First Floor, South Side)

Those who have had the opportunity to travel have, undoubtedly, come across scenes of unforgettable beauty. Who can forget the awe-inspiring sight of the Grand Canyon in the United States; the deeply cut fjords filled with ocean waters in Norway; the picturesque mountains, lakes, and forests of great beauty in Europe, Canada, and the United States; the surging ocean waters breaking over the rocky California and Maine coast lines; the cascading waterfalls of Yosemite National Park in Wyoming; the Presque Isle River's gurgling descent over rocks in Porcupine Mountain State Park in Michigan; the verdant valleys and waterfalls in Kauai and Maui in the Hawaiian Islands; and equally beautiful scenery on other exotic islands of the Pacific? These and a multitude of other magnificent scenes have left their indelible impressions on one's memory. Artists have captured some of this beauty on canvas, a number of these paintings hang in the Landscape Hall of the Museum of American Art of which Thomas Moran's "The Chasm of the Colorado" and "The Grand Canyon of the Yellowstone;" Ralph Blakelock's "Sunset, Navarro Range, California;" and John Kensett's "Mountains in New Hampshire" are just

a very few examples. There are artifacts of great natural beauty
and some created from natural materials in many halls of this Museum
of Natural History, such as many that can be found in the Mineral
Hall, Gem and Carved Jade Hall, Hall of Physical Geology, Hall of
Life in the Sea, Halls of Indians of North America, Halls of Peoples
of Asia, Africa, the Mideast, and of the Pacific Islands, and in the
Insect Hall, among other halls.

Artifacts of great natural beauty that delight the senses
have also been collected from many different sources and exhibited
in this treasure room "Splendors of Nature." These beautiful items
range from selected minerals, shells, corals, scallops, fossil ammonites,
fossil crinoids, and carved ivory tusks, to beetles, butterflies, moths,
feathered baskets, feathered headdresses, feathered skirts and arm-
bands. This hall offers a lovely treat for visitors who stop to look
in on the charming exhibits.

Discovery Room (First Floor, Northwest Corner)

Located on the first floor in the northwest corner of this
building, the Discovery Room is where every visitor can become an
explorer. Geared for interested amateurs, especially children twelve
years and younger, everyone has an opportunity here to handle, taste,
smell, read, or see film strips about natural history dealing with plants,
animals, and minerals of today or in fossil forms or to identify some
they may have found or collected which they may wish to verify.

To find the Discovery Room from the Rotunda (where the
big African elephant stands) go through the Halls of Eskimo and Indian
Cultures (marked on a big banner outside that hall) and follow these
halls all the way through bearing to the left. Just as one leaves the
North American Indian halls he can see the Discovery Room located
near the Rest Rooms.

Before entering the Discovery Room stop for a moment and
look into the room through the large picture window. Through it one
can catch a glimpse of a large salt water aquarium in which are seen
yellow tang fish, arrow crab, hermit crab, blue devil fish, feather
dusters, sea urchins, hydra, painted parrot fish, sponges, algae, and
other things; boxes and terrariums in which are contained much fascinating natural history material; and a multitude of natural artifacts,
all labeled and placed around the room such as mastodon, mammoth,
and dinosaur teeth, and many kinds of stones, woods, fossils, butterflies,
and minerals.

Did you ever see and touch a barnacle? In this room you can
do this. You can also handle many other large objects on display called
"Discovery Room Stumpers" such as whelk egg cases, stalactites,
geodes, a salt lick, a fossil tree stump, whale bones, a stuffed crocodile
head, papyrus, starfish, bamboo, amethyst, garnet, ebony, an elephant
tusk, and dozens of other things.

In "Discovery Room Boxes" can be found collections of objects
like corals, fossils, mollusks, a stone age axe, Indian artifacts, fossil
teeth, mineral crystals, shells that open, shells that spiral, and much
more. There are also boxes to make you think, like "What Is a Fossil?"
"Look Inside a Shell," "Touch a Sound," "Color in Shells," and so on.

While the Discovery Room is open free to the public Monday
through Thursday from 12 noon to 2:30 p.m.; Friday, Saturday, Sunday
and some Holidays from 10:30 a.m. to 3:30 p.m.; and for special hours
during the summer months, it is best to inquire at the Information
Desk in the Rotunda about the availability of space in this small exhibit
room. On Saturday, Sunday, and the holidays when it is open, tickets
obtained at the Information Desk (free) are required. This helps control
the crowds waiting to get into this rather small area. Groups can
be accommodated on Mondays through Thursdays between 10:00 a.m.
and 11:30 a.m. if the group leader will call the Office of Education
(357-2747) to make reservations at least two weeks in advance. This
is also true for handicapped groups for which special arrangements
may have to be provided.

The staff is made up of volunteers on duty to assist children
and adults with their questions and sometimes point out specimens
arranged to show relationships of color, shape, texture or other things;
also to aid them with books, film strips, boxes (arranged by age levels),
and other materials to find answers to their questions. It is recommended that an adult accompany every two or three children.

Hall of Minerals (Second Floor, East Side)

The land areas of the earth are largely composed of various
kinds of rocks that, according to their characteristics, are classified
as sedimentary, igneous, or metamorphic, each consisting of single
elements or elements in combinations. Many different specimens
for each class of minerals found in the rocks are shown in this hall.
These specimens of minerals are housed in well-designed and brightly-lit
exhibit cases grouped according to their class and giving information
about their charactertistic color, shape, hardness, and fluorescence
which are described along with notations of where each specimen
was found. Other exhibits explain what constitutes the mineral world
and simple tests used to identify minerals and the crystalline systems
that occur in nature. Mineral specimens obtained from mines in New
Zealand, Southwest Africa, Mexico, and several areas in the United
States are displayed.

About twenty native elements have been found uncombined
in nature; among these are copper, iron, sulfur, carbon, gold, silver,
platinum, lead, arsenic, bismuth, antimony, diamond, and graphite.
Specimens of these and other elements found in a pure native state
are on exhibit. Another exhibit is devoted to those minerals that
occur in nature as compounds, species that result from combinations
or recombinations of elements or other compounds can be seen, among
them specimens of serpentine, gypsum, tourmaline, dolomite, aptite,
rhodochrosite, and idocrase.

Nature forms minerals in several ways: the cooling and solidifi-
cation of molten rocks or magma; the crystallization of solutions
or gases; the metamorphosis or change of preexisting rocks; and the
decomposition of older rocks through the actions of rain, wind, frost,
and other weathering processes resulting in subsequent recomposition
in new forms. Exhibits discuss these modes of mineral formation
and show specimens of minerals so formed.

Most minerals crystallize in one of six systems. An exhibit describes these systems, with appropriate specimens for each. Pyrite is an example of the isometric system; beryl, the hexagonal system; idocrase, the tetragonal system; topaz, the orthorhombic system; gypsum, the monoclinic system; and axinite, the triclinic system, with additional examples also shown for each system.

Mineralogists now use certain simple tests to help them identify the physical properties of minerals. As discussed in an exhibit, these tests include cleavage, parting, fracture, hardness, specific gravity, luster, refraction, and magnetism. Each test is explained, and specimens shown to demonstrate the nature of each of these properties.

The zinc ore known as smithsonite was first identified by James Smithson, the founder of the Smithsonian Institution. A description of Smithson's discovery and a kelly green specimen of smithsonite from a New Mexico mine are described in an exhibit. Other mineral specimens exhibited here come from private collectors, who have contributed generously to the Smithsonian's mineral collections. Edwin Over found and documented thousands of mineral collections, a selection of them exhibited here. Other donors to the Smithsonian mineral collections were Washington Roebling, Frederick A. Canfield, Isaac Bea, and Leander and Frances I. Chamberlain. An exhibit discusses the work of these and other collectors.

One of the less obvious beauties of the mineral world is the fluorescence of certain minerals when exposed to ultraviolet light (black light). A curtained off, darkened area of the hall becomes the backdrop for the intense colors of the fluorite, calcite, autunite, willemite, wollastonite, kyalite, and other minerals on exhibit when exposed to ultraviolet light. Even without a special display, however, minerals such as hematite, malachite, dioptase, quartz, amethyst, wulfenite, and azurite are beautiful. Specimens of these and other minerals of beauty are on display. An open floor exhibit features a beautifully polished three-foot slab of nephrite from New Zealand. A transparency on display shows a thin slice cut from this slab.

Minerals extracted from the first great copper mine at Bisbee, Arizona are on exhibit. The mine has supplied museums with many fine specimens of copper. Man has known of the mineral mine at Franklin, New Jersey since 1650. The mine supplies zinc, manganese, and other minerals, some of them very rare. A selection of minerals obtained from the mine is on display. There are also mineral specimens from mines in the tri-state district where Missouri, Kansas, and Oklahoma meet. More than half the lead and zinc products produced in the United States come from the mines in this area. A mass of crystalline gold, one of the largest ever found, came from a California mine and is on display along with seventy-eight gold nuggets, other gold crystals, and two platinum nuggets from twelve United States and eight foreign countries. These are of extraordinary beauty. There are minerals, as well, from a Southwest African mine, near Tsumeb. Some fine specimens including azurite, smithsonite, cerussite, calcite, and diplase have been found there.

A diorama, "The Cave of the Swords," recreates an interior view of a limestone cave in the Maravilla mine near Naica, Mexico in which large projecting gypsum crystals have developed formations resembling swords.

There are huge display cases, one or more for each class of mineral in which they are represented by a large number of excellent specimens. Labels indicate the physical properties, chemical composition, crystalline structure, and the location where each specimen was found. Among the mineral classes shown in these brightly lit cases are elements and sulfides, sulfosalts and oxides, carbonates, halides and oxysalts, and (the largest class of all) silicates.

Hall of Gems and Chinese Jades (Second Floor, East Side)

One of the country's finest gem collections resides in the Smithsonian's Museum of Natural History. The famous Hope diamond is on display in the Hall of Gems as is the Victoria-Transvaal diamond. Many visitors on entering the building go directly to the Hall of Gems to see them. There are many beautiful diamonds shown here in addition to the Hope and the Victoria-Transvaal diamonds. There are also exhibited a variety of other gems remarkable for their size, rarity, or exquisite beauty. Many prized jewels are also lavishly displayed in beautiful settings ranging from the elaborate to the simple in rings, bracelets, necklaces, earrings, brooches, and tiaras. In the adjoining Maude Monel Vetlesen Room are featured magnificent Chinese jades carved between the sixteenth and nineteenth centuries.

The Hope diamond is a flawless blue diamond, one of the largest and most beautiful in the world. It was a much larger stone when it was found in the Kollur mine in India and brought to France to become part of the French crown jewels. It was then known as the French Blue diamond. It was stolen after the death of Louis XVI and hidden by the thieves, reappearing on the market many years later as a smaller stone. The diamond was then purchased by an Englishman, Henry Hope, for whom it is named and later by Edward S. McLean, an American. The diamond's wanderings were finally ended when Harry Winston, an American jeweler and its last owner, contributed the Hope diamond to the Smithsonian. It is now displayed in this hall in a special vault with an automatic burglar alarm. The Victoria-Transvaal diamond donated by Leonard and Victoria Wilkinson is a pear-shaped 67.89 carat, champagne-colored gem set in a yellow gold necklace containing one hundred eight additional diamonds that add 44.67 carats to the weight of the necklace. The Wilkinsons have donated seven other great pieces of jewelry to the Smithsonian, all containing diamonds—some of unusual kinds.

Among the unusual, rare, and very beautiful gems shown in this hall are the Gachala emerald (858 carats); the Bismarck sapphire (98.6 carats); the Rosser Reeves ruby, the world's largest and finest star ruby (138.8 carats); the Star of Asia, a blue star sapphire (330 carats); the Logan sapphire, the largest and finest blue sapphire (426 carats); and the Minas Gerais (Brazil) blue topaz (327 carats). A smoky quartz egg shown here weighs 7,000 carats; another of 4,500 carats is mounted on a small gold and jeweled stand.

Beautiful gemstones are exhibited in an adjoining hall, among them opals, a chrysoberyl cat's eye, malachites, rose quartz, emeralds, ambers, amethysts, turquoise, tourmalines, lapis lazulis, garnets, cornelians, and sapphires. There is also a rare black pearl from the

Gulf of California; the world's largest beryl (2,054 carats); and the world's largest topaz (12,500 carats).

"Jewelry Fit for a Queen" is an exhibit of beautiful jewelry. The pieces range from the very elaborate to the simple—all have been gifts to the Smithsonian, some from anonymous donors. Included in the display are an Indian diamond and Columbian emerald necklace called "the Spanish Inquisition necklace," worn by ladies of the Spanish and later French courts, amethyst herons (quartz herons with amethyst bodies and jasper beaks), a gift of Dr. and Mrs. Richard I. Kloecker; and a ring containing twenty-four diamonds surrounded by sapphires that came from Sri Lanka. Among other gifts are a diamond necklace and a ruby and diamond bracelet, a gift of Harry Winston (who gave the Hope diamond); a sapphire pendant, the gift of Countess Mona Bismarck; and Marie Antoinette's favorite diamond earrings, each weighing thirty-six carats (given to her by Louis XVI and found in her pockets when the royal family was caught fleeing the country), a gift of Mrs. Eleanor C. Barzin. Mrs. Marjorie Merriweather Post in her lifetime gave the Smithsonian many jeweled pieces, among them the diamond and turquoise (originally emeralds) tiara given to Marie Louise by Napoleon in 1811; the diamond necklace given to Marie Louise in 1811 to celebrate the birth of a son; the Emperor Maximilian ring containing a 21 carat emerald; another diamond tiara and matching brooches, the diamonds coming from India; an Indian emerald necklace; and a chalice lined with twenty-four carat gold, studded with intaglios, cameos, and over thirteen hundred diamonds—originally a gift from Catherine the Great of Russia to Potemkin. A more recent acquisition is a gold and enameled sculpture of St. George and the Dragon done by the Russian Grachev brothers that includes rubies and diamonds.

On exhibit in this hall is the world's largest flawless crystal sphere—twelve and seven-eights inches in diameter and over one hundred pounds in weight. The crystal was cut from a block of unblemished Burmese quartz that weighed over one thousand pounds to begin with. It required eighteen months to polish.

In the Maude Monel Vetlesen Room of Chinese Jades is a treasure house of skillfully carved pieces exquisitely done by artists. Because jadeite and nephrite are extremely hard to carve, the work must be done by a difficult and laborious process of grinding with abrasives instead of being cut by metals. Among the articles displayed are bowls, plaques, screens, jars, scrolls, scroll cases, incense burners, brush holders, candlestick holders, statuettes, scepters, covered and uncovered vessels, covered tortoise shaped vessels, vases, and whole scenes carved of jade on a boulder and on panels. This is one of the finest collections of carved jades in the country.

Hall of the Earth, Moon, and Meteorites: Our Restless Planet (Second Floor, East Side)

The exhibits in this hall not only discuss a theory of the evolution of the solar system and of the earth's origin, but in its several adjoining sections explore the basic structure of our restless planet, Earth, and explain the principles underlying the geologic changes of past eras and phenomena that are still occurring today. Also discussed are extraterrestrial objects like meteorites (large and small) that have fallen on the earth, some that are older than the earth and have helped add to our knowledge of the solar system. Chondrites and tektites and our earth's satellite, the moon, are other extraterrestrial objects described. Much of the earth's crust, made up of igneous, sedimentary, and metamorphic rocks, is described telling how the rocks were formed. The flow of underground water and evaporation are important geologic processes illustrated here. Volcanoes, earthquakes, and weathering are other geologic phenomena featured, as is the formation of the fossil fuels man depends on today. There are specimens of gold, silver, copper, iron, lead, zinc, and other ores, accompanied by sketches of their history and uses. There are displays of great natural beauty—geodes, pegmatites, and cave growth formations. The exhibits are complemented from time to time by films on such aspects of physical geology as active and dormant volcanoes and discoveries in the deep seas. In one area of the hall there is an exhibit of the history of the science of physical geology and some of its leaders.

A mural by Pierre Meonde illustrates a theory about the four stages in the evolution of our solar system. Some estimates put our solar system's age at more than four and one-half billion years.

As an exhibit illustrates, the Earth, one of our sun's planets, is divided into contrasting layers—the atmosphere is the outermost layer, a gaseous envelope; then a layer of water, the hydrosphere; and then the solid earth's rock formations. Each layer is discussed and the earth's rock formations illustrated according to their subdivisions—core, mantle, and crust. An exhibit features fragments of the earth's interior, rocks from the earth's mantle. Some of these, like olivine, green pyroxine, and black chromite occur as much as thirty-five miles below the earth's surface. Also on display are diamonds, which came from very great depths where they were formed under extremely high temperatures and pressures.

A huge rotating globe of the earth indicates not the usual political divisions one generally expects to see on such a globe, but the major geologic features of the world. Rock formations of the same age are keyed by color, and earthquake zones, volcanic regions, and ocean depths, deep sea trenches, and other physical characteristics of the earth are indicated on this globe. The exhibit notes that the earth is constantly changing. Geologists have new knowledge of the movements of continents, and in what predictable patterns these can occur. Two energy sources effective in changing the face of the earth are solar radiation and the earth's internal heat. An exhibit describes how each process operates in the wearing down and the building up of continents.

Volcanoes can be both productive and destructive and range in activity from dormant to violent as described here. Among the products of volcanic eruptions are basaltic hair (spun into fibers), basalt rock, lava, obsidian, and porphyritic lava, specimens of which are on display. A map indicates the geographic distribution of the five hundred most active volcanoes in the world (the majority in the Pacific Ocean belt), and a film records the violence of erupting volcanoes. Descriptions and photographs of the eruption of Mt. St. Helens taken by the National Oceanic and Atmospheric Administration's geostationary satellite "Goes-West" located 22,245 miles above the equator at 135° west longitude are shown. Another activity (sometimes violent) on the earth is the earthquake, whose force can be detected and measured by seismographs similar to the one operating in this hall. Every year one hears of horrible destruction wrought by earthquakes. The almost unbelievable numbers who lose their lives can be found in statistics which show, among others that in

1556 in Shaanxi, China - 830,000 lost their lives
1737 in Calcutta, India - 300,000 lost their lives
1906 in San Francisco - 452 lost their lives
1923 in Tokyo, Japan - 99,330 lost their lives
1927 in Nan Shan, China - 200,000 lost their lives
1936 in Chillan, Chile - 28,000 lost their lives
1960 in Chile - 5,000 lost their lives
1976 in Northeast Italy - 946 lost their lives
1976 in Tangshan, China - 800,000 lost their lives

Also displayed in this hall is a geiger counter, which measures radioactivity.

An exhibit describes the three processes by which rocks (igneous, sedimentary, and metamorphic) are formed, and displays specimens of each rock type. Sedimentary rocks evolve from the sediments of pre-existing rocks, sediments created by the action of water, air, or ice then buried and compacted and cemented and subsequently converted into such rocks as sandstone, limestone, shale, and conglomerate. Igneous rocks began as molten matter which then cooled and solidified either quickly on the earth's surface or slowly beneath it. These rocks, classified according to their mineralogical composition, include lavas, obsidian, basalt (the most common type of rock on the earth's surface), granite, and pumice. Metamorphic rocks evolve from igneous or sedimentary rocks when their original structure has been altered by pressure and heat. Marble, slate, gneiss, idocrase, garnet, mica, and schist are examples of metamorphic rocks.

The vastness of geologic time is illustrated in an exhibit. Geologists have prepared a time chart by correlating similar rocks found throughout the world. An explanation describes how they arrive at "biologic age" and "relative age."

A small diorama recreates a scene in the Rock of Ages granite quarry in Barre, Vermont. The granite in the quarry is estimated to be 333,000,000 years old, a figure arrived at by radioactive dating. This quarry is the largest and deepest monument-granite quarry in the world. Elsewhere on display in this hall is pegmatite found in quarries, a form of coarse-grained granite with large and often beautiful crystals. Pegmatites are often called giant granites. The specimens on exhibit contain mica, quartz, feldspar, topaz, beryl, tourmaline, spodumene, and a rare mineral, samarskite.

An exhibit shows a display of stone tools of different geologic time periods made by ancient man. Stone tools in the different geologic periods have been found in a variety of geographic locations including Nicaragua, Puerto Rico, Mexico, Chile, and Panama. (See Hall of Western Civilization for stone tools found in Asia, Africa, and Europe.)

Next to the air we breathe, water is our most precious resource.

Underground water, as displays here indicate, plays several important roles in the earth's continuing formation. Underground water erodes certain rocks, and carries chemicals that attack or alter the structure of other minerals. It can dissolve limestone, thus producing caves and sink holes. Exhibits note that for Americans it is particularly important because underground waters feed the springs, wells, and artesian water systems that provide twenty percent of all the water used in this country.

Rocks subjected to the action of underground water solutions may eventually show "substitution pseudomorphs," formations in which new substances have gradually replaced all of the original material. Specimens of substitution pseudomorphs are on exhibit, as are stalagmites, stalactites, flowstone, cave pearls, cave bird nests, azurite, rhodocroisite, and other cave deposits. In addition there are some specimens shown of drapery from the caverns of Luray, Virginia. Such cave deposits form when underground water containing chemicals drips through cracks in a cave roof, and deposits tiny crystals.

Evaporation also plays a role in the great mineral-forming process producing compounds such as potash (used for fertilizer) and salt. An exhibit explains what happens when salt water evaporates in such inland basins as the Great Salt Lake.

If the earth gives us common substances like salt, it also gives us noble metals. On exhibit are specimens of gold, silver, and platinum from many parts of the world. The metals were designated "noble" because of their scarcity and their resistance to oxidation and corrosion. A huge specimen of gold ore is on exhibit. It came from the Homestake mine in the Black Hills of South Dakota, the most important gold mine in the United States. It takes a ton of gold ore to make five tenths of an ounce of gold.

At "the richest hill on earth," located in a section of Butte, Montana gold was discovered in 1864, silver in 1874, and in 1955 high grade copper ore. There are thousands of miles of underground passages in this "hill" and on exhibit are specimens of the ores mined here with illustrations shown of some of the mining pits.

Indians worked the copper mines of northern Michigan as early as 3000 B.C. For centuries they worshipped the large Ontonagen copper boulder on display in this hall believing it possessed supernatural powers. A brief, but interesting history of how it got to the Smithsonian is told in a label near the boulder. Jesuit missionaries knew of the existence of copper mines in the Upper Peninsula of Michigan as early as the seventeenth century, but copper was not mined commercially there until 1845. Exhibited are many specimens of copper from the Michigan mines.

Base metals displayed here include iron, lead, and zinc. While iron has been known to man since 4000 B.C., the "iron age" did not begin until about 800 B.C. An exhibit discusses the history of this mineral, the backbone of modern civilization, and displays specimens of iron ore from all over the world. While iron has long been prized for its rigidity, in contrast, lead has been prized for over four thousand years for its malleability; it is the softest, heaviest, and most malleable of the base metals. Another widely used metal is zinc. On display is a variety of lead and zinc specimens from American mines.

A small diorama recreates a scene in a carboniferous coal

swamp forest. The remains of mighty trees that once grew in such forests 350,000,000 to 270,000,000 years ago are found in the fossil fuels so necessary, and on which we depend today.

An exhibit describes three types of uranium deposits: sandstone-type deposits, vein deposits, and conglomerate uranium deposits. Specimens of each are shown. There is a brief explanation given of nuclear fission and atomic power in which uranium plays an important role. (In the Museum of American History an entire hall called "Atom Smashers" would be of interest to those who would like to pursue the subject of atomic energy further.)

Among the most beautiful objects in this hall are the geodes. There are many kinds and sizes, but they are usually spherical and when opened frequently reveal hollow rock nodules and a lining of quartz or calcite crystals. The exhibit explains in which types of rocks geodes generally occur for those seeking to discover some.

Among other specimens displayed in this hall is banded iron ore from some pre–Cambrian beds in northern Michigan. The beds are thought to be about two billion years old. A pothole originally from Riggsville Landing, Maine was formed many thousands of years ago by melt water from a Pleistocene ice sheet long since dried and hardened. It was carefully removed and brought to the Smithsonian for exhibition. Also exhibited are a dumbbell concretion from the Cannonball River, North Dakota; a four hundred pound lodestone (a natural magnet) from southern California; and a geyser cone from Yellowstone National Park; stalagmites and draperies from the Luray Caverns, Luray, Virginia; and a huge sandstone concretion from Kent County, Maryland.

Meteorites are commonly called "shooting stars" because they become heated to incandescence and are momentarily luminous in the course of their swift flight through the atmosphere before falling on the earth's surface or disappearing in the oceans. Some very large meteorites that did not disappear are on display in this hall each accompanied by an account of its composition and where it was found. Often to obtain information about its composition, very small samples are sliced from a boulder to help determine its mineral and chemical makeup. An illuminated map locates meteorites found in the United States. A piece of the only meteorite in recorded history to injure a human being, Mrs. Hewlett Hodges, in Sylacauga, Alabama in November 1954 is on display. Exhibits explain the differences between the impacts on earth of large and small meteorites while other exhibits describe chondrites and tektites. Since meteorites originate in outer space, scientists hope they may prove to be a key that will help unlock information about the origin and evolution of the solar system. Exhibits in an adjoining room discuss theories about the origin of the solar system and the formation of planets while other displays speculate on the origin of the moon and describe the rocks of which it is composed (specimens shown here were brought back by the astronauts). A recording describes the physical features of the meteorite pocked moon represented on a large globe of the moon displayed here.

Every year in the United States between five and ten new meteorites are recovered. Exhibits describe what happens to a meteorite when it encounters the earth's atmosphere and its gravitational pull. A map pinpoints the fall and recovery of about eight hundred of these meteorites that have been recovered through the years. Other displays explain how the size of meteorites determine its impact on the earth. People have visited or seen on television Meteor Crater in Navaho County, Arizona. The meteor that fell there dug a hole one mile in diameter and about six hundred feet deep as it continued far into the depths of the earth.

Exhibits also explore the forms, structures, and mineral content of different kinds of meteorites. There are labeled specimens of hexahedrites, octahedrites (the most common iron meteorite), ataxites, and pallasites, and specimens, as well, of the major classes of chondrites. Chondrites compose about eighty percent of all recovered meteorites. One theory about chondrites suggests they may have originated about 4,500,000,000 years ago as primitive material whose molten drops cooled rapidly. There is also a display of tektites which appear to resemble terrestrial obsidian but actually are quite different. Tektites are found all over the world (in so-called strewnfields), particularly on the southern edge of Australia and on Antarctica. They appear to be between 600,000 and 700,000 years old and many scientists believe they are of terrestrial origin, possibly coming from the heating of meteorite impacts.

Mineral content and location of recovery are listed for each large meteorite displayed in this hall. Among the large meteorites exhibited are Clovis, El Taco, Henbury, Tucson Ring, Grant, Casas Grandes, Oakley Canyon, Diable, the Drum Mountains, Goose Lake, Owens Valley, and Mundrabilla which is a large iron medium octohedrite of unique composition and structure and has feathery materials of fan shape structures interspersed in it.

On exhibit in the adjoining room of Moon Geology is the stony Allende meteorite that fell near Pueblito de Allende in northern Mexico on February 8, 1969. Scientists believe it contains the oldest identified material in the solar system. They also believe the meteorite is composed of material similar to that which condensed from the solar nebula to form the moon and planets.

Another exhibit in the room of Moon Geology provides a theory about the origin of the solar system, some 4,600,000,000 years ago. Many scientists theorize that a complex series of events may have culminated in the thermonuclear explosion of a nebula, an explosion which ejected the material of our sun (and the planets and their moons, the asteroids, and countless comets and meteors) into the vast surrounding space. The outer planets, moons, asteroids, comets, etc., formed by the condensation and accretion of masses of this hot, diffused material, were then all captured by the gravitational pull of the sun and set in motion around it.

Still another exhibit discusses a theory of the origin of the central planets in our solar system. These planets, scientists theorize, may have originated as accretions of interstellar dust that collected into asteroid-sized, orbiting bodies called planetesimals. The gravitational aggregations of these bodies finally produced the central planets and their satellite moons and set them in motion.

The moon and the earth, although similar in origin, have evolved quite differently. The earth is a geologically active planet with an atmosphere that supports life. The moon is geologically inactive, it has no atmosphere and it appears to have no life. Exhibited are specimens of ancient earth rocks from Greenland (3,400,000,000 years old). These were found to have escaped being destroyed by erosion or other earth processes and are specimens that have helped scientists determine certain facts about the evolution of the earth. Exhibits compare these specimens with lunar rock specimens brought back from the moon by the astronauts: anorthosite, breccia, and basaltic. Although there is much that still remains to be learned, these lunar rocks have helped scientists determine that the moon was molten approximately 4,600,000,000 years ago. An exhibit discusses the moon's molten age and features specimens of anorthositic rocks of this period brought back by the astronauts. These anorthositic rocks are considered the oldest rocks, crystallized soon after the moon's formation with breccia and basaltic rocks generated later by partial melting of older rocks. Moon rocks have also helped scientists fix the period of the moon's vulcanism between 3,900,000,000 and 3,200,000,000 years ago from specimens of basaltic rocks of this period. The relative quiet period of the moon has now lasted 3,200,000,000 years to the present although an occasional large and some smaller meteorites strike the moon but with little evidence of any other activity. A very clear broadcast from the moon of a conversation held by the Apollo 17 astronauts to Mission Control is played in this hall describing the beautiful sights on the moon. (Further descriptions of the astronauts' visits to the moon can be found in the National Air and Space Museum.)

The moon may be smaller than the earth, but the moon does influence life on earth. An exhibit, "The Moon Rhythms of Life," notes that the gravitational pull of the moon affects the tides and the rhythmic growth patterns of life in the sea. Scientists studying the growth patterns of fossil organisms have determined that for 600,000,000 years the number of days per lunar month have very slowly been decreasing.

Halls of Prehistoric Peoples of North America and North American Archeology (Second Floor, East Side)

Scientists theorize that between ten and twenty thousand years ago nomadic groups of Asiatic peoples, following the trails of animals they hunted, crossed a then-existing land bridge over the Bering Strait from Asia to North America. Although much of North America was glacier covered, they were able to find a steady supply of large animals, fish, and wild plants which they gathered for food. Over time successive waves of these peoples crossed the Bering Strait and moved down and across the North American continent wherever food was available and life supportable, from the frozen Arctic in North America, to Central America and then to South America, distributing and adjusting themselves to local conditions and establishing settlements. In their digs, archeologists have uncovered a wealth of artifacts that tell about the cultures of these Paleolithic and Archaic peoples and the generations that have followed them. Since they left no written record, their history has had to be reconstructed from their artifacts. Archeologists, aided by geologists, paleontologists, chemists, physicists, botanists, climatologists, and anthropologists have been able to establish their chronology by studies of the material remains of these prehistoric and extinct cultures using a variety of dating methods that are described in these halls. Exhibits taken from deposits give examples of the cultures and diversity of these far flung peoples, some of them beginning 20,000 years ago.

Archaeologists study how men have lived in the past and have reconstructed their history for a better understanding of these peoples. Among the methods they have employed in dating the past cultures of North America are radiocarbon, obsidian, varve, thermo-luminescent, pollen, magnetic dating, and dendrochronology. Each of these methods is explained and its use illustrated in an exhibit.

Among the exhibits providing an overview of prehistoric North American cultures are several that focus on agriculture. There are explanations of the physical and climatic conditions that prevailed in various regions on this continent permitting the growth of particular crops. There are also illustrations of agricultural practices and of the crops grown in these different regions.

Other omnibus exhibits feature the primitive stone-shaping arts of the North American Indians and the tools they used to fashion implements and ornaments, arts that these craftsmen developed prior to the arrival of white settlers. Using simple tools they created elegant masks, sculptures, and other objects from materials they had found close-at-hand such as driftwood washed in by the sea, ivory from long curved tusks of the walrus, pieces of antler and bone, and in the prehistoric cultures of Ohio the Indians were particularly noted for stone-carving of tobacco pipes in the form of animals and birds. The glass and metal artifacts displayed which were found in deposits in different parts of our country were trade goods, unknown before the coming of the Europeans.

Artifacts of the successive cultures of the Kodiak and Aleutian Islands show these peoples to have been highly talented sculptors carving out of stone and soapstone lamps which used seal oil and moss wicks for heating and lighting; tools often beautifully ornamented of ivory or bone, as well as eye shades or snow goggles which gave protection from the fierce glare of the sun reflected from the ice and snow. These and other finely carved objects are on display.

Archaeologists examining the remains of village sites and middens of the Eskimos on St. Lawrence Island (in the Bering Strait) have been able to describe the cultural development of these people from the time of their early settlements until about 1880. They have noted, particularly changes in the toggle-headed harpoon, an important hunting tool of these peoples used for hunting seals, whales, and wal-ruses. On display is the mummy of a male Aleut of wealth or distinc-tion. He was found in his burial wrappings of grass matting, skin parka, and sinew netting interred in a cave on Kagmamil Island. There are other artifacts shown that are frequently found buried with Aleutian dead, including skillfully made and decorated masks used in dances and ceremonials, grass baskets, grass matting, wooden body armor, wooden containers, and other items.

The Indians of northwest California and the lower Columbia River created a highly developed social order, as exhibits in this hall indicate. The display of artifacts of these people show them to have been extremely skilled woodworkers and carvers, and the women equally skilled in basket work. Among the wooden objects fashioned by these men were canoes of red cedar (some nearly one hundred feet long), paddles, totem poles (perhaps their most famous achievements), boxes for cooking (pottery was unknown), traps, bows and arrows, cradles, and large, well-made houses. Potlatches (great giveaways) characterized their festivities, and there was much warfare with neighboring tribes. These peoples lived much of the year in permanent settlements, but did not practise agriculture; their diet consisted chiefly of fish, seaweed, berries, seeds, nuts, and roots.

The prehistoric peoples of California's semi-arid central valleys never practised agriculture either. For hundreds of years they built their villages along streams, marshes, and lakes, subsisting on what they could fish, hunt, and gather. They supplemented this diet with acorns, from which they extracted the harmful tannic acid before pounding them into a flour. Artifacts of their civilization include a portable stone mortar for grinding seeds and nuts, a soapstone bowl, shell ornaments, musical instruments, and other things shown in an exhibit.

The Chumash were an advanced southern California maritime people obliterated by disease and by the persecution of neighboring peoples. Artifacts from the remains of the villages and cemeteries show large soapstone jars, musical instruments, digging sticks, weights of soapstone, a wooden ceremonial sword, fishhooks made of shell and bone, ornaments made of shell and other materials, and an illustration of a Chumash dome-shaped dwelling each occupied by several families.

A display of pottery manufactured by the prehistoric peoples of the American southwest contains items crafted before 300 A.D.; pottery skills reached a peak in the fourteenth century. The cooking pots, pipes, vases, and other pottery pieces shown here are from various locations. Each is identified by the method of manufacture and the types of decoration used. Another exhibit features well-preserved baskets (including a rare, large, round basketry shield from Pueblo Bonito, New Mexico) and textiles that were found in the dry caves of the southwestern United States. Made by the ancient inhabitants of the area, these items show both their early artistry in weaving, and the variety of products they made.

The Pima and Papago Indians excelled in farming. Inhabitants of the middle Gila and the Salt River drainage area of southern Arizona, they are believed descended from the prehistoric Hohokama Indians whose villages and artifacts are illustrated in this hall. The Hohokamas were a farming people, and did basket weaving.

The prehistoric Anasazi are believed to be the ancestors of the modern Pueblo Indians. The Anasazi were prehistoric farmers of mesas and canyons who lived in the area where Colorado, Utah, Arizona, and New Mexico meet. One of their pueblo villages was Pueblo Bonita shown in a diorama in this hall. Some Anasazi artifacts on exhibit include bone daggers, deer bone fleshers, stone hatchet, a stone metate and mano, many shell beads, a digging stick of hardwood, pottery and a bow and arrow.

Folsom man, the nomad of the Ice Age, fashioned the spear points and other tools featured in an exhibit. The tools shown were

found at Lindenmeier site in Colorado, among the bones of some
now-extinct bison, camels, and other animals which these Folsom
men hunted. Archaic Indians of the Black Hills of South Dakota and
eastern Wyoming hunted on foot for bison (horses unknown then were
reintroduced to these areas much later by Europeans). An exhibit
shows how Folsom Man's camp sites may have looked. Illustrations
show how they ambushed bison at water holes.

The peoples who inhabited the western plains (particularly
what is now western Nebraska and Montana) from 2600 B.C. to 1700
A.D. also led a mobile life foraging, but primarily hunting for bison.
An exhibit of the tools and other equipment of these peoples features the
atlatl (an important hunting tool that preceded bows and arrows)
and chipstone drills, scrapers, and knives.

The prehistoric Indians of the Great Plains were generally
not nomadic. They created settlements with a variety of dwellings
in their communities. From about 1150 to 1300 A.D. the Indians in
the central plains of Nebraska and Kansas lived in unfortified houses,
while the middle Missouri Indians of the same period lived in carefully
planned and fortified communities. Between 1750 and 1820 A.D. the
Arikara, Mandan, Pawnee and other corn-growing tribes of the eastern
plains lived in earth lodges behind log stockades, fortifying themselves
against the warlike Sioux and other hunter tribes. Archeologists have
recovered many artifacts from the remains of their villages including
grooved axes, arrowheads, spearheads, adzes, pestles, and tobacco
pipes. Also shown are storage jars, bowls, burial mound vessels all
with incised decorations. These Great Plains Indians were particularly
skilled in handling skins of bison and small game for clothing, tents,
storage bags, and in making clothing soft and supple and embroidering
them with dyed porcupine quills and later with beads.

An exhibit that traces the chronology of Middle Atlantic
cultures begins with the peoples who lived there eight thousand years
ago, the nomadic Paleo-Indian hunters who left behind the Folsom-like
spear points shown here. The Archaic Indians of the next five thousand
years introduced both agriculture and pottery. They were influenced,
during the first thousand years of this era by the mound building cultures of Ohio and Mississippi. About 1500 A.D., the people participated
in a strong religious movement that originated in the southeastern
section of the continent. This religious movement had a great impact
on their lives as did the arrival of Europeans about 1600 A.D. The
items on display here bear witness to the long history and many cultures
of this area.

The prehistoric mounds and earthenworks in Ohio were built
mostly by three cultures: the Adena, the Fort Ancient, and the
Hopewell. Transparencies show details of some of these mounds and
earthenworks and exhibits show utensils and ornaments crafted from
stone, bone, wood, copper, and mica recovered from them. Illustrations
of prehistoric mounds in Ohio show the Great Serpent Mound in Adams
County (the largest known effigy earthenwork, more than 300 feet
long); the Mound City Group in Ross County (23 mounds in a 13 acre
walled enclosure); Newark Work in Bicking County (an octagon and
connected circle, 1055 feet in diameter); Miamisburg Conical mound
in Montgomery County (in an area of three acres, a height of sixty
eight feet, and a diameter of 250 feet); and the Seip Mound in Ross

County (in an area 150 feet by 250 feet and a height of thirty feet).
The Adenas lived at many sites along the Ohio River Valley between 1000 B.C. and 700 B.C. A mound-building people, they lived by hunting, fishing, and gathering and created a highly developed social organization.

The Hopewell people represent the apex of the Burial Mound culture as builders of the Great Earthenworks. The impressive geometrical hilltop enclosures and burial mounds of the Ohio were theirs. The Hopewell culture was highly advanced, reaching its peak in southern Ohio between 500 B.C. and 600 A.D. The people were noted for elaborate and well-executed copper ornaments, flint projectile points of various kinds, and articles of silver, some of which are shown here.

Among the Indians who once populated the Ohio valley were the Fort Ancient and Whittelsey, late prehistoric farmers (1100 to 1600 A.D.) of the Midwest who lived in stockaded villages along the streams of the valley that emptied into the Great Lakes. They were an agricultural people.

Another culture in nearby regions was the Adena-Middlesex culture, derived from the upper Ohio valley partly by migrations of people. The Adena-Middlesex lived at many sites along the Ohio River between 1000 B.C. and 700 A.D. Some artifacts of their culture shown here are stone pipes, projectile points with characteristic Adena lobed base, spearpoints, stone knife, drillpoint and others. The Owasco culture was found in the late Woodland times. They were an agricultural people with corn an important crop. They lived in large fortified villages which held several hundred people in each. Artifacts shown of the Owasco culture include projectile points made from hollowed out antler tips, mat weaving needle, bone awls, flint drills, and hammerstone.

Archeologists now date the archaic hunting and gathering cultures of the northeastern United States between 3500 B.C. and 1000 B.C. basing these dates on retrieved artifacts of the Lamoka, Main Red Paint, Susquehanna Soapstone, Orient, and Laurentian cultures. A selection of artifacts of these cultures is on display. Projectile points used by the early big game hunters of eastern United States resemble those used by Folsom man in the western states, and an exhibit compares the fluted points created at widely separate locations.

The Indians of the Upper Great Lakes region were the continent's first metalworkers, beginning to mine and work the native copper about five thousand years ago. Frequently referred to as the Old Copper Indians, they obtained their food by hunting, fishing, and gathering—perhaps accompanied by their pet dogs. Artifacts of these Indians are exhibited, and a large diorama portrays them digging for copper in the Upper Peninsula of Michigan. (See more about the Old Copper Indians of Michigan in the Hall of Earth, Moon, and Meteorites.)

Another exhibit provides an overview of the Woodland cultures of the northeastern United States, which flourished between 1000 B.C. and 1300 A.D. Among the Woodland cultures are classified the Meadowood of the New York area about 1000-700 B.C.; the Hopewell about 100 A.D.; the Adena-Middlesex about 1000 B.C.; the Point

Peninsula culture introduced from the upper Great Lakes area; and the Owasco culture about 900-1300 A.D. which may have been ancestral to the Iroquois culture.

In upper New York and part of Pennsylvania, the Iroquoian language group: the Cayuga, Mohawk, Onondago, Oneida, and Seneca tribes joined together to form a league known as the Five Nations. They were a powerful group, more advanced than the neighboring tribes and exerted great influence. The Five Nations developed advanced military and political organizations, created their villages inside stockades, and lived in bark-covered community lodges, each of which housed between five and twelve families. The lodges are shown in a diorama. They raised crops, primarily corn, and as shown in an exhibit produced finely wrought items of bone, antler, and occasionally, of stone. The exhibit on the Five Nations includes a selection of their pottery, coil-made and frequently elaborately decorated; claypipes, stone chisels, bone awls, and other artifacts of their culture.

Items recovered from ceremonial centers at Spiro, Oklahoma, at Moundville, Alabama, and at Etowah, Georgia are similar enough to indicate to archeologists the existence of a single widespread religious cult now known as the Southern Cult. Many of the elaborate social and religious customs developed in these cultures were directly connected with the burial of the dead, and at all three sites built between 1000 and 1700 A.D. there are large burial mounds surmounted by temples. Artifacts of the Southern Cult are on exhibit and includes items found in a large burial mound near Spiro, Oklahoma of prehistoric clothing woven from bast and rabbit hair, and large engraved ceremonial shells. Other items displayed are stone and shell beads, pendants, ear spools, pipes, arrowheads and spearheads, knives, and scrapers.

Archaic peoples of the Southeast are dated as living between 5000 B.C and 500 B.C. They were hunters, gatherers and fishermen. Artifacts of tools they used are exhibited such as drills for woodworking, scrapers, knives, and atlatl hooks and weights attached to spears for hunting.

On exhibit are artifacts recovered from the huge middens of the Calusa Indians, woodcarvers who lived in southern Florida's mangrove swamps. Most of their food came from the rivers and the sea, as the large number of shell heaps found in their middens indicate. Displayed are wooden masks, tablets, and net floats they crafted; they also carved bone pins and shell plummets. The solitary figure of a Timucua warrior, represented here in a diorama, commemorates a politically and culturally advanced Florida tribe that was exterminated in the eighteenth century.

A series of dioramas in these halls recreates scenes of Indian life: an eighteenth-century Louisiana village of the Acolapissa Indians; and the Patawomeke village on the Potomac River as it looked prior to the abduction of Chief Powhatan's daughter, Pocahontas. Another shows the Indians of Lake Superior's Keweenaw Peninsula region mining as they did five thousand years ago the large deposits of copper that they fashioned into tools and ornaments. Other prehistoric Indians are shown mining iron in a scene set in what is today Leslie, Missouri. Another is a scene showing Indians at work in an ancient soapstone quarry on Santa Catalina Island, California. A diorama portrays for us Washingtonians of about five hundred years ago working the local quarries to obtain quartzite and other stone for arrow points, spearheads, and knives. The Indian cliff dwellings depicted in an interesting diorama recreate pueblos called Mummy Cave Ruin found in Canyon del Muerto. These dwellings were occupied from the fourth century until drought struck the area in the thirteenth century when they were abandoned. Still another diorama shows a 500 room prehistoric ruin on the canyon bottom, a village of Pueblo Bonita in northwestern New Mexico, which was abandoned in the twelfth century. The Anasazi farmers who built Pueblo Bonita had also constructed dams to collect and store rainfall, and had devised a system of irrigation. Rock carvings reproduced in still another diorama were cut into the sandstone cliffs and ledges of the American southwest by prehistoric Indians.

South America....A Continent and Its Cultures (Second Floor, East Side)

Environment and natural resources are determining factors of human life to which people must adapt in order to survive and prosper. Exhibits in this hall depict the ways in which four principal natural environments of South America have affected the evolution and distinctive human cultures on that continent. Maps, photographs, murals, artifacts, and dioramas depict the mountain valley terrain of the central Andean highlands, the tropical forest of Amazonia, the grasslands or pampas of Patagonia, and the arid central Andean coast which help reveal the story of South American peoples in these four areas from prehistoric to colonial and modern times.

According to a discovery in 1973 and confirmed in 1981, the **New York Times** reported the findings of scientists digging along the central coast of Peru, about 38 miles south of Lima. The skeletons of 7,700 year old humans and other evidence has led them to believe they found the site of one of the oldest known villages in the Americas (Paloma) where the people were no longer nomadic although they continued to hunt animals for food, but had settled in a village kind of life revolving around the planting and growing of crops. Previous excavations had only revealed isolated burials, but at this site they excavated the remains of fifty-six houses finding two hundred twenty skeletons including infants, children, and adults. Before this discovery the oldest known human settlements in the Americas (about 5000 years old) were at Huaco Prieta on the northern coast of Peru.

Because the well-watered Andean mountain valleys are quite narrow, from prehistoric times the inhabitants have terraced parts of the mountainous uplands to make more farmland available. The early peoples, Moche and Chimu farmers on these lands produced a wide variety of crops to support the large population that lived there. The prehistoric Inca roads were superb: two main highways running the length of the empire, and a network of linking highways on which surplus crops from one region could be transported to another. The roads also provided routes for other necessary commodities, and for the highly organized teams of relay runners who carried official messages. Exhibits include maps, a composite mural of several Andean sites, photographs of Inca mountain valley roads and communities, and many artifacts of mountain valley farmlands and their products.

Inca society was higly structured, and life was subject to a highly centralized, all-encompassing bureaucratic socialism. The roads were built and maintained through a labor tax (a requirement that males contribute a specific amount of time and labor to the state); the labor tax also provided workers for state-owned farms and other state projects. The state, in turn, stored and distributed food and goods and cared for its citizens during an emergency. On exhibit are items that, typically, would have been stored and made available in an emergency including llama wool, head bands, agricultural tools (copper knives and axes, copper points and bean sticks), llama wool cloaks, fiber sandals, and llama wool tunics.

Pictured also are Inca temples, palaces, and public buildings that were planned by architects with the work supervised by masons and the labor supplied through labor taxes. Artifacts on exhibit include Inca construction tools: stone hammers, copper and bronze chisels, sand abrasives, ropes, wood or bronze levers, crow bars, and the wooden rollers used on earth ramps in place of wheels.

While the Incas had no written language, they had a most unusual and effective system for calculating and recordkeeping—the quipu—consisting of variously colored cords attached to a base rope, knotted in a special manner to record and transmit information. A special class of trained quipu recordkeepers were in charge of census data, historical accounts, and records of production, storage and distribution. Several quipus are on exhibit with informative labels describing how they were made and used by the recordkeeper.

Everyday Inca life was strongly colored with religious meanings and ceremonies. The people worshipped the sun and believed the Inca, or emperor, to be his son; the Inca, therefore, was also worshipped. The cult of the dead (or ancestor worship) was an important aspect of Inca religion—even today, natives place offerings of food and drink on their ancestors' graves. Exhibited is the "Gold Death Mask," made in Chimu style of the north coast of Peru; the Chimu metalworkers of Cuzco were held in great esteem. A silver figure of a mummy with an impressive death mask is exhibited. Religion was incorporated into the Inca calendar. Rituals connected with the goddesses of earth and sea were regularly observed, and crop cultivation was regulated by a calendar linked to the cycle of corn cultivation and based on observations of the sun, moon, and other natural phenomena. Among other artifacts of the Inca religion exhibited here are such calendars.

Inca ceramic works in many forms and colors shown here reflect the wide regional differences in the far-flung empire. Among the regional ceramics exhibited here are some that retain elements of pre-Inca styling; with others in mixed styles that combine local with Incan features. Ceramics that were found in the graves of pre-Inca peoples show boat models, beige and brick pottery made in Moche Ames (200-800 A.D.), and black pottery of the Chimu Empire which was conquered by the Incas in 1470. Some of the prehistoric pottery shown here features highly realistic renditions of vegetables and fruits.

A large and colorful diorama depicts the plaza of a typical Andean mountain town on market day where people of different surrounding communities meet to sell their products but also to socialize; each woman in the diorama, for example, wears the distinctive costume of her town. The marketplace serves not only as a distribution center for food and other necessities but as a social gathering place for the people from outlying villages. The women in the marketplace sell the fruits and vegetables and other products like coca leaves, lime powder (which is used while chewing coca leaves), other root crops, corn, lemons, sweet manioc, and various forms of chili peppers raised by the men on their farms. Also sold or bartered are alpacas. In the market stalls in which the products of the local merchants and farmers are displayed one can see as well those of professional merchants who travel from market to market in the mountain towns selling pottery, cooking utensils, musical instruments, and trinkets.

In the central Andean coast are arid desert lands. Some of these lands produce good crops through the help of irrigation provided by diverting mountain streams. Mining metals such as copper, tin, platinum, and iron which are found in the mines of this area are other valuable resources. Indeed, for hundreds of years before the Spaniards came to the New World, the Andean people had been working such metals as gold and silver, and copper alloys like bronze. After their conquest of the area, the Spaniards melted down most of the skillfully crafted golden objects, especially the golden jewelry for easier shipping to Spain. Archeologists, however, have recovered metal objects from graves, some of which are on display here and which are dated more than a thousand years old.

An important prehistoric coastal city, Chan Chan, was the capital of the Chimu Empire (1200 B.C. to 147 A.D.) which dominated six hundred miles of the northernmost Peruvian coast. The Chimu kings, absolute rulers believing themselves divine, ruled over farmers, artisans, laborers, and fishermen in a despotic manner. Artifacts of this culture, some with which the dead were buried, include pottery, wool and cotton woven cloth, some metal and wooden objects.

The Pacific coast and islands are rich in chemical resources such as nitrate and guano. An exhibit points out that guano, the dung of sea birds, is a valuable fertilizer. Large colonies of these birds leave immense deposits of guano, accumulating sometimes to depths as great as one hundred feet, on the northern Pacific coast and on the islands of South America on which they live. These were heavily mined in the nineteenth century with almost disastrous results. New laws are regulating the mining of this fertilizer.

The colonial period which began with the Spanish conquest of the Inca empire in 1532 lasted more than three centuries in South America. It was characterized by the building of large churches. In a diorama we see the facade of one such colonial South American church, a monument to the religion established by the early Spanish conquerors. The Spaniards used native Indians to build these churches and in all aspects of their economy. Specimens are shown of copper pins, pendants, gold, silver, and bronze artifacts that these natives made. We see specimens of their weaving, saddles, and lacquered wooden drinking cups which they made. The Spaniards brought horses with them (reintroducing them to South America). The military might of the Spanish troops on horseback was an effective weapon in their conquest of the land.

The lush vegetation of the tropical forests appears to spring from inexhaustible fertile land, but actually the hot climate and heavy rainfall combine to leach nutrients from the top soil, and so restrict its fertility. The peoples who cultivate sections of these forestlands clear them first by slashing and burning, an efficient procedure for preparing fields under these conditions. After cultivation depletes the soil, the farmers abandon the old fields for new ones. Pictures of slashed and burned tropical forest areas are shown here.

The flood plains of the Varzea (a river that joins the Amazon in Brazil) has very rich soil because annually it receives new silt from the river, and crops planted there yield double or triple the harvest of nearby lands. Archeologists have found evidence that is shown and discussed here of dense aboriginal populations that once flourished on the Vargzea flood plains, but that by 1700 A.D. their cultures had been destroyed by warfare, disease, and the slave trade. Archeological excavations of midden heaps provide evidence of the fish, birds, and other foods these people consumed. Unfortunately, such works by archeologists and early explorers are the sole sources of information about these aboriginal peoples. The hot, humid climate has destroyed much evidence of their presence here.

Other archeological findings reveal that the Marajoara Islands which lie at the mouth of the Amazon River, had a rather dense population between 400 and 600 A.D. The earth mounds found on the island reveal a pattern of marked class differences: the dead of ordinary people were buried directly in the ground without benefit of grave goods, while the bodies of high-ranking individuals were placed in large urns which were accompanied by grave goods of which some are shown in an exhibit. Other artifacts of this culture include prehistoric ceramics and shards of some that show several styles, of which polychrome is perhaps the most important.

A mural depicts a contemporary Wai Wai village in Guyana. It shows several related families living together in a large communal house surrounded by small work shelters. The mural shows a farmer in one field planting manioc, the staple crop. In another area men are seen slashing and burning the field. Most villages have several fields in different stages of development. Wai Wai natives hunt for wild plants, fish, and game to supplement their food supply. They catch fish by poisoning the waters or shooting them with harpoon-like arrowheads. Arrowheads are also used to stun birds, and those with broad blades are used for shooting agouti, tapir, and peccary. They eat Brazilian nuts which contain more protein than corn, sweet manioc and other tubers, and from the bitter manioc which they grow they extract the poisonous acid by grating and squeezing before making bread and meal. On exhibit are the male Wai Wai dance costumes, as well as Wai Wai everyday scanty clothing.

The pampas grass upon which the animals of the area graze is Patagonia's greatest natural resource. For thousands of years nomadic peoples hunted the animals that fed upon the open plains of the grasslands. A large open floor diorama shows a nineteenth-century Tehuelche Indian who with others shown in a mural is hunting using a bola to capture such game animals as the rhea (a flightless, ostrichlike bird) and the guanaco (a relative of the llama) in the Argentine grassland. Bolas, exhibited here, are weighted throwing weapons that entangle the prey. They are still used by the primitive hunters of

Tierra del Fuego, and are said to have originated sometime between 5000 and 3000 B.C.

Today, instead of hunting guanacos and rheas, pampas ranchers stock their grasslands with herds of cattle and sheep. The animals graze on the pampas grass and then are shipped by rail to coastal ports. From there, ships carry the meat abroad, mainly to Europe.

Hall of Human Origin and Variations (Second Floor, West Side)

This hall examines the science of physical anthropology, which is particularly concerned with the biology of humans, their evolution and the range and variety of groups within their populations. The exhibits describe how we differ from other primates and from our own evolutionary forebearers. Diets, genetics, and disease have affected the health and welfare of individuals and even whole populations. Differences that exist between the sexes and among people of different racial stocks are also subjects discussed. Human fetuses are displayed to show different stages in their development. Certain practices (evolved in several cultures) for modifying the appearance of human heads, feet, skin, and teeth are shown. Exhibits of great interest are those showing people who have been mummified in highly unusual ways.

An eye-catching exhibit of human skulls mounted against a black background is attention-getting the moment one enters this hall. It effectively dramatizes the population explosion in this country. This exhibit's base population figure is set at the time of the earliest European settlements in America, about 1560. Three hundred years later, by the time of the Civil War, the population in America had doubled; one hundred years after that, or by 1960, the population had tripled. One thousand year old human Peruvian skulls are mounted eerily against a solid black background to emphasize America's population explosion. Eventually this will not only result in an American problem, but is already a world problem in some regions where the major threats to humanity (along with the population explosion and nuclear war) are the destruction of the eco system by overgrazing, plowing under, paving over, and the pollution of the air and water.

In the complex process of man's primate heritage, scientists have found that one favorable change or development is often what has promoted others. Exhibits in this hall discuss the effect of our evolutionary ancestors' upright posture on the development of human brains and speech. Paleoanthropologists, who study fossil remains to reconstruct evolutionary history, discovered that our ancestors by the time they were bipedal were way ahead of the apes in the use of tools. They found that about 1.5 million years ago the stone tools made and improved by these primitive ancestors and some form of speech they began to use to communicate resulted in brain size increase. Models compare the brain sizes of men (homo sapiens) and other primates. Other exhibits compare primates and selected non-primates in such details as shoulder structure, eye sockets, horny plates (finger and toe nails), teeth, and pre-natal development.

Paleoanthropologists now believe that about two million years ago in Africa the pre-human species Paranthropus and Australopithecus had grinding teeth, not the teeth of carnivores, and achieved erect postures. It is believed that even earlier, perhaps 3.5 million years ago, these creatures began making tools and started their change toward bipedalism. The anthropologists believe, further, that Australopithecus (or Homo habilis) later evolved into an early form of man, but that Paranthropus did not survive. An exhibit illustrates some of the activities in which these pre-men may have engaged. Instead of getting close to their enemy to bite him our ancestors may have used stone tools to bop him on the head. They may also have used tools for butchering animals to eat. This may have resulted in the survival of the more intelligent creatures.

An exhibit has a replica of the skull and lower jaw of Zinjanthropus that Dr. Louis Leakey and his wife, Mary, discovered in 1959 in Tanganyika. The original specimen of Zinjanthropus was estimated to be between 1,760,000 and 1,900,000 years old. A cast of his brain cavity is compared with that of a gorilla and human brain cavities.

Many tools used by anthropologists in their research are displayed. Such instruments for measuring and comparing anatomy and skeletal structure such as an anthropometer, many kinds of calipers, a craniometer, an occipital goniometer, a parallelometer, and head spanners are among others shown. Some of these measure body fat, chest breadth and depth, and head diameters. Other instruments shown are used for medical purposes.

Absorbing exhibits discuss and illustrate the development of human bones which is a complex process that is controlled both by genes, nutrition, hygienic conditions, and by the hormones secreted at different stages of growth. While human bone structures naturally vary, and although genes and hormones play the major roles, nutrition and hygiene can also affect bone development. Records kept in many parts of the world, with some shown here, indicate that the ages differ at which different developmental stages of bone occur, and that even these can change from generation to generation. This is reflected in the specimens shown of teeth, skulls, hip, shoulder, wrist, and other bones. Fetal specimens, ages eight, twelve, fourteen, fifteen, and eighteen weeks, which reflect the normal skeletal changes, are on exhibit and attract a great deal of interest.

The bone injuries and diseases of prehistoric men can often be traced in their skeletons. An exhibit explores the causes of certain bone defects in the backs of Eskimos. On display are various bones of people who suffered arthritis, tubercular lesions, and other illnesses affecting the skeleton. In some cases X-rays have helped establish proof of these defects.

Major genetic mutations may provide an advantage or disadvantage to an individual. Such individual variations may lead in time to variations in the population, and to survival advantages or disadvantages for the group. The Eskimo back defects mentioned above, for example, increased with interbreeding. Specimens shown here of shoulder blades, sacrums, and thigh bones indicate genetic variations.

Another important characteristic of the individual, his or her sex, is a matter of genes. An exhibit explains the role of chromosomes in determining both the sex of a child and his or her sexual development. Other material discusses sex-linked characteristics:

sex differences are noted in the skulls, hip bones, sacrums, and joints displayed. Secondary characteristics are usually affected by health and nutrition.

Another exhibit discusses the characteristics of body types (endomorph, mesomorph, and ectomorph) that are described with revolving sculptures that depict each of these body types. This body typing is called somatotyping. There is a description of particular temperaments, specific diseases and other factors that may be more likely to occur in certain body types than in others.

The general character of facial features and body build in a given population is also genetically transmitted. Models of people from different geographic areas, placed on a large world map, indicate the variations in types of facial features, body heights, and silhouettes among modern populations. Other exhibits discuss differences in physical characteristics such as blood groupings among peoples of Mongoloid, Caucasoid, and Negroid racial stocks. The Caucasoid racial stock is believed to have originated in Europe, the Negroid in Africa, and the Mongoloid in Asia. Exhibits explore theories on the evolution of the distinguishing physical characteristics of each racial stock; skulls from each group are displayed.

Human beings do not seem to rest content with their appearances, however rich the mix of factors that have contributed to them. A large mural shows some of the ways human beings have modified their appearances, usually for decorative purposes: tattooing practices by various cultures; binding the feet practiced until about 1911 by Chinese women; and African lip deformation, and piercing and stretching of ear lobes. Some African tribes filed their teeth to a point, and prehistoric Mexicans altered their front teeth by drilling small holes, in which they placed semi-precious stones, and chipped and notched their teeth for cosmetic purposes. In various cultures, including modern western ones, ear lobes or rims are pierced and rings of various sizes are attached. Certain Indian tribes practiced head deformation and exhibited in this hall is the mummy of a prehistoric Peruvian child whose head was so deformed. Also displayed are artificially deformed human skulls from North and South America, as well as head-shaping devices from South America.

Illness and hardship left their marks on human skeletons. Models of the toothless jaws of prehistoric Eskimos and Indians indicate how coarse food they ate had to be chewed very hard before they could ingest it. The chewing along with the grit in the vegetation which was not removed by washing wore down the surfaces, beginning a process that eventually resulted in tooth loss. Children's teeth that have been found were usually in good condition, which demonstrates the progressive character of the problem.

A large mural depicts skull surgery (trephination) as practiced by prehistoric Incas at Machu Picchu in the Peruvian Andes. In a nearby exhibit case are shown ancient Peruvian skulls that had undergone such surgery. The ancient Peruvian surgeons excelled in trephination.

A glass exhibit case houses the remains of four mummified men. We see an Aleutian preserved in the cold of his burial cave; a seated mummy preserved by the high, dry heat of a coastal Peru; the body of Wilhem Von Ellenbogen of Pennsylvania preserved in a most unusual way (which we leave to the visitor to discover); and a fourth body, an Egyptian preserved from exposure to the air and from decay by the protection of linen wrappings.

Halls of Western Civilization, Origins and Traditions (Second Floor, East Side)

Changes people made in their life styles at the end of the last Ice Age, approximately 12,000 years ago, eventually affected all primitive societies living in areas of southwestern Asia, northeastern Africa, and southeastern Europe. Earlier primitive bands of families moved about constantly changing locations while foraging for plants, seeds, nuts, roots, fruits, and occasionally gathering insects, invertebrates, and other small animals for food. At the time of these early primitive bands the population was scattered, isolated, and sparse. In areas where it was cold they hunted, sometimes groups joining forces, for large animals for food and skins for clothing, while finding shelter in caves. In warmer areas such as the valleys of the Nile in Egypt and the Tigres and Euphrates in Mesopotamia where soil and climate produced conditions favorable for the development of an agricultural life, people settled, often in small groups that later developed into farming villages. Advancing cultural changes found people moving together in larger groups, large enough to form towns for defense where they established social classes. Archeologists have unveiled artifacts, some shown in these halls, about the economic growth and eventual complex governments they set up that show organized groups centered around priests and kings.

In the Fertile Crescent, while not as rich in agricultural lands, there were broad grasslands which were excellent for pasture land. Along the Mediterranean the Phoenicians with an advantageous geographic location became the middlemen of the Near East, obtaining their livelihood from trade and manufacture. It was around some of these ancient permanent sites that city-states eventually were created. In these halls are collections of artifacts retrieved by archeologists which reveal the transitions that took place in cultural advancements from one era to another in different geographical regions. These earliest western civilization builders represent a medley of peoples whose achievements shown in these halls began with stone-age cultures.

During the last part of the Ice Age between 37,000 and 10,000 B.C. the peoples who lived in Europe, northern Africa and southwestern Asia, developed skills in making blade tools for hunting and killing big game. Skeletal parts of these animals have been found in caves and with them the stone and bone tools people made that archeologists have dated as belonging to the period of the last Ice Age. Not only are some of these tools and bones exhibited, but also excellent Ice Age cave paintings (shown in photographic reproductions) made for various reasons by skillful artists that include: a horse and mammoth from Pechmerle, a deer from Laschimenes, a horse, bison, and ibex from Niaus, and another bison from Altamira.

It is believed that some ideas about crop cultivation that began in the Near East spread from there to all parts of the known world. Agriculture helped lead the transition of western civilization from a nomadic life to a more settled one. A diorama of Ali-Kosh, a permanent site of sun-dried brick houses located in the foothills of the Zagros Mountains in what is today southwest Iran, existed between 7500-5500 B.C. A section of it is recreated in this hall that should be of interest to the viewer. The people of this village relied basically on their own local resources chiefly as settled farmers raising crops, but also as herdsmen and hunters. We see the village and the fields from which wheat and barley has been harvested; a part of the land on which a flock of sheep and goats is held in a brush enclosure; a marsh from which a girl has captured a duck; and in the distance the plains on which we can see running the gazelles and other animals the villagers hunted for additional meat.

Pottery is a method archeologists use to distinguish the different period of prehistoric and historic times. Pottery was a major technique invented probably in the Near East that spread from there to Europe. Made from a combination of earth, water, and probably straw or grit, it was first fired in an open pit, but later (probably before 3000 B.C.) replaced by the kiln method. Styles of decoration, make-up of clay, and shape of the bowls differed at various sites and during different periods. Shards of pottery have been recovered where both the open-pit and kiln methods for firing were used and dated by archeologists, and some are displayed here. Some of these had been used for cooking, eating, carrying and storing food in what is now France, Spain, Holland, Switzerland, and Czechoslovakia.

The earliest European settlements made tools for hunting and warfare from stone, bone, and wood. They used stone axes with wooden handles to clear forests for agricultural lands, chop wood, and perhaps for weapons against the enemy. By 10,000 to 9,000 B.C. along the eastern Mediterranean coast the transition from hunting to farming is reflected in the tools they made. Among stone, bone, and wood tool artifacts exhibited here are some found in prehistoric caves that are important evidence that help us see links in the history of mankind.

The introduction of metal opened the way for more effective tools that were greater in number and variety than stone tools, although stone tools continued to be used. Copper had been used from as early as 8,000 B.C. but at that time natives simply cold-hammered the copper they found. It was not until about 5,500 B.C. when people began to smelt or melt copper ore and gold ore and craftsmen became skilled in making tools, weapons, and jewelry that the usefulness of these metals was increased. A diorama shows the figure of a man working as a metalsmith outside the city of Larsa in Mesopotamia. He is casting a large number of bronze spearpoints and arrowheads. Because he is a skilled worker, he is employed to make these weapons for King Rim-Sin who is preparing to march against the nearby city of Uruk. Bronze metallurgy was an important step in the development of metals. An exhibit describes the technique of bronze metallurgy made from 90% copper and about 10% tin or arsenic. It was first produced about 3,500 B.C. Specimens of bronze, that had been annealed and hammered making it a harder and stronger metal than copper, show spearheads, arrowheads, daggers, etc., for weapons as well as for bowls, jars, and tools. In addition to pottery and metallurgical artifacts, there are related objects like seals and coins, as well as textiles and glass displayed in these halls, each group of artifacts contributing information about succeeding civilizations in the geographical regions where they were found.

In Mesopotamia King Rim-Sin reigned for sixty-six years in the town of Larsa (1822-1763 B.C.). Not only did Rim-Sin reign over a large part of southern Mesopotamia, including the city of Uruk, but he had constructed large public buildings and defensive fortifications in which bronze figurines of Rim-Sin were buried in the foundations and on which information about Rim-Sin and his reign was recorded with Sumerian inscriptions, pictographic and cuneiform writing, the first writing system known in Mesopotamia. Although the Sumerian language was later replaced by Akkadian in the Mesopotamian area, Sumerian remained a literary language for centuries. A very large diorama of an area in or near the city of Larsa in about 1801 B.C. recreates a section of what might have taken place in this area. Soldiers stand guard at the city gate of Larsa. A group of soldiers are preparing to make morning rounds. A small market place along the city wall shows food products and crafts for sale. In the distance one gets a glimpse of a pyramidal Ziggurat or temple in the city of Uruk. Flowing past Larsa from the direction of Uruk is a large irrigation canal, a branch of the Euphrates River. One can see a barge loaded with mud bricks being towed up the canal by a team of oxen. Some of the king's workmen are getting ready to plant onions; a woman is watering a vineyard with a water-lifting device; and the barley which had been cut is being threshed.

Rim-Sin's kingdom was conquered by Hammurabi who became known as "the king of justice." A model of a famous monument shown in this hall depicts Hammurapi at the top of the monument receiving divine sanction from the Sun God, who is also the god of justice, giving Hammurapi powers to establish the laws of the land. The long, cuneiform inscription carved on the monument gives information about the common laws Hammurapi established and sometimes about the several classes of stratified society in the kingdom.

Graves yield important information about ancient civilizations. Two tombs from Bab edh-Dhra, Jordan, dating from 3100 B.C., have been recreated in these halls showing not only the skeletal remains of those buried, but the grave goods buried with them. Early settled Europeans wore beads and pendants and ornaments of beads, shell, and stones that have been found in their graves. Many of these artifacts are exhibited in reproduction in the graves and in nearby cases.

Not only in the Nile valley and in the Tigres and Euphrates valleys did great civilizations have their beginnings, but another, the Indus civilization, arose in the valley of the Indus River, a river about 1900 miles long which today is the chief river of Pakistan. The Indus Valley civilization arose about 2500 B.C. in this area of fertile soil and favorable climate where fine agricultural crops like wheat, corn, rice, and millet as well as dates and fruits could be grown. This civilization, too, developed large urban centers, political centralization, class stratification, monumental architecture and, very important, a writing system. A large diorama recreates a section of a Pakistani bazaar located in the center of a city. Although this one appears rather modern looking, it shows, as did such bazaars of the past, agricultural goods for sale grouped in one area, and craft artifacts grouped for sale in another. One can find here the simplest of requirements as well as luxurious goods; groups of people are seen visiting, others are listening to the news of the town crier, while still others conduct legal business.

The work of Henry Rawlinson, a translator, who risked his life to read an inscription carved above the cliffs of Disotun in West Iran, is described in these halls. The inscription high on the cliffs began "I am Darius, the great king...," and goes on about his kinship. It was written in cuneiform (about 400 lines of the Persian part) with the same message inscribed in Elamite and Babylonian which Rawlinson was able to translate in 1846. This was a key to cracking the cuneiform writing system.

The Egyptian religion developed from a belief in a life after death based on one's actions in this life. This interest in a future life can be seen in their pyramids and other monumental tombs which are enduring witnesses of a belief in a life after death. They were careful to preserve the bodies of the dead of wealthy or highly placed individuals, taking seventy days for the embalming procedure (stuffing the body with linens to preserve its shape, washing it in a salt solution and wrapping it with linen cloth soaked with oils and resin), meanwhile placing the internal organs in a coptic jar. In these halls are exhibited many mummy cases, coptic jars, and many masks provided for the dead, but no mummies. (However, one Egyptian mummy and other mummies can be seen in the Hall of Human Origin and Variations.) Exhibited also are examples of Egyptian writing, the best known is hieroglyphics in which pictographic symbols stand for syllables. Very often hieroglyphics are found in mummy wrappings, as shown here in exhibits of mummy cases.

The benefits derived from the Nile River's annual overflow played an important role in the life and politics of the people of Egypt. In an early monument the Pharaoh is represented as chief benefactor of the land because he engineered the digging of ditches from which the Nile's water flowed to benefit the land. A section of these halls describes Egyptian monumental architecture of which the pyramids are the most famous. There are other massive tombs and temples along the Nile which are pictured and described here.

During his reign King Solomon had control of the port city of Ezion Geber from which he could command both the land and sea routes south toward Arabia and to the north, east, and west. In the 1930s Rabbi Gleuck, an archeologist, uncovered artifacts (bone tools, incense cups, ropes of palm tree fibers, and others shown here) at the site of Tel El-Kheleifeh in the Negev Desert, which may have come from Ezion Geber, a fortified industrial town containing ware-houses that were located on the major trade routes of King Solomon's time and in later periods.

A large map labeled "Controlling Trades" shows the power states of that time, Arabia, Tyre, Damascus, Syria, Egypt, and Ezion Geber (among others) where these governments controlled the flow of goods in trade networks. Governments constructed fortified settle-ments at crucial points and their officials and trade businessmen kept track of their accounts with written records (some shown). The map shows trade routes which King Solomon of Israel (who joined with King Hiram of Tyre) took when his fleets sailed from the port city of Ezion Geber to Ophir, the legendary source of gold, precious wood and precious stones, and to other lands to the south. As trade networks developed among the Assyrians, Persians, Greeks and Romans, they formed important lines of communications with the rest of the known world to spread ideas and craft skills as well as goods to the people. A large open floor exhibit shows some of the merchandise that was traded: pottery, lumber, gemstones, jewelry, textiles, ivory, basalt, obsidian, flint, and gold.

Another map shows where Greek colonies, Phoenician colonies, and Syrian colonies were established. Here, too, the introduction of ideas, techniques, and goods were spread through trading. Other regions—Egypt, Palestine, Syria, and Cyprus each had goods, techniques, and ideas to trade. The islands of Cyprus, especially, with its supply of copper deposits and timber was important in trading. Cyprus also exported pottery exhibited here. During the period from 1500 to 1100 B.C. of the late bronze age the Mycenaeans of southern Greece were very active traders, keeping good economic records and establishing colonies to support their trade. Artifacts of this civilization include figurines and jars, among other things that are shown.

Some ancient peoples of the steppes in what is today part of West Siberian USSR built small burial mounds called kurgans over graves. They were an Indo-European speaking people known to have been warlike nomads with a religion based on sun worship. Artifacts of this culture exhibited here include bone pins, bone beads, bronze bracelets and some pottery.

It is thought Anatolians were attracted to Cyprus in the early bronze age between 2300-1850 B.C. because of the island's rich copper deposits. These peoples brought new ideas about pottery making and other crafts to Cyprus, and some of the Cypriot pottery painted with geometric designs they made are shown here.

An exhibit of the bronze age in Europe shows one that was part of the Swiss Lake Dwellers. These people cleared large forest areas for pasture lands and constructed hill forts for defense and the control of trade. Eventually their lakeside villages were covered by rising waters which destroyed their villages but helped preserve the contents of midden heaps left there. From these midden heaps archeologists have been able to determine that these people ate fish and water mammals from the lakes, fishing for them in dug-out canoes with fishing tackle we see exhibited that includes bronze fish hooks and net floats, fish scales and other equipment which replaced those of stone. Hunters used dogs to hunt for bear, deer, wild pigs for meat with exhibited weapons of bronze. Among remains found in the middens were jaws of many of the animals they hunted, some shown here.

Eastern cultures spread westward and were among the important contributions in the rise of western civilizations in Europe. It probably came first to the areas around Greece, later throughout the Mediterranean area, and ultimately into Europe. Greek civilization flourished as the result of a number of local and foreign factors. Locally the city-states constantly engaged in economic, ideological and military competition. Historians have suggested that this kind of competition laid the groundwork for the acceleration of cultural life in the arts and sciences, and in political and social achievments. Descriptions are given of some of their political activities, social life, and economic activities. There is much evidence of their skills as artists which are shown in exhibits of Greek pottery of outstanding beauty and in the remains of equally beautiful Greek sculpture.

Historians have also determined that the Etruscans, the fore-runners of the Romans, played an extremely important part in the ancient world. In exhibits displaying the abilities of Etruscan craftsmen we see examples of ceramics and metalworkings accomplished with great skill. Among some shown are a bronze mirror, gold-plated beads, a bronze device for scraping oil from the skin, a bronze razor, and various kinds of pottery. Some of the Etruscans buried their dead in spectacular tombs. Exhibits here show examples of funerary art that was practiced for this purpose. A beautiful spirit boat dated about 1500 B.C. is a product of a bronze industry centered in Sardinia. The spirit boat probably served as a lamp. Traders such as the Phoenicians and others probably brought such crafts to the Etruscans.

Rome, too, from early times was in contact with the East. From the Etruscans the Romans learned many skillful techniques. As a result of Roman conquests there came streams of slaves from the east who brought with them, among other things, their religions and their superstitions, but also new techniques for crafts. Trade with the colonies introduced the use of metal coins and we see in exhibits many of these that were used throughout the Roman empire during various periods. Glass was one of the major items of trade with the Romans. Examples of glass of many periods are shown beginning with the earliest glass made before the invention of glass blowing. When glass blowing made possible greater production of glass, in many cases it took the place of pottery. The exhibits which show iridescent glass have some especially beautiful pieces, the iridescence caused by moisture penetrating the glass and leaching out soda and lime, leaving thin layers of amorphous silica which produce the attractive colors.

Hall of Cold-Blooded Vertebrates (Second Floor, West Side)

A thirty-one year old man entered the Hall of Cold-Blooded Vertebrates in 1969 armed with a hatchet and butcher knife, smashed the glass of two snake exhibit cases and proceeded to "kill" the snakes by decapitation. When he was apprehended he protested that a snake had robbed him of $20,000 and he wanted "revenge!"

Some of the most absorbing exhibits in this hall describe the life cycles of reptiles and amphibians. Among some species of lizards (by no means all) the females can produce babies without any male lizard ever becoming involved. Also absorbing are exhibits that trace how reptiles and amphibians obtain their food, how they move from place to place, and in what ways they defend and protect themselves. While some of these animals are beneficial to man, others are definitely harmful: exhibits describe animals in each category. Displays and dioramas show cold-blooded vertebrates in a variety of habitats—one diorama recreating an area of the Florida Everglades that is a veritable paradise for them.

The display on the life cycle of amphibians follows their develop-ment from fertilization to adult form, emphasizing the biological changes called metamorphosis. Exhibits on the anatomy of an adult frog include material on its circulatory and nervous system. Models of the skulls of frogs and salamanders help further explain the physiology of these animals.

Like amphibians, most reptiles are hatched from eggs that are laid externally, but there are a few species of reptiles that are born alive. An exhibit describing the life cycle of such reptiles as turtles, crocodilians, snakes, and lizards features models of their eggs, and of their newborn or newly hatched young. Models also show the heart and blood vessels of turtles, snakes, and crocodiles; the brains of vipers and tortoises; and of the European lizard (greatly enlarged). Other material explains the changes that occur in the color and form of snakes and turtles; and a chart shows the growth and maximum size obtained by large reptiles.

Most reptiles and amphibians are carnivorous, although lizards are vegetarians as are amphibians in the tadpole stage. Tadpoles eat the algae that clings to submerged vegetation or debris. An exhibit describes what reptiles and amphibians eat and how they obtain their food.

An exhibit describes the various forms of amphibian and reptilian locomotion. These include gliding (certain lizards and snakes), climbing (many amphibians and reptiles), walking and running (various frogs, toads, turtles, salamanders, and lizards), and hopping (toads and frogs). Some reptiles and amphibians swim (there are those that never leave the water or do so only briefly), and many of the smaller and weaker amphibians and reptiles burrow for defense, some hibernating where winters are severe. Legless reptiles and amphibians, such as the glass lizard, some salamanders, and most snakes crawl.

Reptiles and amphibians defend and protect themselves by several methods. An exhibit explores these methods: concealment, a device of the smaller and weaker reptiles and amphibians; burrowing to protect from danger but also to prevent drying out during periods of drought; and secretion of poisonous substances, an ability of some amphibians and snakes. Thick scales and large size protect sea turtles, large land turtles, and most crocodiles from their enemies. Other defenses include mimicry of stronger species and speed in escaping from threatening species.

While reptiles and amphibians have developed an unfortunate reputation, some of them provide humans with genuine benefits and should be protected rather than destroyed. Some snakes prey on troublesome rodent populations and other mammals that destroy farmers' crops, while certain amphibians and snakes prey on harmful insects. Purses, shoes, and leather trim are made from the valuable skins of snakes and alligators. The eggs and the flesh of some large turtles and lizards as well as the legs of certain frogs provide humans with food. Of course, contact with certain reptiles and amphibians can be harmful to humans: poisonous snake bites can result in death, and severe cuts can be sustained from contact with crocodiles and large lizards. Diseases are spread by the mites and ticks carried by some lizards, snakes, and toads; game fish eggs are preyed on by aquatic turtles and salamanders; and ducks, fish, and muskrats are sometimes killed by snapping turtles.

Several dioramas in the hall show natural habitats of cold-

188   National Museum of Natural History

blooded vertebrates. An Arizona desert diorama features native reptiles and amphibians living there that include the western diamondback rattlesnake and Couch's spadefoot toad. The southwest African desert is one of the driest places on earth. A diorama in this hall shows that the most numerous animals living there are lizards (shovel snouted and Skoog's), and the Namagua chameleon. A large diorama depicts the sub-tropical environment of the Florida Everglades. Among the animals which make their home in its swampy areas are reptiles and amphibians; alligators; harmless snakes like the rat and king snakes; poisonous snakes like the diamondback rattlesnake and the cottonmouth; softshell and mud turtles; American chameleons; tree and bull frogs; and salamanders. Another diorama shows marine iguanas which actually are true sea lizards that can achieve a length of six feet and are found only on the Galapagos Islands.

In an exhibit of the Malayan jungle are shown a number of reptiles: the king cobra, the largest poisonous snake known; the reticulated python which reaches a length of thirty feet; forest lizards and skinks; bronzeback and mangrove snakes; the green whipsnake and the tree viper. In an exhibit of a scene along the Amazon River is shown the matamata and tartaruga turtles, caimans, and such snakes as the anaconda (the largest living snake), coral, cotiara, and boa constrictor.

Other cold-blooded vertebrates shown in small exhibits include the true marine toad (Busomarinous), the Surinam toad, the bicolored terereca, the tegu, the Florida gopher tortoise, the Indian cobra, the mangrove snake, the bamboo viper, and the black iguana. There are, as well, examples of the only lizards known to be poisonous, the Gila monster of the American southwest, and its relative, the Mexican bearded lizard. The exhibits discuss the living habits and territory occupied by each of them.

Still another lizard which is featured in an exhibit is the Komodo Dragon or Komodo Monitor, a carnivore. This large dragon lizard of Indonesia is the world's largest lizard, reaching a length between ten and eleven feet and a weight of 150 to 200 pounds.

Hall of Osteology (Second Floor, West Side)

Most animals could not maintain their shape without a thickening and hardening of certain parts, the framework called the skeleton made up of bones, to form a support for its body. The skeleton not only gives shape and support to the body, but protects vital organs, and by means of muscles attached to it permits movements of its various parts such as for locomotion. Exhibits in this hall give us an opportunity to examine, compare, and (to whatever degree possible) understand the skeletal characteristics of vertebrates (animals with a backbone) from fish to man. In some cases the exhibits indicate how bones function as the producer of cells for the body and how they serve as a basis for the classification of some species. The skeletal exhibits include water mammals, edentates, insectivores, bats, rodents, carnivores, reptiles, birds, primates, and others. There are exhibits that show teeth, jaws, vertebrate columns and other bony structures of a number of animals which one can examine.

Among the most informative exhibits in this hall are those describing the structure of cartilage and bone which together with the tendons, ligaments, and connective tissues support the organs and muscles of the body. Bones also, we learn, have a protective function: the skull, for example, protects the brain, eyes, and ears. The vertebral column not only supports but protects the spinal column. Bones also aid in the transmission of vibrations, the production of red and white blood corpuscles (enlarged transparencies illustrate this), and the control of specific gravity, reproduction and in other body functions. Models of various bones and enlarged slides of cartilage displayed here help explain the functions of these body parts.

Bones originate in embryonic connective tissues; an exhibit here traces how bones develop and grow. Another exhibit demonstrates the remarkable way in which the skeletons of land vertebrates support the animal's weight, and an illustration compares a human's bones to a cantilever bridge. Bones do more than support weight, however—they help move it. An exhibit illustrates how skeletal structure, in combination with muscles, creates motion in various parts of the body.

Of all the chordates, fishes are the simplest in skeletal structure. An exhibit describes the skeletal characteristics of flat-fishes, herring-like fishes, carps, catfish and their relatives, lampreys and hagfish, Australian lungfish (which are offshoots of an ancient group of fishes that are ancestors of land dwelling vertebrates), spin-rayed fishes, sharks, rays, flying fishes, chimaeras, and peciform fishes that include sailfish, swordfish, sea bass, and dolphins.

The exhibits on reptiles feature the skeletal structures of crocodiles, tuataras (which have skull features different from all other reptiles), and snakes (constrictors, poisonous, and nonpoisonous). Among the amphibian skeletons are those of caecilians (wormlike and almost blind tropical amphibian), salamanders, frogs, and toads. Several exhibits show skeletal specimens of turtles. Among the turtles shown here are leatherback (the largest living turtle), soft-shelled, and sea turtles. Among the turtle families featured are side-necked turtles, the turtles which have concealed necks and draw their heads straight back into their shells, and the pond, wood, box, loggerhead, green and painted turtles.

Ornithologists use a combination of skeletal characteristics as criteria for the classification of birds. An exhibit discusses some of these characteristics such as nasal openings, sternum shape, palate type, and toe number and arrangement. Other exhibits display skeletal structures of birds according to type: land types (parrot, dove, owl, grouse, trumpeter), terrestrial (ostrich, cassowary, tinamou), running (rhea, cariama, bustard, roadrunner), arboreal (to which more than half of the world's birds belong), and aquatic, semi-aquatic, or underwater swimmers. Birds underwent many skeletal modifications that prepared them for flight; among these were a reduction in the number of bones through fusion and loss, a shortening of the trunk and bony tail, the development of a keeled breastbone (sternum), and a strengthening of the rib cage and shoulder supports. Among specimens exhibited and labeled to help explain such changes are a frigate bird and a hummingbird.

Almost all vertebrates except birds have teeth or tooth-like

190   National Museum of Natural History

structures. Teeth perform such functions as seizing and manipulating food, and are used in defense, offense, and grooming. Teeth vary greatly, of course, in form, size, number, and position, as shown in specimens of fish, amphibian, reptilian, and mammalian species. Jaws evolved from filtering mechanisms like that found in lancelets, a primitive vertebrate. Skeletal specimens of fish, amphibian, reptile, bird, fox, and human jaws are displayed for comparison. (When examining skeletons of sea mammals take note of the interesting label that tells about the manatee which lives in the Atlantic and possesses "traveling teeth.") Cottontail rabbits look like rodents but have two pairs of upper incisor teeth (rodents have only one pair).

The most widely distributed mammals in the world are the carnivores. Skeletal specimens are displayed of cats (wildcat, caracul, tiger, cheetah, and Maylay civet); and dogs (jackal and collie). Other skeletal specimens of the Order Carnivora shown are coatimundi, raccoon, bear, fox, and badger. The harp seal, fur seal, sea lion, Pacific walrus and other water mammals are aquatic carnivores which in their evolutionary development represent two distinct lines of evolution: the sea lions and walruses are believed to be derived from the same ancestors as bears, while the true seals are descendants of the otters.

The monotremes, echidnas and platypus, found in Australia and New Guinea are primitive egg-laying mammals. Their skeletal characteristics which retain features of reptilian ancestors are described and specimens of each are shown.

Although marsupials differ from one another in many ways, they share certain distinctive characteristics, as discussed in an exhibit. Among the marsupials shown are the brushtail possum, the great kangaroo, the American opossum, marsupial mole, the Australian bandicoot, the great flying phalanger, and the koala.

Edentates (toothless mammals) are found in three distinct orders of mammals but nevertheless have certain skeletal characteristics in common. On view are skeletal specimens of a variety of edentates: two and three toed sloths, pangolins, aardvarks, hairy and nine-banded armadillos, and the great anteater.

Hoofed animals are likewise found in more than one order. Artiodactyles are even-toed, cloven-hoofed mammals and exhibited are skeletal specimens of their order that include musk-ox, big horn sheep, pronghorn antelope, American buffalo, camel, llama, giraffe, deer, pigs, peccaries, and others. Perissodactyles, on the other hand, are odd-toed, hoofed mammals such as the horse, tapir, and Indian rhinoceros whose skeletal specimens are also exhibited.

Rodents are the most abundant mammals in the world. There is an enormously large number of rodent species, but whether amphibious, gliding, burrowing, or leaping all rodent species share certain common skeletal characteristics. Exhibited are skeletal specimens of the mountain beaver, western chipmunk, the kangaroorat, Norway rat, woodchuck jerboa, white-footed mouse, jumping mice, African dormouse, capybara, and many more. The label explains what skeletal structure these rodents share in common.

The animals in the order that includes whales and porpoises have bones that are porous, soft, and less dense of surface than the bones of land mammals. Animals in this order are the only completely aquatic mammals. Skeletal specimens of the grey whale, LaPlata dolphin, and the Harbor porpoise are also shown. Other large animals on exhibit whose home is in the sea show skeletons of a Stellar sea cow (a sea cow is more closely related to elephants than to whales), dugong, which live in the shallow waters of the Indian Ocean around the East Indies and in the western Pacific, and the manatee which lives in the Atlantic. Exhibits explain how these huge animals exist in the waters of the world.

Another exhibit describes the skeletal characteristics of bats and insectivores. While bats differ from one species to another in food habits, they have similar skeletal structures, as shown in the various skeletal specimens on display. Bats are the only mammals that can fly. They use their hands which are like the ribs of an umbrella covered by a thin membrane which expands when in flight and folds up when not in flight. Also displayed here are skeletal specimens of shrew, mole, tenrec, hedgehog, and other insectivores, primitive mammals thought to be ancestors of carnivores, bats, and primates.

Exhibits indicate that several primitive primates are clearly modern survivors of older kinds of primates. Such animals now live in tropical regions of Africa and Asia. Skeletal specimens shown here include bush baby, tree shrew, tarsier, loris, lemur, and aye-aye.

The primate order, of course, includes monkeys, all of whom have certain characteristic skeletal structures. Shown are Old World monkeys including proboscis and mandrills. Also seen are New World monkeys (which are generally smaller and more primitive) with skeletal specimens that include the spider monkey, howler, capuchin, squirrel monkey, pigmy and cottontail monkeys. Among the larger primate skeletons are shown ground dwelling apes like the gorilla and chimpanzee which more closely resemble man than tree dwellers (skeletal specimens also shown) like the orangutan and the gibbon. From these primate skeletal specimens an alert observer can note similarities and differences.

Man's skeletal structure is compared to other higher primates like the chimpanzee, gibbon, orangutan, and the gorilla. All are alike in certain skeletal characteristics (the large brain cavity, the number of teeth, and lack of a tail), but differ in other skeletal features which have been effected by their particular ways of life.

Insect Zoo (Second Floor, West Side)

Sometime ago an article appeared in **National Geographic** that reported that the Insect Zoo was used in a therapy program to help rid a young woman of her phobia—a fear of insects. Insects and their arthropod relatives busily live their lives in, as nearly as possible, natural habitats provided for them by curators, entomologists, and rearing room aids assisted by volunteers who help the entomologists with rearing procedures, feedings, clean up and with the collections of arthropods and plant specimens. There are such absorbing exhibits in this hall, people have frequently remained four or five hours observing them.

Arthropods (animals with jointed legs, segmented bodies and appendages, and external skeletons that are shed during periods of growth) are the world's most successful animals. They have been in existence for over five hundred million years and now account for nearly eighty percent of all of the earth's creatures. Their life histories have been diverse resulting in diverse habitats, feeding techniques, structures, shapes, and colors. Five classes of arthropods are featured in this hall. Class Insecta, the most numerous of the Arthropods contains insects with six legs, two antennae, usually one or two pairs of wings, segmented bodies (head, thorax, and abdomen) and lives all over the world except the oceans. Class Insecta is divided into many orders which include bees, beetles, moths, butterflies, ants, cockroaches, dragonflies, mosquitoes, waterstriders, praying mantis, crickets, locusts, grasshoppers, and many others. Class Crustacea consists of sowbugs, crabs, shrimps, crayfish, lobsters, barnacles, and many others. Class Arachnida encompasses spiders, scorpions, mites, ticks, and tarantulas, among others. Class Diplopoda includes the millipedes, and Class Chilopoda, the centipedes. The exhibits are anything but static: webs are being spun and flies caught, eggs are hatching and larvae changing to adult forms. The Insect Zoo boasts about 5,000 specimens of 100 species, but the mortality rate is high. Some of the inhabitants, somehow, manage to eat some of their neighbors. Feeding schedules for some of the arthropods are posted, and white-coated volunteer docents courteously answer visitors' questions about the animals on display, give public demonstrations and monitor the Insect Zoo. Insects play valuable roles as well as pestiferous ones, as the exhibits here point out. But visitors need have no fear—all of the animals are safely contained behind plexiglass walls.

Many extant species bear strong resemblances to their ancestors, as shown in the models of these ancient animals which have been reconstructed. A diorama "Life in a Swamp Three Hundred Million Years Ago" depicts such arthropods of past ages as scorpions, spiders, giant dragonflies, centipedes, shrimp, horseshoe crabs, and cockroaches. It also shows models of a great scale tree, tree ferns, and other fossil vegetation which grew at that time. One insect that appears to have remained intact, unchanged throughout the ages, is the venerable cockroach.

"Where Arthropods Live" is a fifty-foot long display of simulated insect habitats safely enclosed behind plexiglass walls. Whirligig beetles, water beetles, damselfly naiads, young dragonflies, water scorpions, and other arthropods inhabit (some permanently, some temporarily only in their immature stages; some underwater, others on the water's surface) a simulated pond setting. In the simulated grassland environment there are fireflies, doodlebugs, ant lion larvae, and spittle insects, among others, at home in burrows underground or above ground. A simulated tropical forest setting provides comfortable quarters for most terrestrial arthropods including walking sticks, termites, beetles, centipedes, cinch bugs, mosquitoes, and others.

The exhibit "How Arthropods Grow," describes three types of metamorphosis (in which the animals molt or shed their external skeltons to make room for new growth). The display traces the complete metamorphosis (from egg to larva to pupa to adult) of such arthropods as beetles, flies, moths, butterflies, ants, bees, wasps, and others;

the gradual (or incomplete metamorphosis) of such terrestrial and non-gill-bearing insects (in their immature stage called nymphs) as grasshoppers, earwigs, stink bugs, assassin bugs, and squash bugs (the latter three known as "true bugs"); and the gradual metamorphosis of such gill-bearing insects (in their immature stage called naiads) as dragonflies, mayflies, damselflies, and stoneflies. There is still another type of change illustrated here. This takes place in the growth patterns of scorpions, centipedes, and spiders, and a few primitive species of arthropods where the young as they hatch from the egg resemble the adult—molting their exoskeletons several times in the process of becoming an adult.

"How Arthropods Eat" depicts feeding habits of these animals. Some herbivorous arthropods suck plant fluids, others, which are carnivorous chew and eat other animals, and still others which are omnivorous chew and or suck both plant and animal matter. Among these latter two types are scavengers that feed on dead matter. There are others which suck blood. It will come as a surprise to some to learn that some arthropods over a period of five hundred million years have evolved modified legs that became mouthparts for slashing, chewing, sucking, and filtering desirable food; while still others have no mouth parts at all but absorb nutrients found in the waters in which they live through their skin. Rather uncommon in diet, and in other ways, are two species of beetles represented in the Insect Zoo: the Harlequin Longhorn beetle from Trinidad feeds only at twilight and, in this zoo, exclusively on bananas. The other, also from Trinidad, is the Hercules beetle—the longest beetle in the world. It also eats fruit, but is most remarkable for the long horns sported by the males and used in masculine combat.

Camouflage plays a vital role in the lives of many arthropods. Some species have evolved mimic coloration: the coloring of the tasty Viceroy butterfly, for example, mimics the coloring of the Monarch butterfly, whose taste is repugnant to birds and other animals. Other arthropods have evolved a particular color that blends almost completely with the plants or objects upon which they usually rest; still others, as a means of escaping detection, camouflage themselves by shape (dried-up leaves, tree bark, or thorns, for example). Each type of camouflage, for the most part shown with living specimens, is illustrated in this hall.

Given the number and variety of arthropod species, it is not surprising to find there is such great variety in size. The Insect Zoo has a mounted specimen of the largest living arthropod, the Japanese spider crab, which lives at some depth in the ocean, and can achieve a length of nine feet. By contrast, there is a display of such minute arthropods as flour beetles, mites, and springtails for which visitors will need to use the magnifying glasses provided. Arthropods of intermediate sizes include the inch-long beetles and bugs, and the three-foot spiny lobster on display.

Two particularly absorbing exhibits feature insect societies that demonstrate cooperation among their own kinds—live bees and live leaf-cutter ants. Visitors can see the live bees in their own hive behind the glass panes where the queen (identified by the large red dot placed on her back) and the worker bees carry on their numerous activities as they work for the success of the hive. The leaf-cutter or fungus ants methodically harvest leaves, chop them into portable pieces, and drag them down (here shown through long transparent tubes) into underground gardens. In these gardens a fungus grows on the leaves, which the leaf-cutter ants tend and when ready use for food. The leaf-cutter worker ants put the eggs laid by their queen on the fungus which the young eat when they hatch from the egg. The leaf-cutter ants maintain a caste system which includes the queen, males for reproduction, and workers divided into scout ants (which discover sources for food); workers which bring in the petals and leaves; soldiers; nursery attendants; and workers which maintain the cleanliness of the underground establishment.

4

The National Air and Space Museum

The Smithsonian has received many retired crafts, missiles, rockets, engines, and other equipment from the National Air and Space Administration as well as many donated by other institutions and individuals that are now part of the National Air and Space Museum's collections. Selections of these exhibited are such spectacular sights as the **Columbia Command Module** in which the astronauts of **Apollo 11** returned to Earth from their lunar mission; and a back-up model of the **Eagle,** the golden lunar module in which two **Apollo 11** astronauts rode down to the moon's surface using it for scientific work and as "a home away from home" in the upper part of the **Eagle.** Later abandoning the **Eagle's** lower stage on the moon, the two astronauts lifted off in the upper stage to rendezvous with Astronaut Collins in the **Command Module** that had been circling around the moon while awaiting their return. (When the three astronauts were safely inside the **Command Module** the upper stage of the **Eagle** was released and dropped back on the moon, its impact recorded on scientific instruments left on the moon for that very purpose.) Other exhibits of absorbing interest are replicas of the **Apollo-Soyuz** spacecrafts docking; the back-up of the huge **Skylab Orbital Workshop;** the chronological steps taken prior to the **Apollo** flights; the men, crafts, equipment, and reenactments of the **Apollo** flights; and scores of other engrossing exhibits.

Among the historic planes shown here are the Wright brothers' **Kitty Hawk Flyer,** the first manned airplane to fly; Lindbergh's **Spirit of St. Louis,** the first plane to fly non-stop across the Atlantic; planes of World War I and II, and others that were landmarks in the evolution of civilian and military aircraft. A profusion of aircraft abound in the galleries and around the balcony where visitors find such craft as the **Gossamer Condor,** a lightweight craft of seventy pounds, built of mylar, balsa, cardboard, thinned-down tubing, and piano wire, which was pedaled to victory on August 23, 1977 near Bakersfield, California winning a British prize of 50,000 pounds; the **Lockheed F-104 Starfighter,** the first fighter capable of operating at Mach 2 (twice the speed of sound); and a **Douglas D-558-2 Skyrocket** that could also go that speed. When exploring other galleries visitors are better able to imagine themselves participating in events pilots and astronauts experienced. For example, visitors can enter the back-up **Skylab Orbital Workshop** from the balcony and see at first hand where three different crews who manned the spacecraft worked, exercised, and slept; they can walk out on a hangar deck in the gallery Sea-Air Operations and be piped on board as if they are VIPs; and they can listen in on a conversation that might have taken place between aviators in a World War I American military airfield near Verdun. Large dioramas give fascinating pictures of the preparation for and landing on the moon using mannequins dressed as astronauts; the Land Rover used to carry them and their equipment distances on the moon; and the equipment the astronauts took with them for exploratory work, scientific work, and gathering rocks on the moon.

Films moving across an IMAX screen five stories high and seven stories wide in the Samuel P. Langley Theater on the first floor create some awesome and spine tingling scenes of flight. The first film shown here, "To Fly" was seen by well over four million viewers. Another film "Living Planet" carried its viewers all over the globe—to Africa, India, Venezuela, and the North Pole and gave them a fresh perspective of our planet Earth. It takes only forty-five minutes for a visit in the Albert Einstein Sky Theater on the second floor and it is time well spent. Here the Carl Zeiss instrument (a Bicentennial gift from the Federal Republic of Germany) projects onto the domed ceiling sights not unlike those which might have been seen by the astronauts on their journeys to the moon. Visitors seated in this auditorium can hear an accompanying talk (on headphones programmed to receive selected foreign language broadcasts, or listen to an English talk without headphones) describing the scenes they are passing. It is not uncommon for patrons to imagine themselves seated in a real spacecraft, looking out at a majestic sky, and moving through time and space beyond our galaxy, the Milky Way, to future worlds. Admission to each theater is minimal.

Before visitors enter the building, they may want to take a turn around its outside to examine some fine sculptures. Among them Richard Lippold's "Ad Astra" (To the Stars), Charles Perry's "Continuum," and especially Alejandro Otero's "Delta Solar" on the Seventh Street side which is forty-eight feet by twenty-seven feet and includes rotary sails turning with the slightest breeze.

Those enjoying art seek out the fine artworks inside this building, beginning with two large murals facing each other in the south lobby. While art works are displayed throughout the building and outside around the building's grounds, most are on exhibit in Gallery 211 "Flight in the Arts." Among many drawings, prints, paintings, and sculptures are art works by such well known artists as Norman Rockwell, Robert Rauschenberg, Jamie Wyeth, Alexander Calder, Jim Dine, Robert McCall, Georgia O'Keeffe, and others shown on a rotating basis.

The museum's public services division is constantly engaged in creating programs that appeal to the public, which include lectures, symposiums, films, and tours. Most of these are free. Some are given during daytime hours while others are held at night. To learn more about current programs available while you are in the building, inquire at the Information Desk.

In the south lobby is a large display of trophy and medal awards for many kinds of achievements in air and space. In this lobby, too, is the Information Desk where museum personnel courteously answer many, many questions about the museum—particularly about exhibits mentioned in this chapter which may have been rotated or in storage since the completion of this guide to make room for newer exhibits of crafts or artifacts contributed by NASA or other donors.

According to **Newsweek** the National Air and Space Museum has become the most visited museum in the world. Anyone planning to go there is advised to browse through the following directory and chapter while still at home to get an overview of the galleries and the exhibits contained in them in order to select those that would interest him the most. Each gallery is introduced by a paragraph or two indicating its theme and is then followed by examples of selected exhibits in it.

Part of the National Air and Space Museum's restoration facilities in Suitland, Maryland located about eight miles from the National Air and Space Museum is now an adjunct museum housing a great many aircraft, spacecraft, and a variety of flight-related objects. It is known as the Paul E. Garber Preservation, Restoration, and Storage Facility in honor of Paul E. Garber's devoted service in acquiring much of the Smithsonian's aeronautical collections. There is much of interest that can be seen here for visitors interested in aircraft, rockets, missiles, and spacecraft for which, at present, there is no room on the Mall. Free tours to this facility are given Monday through Friday at 10 a.m.; and Saturday and Sunday at 10 a.m. and 1 p.m. by trained guides, but visitors must make reservations, if possible two weeks in advance to arrange for them. Call (202) 3571400 between 9 a.m. and 4 p.m. Monday through Friday or write to the Tour Scheduler, Education Services Division, National Air and Space Museum, Smithsonian Institution, Washington, D.C. 20560. Children under ten are not permitted on the tours. Special tours for the handicapped can be arranged.

Directory of Galleries and Popular Exhibits

FIRST FLOOR

Gallery 100: Milestones of Flight, p. 206
Langley's Aerodrome #5, 1896
Wright Brothers' 1903 **Kitty Hawk Flyer**
Model of **NC-4** biplane, first plane to cross Atlantic, 1919
Copy of Goddard's 1926 rocket
Lindbergh's **Spirit of St. Louis,** 1927
Goddard's unsuccessful 1941 rocket
Bell X-1, Glamorous Glennis, first plane to fly faster than sound, 1947

Replica of Sputnik, 1957
Back-up of **Explorer I** satellite, 1958
North American X-15, 1959, first plane to fly at Mach 4, 5, 6+
Mercury spacecraft **Friendship 7,** 1962, in which Glenn circled the Earth
Back-up of **Mariner 2,** interplanetary spacecraft, 1962
Gemini 4 spacecraft, 1965 and gold "umbilical cord" of Edward White's first American spacewalk
Apollo 11's Command Module, Columbia, first to land astronauts on moon, 1969

Moonrock brought back by astronauts, 1972
Back-up of **Pioneer 10** spacecraft
launched 1972 to go to outer
planets and its plaque descriptive of Earth
Back-up of **Viking Lander** launched
1976 to make probe of Mars

**Gallery 102: Air Transportation—
Mobility for Mankind,** p. 209
Among other artifacts shown in
this hall are:
Douglas M-2, 1920s
Fairchild FC-2, 1928
Ford Tri-Motor "Tin Goose", 1930
Boeing NC-13369 – "Tuck"
Pitcairn PA-5 Mailwing, 1929-
1934
Northrop Alpha, passenger and
later freight plane
Boeing-247D, United Airlines
passenger plane
Douglas DC-3, United Airlines
passenger plane
Beechcraft, used for local air ser-
vices to supplement services of
larger lines
Cockpit of a **DC-7,** American Air-
lines plane that flew non-stop
across U.S.
Engines used on transport aircraft
Uniforms of air personnel

Gallery 103: Vertical Flight,
p. 211
Replica of Chinese Flying Top,
1100 A.D.
Replica of Leonardo's Helix De-
vice, an artifact for flying
Reconstruction of Cayley's **Con-
verta Plane,** 1843
Model **AC-35,** Pitcairn Rotobile
Auto-Giro, 1936
Model of Sikorsky's **XR-4** Heli-
copter, 1942
Sikorsky **UH-34D** Helicopter
Kellett Autogiro Co. **X0-60** Auto-
giro, 1943
Hiller-Copter **XH-44** Helicopter,
1944
Benson Gyro-Glider, 1954
Reprod. of Bensen Gyro-Copter,

1955
Reprod. Pentecost Hoppicopter
Reprod. Focke-Achgeles **FA-330**
Bell Ranger BH-13-J (Pres. Eisen-
hower flew in it)
Piasecki **PV-2**
Illustrations of other vehicles of
vertical flight:
**Convair X-FY-1; Curtiss-
Wright X-100; Bell ATV,** 1953;
McDonnell XVI-1, 1954; **Ryan
X-1; Hawker-Siddley P.1127;
Kestrel,** 1965, and others
Illustrations of turbine-powered
engines for helicopters; Pratt
and Whitney turbine engine
Film showing the Coast Guard's
use of helicopters for rescue
missions

**Gallery 104: Flying for Fun and
some Significant Military Planes,**
p. 212
This colorful gallery explains the
history of each sport or activity
along with the type and variety
of equipment and techniques
used by those flying different
aircraft or utilizing other equipment. There are kites, plastic
discs, frisbees, boomerangs,
model airplanes of all types and
sizes, parachutes, and hang
gliders. Aerobatics (illustrated)
include wing walking, looping,
rolling overhead, snap rolling,
topple blooping, tail sliding.
Wittman's **Chief Oshkosh**
Turner's **RT-14 Meteor,** and Turner's 1937-39 Special Racer
Models of planes that flew in
Schneider, Thompson, Pulitzer,
and Bendix races and trophies
won
Stunt flying (aerobatics) planes:
Bucker 133 Jungmeister, flown
by "Bevo Howard; Pitts Special;
Curtiss Jenny; Waco 9; Grumman G-22 Gulfhawk II
Fighter planes:
Boeing P-26-A "Peashooter,"
1930s
Grumman G-22 Gulfhawk II

Mustang P-51C "Excalibur III"
Vought F4U-1D Corsair
Film of Colonel Turner and his
pet lion, Gilmore

Gallery 105: General Aviation, p. 214

Planes used for non-airline commuter services, sports, and
business; also films of what is
involved in the basics of flying
Piper PA-12 "City of Washington,"
1946
Beechcraft Bonanza 35 "Waikiki"
flown by Captain Bill Odom
Cessna 180 "Spirit of Columbus"
flown by Geraldine Mock
Gates Learjet
Models of historic planes
1910-1919; 1920-1929;
1930-1939; 1940-1949;
1950-1959; 1960-1969
Engines of a variety of aircraft

Gallery 106: Jet Aviation, p. 215

Large mural in which Keith Ferris
depicts evolution of jet air-
planes with 27 significant planes
Among pioneers of jet propulsion
for military and commercial
purposes; Hans von Chain, Ger-
many; Sir Fred Whittle, Gr.
Britain; others from Japan,
Sweden, France, USSR, Italy,
Hungary, Canada and USA
Among models and some jet planes:
HE-178; Gloster 28/29;
DeHaviland DH-106; Comet 3;
Hawker-Siddeley Tridente; Rock-
well International B1; Bede B-D;
MacDonald-Douglas DC-10;
MacDonald FH-1 and F-4 Phan-
toms; North American P-51
Mustang; Messerschmidt ME-262
Schwalbe; Lockheed XP-80
Among important engines shown
are those for turbojets, turbo-
props, ramjets, and turbofans
from many countries
Mock-up of an advanced flight
deck
Film "Sneaking Through the Sound
Barrier

Changes in apparel worn by personnel
Exhibit with explanation of historic propellers

Gallery 107: Early Flight: From Dream to Reality, p. 217

Scenes in a commercial indoor
aereo show with Wright, Cur-
tiss, Bleriot, and other U.S. and
European companies promoting
their planes with talking man-
nequins, movies, music, posters
Reprod. of Lilienthal Hang Glider,
1894
Photographs of world's great aviators and their planes of early
1900s:
Eugene Lefere, Leon Dela-
grange, Henri Farman, Hubert
Latham, Glenn Curtiss, Eugene
Ely, Hugh Robinson, Calbraith
P. Rodgers, Captain Albert
Berry
Illustrations of "firsts" in aviation
history: Wright brothers Type A
Military Flyer, 1909; Bleriot
Aeronautics, 1909—the first
plane to fly across the English
Channel; Eugene Ely's landing
his plane on U.S.S. Penn., 1911;
Hugh Robinson's air-sea rescue,
1911; Rodger's transcontinental
trip, 1911; Berry's parachute
jump, 1912; Sperry's automatic
pilot, 1912; Sperry's gyroscopic
stabilizer, 1914; A.V. Roe (Eng.)
who designed first enclosed
cabin, 1912; Fabre (Fr.) who designed first planes to take off
and land on water
Illustrations of "Women in Flight":
Mme. Thible (Fr. 1784) first
woman to fly in a balloon,
Therese Petier, Raymonde de la
Roche, Helene Dutrieux, Harriet Quimby, Bernetta Miller,
Alys McKey Bryant, Marjorie
and Katherine Stinson, Ruth Law
Models, illus. or the actual engines
of early aeronautical engine
builders: John Stringfellow,
Samuel Langley, Wright brothers,

Glenn Curtiss, Seguin brothers

Gallery 109: Flight Testing,
p. 219
Design theories of aircraft including wind tunnels used;
working wind tunnels explained;
cross-section of a subsonic wind
tunnel; blueprints for aircraft
designs
Large exhibit with models, illustrations and apparel worn for
"Flight Testing from the Wright
Brothers Through World War II"
Comparison of test pilot clothing
worn in 1935 and in 1965
Wiley Post's **Winnie Mae** and pressure suit he designed
Films of flight testing done by
courageous pilots
X-P-59-A **Aircomet,** 1942, first
American experimental turbo-
jet
Hawker-Siddeley **XV 6A Kestrel,**
vertical flight craft using rotors
or direct jet thrust to lift off
directly and then move horizontally
Scale model of **Consolidated NY-
2,** 1929, Doolittle made first
blind flight in it
Large exhibit with models, illustrations, and devices showing:
telemeter transmitter, oscillator, power supply
Bell XS-1 equipment showing pressure recorder, film drums, other
artifacts
Radio jeep—an air ground flight
test communication vehicle
Tomahawk Cruise Missile, 1975, a
U.S. naval guided missile

**Gallery 110: Satellites and Sound-
ing Rockets,** p. 220
Chronology of U.S. satellite and
sounding rocket development
for scientific and astronomical
research; weather forecasting
and tracking; military reconnaissance; exploration; surveying of crop lands, forests and
minerals; distress calls by

downed planes; relaying telephone calls; others
All exhibits of satellites and
sounding rockets in this gallery
are usually back-up or scale
models of launched crafts
Biological satellites carrying
plants, frog eggs, and microorganisms to test radiation,
weightlessness and other factors
Sounding rockets that could parachute or telemeter information
to Earth: **WAC Corporal,** 1945; **Viking
Rocket,** 1954; **Aerobee 150,**
1954; **Nike Cajun,** 1956; also
**Honeybee; Farside; Loki Dart;
Cricket; Arcas; Nike Smoke;**
others
Satellites: **Explorer I** (cut-away
model), series of **Explorers,
Pioneers, Tiros, Itos, Ariels,
Landsats, Echos, Scores, Couriers, Oscars, Intelsats, Loftis,
Telstars, Relays,** others
Westar (Western Union) can transmit in 12 color television channels, or up to 14,000 one-way
telephone circuits, and in computer data transmissions can
handle 6,000,000 bits per second
(1974)

**Gallery 111: Stars: From Stone-
henge to the Space Telescope,**
p. 223
Mock-up of Stonehenge, the original was set up for celestial
observation by the Druids, 1845
B.C.
Exhibits describe the study of the
sun with telescopes and various
other astronomical instruments
used (some of them operational)
A mock-up of the Sun describing
its chemical elements, its prominences, its solar storms, solar
flares, and sun spots and other
dynamic forces that go on constantly in its interior and at its
surface
A section of a back-up of the
Apollo Telescope Mount (ATM),

a manned solar observatory in space

Scale models of a Space Telescope Satellite and its optical telescope assembly to be launched in 1985 that will record high radiation astronomical images, detect extremely faint objects, collect spectographic data, make very precise measurements of the position of radiant sources in the sky

Suspended from the ceiling is satellite **Copernicus**—that is capable of examining the ultraviolet spectra of stars

Suspended from the ceiling is the International Ultra-violet **Explorer** satellite (IUE) used as a guide for high energy studies

A computer operated glossary of astronomical terms that gives the visitor some definitions of unfamiliar astronomical words and phrases

Gallery 112: East Gallery: Unmanned Lunar Exploration Vehicles, p. 225

Replica of **Ranger** with its cameras that took television pictures of the moon's surface, 1961–65

Back-up of **Lunar Orbiter,** whose cameras took pictures of 95% of moon's surface including the dark side of the moon

Back-up of **Surveyor** that tested lunar surface, sampled lunar soil, did chemical analysis preparatory for selecting landing sites, 1966 and 1968

Back-up of **Eagle** showing upper and lower stages of Apollo's manned golden lunar module, the original lower stage left on the moon

Gallery 113: Rocketry and Space Flight, p. 226

Model of interstellar space ship **Star Trek**

Illustrations of Arabian and Chinese tales told by men who dreamed of space flight

Illustrations of Johannas Kepler's and Francis Godwin's allegories of flying to the moon

Books by Jules Verne displayed: **From Earth to the Moon; Around the Moon**

Schemes of flight devised by Chinese, Leonardo and others illustrated

Rockets for military purposes: model of Englishman William Congreve's rocket; illustrations of German Werner von Braun's V-2 rocket

Rockets for non-military purposes illustrated: harpooning whales; rescuing ships in distress; used by ships, airplanes, and on the ground for distress signals

Work of important pioneers in step-rocketry discussed and illustrated: Roumanian Herman Oberth, Russian Konstantin Tsiolkovsky, American Robert Goddard

Engines used on rockets are displayed: RL-10 to boost **Viking** and **Surveyor** crafts; F-1 Turbopump; LR-87 to power **Titan II CBM**; V-2 German rocket engine; a liquid propellent engine used for Saturn and IBM launch vehicles; a retrorocket engine using asphalt propellant grains used on **Surveyor** to bring lunar module down to the moon; rocket engines of the future

Chronological display of spacesuits worn by astronauts

Gallery 114: Space Hall, p. 228

Exhibits show some original artifacts wherever possible, but those that could not be returned from space are shown here by back-ups, replicas, or models

Back-up of **Skylab Orbital Workshop** showing: systems for solar electrical power; telescope mount; multiple docking adaptor; wardroom, sleeping quar-

202 National Air and Space Museum

ters, workroom, and exercise
Model of Saturn V booster rocket
that launched lunar module
Columbia
Replica of a **Saturn V** engine
cleverly mirrored so there appears to be 5 engines (there
were 5 in the cluster that boosted the **Apollo Command Module
Columbia** to the moon)
Models of other booster rockets:
Atlas-Centaur; Titan 3-C
Models of German rockets; air to
air missiles; ground to air
Rheintochter V-1; and V-2 "buzz
bombs"
Four original American rockets in
a 15 foot pit: **Jupiter-C** launched
satellite **Explorer I** and others;
Vanguard launched three satel-
lites; **Scout D** was first solid-
propellant rocket to launch a
satellite; **Minuteman III**, an in-
tercontinental ballistic missile
Mock-up showing inside of **Lunar
Command Module**
Back-up of Lunar Rover Vehicle
Replica of the docking of **Apollo-
Soyuz**
Models of satellites launched for
planetary research: **Pioneer 11**
launched in 1973 by an **Atlas-
Centaur; Mariner 10** launched
in 1973 by an **Atlas-Centaur;
Voyagers I** and **II** launched in
1977
Model of **Space Shuttle Columbia**

SECOND FLOOR

Gallery 203: Sea-Air Operations,
p. 230
Simulated deck of aircraft car-
rier and hangar deck
Aircraft of World War II:
Boeing F4B-4; Grumman FM-1
Wildcat; Douglas **SBD Daunt-
less;** Douglas **A-4E Skyhawk,**
others
Illustrations of Navy ships:
USS Forrestal CV-59; USS

**Nimitz Cun-68; USS Taraw
LHA-1; USS Lexington CV-2;
USS Essex CV-9; USS Indepen-
dence CVL-22; USS Casablanca
CVE-55; USS Midway CV-41;
USS Enterprise CV-6;** others
Illustrations of Eugene Ely's take
off and landing on carrier; a
first in aircraft history
Models and photographs of:
**Fokker FVII-3M Southern Cross;
Bleriot XI; Fabre Hydravion;
Curtiss Navy Seaplane A-1,**
others
Brief biographies of: Amelia Ear-
hart and the red Lockheed **Vega**
she flew; Lindbergh's brief biog-
raphy
Uniforms of members of U.S. Navy
and Marine Corps
Films showing activities seen from
side of carrier: planes taking off
carrier; mock combat; planes
returning to carrier
On second level balcony:
Primary Flight Control Area
(PRIFLY)
Navigation Bridge
Museum showing artifacts of sea-
air operations

Gallery 205: World War II Aviation,
p. 232
Exhibit describing exploits of Gen-
eral Chennault and the Flying
Tigers
Fighter planes in World War II:
**Mustang P-51-D; Grumman
F6F; Martin B-26 B Flak Bait;
Spitfire Hawker Hurricane; War-
hawk; Mosquito; Defiant; Fol-
gore; Zero; Messerschmitt
Bf.109;** others and models of
others
Bombers of World War II:
Thunderbird (most widely used
bomber); **Halifax; Lancaster;**
models of others
Engines noted for performance in
planes: Pratt & Whitney R2800
Double Wasp; Rolls Royce Mer-
lin—Mark 64; A-65-8 (U.S. Army
standard engine); others

Uniforms of pilots of U.S. and
  German aviation corps
History of Eagle Squadron (an all
  American fighting squadron)

**Gallery 206: Balloons and Air-
ships,** p. 234
History of Montgolfier brothers
  (Fr.) and their pioneering work
  with balloons
Puppet show: humorous story of
  1785 balloon flight across the
  English Channel by an American
  and a Frenchman
Balloons for meteorological and
  other scientific purposes: **The
  American,** first balloon to fly
  across the Rockies; **Explorers,**
  scientific balloons in the upper
  atmosphere
Balloons for military purposes
  during: Civil War, Siege of
  Paris, World Wars I and II,
  WWII Japanese bombs sent
  across Pacific by balloons
Cabin of advertising Goodyear
  blimp **Pilgrim**
Zeppelins: 30 foot model of **Hindenburg,** illustration of **Graf
  Zeppelin;** exhibit showing luxurious furnishings of **Hindenburg** and **Graf Zeppelin**
Double Eagle II (first balloon to
  cross Atlantic); exhibit and
  film tell history of this flight;
  mannequins dressed in clothing
  worn by the pilots; artifacts
  carried on the **Double Eagle II**

**Gallery 207: Exploring the Plan-
ets,** p. 235
History of unmanned space exploration (back-ups, models, or
  illustrations of crafts sent to
  explore the planets) of our
  solar system to gather scientific information and take photographs: **Pioneer 10** and **11**
  sent to explore Jupiter, Saturn,
  Venus, Uranus and take photograph; **Mariner 9** photographed
  surface of the moon; crashed
  on the moon; **Surveyor** series

photographed surface of the
  moon; **Mariner** and **Viking
  Landers 1** and **2** landed on Mars;
  surveyed Mars, sent back photographs; **Viking Landers 1** and **2**
  used robot arms to bring into
  satellite for testing purposes
  samples of soil, air, and gases
  on Mars, information which was
  relayed to Earth; **Mariner 10**
  took photographs of Mercury;
  Venera 9 (Russian) landed on
  Venus, sent back photographs;
  Voyagers 1 and **2** sent back
  spectacular photographs of Jupiter, and outer planets
Exhibit "Mars Overflight Unit"
  gives the visitor an opportunity
  to look through a special lens
  which makes it possible to view
  the Martian surface as an astronaut might see it
Exhibit "Descent to Venus in the
  Year 2250" shows the cladding
  space ships and astronauts would
  need as they descend to the
  900° surface through dense and
  noxious gases
Ptolemy's astronomical ideas are
  discussed in an exhibit
Copernicus, Kepler, and Galileo's
  theories discussed in an exhibit
History of telescopes and the discoveries they helped make of
  planets and their satellites

**Gallery 208: Pioneers of Flight:
Aircraft Used on Famous First
Flights,** p. 238
Gossmer Condor, the first successful self-propelled craft; won
  prize in 1977 (Bryan Allen)
Vin Fiz, made the first transcontinental flight, 1911 (Rodgers)
Fokker T-2, a monoplane that
  made the first non-stop transcontinental flight, 1923 (Kelly
  and MacCready)
Douglass Chicago made the first
  American flight around the
  world (1924) (Smith and Arnold)
Tingnissartoq flown by Charles
  and Anne Lindbergh to survey

first overseas routes for international flights, 1931

Curtiss R3C-2, seaplane in which
Jimmy Doolittle won the Schneider Trophy, 1925

Brief biographies of other pioneers: Grover Loening, developer
of amphibian craft; Jacqueline
Cochran, among many other accomplishments won the Bendix
Trophy, 1938; Amelia Earhart,
among many other accomplishments was the first woman to
make a solo flight across the
Atlantic

**Gallery 209: World War I Avia-
tion,** p. 239

A recreation of part of the military airfield near Verdun,
France

Planes of World War I:
Fokker D VII; Spads VII and
XVI; Albatross D VA

Models of World War I planes:
**Vickers FB-5 Gun Bus; Rumpler
C-B; Moraine Saulman; Bristol
F-2 B** and **DH-4; Fokker E-111;
SE-5A; PF ALZ-D 111, Ansaldo
Sua; Spad XII, Nieuport 28;
Fokker D VII; Sopwith Camel,**
and others

Engines used on World War I
planes: Hispano-Suiza (Fr.);
Gnome **Monosoupipe** (Fr.),
others

Uniforms, decorations, and trophies of armed forces in World
War I

Photographs of fighter aces in
World War I

Bronze statue of General Billy
Mitchell, commander of American Airforces in World War I

Taped conversation (not authentic)
between Americans questioning
German pilot who mistakenly
landed his **Fokker D. VII** on
allied airfield

Gallery 210: Apollo to the Moon,
p. 240

Steps taken prior to Apollo 11's

landing on the moon:
animal and biological experiments in space; Mercury
flights described; astronaut
Alan B. Shepard, Jr.'s first
American orbital flight around
the Earth, 1961, in **Freedom 7**
(exhibited); other Mercury
flights

Gemini flights described: ten unmanned flights; first American
walk in space, 1965, by Astro.
Edward White II from Gemini 4;
Astro. Borman and Lovell, Jr.'s
flight in Gemini 7, 1965 (command module exhibited) and its
rendezvous with Gemini 6 (carrying Astro. Schirra and Stafford)

Apollo flights described: Apollo 7
(Astro. Schirra, Eisile, Cunningham) eleven day flight in earth
orbit, 1968; Apollo 8 (Astro.
Borman, Lovell, Anders) first
craft free of earth's gravity,
1968, went into lunar orbit;
Apollo 8 (Astro. McDivitt,
Scott, Schweickart), 1969, flew
in earth's orbit carrying lunar
module; Apollo 10 (Astro. Cernan, Young, Stafford) went into
lunar orbit and did a rehearsal
of a command and lunar module's rendezvous; Apollo 11
(Astro. Armstrong, Aldrin,
Collins), 1969, tells of Armstrong and Aldrin's landing on
the moon in the lunar module
while Collins circled moon in
the command module; recorded
conversation of Apollo 11's astronauts replayed; other Apollo
landings on the moon (12, 14,
15, 16, 17) described; illustrations of all Apollo crafts and
astronauts shown

Dioramas of Apollo spacecraft
show mannequins dressed as
astronauts on the moon engaged
in work; duplicates of scientific
packages for experiments, tools,
cameras; duplicate of Apollo
14's two wheeled cart to carry

equipment (MET) and of the
Lunar Rover Vehicle (LRV) carried on Apollos 15, 16, 17; other
artifacts include duplicates of
lunar portable magnetometer,
lunar drill, freeze-dried food,
oral hygiene kit, waste disposal
system, sleeping restraint assembly, other artifacts

Engines: Back-ups of: lunar descent engine, lunar ascent engine

Console of simulator used for astronaut training

Exhibit "Snap-Dash 27" describes:
Apollos' radio isotope thermal
electric generator and fuel supply

A re-enactment of Apollo 17's
lunar landing (Astro. Cernan
and Schmitt) describes final descent

Exhibit "Development of Man's
Space Flight" 1957-1980, traces
the chronological development
of space flight

Models of launch vehicles: Mercury
Redstone used in suborbital
flight of Grissom and Shepard;
Mercury **Atlas** used in earth
orbital flights of Carpenter,
Shirra and Cooper; Gemini **Titan**
I used in two-man Gemini earth
orbits; **Saturn IB** used to launch
Apollo 7, the crews of Skylab
Orbital Workshop, and the U.S.
crew of the Apollo-Soyuz dock-
ing **Saturn V** used to launch
Apollos 7 through 17

Models of lunar module designs:
early designs (1963), Apollo
lunar module (1965)

"Apollo Results Exhibit" scientific
results of missions that landed
on the moon

Large exhibit of the moon showing
its physical features: Apollo
landing sites

Gallery 211: Flight and the Arts,
p. 243

Famous artists and some less well-
known have created the art

works display of paintings,
sculptures, prints, and drawings
inspired by air and space exploits and by individuals who
participated in them

In addition to the works in Gallery
211, other art works are located
throughout the building, at entrances, and around the grounds
of the National Air and Space
Museum

The Information Desk in the lobby
on the first floor carries a complete listing of artists and their
art works that are part of the
National Air and Space Museum's collection or those on loan
to the museum

Gallery 213: Flight Technology,
p. 245

Hughes H-1 Racer, the airplane
built by Howard Hughes in 1935
was powered by a Pratt & Whitney Twin Wasp Junior radial
piston engine; the plane had a
revolutionary impact on high
performance aircraft in the
years that followed

A cut-away model of a Pratt &
Whitney R985 radial piston engine has its parts labeled and a
recorded talk that helps explain
its working parts and their functions

Exhibits on the designs of crafts
and the principles of flight include explanations and demonstrations of aerodynamic concepts: lift, drag, thrust, stream-
lining, etc.; in some instance
demonstrated with working
models of wind tunnels.

Workings of a jet propulsion engine is explained using a labeled
model to show its parts and a
cartoon to show how the engine
operates

Films show past and present developments in aerospace technology

Panels around the inside walls list
contributors to flight technology

(beginning with the Wright brothers); their specific contributions to flight technology is recorded on the panels; and, in addition, world events are noted that took place during the time of each individual's contribution.

Around the Balcony, p. 245

There are exhibited many famous aircraft, among them the **Lockheed F-104A Starfighter**, the first fighter craft capable of operating at mach 2 (twice the speed of sound); and a **Douglas D-558-2 Skyrocket** that can also travel at twice the speed of sound.

Two Theaters in the NASM, p. 246

On the first floor in the Samuel P. Langley Theater (Gallery 115) are shown some fantastic films on a five by seven story screen. These are mainly concerned with flight in various craft such as balloon, hang gliders, and airplanes so realistic the visitor feels he has participated in the flight.
Headphones are provided at the seats for languages other than English.
Entrance fees are minimal.
On the second floor in the Albert Einstein Sky Theater (Gallery 215) visitors view some marvels of space travel projected on a domed ceiling which gives a feeling of traveling in a spacecraft and looking out of windows onto scenes one could never experience on earth.
Headphones are provided at the seats for languages other than English.
Entrance fees are minimal.
On Thursdays at noon free illustrated planetarium lectures are given.
On the first Saturday of each month a free monthly sky lecture is given that begins promptly at 9 a.m. Visitors must use the 6th and Independence Ave. entrance, the only one open at that hour.

The Paul Garber Facility, p. 247

Located in Suitland, Maryland (about 8 miles from the National Air and Space Museum). This is a preservation, restoration and storage facility of the National Air and Space Museum; it is also an adjunct museum.
Tours by reservation only can be arranged. (See QuickGuide for further information.)

Bulletin Boards

Visitors are urged to consult bulletin boards for any special presentations that might be available during the time of your visit.
The General Electric Aircraft Engine Group made possible a free series of aviation lectures. One of these was **The Tokyo Raid** given by Col. Robert G. Emmens, USAF (Ret.).
Free films given in the Langley Theater on Space Fiction or other subjects are available, at certain times of the year on a first come, first served basis.
Other film or lecture series are presented free. Consult the bulletin boards.

Descriptions of Galleries and Exhibits

Gallery 100: Milestones of Flight (First Floor)

In this central gallery with its huge windows facing the Mall are some of the most significant and impressive artifacts in the museum. These represent major achievements of man that show planes, rockets, satellites, modules, and models of some not available to be shown. Labels affixed on pylons around the hall describe and help clarify exhibited artifacts.

One of the earliest crafts shown is Langley's 1896 **Aerodrome #5,** a steam-powered unmanned vehicle that was catapulted from a houseboat. It splashed down in the Potomac River after flying about 3,000 feet at 25 miles per hour for less than two minutes. Langley tried unsuccessfully again and again to launch a manned vehicle, the last time in November 1903. Six weeks after Langley's last try, on December 17, 1903 the Wright brothers, with great technical insight and engineering skills, succeeded where Langley had failed. Their **Kitty Hawk Flyer** shown here, a small plane with twin wooden propellers, flew 100 feet in 59 seconds, establishing a first in the history of man-powered flight. Exhibited in a place of honor with nothing to obstruct it from public view (a stipulation the Wright heirs made when donating the plane to the Smithsonian) it attracts a large viewing audience.

A model of the **NC-4,** a Curtiss four engine biplane, is shown. The original (now located in Pensacola, Florida) was the first plane (1919) to fly the Atlantic, taking fifteen days to cross. It started with its six men aboard from Newfoundland making stops in the Azores, Portugal, and then England.

On May 20-21, 1927 Charles Lindbergh made his historic non-stop flight from New York to Paris in the **Spirit of St. Louis,** a Ryan monoplane fitted with a 220 horsepower Wright 15 Whirlwind radial engine, in 33 hours and 30 minutes. While Lindbergh was still in flight a cable was dispatched from the Smithsonian to the Le Bourge Airfield asking him to donate the **Spirit of St. Louis** to the Institution. Lindbergh consented and that made it possible for millions to see this renowned plane displayed in this hall.

Robert H. Goddard, known as the "father of American rocketry," was responsible for the first American designs to incorporate the principles of rocket flight, which were later applied to long-range rockets and space boosters. His work was as important to space exploration as the Wright brothers' was to aviation. On display in this hall is a copy of Goddard's first (1926) rocket that was propelled by liquid fuel. It flew for just two and a half seconds, but in that time it rose to a height of forty-one feet traveling sixty miles per hour. His 1941 rocket is also shown, but due to some malfunction it did not fly.

A record was made on October 14, 1947 when Captain Charles Yeager (despite two broken ribs he sustained when he fell from a horse) flew the **Bell X-I** plane **Glamorous Glennis** that reached a speed of Mach 1.06. He was the first person to fly faster than sound. This famous plane is shaped like a speeding bullet and has a rocket engine which Yeager was able to successfully maneuver until it flew 700 miles per hour.

The world was electrified when **Sputnik,** a satellite launched by the Soviet Union on October 4, 1957, became the first man-made object placed in orbit around the Earth and which transmitted important space data. It burned up on January 4, 1958 while reentering the Earth's atmosphere. On exhibit is a replica of the original, a model on loan from the USSR's Academy of Sciences. Shortly after **Sputnik I**'s demise, **Explorer I**, a successful American-made research satellite was launched by a Jupiter C rocket on January 31, 1958. The original **Explorer I** (the one shown here is a back-up model) measured cosmic rays and radiation levels, data which led to the discovery of the Van Allen belts, and tracked encounters with micrometeorites monitoring their interior temperatures.

The **North American X-15** plane shown here was launched from a modified **Boeing B-52 Stratofortress** aircraft in 1959. The importance of the X-15 rocket-powered research aircraft lay in its ability to attain speed six times faster than sound. Bridging the gap between manned flight in the atmosphere and manned flight into space, it was the first plane to fly at Mach 4, 5, 6+, roughly 4,500 miles an hour (more than three times as fast as the **Concorde**). The X-15s flew higher than any other plane, one of them reaching a height of sixty-seven miles above the Earth (almost into space).

On February 20, 1962 John Glenn, Jr. became the first American to orbit the Earth in the Mercury spacecraft **Friendship 7** shown here. It circled the Earth three times and splashed down in the Atlantic Ocean four hours and fifty-five minutes after launch. It had been launched from an Atlas launch vehicle and tested the performance of weightless conditions for a pilot flying at a speed of 17,540 miles per hour.

Late in 1962 the original interplanetary spacecraft, **Mariner 2**, was launched from an Atlas Agena launch vehicle. The **Mariner 2** shown here is a back-up craft. The original **Mariner 2** flew past and probed the environment of Venus telemetering back information about that planet and about space on its way to Venus. It is now in orbit around the sun.

Another impressive "first" was achieved in space when Edward White became the first American to walk in space tethered to a "gold umbilical cord" that was attached to the spacecraft **Gemini 4** which had been launched from a **Titan II** booster in June 1965. His fellow astronaut, James McDivitt, had a difficult time persuading White, enchanted with the sights, to return to the spacecraft. Both the **Gemini 4** and the gold support line are exhibited.

The **Apollo 11 Command Module Columbia** was part of the space vehicle which took three astronauts (Neil Armstrong, Edwin Aldrin, and Michael Collins) to the moon in July 1969. While Collins stayed in this space capsule orbiting the moon, Armstrong and Aldrin took the lunar module **Eagle** (see the back-up model in Gallery 112) down for a soft landing on the moon. As he got out to walk on the moon the world heard Armstrong (with the help of television) say, "That's one small step for man, one giant leap for mankind." Later, when their work on the moon was completed, they returned in the upper part of the **Eagle** to rendezvous with the **Columbia** (see more in Gallery 210). The three astronauts then returned to Earth in the **Command Module Columbia**, an adventure which was certainly more electrifying than **Sputnik** and which held the world enthralled as they watched the American astronauts on television. Exhibited in this gallery is the **Columbia Command Module** with a mannequin representing Michael Collins inside lying on his back dressed in a white spacesuit while in front and above him are all of the instruments the astronauts needed to guide the craft. While on display in this hall the **Columbia Command Module** is protected by a plexiglass covering, but one of the rocks brought back from the moon in 1972 and displayed here has no covering—visitors are invited to touch this ancient rock and then they can go back and tell their friends, "I touched a piece of moon rock over four and one-half billion years old."

Pioneer 10 (the satellite displayed here is a back-up model), the craft that was sent in March 1972 on a space probe of Jupiter, was the first spacecraft to go to the outer planets. It reached Jupiter in 1974 gathering scientific data and sent back photographs of the planet. Its sensors were able to detect and send back the first readings of Jupiter's environment; in 1976 it sent back information about Saturn; in 1979 information about Venus. In 1987 it is expected to send back information about Uranus and Pluto after which it is expected to leave our solar system. On the remote chance that the satellite might some day come close to another star system and eventually be found by other beings, there is attached to **Pioneer 10** a plaque engraved with images of a man and a woman, the location of our planet, Earth, and other basic scientific information that could conceivably be understood by intelligent beings. Later satellites (not shown here but some shown as models in Gallery 114) are **Pioneer 11** and **Voyagers I** and II which probed the planets Jupiter and Saturn and sent back even more spectacular photographs with far sharper images and greater details than those ever made of these planets.

Viking Lander I (a twin of the satellite shown here) landed on Mars in 1976. **Viking I** was launched to test for positive signs of life on the planet's surface (none were detected), and to check out geological and meteorological conditions on Mars. One of the testing devices was a small shovel which moved out from the vehicle and scooped up soil from Mars's surface, returning it to the inside of the craft, analyzing that soil with chemicals programmed to perform this task and telemetering the results back to Earth.

Gallery 102: Air Transportation: Mobility for Mankind (First Floor)

The vehicles in this hall were landmarks in the evolution of civilian aircraft, planes that transported passengers, mail, and cargo. The history of commercial flights began with the St. Petersburg-Tampa Airboat Line in 1914 using a Benoit Type XIV biplane flying boat, but it was short lived. It was not until 1919 that irregular periods of commercial flights using Curtiss F-5L flying boats began with U.S. Aeromarine flights. Later Ford **Tri-Motors** came on the scene.

Ford **Tri-Motor** all-metal planes began service in this country as passenger planes in 1926. They have since been used all over the world. The original planes seated fourteen passengers in wicker seats. Known as the "**Tin Goose**," Ford **Tri-Motor** planes served on regular United States routes for transportation in the early 1930s, and after World War II they were used in Nicaragua and Mexico for passenger and cargo hauling. Later they were used for crop dusting. The plane in this gallery is a 5-AT-B, NC 9683, a plane built by Ford and owned and used by American Airlines. This company donated the plane to the National Air and Space Museum.

The need for quick delivery of mail caused the U.S. Post Office Department to purchase some Douglas M-2s in the late 1920s for use as mail planes. These carried Liberty engines. One of the Douglas M-2s of that era is exhibited. In 1928 a Fairchild FC-2, which had wings that could fold for easy storage, made the first international airmail, passenger, and freight flight from Lima, Peru to Guayaquil, Ecuador. The Boeing NC-13369, shown here, was used for mail on express service in the United States and bore the nickname "Tuck." The Pitcairn PA-5 **Mailwing**, a pioneer single seat biplane shown in this gallery was especially designed to carry mail stowed in a compartment forward of the cockpit. Between 1929 and 1934 these planes helped establish major airmail routes. These planes were later used as passenger planes, and, still later, as crop dusters.

The designer of the Northrop Alpha shown here made quite a change for the better comfort of the four passengers it carried enclosed in heated cabins. He also designed new types of wings, fuselage, landing gears, and other useful features. Although at first a passenger plane, the Northrop Alpha later became a freight carrier which was important for swift coast to coast flights of perishable merchandise.

The Boeing-247D shown here was another important passenger airplane. It was fast enough to have been flown in various air races. The Boeing-247D plane was used as a passenger plane by United Airlines beginning in 1933, and succeeded in making at that time the flight from San Francisco to New York in nineteen and one half hours, about eight hours less than its competitors.

The Douglas DC-3s, propeller-driven planes made by the Douglas Aircraft Company, were called "work horses." These planes were to the history of the airplane what the early Fords were to automobiles. They were used not only as passenger planes, but were also used as military planes (the C-47 was called the "Gooney Bird"). The Douglas DC-3s began flying in 1935. By 1942 they carried at least eighty percent of the world's air traffic. They were retired from service by Eastern Airlines in 1952, but are still found in use around the world. The DC-3 which hangs from the ceiling in this gallery has painted on it the red and white Eastern Airline logo. It had clocked more than 56,000 hours in the air before it was retired.

Another very useful plane exhibited in this gallery is the Beechcraft Model 18 first produced in 1937 and manufactured for about thirty years because it was considered the best small twin engine transport in the world. It was a strong, fast plane that was easily maintained, especially useful for smaller airlines for local air service that covered every one of the 48 contiguous states as well as for Alaska and Hawaii. The Beechcraft Model 18s were used to supplement services offered by larger airlines.

The cockpit of a DC-7 shown in this gallery was on a plane belonging to American Airlines that went non-stop across the country, the first airline to offer such a service. Their piston engine planes were later replaced by turbine-engine powered ones.

In a very large diorama visitors can see a mannequin sitting before a panel board testing control conditions for a General Electric CF-6 turbo-jet fan engine. Other exhibits in this area, called "Propulsion for Air Transportation", show three types of engines on transport aircraft: the liquid-cooled in-line, the air-cooled radial, and the turbo-jet. Among the engines displayed are a Rolls Royce Dart Turboprop engine; a Rolls Royce RB 211 Turbofan engine; Wright R-3350 "Cyclone 18" Piston engine; Pratt & Whitney R-1830 Twin Wasp Piston engine; and a Liberty Piston engine.

The uniforms of some of the air personnel are exhibited in this hall. Included among these historic uniforms are: that of a pilot on the Transcontinental & Western Air, Inc., 1931; a stewardess of Transcontinental & Western Airlines, 1934; a stewardess of American Airlines, 1936-37; a flight steward on Eastern Airlines of the 1940s; a maintenance man on Western Airlines of the 1960s; a Captain in the service of Lufthansa German Airlines; a sales agent of Continental Airlines of 1979; and others.

Gallery 103: Vertical Flight: Helicopters, Autogyros, and Special Vehicles (First Floor)

The Chinese in 1100 had devised a top that was designed to fly. It was more of a toy, but it could fly. A replica of one of these Chinese flying tops is shown. It was Leonardo da Vinci who had an idea four hundred years ago of a helix device that could fly, but it proved unable to do so. A replica of it is shown in this hall. It took modern technology and materials that were not available earlier, but were required to construct and fly the vertical flight craft so much in use today. Exhibits in this hall represent some of the signposts in the evolution of these craft.

Cayley's **Converta Plane** was an early attempt at vertical flight. Suspended from the ceiling of this hall is a reconstruction of Cayley's 1843 model. Almost a hundred years later, in 1936, the Pitcairn Autogiro Company flew its AC-35. Called the **Rotobile Autogiro**, the craft made its first landing in a small park in Washington, D.C. It could not only fly, but could be used (with minor adjustments) as a road vehicle, the front wheels being used for steering. A model of this Pitcairn AC-35 is shown in this hall.

Igor Sikorsky's name is very prominent in the design of flight craft. Sikorsky designed not only the 1938 lift and tort device shown here but also the XR-4 helicopter, a model which Sikorsky built in 1942 for the army which is shown. An XR-4 made the first successful American cross-country helicopter flight. A Sikorsky UH-34D, used chiefly by the marines, is also shown. One of them played an important role in recovering Allen Shepard when he splashed down in **Freedom 7** in 1961.

Also in 1942, the Kellet Autogiro Corporation designed the X0-60 **Autogiro** for the Army Air Force. The X0-60 could take off and land almost vertically, and could remain close to the ground hovering at slow speeds. A 1943 X0-60 craft is on display here.

A year later the first Hiller-Copter craft was built. The 1944 Hiller-Copter shown here was the first helicopter to use all-metal rotor blades and the first to successfully fly in western United States. Also shown are the Bensen **Gyro-Glider**, first airborne in 1954, and the Bensen **Gyro-Copter** that followed in 1955. Like the **Rotobile Autogiro**, these craft could be driven as cars on the road and used by laymen, and then stored in a garage.

Pentecost's **Hoppicopter** was a not very successful vehicle consisting of a small engine, a pair of coaxial counter-rotating blades, a control stick and other parts which all fitted over a pilot's shoulders and were attached to his body by harnesses. Hiller's **Flying Platform** was a small circular vehicle on which a pilot stood. It was designed to be a sort of airborne motorcycle. It, too, was unsuccessful. The **Focke-Achgeles FA-330** was a German collapsible helicopter flown in World War II which could be stored in a watertight hatch on board a ship. All of these are shown in reproductions in this hall.

Illustrations of other forms of vertical flight shown here include: **Convair X-FY-1; Curtiss-Wright X-100; Bell ATV,** 1953; **McDonnell XV-1,** 1954; **Ryan X-1, 3 Vertijet,** 1955; and **Hawker Siddley P.1127 Kestrel,** 1965. Turbine power for helicopter illustrations show those for a Sikorsky **S-64E Skycrane; Kaman K-5; Boeing-Vertol CH-47;** and a turbine engine conversion that was used in a Sikorsky **J-58J.**

The honor of the first helicopter to carry a president belongs to the 1957 **Bell Ranger BH-13-J** shown here. The president was Eisenhower who made the trip as part of a military exercise.

Other exhibits feature a 1968 Pratt & Whitney **PT 6T-6 Twin Pak** turbine engine, as well as descriptions of helicopter controls with the principles of autogiro operation.

A **Piasecki PV-2** helicopter is displayed and a special exhibit shows the many life-saving roles played by United States Coast Guard helicopters.

Gallery 104: Flying for Fun, and Some Significant Military Airplanes (First Floor)

The colorful exhibits in this gallery show examples of flights participated in by pilots for entertainment, sports, and competitions. The exhibits feature planes, sailplanes, balloons, dirigibles, kites, parachutes, flying discs, hang gliders, boomerangs, frisbees, model airplanes of all types and sizes, and some show historic specimens of those which participated in particular sports or activities. There are dioramas and films of sport flying, barnstorming aerobatics, air racing, and air shows. In the early days pilots added glamour to carnivals and fairs by performing aerobatics and taking passengers for rides—even today some do these things. The gallery also features, temporarily, examples of some military planes that are of historic significance.

Balloon and dirigible pilots were among the first to begin competing for records, and to attend carnivals and fairs for exhibition flights. A diorama portrays some of the activities of these pilots and their flights and a film screened in a little theater in this hall shows other examples.

One of the small airplanes on exhibit is Wittman's **Chief Oshkosh** (also known as **Buster**), which won innumerable races, set many records, and won an armful of trophies—including two for wins in the Goodyear Trophy Races. Turner's **RT-14 Meteor,** displayed here, also won many trophies. In this plane Roscoe Turner won the Thompson Trophy Race three times.

A film screened in this gallery shows Colonel Roscoe Turner with his pet lion, Gilmore. The preserved skin of Gilmore was stuffed and is shown near Turner's 1937-39 Special Racer. Other trophy races featured in exhibits here include the Schneider, the Pulitizer, and the Bendix races with models of planes that flew in these competitions.

There have also been competitions in aerobatics, or stunt flying. The daredevil stunt flyer "Bevo" Howard, an aerobatic champion, flew the **Bucker 133 Jungmeister,** shown here, in aerobatic demonstrations across the country. The **Pitts Special** on exhibit is another that had been flown in aerobatic competitions in this country and abroad. The **Pitts** plane was donated to the Smithsonian by Dawson Ransome, a member of the world champion team that once piloted it.

In other days, daring pilots would visit carnivals or fairs and, in small planes like the old Curtiss **Jenny** shown here, perform such aerobatics as wing walking, looping, rolling overhead, snap rolling, topple blooping, and tail sliding—all illustrated and described in this hall. Pilots in the barnstorming era of the 1920s would land their small planes on fields, wherever they saw a gathering of people, and offer five dollar rides. Exhibits and dioramas depict these great rural events. Some of the planes had several lives: the **Waco 9** shown here was flown not only as a "barnstorming" plane, but for crop-dusting. In its early days it was even used as a passenger plane.

Displayed in this hall is the first all-metal American monoplane fighter, the **Boeing P-26-A,** nicknamed the **Peashooter.** During the 1930s it was one of the best-known fighter aircraft, and the last to have an open cockpit, a fixed undercarriage, and externally braced wings.

The Gulf Oil Company purchased the Grumman G-22 **Gulfhawk II,** on display here, in 1936. Major Alford Williams, head of Gulf's aviation division and a former naval aviator, piloted this plane, demonstrating its ability in precision aerobatics and dive-bombing. The plane was also used to test oils, fuels, and lubricants.

The Curtiss P-40-E **Warhawk** shown here was a first-line American fighter at the beginning of World War II. The famous Flying Tigers led by General Chennault flew these planes in China. **Warhawks** were also used as fighters by Great Britain, Canada, France, New Zealand, China, Russia, South Africa, Australia, and Turkey. More than 14,000 of these planes were built and some are still flying today.

The red P-51C **Mustang** "Excalibur III", 1943, a fighter plane developed for use in World War II, is shown. The one on exhibit was used by a stunt pilot who also won a Bendix Trophy flying this **Mustang.** Another trophy was awarded a pilot of this plane for a flight he made first from New York to London and then via Norway, Alaska, to the North Pole.

The Vought F4U-ID **Corsair,** a plane developed for war, saw service in Guadalcanal in February, 1943. These **Corsairs** became very important carrier-based fighters for the United States Navy and the Marine Corps. In the Pacific War it was also used by the Royal Navy.

Gallery 105: General Aviation (First Floor)

General aviation is used by individuals for nonairline commuter services, sport purposes, and for many business purposes. Their craft include several types of conventional, private, and non-military craft, such as one might find around small airports. On the floor of this hall and suspended from the ceiling are selected specimens that show a **Piper Cub**, a **Cessna**, a **Lear Jet**, and a **Beechcraft Bonanza.** An exhibit discusses the world's vast network of airports. The hall's primary purpose is to give the individual an idea of what is involved in learning to fly.

The **Piper PA-12 City of Washington** shown here was developed in 1946. It was one of two Super Cruisers to fly around the world in 1947, leaving from Teterboro, New Jersey and returning to the same airport four months later, thus becoming the first airplane of less than one hundred horsepower to successfully complete a world flight.

A successful craft from its first flight in 1947, the **Beechcraft Model 35 Bonanza,** with modifications, is still in production today. A single-engine light plane designed with the "V" tail configuration, it is both efficient and dependable. Captain Bill Odom piloted the **Waikiki Beechcraft** displayed here and established records for this plane in several flights.

Geraldine (Jerrie) Mock made her solo flight globe-circling the world in the **Cessna 180 Spirit of Columbus** displayed here. Her April 18, 1964 around the world flight was a first for women; her airtime was twenty-nine days, eleven hours and fifty-nine minutes. Her **Cessna 180** with a Continental 225 horsepower engine was not new (eleven years old) but it was well equipped; dual VHF and ADF radios and a ten channel HF radio; special automatic direction finders, a drum altimeter, a vertical reading compass, and an aidopilot, among other equipment.

Suspended from the ceiling is a very different sort of plane, a sleek **Gates Learjet.** It is considered a luxury plane, and can carry a crew of two and six passengers at speeds of up to 570 miles per hour. The plane is air-conditioned and pressurized and carries oxygen, radar, and navigational systems.

On exhibit are models of historic general aviation planes. They are divided in the following groups: 1910-1919; 1920-1929; 1930-1939; 1940-1949; 1950-1959; 1960-1969.

An exhibit in this gallery is devoted to the basics of flying. It gives the interested visitor some ideas of what is involved in getting a pilot's license. Films and trained instructors at simulators in this hall include three GAT-1s "flying over" photomural landscapes including a cockpit view of the approach to Washington's National Airport. These permit the visitor to try his skills in the mock-up cockpit of a plane. In addition to being in good physical condition, one must pass certain courses that are related to the safe operation of a plane, and pass written and oral exams required by the Federal Aviation Administration. Americans love quiz games. A computer with aviation quizzes attracts many visitors to test their knowledge on aviation subjects.

Aviation advanced with the development in propulsion technology. Engines on exhibit include those for piston turboprop, turbojet, and airbofan craft. Among them are: Pratt and Whitney JT 15 D-1, the Turbo of a 1971 engine designed to power General Aviation aircraft; General Electric CJ 610 Turbojet 1964 engine; Continental A-65-8 engine, 1939; Porsche 678 engine, 1958; Garrett TPE 331 engine, 1965; Curtiss OX-5 engine, 1914; Lycoming R-690 engine, 1930; Ranger L-440-3 engine, 1942; and others.

Gallery 106: Jet Aviation (First Floor)

Squids, octopus, nautilus, and cuttlefish forcibly expel water in jets through a funnel or siphon causing them to move forward or backward using a kind of jet propulsion that men observed but did not, for a long time, emulate to move vehicles. The ancient Chinese did build small rockets that utilized principles of jet propulsion. Much, much later, before World War I, ingenious inventors began working on devices that would propel a vehicle by jet propulsion, laying the groundwork for its utilization in flight. This hall traces the evolution of jet aviation for military and commercial purposes.

As shown in an exhibit describing pioneers of jet propulsion, there were many individuals of many countries whose successes and failures in research advanced the work in jet propulsion. Among these were Hans von Ohain of Germany and Sir Frank Whittle of Great Britain who are regarded as inventors of the first practical jet engines for planes. The very first jet airplane in the world to fly, HE 178, was designed by Hans von Ohain for the Heinkel Company of Germany in which Eric Warsity, a Heinkel test pilot, flew a thousand feet in several seconds (August 27, 1939). A model of it is shown, as well as a model of another successful jet plane, a Gloster 28/39. Models of early turbojet planes shown include some from Japan, Sweden, Germany, England, France, USSR, Hungary, and Italy.

The engines used to propel the various types of jets are explained in exhibits in this hall. Major jet propulsion engines developed for planes in this general order: turbojets, turboprops, ramjets, and turbofans. Turbojets carry an air-breathing propulsion engine that for better propulsion use some of the principles of a combustion engine and a supercharger for the power developed in a turbine to drive a compressor that eventually gives the vehicle a forward thrust; they are used in most military fighters, bombers, and modern commercial transport planes. A turboprop engine has a compressor, combuster, turbine, and a power turbine with a single shaft engine power to drive a conventional propeller. A ramjet engine has an air-breathing propulsion system compressing air in its inlet diffuser as it travels at high velocity burning fuel in the air and discharging it through a jet nozzle; it is used primarily in guided missiles. A turbofan has an air-breathing turbine engine consisting of a compressor-combustor-turbine unit called a core or gas generator, and a power turbine which drives a fan. On exhibit are examples of these engines that include a model of a General Dynamics S-16 shown to illustrate the general understanding of the gas turbine engine and the Pratt & Whitney J T-3 (J-57), a very important engine which was the first to reach and exceed 10,000 pounds of static thrust and was used in the North American

F-100s to become the first mass-produced fighters to reach supersonic speeds in level flight (this engine was also used in MacDonald F-101s, Conveyor F-102s, Douglas A3Ds and F-4Ds, Chance Vought F 8Us, Boeing B-52s, Kc 135s, 707s, and in the Douglas DC 8s). A Lycoming T-53 turboprop/turbo shaft engine built in Germany is shown which powered Bell 204, 205, and 209 helicopters. The Whittle WIS engine, 1941, is shown that was designed by Sir Frank Whittle and powered the British Gloster E 28/29 aircraft. A General Electric J-79 (C-J805), the first high compression variable Stator turbojet, carried an engine that was developed under a U.S. military requirement for a reliable high thrust, low weight, mechanically simple jet engine which could perform efficiently at mach 9 cruise and at mach 2 combat speed (the J-79 was produced overseas for the Lockheed F-104 Starfighter by many countries: Canada, Japan, Germany, Italy, and Belgium). The Pratt & Whitney J-T-9D and the Williams WR-19 engines are exhibited together so that one can compare them.

A large mural in this gallery painted by aviation artist Keith Ferris in 1981 features twenty-seven significant planes of the jet age. It shows the evolution of jet aviation. There is a key identifying those planes on a nearby chart.

Among the models, illustrations, and some jet planes shown in this gallery are found: De Haviland **DH-106 Comet 3,** Hawker-Siddley **Tridente,** Rockwell International **B 1;** Bede **B-D;** a general aviation aircraft; McDonnell-Douglas **DC-10** with a single General Electric engine located at the base of the vertical fin; McDonnell **FH-1 Phantom,** the world's first shipboard jet fighter (below it is given an explanation of how it operates with a film further illustrating its operation); McDonnell **F-4 Phantom 2;** North American **P-51 Mustang,** considered the best fighter plane of World War II; a Messerschmidt **ME-262 Schwalbe,** the world's first operational jet fighter; and the Lockheed **XP-80,** the first U.S. operational jet fighter.

An exhibit shows an advanced flight deck mock-up. This mock-up is similar to the British aerospace advance flight deck simulator in England; however, the instruments in this mock-up are not operable with the exception of the cathode-ray tube displays which are numbered for ease of reference. A McDonnell-Douglas F-18 instrument panel is shown and along with it a moving picture to clarify what the instruments on the panel mean and how they operate.

A little theater in the hall features a film, "Sneaking Through the Sound Barrier." It stars Sid Caesar, Imogene Coca, Carl Reiner, and Howard Morris. It runs for about twelve minutes.

An exhibit labeled "The Latest in Flying Togs" describes some outfits that men and women both used in the early days of flying. Also shown in an exhibit are military jet crewmen's equipment: a pressure suit, 1942; a Lamport pneumatic suit of 1945; a Soviet anti-G garment, type PPK-1U; a U.S. Air Force fighting pilot of 1965 of S.E. Asia; the U.S. Navy fighter pilot of 1979 in his uniform; and helmets that are chronologically arranged.

An exhibit shows nine historic propellers of different types with some that are used today. A propeller driven by an engine is a device that provides a thrust to move an airplane through the air. The Wright brothers demonstrated that a propeller should be regarded as a rotary wing. The lift generated as the propeller revolves is the thrust that pulls the machine forward. A wing of a jet plane in operation is also shown and explained.

Gallery 107: Early Flight: From Dream to Reality (First Floor)

To fly had always been a dream of men. So many creatures accomplish this feat (insects, birds, bats) but for ages mankind, despite many attempts, remained frustrated. Flight evaded him. The great Leonardo da Vinci was convinced that someday men would fly; in his preserved notes are found sketches he made for many aeronautical devices that his fertile mind created for flight. There were men who tried and failed at designing and operating devices that could emulate the birds. Sir George Cayley, an Englishman, experimenting first with small devices, later constructed several full scale gliders that he flew in 1804. These inspired other inventors, among them J. Stringfellow and W.S. Henson, who in 1843 designed flying machines which were the earliest attempts at aviation on a great scale. The names of Hiram Maxim, Clement Ader, A. Santos Dumont, Octave Chanute are among others in the history of early flight who experimented.

Otto Lilienthal in Germany designed the 1894 glider suspended from the ceiling of this hall. Lilienthal controlled his craft by swinging his legs and his torso, thus altering the center of gravity. The work of Lilienthal and Percy Pilcher of England, who was also well known for his hang gliders, unfortunately ended in accidental deaths for each.

The third Secretary of the Smithsonian, Samuel P. Langley, also experimented, but was unsuccessful. It was the Wright brothers who after experimenting with hang gliders built the first successful airplane. It made the first flight in a manned, gasoline powered heavier-than-air machine at Kitty Hawk, North Carolina on December 17, 1903. (See Gallery 100)

Visitors entering this colorful gallery are immediately drawn into scenes which may have taken place in an indoor aero show of about 1913 where some of the top aviation companies of those days (Wright, Curtiss, Bleriot and others) display planes they made in order to interest investors in buying them. One gets a "you are there in 1913" feeling from the posters promoting various kinds of planes, mood setting jazz "played" by a band of three mannequins on a balcony, and flags, plants, marvelous silent movies of early planes, and trade show advertisements for their products.

Booths are scattered around the perimeter of the hall with mannequins inside giving sales pitches about their products. In one booth a mannequin is talking about the Bleriot **Aeronautique** designed by Louis Bleriot and manufactured by his firm. This plane we are told was the first heavier-than-air machine to fly across the English Channel in 1909. The Bleriot company went on to make other models and by 1913 the Bleriot XI shown here was one of the most copied planes in the world.

The Wright Company of Dayton, Ohio advertises itself here as the "sole makers and exhibitors of the famous Wright Flyers." The advertising poster also states that "both planes and motors are built entirely in our own factory." In 1909 the Wright brothers sold

their Type A Military Flyer shown here to the U.S. Army. This, the
world's first military aircraft, was built for the U.S. Army Signal
Corps and was used for reconnaissance operations.

Photographs of the world's great aviators of this period are
displayed in the hall, among them Eugene Lefere, Leon Delagrange,
Henri Farman (who won the distance competition at a meet in Rheems,
France in 1909), Hubert Latham (who won the altitude contest at
the same meet), and Glen Curtiss (who won the speed competition
at this meet). The aircraft in which some of these events took place
are also displayed in photographs.

A section of this gallery discusses with audio-visual material
U.S. Aeronautics, 1910-1914. Air meets held in 1910 and 1911 in
the United States drew aviators from around the world competing
for speed, distance, and altitude flights. In 1911 Eugene Ely, flying
a Curtiss plane from San Francisco, made a landing on the deck of
the ship U.S.S. Pennsylvania thirteen miles away and then returned
to San Francisco. This outstanding achievement was a "first." The
Curtiss Company achieved another "first" in 1911 when it introduced
the first practical seaplane in history, a modified **Goldenflyer** with
a central float and stabilizers under the wingtips. It soon proved its
worth when with this plane Hugh Robinson, a pilot, rescued a pilot
who had crashed in Lake Michigan—a "first" for an air-sea rescue.
Still another "first" in 1911 discussed here was the United States
transcontinental flight of the Wright brothers EX plane, the **Vin-Fiz**
piloted by Calbraith P. Rodgers (the plane is on exhibit in Gallery
208). Other "firsts" discussed in this section of the gallery describe
radio transmission between an airplane and the ground; the first
parachute jump from an airplane in 1912 by Captain Albert Berry;
the first automatic pilot built by Lawrence Sperry and demonstrated
by him in 1912, followed two years later by his gyroscopic stabilizer
and turn and bank indicator.

Just as there is a U.S. section of aeronautics 1910-1914 in
this gallery, there is a comparable European section for the same
period which discusses and illustrates European achievements. In
England the Royal Flying Corps (RFC) and the Royal Naval Air Service
(RNAS) were created to meet military aviation needs.
A. V. Roe, an English aircraft designer, built the world's first
enclosed cabin airplanes in 1912. (It was, however, the C.F. Bellanca
Company of the U.S. which designed and built the first successful
line of cabin monoplanes. These efficient planes significantly advanced
commercial aviation and won first places in many aviation meets.)
Other English designers of this period include T. Sopwith, Harry
Hawker, and G. de Haviland whose works are discussed and illustrated.
In France Bleriot continued to produce aircraft as did Henri Fabre
who developed the first planes to take off and land on water. Building
planes in Berlin was Anthony Fokker (of Holland) and in Italy Gianni
Caproni who owned the Caproni Company and designed and patented
his planes and their parts. There were many aviation meets that took
place in European countries including England, France, Germany,
Italy, Spain, Switzerland, Hungary, Denmark, Belgium, and Russia
that are discussed in the gallery.

Still another section in this hall is devoted to "Women in
Flight." It seems that French women were among the first to venture

into aeronautics. Some noted names include Mme. Thible who in 1784 was the first woman to fly in a balloon; Therese Petier in 1908 was the first woman to fly in a heavier-than-air craft; Raymonde de la Roche received the first pilot license given to a woman in 1910; and, perhaps the most famous French woman, Helene Dutrieu, who flew in air meets in Europe and the United States as early as the 1900s. In the United States there were equally courageous women who were among the early fliers. Harriet Quimby received a pilot's license in 1911 and was the first woman to pilot an airplane across the English Channel. Other well-known names among the early U.S. women pilots discussed here were Bernetta Miller, Alys McKey Bryant, Marjorie and Katherine Stinson. Outstanding was Ruth Law who did exhibition flying and held records for distance flying.

A section in this hall is devoted to exhibits of early aeronautical engines. John Stringfellow built a small steam engine that generated one horsepower and is illustrated here. It was Samuel Langley who succeeded in flying a small model of his aerodrome propelled by a gasoline engine. When he tried the larger, full-scale craft propelled by a water-cooled radial gasoline engine it failed. The Wright brothers succeeded when they flew their 1903 Wright Flyer using a Wright inline engine shown here. So did Glenn Curtiss with his early inline aeronautical engine, as did other lesser-known manufacturers using inline engines discussed here. Other, later engines displayed show the radial design with cylinders arranged in a circle around the crankshaft that propelled the aircraft. Such engines were first developed successfully by the Seguin brothers in France for their Gnome engine which is illustrated here.

Gallery 109: Flight Testing (First Floor)

This gallery is dedicated to the highly skilled test pilots without whom aviation could not have progressed. Before they can be considered safe for use, aircraft must be carefully researched and tested. The exhibits in this hall recount the history of flight research, describing flight testing, ground testing, design theories, and the constantly improved equipment that advanced the capabilities of aircraft—even the suiting for pilots. Films of flight testing are screened in this hall.

A large exhibit with models and illustrations describes "Flight Testing from the Wright Brothers Through World War II." It explains the development of test piloting as a highly specialized branch of aviation with work that was often hazardous and needed the competence of highly skilled and trained individuals. Flight research involves studying the problems of high altitude flight including the use of pressurized suits, pressurized cabins, and other necessary equipment.

Aircraft designers have been aided by wind tunnels, valuable tools of flight research. Wind tunnels used with plane models help demonstrate useful information that plane designers in their research gain for designing new planes or modifying older ones. An exhibit shows a cross section of a subsonic wind tunnel at the Edgewood Arsenal in Maryland and above it the Bell X-2 wind tunnel model that was used in designing new experimental aircraft. A small working model is shown in which a section of wing rises to show lift. There are two other working wind tunnels, one demonstrating streamlining, the other showing how a tightly fitted, specially contoured engine cover can increase the speed of an aircraft. (See other wind tunnels in Gallery 213.) Other models, and blueprints of designs, are displayed in an exhibit called "Flight Research Confirms New Design Theories."

In his **Lockheed 5C Vega,** named for his daughter the **Winnie Mae,** pilot Wiley Post flew twice around the world; the second time he soloed. Post also made high altitude flights in the substratosphere in 1934 and 1935 for which he designed a pressure suit that provided necessary oxygen. Both the **Winnie Mae** and the suit Post designed are on exhibit in this hall. An exhibit shows the changes in apparel worn by test pilots from the 1930s to the 1960s and describes how needs for better suiting were met. One of the exhibits shows the clothing and equipment used by a test pilot when he flew in an open cockpit plane in 1935, and this is compared to the clothing worn by a test pilot testing a **Convair B58 Hustler** in 1965.

Flight testing contributed much toward the outcome of World War II as indicated in an exhibit in this gallery with illustrations of planes that helped the Allies in its victories. An open floor exhibit shows the 1942 **XP-59-A Aircomet** developed by the Bell Aircraft Corporation. It was the first experimental American turbojet. During World War II, in order to keep research on this jet a secret, both this and a second XP-59-A were disguised with dummy propellers so that onlookers would think them conventional planes. Mechanics removed the dummy propellers before flight and reinstalled them immediately after landing. Another aircraft carefully tested was the **Hawker-Siddeley XV 6A Kestrel** shown here. It was a vertical flight aircraft that used rotors or direct jet thrust to lift itself straight up off the ground and then could move horizontally in flight. Other accomplishments done then and later in research work by these skilled and brave test pilots included blind flying turbojets and flights into the stratosphere. There is a scale model of the **Consolidated NY-2** in which Jimmy Doolittle made the world's first blind flight on September 24, 1929 at Mitchell Field, Long Island.

A large wall exhibit describes with models and illustrations the devices of telemeter transmitter, telemeter oscillator, telemeter power supply, NACA three component accelerometer installed in the **Bell XS-1,** pressure recorder and film drum installed in the **Bell XS-1,** and the supersonic breakthrough from subsonic to supersonic and beyond.

A radio jeep that acts as an air-ground flight test communications vehicle, an important link between the test pilot and the ground, is shown here. There is a torpedo shaped **Tomahawk Cruise Missile** of 1975 exhibited. This is a guided missile the United States Navy developed which is capable of being launched from either an aircraft, surface ships, submarines or land platforms. This Tomahawk can carry either conventional or nuclear warheads.

Gallery 110: Satellites and Sounding Rockets (First Floor)

Most laymen are unaware of the vast array of launched

satellites and sounding rockets that have been and continue to be useful to scientists, to commerce and industry, to various branches of our government, and directly or indirectly to each of us. The exhibits in this hall feature all types of satellites and sounding rockets used for scientific research in meteorological services such as in weather forecasting, hurricane tracking, and severe storm warnings that began with kites and balloons then sounding rockets and finally satellites. Data gathered for military reconnaissance and surveillance are among other uses as are research, exploration, and services to society in peaceful pursuits such as surveying croplands, forests, and locating minerals. Satellites have proven saviors for plane crash victims by picking up distress calls from downed planes and pinpointing their locations for rescue. A very important use is in the field of communications where they can relay hundreds of telephone calls, store messages, play them back on command and relay teleprints, photovision and other data. Deep space probes by satellites have provided wider understanding of the planets in our galaxy and have helped unveil greater knowledge of the universe than men were ever able to learn since the time they first began to search for answers thousands of years ago. These satellites and sounding rockets carry scientific instruments for research that are unhampered by atmospheric distortions frequently encountered with land-based instruments.

Normally satellites and sounding rockets are not recovered from space, but some, like **Discoverer II** and **Biosatellite II** which carried plants, frog eggs, and microorganisms to test the effects of weightlessness, radiation and other factors, have released them in capsules from the satellites while in orbit, reentered the earth's atmosphere and were recovered. The satellites and sounding rockets in this gallery, for the most part, are back-up or scale models of launched craft.

Robert Goddard, one of the fathers of modern rocketry, has his work explained in this gallery with the rockets or back-up models of those he devised to carry scientific instruments to gather information about the upper atmosphere shown. One of the 1935 Goddard A series rockets is on exhibit (its parts labeled). Also exhibited are scale models of or back-up contemporary sounding rockets which could go high in the atmosphere (higher than balloons previously could) to gather information with devices on them that could parachute down or telemeter the information. Among the replicas or models of sounding rockets shown are: the **WAC Corporal,** the first successful sounding rocket (1945) to reach significant altitude; the **Viking Rocket** (1954) with instruments that measured air temperature, density, pressure, composition of atmosphere, and gathered data on cosmic and solar radiation and, in addition, cameras that could photograph Earth from high altitudes; the **Nike Cajun** (1956) that carried instruments for weather photography and weather forecasting; the **Aerobee 150** (1954) that did a variety of tasks in the atmosphere and ionosphere for weather forecasting and research; and other back-up models of sounding rockets used for meteorological data, among them **Honeybee, Farside, Loki-Dart, Cricket, Arcas,** and **Nike Smoke.**

An introductory exhibit gives an illustrated chronology of satellite development. The first **Vanguard** (1955), the size of a grapefruit, exploded on the pad; however, later **Vanguards** launched in 1958 and 1959 were successful in testing for temperatures and the shape of Earth; **Vanguard III** made studies of solar X-ray radiation, air density, and micrometeorite studies of the atmosphere.

Sputnik (the Russian satellite) jarred the United States aeronautical scientists to action and led them six months later to launch **Explorer I** in 1958 (a cut-away model is shown). There were a series of **Explorers** (scale models or back-ups shown) which transmitted valuable information on the relationship between terrestrial and interplanetary magnetic fields, the sun's magnetic fields as well as solar winds and solar flares. **Explorer VI** was able to televise cloud cover of the Earth's surface, measure radiation levels in the Van Allen belts, map the Earth's magnetic field, and study radio waves in space.

A series of **Pioneers** (scale models or back-ups shown) were launched to make deep space probes (**Pioneer I** was not successful, however, later **Pioneers** did better). **Pioneer IV** (1959) was the first American spacecraft to pass beyond the moon into interplanetary space and on its way to sample radiation levels in space and near the moon telemetering back the information to ground stations. **Pioneer V** (1960), a joint U.S. and United Kingdom satellite, tested long-range communication systems that measured astronomical distances, and studied the effects of solar flares.

Shown also are scale models or back-ups of the meterological satellites **Tiros** (television infra red observation satellites) of which there were a series from 1-10 which sent hundreds of photographs of Earth cloud cover and infra-red radiation measurements by telemeter to ground tracking stations, which the U.S. Weather Bureau used for daily weather analysis. **Tiros** also transmitted photographs of atmospheric and oceanic conditions to major receiving centers. A back-up model of the improved **Tiros** called **Itos** was given to the National Air and Space Museum by the Astro Electronics Division of RCA. Other satellites displayed here that were launched for scientific research were **Ariel I** and **Ariel II** (another joint U.S. and United Kingdom satellite) that investigated the layer of ozone surrounding the Earth, galactic radio noises, and micro meteoroids; **Lofti I, Atmosphere Explorer-A,** and **Interplanetary Monitoring Platform-E (IMP-E).** Back-ups are shown of the **Landsat** series of satellites, launched to monitor Earth's resources, that orbit Earth every sixteen days producing pictures of great resolution which can discern under computer analysis some things as small as a one acre plot of woodland, discern changes in the world's forests and can forecast crop yields. The back-ups of **Voyager I** and **II** satellites shown here were launched from Cape Canaveral in August and September 1977 to study Jupiter and Saturn and their planetary systems. They sent back spectacular pictures.

Some examples of back-ups of early communication satellites shown include **Echo I** and **Echo II** (the first satellite used in cooperative communication experiments by the U.S. and the Soviet Union); **Score** launched to study the ability of a satellite to relay voices and teletype communications (1958); **Courier I-B** (a cut-away model is shown) that tested the use of a "delayed repeater" method for global military communication by storing messages and later repeating them as the satellite passed over a ground station (1960); **Oscar I** (orbital satellite carrying amateur radio) designed and constructed by American ham radio operators to relay voice, slow scan television, teletype, radio and Morse code; **Telstar** I and II which were used in making the first trans-Atlantic television broadcast (1964); **Relay I,** an active repeater satellite that broadcast television pictures of Pope Paul VI's funeral, John Kennedy's funeral, the opening of the UN General Assembly, and military parades in Moscow (1962); **Intelsat** I and II which provided communication support for the Apollo missions to the moon; **Intelsat III** which made possible global communication coverage; and **Intelsat IV-A** which provides 3,000 to 9,000 one-way telephone channels or combinations (and, in addition, can provide twelve TV channels); **Anik,** the first Canadian communication satellite that was designed for television and telephone service in Canada; **Westar** operated by Western Union that can transmit in twelve color television channels, or up to 14,000 one-way telephone circuits, and, in addition, can handle computer data transmissions at the rate of six million bits per second (1974).

Finally, a television screen set in a small niche near an exit in this gallery carries a taped report on satellites that is presented by Walter Cronkite who tells what satellites can accomplish and some things they cannot do yet.

Gallery 111: Stars: From Stonehenge to the Space Telescope (First Floor)

In this gallery visitors are given an opportunity to follow astronomy's historic developments from ancient times when the sites for many temples and ancient monuments like Angora Wat in India, Chichen Itza in Mexico, the temple of the Anasazis in southwest America and Stonehenge in England, among others, were carefully located for celestial observation to catch the first rays of the sun at solstice. Shown also are some major advancements in astronomy since these times. The discipline of astronomy took a major leap forward when in 1608 a Dutch optician called Hans Lippershey invented the first telescope which inspired Galileo, the Italian astronomer, and led him in 1610 to build a telescope with which he was able to see the rings of Saturn, four of the satellites of Jupiter, and the mountains and craters on the moon. Sir Isaac Newton's invention of the refracting telescope was another of great importance to astronomers. With the help of land-based telescopes of all kinds, of orbiting satellites carrying telescopes, and with other kinds of astronomical instruments astronomers have learned a great deal about our sun and the stars in our galaxy, the Milky Way, other galaxies, and about extra galactic space. These are among some of the major exhibits which fill this hall.

A visitor enters this gallery through a nearly full-scale recon-struction of an arch of which the original, according to radio-carbon dating, was built in about 1845 B.C. in Wiltshire, England and was known as Stonehenge. Some archeologists believe Stonehenge was a temple for a group of sun-worshipping people, the Druids, who placed some of the stones to form an altar with a nearby soltice marker, the heelstone, set to cast a shadow on the altar at midsummer's day, the longest day of the year marking the summer soltice. In the hall beyond the arch through which the visitor enters lies the heelstone, the soltice marker, which points to a "sun" located in the gallery.

A major portion of exhibits in this gallery focus on what astronomers, astrophysicists, and astrochemists using a variety of telescopes and other types of astronomical instruments have learned about our sun and other stars. Some of the exhibits using mini-computer systems and video disc technology are geared for visitor participation, which can clarify and help him understand some of the complex scientific information being presented.

Fusion is a process which goes on continuously on our sun. Children and adults will have fun playing a game called "Fusion" which illustrates the hydrogen fusion process occurring in its central region. The player aims an atom-shooting gun at a field of oncoming atoms. If he makes a "hit" fusion occurs. The trick of the game is to stimulate fusion at the lowest possible temperature which rises one million degrees every three seconds.

It is not altogether surprising that early people worshipped the Sun, because light and heat from it makes all forms of life on Earth possible. A spectroscope, an instrument which analyzes sunlight, has been able to tell us of the chemical elements of the Sun. We learn of the gases which are much more dense at the center but lighter at the surface, and of their "prominences" or solar flares which some-times burst from the Sun's surface to more than 250,000 miles high. When looking at the Sun through a suitable telescope, one can often see dark specks or sun spots, which are actually huge storm centers in the Sun's atmosphere and magnetic fields and which often can cause interference with radio and television broadcasts here on Earth. An exhibit of our sun shows large images of its surface in polar motion (a special effect illustration of solar flares and sun spots) and as we walk past an exposed core of the Sun some sixteen feet in diameter, we learn of the dynamic balance of forces that go on there.

A section of a back-up of the Apollo Telescope Mount (ATM) used on the Skylab Workshop in the early 1970s is shown. The ATM was the first manned solar observatory in space from which the Sun was monitored. This back-up ATM is displayed in the gallery against a twenty-foot mural of the Skylab Workshop in space. Using remote control the astronauts working the telescope mount in space could examine the Sun through a cluster of eight telescopes in the mount and in a wide range of the spectrum (from X-rays and ultraviolet, through the visual and into the near red regions) could gather an enormous among of data about the Sun, far more than any land-based telescopes had ever been able to do.

There are also shown scale models of the Space Telescope satellite and its optical telescope assembly which was launched to an altitude of 300 miles in 1985 on a Space Shuttle mission. It will be the largest astronomical telescope ever orbited and will be equipped with an assortment of scientific instruments for recording extraordinary high-resolution astronomical images, for detecting extremely faint objects, for collecting spectographic data, and for making very precise measurement of the position of radiant sources in the sky.

Suspended from the ceiling (that had been carried in the third Orbiting Astronomical Observatory (OA)-III) is Copernicus, the proto-type of the Princeton telescope (a 32-inch reflecting telescope). It is capable of examining the ultraviolet spectra of stars, galaxies, a nova, and the interstellar regions. For nine years it provided astronomers with information about the formation and evolution of stars.

Also suspended from the ceiling in this gallery is the International Ultraviolet Explorer satellite (IUE), a full-scale engineering model of the original launched in 1978 to study celestial objects in ultraviolet light and which produced an X-ray map of the sky used by astrophysicists as a guide for all later high energy studies.

There is a room in this gallery in which visitors standing "outside" the Milky Way can look out into an area of simulated extragalactic space. Imagining themselves as astronauts working a telescope in an orbiting satellite they can see, when a button is pressed, galaxies, stars being formed, and exploding stars on a screen set into the original shell of the IUE's control console.

In the gallery there is a computer-operated glossary of astronomical terms which can give definitions of words and phrases for the visitor who is not familiar with these terms. Artifacts on display with a star or sun theme include flags, record albums, license plates, beer labels, car insignias, etc. Astrological charts and large photo murals of galaxies, the Sun, and the stars are also on view.

Gallery 112: East Gallery: Unmanned Lunar Exploration Vehicles (First Floor)

Apollo 11's flight to the moon (July 16-24, 1969) was such an awesome event, practically everyone in this country who was able to snatch time off to get near a radio set or watch its progress on television did so. (See Gallery 210 for fuller details of the **Apollo** flights, milestones in man's history.) The golden moon lander **Eagle,** shown here, and all other spacecraft in this gallery are replicas, backups or models used prior to the **Apollo** missions to the moon. Among the unmanned exploratory craft shown are **Ranger, Lunar Orbiter,** and **Surveyor.**

Between 1961 and 1965 an Atlas Agena rocket launched unmanned **Ranger** spacecraft on sixty-five hour journeys to the moon. Cameras on board these craft transmitted television pictures back to earth; the pictures enabled American scientists to get their first close look at the moon's surface. These pictures helped scientists evolve most of the basic techniques and flight operating procedures later used in manned lunar-orbital flights. The **Ranger** spacecraft shown here is a replica of those that went to the moon and crash-landed on its surface.

Five unmanned **Lunar Orbiters** were then sent to the moon between 1966 and 1967 to photograph its surface preparatory to selecting landing sites for the **Apollo** missions. The cameras on board surveyed and photographed about ninety-five percent of the moon's surface, sending pictures back to earth by electrical signals. There were now pictures of the far side of the moon, which had never been seen before. The **Lunar Orbiter** shown here is a back-up model.

Between 1966 and 1968 seven unmanned **Surveyor** missions were sent to the moon; five landed successfully. The **Surveyors** were sent to test lunar soft-landing techniques and to survey potential **Apollo** landing sites. Television pictures sent back by the **Surveyor** cameras showed lunar surfaces. Lunar soil was sampled by means of a small scoop sent out from the vehicle (for the **Surveyors** were programmed to perform chemical analyses of the soil and do other scientific experiments). The **Surveyor** shown here was used for ground tests on Earth.

The **Apollo** 11's golden lunar module **Eagle** shown here is one of twelve built to place men on the moon. The lower descent stages of the lunar modules that landed on the moon were left there. The back-up module on display shows both the upper and lower stages of the lunar module. Its shiny gold exterior is aluminum thinly coated with a plastic (mylar) film. Each lunar module has two stages (each section containing rocket engines or clusters of engines). The descent or lower stage contains both a rocket motor to slow the descent to the lunar surface for a soft landing, and the exploration equipment the astronauts would need to use. This lower stage remained on its landing site on the moon when the astronauts left. The ascent or upper stage contained the pressurized compartment in which the astronauts lived and slept, and a rocket motor that enabled them to blast off from the moon and return to the Command Module circling the moon. When the astronauts had safely docked with and returned inside the Command Module, the Service Module (ascent stage) was discarded and in three of the **Apollo** missions fell back to the moon where their impact was monitored by instruments left on the moon for this purpose and by the electrical signals they sent back to Earth.

Gallery 113: Rocketry and Space Flight (First Floor)

At the entrance to this hall is a studio model of an interstellar space ship that had been used in the filming of the science fiction television series "Star Trek." Many of the episodes of this series dealt with the problems and results of possible human contacts with extraterrestial life forms and civilizations. This model was a gift of Paramount Television, a division of Paramount Pictures.

Man dreams and sometimes these dreams become realities, like the dream to fly like the birds. This gallery's exhibits trace the evolution of rocket propulsion and rocket engines from their beginnings in the seventeenth century to their present state. The corollary history of space suits is also recounted here.

People have dreamed of space travel from ancient times; as exhibits here illustrate, a wealth of stories about leaving this planet, voyaging off into space and reaching the moon have been created. There are illustrations in this gallery of Arabian tales and Chinese tales, the 1643 allegorical tales of the great scientist Johannes Kepler, and of Francis Godwin's 1638 story of a man who trained a flock of birds to fly him to the moon (in this hall illustrated by a wire sculpture depicting the hero of the story "The Man in the Moon"). Cyrano de Bergerac devised systems for carrying people into space, and Jules Verne's well-known and in part prophetic books, **From the Earth to the Moon** and **Around the Moon** are shown. These inspired scientists and engineers alike.

Exhibits describe the eleventh century Chinese discovery of gunpowder. By the thirteenth century they had devised black-powder rockets by stuffing gunpowder into bamboo tubes to make effective weapons for military purposes. In the Middle East during the fourteenth century men were devising schemes for rocketry use, and in the fifteenth century Leonardo da Vinci was one who thought in terms of rocketry for war machines, as did others in the sixteenth and seventeenth centuries, as weapons to be used against fortresses and ships.

The powder rocket came into frequent use as an instrument of war during the nineteenth century. Later in the century, as technology improved the propellent efficiency of rockets, some European armies established corps of rocketeers. Francis Scott Key observed "the rockets' red glare" that he wrote about in the Star Spangled Banner having observed it from a ship at Fort McHenry during the War of 1812; the rockets he saw were developed by William Congreve. A model of one of Congreve's rockets is shown. The V-2 rockets fired on England by the Germans during World War II were the first large-scale step rockets used and they are illustrated in this gallery.

Rockets have been used not only for war but for such peacetime purposes as harpooning whales and saving lives: they have been used to shoot rescue lines to ships in distress, and as distress signals from ships, airplanes, and the ground. Examples of these kinds of rockets are on exhibit.

Scientists soon realized that rockets were the only vehicles capable of taking man into space. Several exhibits in this gallery describe and illustrate the works of great pioneers in the early development of step rockets in the early twentieth century. Step rockets were placed one on top another in successively smaller sizes so that when fuel in the one underneath was consumed it dropped off and, in stages, the engines on the next rocket above fired upward causing it to travel at increased speed and eventually place the satellite the rockets carried upward into orbit or into deep space. Among the early twentieth century pioneers whose works are described and illustrated are the Roumanian Hermann Oberth, the Russian Konstantin Tsiolkovsky, and the great American physicist Robert H. Goddard, "the father of American rocketry." On exhibit is a replica of Goddard's liquid propellant rocket of 1926 which carried an eight pound thrust, and his "Hoopskirt" rocket that used gasoline and liquid oxygen for fuel: it flew successfully in December of 1928. Goddard developed innumerable rocket devices and suggested electric rocket motors as early as 1906, but they were not tried in space until 1964. Goddard was one of the first to develop a general theory of rocket action and to prove, experimentally, rocket propulsion in a vacuum which became the basis for rocketry around the world including the German rocket program used in World War II. At the close of World War II Wernher von Braun came to the United States from Germany where he had been responsible for the successful development of the V-2 liquid fuel rocket. In this country he became associated with the space program, developing rockets for the manned lunar program. Earlier, in 1957, when Sputnik I (see replica In Gallery 100) was launched it was carried into space by a modified three-stage Soviet

Intercontinental Ballistic Missile. The success of Sputnik acted as a goad stimulating American scientists into greater action in their rocketry program.

In the multiple steps used in rockets, each of the steps carries its own engine and performs independently when separated. To explain "What Is a Rocket" a full-sized RL-10 engine (which serves as an upper stage propulsion system to power the Centaur stage that boosted the **Viking** and **Surveyor** craft into space and was developed by Pratt and Whitney Aircraft Florida Research Center) is displayed. Diagrams explain how it functions. There is also an F-1 Turbopump displayed (opened to show its parts) with diagrams and explanations for each of its parts. Various engines have played key roles in rocket and space flight. Among other engines displayed are the LR-87 used to power the **Titan II CBM**; the H-1 engine; a German V-2 rocket engine contained in the tail section of the rocket; a liquid propellant rocket engine used in the first stage of the **Saturn** and the IBM launch vehicles; a **Surveyor** retrorocket motor with an engine using asphalt propellant grains instead of liquid fuel and used to bring the **Surveyor** down to the Moon. Scientists are considering new forms of propulsion for the future. Exhibits describe the nuclear rocket motors, which would use atomic fission instead of chemical combustion, and electrorocket motors that would use electrostatic or electromagnetic forces to accelerate propulsion.

Up until now, and probably for quite some time to come, space travelers will need spacesuits for protection. The original space-suits were modeled on the pressure suits used by deep sea divers, but with increased demand, spacesuit design has undergone many changes. Glass exhibit cases house a chronological display of these suits; descriptions note how the suits evolved into the sophisticated garments astronauts now wear to protect them from the inhospitable environment of space. A space suit valued at $6,000 that had been worn by Alan Bean during his Apollo 12 mission was loaned by the Smithsonian to the Kingsman Museum in Battle Creek, Michigan. It is believed it may have been an avid future astronaut fascinated with ideas of space travel who smashed a window and cut through security locks to steal it. It was recovered when an anonymous telephone tip gave the FBI a clue as to where it could be recovered: stuffed inside a green bag in front of a mausoleum at an Albion, Michigan cemetery.

Gallery 114: Space Hall (First Floor)

This fascinating hall is filled with monumental exhibits of guided missiles, launch vehicles, spacecraft, and a model of the space shuttle **Columbia**. Many of the exhibits are original, but items that could not be returned from space are represented here by back-ups, replicas, or models.

The largest item in the entire National Air and Space Museum is the **Skylab Orbital Workshop** displayed in this hall with one of its solar panels standing on the floor beside the craft. There were two systems of solar electric power—one wing supplied power in the Orbital Workshop, and four panels were used for the Apollo Telescope

Mount which had astronomical instruments to obtain information about the sun. Each panel contains some 150,000 solar cells for supplying solar energy that powered Skylab. The original Skylab was a research workshop for three changing astronaut crews wearing special shoes to help anchor them to the grid against weightlessness and who also lived aboard in quarters that were provided. The original Skylab was sent into space in 1973 as the third stage of a Saturn V rocket and fell back to Earth in 1979. The Skylab shown in this gallery is a back-up model of the one that had been in space. What looks like a windmill in the model displayed on the floor beside it is a telescope mount with one of its panels that contains solar silicon chips for generating electricity to run the telescope. On the very top of the model of Skylab one can see the Multiple Docking Adapter that very much resembles the Apollo Command Module. It was this Multiple Docking Adapter the astronauts used to rendezvous with Skylab and dock at its port on top to change crews and resupply Skylab. What missions were the Skylab crews performing? Among other things they were able to obtain data and photographs valuable in planning possible future space habitats. Testing for microorganisms included extensive microbiological sampling of the crews and the spacecraft. Also tested was the crew's ability in a weightless environment to observe the Earth with instruments and obtain photographs of areas of the Earth for further knowledge of its natural resources. Skylab crews also made studies of the Sun and its influences on the Earth. Visitors entering this back-up of Skylab's hugh cylinder (about 118 feet long, 22 feet in diameter) from the balcony above the hall can see, divided in two major portions, the wardroom, sleeping quarters, workroom and exercise area for a crew of three astronauts.

Aided by a scale model figure of a man standing beside the scale model of a Saturn V booster rocket (which launched the lunar module **Columbia** into space) one manages to get some idea of the true size of this tremendous rocket. The actual Saturn V rocket is four times taller than the height of the National Air and Space Museum. Visitors can also see a replica of one of Saturn V's five engines cleverly mirrored so as to give the illusion of five Saturn V engines, the number used in the rocket cluster to boost the **Apollo** to the Moon. One of the treads of the enormous mobile platform that took the Saturn V from the vehicle assembly building to the launch pad can be seen. On the launch pad the original Saturn V was supported by gantry arms which provided for fueling and for entry of the astronauts into the Multiple Docking Adapter near the top.

Models also depict other booster rockets, including an Atlas-Centaur and a Titan 3-C. There are also several models of German rockets: air-to-air missiles, the ground-to-air Rheintochter, the V-1 "buzz bomb" of World War II, and the large V-2, the first long-range ballistic missile. After World War II, the V-2 was used as a sounding rocket for high altitude research; both the V-1 and V-2 were progeniters of our Saturn V rockets.

There is a mock-up of the inside of the Lunar Command Module (the original can be seen in Gallery 100) launched by the Saturn V: visitors can see the guidance navigational system and the types of instruments carried to the moon for seismic and laser experiments. Among other items in this gallery is the back-up model of the Lunar

Rover Vehicle, the dune buggy, the world's first extra-terrestrial car (another can be seen in Gallery 210).

There is a replica of the **Apollo-Soyuz** test project (of which there is an identical exhibit in the Moscow Museum) as they appeared in space in 1975 docked together high above the Atlantic drifting in orbit about 140 miles west of Portugal. They are shown here in docked position, an airlock adapter between the two crafts that equalized air pressures because of the differences in atmosphere. In this position, the astronauts and cosmonauts could move back and forth between the two crafts frequently eating together and conducting some scientific experiments. The exhibit was installed by American and Soviet technicians.

A fifteen-foot pit was excavated in this gallery's floor in order to provide sufficient height for four towering rockets: a Jupiter-C rocket that launched the first successful American satellite **Explorer** I and later several other Explorer satellites; a Vanguard rocket that launched three satellites; a Scout-D that was the first solid-propellant rocket to launch a satellite; and a Minuteman III, an intercontinental ballistic missile, a major strategic defense missile that can be launched from either an underground or an airborne launch control center.

Models are shown of the following spacecraft launched for planetary research: (1) **Pioneer 11** that was launched by an Atlas Centaur in April 1973 to investigate the asteroid belt and, reaching Jupiter, (closer than Pioneer 10 did) relayed back to earth many pictures of that planet including the polar regions. It reached Saturn in 1979 and like **Pioneer 10** will eventually leave the Solar System; (2) **Mariner 10**, an interplanetary spacecraft that was launched on November 4, 1973 by a combination Atlas/Centaur rocket, whose mission was to collect valuable scientific data and pictures about Venus and Mercury, particularly their atmosphere, and relay them back to earth; (3) **Voyagers** I and II that were launched from Cape Canaveral to give comparative studies of the Jupiter and Saturn planetary systems, each picking up spectacular photos and data about these planets which they relayed back to Earth (Voyager I, launched September 5, 1977, made a flyby of Jupiter and Saturn and will reach Uranus in 1986 while Voyager II, launched September 20, 1977, followed Voyager I to Jupiter and Saturn and took equally spectacular pictures of these planets and their moons and now will go on to Neptune).

A model of the manned space shuttle **Columbia,** the craft that was carried piggyback to high altitudes by a Boeing 747 then released to glide to a landing, is shown in this gallery. This shuttle will eliminate the need for costly launch vehicles. The model of the **Columbia** is sixteen feet and shows the thermal protection tiles for its exterior. The space shuttle is one of the most complex machines ever built, and the 1980s will see four of these reusable manned space vehicles that are capable of reentering the atmosphere after completing its mission in space, and landing on a runway like an ordinary aircraft.

Gallery 203: Sea-Air Operations (Second Floor)

As visitors reach the quarter deck of the **USS Smithsonian**

CVM-70, the simulated aircraft carrier in this gallery, they hear the sound of bo's'n pipes welcoming them on board as if they are VIPs. Although an actual hangar deck is about two acres in size, this one is foreshortened. A real hangar deck, which serves as a protected space for working on planes, is divided into sections or bays, separated by large retractable, watertight doors, which are shut in case of fire or other emergency. Aircraft are transferred from the flight deck to the hangar deck or vice versa by means of elevators which extend out from the side of the ship. Visitors looking out toward the sea from the deck can watch (courtesy of a film loop) escort destroyers and several other ships that accompany carriers. On the deck itself are numerous U.S. Navy and Marine Corps aircraft, primarily of World War II vintage that saw service in the Pacific theater of war, as well as some of the weapons they carried. Also in this hall one can see United States Navy and Marine Corps uniforms and illustrations of modern carriers of other years; an exhibit explains how some of these carriers are modernized. A section of this gallery, dubbed the "ship's museum," is devoted to a history of flight over water. In this museum, among illustrations of Navy ships with information about them, are included: **USS Forrestal,** CV-59; **USS Nimitz,** CVN-68; **USS Tarawa,** (LHA-1); **USS Lexington,** CV-2; **USS Essex,** CV-9; **USS Independence,** CVL-22; **USS Casablanca,** CVE-55; **USS Midway,** CV-41; and **USS Enterprise,** CV-6.

Temporarily removed, but hopefully restored now, is the Boeing F4B-4, a stubby little biplane fighter built for the Marine Corps in the late 1920s and early 1930s. This F4B-4 served in the Marine Fighting Squadron until July 1933 when it was replaced by the Grumman F3F-2.

The Grumman FM-1 (F4F-4) **Wildcat** shown on the hangar deck was a United States Navy and Marine Corps basic fighter craft during World War II. The French and the British also used FM-1s, although they gave them different names. It is perhaps best remembered for its 1941 role in the defense of Wake Island.

Suspended above the Grumman FM-1 is a Douglas SBD **Dauntless,** a dive bomber (Scout Bomber Douglas) that made an impressive record in World War II, particularly in the 1942 Battle of Midway to which a special section has been allocated in this gallery. Some experts believe the assistance provided by the **Dauntless** helped bring about a turning point in the Pacific war. The Douglas SBD was later replaced by the Curtiss SB2C. The Douglas A-4C **Skyhawk** displayed here proved its worth in Southeast Asia during the Vietnam War; the plane, a jet, was used by both the Navy and the Marines. In this gallery it is displayed to show part of the large bomb load that was carried on combat missions and its external fuel tank.

From a bridge on the **USS Smithsonian's** CVM-70 deck, visitors can watch a (filmed) aircraft land on a carrier; from the other end of the carrier they can see a plane take off, assisted by an initial boost from a steam catapult. An exhibit recounts the history of the first shipboard take off and the first shipboard landing, with photographs of Eugene Ely's take off and two months later his landing on a flight deck in 1911, two very important historic events. Other exhibits illustrate the history of aircraft carrier development.

Displayed in a small museum in this gallery are models and photographs with their histories of historic planes such as: Fokker

FVII-3M **Southern Cross;** Bleriot XI, which flew across the English
Channel on July 25, 1909, the first heavier-than-air machine to do
so; a 1910 Fabre Hydravion, and a Curtiss Navy A-1, an early seaplane.
There are also stories with illustration of ten record overwater flights
that include those by Amelia Earhart, whose red Lockheed **Vega** hangs
in this gallery, Lindbergh and others. Uniforms of the U.S. Navy
and Marine Corps are displayed in this museum.

There is a restored ready room which is the pilot's living
room while on board an aircraft carrier. From here the visitor can
get a pilot's eye view of activities on a carrier including taking off
(strapped behind the pilot), taking part in a mock combat aloft, and
then returning to the carrier and landing on it with the tail hook
catching the hook on the plane and bringing it to a stop (all by courtesy
of film).

On this gallery's second level balcony, one can go into the
Primary Flight Control Area (PRIFLY), the nerve control center
of a carrier during day operations; and to the Navigation Bridge,
usually located high on the forward edge of the carrier's superstruction.
Both are equipped with electronic equipment, telephones, and radio
equipment to monitor each craft's launching and return to the carrier
when it is secured on board.

Gallery 205: World War II Aviation (Second Floor)

As one enters the hall a display tells about the Flying Tigers,
describing the operations of this group of American volunteers who
participated under the leadership of General Claire Chennault. Shown,
among other things, are the flag General Chennault flew over his
headquarters, the Air Force shoulder patches, illustrations of the
crew, and General Chennault's medals and decorations.

In the hall are some sad remembrances of the most destructive
war in history with more than 35,000,000 lives lost. At first it was
confined to Europe (for the first two years), but with the Japanese
attack on Pearl Harbor (December 7, 1941), it spread to the Pacific.
The airplane played an important role in the conduct of the war.
There were hundreds of new aircrafts developed and advances in
propulsion systems and aerodynamics were very rapid and extraordinary.
Because of space limitations this gallery shows only a few of the
best-known fighter aircraft of some of the participating nations.
The display of fighter planes, photographs of many bombers, the large
mural by Keith Ferris of the **Thunder Bird** Boeing B-17 G, the most
widely used bomber in World War II, and the nose sections of some
actual bombers can be seen in this gallery. The engines displayed
are all authentic; they were used on fighter planes and other craft
by different nations during World War II which began on September
1, 1939 and ended on August 15, 1945.

Many considered the North American P-51-D **Mustang** shown
here the best fighter plane of World War II; because of its speed, range,
firepower, and maneuverability, the **Mustang** was extremely versatile.
It provided escort support for bombing and strafing missions in every
major theater of the war. The **Mustang**s proved especially effective
when earlier engines, the Allison P-51s, were replaced by Rolls-Royce

Merlin engines and when the three bladed propellers were replaced by four bladed propellers. The Grumman F6F, another great United States fighter, is also shown here, as is the Norden Bombsight used for high precision bomb sighting.

Another allied fighting plane was the British Supermarine Mark VII **Spitfire,** shown here. Designed as an interceptor for the German fighters and bombers invading England, it was later used as a fighter plane, escorting bombers into Germany. It was also used for aerial photography, and in rescuing pilots downed in the English Channel. Other World War II allied fighter planes shown here include the **Hurricane, Warhawk, Mosquito,** and **Defiant.**

The cockpit section of the Martin B-26B Marauder **Flak Bait** shown here was part of a twin engine World War II American bomber. It flew many missions in the European theater, served in the African campaign, and returned safely from all of its many spectacular encounters. Other World War II bombers are illustrated here, including the **Halifax** and the **Lancaster.**

The Messerschmitt Bf.109 (with a B-505 engine) was one of the best German fighters of World War II. It had great speed, maneuverability, and other virtues, but in the long run was no match for American fighter planes. The Messerschmitt is displayed in this gallery with another important German fighter plane, the Focke-Wulf FW 190.

A well-engineered Italian fighter plane, the Macchi C.202 **Folgore** (meaning "Lightning") is the only example of its type remaining in the world. It is suspended from the ceiling in this hall. The **Folgore** gave stiff competition to both the American Curtiss P-40 and the British **Hawker Hurricane** fighting planes, but was decidely outflown by the late-arriving **Spitfires** and **Mustangs.**

A Japanese Mitsubishi **Zero,** a fighter plane, is suspended from the ceiling of this hall: **Zeros** such as this one escorted the bombers that attacked Pearl Harbor. The swift and maneuverable **Zero** was a force to be reckoned with, and it was not until planes like the **Mustang** appeared that the **Zero** began to lose ground.

In addition to the aircraft displayed here, there are several engines noted for their performance in World War II planes. Among these are a Pratt and Whitney R-2800 Double Wasp engine, which is shown with an explanation about this radial engine and the aircrafts in which it was carried; a Rolls Royce Merlin Mark 64, which was built for England in the United States by Packard Motors and Continental Motors; and the A-65-8, which was the United States Army's standard engine for all light liaison aircraft.

There is a series of glass cases exhibiting uniforms. These were the uniforms worn by World War II pilots of the United States and Germany.

The Eagle Squadron, an all-American fighter squadron that began flying with the Royal Air Force and the French Lafayette Squadron in October of 1940, is described in exhibits. When the United States entered the war, many of these men resigned from the Royal Air Force and the Lafayette Squadron to join American Air Force 4 Pursuit Group. The history of the Squadron is recounted with illustrations and artifacts.

Gallery 206: Balloons and Airships (Second Floor)

"May the wind welcome you with softness; may the sun bless
you with his warm hands; may you fly so high and so well, God joins
you in laughter, and may He set you gently back again into the loving
arms of Mother Earth."*

The exhibits in this hall describe the history of lighter-than-air
flight. Balloons preceded by nearly two centuries any other type of
man-made aircraft. Even though man's thoughts had traveled in that
direction many centuries earlier, it was not until the Montgolfier
brothers of France began experimenting that ballooning actually
began in 1783. In August of that year the Montgolfier brothers successfully flew a balloon lifted by hot air carrying a sheep, a duck, and a
rooster in the basket beneath the bag they had devised and later brought
the animals safely back to Earth after a flight of eight minutes. Their
success spurred on more experiments, and later that same year (1783)
men began to fly the balloons lifted by hot air from a central grate
in the basket resulting in ballooning to be used for military purposes,
and still more years for its use in science. On an overhead grid in
this gallery are examples of bright-colored modern balloons which
today use propane burners to control the temperature of the air within
the balloon and can control the height to which the balloon can rise.
A modern wicker balloon basket with its shroud lines and its burner
controls on top can be seen as one enters the gallery.

President Lincoln used balloons for reconnaissance services
during the Civil War. Later balloons were used in the siege of Paris,
World War I and II to airlift people and mail. **Explorer II** whose gondola
is shown here was a balloon doing scientific work in the upper
atmosphere for the National Geographic Society. Balloons continue
to be used by meteorologists to gather information about the upper
atmosphere and for other scientific purposes discussed in an exhibit.
An outgrowth of the development of balloons was the zeppelin used
for the transportation of people and for commercial uses, but later
discarded as dangerous.

An exhibit explains the work of the Montgolfier brothers,
of France who used their knowledge of the laws of buoyancy and
what they had learned in their paper manufacturing business to make
hot air balloons of linen bags lined with paper 10.7 meters in diameter.
Small dioramas illustrate their experiments. There is also a one-quarter
scale model of a Montgolfier type of balloon that has the air heated
by a disguised heater in its base. The balloon rises as the air is heated
then settles down as the air cools. On August 27, 1783 the ascent
of a Montgolfier balloon that sailed over Paris was witnessed by
Benjamin Franklin who was at that time the U.S. Minister to France.

In a "balloon room" a puppet show tells the humorous story
of the 1785 flight across the English Channel by French Jean-Pierre
Blanchard and American Dr. John Jeffries in a hydrogen balloon.
The balloon traveled thirty-one and one half miles, leaving Dover,
England at one p.m. and arriving at Calais, France two hours later.

*This balloonist's prayer was heard on CBS's Morning News June 24,
1983, the 200th anniversary of ballooning. Source and author unknown.

A section of this hall illustrates balloons used for military purposes. T.S.C. Lowe successfully persuaded President Lincoln to make use of balloons for observing the movements of Confederate troops during the Civil War; balloons were used in the siege of Paris during the Franco-Prussian War of 1870-71 providing the first air lifts; during World War I and II blimps were used for coastal patrol—flying above the ships when they got close to the coast so there would be less opportunity for enemy aircraft to get down close to the ships on their bombing raids; and balloons were also used for anti-submarine warfare. Also shown is an example of a Japanese balloon bomb sent over from Japan on the jet winds. The one exhibited was picked up in Mexico. The first balloon to fly over the Rockies, **The American,** is displayed in this hall. Unmanned balloons carrying scientific instruments is used in research in the upper stratosphere where human observers are unable to travel. Often information from these balloons are dropped to the ground from parachutes.

An exhibit shows the cabin of the advertising Goodyear blimp **Pilgrim.** It was completed in 1925, the first commercial helium filled blimp. Its design was later incorporated in many blimps.

Zeppelins, rigid giant airships like the **Graf Zeppelin** and the **Hindenburg,** were used to fly across the Atlantic Ocean until the catastrophic burning of the Hindenburg at its mooring mast at Lakehurst, New Jersey in 1937. A thirty foot model of the Hindenburg and its control gondola are shown. They were made and used by Universal Studios in filming a story about the Hindenburg. An exhibit displays the furniture, chinaware, silverware, and place settings that were typical in the dining rooms of the Hindenburg and the Graf Zeppelin. Luxurious passenger accommodations on these zeppelins for which passengers paid $720 round trip were comparable to those provided in first class ocean-going liners.

An eye-catching exhibit shows the **Double Eagle II** with its red and yellow gondola, the first balloon to cross the Atlantic and land near Paris in 1978. This balloon was piloted by Max Anderson (who was killed in 1983 when his balloon crashed in Germany), Ben Abruzzo, and Larry Newman. The flight originated in Presque Isle, Maine and landed in a field near Miserey, France about sixty miles from Paris. In all it took 137 hours and 6 minutes for this first success-ful balloon flight across the Atlantic. Mannequins in this balloon representing the pilots wear the clothes the pilots wore during the flight. Colorful bags of sand, a table on which is seen a teapot and a water bottle, chairs, radio, a satellite transmitter and other artifacts they took can all be seen. A moving picture describing their take off and landing is shown in this gallery. Like a similar request for Lindbergh's plane, **The Spirit of St. Louis,** a cable was dispatched requesting that the **Double Eagle II** be given to the National Air and Space Museum; an affirmative response has made it possible to show the **Double Eagle II** in this gallery.

Gallery 207: Exploring the Planets (Second Floor)

Recent planetary explorations have answered many questions

about our solar system and have, in turn, raised many more. Exhibits in this gallery describe various telescopes able to detect light from sources at great distances from the Earth. Some of these traveling to Earth started, in some cases, before the Earth was formed. Among the questions discussed in this hall that are still puzzling our astronomers are how was the universe formed and when, and is the universe expanding and, if so, how long will it continue to do so? In our own Milky Way galaxy there are estimated to be over 100,000,000,000 stars. Based on the planets found in our solar system it is believed by some astronomers that there could be other planets in orbit around the stars in our galaxy and similar solar systems in other galaxies. The reader is referred to the back-up satellite **Pioneer 10** in Gallery 100 which was sent on a space probe of Jupiter, Saturn, Venus, and later Uranus and Pluto. Before it was rocketed into space, there was attached to it a plaque engraved with images of a man and a woman, the location of Earth in our solar system along with other scientific information in the hopes that it might be recovered and understood by intelligent life that exists elsewhere in the universe.

Important exhibits in this gallery discuss spacecraft that have been sent from the United States with a few from Russia to explore our own solar system and gather information about it which land-based instruments are unable to discern. The United States succeeded in landing six crews of astronauts on the moon who brought back much that was not known about our Earth's satellite. In addition, unmanned satellites sent on missions before the Apollo missions to flyby, orbit, land, and impact on the moon relayed information about it that was relayed to Earth with photographs and by radio. These were preparatory missions to a landing on the moon. Examples include the **Ranger 9** which photographed and sent back pictures of the lunar surface as it descended and crashed on the moon in 1965. A selection of photographs taken from the Surveyor series is shown here.

Exhibits tell about the earliest known planets, Mercury, Venus, Mars, Jupiter and Saturn, which were named for important Roman gods. Because of their relative nearness to Earth these planets were thought, at one time, to move around our planet, Earth. An historical exhibit describes and illustrates the ideas of planetary motion. Ptolemy, a famous Egyptian astronomer and geographer who flourished in the second century A.D., devised a rather complex system in which the motionless Earth was, as he saw it, at the center of the universe with the sun, moon, and known planets going around it. He devised cycles and epicycles to account for the irregular motions of the planets (name given by the Greeks for wanderers) going around the Earth. Ptolemy's astronomical ideas were accepted for hundreds of years. Copernicus (1473-1543), dissatisfied with Ptolemy's explanations of planetary motion disproved them and promulgated the theory that the sun was the center of the solar system and that the Earth and other planets revolved around it. Kepler (1571-1659) added to this knowledge when he developed Kepler's Laws of Planetary Motion. Galileo (1564-1642) added support to the Copernican theory. He was intimidated and condemned for the heliocentric theories he advocated, only retracting when threatened with the rack, an instrument of torture.

Exhibits discuss and illustrate telescopes which have played major roles in learning so much about our planets. Galileo devised telescopes which he was able to fix on the moon and other planets and with increased power to see things never discerned before. Since Galileo's time greater numbers and more highly powered telescopes were developed to examine the sky of Copernicus, Kepler, Galileo and others verifying and exonerating their theories and continuing to reveal evidence of additional revelation about our solar system. The exhibits discuss and illustrate how the early telescopes helped discover four of Jupiter's moons, later five of Saturn's moons, and later revealed two more of Saturn's moons. Other discoveries made in the 19th century discussed and illustrated in exhibits include the planet Uranus in 1801 and two of its moons, and the planetoids in the asteroid belt. In the 1840s the planet Neptune with one of its two moons was located. In 1848 another of Saturn's moons was discovered; in 1877 two of Mars' moons; in 1892 a ninth moon of Saturn. In the 20th century seven more satellites of Jupiter were discovered; in 1930 the planet Pluto (the ninth planet in our solar system) was discovered and photographs of it are shown and discussed. In 1948 a fifth moon of Uranus, and in 1950 a second moon belonging to Neptune were located, all illustrated with labeled explanations.

The surface area of Mars is approximately the same as Earth. Exhibits in this hall discuss this planet. The **Mariner, Viking I** and **II**, and **Mars Landers** (1976), which surveyed Mars opened vistas for astronomers about the surface and climate of that planet. The photographs taken by their cameras and relayed to Earth showed unbelievable high volcanic cones and rocky surfaces. A selection of them are shown in this gallery. Particularly interesting are the sites where Viking I Lander came down on July 20, 1976 on Chrysae, and Viking II's landing site on Utopia. At both landing sites the Viking Landers put out mechanical arms that dug out sand and brought it back into the space-craft for analysis. These red sands of Mars were analyzed very carefully. The experiment found the soil of Mars did not appear to contain organic material—no trace of any living matter was found. These unmanned spacecraft with their robot arms and indoor chemical plants were programmed to analyze soil, air, and gases on Mars, information which they relayed back to Earth along with photographs, thus contributing much that was revolutionary about our knowledge of that planet. Many impact craters were found by meteors, but no canals as Percival Lowell had believed existed there. A huge Martian valley was seen (if it were on Earth it would have stretched from Los Angeles to New York). Evidence showed signs of high winds that blew sand all over the Martian surface. These blown sands have built up in pyramid forms, some that are ten times larger than the pyramids on Earth.

The United States sent **Mariner 10** three times to Mercury to take photographs of its barren and cratered surface; selections of them are shown in an exhibit. Russia sent **Venera 9** that soft-landed on Venus and sent back photographs of this most uninviting planet.

Pioneer 10 and **11** spacecrafts both sent back good photographs of Jupiter, but it was **Voyager 1** (a model of it shown in this gallery) which sent back spectacular photographs of Jupiter in March 1979. Shown on a monitor in this hall are not only its red spot (huge storms brewing on Jupiter) and its four largest moons, but even the first sight (until then unknown) of Jupiter's ring, and of a volcanic explosion on Io, one of Jupiter's moons. **Voyager 2** picked up even more spectacular pictures of the outer planets, selections of which are shown.

Gallery 208: Pioneers of Flight: Aircraft Used on Famous First Flights (Second Floor)

The dream of men for centuries of a human self-propelled craft that could take off and sustain flight was realized on August 23, 1977 when the **Gossamer Condor** flew around the figure eight course 1.15 miles in seven minutes and thirty seconds. The craft designed by Paul MacCreedy is built of mylar, balsa, thinned-down tubing, piano wire, cardboard and Scotch tape and has a 96 foot wing-span but weighs only seventy pounds and has gears under the seat with which the pilot can change the shape of the wings and help turn the plane around. It won a British prize the equivalent of $100,000 at Shafter Airport in California, piloted by Bryan Allen, a bicycle racer, who supplied the manpower by energetically and skillfully pedaling the craft to a safe and happy victory. The **Gossamer Condor** can be seen just outside this gallery.

Inside the gallery are featured rotating exhibits of historic craft, among them the Wright Brothers' **Ex Vin Fiz** (named for a soft drink), flown from Sheepshead Bay, New York to Longbeach, California in 1911 as an advertising stunt. Pilot Calbraith Perry Rodgers' memorable achievement was the first transcontinental flight. The plane made seventy landings for repairs, aided en route by a train that followed the plane (the path went along a train route) carrying mechanics and spare parts. Since the plane had to be rebuilt several times over the course of the journey, very little of the original plane was left by the time it arrived in California. Another pioneer aircraft on display is a Fokker T-2 monoplane with wing surfaces of plywood that made the first American non-stop transcontinental flight on May 2-3, 1923 in less than 27 hours. It was piloted by Lieutenants Oakley Kelly and John MacCready. In addition to these crafts, other changing exhibits show important aircrafts described below. Museum personnel will be happy to answer questions about the location of these or other exhibits that may have been relocated.

Among the first planes to circumnavigate the globe was a Douglas single-engine biplane, the **Chicago**, exhibited here. The April 6-September 28, 1924 round the world flight was an American first accomplished in 175 days. The **Chicago** was one of two Douglas World Cruisers to complete this 27,533 mile flight around the world. The aircraft has an open cockpit and is a two place biplane of tubular steel and wood framework covered by fabric. The 420 horsepower, 12 cylinder water-cooled Liberty engine was used to power the plane. A compass, an altimeter, and a turn and bank indicator on board were the only navigational aids—not even a radio. Photographs, newspaper accounts and other artifacts commemorating this flight are exhibited.

In the Lockheed Sirius monoplane **Tingmissartoq**, shown here, Charles Lindbergh and his wife Anne made two flights to survey possible

oversea routes for international air travel. Their 1931 flight took
them from Maine over Canada, Alaska, and Siberia to Japan, and
proved that the Great Circle route to the Far East was a feasible
one. The Lindberghs' 1933 flight surveyed a possible route from
Newfoundland to Europe by way of Greenland. The information they
gathered was of inestimable value in planning commercial air routes
for the North and South Atlantic. A boy in Greenland named the plane
Tingmissartoq, an Eskimo word meaning "one who flies like a big
bird."

Other exhibits about famous pioneers and planes shown in
this gallery include the many and varied accomplishments of General
James H. Doolittle, race pilot, test pilot, engineer, and leader of
the Tokyo Raid. The Curtis R3C-2 seaplane shown here was flown
by Lt. James H. Doolittle when he won the race for the Schneider
Trophy on October 25, 1925. The career of Grover Loening, aircraft
developer of amphibian aircraft, is described here. Jacquelin Cochran,
who at the time of her death held more speed, altitude, and distance
records than any pilot in aviation history, received her pilot's license
in 1932, and in 1938 won the Bendix Trophy. During World War II
she organized and was the director of the Women Airforce Service
Pilots. A red Lockheed Vega shown here was used by Amelia Earhart
to make the first solo flight by a woman across the Atlantic. She
also made the first solo flight by a woman across the United States.
She was the first person to fly from Hawaii to the United States.

Gallery 209: World War I Aviation (Second Floor)

An indescribable feeling of "you were there" attends some
visitors going through this hall. This gallery contains the re-creation
with authentic artifacts of an advance military airstrip near Verdun,
France, as it appeared on November 9, 1918, just two days before
the Armistice was declared. On that day a German fighter pilot
mistakenly landed his Fokker D.VII, **U-10** on the airstrip. He
immediately recognized his error and attempted to burn the plane,
but was prevented by three alert American airmen. The Fokker D.VII
single-seat fighters had scored many German victories in the summer
of 1918 and contributed to the marked increase in Allied casualties.
One of the Armistice terms stipulated that all Fokker D.VIIs had
to be surrendered. A taped, imaginative re-creation of conversations
between the Americans questioning the German pilot, and filmed
silhouettes moving on the ready room wall give visitors an impression
of the ongoing discussions.

The **Spad VII** fighter plane suspended from the ceiling in this
gallery appears to be coming in for a landing; it is upside down in
the "victory roll" indicating a successful mission. It has painted on
its side the Indian-head insignia of the famed Escadrille Lafayette
N.124 group. The French-built Spad was used by most of the Allied
Forces because it could score heavily against the enemy. A restored
Albatross D.Va fighter is displayed in this gallery, too. The Albatross
D.Va was another fighter plane used successfully during 1918.

Another Spad, **Spad XVI**, shown here, was a two-seat fighter
and reconnaissance plane used by General Billy Mitchell, commander

of the American Air Forces who flew this plane on many World War
I missions, including the battles at Chateau Thierry and the Argonne.
A larger than life bronze statue of Brigadier General William Mitchell
stands in full uniform on a pedestal in this hall. It was sculpted by
Bruce Moore. On one occasion General Mitchell took the Prince of
Wales (later King Edward VIII) with him in this plane on a tour of
the Rhine River in Germany that was then occupied by American
troops. When Charles, the present Prince of Wales and himself a pilot,
visited the National Air and Space Museum, he was shown the Spad
XVI in which his great uncle King Edward VIII flew in 1916. It is said
that he jokingly remarked, "It was very thoughtful of you to have
it hanging there for me to see on my visit to the National Air and
Space Museum."

One can hear via taped broadcasting from a nearby hangar
on the airfield mechanics being bawled out by a sergeant for their
shortcomings in preparing engines for flight. Le Rhone Manufacturing
Company made light weight engines in France which were rotary
radial engines. A model of one is shown in the hall. This engine was
used in Allied aircraft during World War I in the **Bleriot XI**, the **Caudron
G-4**, the **Nieuport 82**, the **Thomas-Morse S-4c**, and others. Other
engines shown here are Hispano-Suiza (French) and the "Gnome
Monosoupipe," also French.

Uniforms of some of the troops of World War I are shown
in cases. Memorabilia displayed include orders, decorations, and medals
awarded for heroism to aviators, as were aviation badges of the Allied
and Central Powers. Photographs of Fighter Aces include those from
Britain, Germany, Russia, United States, Italy, and Belgium.

Models of World War I fighter planes shown in this gallery
include: a **Vickers FB-5 "Gun Bus"**, **Rumpler C-B**, a **Morane Saulmer
Monoplane** (1912), **Bristol F-2B** and **DH-4**, **Fokker E-111**, **SE-5A**, **Pfalz
D-111**, **Ansaldo Sua**, **Spad XII**, **Nieuport 28**, **Fokker D-VII**, **Sopwith
Camel**, and others.

Gallery 210: Apollo to the Moon (Second Floor)

For several years before Gargarin's one orbital flight on April
12, 1961, NASA engineers had studied the possibility of a lunar mission
and had assured President Kennedy that sending men to the moon
was technically feasible. Yuri Gargarin, the Russian cosmonaut, was
the first man in space but our series of Mercury, Gemini, and Apollo
missions (described in this gallery) succeeded in landing men on the
Moon.

Sending astronauts to the Moon marked a major milestone
in space history. Preparing for it was a tremendous task involving
thousands and thousands of people and resulted in a remarkable human
achievement. It seems almost everyone around the world watched,
whenever possible, as did we in the United States, proud that American
astronauts six times succeeded in getting to the Moon and exploring
it, then coming back to Earth to tell the world about it. The exhibits
in this hall trace the steps taken from its inception beginning with
the Mercury and Gemini missions through the Moon landings of the
Apollo programs.

Before humans were sent into space animals were sent to determine the nature of the space environment and the effects of rocket travel. On May 28, 1959 Abel, a seven pound Rhesus monkey, along with Baker, an eleven ounce Spider monkey, made a suborbital flight of sixteen minutes and were returned to Earth. After her death Abel was preserved and can now be seen in the cradle that carried her on this flight. Among other biological experiments described before humans were sent into space were the effects of radiation on three batches of sea urchin eggs; the effect of possible damage of cosmic rays on human blood cells, mustard seeds, yeast, onion skins, mold spores, corn seeds and fruit fly larvae. These flights helped determine that man could physically endure trips in space.

To help determine the technology of flights for humans in space the exhibits trace the Mercury, Gemini, and Apollo flights that preceded **Apollo 11**, the first craft that landed men on the Moon on July 20, 1969 and ended with the flight of **Apollo 17** launched December 7, 1972. In that time twelve astronauts in six trips had landed on the Moon and explored it. Only the flight of **Apollo 13** had to be aborted because of a malfunction in the switching system. The scientific data collected during these manned Apollo flights has yielded important data about the solar system. A wall exhibit discusses the importance of the pioneer work of Robert Goddard (1882-1945), the "father of American rocketry." Without huge rockets to launch them, space vehicles could not have left Earth's orbit for space.

Shown in this gallery is **Freedom 7**, the Mercury spacecraft in which on May 5, 1961 Astronaut Alan B. Shepard, Jr., was carried on the first American space flight from Cape Canaveral lifted from the launch pad by a Redstone booster rocket. On February 20, 1962 John Glenn, Jr. became the first American to orbit the Earth. He accomplished this feat in the Mercury spacecraft **Friendship 7** (seen in Milestones of Flight Hall) splashing down in the Atlantic four hours and fifty minutes after launch. After these flights there were three more Mercury flights, each yielding further information for scientists. There were ten unmanned Gemini flights followed by ten manned Gemini missions. From each of these missions new ideas about space flight were learned and further technological improvements made. **Gemini 4** from which Astronaut White made a space walk is shown in Milestones of Flight Gallery. Exhibited here is the **Gemini 7** command module that was boosted into space on December 1965 by a Titan rocket and carried Frank Borman and James Lovell, Jr. During this flight Borman and Lovell participated in medical, technological, and scientific experiments. Their flight lasting fourteen days was the longest flight of Americans up to that point in time. They also accomplished a rendezvous in space with **Gemini 6** which carried Wally Schirra and Tom Stafford.

The Gemini missions were followed by the Apollo missions. **Apollo 7**, the first three-manned American craft carrying Schirra, Eisile, and Cunningham went into an eleven day flight in Earth orbit in October 1968 carrying the command module. Two months later **Apollo 8** carrying Borman, Lovell, and Anders went into lunar orbit, becoming the first craft to carry men free of the Earth's gravity. In March 1969 **Apollo 9** carried McDivitt, Scott, Schweickart with a lunar module to test the craft in the Earth's orbit, and in May of

1969 **Apollo 10** carrying Cernan, Young, and Stafford went into lunar orbit preparatory to the **Apollo 11**'s landing (a dress rehearsal of a Moon landing and rendezvousing with the command module). Finally on July 20, 1969 the **Apollo 11** mission took place carrying Neil Armstrong, Edwin Aldrin, and Michael Collins. In the landing craft Armstrong and Aldrin went down to the Sea of Tranquility on the Moon and in order not to make too hard a landing fired a rocket that checked a possible too rapid descent. (A back-up model of the landing craft **Eagle** can be seen in Gallery 112.) Michael Collins circled the Moon in the Command Module awaiting the return of those on the Moon. (This Command Module **Columbia** can be seen in Gallery 100.) The **Eagle** on its return would rendezvous with **Columbia**, the Command Module. Recorded conversations of this mission are replayed here. Illustrations of all Apollo craft and the men who flew in them are exhibited.

Several large dioramas give vivid portraits in close-up views of the activities of the astronauts on the Moon. Life-size mannequins are dressed in the space suits (or replicas) worn by the astronauts on the successful Apollo missions. We also see duplicates of early scientific experimental packages (EASEP), a multiple purpose tool used to clean specimens, examine, and mark them; stereo and other cameras that took photographs of the lunar surface and the astronauts; the Modularized Equipment Transporter (MET); a two-wheeled hand-drawn vehicle used by **Apollo 14** crew to carry their equipment; a duplicate of the Lunar Rover Vehicle (LRV) carried by **Apollos 15, 16,** and **17** crews and left on the Moon, which was designed to carry two astronauts of each crew approximately fifty seven miles with their life support systems, cameras, scientific equipment, and then carry them back to the moon lander with the scientific equipment, etc. and with the rocks the astronauts had marked and collected to be stored in the ascent stage of the moon lander for later return to the command module and then to Earth. Other artifacts that can be seen in this gallery (all are back-ups or duplicates of those left on the moon) are a lunar portable magnetometer to measure the magnetic field of the moon; an Apollo lunar drill, which is electrically powered to drill holes as deep as fifteen feet below the surface to make probes and collect core samples; items carried by **Apollo 11** (freeze-dried space food, a contingency feeding system, an oral hygiene kit, a waste disposal system for urine and fecal matter, and a sleeping restraint assembly designed to hold the sleeping astronaut in place and prevent him from floating about in the spacecraft).

Two engines (back-ups of the ones actually used) are suspended from the ceiling of this gallery. The first is a lunar module descent engine. This descent engine supplied power for complex maneuvers to take the lunar module from lunar orbit down for a soft landing on the moon and also fired a retro-rocket to slow the module so it would come down gently on the Moon. The second engine suspended from the ceiling is a lunar module ascent engine which lifted the ascent stage (upper section of the lunar module) off from the lower stage. The ascent stage had to rendezvous with the Command Module orbiting the Moon and dock with it, the engine had to perform with absolute reliability.

A console of the simulator which was used for astronaut

training can be seen in this gallery. It contains switchers, dials and meters used to control the spacecraft and monitor its performance. While lying on the couches of the Apollo Command Modules, the astronauts faced a similar console.

An exhibit called "Snap-Dash 27" describes the Apollo radio isotope thermal electric generator and fuel supply. This thermal electric generator converted the heat energy from radioactive decay to electrical power for the Apollo lunar experimental packages left on the Moon by **Apollos 12, 14, 15, 16,** and **17.** These packages (stations) are still transmitting information about Moon quakes and meteor impacts, lunar magnetic and gravitational fields, the Moon's internal temperatures and the Moon's atmosphere.

In a little theater is reenacted the **Apollo 17** lunar landing that started from Kennedy Space Center on December 7, 1972. Through the windows of the lunar landing cockpit we see the lunar landing of Ceranan and Schmidt, their voices describing the flight as they come down at a final descent rate of two feet per second to touch down on the Moon.

As the visitor enters this gallery he will see a very large wall exhibit labeled "Development of Man's Space Flight, 1957-1980." It traces the chronological development of space flight.

A glass case exhibit shows two types of models. In the first place the models of launch vehicles are shown. These include a Mercury Redstone Launch Vehicle used in the suborbital flight of Grissom and Shepard; a Mercury Atlas Launch Vehicle used in the Mercury programs of the Earth orbital flights of Glenn, Carpenter, Schirra, and Cooper; a Gemini-Titan II Launch Vehicle used to boost the two-man Gemini spacecraft into Earth orbit; a Saturn IB Launch Vehicle used to launch **Apollo 7,** the first manned Earth orbital Apollo mission and also used to launch the crews of Skylab Orbital Workshop as well as the U.S. crew of the Apollo-Soyuz docking; a Saturn V Launch Vehicle used to launch crews of Apollo missions 8 through 17. The second group of models shown in this case are those of lunar module designs. These include the early designs (1963) of Apollo Lunar Excursion module with five landing legs, and the 1965 Apollo Lunar Module with a four-legged final version.

In an exhibit labeled "Apollo Results Exhibit" the visitor will see some of the actual scientific results of the six successful Apollo missions that landed on the Moon and returned to Earth with over 800 pounds of lunar rocks (basalt, breccia, anorthrocite, plagioclase, and others, some of these are as much as 4.5 billion years old) and lunar soil which contained particles of many fragments of rock types.

In a niche in this hall the near and far sides of the moon are represented on a large revolving disc. The near side is distinguished by the smooth areas called "marias" (plural of a Latin word meaning sea), which are smaller and rarer on the far side. Some of the more prominent features of the Moon are identified along with the six Apollo landing sites.

Gallery 211: Flight and the Arts (Second Floor)

Space and flight—their possibilities, their technology, the

244   National Air and Space Museum

minds that inquired into them—inspired the drawings, prints, paintings, and sculptures exhibited in this gallery. As Dr. H. Lester Cooke who guided the NASA Art Program during the Apollo moon launchings said, "Painting is the most lasting of all visual records. Perhaps this project will help to prove the United States produced in the sixties not only engineers and scientists capable of shaping the destiny of our age, but also the artists worthy to keep them company." Some of the art works belong to the permanent collection of the National Air and Space Museum; others are on loan from art galleries, institutions, or private individuals. As art works are generally rotated more frequently than other exhibits in the National Air and Space Museum, visitors who cannot locate works they wish to see should inquire at the Information Desk in the lobby.

Among artists whose works have been exhibited in this gallery are Norman Rockwell's portraits of Astronauts Gus Grissom and John Young; William Crutchfield's watercolor rendering of a space countdown; Georgia O'Keeffe's "Blue A;" Robert Handville's portrait of Albert Einstein; and Guy Gladding's "Second Shield of Venus." There is also Robert Rauschenberg's silkscreen of a rocket at liftoff; and Paul Calle's "The Centerfuge" and "Launch Morning." Richard Lippold's gold-filled wire sculpture, "Variations On A Sphere," is suspended over a platform near the gallery's entrance; and Lowell Nesbitt's steel sculpture of a rocket service gantry is shown here too. Among other artists that are now or have been represented in this gallery are works of Jamie Wyeth, Alma Thomas, Michael Ayrton, Nancy Graves, Jim Dean, Yeffe Kimball, Chesley Bonestell, Peter Hurd, Jack Perlmutter, Nicholas Solovioff, Frank Wootton, Paul Sample, George Curtis, Lamar Dodd, Lowell Nesbitt, William Thon, Ted Wilbur, Robert Vickrey, Clayton Pond, Rowland Emmet, Dong Kingman, Paul Landowski, Wilson Hurley, Tom O'Hara, Arthur Shilstone, Henry Casseli, Robert Shulman, Morton Kunstler, Andreas Nottenbohm, Alan Cober, and many others.

Art works are not confined to this gallery but can be found inside the museum building in many galleries and places as well as at its entrance and on the museum's grounds. Visitors may come upon the sculpture "Delta Solar" on the Seventh Street grounds, a monumental and extraordinary piece of work done by Alejandro Otero and given to the United States as a Bicentennial gift from Venezuela. The sculpture is forty-eight feet wide, twenty-seven feet high, and has rotary sails that turn in the slightest breeze. It is mounted on short stone pylons that are fixed into the bed of the pool. A sculpture by Richard Lippold, the monumental gilded sphere "Ad Astra" rises slightly above the museum's roof at the Mall entrance to the building. Another sculpture by Lippold is "Triple Hero to the Sun." Charles Perry's sixteen-foot globe of cast bronze "Continuum" stands on the south side entrance to the museum, and the sculpture called "Icarus" by Michael Ayrton depicts the mythical god who appears to be taking off on a flight and is at the entrance to Gallery 221.

There are several large murals that attract visitors, among them "The Space Environment—A Cosmic View," by Robert McCall and "Earth Flight Environment," by Eric Sloan, huge murals which face each other on opposite walls of the Independence Avenue (south) lobby, each painted with acrylic paints on Belgian linen; a mural in

Gallery 205 of the B-17 **Thunderbird** by aviation artist Keith Ferris who did another painting "The 19th Hour" in Gallery 208; and three paintings about World War I by Henri Farre at the entrance to Gallery 209.

Gallery 213: Flight Technology: How and Why Airplanes Fly (Second Floor)

Visitors are introduced to the exhibits in this gallery by the cut-out puppet figures of two young boys, Wheeler King and Ace Blue, dressed in early 1900 clothing, who are watching the flight of a 1908 Wright brothers aircraft. As one moves through this hall these boys whose puppet figures act as guides in the gallery and while growing older are joined by other puppet figures who are specialists in their fields of aeronautics (Bulldog Powers in propulsion, Reginald Pick, a structural engineer, and Slick Camber whose work is in streamlining planes), explain their specialties and introduce us to fundamental concepts about the mechanics and the building of a plane.

There is a center for live demonstrations located in this gallery that provides instructions on aerospace subjects difficult to explain by graphic or audio-visual means alone. Members of the education staff present programs to help both children and adults to understand why an airplane flies, how it is controlled, and why a rocket was used to get our astronauts to the Moon. The program explains orbiting satellites and what jobs they perform; also other important aspects of flight such as supersonic flight, hypersonic flight and reentry.

The exhibits on certain basic design concepts of aircraft give the visitors a clearer understanding of the significance of these designs and their relationship to the craft. Detailed displays show how an airplane is conceived and built, as well as some ideas about the mechanics of plane flight. A film in a small theater in this gallery reviews the developments in space flight technology.

In 1935 Howard Hughes, flying the H-1 **Hughes Racer,** smashed all previous speed records for land planes. It had features such as flush riveting, butt-joined skin, bell cowling, retractable landing gears, and other concepts which were revolutionary and influenced aircraft designers all over the world. This monoplane is now on exhibit in the gallery's rotunda after having been kept in storage for over thirty years. When it was built it had a tremendous impact on the design of high performance aircraft. It was powered by a Pratt and Whitney Twin Wasp Junior radial piston engine, whose workings are explained and demonstrated in a nearby exhibit. The cut-away model of a Pratt and Whitney Twin Wasp Junior radial piston engine R985 is color coded to reveal its working parts in motion, which include the drive of the pistons, the opening and closing of valves, and the steady rotation of the crankshaft. The labeled parts are further explained by a recorded talk in this exhibit.

A scale model is shown of a Curtiss JN-4D **Jenny** (1918) with its cover removed to show structural details. The Jenny was used by the United States Air Force to train pilots in World War I.

Around the perimeter of the hall are exhibits and short animated films that explain and demonstrate some of the principles

246   National Air and Space Museum

of airplane flight, the proper application of the forces of lift, thrust, weight and drag necessary for powered flight, and the design of wings and propellers that provide increased efficiency for the plane. Lift and drag are demonstrated in small, working model wind tunnels. On one small working model, a section of the wing rises to show lift with another working model wind tunnel that demonstrates stream-lining. Another shows how a tightly fitted, specially contoured engine cover can increase the speed of an aircraft. Other model wind tunnels demonstrate other basic aerodynamic concepts. A wind tunnel model of the XB-70 bomber built for supersonic flight shows where the wind tunnel force and pressure sensors were placed. Also explained are jet and rocket propulsion. A model of a turbo-jet engine is carefully labeled to show its parts and a cartoon show explains how a jet engine works. Other models and blueprints are displayed in exhibits.

In a small space technology theater, films provide visitors with a sketch of past and present developments in space flight technology. Two exhibits illustrate, with the aid of models and films, the chronology of aerospace development. The first exhibit covers the period 1908-1938, the second 1939-1956. Panels around the inside wall of this gallery list contributors and their great contributions to flight technology beginning with the Wright brothers, and below each panel is a list of what was happening in the world at the time of that individual's work.

Samuel P. Langley Film Theater (Room 115, First Floor)
Albert Einstein Sky Theater (Room 215, Second Floor)

Two theaters provide enjoyment, welcome rest and relief for the weary, footsore visitors. The absorbing programs offered in each are quite different from one another, and definitely worth seeing.

In the 485 seat Langley Film Theater museum visitors will find an opportunity to rest and be refreshed (at nominal fee) by some high quality films projected by an IMAX motion picture projector system on a screen five stories tall and seven stories wide. The initial presentation in this theater (and still shown at times) is the spectacular film "To Fly" in which visitors are treated to a trip down Niagara Falls in the basket of a balloon; a plane trip over Manhattan and through the St. Louis' Arch; and finally soaring past the cliffs and islands of Hawaii in a hang glider. The second film, "The Living Planet," offers an exciting overview of our Planet Earth; while the third film "Hail Columbia" is an acclaimed film about the Space Shuttle.

The second theater is the Albert Einstein Sky Theater. Inside this great domed theater visitors can witness marvels brought to them by means of a Zeiss projector, a Bicentennial gift from the Federal Republic of Germany, and also by the use of additional projectors. In the initial offering, "Cosmic Awakening," visitors find themselves seemingly traveling through space much as our astronauts actually did when visiting the Moon. As in other planetarium showings, there is a night sky with the Moon, the Milky Way, and stars in remote galaxies seen, but here museum visitors become armchair explorers by going further than the astronauts and by traveling in this "airship" visit the barren landscapes of one of Saturn's satellites and to quasars, pulsars, and black holes. The second presentation was "Worlds of Tomorrow." Other multi-media presentations in this auditorium have been "Probe" and "A Celebration of Flight" that dramatized the colorful history of flight.

Headphones available at each seat in the Albert Einstein Sky Theater give the visitor an opportunity to listen to the narrative presented in French, German, Spanish, or Japanese. For the English narrative headphones are not necessary. The charge in this theater is also a nominal one.

Every Thursday at noon there is a free weekly planetarium lecture, part of a series called "Noontime With The Stars" given in the Albert Einstein Sky Theater. It provides in thirty minutes a view of the seasonal constellations and planets currently on view in the night sky. There is no charge for the planetarium lecture.

Suspended from the ceiling in front of the Albert Einstein Sky Theater is a Lockheed F-104 **A Starfighter,** with its unusually thin underswept wings. This Starfighter was the first fighter plane in the world capable of operating at Mach 2—twice the speed of sound and used in many scientific research missions.

Monthly Sky Lectures are given free on the first Saturday of the month by staff members of the National Air and Space Museum in the Albert Einstein Sky Theater. In addition to the scheduled lecture upcoming celestial events due to occur in the weeks ahead are highlighted using the Zeiss planetarium instrument. These lectures, which begin at 9 a.m. sharp, are free but visitors are admitted at that hour only through the Sixth Street and Independence Avenue entrance. Be on time since no late admissions are permitted.

Paul E. Garber Preservation, Restoration, and Storage Facility

Part of the National Air and Space Museum's restoration facilities are located about eight miles from the National Air and Space Museum in Suitland, Maryland. It is an adjunct museum housing a great many aircraft, spacecraft, and a great variety of flight-related objects from the Smithsonian's astronautical collection. This facility, known as the Paul E. Garber Preservation, Restoration, and Storage Facility, honors Paul E. Garber for his devoted service in acquiring much of the Smithsonian's aeronautical collection.

Since 1977 visitors coming here have seen displayed in three Quonset hut type buildings restored planes, missiles, rockets, engines, and launch vehicles for which there is, at present, not exhibit space at the museum on the Mall. Other craft are being restored here. Among the aircraft displayed are: a Hawker Hurricane II CB, a British fighter plane used in the Battle of Britain; a Messerschmidtt 163B (the first rocket-powered aircraft); a tiny Martin Kitten made in 1918 which had the first retractable landing gears still used on planes today; a Curtiss JN-4D Jenny which was a World War I trainer, later used by some pilots in barnstorming demonstrations; a Stinson Reliant which made the first human pickup from the ground by an aircraft in flight; and a Spad XIII World War II fighter airplane.

There are numerous space artifacts exhibited, among them:

the Abel-Baker Missile Nose Cone (original) of the Jupiter launch vehicle which carried two monkeys (Abel and Baker) into space on May 28, 1959 so that scientists could obtain data on weightless conditions; one of the J-2 engines for the Saturn launch vehicles; a model of Surveyor (the original soft-landed on the moon preparatory for Apollo flights); and many other space artifacts. Among other interesting things to see are: a Bell Model 30, the first successful two-bladed helicopter, and some Chinese kites that were donated after the Centennial Exposition in Philadelphia in 1876.

Trained guides conduct the free tours, which last between two and three hours. These tours are made on Mondays through Fridays at 10 a.m.; and Saturdays and Sundays at 10 a.m. and at 1 p.m. by reservation only. These reservations must be made two weeks in advance by either calling 1-202-307-1400 between 9 a.m. and 4 p.m. Monday through Friday or writing the Tour Scheduler, Education Services Division, National Air and Space Museum, Smithsonian Institution, Washington, D.C. 20560. Special tours for the handicapped can be arranged by calling or writing, but children under ten are not permitted.

5

The Arts and Industries Building

By 1876 pressure for exhibit space in the original Smithsonian building (the Castle) had increased tremendously. Spencer Baird, who at that time was the Assistant Secretary, had solicited the donation of many artifacts from the Centennial Exposition in Philadelphia for the Smithsonian Institution. In response to Baird's request, forty-two carloads of mostly natural history specimens, but also Indian artifacts, ordnance, pharmaceuticals, machinery, and consumer products from U.S. agencies and from different areas of this country, as well as exhibits donated by many foreign countries, were delivered to the Smithsonian by rail. Selections of the Centennial artifacts were displayed with other exhibits already in the Smithsonian's possession, crowding the limited space with almost bulging walls. Congress, finally recognizing the need for greater display and storage space that the Castle was unable to provide, authorized an appropriation for what, at the time, was considered a temporary building. The Arts and Industries Building which was then constructed was called the Annex to the Smithsonian and was also known in its early days as the U.S. National Museum. It was inexpensively constructed of red bricks and Ohio sandstone and was completed just in time for President James A. Garfield's inaugural ball held in it in 1881.

For many years this building continued to display selected artifacts from the Philadelphia Centennial. In Philadelphia, that exhibit had drawn over ten million viewers who had come to gape in wonder at the telephone, the typewriter, steam engines, electric communication systems and hundreds of primarily commercial artifacts as well as exhibits of silver, ceramics, glassware, scientific apparatus, pharmaceuticals and tools among a multitude of other things of the 1876 period. In this building, too, among other displays were exhibits of the First Ladies' Gowns, natural history specimens, and air and space artifacts. These last three groups were later moved to permanent quarters in other Smithsonian museums.

The Arts and Industries Building also housed excellent special exhibits such as "Drugs, Their Uses and Effects," and "Photography and the City," which were called "continuing exhibits" remaining on display for a year or more. The largest special exhibit ever staged in the Arts and Industries Building is "1876," an exhibition displaying a number of artifacts which were part of those shown at the Philadelphia Centennial, but also others not shown at that exposition but which were of the 1876 period. This "1876" exhibit was mounted as a part of the Smithsonian's Bicentennial celebration observed throughout our country in 1976. Artifacts from the Philadelphia Centennial plus many more items of the 1876 period (many of which had never appeared in the Philadelphia Centennial) were resurrected from storage and displayed with some artifacts of that period that the Smithsonian borrowed from corporations, institutions, and individuals to create this "1876" exhibit. Of the 30,000 artifacts exhibited in this building only about 15% had been displayed in the Philadelphia Centennial. These are noted in this "1876" exhibit by a gold star.

The exhibition, occupying a good part of the building, was scheduled to remain for only one year, but proved so popular that plans were changed and it is now considered a permanent exhibit. Its unique display of American ingenuity and achievement helps prove that by 1876 in this country industry, technology, science, and agriculture had inventive people who were rapidly increasing America's ability to create, manufacture, and buy and sell products on a world-wide scale.

The visitor coming into the Arts and Industries Building is immediately drawn into a world of artifacts that carry one back in time to another age quite different from what he encounters in his own daily life. He finds here Victorian-style consumer goods of the 1876 period ranging from clothing, silver, glass, ceramics, furniture, organs and pianos, clocks, and even Butterick sewing patterns. There are also foot-powered machines such as sewing machines, products of machinery that operated to produce brass castings, machines for cotton picking and other agricultural implements, and machines for making shoes and boots. Also shown are machines for draining sugar, a machine for manufacturing starch, one for making candy, another for making snap hooks, belt clasps, and buttons, and one for folding paper.

The "1876 Centennial Exhibition" is shown in four very large halls laid out in the form of a cross. These halls radiate from a central plaza on which a large, gently spraying fountain is encircled by seasonal plants and flowers. Nearby benches make this a delightful rest area for the foot-weary.

The visitor entering the Arts and Industries Building from the Mall finds himself going first into the North Hall. The original Centennial Exposition in Philadelphia was primarily a commercial trade fair in which merchants eager to acquaint potential customers with their products showed their finest and newest wares. So one finds in the North Hall the merchandise of furniture makers tastefully displayed, and of musical instrument makers (of pianos and organs and others) placed in home settings. The names and addresses of the makers (or sellers) are prominently displayed so that, if interested, the customer could contact them to make purchases of these or other merchandise. There are also displays of timekeeping equipment (clocks, watches), flat silverware, ceramics, bookcases filled with the books of various publishers. Men whose interests might be engaged by exhibits of surveying instruments, photography equipment, foot-powered tools, steam engines, and axes will find each displayed in its own niche in this hall. Women might be interested in examining the lovely dresses displayed in glass cases and the Butterick patterns for making some of the 1876 models displayed. To add a touch of humor and lightness to these otherwise serious showings there is the large statue of Gambrinus, a mythical Flemish king, who was said to be the inventor of beer. He stands in a slightly inebriated condition, holding a mug of beer.

As the visitor makes his way from the North Hall across the central plaza to the South Hall, he finds almost at its entrance the forty-two foot model of the loop-of-war "Antietam." This model was used for many years to help Annapolis students learn the art of rigging. Nearby are smaller models showing a variety of naval vessels contributed by the Navy Department. In niches in this hall are exhibits of many mammals, birds, and minerals found in North America as well as exhibits on fishing and whaling there. The Patent Office shows examples of some early inventions created by inventors who, at that time, were required to submit a model of their patent along with a written description and a statement of purpose. Other armed forces are represented in this South Hall by artifacts of the 1876 and earlier periods contributed by the War Department. Among these are ordnance material (Rodman guns, cannons, Colt firearms, etc.) and historic uniforms worn by all ranks and branches of the services. The Lighthouse Board and Coast Survey is also represented in this South Hall, one of the items being a huge Fresnel lighthouse lens. Displays of ethnological material in the South Hall show some of the crafts, social life, customs, and cultures of some of the Indian tribes living in America. Among these are some very interesting totem poles, and beautifully crafted baskets.

In the East Hall are exhibited many kinds of vehicles used for land transportation in the 1876 period made by several well-known companies. One of them, the Jim Eisenberg Company of Alexandria, Pennsylvania, shows examples of their carriages, buggies, and carryalls. There is also historic fire fighting equipment shown. A huge railroad locomotive takes up a large part of the central area in this hall. Other exhibits in the East Hall show artifacts from foreign countries and some that were typical of various states in this country. From France we see a beautiful 1876 dress, shoes, and jewelry. A Japanese display shows large porcelain jars, urns, a breakfront case and other furniture with woodcarvings. Chinese objects include furniture typical of that country that also have woodcarvings (chairs, a screen, a room divider), and sample shoes, basketry and pewter objects. Great Britain's exhibit shows silverware, jewelry, and a cosmetic box. From Siam there are masks, bronze works, models of sampans, and drugs. Russia exhibits some sculpted figures on horseback and some pottery. Italy's exhibit includes some sculpted figures, jewelry, pottery, and textiles. Germany's exhibit displays elaborate bronze fruit bowls, glass window panes that are leaded and colored, and jewelry. Denmark's exhibit shows a model of a ship, some playing cards, and some pottery. Switzerland displays a very intricate music box that is about a yard long, watches, and watch movements. Austria-Hungary shows a woven rocking chair, some glassware and jewelry, and a small writing desk. Spain's exhibit shows some swords and ceramics.

Exhibits of the following states in the East Hall display interesting crafts and natural history specimens found in each: New

Jersey, North Carolina, California, Maryland, Virginia, Pennsylvania, Connecticut, Mississippi, Michigan, Massachusetts, Wisconsin, Tennessee, New Hampshire, West Virginia, New York, Iowa, Kansas, and Illinois. In one niche in this hall there are displays of medical, surgical and dental instruments, as well as a wide variety of pharmaceuticals used during the 1876 period.

In the West Hall are exhibits of all kinds of machinery. Among those shown are a watertube steam boiler, woodworking and metalworking machines, special steam pumps (including a model of a compound steam pumping engine), and an atmospheric gas engine. (Those interested in this type of equipment might like to supplement what they find here with the halls of Hand Tools and Machinery and Power Machinery found on the first floor of the Museum of American History.) Additional West Hall exhibits display mill supplies, an elevator, a wind mill, steam hammers, other boilers, a refrigeration compressor, some rotary type fans, agricultural tools (a large display of shovels), wagons, electrical communication artifacts, and a welter of other artifacts including printing presses, pamphlets, books, and telegraphic equipment.

The second largest museum shop in the Smithsonian complex is found in the Arts and Industries Building. One can purchase films, postcards, models of boats, railroads, aircraft, toys of all sorts and a multitude of other items for gift giving. In this museum shop there is a tintype photographer's studio "Discover the Old You." Here the photographer lets the customer (young or old) select the "1876" clothing in which he chooses to pose for the camera.

The Discovery Theater, under the auspices of the Resident Associate Performing Arts Program working with the Department of Performing Arts, shows live performances in the Arts and Industries Building which, in addition to puppet farces and classical marionette shows, gives children's theater productions. At the close of the puppet and marionette performances the puppeteers demonstrate their puppets and artistry to the audience and answer questions. The theater puts on children's education shows, particularly fine ones for the deaf. Tickets can be purchased at the Box Office of the Discovery Theater in this building or one can call for information about days and hours of performances as well as the prices of tickets.

6

The Art Galleries of the Smithsonian

In Europe collecting art, in most cases, had a much earlier start than it did in the United States. One finds palatial art galleries in large cities in Europe filled with great art. However, the Metropolitan Museum in New York, the Museum of Fine Arts in Boston, the Albright-Knox Art Gallery in Buffalo, the Detroit Institute of Arts in Detroit, the Art Institute in Chicago, the Fogg Art Museum of Harvard University, the DeYoung Memorial Museum in San Francisco, the Freer, the Hirshhorn, and the National Gallery of Art in Washington are among other outstanding museums of excellent quality in this country in which we Americans take great pride.

Washington, D.C. has within the city borders and its suburbs some of the finest art museums in the country, including a few that are world-renowned. Among these art museums, eight that are affiliated with the Smithsonian offer the public an astonishing wealth of beauty and artistic achievement not often encountered within such a relatively small geographic area. A ninth is in the process of construction. Some of the works displayed in these Smithsonian art galleries have roots in the past, while others are very contemporary, yet all indicate the presence of great creative abilities. In these facilities the public has an opportunity to observe artworks in many media from many different countries that were produced during different periods in time. Best of all, admission to each gallery is free.

Just to see Rembrandts, Manets, El Grecos, Degas, Copleys, Calders, Turners, Raphaels, Stuarts, O'Keeffes, Noguchis, Moores, and works of hundreds of other well-known artists affords the greatest pleasure to visitors of these great galleries; while for others, perhaps more knowledgeable in art, what frequently proves most enjoyable is the opportunity to carefully examine and study the techniques of these famous artists. The visitor services in each facility offer illustrated lectures, films, tours, publications, etc., which help enrich the public's knowledge of the treasures found in each gallery by interpreting for them some of the exhibited artworks and serve to further a greater appreciation of the artists and their works.

Much has been written about these museums and their particular collections. Information about them is found in catalogs, or other publications that one can purchase in the Publication Shops or as reference material that is part of the holdings of large libraries or special art gallery libraries. The descriptive summary of each Smithsonian art gallery in the ensuing pages provides a brief history of the museum and a representative selection of famous or noteworthy works found in each.

There are a number of artists whose works can be seen in more than one Smithsonian art gallery. For example (and only a few artists are cited, among others who might be mentioned), we can see in both the Hirshhorn and the Museum of American Art works by: Albers, Anshutz, Archipenko, Avery, Calder, Cassatt, Chase, Cornell, Davies, Stuart and Gene Davis, de Kooning, Dickinson, Diebenforn, Dine, Eakins, Eilshemius, Evergood, Frankenthaler, Gabo, Gatch, Gorky, Gottlieb, Graves, Groves, Gropper, Hartley, Hassam, Henri, Hoffmann, Hooper, Indiana, Inness, Johns, Johnston, Kelly, Kepes, Kline, Lawson, Luks, MacIver, Marc-Relli, Metcalf, Mitchell, Motherwell, Myers, Nadelman, Nakian, Noguchi, Noland, O'Keeffe, Olitski, Oliveira, Pousette-Dart, Powers, Prendergast, Rauschenberg, Ray, Rickey, Rivers, Roszak, Rothko, Ryder, Sargent, Segal, Sheeler, Shinn, Sloan, Smith, Stella, Still, Tobey, Twachtman, Warhol, Whistler, Wyeth, and Zorach. Among artists whose works are in the Hirshhorn and in the National Gallery of Art (and again only some are cited) are: Bellows, Blakelock, Braque, Calder, Eakins, Francis, Gaugin, Hartley, Hassam, Henri, Homer, Houdon, Innes, Johnston, Kline, Luks, Maillol, Matisse, Miro, Modigliani, Motherwell, Noguchi, O'Keeffe, Picasso, Renoir, Rodin, Ryder, Sargent, Twachtman, and Whistler. A few artists represented in the Hirshhorn and in the National Portrait Gallery (again more could be cited) are: Epstein, Henri, Houdon, Johnston, Sargent, Shahn, and Sloan. Several artists in the Hirshhorn are also represented in the Freer Gallery of Art: Hassam, Homer, Metcalf, Sargent, Thayer, Twachtman, and Whistler.

For the individual who wishes to pursue the works of a particular artist, the Information Desks in each facility are very helpful, and Publication Shops carry catalogs or other publications, and sometimes reprints of an artist's works. The Information Desks are a also a good source for current information about illustrated lectures, films, tours, and concerts. Bulletin Boards are another good source for information, for they, too, announce current services. These services, most of them free, should prove very attractive to inquiring minds interested in art.

Three galleries are on the Mall within fairly easy walking distance of one another. The National Gallery of Art's West Building is on the north side of the Mall (east of the Museum of Natural History) with its East Building close by at Fourth and the Mall and is entered from off the National Gallery Plaza. The Hirshhorn Museum and Sculpture Garden, with some of its art in the garden and the rest in the easily recognizable circular building, is on the south side of the Mall across from the National Gallery. Also on the south side of the Mall is the Freer Gallery of Art in its Florentine Renaissance building west of the Castle, the Smithsonian's original building. On Pennsylvania Avenue (almost across from the White House and next door to Blair House, the guest house for important visiting dignitaries) is the Renwick Gallery of Art (the original Corcoran Gallery of Art), which is today administered by the Museum of American Art. About three-quarters of a mile north of the Mall is the Fine Arts and Portrait

Gallery Building housing in this single, large structure (formerly the
Old Patent Office Building) the Museum of American Art and the
National Portrait Gallery, each a separate museum with its own staff.
In the Barney Studio House at 23056 Massachusetts Avenue N.W.
one can visit the former home of Alice Pike Barney, who lived in
it for twenty-four years in the early part of the twentieth century.
Evidence of her many artistic interests and those of some of her
friends have been gathered and shown here. This Barney Studio House
is, like the Renwick, administered by the Museum of American Art.
The Museum of African Art exhibiting art from that continent is
presently located at 316 A Street N.E., but will be moving, when
construction is completed, into an area that was formerly occupied
by the Victorian Gardens on Independence Avenue and in back of
the Arts and Industries Building and the Castle. Another art museum
on Independence Avenue will open, when construction is completed,
as the Sackler Center for African, Near Eastern, and Asian Cultures.
It will not be a part of the Freer Gallery nor the Museum of African
Art but will have access to them just as the Museum of American
Art and the National Portrait Gallery (entirely independent museums)
in the Fine Arts and Portrait Gallery Building do.

Each of the above mentioned museums, except the Sackler,
is briefly discussed in the pages that follow in this chapter.

National Gallery of Art—West Building

The National Gallery of Art's original building, today called
the West Building, a handsome rose-tinted marble building of classical
style, stands east of the Museum of Natural History on the north
side of the Mall. It was designed by John Russell Pope (who, among
other places, had designed the Jefferson Memorial in Washington).
Its equally handsome East Building, in a contemporary style, was
designed by I.M. Pei and stands east of this original building just across
Fourth Street. When the East Building opened in 1978 space available
for use in the National Gallery of Art nearly doubled.

Funds for the West Building and the land on which it stands
were provided by former Secretary of the Treasury Andrew Mellon
through the Andrew Mellon Educational and Charitable Trust. Ground
for the gallery was broken in 1936. Mellon died shortly before the
building was completed in 1941, but he had already made arrangements
for the transfer to the National Gallery of Art of his magnificent
art collection consisting of paintings and sculpture representing several
European schools of art from the eleventh to the eighteenth centuries,
including some world-renowned masterpieces, and, in addition, some
fifty great American paintings. Shortly after the opening of the
National Gallery of Art in 1941 the donations to the museum's holdings
by Samuel and Rush Kress (brothers) added superb Italian paintings
and sculpture as well as important eighteenth century French paintings
and sculpture. Still another magnificent collection containing many
famous masterpieces came from Philadelphia donated by Joseph
Widener which were later added to by his son, Peter. The Lessing
J. Rosenwald's splendid collection that included notable engravings,
woodcuts, etchings, aquatints, and drypoints which were, in some| cases,

done by old masters like Durer, Cranach, Van Leyden, Rembrandt, Rubens, Nanteuil, and later artists like Daumier, Blake, Forain, Milles, Picasso, Cassat, Vuillard, and Gaugin. At the time of Rosenwald's original gift there were over 10,000 prints and drawings, but he later added many more so the contributions he made came closer to 20,000. Among other large contributors of notable artworks have been Chester Dale, Paul Mellon, Ailsa Mellon Bruce plus over four hundred public-spirited friends who donated single artworks or their entire collections to the National Gallery's holdings, while others gave funds with which to purchase artworks now exhibited in its galleries.

As a visitor enters the foyer of the West Building from the Mall, he will see on his left a Reception Room in which a lighted Bulletin Board announces free tours, films, lectures, and concerts; and an Information Desk manned by art-trained men and women who graciously answer all visitor questions. These people will also give the visitor a free booklet containing information about this West Building that includes a map and examples of some exhibited artworks. In this same Reception Room a visitor can rent taped guided tours of many of the galleries, some in foreign languages as well as in English. This allows the visitor, if he chooses, to see the galleries at his own pace rather than to take a docent-led tour (by trained art specialists) with twenty or thirty people moving rapidly through the galleries. On the right of the foyer is a lounge room and a free check room. A visitor accompanied by a young child can obtain from one of the guards a stroller (free) for the child's use while in the building in which he/she can ride while the adults tour the galleries. There are also wheelchairs available (free) from the guards for those who need to use them while in the building.

A word of caution should be inserted here for visitors who might find it difficult to climb the steep steps of the West Building on the Mall side—go around to the Constitution Avenue side of the building (there is a ramp for handicapped visitors) where you will enter on the ground floor, and where nearby elevators can carry one effortlessly up to the first floor. At this entrance on the ground floor there is also an Information Desk where art-trained people can supply one with information and booklets about this West Building. Two additional entrances are available to the West Building—one on the Seventh Street side which takes one to the ground floor, and another off of Fourth Street.

The visitor entering the West Building of the National Gallery from the Mall will see straight ahead a large rotunda covered with a spacious dome (reminiscent of the Pantheon in Rome) which is supported by huge green-black marble columns. In the center of the Rotunda is a large fountain and mounted high in this fountain is a bronze figure, the wing-footed god Mercury (attributed to Adriaen de Vries). This rotunda is used as a gathering place and starting point for all docent-led tours in the West Building. On either side of this rotunda, going east and west, are long halls. At the end of each hall is a garden court with fountains, plants, and changing seasonal flowers grown by the National Gallery's own horticulturalists in greenhouses that supply plants and flowers throughout the year to both the East and West Buildings.

Leading off from the west hall or west garden court on the

first floor of the West Building are galleries in which are generally displayed Flemish, German, Dutch, Spanish paintings and sculpture of many centuries (some as early as the fifteenth, and one or two galleries of French art of the seventeenth, eighteenth, and early nineteenth centuries. There are, as well, Italian paintings and sculpture from the twelfth through the eighteenth centuries for which the National Gallery of Art is especially noted. Among these is Leonardo da Vinci's "Ginevra de'Benci," the only one of his paintings completely done by him known to exist in the western hemisphere. Other representative artworks found on this side of the West Building include: (paintings) "The Adoration of the Magi" by Fra Angelico and Fra Filippi Lippi; "Saint Jerome Reading," "The Feast of the Gods," and "Portrait of a Venetian Gentleman" all by Bellini; "Passion and the Miser" by Bosch; "The Square of St. Marks" by Canaletto; "The Youthful David" by Castagno; "Diane de Poitiers" by Clouet; "The Maas at Dordrecht" by Cuyp; "The Sacrament of the Last Supper" by Dali; "Portrait of a Clergyman" by Durer; "Queen Henrietta With Her Dwarf" by van Dyck; "The Holy Family" by Giorgionne; "Dona Teresa Sureda" and "Victor Guye" both by Goya; "Saint Jerome" by El Greco; "The Small Crucifixion" by Grunewald; "William Coymans" and "A Young Man in a Large Hat" both by Hals; "Edward III As A Child" by Holbein; Series of Cephalus paintings by Luini; "Portrait of a Lady" by Neroccio; "The Alba Madonna," "St. George and the Dragon," and "The Small Cowper Madonna" all by Raphael; "Self Portrait," "A Girl With a Broom," "Joseph Accused by Potiphar's Wife," "The Mill," and "Saskia" all by Rembrandt; "The Meeting of Abraham and Melchizedek," "Marchesa Brigida Spinola Doria," and "Daniel in the Lion's Den" all by Rubens; "St. George and the Dragon" by Sodoma; "The Suitor's Visit" by Ter Borch; "Madonna of the Goldfinch" by Tiepolo; "The Worship of the Golden Calf" by Tintoretto; "Venus With A Mirror," "Venus and Adonis," "Doge Andrea Gritti" all by Titian; "The Needlewoman" and "Pope Innocent X" both by Velazquez; "A Woman Weighing Gold" and "The Girl With a Red Hat" both by Vermeer; and "Portrait of a Lady" by van der Weyden.

Representative sculptures on the west side of this building include "Madonna and Child" by Duccio; "Kneeling Angel" by Amadeo; "Monsignor Francesco Barberini" and "Louis XIV" both by Bernini; "Neapolitan Fisherboy" by Carpeaux; "Bust of a Little Boy" and "Madonna and Child" both by Desiderio; "The David of the Casa Martelli" by Donatello; "Ferdinand II" and "de'Medici and His Wife" both by Foggini; "Emperor Charles V" by Leoni; "Charity" and "Faith" both by Mino da Fiesole; "Angel with Hurdy Gurdy" and "Angel with Tamborine" both by Orcagua; "The Virgin In Adoration," "Saint Peter," and "Adoration of the Child" all by Andrea della Robbia; "Pieta" by Giovanni della Robbia; "Madonna and Child" and "Nativity" both by Luca della Robbia; "Bacchus and A Young Faun" by Sansovino; "Cherubs Playing With a Swan" by Tubi; "Putto Poised on a Globe" and "Lorenzo de'Medici" both by Verrocchio (teacher of Leonardo); "Virtue and Vice" by DeVries.

Leading off from the east hall or east garden court on the first floor of the West Building are these representative British, American, French 19th and 20th century paintings: "Venus Consoling Love" and "The Love Letter" both by Boucher; "Return of the

Terre-Neuvier" by Boudin; "The Finding of Moses" by Bourdon;
"Landscape in Provence," "The Artist's Son, Paul," "Le Chateau Noir"
all by Cezanne; "The House of Cards," "Soap Bubbles," and "The
Attentive Nurse" all by Chardin; "The Herdsmen" by Claude Lorraine;
"Both Members of the Club" by Bellows; "The Voyage of Life Series"
by Cole; "A View of Salisbury Cathedral" and "Wivenhoe Park, Essex"
both by Constable; "Watson and the Shark" by Copley; "Agostina"
and "A View Near Volterra" both by Corot; "A Young Woman Reading"
by Courbet; "Wandering Saltimbanques" by Daumier; "Napoleon in
His Study" by Jacques-Louis David; "Madame Camus," "Ballet Scene,"
and "Mademoiselle Malo" all by Degas; "Columbus and His Son at
LaRabida" by Delacroix; "Circe and Her Lovers in a Landscape" by
Dosso; "Still Life" by Fantin-LaTour; "A Young Girl Reading,"
"Blindman's Buff" and "The Swing" all by Fragonard; "Mrs. Richard
Brinsley Sheridan," "Landscape With a Bridge," and "Master John
Heathcote" all by Gainsborough; "The Bathers" and "Haystacks in
Brittany" both by Gaugin; "The Lute Player" by Gentileschi; "Trumpters
of Napoleon's Imperial Guard" by Gericault; "LaMousme" and "Self
Portrait" both by van Gogh; "The Franklin Sisters" and "The Hoppner
Children" both by Hoppner; "Madame Moitessier" by Ingres; "Elizabeth
Throckmorton" by Largilliere; "Landscape With Peasants" by Le
Nain; "The Dead Toreador," "Gare Saint-Lazare" and "The Old Musician"
all by Manet; "La Coiffure," "Pot of Geraniums" and "Odalisque with
Raised Arms" all by Matisse; "The Bather" by Millet; "Nude on a
Blue Cushion" by Modigliani; "Rouen Cathedral, West Facade,"
"Madame Monet Under the Willows" and "The Scene at Giverny" all
by Monet; "The Sisters" and "The Dining Room" both by Marisot;
"A Girl and Her Duenna" by Murillo; "The Lovers," "Harlequin on
Horseback" and "Family of Saltimbanques" all by Picasso; "Peasant
Woman" by Raeburn; "Woman With a Cat," "Girl with a Hoop," "A
Girl with a Watering Can" all by Renoir; "Lady Caroline Howard"
by Reynolds; "Miss Willoughby" by Romney; "The Equatorial Jungle"
by Rousseau; "The Banks of the Oise" by Sisley; "The Skater" by Stuart;
"Queen Victoria" by Sully; "Quadrille at the Moulin Range" by
Toulouse-Lautrec; "Mortlake Terrace" and "Keelman Heaving in
Coals by Moonlight" both by Turner; "The Marquise DePeze and the
Marquise DeRouget With Her Two Children" by Vige-Lebrun; "Theodore
Duret" by Vuillard; "Italian Comedians" and "Cerces (Summer)" both
by Watteau; and "The White Girl" by Whistler.

Some representative British, American, and French sculpture
on the east side of this building include: "Neopolitan Fisherboy" and
"Girl With a Shell" both by Carpeaux; "Monumental Urn," "Poetry
and Music" and "Bacchant" all by Clodion; "Alexandre Brongniard"
and "Voltaire" both by Houdon; and works by Maillol and Prou.

Special exhibits that have been shown in the West Building
in the past included: "Drawings from the Holy Roman Empire, 1540-
1680: A Selection from North American Collections;" "Alfred Stieglitz,
Photographer: A Retrospective Exhibition;" "Prints of Paris: the 1800's;"
"Gallery of the Louvre by Samuel F.B. Morse;" "Lucas van Leyden
and His Contemporaries;" "Night Prints;" and "Gainsborough Drawings."

In the East Garden Court free concerts by fine artists or
the National Gallery Orchestra are given every Sunday at 7 p.m.
beginning in October and going through May.

Galleries on the ground floor of the West Building display an array of Renaissance bronzes, collections donated by the Kress brothers; a Treasure Room where one can see, among other things, a group of ancient treasures that include the Chalice of the Abbot Suger and a reliquary in the shape of a cross which is purported to a contain a splinter of the true cross; and displays of magnificent Chinese porcelains. In addition, there are examples of Renaissance furniture, jewelry, tapestries (including a Mazarin tapestry), ceramics, rock crystals; and French eighteenth century furniture, decorative arts, books, paintings and engravings. From the Rosenwald collections are displayed prints and drawings of old and new masters of these arts. There is also on the ground floor a sculpture garden showing many famous sculpture, some relocated from the first floor.

The Index of American Design located on the ground floor of this building has in its holdings a collection of watercolor renderings and photographs of popular arts in this country dating from about 1700 and up until about 1900. This Index was established to record designs of significant historical items: ceramics, costumes, furniture, glassware, metalware, textiles, tools, utensils, woodcarvings, and other types of American craftsmanship which might otherwise get lost. Artists, designers, art schools, libraries, museums, etc. with a need to examine these types of designs may do so by calling and making an appointment with the Index of American Design in the National Gallery.

There is a Garden Cafe on the ground floor located in the Central Lobby around a fountain. It offers soups, sandwiches, and desserts.

National Gallery of Art—East Building

The East Building of the National Gallery of Art opened on June 1, 1978 amid much fanfare in the national press. Simultaneous showings of major special exhibits (which generally remained for a limited time) were displayed on different levels (concourse, ground level, mezzanine, upper level and tower), among these: "The Splendor of Dresden," "Master Drawings and Water Colors," "Small French Paintings," "European Paintings and Sculpture," "Aspects of Twentieth Century Arts," and "American Art of the Mid-Century." Among other well attended special exhibits since 1978 in the East Building have been: "John Hay Whitney Collection," "Art of Aztec Mexico: Treasures of Tenochtitlan," approximately thirty paintings, drawings, watercolors and prints assembled from European and American collections that illustrated "The Improvisations of Kadinsky," and "The Search for Alexander" that included objects from Greek museums.

Like their father, Andrew Mellon, Paul Mellon and his sister, the late Ailsa Mellon Bruce, contributed, with the Mellon Foundation, funds amounting to over ninety million dollars toward the construction of the beautiful contemporary East Building and, in addition, donated a great many excellent works of art which they had collected.

For this East Building architect I.M. Pei designed a trapezoidal building in the form of two triangles which join at a huge skylighted exhibition area. One can enter the East Building directly from Fourth Street by way of a rough, granite-block paved plaza or from the West Building by way of a "Connecting Link" that runs from the ground floor of the West Building to the Concourse Level of the East Building on a moving walkway that connects these two buildings. Found in the "Connecting Link" are Publication Shops that sell art books, cards, prints, etc. The building has provided much needed exhibition space for the National Gallery of Art as well as space for research, educational and service programs that are carried on by a national art museum. The Mall side of the East Building is seven stories tall, and houses the Center for Advanced Studies on its first five stories. In this area one finds an extensive art library, a comprehensive photographic-art archive center, and rooms in which the staff of the National Gallery along with American and European art fellows and professors-in-residence can meet for colloquies on art. On the three upper floors of the East Building's Constitution Avenue side of the triangle are galleries of various proportions. Modern works of art are generally shown in large, high-ceilinged rooms where these large works have the advantage of adequate display space; the smaller galleries in this building frequently exhibit old masters or other works that are seen at their best advantage in a more intimate setting.

Among the permanent exhibits in the East Building are an Alexander Calder mobile specifically designed by him for its place in the skylighted court; Robert Motherwell's painting "Reconciliation Elegy, 1978" which is displayed on the upper level; and James Rosati's sculpture "Untitled, 1978" which is displayed on the Mezzanine. Among other permanent works on display are: Joan Miro's tapestry "Femme 1977," another tapestry based on a mural by Jean Arp called "Variation Sur 'Aubutte'," Isamu Noguchi's "Great Rock of Inner Seeking, 1974," Henry Moore's "Knife Edge Mirror-Two Pieces, 1977-1978," and David Smith's "Circle I, Circle II, Circle III." Others in the permanent collection are: a collection of impressionist and post impressionist paintings that were a gift from Ailsa Mellon Bruce, American prints and drawings that include works by Andrew Wyeth, Jasper Johns, Claes Oldenburg, Jim Dine, Archile Gorky, Robert Rauschenberg, Andy Warhol, and others; and an exhibit shown in a hall on various levels of artworks by the influential and prolific sculptor David Smith. There is, as well, an exhibit of paper cut-outs by Matisse which because of their fragility are shown only on certain days and at scheduled hours in a room in the Tower of the East Building. Inquire at the Information Desk for times when this exhibit can be seen. An auditorium for five hundred and a smaller one seating about one hundred are used for illustrated lectures, films, and conferences.

Many of the artworks in the East Building are brought in for Special Exhibitions on loan from other institutions, individuals, or to fit in with special exhibits from the West Building. One of the largest that drew thousands of viewers to the East Building was the "Rodin Rediscovered" exhibit with 350 works shown from June 28, 1981 to January 31, 1982. It was divided into ten sections and shown on four floors of the East Building. On the Upper Level was displayed "Rodin and the Paris Salons of the 1870s," on the Mezzanine "In Rodin's Studio" and "Creations and Creators," on the Ground Level "The Marbles," "Rodin and Photography," "Early Drawings," and "Studies

for the Gates of Hell," and on the Concourse Level "The Gates of
Hell and Their Offspring," "The Partial Figures and the Late Drawings,"
"The Figure in Motion," and "Rodin and the Beginnings of Modern
Sculpture." Another special exhibit was "El Greco of Toledo" which
was organized with art works from the Museo del Prado, the Dallas
Museum of Fine Arts, and the El Greco artworks from the West
Building. Still other special exhibits have included: "Lessing J.
Rosenwald, A Tribute to a Collector," "Berenson and the Connoisseur-
ship of Italian Paintings," "Grandma Moses: Anna Mary Robertson
Moses (1860-1861)," "The Four Moments of the Sun: Kongo Art in
Two Worlds," "Sixteenth Century Italian Maiolica," "Bellows, the
Boxing Pictures," "Manet and Modern Paris," "Raphael and America,"
"Paintings in Naples from Caravaggio to Giordano," and "Five Surrealists
from the Menil Collections (Rene Magritte, Giorgio de Chirico, Max
Ernst, Yves Tanguay, and Victor Brauner).

Other outstanding special exhibitions have included two from
private collectors "An American Perspective: Nineteenth-Century
Art," from the collections of Jo Ann and Julian Ganz, Jr.; and
"Twentieth Century Masters" from the Thyssen-Bornemisa Collection.
Another excellent special exhibit came from the Hague, "Mauritshuis:
Dutch Paintings of the Golden Age from the Royal Picture Gallery,
the Hague."

Because far too much is there for the average visitor to see
and savor in the two buildings of the National Gallery of Art, many
people (who numbered over six and one half million in 1981) feel
the need, whenever possible, to return time and again. A single visit
can hardly suffice to observe and absorb all that one may wish to
see. Such a wealth of beauty and artistic excellence is available to
everyone in the National Gallery of Art, one should take advantage
of visiting its two buildings.

The National Gallery of Art was established in 1936 as a
bureau of the Smithsonian and is therefore affiliated with it. It is,
nevertheless, governed by its own board of trustees just as is the
Kennedy Center of the Performing Arts.

Hirshhorn Museum and Sculpture Gardens

The Hirshhorn Museum and Sculpture Gardens opened its
doors on the Mall on October 4, 1974 bringing a distinctly new element,
contemporary art, to the Smithsonian's art complex in Washington.
While the museum's collections emphasize modern arts, there are
some late eighteenth and early nineteenth century works displayed
as well. However, by far, the greatest number are by artists of the
late nineteenth and twentieth centuries. One of the goals of this
museum is to popularize modern art by helping the public learn more
about it, increasing their understanding of it, and thus enriching their
lives through a greater familiarity with contemporary works.

As a collection these contemporary compositions represent
some of the major movements of the Western world in art. Some
of the modern movements (but by no means all) are shown in the
Hirshhorn with a few representative artists in each category exhibited
that include: Cubism (George Braque, Joseph Albers, Pablo Picasso,

Alexander Archipenko, Max Weber, Ferdinand Leger); Surrealism and/or Dadism (Salvador Dali, Alberto Giacometti, Joan Miro, Jean Arp, George Crosz, Man Ray, Max Ernst); Futurism (Giacomo Balla, Hugo Robus, Frank Stella); Fauvism (Ben Benn, Arthur Carles, Robert Delaunay); three types of realism: (1) "dark" impressionism (William Chase, Abbott Thayer, Edwin Dickinson); (2) urban realism (Ralph Soyer, Moses Soyer, Reginald Marsh); and (3) social realism (Ben Shahn, Philip Guston, Philip Evergood, William Gropper); Ashcan School (Everett Shinn, John Sloan, William Glacken, George Luks); Expressionism (John Martin, Walt Kuhn, Yasuo Kuniyoshi, Jacques Lipchitz); Classicism (Artistide Maillol, Charles Despiau); Regionalism (Thomas Hart Benton, Grant Wood, John Steuart Curry); Optical or Op Art (Victor Vasarely, Yaacov Agam, Richard Anuszkiewicz, Larry Poons); Pop Art (Robert Morris, Ad Reinhardt, Andy Warhol, Jasper Johns, Robert Rauschenberg, Kenneth Noland, Donald Judd); Action Painters or Abstract Expressionism (Robert Motherwell, Willem de Kooning, Franz Kline, Clyfford Still, Hans Hoffman, Adolph Gottlieb, Jackson Pollock); and Minimal Art (Mark Rothko, Ellsworth Kelly, Barnett Newman). While European artists created some of the paintings in the collection, most of them were done by American men and women. On the other hand, the sculpture collection at the Hirshhorn, which some critics regard as an even more distinguished group than the paintings, is more international in scope.

Joseph Hirshhorn's collection, which had been sought after by many governments for their art museums, is considered one of the most impressive ever assembled by one individual in modern times. The donation of his collection (estimated to be worth between $65,000,000 and $100,000,000) to the Smithsonian was a munificent gift and for the American people a most fortunate one. Congress accepted the gift in 1966 authorizing a site and later appropriating funds for a building on the Mall. Mr. Hirshhorn helped support the museum's construction and continued to donate important works of art until his death. The museum has received gifts of art from many other donors, and with funds donated by generous friends of the Hirshhorn Museum has been able to purchase other works by contemporary artists.

The site Congress authorized for the Hirshhorn is on the south side of the Mall, between the Arts and Industries Building and the National Air and Space Museum. The circular concrete and granite museum structure stands fourteen feet above the ground on four hollow piers. Gordon Bunshaft's design for the building stirred considerable controversy at first, but most critics today agree it admirably serves its purpose—effectively displaying exhibits from its collections of fine modern paintings and sculpture as well as special exhibits, which generally remain for a limited time.

Galleries, called ambulatories, ring the second and third floors of the building; visitors can take either the escalator from the lobby or the elevators in one of the piers to reach them. The inner ambulatories provide splendid spaces for the exhibits, generally, of sculpture; the outer ambulatories do as well for the display of both paintings and drawings. Glass window walls enable visitors to look down into the inner garden court, whose plaza holds a sixty-foot bronze fountain. On the plaza around the museum are found such fine pieces of modern sculpture as Alexander Calder's "Two Discs," Michael Steiner's "Flingtime," Laura Ziegler's "Eve," Kenneth Snelson's "Needle Tower" and "Lorraine," and Menashe Kadisma's "Open Suspense" and "Segments." Among other pieces exhibited in this garden near the museum are Beverly Pepper's "Open Sky," Antoine Poncet's "Corporeal," Sorel Etrog's "Mother and Child," and Norbert Kricke's "Space Sculpture."

Visitors are able to reach the other garden, sunken and terraced, via a passageway from the museum building that goes under Jefferson Drive. Once there they can wander at leisure around an acre of sculpture-strewn land. Here one can find Rodin's "Burghers of Calais" and his "Crouching Woman," "Monument to Balzac," and "Walking Man;" Henry Moore's "King and Queen," "Falling Warrior," and "Draped Reclining Figure;" and Picasso's "Baby Carriage." Visitors can gaze into the garden's reflecting pool, relax on the stone benches, and then walk around some more to see other pieces of great modern sculpture including: Jean Arp's "Human Lunar Spectral," Jean Ipousteguy's "David and Goliath," and "Man Pushing the Door," William Trumbull's "Head," Elizabeth Frink's "Fallen Bird Man," Fritz Wotruba's "Figure With Raised Arms," Menasha Kadisma's "Wave," Eduardo Chillida's "Ikaraundi" and Alberto Giacometti's "Monumental Head." Among many other pieces of artwork in this garden are Aristade Maillol's "Nymph," Marino Marini's "Horse and Rider," and David Smith's "Agricola I," "Cube XII," and "Pittsburgh Landscape."

Below is a short list of some of the better-known works at the Hirshhorn. Please note that because exhibit space is limited, all works in the museum's collection cannot be exhibited at the same time, and so are generally rotated in and out of storage. The locations of works in the museum, therefore, are not given below; visitors may inquire about the location of a work from personnel at the Information Desk on the first floor.

An (S) after the title of the work indicates sculpture; a (P) indicates a painting.

Yaacov Agam
(Israeli, 1928-)
Transparent Rhythms (S)

Joseph Albers
(American, 1888-1976)
Homage to the Square: Chosen (P)
Homage to the Square: Glow (P)

Thomas Anshutz
(American, 1851-1912)
Portrait of a Girl in a White Dress (P)

Alexander Archipenko
(American, 1887-1964)
Sorrow (S)
Woman With Fan (S)

Milton Avery
(American, 1893-1965)
Interior With Figure (P)
Ruffled Pigeon (P)

Saul Baizerman
(American, 1889-1957)
The Miner (S)

Antoine-Louis Barye
(French, 1796-1875)
Tiger Devouring An Antelope (S)

Leonard Baskin
(American, 1922-)
The Guardian (S)

William Baziotes
(American, 1912-1963)
Green Night (P)

George Bellows
(American, 1882-1925)
Hudson River: Coming Squall (P)

Thomas Hart Benton
(American, 1889-1975)
Field Workers (Cotton Pickers) (P)

Albert Bierstadt
(American, 1830-1902)
Shady Pool, White Mountains, New Hampshire (P)

Ilya Bolotowsky
(American, 1907-)
Trylon: Blue, Yellow, and Red (S)

Pierre Bonnard
(French, 1867-1947)
Bather (S)

Emile-Antoine Bourdelle
(French, 1861-1929)
Bust of Ingres (S)

Constantin Brancusi
(Rumanian, 1876-1957)
Prometheus (S)

George Braque
(French, 1882-1963)
Hesperis (S)

Alexander Calder
(American, 1898-1976)
Crank-Driven Mobile (S)
Fish Mobile (S)

Anthony Caro
(English, 1924-)
Monsoon Drift (S)

Jean-Baptiste Carpeaux
(French, 1827-1875)
The Negress (S)

Mary Cassatt
(American, 1844-1926)
Woman in a Raspberry Costume Holding a Dog (P)

Cesar (Cesar Baldaccini)
(French, 1921-)
Cesar's Thumb (S)

William Merritt Chase
(American, 1849-1916)
Interior: Young Woman Standing at Table (P)

Clodion (Claude Michel)
(French, 1738-1814)
Female Satyr Group (S)

Joseph Cornell
(American, 1903-1972)
Shadow Box (S)

Salvador Dali
(Spanish, 1904-)
Skull of Zurbaran (P)

Honore Daumier
(French, 1808-1879)
The Confidant (S)
Dr. Prunelle (S)
Toothless Laughter (S)

Arthur B. Davies
(American, 1862-1928)
Beauty and Good Fortune (S)

Gene Davis
(American, 1920-)
Bartleby (P)

Stuart Davis
(American, 1894-1964)
Lucky Strike (P)

Edgar Degas
(French, 1834-1917)
Woman Stretching (S)
Woman Arranging Her Hair (S)

Willem de Kooning
(American, 1904-)
Queen of Hearts (P)
Two Women in the Country (P)

Robert De Niro
(American, 1922-)
Seated Nude (S)

Jose de Rivera
(American, 1904-)
Construction #76 (S)

Richard Diebenkorn
(American, 1922-)
Man and Woman in Large Room (P)

Jim Dine
(American, 1935-)
Flesh Striped Tie (P)

Mark Di Suvero
(American, 1933-)
Homage to Martin Luther King (S)

Jean Dubuffet
(French, 1901-)
Actor in a Ruff (S)
Oberon (S)

Raymond Duchamp-Villon
(French, 1876-1918)
Head of Baudelaire (S)
Torso of a Young Man (S)

Thomas Eakins
(American, 1844-1916)
Mrs. Thomas Eakins (P)
A Youth Playing the Pipes (S)

Louis Eilshemius
(American, 1864-1941)
Mother Bereft (P)

Sir Jacob Epstein
(English, 1880-1959)
Joseph Conrad (S)
The Visitation (S)

Philip Evergood
(American, 1901-1973)
American Shrimp Girl (P)

Alexandra Exter
(Russian, 1882-1949)
Grey Harlequinn (S)

Sam Francis
(American, 1923-)
Blue Out Of White (P)

Helen Frankenthaler
(American, 1928-)
Indian Summer (P)

Naum Gabo
(American, 1890-1977)
Linear Construction No. 2 (S)

Paul Gauguin
(French, 1848-1903)
Torso of a Tahitian Woman (S)

Alberto Giacometti
(Swiss, 1901-1966)
Annette (P)
Reclining Woman Who Dreams (S)

Arshile Gorky
(American, 1904-1948)
**Portrait of Myself and My Imagin-
ary Wife** (P)

Adolph Gottlieb
(American, 1903-1974)
Two Discs (P)

William Gropper
(American, 1897-)
Tailor (P)

Philip Guston
(American, 1913-)
Oasis (P)

Marsden Hartley
(American, 1877-1943)
Christ Held by Half-Naked Men (P)

Childe Hassam
(American, 1859-1935)
**The Union Jack, New York, April
Morn** (P)
Vesuvius (P)

Robert Henri
(American, 1865-1929)
Blind Singers (P)

Dame Barbara Hepworth
(English, 1903-1976)
Figure for Landscape (S)

Hans Hofmann
(American, 1880-1966)
Composition No. III (P)

Winslow Homer
(American, 1836-1910)
Scene at Houghton Farm (P)

Edward Hopper
(American, 1882-1967)
First Row Orchestra (P)

Jean-Antoine Houdon
(French, 1741-1828)
**Jean Louis Leclerc, Comte de
  Buffon** (S)

Robert Indiana
(American, 1928-)
**The Beware-Danger American
  Dream** (P)
Love (S)

George Innes
(American, 1825-1894)
Niagra (P)

Jasper Johns
(American, 1930-)
Number 0-9 (P)
Flag (S)

Eastman Johnston
(American, 1824-1906)
Mrs. Eastman Johnston (P)

Ellsworth Kelly
(American, 1923-)
Red White (P)

Franz Kline
(American, 1910-1962)
Delaware Gap (P)

Gaston Lachaise
(American, 1882-1935)
**Reclining Woman with Arms Up-
  raised** (S)

Henri Laurens
(French, 1885-1954)
Maternity (S)

Fernand Leger
(French, 1881-1955)
Nude on a Red Background (P)
Sunflower (S)

Roy Lichtenstein
(American, 1923-)
Modern Painting with Clef (P)
Modern Sculpture with Black Shaft
  (S)

Jacques Lipchitz
(American, 1891-1973)
Still Life (P)
Reclining Nude with Guitar (S)

Seymour Lipton
(American, 1903-)
Mandrake (S)

Morris Louis
(American, 1912-1962)
Point of Tranquility (P)

George Luks
(American, 1866-1933)
Girl in Orange Gown (P)

Loren MacIver
(American, 1909-)
Skylight Moon (P)

Aristide Maillol
(French, 1861-1944)
Kneeling Nude (S)

Giacomo Manzu
(Italian, 1908-)
Praying Cardinal (P)
The Execution (S)

Conrad Marca-Relli
(American, 1913-)
The Picador (P)

Marino Marini
(Italian, 1901-)
Susanna (S)

Henri Matisse
(French, 1869-1954)
Heads of Jeannette I, II, III, IV, V
  (S)

Constantin Meunier
(Belgian, 1831-1905)
The Coal Miner (S)

Joan Miro
(Spanish, 1893-1983)
Circus Horse (P)
Lunar Bird (S)

Joan Mitchell
(American, 1926-)
Lucky Seven (P)

Amedeo Modigliani
(Italian, 1884-1920)
Head (S)

Piet Mondrian
(Dtuch, 1872-1944)
**Composition with Blue and
   Yellow** (P)

Henry Moore
(English, 1898-)
King and Queen (S)
Falling Warrior (S)

Grandma Moses
(American, 1860-1961)
The Old Oaken Bucket (P)

Robert Motherwell
(American, 1915-)
Black and White Plus Passion (P)

Elie Nadelman
(American, 1882-1946)
Standing Female Nude (P)
Two Acrobats (S)

Reuben Nakian
(American, 1899-)
Head of Marcel Duchamp (S)
Goddess of Golden Thighs (S)

Louise Nevelson
(American, 1899-)
Black Wall (S)

Isamu Noguchi
(American, 1904-)
Lunar Landscape (S)

Kenneth Noland
(American, 1924-)
Bend Sinister (P)

Georgia O'Keeffe
(American, 1887-)
Goat's Horn with Red (P)

Claes Oldenburg
(American, 1929-)
**Geometric Mouse, Variation I
   Scale A** (S)

Jules Olitski
(American, 1922-)
The Greek Princess – 8 (P)

Barnett Newman
(American, 1905-1970)
Covenant (P)

Nathan Oliveira
(American, 1928-)
Man Walking (P)

Philip Pearlstein
(American, 1924-)
**Male and Female Nude With Red
   and Purple Drape** (P)

Antoine Pevsner
(French, 1886-1962)
Column of Peace (S)

Pablo Picasso
(Spansih, 1881-1973)
Smoker (Color aquatint) (P)
Head of a Jester (S)

Jackson Pollock
(American, 1912-1956)
Number 3, 1949 (P)
Water Figure (P)

Richard Pousette-Dart
(American, 1916-)
**Cavernous Earth with 27 Folds of
   Opaqueness** (P)

Hiram Powers
(American, 1805-1873)
Proserpine (S)

Maurice Prendergast
(American, 1859-1924)
Beach at Saint-Malo (P)

Robert Rauschenberg
(American, 1925-)
Whale (P)

Man Ray
(American, 1890-1976)
Chess Set (S)
The Hill (P)

Pierre-Auguste Renoir
(French, 1841-1919)
Boy with a Flute (S)
The Judgment of Paris (S)

Larry Rivers
(American, 1923-)
The History of the Russian Revolution: From Marx to Mayakovsky
(P)

Auguste Rodin
(French, 1840-1917)
The Burghers of Calais (S)
Mask of the Man with the Broken Nose (S)

Mark Rothko
(American, 1903-1970)
Blue, Orange, Red (P)

Albert Pinkham Ryder
(American, 1847-1917)
Pegasus (P)

John Singer Sargent
(American, 1856-1925)
Betty Wertheimer Salaman (P)

George Segal
(American, 1924-)
Bus Riders (S)

Ben Shahn
(American, 1898-1969)
Supreme Court of California: Mooney Series (P)

Everett Shinn
(American, 1876-1953)
Acrobat Falling (P)

John Sloan
(American, 1871-1951)
McSorley's Saturday Night (P)

David Smith
(American, 1906-1965)
Cubi XII (S)
Agricola I (S)
Voltri I (S)

Raphael Soyer
(American, 1899-)
Moses Soyer (P)

Frank Stella
(American, 1936-)
Honduras Lottery Company (P)

Clyfford Still
(American, 1904-)
1960-R (P)

Abbot H. Thayer
(American, 1849-1921)
Study for Seated Angel (P)

Mark Tobey
(American, 1890-1970)
Plains Ceremonial (P)

Prince Paul Troubetzkoy
(Italian, 1866-1938)
Seated Woman (S)

John Twachtman
(American, 1853-1902)
The Waterfall (P)

Victor Vasarely
(French, 1908-)
Arcturus II (P)

Andy Warhol
(American, 1928-)
Marilyn Monroe's Lips (P)

Max Weber
(Russian, 1881-1961)
Stiff Life (P)

James Abbott McNeill Whistler
(American, 1834-1903)
Girl in Black (P)

Frank Lloyd Wright
(American, 1869-1959)
Two Stained Glass Windows

Andrew Wyeth
(American, 1917-)
Waiting for McGinley (S)

Francisca Zuniga
(Mexican, 1913-)
Yucatan Woman (S)

William Zorach
(American, 1887-1966)
Eve (S)

Mark di Suvero
(American, 1933-)
Isis (S)

Freer Gallery of Art

A Florentine Renaissance building designed by Charles A. Platt houses the Freer Gallery of Art on the south side of the Mall west of the Castle, which opened its doors in 1923. A major part of the collections that reside in it, and an endowment fund for the study and further acquisitions of art from the Near and Far East as well as the building were given in trust to the Smithsonian by Charles L. Freer, a wealthy Detroit industrialist. The regents of the Smithsonian were hesitant at first to accept Mr. Freer's offer but were persuaded by the urging of President Theodore Roosevelt to do so. This decision was a most fortuitous one, for Mr. Freer's gift at that time enormously enriched our country's art collections. Almost until his death in 1919, Charles Freer continued to purchase and give Oriental artworks to the Freer. The Oriental collection he gathered (with more obtained by the gallery after Freer's death) is considered one of the most outstanding of its kind in the western world.

The Freer Gallery of Art provides each interested visitor with a magnificent display of treasures from the Near and Far East. In its collections are hand and hanging scrolls, bronzes, screens, and religious sculptures; metal, lacquer, and stone works; works in ceramics, glass, and jades; manuscripts, and many examples of Chinese, Japanese, and Arabic calligraphy. Seven exhibition galleries usually display Chinese works, five galleries generally show works from Japan, and an exhibit hall features Buddhist and Shinto art. The remaining galleries are devoted to the works of other Near and Far Eastern lands, among these the art of Turkey, Korea, as well as the Arab and Persian world. There are also displayed the works of a number of American artists.

The one American artist whose works Mr. Freer collected extensively were those of James Abbott McNeill Whistler. Whistler had become a close friend of Charles Freer and it was he over the years who encouraged Freer's interest in oriental art, guiding his purchases of the art objects he collected. Whistler's works in the Freer Gallery are probably the largest in the world, although only a sampling of them is shown at any one time. The collection includes many of Whistler's oil paintings (the best known **Arrangement in Grey and Black No. 1: The Artist's Mother** is not here, however, but in the Louvre), but also watercolors, pastels, and etchings. Some cancelled copper plates, among them a survey plate made while he was briefly employed in the United States Coast Guard Survey Department are also in the collection.

Among the other American artists whose works Freer collected and which were shown on a rotating basis in two galleries are the works of John Singer Sargent, Abbott Thayer, Gari Melcher,

Winslow Homer, George DeForest Brush, Thomas Dewing, Willard Metcalf, John F. Murphy, Dwight Tryon, Childe Hassam, and John Twachtman. Most of these American works are oil paintings, but there are also drawings and prints. According to the trust agreement, no further American art works may ever be added in the Freer.

While only eight hundred to a thousand art works are displayed in the galleries at any one time, exhibits are not static but are slowly rotated with those in reserve collections. The staging of special exhibits at times will cause a more rapid relocation of exhibits. Special exhibits in the past have included among many others: "Ukiyo-e, 16th Century School of Japanese Paintings;" "Chinese Figure Paintings;" "Ceramics from the World of Islam;" "2500 Years of Persian Art;" "Early Christian Art;" "Chinese Art of the Warring States Period: Changes and Continuity, 480-222 B.C.;" "Nastaliq Calligraphy: Examples of the Most Celebrated Artists of the Islamic World;" "Japan and Chinese Lacquer: Containers, Utensils, Furniture from China and Japan, 10th through 19th Centuries;" "Boxed In: Japanese Ceramics and Their Storage Boxes. Edo Period (1615-1868): Teaware and Other Ceramics;" "Historical Survey of Japanese Ceramics;" "Chinese Flower Paintings. Hand and Wall Scrolls, Album Leaves—14th through 19th Centuries;" "Japanese Portraiture by Japanese Painters: 13th through 19th Centuries;" "Pre-Islamic Metalwork from Iran and Egypt, 5th Century B.C. through 6th Century A.D.;" and "Japanese Ceramics: Glazed and Unglazed Earthenware, and Porcelains from 3000 B.C. to late 19th Century."

These special exhibitions are usually quite special, and very much worthwhile seeing. Consult the Freer Gallery Information Desk, Bulletin Board, or phone the Freer for information about current offerings.

On Monday through Friday the gallery offers free tours (call the Freer to check for the time of these tours). Guided tours for groups are available, but such groups should make prior arrangements by writing or calling the Freer. The gallery also offers spring and fall illustrated Oriental art lecture series. The lectures are held in the ground floor auditorium at 8:30 p.m. Again, consult the Information Desk, Bulletin Board, or call the Freer for further information. Between September and May the Freer offers an authentication or identification service at which time consultation services are offered to those who wish to submit objects for examination. Visitors are advised to write the gallery for an appointment.

The Freer permits photography, but photographers planning to use tripods and flash bulbs should obtain permission first from the administration office; any copying of objects also requires permission.

Visitors who have an authentic need to consult the library on the ground floor may do so, but are not permitted to withdraw books.

The works not on display are available to students of Oriental art and to scholars who are studying the civilizations of the Near and Far East through their artistic achievements. Permission for access to these study collections must be obtained from the administration: write or call the Freer.

A Museum Shop in the Freer's lobby offers publications and

museum prints, postcards, slides, photographs, and objects in the round. Please see the QuickGuide for further information about other services and schedules at the Freer.

The following brief descriptions of items in the collections are only representative of some of the works that have been displayed in the various galleries. Visitors interested in the location of particular works they cannot find are advised to consult museum personnel at the Information Desk in the lobby.

Gallery I and the hallway before it feature Japanese art of several of the earlier periods: The Hakuho in the seventh century, the Tempyo in the eighth, the Heian period in the ninth and tenth, the Fujiwara in the eleventh, and the fruitful Kamakura period that extended from the late twelfth through the fourteenth century. In the hallway are wooden sculptures of two Guardian Figures (Kamakura period) and the Bodhisattva Miroku (late Fujiwara-early Kamakura period).

Unless they are displaced by special exhibits, Gallery I generally displays Japanese artworks, among them scrolls executed on silk or on paper then mounted with a backing of layers of paper and enhanced with borders of plain or figured silk that acts as a frame to protect the picture. Traditionally the scroll is hung by a cord with the bottom affixed to a roller of ivory, porcelain, or stone to make it easy to roll up and store. Among some hanging scrolls in the collection that have been exhibited here were: "Gohimitsu Bosatsu, The Five Secret Bodhisattva of the Shingon Sect," (Kamakura period); "Emma-Ten Mandara, Two Aspects of the King of Hell and Attendant Divinities," (Fujiwara period). Sculptures in the collection that have been displayed in Gallery I showed: a wooden eleven headed Kannon in the Danzo technique, (Fujiwara period); a dry lacquer Bodhisattva, (Tempyo period); a bronze Miroku-Maitreya, (Hakuho period); and a wood Amida Buddha, (Heian period).

Unless they are displaced by special exhibits, Galleries II, III, IV, and V generally display Japanese art. Among selections of Japanese hanging scrolls in the collection that have been exhibited in Gallery II were several by artists of the Muromachi-Suiboku School: "Landscape" by Gakuo (active about 1500); "Orchids and Rocks" by Gyokuen-Bompo (died about 1420); "Boy on a Water Buffalo" (attributed to Sekkyakushi); and "The Monk Kanzan" by Kao (active in the Kamakura period). "The Hermit Gama" by Soga Shokau (died 1781) was done in the Edo period. Also of the Muromachi-Suiboku School and the Edo period were two small, six-panel screen landscapes by Sesshu (1420-1506). Ceramic ware in Gallery II has included such pieces as a Sue ware jar of the Tumulus period (c. fifth century), a jar by Nonomura Ninsei (early seventeenth century), and an Oriba tray (Mino ware, Momoyama period, 1568-1615).

Unless displaced by special exhibits Gallery III has displayed artworks from the Japanese collections that included hanging scrolls, small painted wooden screens, and some decorated fans of the Rimpa School, chiefly of the Momoyama-Edo periods (first half of the seventeenth century) and of the Edo period (mid-seventeenth to the eighteenth centuries). In this gallery too, selections of calligraphy from the Japanese collection have been displayed: several poems written over floral designs by Kojima Soshin (1580-c. 1655); the "Priest in a Boat" by Shokado (1584-1639), calligraphy by Kogetsu Shugen, (Momoyama-Edo period); "The Tale of Genji" by Tosa Mitsunori (1583-1638); and "Poems of the Thirty-Six Master Poets" by Hon'Ami Koetsu (1558-1637). There have also been selections of ceramic ware exhibited: a plum branch decorated vase by Tanomura Chikuden (1777-1835) and a pottery tray by Kenzan (1663-1743) are examples.

Unless displaced by special exhibits much of the art that has been displayed in Gallery IV belonged to the Ukioyo-e School of the Edo period in Japan. Included have been pieces from the early seventh through the late eighteenth centuries. There have been both hanging and hand scrolls and fine examples of ceramic ware, especially Kakemon, Kutani, Imara, Nabeshima, and Arita ware displayed. "Landscapes of the Four Seasons" by Gyokuran (1728-1784) were among the hanging scrolls shown, while among the ceramics were a tiered food box (Kyoto, Old Kiyomizu ware, Edo period); a molded porcelain figure of a lady (Kakemon-type, overglaze enamels, Edo period); and a pottery urn with applied, carved and incised decoration of the middle Joman period (c. 3000-2500 B.C.). Two small six-panel screens showing children at play were also done by artists of the Ukioyo-e School (Kanei era, 1624-1643).

Gallery V generally features large, lightweight but sturdy Japanese folding screens beautifully decorated, the original ideas for which were introduced from China and Korea. Some screens are embellished with applied gold leaf to form a background for the paintings and on which the artist drew a landscape or a body of water, or a group of people, birds, or animals across the screen uniting the panels into a single unit. The screens vary from two or three panel widths to as many as twelve panel widths. Examples of some of the screens shown on a rotating basis have included: "Dragons" by Nonomura So Tatsu (Rimpa School); "Cranes" by Ogata Korin (Rimpa School); "Camellias" by Suzuki Kiitsu (Rimpa School); and "Coxcombs, Maize and Morning Glories" (Koetau School).

Unless displaced by special exhibits Galleries VI and VII generally display a variety of Near Eastern art works in several mediums created by Persian and Arabic artists over more than a millenium. In the collections, displayed on a rotating basis, have been Persian illustrated manuscript pages of the Inju period (mid-fourteenth century), and of the Ilkhanid period (early fourteenth century). There have also been displayed a silver head of a lady from the Parthian period (first century B.C.-first century A.D.); a bowl with Dionysiac, Sassanian period (fourth century); a silver bowl with scenes from Euripedean dramas of the Bachtrian period (first century B.C. to first century A.D.); a silver bust of a king, from the Sassanian period (mid-sixth century); and a carved limestone pediment from a double window, Kubatcha, Daghestan (twelfth-thirteenth centuries). Among the Arabic art works in the collections that have been displayed in Gallery VI were numerous manuscript illustrations copied from the "Materia Medica" copied by artists in Iraq and dated 1224, and many taken from pages of various Korans: from Iraq (ninth-tenth centuries), from Egypt (late fourteenth century), and from North Africa (thirteenth century). Arabic writing or calligraphy considered a major art form in the Islamic world is used in many different styles such as angular and cursive scripts for copying the Koran, for other manuscripts, and for decoration on monuments, ceramics, glass, metalwork, wood-work and even textiles. There have also been displayed examples of medieval Arabic metalwork such as a brass ewer inlaid with silver made by Ibn Ali for Amir Shihab Al-Din, (Syria, 1232). The artistry of Islamic ceramists showed beautiful objects of utilitarian use and of great artistic quality. Some of them included: an Egyptian bowl with an overglaze painted in golden and reddish luster of the twelfth century; an overglazed painted beaker of the thirteenth century from Iran; and from Iraq of the ninth century a molded plate glazed in a golden luster with overglaze of green splashes.

Among the Persian works in the collections that have been shown on a rotating basis in Gallery VII have been framed miniatures and portraits (fifteenth and sixteenth centuries); illuminated books; and examples of ceramic lusterware, overglaze pottery, slip painting, and polychrome glazes. Among the Arabic works in the collection also shown on a rotating basis in Gallery VII have been a carved tomb-stone made for Sadullah (twelfth-thirteenth centuries); a glass mosque lamp, enameled and gilded, made for Sultan Al-Malik Al-Nasn (Egypt, c. 1360); and a glass bowl, enameled and gilded, made for a Rasulid Sultan of Yemen (Syria, second quarter of the fourteenth century). There have also been shown in this gallery Egyptian, Syrian, and Iraquian glass bowls; beakers, vases of lusterware, underglaze pottery, overglaze pottery and pieces showing combinations of these. Many illuminated manuscript pages from the "Ajaib-Al-Makhouat of Al Kazwini" (Iraq, late fourteenth century) have also been displayed.

Unless displaced by special exhibits, Gallery VIII features the art of India and Pakistan. From the collections and displayed here on a rotating basis have been many examples of illuminated manuscript pages: Amir Khosrow Dehlavi's "Khamser" (Sultanate period, fifteenth century); "Rasikapriya" (Central India, Malwa, seven-teenth century); "Chingiz-Nameh" (Mughal period, school of Akbar, c. 1590-1600); and "Babar-Nameh" by Kanha and Mansur "Mughal school, 1610-1620); and leaves from an album of Emperor Jahangir (Mughal school, 1610-1620). An ivory throne leg in the form of an elephant-lion mauling a warrior (Orissa, thirteenth century); a bronze cast of the Hindu goddess Parvati (Cola dynasty, tenth century); and a bronze shrine of Vishnu with Attendants (Pala dynasty, eleventh-twelfth centuries) have been shown. Also shown from the collections have been a stone frieze depicting scenes from the life of Buddha: his birth, enlightenment, first preaching, Nirvana (Indian Gandhara school, c. second century A.D.); and part of a fence rail from the Buddhist Stupa at Bharhut (Sunga period, early second century B.C.) showing the "Great Miracle of Sravasti;" and a stone Vishna with Consorts (Sena dynasty, twelfth century) from Bengal.

Gallery IX generally houses a rotating display of American paintings from the Freer collections. Among some that have been shown were: "White Lilacs" by George DeForest Brush (1855-1941); "La Comedienne" by Thomas W. Dewing (1851-1938); "A Fisherman's Day" and "Waterfall in the Adirondacks" by Winslow Homer (1836-1910); "A Sailor and His Sweetheart" by Gari Melcher (1860-1932). There was also shown "Breakfast in the Loggia" by John Singer Sargent (1856-1925); "Capri" by Abbott Thayer (1848-1925); "Nocturne: Blue and Gold-Valpariso" and "The Thames in Ice, 1860" by James Abbot

McNeill Whistler (1834-1903); "The Rising Moon" by Dwight W. Tryon (1849-1925); and "Drying Sails" by John Twachtman (1853-1903).

Galleries X and XI have often shown some of the Freer's many paintings by Whistler, among them: "Caprice in Purple and Gold #2;" "The Golden Screen;" "The Music Room, Harmony in Green and Rose, 1860;" "Dorsetshire Landscape;" "Portrait of Charles L. Freer;" "The Little Red Glove;" and "Nocturne: Trafalgar Square."

Gallery XII is Whistler's Peacock Room, originally designed as a dining room for the home of Mr. F.R. Leyland, a wealthy Englishman. It was intended to include fine blue and white porcelain and Whistler's painting "Rose and Silver: The Princess from the Land of Porcelain" as its focal point of interest. Whistler was the last interior decorator to work on this room and he completely redecorated it, even painting over some very fine and costly Spanish leather that a previous decorator had mounted as a wall covering. He added a motif of peacocks, in blue and gold paint to the walls and shutters. A museum booklet describes the controversy that ensued over the decoration of the Peacock Room by Whistler that gives some details of many articles that appeared in the English press about it. The booklet also describes various details of the room. It can be purchased at the Sales Desk in the lobby of the Freer Gallery.

Unless displaced by special exhibits, Galleries XIII through XVIII generally feature items from the Freer's extensive collections of Chinese art. As is true of other galleries in the Freer, the Chinese art works mentioned below are only representative of the collections and their display locations have not been static. Gallery XIII has generally featured scrolls of the eleventh century; the Sung Dynasty (thirteenth century); the Ch'in Dynasty (twelfth-thirteenth centuries); the Yuan Dynasty (fourteenth century); the Ming Dynasty (fourteenth-sixteenth centuries); and the Ch'ing Dynasty (seventeenth century). There have been such beautiful items as the prose poem on the "Nymph of the Lo River" (regular script) by P'eng Nien (1505-1566, Ming Dynasty); a memorial to the "Taoist Immortal Maku" (regular script) by Lu Shih-Tao (c. 1510-1570, Ming Dynasty); an encomium in cursive script by Kung Hsien (c. 1672-1718); and an "Ode on the Red Cliff" in semi-cursive script, by Wen Chen-Ming (1470-1559, Ming Dynasty). Also shown in the past in this gallery have been many rubbings of steles (upright sculptured stones or slabs) including one engraved in formal script with the "Classic of Filial Piety" by T'ang Hsuan-Tsung (T'and Dynasty, dated 745); another engraved in regular script with "The Epitaph of Priest Tuan-Fu" by Liu Kung-Chuan (T'an Dynasty, dated 842); another engraved in regular and semi-cursive scripts "The Thousand Character Classic" by Monk Chih Chih-Yung (Ch'enor Sui Dynasty, 550-600 A.D.); and one recording the spread of Nestorian Christianity in China engraved in regular script by Lu Hsiu-Yen (T'ang Dynasty, dated 781).

The hallway between Galleries XIII and XIV has often displayed special exhibits. Among some shown in the past have been Korean exhibits of scrolls and pottery of several dynasties including the Unified Silla Dynasty (668-935 A.D.); the Koryo Dynasty (918-1392 A.D.); and the Yi Dynasty (1392-1910 A.D.).

Other Chinese art in Galleries XIV and XV in the past have shown additional rubbings of steles engraved by master calligraphers.

From the Chinese collections of ceramics there have been displayed in the past in these galleries examples of polychrome ware of the Ming Dynasty (1368-1644); Ting ware from Ting Chou, Hopei Province (Sung Dynasty, 1368-1644); Tz'u ware from Honan or Hopei (Northern Sung Dynasty, 960-1127); Northern Celadon ware from Shensi Province (Northern Sung Dynasty, 860-1127); and Kuan ware from Hang-Chou Chekian Province (Southern Sung Dynasty, 1127-1279). There were also displayed a pottery funerary urn from the late Neolithic period (c. 2000 B.C.) and a funerary model of a fortified tower in earthenware with green lead glaze, North China, Honan area (Eastern Han Dynasty, second century A.D.). Gallery XV, particularly, has featured in the past many Chinese porcelains of the fourteenth, fifteenth, and sixteenth centuries decorated with underglaze blue.

Additional Chinese scrolls have been featured in the past in Gallery XVI, such as "A Vaisravana, Guardian of the North" (fourteenth century); "Lohans Laundering" by Lin T'ing-Kuei, and "Lohans and the Bridge of Heaven" by Chou Chi-Ch'and (both dated 1178); and a Bodhidharma of the fourteenth century. Many Chinese sculptures have been featured in the past in Galleries XVI and XVII. Among some shown were Buddhist votive images made of gilt bronze; a Bodhisattva in dry lacquer (Yuan Dynasty, thirteenth century); and a large wooden Kuan-Kin "Bodhisattva of Mercy" (Sung Dynasty, twelfth-thirteenth centuries). Other Chinese sculptures made of stone from the sixth to the early thirteenth centuries have included pieces such as a base for a sarcophagus (Northern Ch'i Dynasty, 550-557 A.D.); pillar bases from the Hsing'T'and-Shan caves, Honan province (sixth-seventh centuries); a Bodhisattva, "Pu-Sa" (Sui Dynasty, late sixth century); "Eleven-headed Kuan-yin" (T'and Dynasty, eighth century); and a stele of the Northern Wei Dynasty dated 534.

The Freer collections are rich in carved pieces of jade (nephrite and jadeite). The Chinese have always regarded the carving of these difficult minerals as a major art form. Some that have been displayed in Gallery XVIII included jade ceremonial weapons, carved ornaments, thumb rings, and sword fittings. Also displayed in this gallery have been bronze and other metalworks. Among some of those displayed in the past have been a bronze bell, the late Chou Dynasty (sixth century B.C.); a bronze quadruped of the late Chou Dynasty (fourth century B.C.); a bronze ceremonial vessel (type cheuh), Shang Dynasty (twelfth century B.C.) in which to heat and pour ceremonial wine; and sleeve weights of iron overlaid with sheet gold and inlaid with jade (late Chou Dynasty, fifth-third centuries B.C.). There have also been displayed bronze mirrors of the Han Dynasty (200 B.C.-200 A.D.) and jade ceremonial instruments of the Shang and Chou Dynasties (eleventh and tenth centuries B.C.). Shown in special exhibits in this gallery have been additional calligraphies obtained from rubbings.

A hallway between Galleries XVIII and XIX has featured in the past Chinese sculptures, frequently of the T'and Dynasty (seventh through the ninth centuries).

Gallery XIX has for many years displayed bronze ceremonial items and continues to show these unless displaced by special exhibits. Among bronze ceremonial items shown have been some used as ritual food containers, wine containers, and as containers for sacrificial food. Examples of some shown were: type huo of the Chou Dynasty (late eleventh-early tenth centuries B.C.); type huo, Shang Dynasty (twelfth century B.C.); type ku, Shang Dynasty (twelfth-eleventh centuries B.C.); type kuei, Shang Dynasty (twelfth-eleventh centuries B.C.); and type chih, Shang Dynasty (twelfth-ninth centuries B.C.). Two bronze tigers of the Chou Dynasty (c. ninth century B.C.) are other interesting items of these early periods.

National Museum of American Art

Harriet Lane Johnston was President James Buchanan's niece and his White House hostess. She also collected paintings. When Harriet Johnston died she left several of her paintings to the Corcoran Gallery of Art with a proviso in her will that when the government established a National Gallery of Art her paintings were to revert to it. The courts decided in 1906 when her will was contested that indeed there was a National Gallery of Art and Harriet Lane Johnston's pictures belonged to it. In this rather curious way a national collection was "officially" born. Although christened the National Gallery of Art it lost its "official" name to Andrew Mellon's new art museum in 1937. The former National Gallery was renamed the National Collection of Fine Art but it later once again underwent a name change to the National Museum of American Art. The museum is the national center for American art rich in American works from the nineteenth and twentieth centuries, and features eighteenth century works as well. Artists both famous and little-known are represented in its holdings.

Despite its laudable purpose, until 1968 the national center for American art had no facility of its own, exhibiting its works in existing Smithsonian museums. In 1968 it was at long last moved into a permanent home, sharing quarters with the National Portrait Gallery in the former old Patent Office Building. This building has served not only as the United States Patent Office but as the scene of Lincoln's inaugural ball, a Civil War hospital, and the administrative center of the United States Civil Service Commission. Greek Revival in style, renovated and beautiful, the building is now called the Fine Arts and Portrait Gallery Building. The National Museum of American Art has large exhibition galleries that are located on three floors on the north side of this building, as well as storage areas in it for reserve collections. This art museum also shares a library (in which the collection Archives of American Art is stored), and facilities for scholars and for conservation work with the National Portrait Gallery.

The collections have been enriched since their inception by the generosity of many donors. William T. Evans gave many important American works; Henry Ward Ranger, a landscape painter, left a large bequest for the purchase of paintings by living American artists. Among others who have contributed funds or art works to the Museum of American Art were Ralph Cross Johnson, Irene and Herbert Johnson, S.C. Johnson and Son, Inc., Paul Manship, and Doris K. Magowan who donated her collection of miniatures (most done on ivory with water-colors) selections of which are exhibited in a special gallery of which most are in frames but some of these miniature portraits are incorporated into pendants, rings, and bracelets.

John Gellatly contributed a large collection of paintings (among them Ryders, Sargents, Hassams, Thayers, and Whistlers), sculptures, and many other beautiful objects—reputedly valued at over four million dollars. A rather amusing story is told by Geoffrey Hellman in **The Smithsonian: Octopus on the Mall** about how Gellatly outfoxed his greedy second wife who was more than a little anxious to lay her hands on these artworks. A permanent gallery that exhibits precious items, which for the most part came from the John Gellatly collections, is called the Treasure House. Here one can find, among scores of other exquisite items, a changing panorama that often includes a diamond-studded, gold-enameled box that had been owned by Catherine the Great; thirteenth and fourteenth century ivories and alabaster some in the form of reliquary crosses; Chinese jades; Chinese glass; and sixteenth century Renaissance jewels; ritual vessels; medallions; sculptures; and ceramics.

Among this museum's objectives is the presentation of the great achivments of American art to the nation and the world. It, therefore, loans exhibits of the works of outstanding modern American artists to other art museums throughout the country, to our embassies abroad, and to the Executive Wing of the White House. As one of the participants in the International Arts Program, it also sends contemporary American art to such international exhibitions as the Biennials at Venice and Sao Paulo. The National Museum of American Art also serves as a repository of government-owned art such as made by artists working in the Works Progress Administration (WPA) program.

The renovated museum now displays on its first floor paintings and sculptures in chronological sequence from colonial times through the mid-nineteenth century. In an Art of the West Gallery on the first floor there is displayed selections from over four hundred paintings by George Catlin owned by the Museum of American Art as well as some by John Mix Stanley and Charles Bird King. The Explore Gallery especially designed as an introduction to art for children from three to twelve, and the Discover Gallery designed to make high school students more aware of interesting, different art forms are also on the first floor.

A sculpture gallery on the second floor shows the studio of Hiram Powers, an American sculptor who lived and worked in Italy. The studio contains authentic Powers' artifacts as well as examples of some of his beautiful sculptures. A number of these are also displayed in the hall just before one enters the studio, including "The Greek Slave" which was originally intended to be shown in the Octogon Room of the Renwick Gallery of Art. On the second floor, too, there is a Small Folk Art Gallery; selections exhibited from the works of American impressionists; Hudson River landscape artists are displayed; and works by American artists through the nineteenth century like Winslow Homer, Albert Pinkham Ryder, and George Innes.

In the Lincoln Gallery and other galleries on the third floor are shown twentieth-century paintings and sculptures. Here a visitor will find works by some of our great contemporary artists, among them Willem de Kooning, Ellsworth Kelly, Isamu Noguchi, Louise Nevelson, Georgia O'Keeffe, Claes Oldenberg, Man Ray, Robert Rauschenberg, Robert Motherwell, Helen Frankenthaler, Conrad Marca-Relli, Joseph Stella, Ralph Soyer, Anthony Padovano, plus many others. In 1984 a most generous gift, a multi-million dollar art collection containing 169 works of twentieth-century American realist artists, was presented to the Museum of American Art by the Sara Roby Foundation of New York that includes works by such artists as Reginald Marsh and Edward Hopper, among others. Selections from the Sara Roby Collection are exhibited on the third floor among other realist American works of the twentieth century.

Sculpture set in the courtyard between the National Museum of American Art and the National Portrait Gallery include David Smith's "Cubi 14;" Lacques Lipschitz's "Bellerophon Taming Pegasus;" a stabile by Alexander Calder, and a copy of Augustine Saint-Gaudens' "Grief." In this courtyard are tables and chairs which in fair weather are occupied by diners who bring their trays from the "Patent Pending Cafeteria" out there to enjoy its peaceful setting.

Below is a representative list of some of the American paintings and sculpture exhibited on the three floors of the National Museum of American Art. A (P) indicates a painting, and (S) a sculpture. Consult the Information Desk for locations of these or other works by artists in the collections.

Joseph Albers
(1880-)
Homage to the Square—Insert (P)

Thomas P. Anshutz
(1851-1912)
Checker Players (P)

Milton Avery
(1893-1965)
Spring Orchard (P)

Saul Baizerman
(1889-1957)
Primavera (S)

Peggy Bacon
(1895-)
The Elevated (P)

Cecelia Beaux
(1855-1942)
**Henry Sturgis Drinker
   Man with the Cat** (P)

William Baziotes
(1912-1963)
Scepter (P)

George Bellows
(1882-1925)
Mr. & Mrs. Philip Wase (P)

Thomas Hart Benton
(1889-1975)
Gateside Conversation (P)

Albert Bierstadt
(1830 Germany-1902 USA)
Alaskan Coast Range (P)

Ralph Blakelock
(1847-1919)
Sunset, Navarro Ridge, California
   (P)

Ilya Bolotowsky
(1907-)
Vibrant Reds (P)

Solon H. Borglum
(1868-1922)
**The Command of God to Retreat,
   Napoleon at Moscow** (S)

Romaine Brooke
(1874-1970)
**Jeune Fille Anglaise Yeux, et
   Rubans, Verts** (P)

George Loring Brown
(1814-1889)
Italian Landscape Near Florence (P)

Henry Kirke Brown
(1814-1886)
La Grazia (S)

Charles Burchfield
(1893-1967)
Orion in December (P)

Mary Cassatt
(1844-1926)
The Caress (P)
**Spanish Dancer Wearing a Lace
    Mantilla** (P)

George Catlin
(1796-1882)
Eagle's Rib, A Pigeon Chief (P)
**Buffalo Chase in Winter, Indians
    on Snow Shoes** (P)
**River Bluff, 1320 Miles Above
    St. Louis** (P)

William Merritt Chase
(1849-1916)
Chinnecock Hills (P)

Frederick E. Church
(1826-1900)
Cotopaxi (P)
Aurora Borealis (P)

Thomas Cole
(1801 England-1848 USA)
**The Pilgrim of the Cross at the
    End of His Journey** (P)

Jasper Cropsey
(1823-1900)
Indian Summer (P)

Leon Dabo
(1868-1960)
Evening on the Hudson (P)

Gene Davis
(1934-)
Raspberry Icicle (P)

Stuart Davis
(1894-1964)
International Surface No. 1 (P)

Arthur B. Davies
(1862-1928)
Evensong (P)

Willem de Kooning
(1904-)
Woman VIII (P)
The Wave (P)

Thomas Dewing
(1851-1938)
A Reading (P)

Henry Dexter
(1806-1876)
James Buchanan (S)

Edwin Dickinson
(1891-)
The Cello Player (P)

Richard Diebenkorn
(1922-)
View of Oakland (P)

Jim Dine
(1935-)
Five Paintbrushes (Fourth State) (P)

Asher B. Durand
(1796-1886)
Mary Louisa Adams (P)

Frank Duvneck
(1848-1919)
Water Carriers of Venice (P)

Thomas Eakins
(1844-1916)
Mother (Annie Williams Gandy) (P)

Ralph Earl
(1751-1801)
Mrs. Richard Alsop (P)

Jacob Eichholtz
(1776-1842)
Portrait of a Man (P)

Louis M. Eilshemius
(1864-1941)
Standing and Reclining Nymphs (P)

Philip Evergood
(1901-)
Woman at Piano (P)

Paul Feeley
(1913-1966)
Jack (S)

Robert Feke
(ca. 1705-1750)
Thomas Hopkinson (P)

Alvan Fisher
(1792-1863)
Niagra Falls with Rainbow (P)

Sue Fouller
(1914-)
Plexiglass & Nylon String
  Sculpture

Sam Francis
(1923-)
Blue Balls (P)

Helen Frankenthaler
(1928-)
Blessing of the Fleet (P)
Small's Paradise (P)

Lee Gatch
(1902-1968)
Herodiae (P)

Adolph Gottleib
(1903-1974)
Three Discs (P)

Morris Graves
(1910-)
Norse V (S)

Horatio Greenough
(1805-1852)
Samuel F.B. Morse (P)

Red Grooms
(1937-)
Gertrude (P)

William Gropper
(1897-)
Construction of a Dam (P)

Chaim Gross
(1904-)
Three Acrobats on a Unicycle (S)

Dimitri Haezi
(1921-)
Terra III (S)

Marsden Hartley
(1877-1943)
Untitled (P)

William S. Haseltine
(1835-1900)
Lago Maggiore (P)

Childe Hassam
(1855-1935)
Celia Thaxter in Her Garden (P)
Sunny Blue Sea (P)

George Peter A. Healy
(1813-1894)
Vinnie Ream (P)

Robert Henri
(1865-1929)
Blind Spanish Singer (P)

Hans Hofmann
(1880 Germany-1966 USA)
Fermented Soil (P)

Winslow Homer
(1836-1910)
A Visit from Old Mistress (P)
The Bean Picker (P)
High Cliffs, Coast of Maine (P)

Edward Hopper
(1882-1967)
People in the Sun (P)

Harriet Hosmer
(1830-1908)
Puck (S)

Robert Indiana
(1928-)
The Figure 5 (P)

George Innes
(1825-1894)
Niagra (P)
September Afternoon (P)

Chauncy B. Ives
(1810-1894)
Pandora (S)

John Wesley Jarvis
(1780 England-1880 USA)
**Baron John Cornelius van den
Heuvel** (P)

Jasper Johns
(1930-)
Periscope (Hart Crane) (P)

Eastman Johnson
(1824-1906)
The Lord Is My Shepherd (P)

Morris Kantor
(1896-1938)
Synthetic Arrangement (P)

Ellsworth Kelly
(1923-)
Blue On White (P)

John F. Kensett
(1816-1872)
Mountains in New Hampshire (P)

Gyorgy Kepes
(1906 Hungary-)
Earth Archive (P)

Charles Bird King
(1785-1862)
Young Omawhaw, War Eagle (P)

Franz Kline
(1910-1962)
Merce C (P)

Leon Kroll
(1884-1974)
Summer, New York (P)

John LaFarge
(1835-1910)
Visit of Nicodemus to Christ (P)

Alexander Liberman
(1912 Russia-)
Equipoise (S)
Green Diagonal (P)

Seymour Lipton
(1903-)
The Defender (S)

Morris Louis
(1912-1962)
Beta Upsilon (P)

George Luks
(1867-1933)
The Polka Dot Dress (P)

Loren MacIver
(1909-)
Downstairs (P)

Paul Manship
(1855-1966)
Dancer and Gazelles (S)

Conrad Marca-Relli
(1913-)
Steel Grey (P)

Frank B. Mayer
(1827-1899)
Independence-Squire Jack Porter
  (P)

Frederick MacMonnies
(1863-1937)
Bacchante and Infant Faun (S)

Gari Melchers
(1860-1932)
The Sermon (P)

Willard Metcalf
(1852-1925)
A Family of Birches (P)

Joan Mitchell
(1926-)
Marlin (P)

Thomas Moran
(1837 England-1926 USA)
The Chasm of the Colorado (P)
Grand Canyon of the Yellowstone
   (P)

Samuel F.B. Morse
(1791-1872)
The Goldfish Bowl (Mrs. Richard
   Cary Morse and Family) (P)

Robert Motherwell
(1915-)
Monster (for Charles Ives) (P)

William S. Mount
(1807-1868)
Saul and the Witch of Endor (P)

Elie Nadelman
(1882 Poland-1949 USA)
Dancer (S)

Ruben Nakian
(1897-)
Le Chambre a Coucher de l'Emper-
   eur (P)

Isamu Noguchi
(1904-)
Grey Sun (S)

Louise Nevelson
(1900 Russia-)
Untitled #1 (P)

Georgia O'Keeffe
(1887-)
Only One (P)

Claes Oldenburg
(1929 Sweden-)
Pile of Erasers (P)

Jules Olitski
(1922-)
Verticle (P)

Anthony Padovano
(1933-)
Sentinel (S)

Raphaelle Peale
(1774-1825)
Melons and Morning Glories (P)

Rembrandt Peale
(1778-1860)
The Roman Daughter (P)

Philip Pearlstein
(1924-)
Girl on Orange and Black Mexican
   Rug (P)

Ferdinand Pettrich
(1798 Germany-1843 USA)
Dying Tecumseh (S)

Jackson Pollock
(1912-1956)
Going West (P)
Peddler (P)

Richard Pousette-Dart
(1916-)
White Gothic #5 (P)

Hiram Powers
(1805-1873)
Fisher Girl (S)
The Greek Slave (S)
Eve Tempted (S)

Maurice Prendergast
(1859-1924)
Summer, New England (P)

Henry Ward Ranger
(1858-1916)
Entrance to the Harbor (P)

Man Ray
(1890-1976)
Untitled (P)

Robert Rauschenberg
(1925-)
Reservoir (P)

Frederick Remington
(1861-1909)
Fired On (P)

George Rickey
(1907-)
Stainless Steel Mobile
24 Lines (S)

William Rimmer
(1816 England-1879 USA)
The Falling Gladiator (S)

Larry Rivers
(1923-)
The Athlete's Dream (P)

Albert Pinkham Ryder
(1847-1917)
Moonlight (P)
Flying Dutchman (P)
Christ Appearing to Mary (P)

Augustus Saint-Gaudens
(1848 Ireland-1907 USA)
Robert Louis Stevenson (S)
Diane (S)

John Singer Sargent
(1856-1925)
Betty Wertheimer (P)
Simplon Pass (P)

Millard Sheets
(1907-)
Family Flats (P)

John Sloan
(1871-1951)
Gwendolyn (P)
Traveling Carnival, Sante Fe (P)

Moses Soyer
(1899-1974)
Artists on WPA (P)

Raphael Soyer
(1899-)
Two Girls (P)

Lilly Martin Spencer
(1822 England-1902 USA)
Peeling Onions (P)

John Mix Stanley
(1814-1872)
Black Knife, An Apache Chief (P)

Joseph Stella
(1827 Italy-1946 USA)
Metropolitan Port (P)

Frank Stella
(1936-)
River of Ponds (P)

Clyfford Still
(1904-)
Row of Elevators (P)

William Wetmore Story
(1819-1895)
The Libyan Sibyl (S)

Gilbert Stuart
(1755-1828)
John Adams (P)
Portrait of a Lady (P)

Thomas Sully
(1783 England-1872 USA)
Mary Abigail William Coale (P)

Agnes Tait
(1896-)
Winter Afternoon, Central Park (P)

Henry O. Tanner
(1859-1937)
Palace of Justice, Tangiers (P)

Edmund C. Tarbell
(1862-1938)
Mary Reading (P)

Abbott H. Thayer
(1849-1921)
Angel (P)
Virgin Enthroned (P)

Mark Tobey
(1890-)
Autumn Field (P)

John Trumbull
(1756-1843)
Dr. Hugh Williamson (P)

Dwight W. Tryon
(1849-1925)
November (P)

John H. Twachtman
(1853-1902)
The Brook (P)

Jack Tworkow
(1900-)
Friday (P)

Elihu Vedder
(1836-1923)
The Cup of Death (P)

Andy Warhol
(1930-)
Orange Disaster (P)
Marilyn (P)

Adolph A. Weinman
(1870 Germany-1952 USA)
Descending Night (S)

J. Alden Weir
(1852-1919)
Upland Pasture (P)

Benjamin West
(1738-1820)
Helen Brought to Paris (P)

James A.M. Whistler
(1834-1903)
Head of a Young Woman, Leonora
  (P)
Valpariso Harbor (P)

Worthington Whittredge
(1820-1910)
Seconnet Pointe, R.I. (P)

James Wines
(1932-)
Disc V (S)

John Wollaston
(England, active 1736-1767)
Mrs. Lucy Parry (P)

Andrew Wyeth
(1917-)
Dodges River (P)

William Zorach
(1889 Lithuania-1906 USA)
The Artist's Daughter (S)
Victory (S)

Renwick Gallery of Art

The story of the building that now houses the Renwick Gallery of Art begins with William W. Corcoran, a wealthy merchant, banker, and art collector. Desirous of creating a museum worthy of his collections of paintings, sculptures, and ceramic ware, Corcoran engaged the services of architect James Renwick, Jr. who had designed the original Smithsonian building (the Castle). Renwick designed a French Second Empire style building for the original Corcoran Gallery located on Pennsylvania Avenue next door to what is now Blair House. During the Civil War the building—its interior not yet completed—was commandeered by the Union Army for administrative offices and as a storehouse for records and uniforms. It was restored to Mr. Corcoran at the conclusion of the war and opened as the Corcoran Gallery in 1874. Before Mr. Corcoran died in 1887 his collections had not only greatly increased, but he had made plans for an art school. For both of these uses the building would prove inadequate, so in 1890 ground was broken for a larger facility just two blocks south of the original gallery. The federal government purchased what is today known as the Renwick building, remodeling and partitioning it into courtrooms. For sixty-five years this building housed a Court of Claims.

It was almost its last function, for by the middle of the

twentieth century the old Court of Claims Building (as it had by then come to be known) was scheduled for demolition in anticipation of a large renovation project. It was happily rescued by President John F. Kennedy and the Commission of Fine Arts, which subsequently undertook the restoration of this building and all the other outstanding examples of period architecture on nearby Lafayette Square. The Court of Claims was transferred to new quarters, and the restoration of what was to be known as the Renwick Gallery was begun. In 1965 the building was assigned to the Smithsonian Institution, to be used as a showcase for past and present achievements in American decorative arts, design, and crafts, and to host changing displays of arts and crafts exhibited from other lands. At the time it was established it was commissioned a department of the National Museum of American Art. The building was restored "in the spirit of Renwick's time," renamed the Renwick Gallery of Art in honor of its architect, and opened to the public in early 1972.

Special exhibits have remained on display in the Renwick from one or two months to two or more years. An exhibition of contemporary designs showed utilitarian and functional objects, including such items as household articles, medical instruments, and even fire plugs. Other exhibits here featured decorated American furniture since the seventeenth century (including chairs, tables, clocks, boxes, and washstands), and contemporary fabric designs. Another exhibit typical of the Renwick's offerings was a show of Frank Lloyd Wright's decorative designs—the furniture, windows, architectural ornaments and decorative accessories that enhance a structure he had designed. The exhibit "200 Years of Royal Copenhagen Porcelain," featured the artistic achievements in porcelain, stoneware, and faience of this old Danish manufactory.

Among other exhibits that have been mounted at the Renwick were notable displays of glass including some of Frederick Carder's (a noted glass designer for Steuben) and those of Dale Chihuly's (who also demonstrated his art); and French playbills of the 1890s including works by Munch, Bonnard, Lautrec, and Vuillard, among others. There were exhibits of Shaker furniture, and one of glass sculptures by more than thirty American craftsmen. "Paintings from Pakistan" honored Pakistan's twenty-fifth anniversary of nationhood, while "Man-Made Mobile" traced the humble history of saddle design in America. A show of decorated containers made by nineteenth century Haida, Tlingit, Bella Bella, and Taimahian Indian artists revealed an aspect of North American Indian crafts not very familiar to many. Another Indian exhibit featured over one hundred pieces of pottery by Maria Martinez, the famous potter of San Ildefonso, and her husband, Julian. Yet another display highlighted the work of North American goldsmiths showing contemporary jewelry, tableware, and other pieces accompanied with demonstrations and films of these arts. One of the loveliest exhibits was of "Venini Glass" that showed plates, figurines, sculptures, stemware, vases, bowls, and bottles of delightful color tones sometimes subtle, sometimes brilliant created by the Venetian factory located on the island of Murano.

Indeed, demonstrations, films, slide shows and lectures are a vital part of the Renwick's offerings. Demonstrations are often given in conjunction with some exhibits; among these have been included such diverse crafts as traditional Polish paper cutouts, off-loom fiber techniques, quilting, basic jewelry techniques, and a demonstration of guitary-making. There have been informal demonstrations of American musical instruments co-sponsored by the Renwick and the Smithsonian's Division of Performing Arts.

The Grand Salon and the Octagon Room on the second floor of the Renwick Gallery have more or less permanent exhibits of late nineteenth century design that recall the French Second Empire style of the building. In the Grand Salon are gilt chairs and sofas and marble-topped, boulle work (inlaid brass and tortoise shell) cabinets with gilded bronze fittings. Red velvet-covered benches are arranged around pedestals displaying huge vases originally exhibited in the 1876 Philadelphia Centennial Exposition. There are, as well, four large exhibit cases holding Limoges vases and pate-sur-pate (low relief, surface decorated) works by Marc Louis Solon and Alboine Birks of the Minton factory in England. Also displayed are pate-sur-pate decorated candelabras.

The Octagon Room was originally designed to display Hiram Powers' sculpture, "The Greek Slave," but "The Greek Slave" is now exhibited in the National Museum of American Art with other works by this famous sculptor. "The Berlin Vase" which now stands in its place in the Octagon Room is a German work considered a technical masterpiece of color and detail.

The paintings listed below are on exhibit in the Grand Salon or in the Octagon Room (an asterisk preceding the name of the painting indicates the Octagon Room). Many of these works are on permanent loan from the Corcoran Gallery; others are from the William A. Clark Collection, or are the gifts of individual donors, or were purchased through the Gallery Fund. Only five paintings are by American artists.

Edwin Austin Abbey
(American, 1852-1911)
The Trial of Queen Katharine

Amati (possibly Carlo Amati)
(Italian, 1776-1825)
Scene on the Coast of Calabria

Theophile de Bock
(Dutch, 1851-1904)
The Poudon Commons

William A. Bouguereau
(French, 1825-1904)
*La Petite Berceuse

Michel Bouquet
(French, 1807-1890)
**Halt of the Hunters at
    Fontainebleau**

Ferdinand de Braekelleer
(Belgian, 1792-1883)
**The Unhappy Family
The Happy Family**

Jules Adolphe Breton
(French, 1827-1906)
**The Colza Harvest
*Brittany Widow**

Richard Burnier
(Dutch, 1826-1884)
**Cattle on Seashore Near
    Scheveningen**

Jean Charles Cazin
(French, 1841-1901)
**Ecouen on the Cliff: Low Tide
Moonlight in Holland
*Great Windmill and the Rainbow
*Home of the Artist at Ecouen**

Luigi Chialiva
(Swiss, 1842-1914)
The Old Shepherd
The Shepherdess

Emile Couder
(French, d. 1903)
Flower Piece With a Cat

Jean Baptiste Detaille
(French, 1848-1912)
General of the First Empire

Narcisse Virgile Diaz de la Pena
(French, 1808-1876)
The Approaching Storm

Jules Dupre
(French, 1811-1889)
Stormy Landscape

Pierre Edouard Frere
(French, 1819-1886)
Preparing for Church

C. Fribel
(Swiss, active ca. 1850)
Swiss Mill Scene

Jean Jacques Henner
(French, 1829-1905)
Joan of Arc
Woman Standing

Leon Augustin L'Hermitte
(French, 1844-1905)
Washerwoman on the Banks of
**   the Marne**

Eduard Hildebrandt
(German, 1818-1869)
Moonrise in Madeira

Edwin Landseer
(English, 1802-1893)
Duke of Devonshire and Lady
**   Louisa Egerton**

Louis Lang
(American, 1814-1893)
Norma

Philip de Laszlo
(English, 1869-1937)
Head of an Indian Prince

Emanuel Leutze
(American, 1816-1864)
Cromwell and Milton

Franz Linder
(German, 1736-1802)
The Butterfly

Louis Charles Moeller
(American, 1855-1930)
Disagreement

George Morland
(English, 1763-1804)
The Warrener

Aime Nicholas Morot
(French, 1850-1913)
El Bravo Toro

Charles Louis Muller
(French, 1815-1892)
Charlotte Corday in Prison

Johann Wilhelm Preyer
(German, 1803-1899)
Fruit

Louis Robbe
(Belgian, 1806-1887)
Landscape and Cattle

Emile Renouf
(French, 1845-1894)
The Helping Hand

Thomas Prichard Rossitar
(American, 1818-1871)
Rebecca at the Well

Gaston Saint-Pierre
(French, 1833-1916)
Nedjma-Odalisque

August Schaeffer
(Austrian, 1833-1916)
Sunset in a Hungarian Forest

Adolf Schreyer   Constant Troyon
(German, 1828-1899)   (French, 1810-1865)
The Watering Place   **Moving with the Flock**

William Oliver Stone   Claude Joseph Vernet
(American, 1830-1899)   (French, 1714-1789)
William Wilson Corcoran   **Seaport**

Barney Studio House

Alice Pike was born in Cincinnati in 1858. She enjoyed all of the advantages and benefits made available to a privileged child in the wealthy home of her successful and culturally interested father, who had built the first Opera House in Cincinnati the year Alice was born and ten years later the Grand Opera House in New York. As an intelligent, beautiful, charming and socially aware young person endowed with many talents including the ability to paint (Alice studied with some of the leading painters of her day, one of them James Abbot McNeill Whistler), she attracted almost everyone she met including many eligible men; one of them, Sir Henry Morton Stanley, she almost wed. Instead she married a very wealthy man (Albert C. Barney) and with him traveled extensively both in this country and abroad. They established homes in Bar Harbor, Maine and in Washington, D.C. where Alice Pike Barney became well-known as a brilliant society leader in some of the highest social circles. The home in Washington on Sheridan Circle, which she called Studio House, became known as a center for the cultural set of her day. It was completed after the death of her husband in 1902 but she continued to live there for twenty-four years bringing culture, as she put it, "to a provincial town" by influencing the life of Washington in the early 1900s in painting, dance, theater and even architecture, in all of which she was accomplished. The building served not only as her home but also as her studio and salon. In it are hung selections from a collection of over 400 of her paintings as well as paintings of some of her friends. In her home, Studio House, she held poetry readings, dramas, and gave concerts of salon music and dance. Her stage set has been preserved in Barney Studio House and the house still reflects the Bohemian character it showed during the days when Alice Pike Barney was its mistress.

Among entertainers who visited her home were Ruth St. Denis, Sarah Bernhardt, and Anna Pavlova (for whom Alice P. Barney wrote the scenarios and designed the set and costumes of a one act ballet; she also painted a portrait of Pavlova. Among some of the highest echelon in government circles who were guests in her home were Eleanor and Franklin Roosevelt, Alice Roosevelt Longworth, and the Cabot Lodges. She held soirees in her home which she called "Evenings at Barney Studio House" and entertained her guests with concerts of salon music and the dance, poetry readings and dramas. Today these soirees are being revived in the same spirit in which they were held then, with these "Evenings at Barney Studio House" given in a series of monthly programs. However, today (unlike then) each performance, limited to fifty people, carries a charge of $10

per person. These programs are followed by a reception for the artists
and guests. To obtain information about how to reserve the limited
number of tickets available for these performances call (202) 357-3111
or write to Barney Studio House, Room 253, Museum of American
Art, Washington, D.C. 20560.

Mrs. Barney was interested in charitable causes, for one of
which, a settlement house called Barney Neighborhood House, she
contributed four buildings that included an art center. She also taught
children and adults certain art forms like tie dying, and because she
was interested in dramatics (she directed children's plays) she
participated in the creation of the first federally supported outdoor
theater on the Washington Monument grounds. She wrote and produced
plays, as well, for charity.

Limited informal tours of Barney Studio House are offered
to those who make reservations in advance. (See QuickGuide.) Among
objects visitors will see on their tours there are some of Alice Pike
Barney's paintings (among them portraits of Ruth St. Denis, Anna
Pavlova, actress Mrs. Patrick Campbell, Albert Hunter, Aman Jean,
and James Abbot McNeil Whistler); original furnishings, jewelry that
includes the "Peacock Necklace" designed by Moubisson, and a diamond
necklace designed by Romaine Brooks; Tiffany candelsticks; Quetzl
lamps; silver decorative objects; china she had used; textiles; Oriental
rugs; and various studio props that she had used in some of the plays
she produced.

Her two daughters donated the house and its contents to
the Smithsonian Institution. Some paintings, which had been loaned
to museums and institutions, were returned at the request of her
daughters and are now included by the donors as gifts to the Smithsonian.

The Barney Studio House is administered by the Museum
of American Art. Further information about Barney Studio House
can be obtained by calling (202) 357-3176 or addressed to Barney
Studio House at the Museum of American Art, 8th and G Streets
N.W., Washington, D.C. 20560.

National Portrait Gallery

The National Portrait Gallery opened in October of 1968,
on the south side of the Fine Arts and Portrait Gallery Building. The
structure formerly known as the old Patent Office Building was a
famous landmark, narrowly rescued from demolition. The Post Office
issued a special stamp in commemoration of the gallery's opening.
The stamp pictured Chief Joseph, a leader and chief of the Nez Perce
tribe of eastern Oregon. (The peaceful Nez Perce were given thirty
days to move to another reservation when gold was discovered on
their land. Before the tribe could move out, however, gold prospectors
moved in and started trouble. A war broke out, which the beleagured
Indians lost. The survivors were shipped off to prison camps, where
they were decimated by ill treatment and disease. Among the dead
were Chief Joseph and his six children.) The original portrait of Chief
Joseph copied for the commemorative stamp is one of the many works
in the gallery tracing American history through portraits.

The National Portrait Gallery is the only museum of its kind in the Americas. In its collections are the portraits of individuals whose contributions to the country—whether political or cultural, religious or technological, scientific or humanitarian, noble or base— have been in some way distinctive.

The process of selection to the National Portrait Gallery is a careful one. Each name proposed for admission is first presented by a subcommittee to the Director of the National Portrait Gallery. The proposal is then reviewed by the National Portrait Gallery Commission. Finally, the candidate's name is submitted to the Board of Regents of the Smithsonian Institution, who make the final decision. Most of the individuals whose names are considered have been dead ten or more years, and have been noted in the **Dictionary of American Biography** or a comparable biographical list.

While some of the portraits (the term encompasses paintings, sculpture, drawings, photographs, and the like) are the work of famous artists like Gilbert Stuart, John Singleton Copley, Jo Davidson, Hiram Powers, and Augustus Saint-Gaudens, many are the work of lesser-known men and women. The gallery staff's chief interest is in acquiring a good likeness of an individual for its records. Life portraits are preferred, but if none is available, a copy of an existing portrait or a photograph is acceptable if the likeness is a good one.

The National Portrait Gallery's Hall of Presidents on the second floor has always attracted many visitors. The incumbent president's portrait is displayed in a special room with the presidential seal affixed above it.

Also in the National Portrait Gallery are many popular group portraits such as "Washington Irving and His Friends at Sunnyside," (Irving numbered among his friends some of the leading writers of his era), "Grant and His Union Generals," and "Inventors and Their Inventions: Men of Progress," a portrait of a remarkable group of men who had made great technological contributions to America and to the world. Among other highlights in this Gallery are a sinopia (a preliminary guide, an underdrawing for a fresco done on plaster) done by Ben Shahn, and selections of the hundreds of Saint-Memin engravings donated to the National Portrait Gallery by Mr. and Mrs. Paul Mellon. A small gallery on the first floor displays changing exhibits of documentary records, including photographs, scrapbooks, letters, diaries, etc. from the Archives of American Art.

The hundreds of portraits not on exhibit are kept in a study collection, a research center for American biography and portraiture to which scholars and students of American history have access. The library, shared with the National Museum of American Art, contains in addition to bound volumes a large clipping and pamphlet file, a manuscript collection, and a lending collection of slides.

No other facility of the Smithsonian seems to mount special exhibits with quite the flair that the National Portrait Gallery achieves. Their skilled designers' innovative handling of color, labeling, and associative artifacts makes each special exhibit a visual feast. Special exhibits in the past have featured "This New Man: A Discourse in Portraits" as an outstanding opening exhibit. Others depicted with great skill the "Works of Saint-Gaudens," "Life Portraits of John Quincy Adams," "Portraits of Black Leaders," "Notable Women in the Gallery's Collection," "Afro-Americans in the Age of Revolution," "Unsuccessful Candidates for the Presidency," and "Members of the Brook Farm Community." The exhibit called "Facing the Light" captured over one hundred notable Americans in photographs that were made by the earliest photographic processes. A Helen Keller exhibit marked "Better Speech and Hearing Month," and "The **Time** of Our Lives" featured over one hundred original oils that were reproduced on covers of **Time** magazine. Most of the National Portrait Gallery's major exhibitions are accompanied by lectures featuring prominent speakers. The QuickGuide (an appendix) gives further information about this gallery's services.

Gallery personnel at the Information Desk will happily supply information on the location of any portrait. Following is a representative list of portraits in the National Portrait Gallery.

John Adams (1735-1826)
second American president
 Painting by
 Gilbert Stuart (1755-1828),
 finished by Jane Stuart, n.d.
 Painting by
 Thomas Spear (1789-1863)

John Quincy Adams (1767-1848)
sixth American president
 Painting by
 George C. Bingham (1811-1879)
 Daguerrotype by
 Bishop and Gray, n.d.

Jane Adams (1860-1935)
social worker
 Marble sculpture by
 unidentified artist
 Painting by
 unidentified artist

Louis Agassiz (1807-1873)
biologist, teacher, collector
 Painting by
 Walter Ingalls (1805-1874)

Louisa May Alcott (1805-1888)
author
 Bronze sculpture by
 Frank E. Elwell (1852-1922)

Ira Aldridge (1804-1867)
black Shakespearean actor
 Painting by
 Henry P. Briggs (1791-1844)

Alexander Graham Bell (1847-1922)
teacher, inventor
 Marble sculpture by
 Moses W. Dykaar (1884-1933)

Mary McLeod Bethune (1875-1955)
educator, black leader
 Painting by
 Betsy Graves Reyneau (1888-
 1964)

Black Hawk (1767-1838)
Sauk war chief
 Painting by
 George Catlin (1796-1872)

Mathew B. Brady (ca. 1823-1896)
Civil War photographer
 Painting by
 Thomas LeClear (1818-1882)

Heywood Broun (1888-1939)
journalist, author
 Painting by
 Ben Shahn (1898-1969)

John Brown (1800-1859)
abolitionist
 Bronze sculpture by
 Joseph-Charles de Blezer

William Cullen Bryant (1794-1876)
poet
 Marble sculpture by
 Henry Kirke Brown (1814-1886)

John C. Calhoun (1782-1850)
senator, American vice-president
    Painting by
    Charles B. King (1785-1862)

Joseph G. Cannon (1836-1926)
speaker of the House
    Sculpture by
    Jo Davidson (1883-1952)
    Painting by
    Harriet Murphy

George Washington Carver
(1864-1943)
botanist
    Painting by
    Betsy Graves Reyneau (1888-
    1964)

George Catlin (1796-1872)
painter
    Painting by
    William Fisk (1796-1872)

Carrie Chapman Catt (1859-
1947)
leader, women's suffrage movement
    Painting by
    Mary Foote (1872-1968)

William Clark (1770-1838)
explorer
    Painting by
    George Catlin (1796-1872)

Henry Clay (1777-1852)
orator, statesman
    Pressed paper sculpture by
    Frederic Key (active 1844-
    1864)
    Painting by
    George A.P. Healy (1816-1894)

Samuel L. Clemens (Mark Twain)
(1835-1910)
author
    Miniature on ivory by
    Eulabee Dix (1878-1961)

Stephen Grover Cleveland (1837-
1906)
twenty-second and twenty-fourth
American president
    Painting by
    Eastman Johnson (1824-1906)
    Painting by
    Sir John Tenniel (1820-1914)

William W. Corcoran (1798-1888)
banker, art collector
    Painting by
    George A.P. Healy (1813-1894)

David ("Davy") Crockett (1786-
1836)
frontiersman, representative
    Lithograph by
    Cephas Childs (1793-1871) and
    George Lehman (d. 1870)

Clarence S. Darrow (1857-1938)
attorney
    Bronze sculpture by
    Jo Davidson (1883-1952)

Eugene V. Debs (1834-1928)
labor leader, presidential candidate
    Bronze sculpture by
    Louis Mayer (1869-1969)

Dorothea L. Dix (1802-1887)
educator, reformer, author
    Sculpture by
    Samuel B. Waugh (1814-1885)
    Painting by
    Samuel B. Waugh

Stephen A. Douglas (1813-1861)
senator, orator
    Painting by
    Duncan Styles, n.d.
    Polychrome wood carving by
    unidentified artist

Frederick Douglass (1817-1895)
editor, consul-general to Haiti
    Painting by
    Charles Wells (b. 1935-)
    Painting by
    Elisha Hammond, n.d.

William E.B. Du Bois (1868-1963)
educator, sociologist, Civil War
activist
  Painting by
  Winold Reiss (1886-1953)
  Painting by
  Laura Waring (1887-1948)

Isadora Duncan (1878-1927)
dancer
  Painting by
  John Sloan (1871-1951)

Mary Baker Eddy (1821-1910)
founder of Christian Science
  Marble sculpture by
  Luella Varney Serrao (1865-
  1926)

Thomas Alva Edison (1847-1931)
inventor
  Painting by
  Abraham A. Alexander (1847-
  1940)

Albert Einstein (1879-1955)
physicist
  Painting by
  Joseph Scharl (1896-1954)
  Painting by
  Ben Shahn (1898-1969)

Dwight D. Eisenhower (1890-
1969)
thirty-fourth American president
  Painting by
  Thomas E. Stephens (1894-
  1947)

Ralph Waldo Emerson (1803-1882)
poet, essayist
  Sculpture attributed to
  Daniel C. French (1850-1931)

John Ericsson (1803-1899)
engineer, inventor
  Marble sculpture by
  Augustus Saint-Gaudens (1848-
  1907)

Edward Everett (1794-1865)
clergyman, statesman
  Marble sculpture by
  Hiram Powers (1805-1873)

David G. Farragut (1801-1870)
Civil War admiral
  Painting attributed to
  William Swain (1803-1847)

William Faulkner (1897-1962)
novelist
  Painting by
  Soss Melik (b. 1912-)

F. Scott Fitzgerald (1896-1940)
novelist
  Painting by
  David Silvette, n.d.

Henry Ford (1863-1947)
manufacturer
  Bronze sculpture by
  H. Wellner, n.d.

Stephen C. Foster (1826-1864)
composer
  Painting attributed to
  Thomas Hicks (1823-1890)

Benjamin Franklin (1706-1790)
printer, inventor, scientist,
statesman
  Marble sculpture by
  unidentified artist
  Painting by
  Edward Savage (1761-1817)

Robert Frost (1875-1963)
poet
  Bronze sculpture by
  Walker Hancock (b. 1901-)

Robert Fulton (1765-1815)
inventor, engineer, portrait painter
  Bronze sculpture by
  Jean-Antoine Houdon (1741-1828)

George Gershwin (1898-1937)
composer
  Self-portrait

James Cardinal Gibbons (1834-
1921)
Roman Catholic prelate
  Sculpture by
  Marie DeF. Keller, n.d.

Ulysses S. Grant (1822-1885)
eighteenth American president
  Painting by
  Ole P. Balling (1823-1885)

William F. Halsey (1882-1959)
Admiral of the Fleet
  Painting by
  Albert K. Murray (b. 1906-)

Alexander Hamilton (1755-1804)
Secretary of the Treasury
  Marble sculpture by
  Giuseppe Ceracchi (1751-1801)
  Painting by
  James Sharpless (1751-1811)

Nathaniel Hawthorne (1804-1864)
author
  Painting by
  Emanuel G. Leutz (1816-1868)

Roland Hayes (b. 1887-)
singer
  Painting by
  Winold Reiss (1886-1953)

Ernest Hemingway (1898-1961)
author
  Painting by
  Soss Melik (b. 1912-)

Robert Henri (1865-1929)
painter
  Self-portrait

Joseph Henry (1797-1878)
scientist, first Smithsonian
Secretary
  Painting by
  Thomas LeClear (1818-1882)

Sidney Hillman (1887-1946)
labor leader
  Painting by
  Ben Shahn (1898-1969)

Herbert C. Hoover (1874-1964)
thirty-first American president
  Painting by
  Edmund Tarbell (1862-1938)

Julia Ward Howe (1819-1910)
author, leader, women's suffrage
  Painting by
  John Elliott (1858-1925)
  finished by
  William Cotton (1880-1958)

Langston Hughes (1902-1967)
author, poet
  Painting by
  Winold Reiss (1886-1953)

Cordell Hull (1871-1955)
Secretary of State
  Painting by
  Casimir G. Stapko (b. 1913-)

Andrew Jackson (1767-1845)
seventh American president
  Ivory miniature by
  James Tooley, Jr. (1816-1844)

Henry James (1843-1916)
author
  Painting by
  Jacques-Emile Blanche (1861-
  1942)

Thomas Jefferson (1743-1826)
third American president
  Painting by
  Mather Brown (1761-1831)

Lyndon B. Johnson (1908-1973)
thirty-sixth American president
  Painting by
  Peter Hurd (b. 1904-)

John Paul Jones (1747-1792)
naval commander
  Bronze sculpture by
  Jean-Antoine Houdon (1741-
  1828)
  Painting by
  Johann-Elias Hard (1739-1809)

Mary Harris "Mother" Jones (1830-
1930)
labor leader
  Sculpture by
  Jo Davidson (1883-1952)

John F. Kennedy (1917-1963)
thirty-fifth American president
   Painting by
   William F. Draper (b. 1912-)

Martin Luther King, Jr. (1929-1968)
minister, Nobel Peace Prize winner
   Marble sculpture by
   Charles Wells (b. 1935-)

Marquis de Lafayette (1757-1834)
statesman
   Bronze sculpture by
   William Rush (1756-1833)

Henry Laurens (1724-1792)
president, Continental Congress
   Painting by
   John Singelton Copley (1735-1815)

John L. Lewis (1880-1969)
labor leader
   Painting by
   Ben Shahn (1898-1969)

Robert E. Lee (1807-1880)
Civil War general
   Pastel by
   D.H. Anderson, n.d.

Sinclair Lewis (1885-1969)
author
   Bronze sculpture by
   Jo Davidson (1883-1952)

Abraham Lincoln (1809-1865)
sixteenth American president
   Painting by
   George P.A. Healy (1813-1894)
   Death mask by
   Clark Mills (1810-1883)

Henry Cabot Lodge (1850-1924)
legislator, author
   Painting by
   John Singer Sargent (1856-1925)

Douglas MacArthur (1880-1964)
general in World War II
   Painting by
   Rudolph Kiss (1889-1953)

James Madison (1751-1836)
fourth American president
   Painting by
   James Frothingham (1786-1864)
   Painting attributed to
   Chester Harding (1792-1866)

George C. Marshall (1880-1959)
general, ambassador, Secretary of State
   Painting by
   unidentified artist

Andrew Mellon (1855-1937)
ambassador, Secretary of Treasury, donor, National Gallery of Art
   Painting by
   Oswald Birley, n.d.

Edna St. Vincent Millay (1892-1950)
poet
   Painting by
   Charles Ellis (b. 1892-)

James Monroe (1758-1831)
fifth American president
   Painting attributed to
   James Herring (1794-1867)

John Muir (1838-1914)
naturalist, conservationist
   Sculpture by
   Edwin K. Harkness (d. 1934)

Thomas Nast (1840-1902)
cartoonist, consul to Ecuador
   Painting by
   John W. Alexander (1800-ca. 1880)

Richard M. Nixon (b. 1913-)
thirty-seventh American president
   Painting by
   Norman Rockwell (1894-1978)

Eugene O'Neill (1888-1953)
dramatist
   Charcoal sketch by
   Soss Melik (b. 1912-)

Oliver H. Perry (1785-1819)
naval commander
    Painting by
    Martin J. Head, n.d.

John J. Pershing (1860-1948)
World War I general
    Sculpture by
    Moses W. Dykaar (1884-1933)
    Painting by
    Sir William Orpen (1878-1931)

Pocahontas (c. 1595-1617)
Indian princess
    Painting by
    unidentified artist
    Engraving by
    unidentified artist

John Wesley Powell (1834-1902)
ethnologist, explorer, writer
    Painting by
    C. Messer (1842-1919)

Sam Rayburn (1882-1961)
speaker of the House
    Bronze sculpture by
    Jimilu Mason, n.d.

Paul Robeson (b. 1898-)
singer, actor
    Painting by
    Winold Reiss (1886-1953)

John D. Rockefeller (1839-1937)
businessman, philanthropist
    Plaster sculpture by
    Paul Manship (1885-1966)

Will Rogers (1879-1935)
actor, humorist
    Bronze sculpture by
    Jo Davidson (1883-1952)

Franklin D. Roosevelt (1882-
1945)
thirty-third American president
    Painting by
    Douglas Chandor (1897-1953)
    Sculpture by
    Jo Davidson (1883-1952)

Theodore Roosevelt (1858-1919)
twenty-sixth American president
    Painting by
    Adrian Lamb (b. 1901-)

Richard Rush (1789-1859)
Secretary of State, public servant
    Painting by
    unidentified artist

Lillian Russell (1861-1922)
soprano
    Pastel by
    Adolph Muller-Ury (1862-1947)

Carl Sandburg (1878-1967)
writer, historian
    Painting by
    Emerson Burkhart (1905-1969)

William H. Seward (1801-1872)
Secretary of State
    Marble sculpture by
    Giovanni M. Benzoni (1809-1873)

Joseph Smith (1805-1844)
founder of the Mormon Church
    Painting by
    Adrian Lamb (b. 1901-)

James Smithson (1769-1829)
scientist, Smithsonian benefactor
    Miniature by
    H. Johns, n.d.

John Philip Sousa (1854-1932)
conductor, composer
    Painting by
    H. Waltman (1871-1951)

Gertrude Stein (1874-1946)
writer, art patroness
    Sculpture by
    Jo Davidson (1883-1952)

Harriet Beecher Stowe (1811-1896)
author
    Painting by
    Alanson Fisher (1792-1863)

Henry David Thoreau (1817-1862)
author
    Maxham daguerreotype by
    Maxham, n.d.

Harry S. Truman (1884-1972)
thirty-third American president
  Painting by
  Greta Kempton (b. 1903-)

Harriet Tubman (c. 1820-1913)
black leader, humanitarian
  Painting by
  Robert S. Pious (b. 1908-)

George Washington (1732-1799)
first American president
  Two paintings by
  Rembrandt Peale (1778-1860)
  Painting by
  Gilbert Stuart (1755-1828)
  Life mask by
  Jean-Antoine Houdon (1741-
  1828)

Daniel Webster (1782-1852)
orator, statesman
  Painting by
  George P.A. Healy (1813-1894)
  Daguerreotype by
  unidentified artist

Noah Webster (1758-1843)
lawyer, teacher, lexicographer
  Painting by
  James Herring (1794-1867)

James Abbot McNeill Whistler
(1834-1903)
artist
  Terra Cotta sculpture by
  Joseph E. Boehm (1834-1890)
  Painting by
  Giovanni Boldini (1845-1931)

Woodrow Wilson (1856-1924)
twenty-eighth American president
  Painting by
  Edmund C. Tarbell (1862-1938)
  Sculpture by
  Bryant Baker (1881-1970)

Alexander Woolcott (1887-1943)
journalist, author
  Charcoal sketch and a
  Painting by
  Soss Melik (b. 1912-)

Brigham Young (1801-1877)
Mormon leader
  Lithograph by
  Hartwig Borneman (active ca.
  1875)

Florenz Ziegfeld (1869-1932)
theatrical producer
  Bronze sculpture by
  Cesare Stea (b. 1893-)

Museum of African Art

Second only to Asia in size, the continent of Africa lies, for the most part, in the torrid zone (only its northern edge and southern tip are more or less in the temperate zones). It has the world's largest desert, the Sahara, huge expanses of tropical rain forests, savannahs (grasslands) where a wide variety of wild animals live including the hippopotamus and giraffe found nowhere else on earth. Climates ranging from extremely hot on the desert and in the rain forests to very cold on the high mountains have influenced the lives of the people who inhabit those regions. The result is a diverse continent with a variety of cultures where great dissimilarities are found in architecture, crafts, clothing, food, religions, folklore, governments, customs and ceremonies, languages or dialects, and arts. In the Museum of African Art there are changing exhibits of artistic works of selected African peoples in major environments where they have enjoyed a long and rich history.

The only parts of Africa known in the ancient world were Egypt, Ethiopia and Libya. Most of the rest of this huge continent was called "the dark continent" and Americans and most Europeans believed the Africans were uncivilized people with nothing of importance to offer the rest of the world. They failed to recognize how creative and talented African people really were. By showing African art, music, dance and by explaining the beliefs and human values of these peoples, the Museum of African Art gives both black and white Americans an opportunity to understand, appreciate and respect African peoples.

The Museum of African Art opened in 1964 with a small collection and little money, but has since grown so that its collections have been greatly increased, numbering among its objects textiles, baskets, furniture, jewelry, costumes, masks, grass mats, money, some paintings, but mostly sculpture, which in the absence of a written language the people of a particular community or cultural group frequently use to convey their beliefs and values. In 1978 Congress passed a bill making this museum a part of the Smithsonian. As soon as construction is completed the museum will move from its present location on Capitol Hill at 318 A Street, N.E. (in a row of townhouses, one of which was occupied by Frederick Douglass, the great 19th century black orator and statesman) to its new location, built mostly underground, as part of the Quadrangle with the Sackler Museum of Oriental Art, with its main entrance on Independence Avenue. It will stand between the "Castle," the original Smithsonian building, and the Freer Gallery of Art (both of these on the Mall).

Warren Robbins, the former director of the Museum of African Arts said, "The purpose of the Museum of African Art is to help people in America understand more about African art and culture. Each piece of sculpture, mask, etc. in the museum has a story to tell from which you can gain some insight into the values and beliefs of the African people." By showing the arts, music, dance, and explaining the beliefs and human values of its peoples, the Museum of African Art hopes to help its visitors understand, appreciate, and respect Africa more.

African art forms have influenced many great European artists, among them Picasso, Modigliani, Derain, and Vlaminck who recognized the aesthetic values of African art, particularly its sculpture. Figures carved of wood or made of other materials are part of the rituals used in religious services. Exhibits of some of these are shown from Western Sudan and the Guinea Coast that are highly abstract. In some figures distortion is often used to emphasize features of cultic significance. Not all figures, however, are for ritual purposes—some like Dahomey figures, shown here, were done in brass by the lost wax process, made for aesthetic purposes, and generally reserved for the enjoyment of royalty. Some figures made in Gabon among the Fang tribes are believed by them to act as guardian spirits over ancestors whose bones are kept in boxes. In the West Congo region the Bapende sculptors make ivory pendants, a few of them in the collection, which portray human faces. Another great art form is textiles. Some beautiful textiles made by the Yoruba tribe of southwest Nigeria and other tribes are among the textiles in the collections.

The African art, rituals and ceremonies described in this museum, for the most part, reflect the universal phenomenon of celebrations. The art works include spears, shields, fighting bracelets, textiles, sculpture of all kinds, masks, costumes, and musical instruments of various sorts related to music and dancing. Messages are often sent by drums (in some areas "talking drums" with pitch variations that can stimulate patterns of speech) and other types of signaling devices. Illustrated in exhibits are examples of games and sports, and ceremonial rites of passage that include ceremonies for births, coming of age, weddings, and deaths, and others for success in hunting or war.

Africa is famous for its masks which are admired the world over for their beauty of design and form. Some, however, more awesome than beautiful are made with the intent of frightening away evil spirits bent on destruction of property, food supplies, or health. Three basic types of African masks can be seen in a variety of forms in the Museum of African Arts: the face mask, which covers only the wearer's face; the helmet mask, which covers the entire head of the wearer; and the headdress mask, which rests on top of the wearer's head on a small support made of basketwork or wood. These masks are made from many different materials, most commonly wood, but also of metal, palm leaf fibers, or bark cloth. They are often painted with natural pigments and some decorated with shells, beads, fibers, or feathers. These masks play an important role in African religious and social life. In religious ceremonies they are worn by a dancer as part of a costume that often covers the entire body of the dancer. The Africans who use this type of mask believe that when the mask is used in this way it takes on special powers that enable it to communicate with the gods, the mask serving as the connecting link with the spirit world. In an exhibit large carved masks are shown made by the Bobo people of the upper Volta, a country in West Africa just south of the Sahara Desert. The Bobos wear these masks in special ceremonies in which the people are reminded of the teachings of their ancestors and implore these departed ancestors for guidance and support for the living relatives. Human and animals figures are often mixed in these masks to express the relationships existing between all living beings and the respect that African people have for the animal world.

The gallery walls are painted in warm brown colors with spotlights that focus on the exhibits just in front of these walls. There are beautiful photographs (large, mural size) mounted on walls depicting African peoples in various environments. The political status of individual countries on this large continent is diverse. Before the middle of the 19th century the European countries with the greatest concentration of power in Africa were France, Portugal, and Great Britain. Further exploration and conquest of parts of Africa resulted in partitioning among these parts by additional European nations seeking that continent's vast natural resources with the possibility of commercial development, new markets for their growing industries, and building up colonial empires. The jurisdiction of European powers has, for the most part, disintegrated, resulting in more groups of independent, sovereign nations. Some like Chad, Cameroon, Zaire, Dahomey, Ghana, Nigeria and others have become members of the United Nations. In some nations, even today, leadership is vested in a king, as we find with the Ashanti people who live in Ghana and the Gold Coast, and his symbol of sovereignty is the gold encrusted stool. Stools (although not always as elaborate) are symbols of authority with other groups of people in Africa as well and no other individual except the leader in the community has the privilege of using it. In the Museum of African Arts are displayed stools carved of wood.

School children brought to the Museum of African Art by bus are led through the museum by a guide (usually a staff member or volunteer) who will speak to them in the auditorium on the third floor about community life in Africa. Sometimes the talk is given by a visiting intern from Africa, familiar with the rituals and ceremonies, costumes, dancing, masks, and other artifacts of several communities near his native community. Oral tradition among the non-white communities is strong in Africa and much teaching is done by means of fables, stories, proverbs, and riddles.

In Gallery 2 on the first floor there are shows presented by slides, photographs and films which photographer and film maker Eliot Elisofon bequeathed to the Museum of African Arts. Often these are accompanied by African music or the recitation of African poetry.

7

The National Zoo

The kiwi of New Zealand is a nocturnal, flightless, and almost extinct bird. In proportion to its four or five pound weight, the kiwi bird lays an enormously large egg (between fourteen and sixteen ounces in weight), which the male incubates for eighty days in a nest burrowed beneath tree roots or in a hollow log. A pair of these rare brown kiwis came to our National Zoo in 1968, a gift from New Zealand's Prime Minister. In the zoo's bird house, a tiny kiwi was hatched. It was the first such birth that occurred outside New Zealand or Australia.

One purpose of the zoo is, of course, the display of animals for the pleasure of visitors who might otherwise never have an opportunity to see a wildebeest, tiger, spider monkey, crocodile, Indian peafowl, kudu, hippopotamus or hundreds of other species, and get the sense of wonder one feels when he views the diversity of animal life from all over the world that this great zoo exhibits. An equally important purpose is the preservation for future generations of wildlife that is likely to become extinct. A recent federal government study found the world is losing an animal, insect, or plant species at the rate of one per day. It is important to save many of these because they are pivotal species in the preservation of their own and other lives. The National Zoo has a Conservation and Research Center at Front Royal, Virginia 75 miles from the National Zoo large enough for animals to be kept in natural herds for breeding and research purposes.

Members of a rare species, a pride of Atlas lions received by our government (on loan) in 1976 from the Rabat Zoo in Morocco, are on view in the Mann Memorial Lion and Tiger Building. In the winter of 1977 the first set of Atlas lion cubs were born and joined the lion exhibit. Among other rare or endangered animals the zoo houses are animals that American government officials received as gifts and placed in the National Zoo for safekeeping. Such was a pair of giant pandas given to President Nixon in 1972 by the People's Republic of China. The giant pandas proved so popular that after their arrival attendance at the Zoo nearly doubled. The pandas come from northern China where it can be quite cold, so they are housed in special, climate-controlled quarters and are kept indoors on hot days. For those interested in seeing Ling-Ling and Hsing-Hsing follow the Crowned Crane Trail with its green crane footprints to their quarters where they are fed at 11 a.m. and 3 p.m. After this they

301

are playful for a few hours, but spend most of the day snoozing. The Zoo has been home for animal celebrities, too: Ham, the Chimpanzee who was rocketed into space in 1961; Smokey, the son of the original Forest Fire Prevention Bear; and the offspring of the rare white tiger, Mohini Rewa, brought from India in 1961.

Near the Connecticut Avenue pedestrian entrance to the Zoo is the Pelzman Memorial, a thirty-five bell carillon tower called a Glockenspiel that was donated by Dr. Ivy A. Pelzman in memory of his wife, Katherine. The tower contains a clock and a mechanism programmed to play fifty taped melodies. The bells chime every quarter of an hour. The musical tower delights the many visitors who stop to watch at regular intervals the movements of animals four feet tall made of fiberglass that include a bear, lion, giraffe, and an elephant, as well as birds which seem to fly in the breeze.

The main walkway in the National Zoo is called Olmsted Walk. It has a broad red stripe painted along its entire length. All of the Zoo's six trails begin and end at Olmsted Walk. To help orient the visitor so that he can become acquainted with the six trails and with the animals that reside along each of them, a free map is offered at the Education-Administration Building, the first building located just beyond the Connecticut Avenue entrance.

Many animals live in areas that have moats and glass as barriers rather than cages. To get to the one thousand foot long ravine called Beaver Valley follow the Polar Bear Trail with the blue footprints of a polar bear. In this Beaver Valley Ravine lives such aquatic animals as grey seals, California sea lions, North American otters, river beavers, and manatees. In this area also are found crab-eating foxes, bush dogs, and timber wolves in natural settings.

The National Zoo has one of the finest small mammal facilities in the country. To get there follow the Lion Trail with the orange footprints of a lion. Among some of the species a visitor will find exhibited in the small mammal building are: marmosets (small South American monkeys); southern potoroos (rat kangaroos); mongooses (noted for their ability to kill cobras and other venomous snakes); chinchillas; Orabissu titi monkeys; binturongs (southern Asian arboreal carnivores related to civets); oriental small-clawed otters; elephant shrews; golden lion tamarins; giant squirrels; and South American cavies (agouti, capybara, guinea pig, rodent). A nocturnal exhibit has a red light that reverses the day-night cycle of the nocturnal species shown in this special closed-off-from-daylight area. The animals cannot see the red end of the light spectrum. When the red lights are turned on, they assume it is "night" and become active. During our night bright white lights are used to make the animals believe the sun has come up, and they go to sleep. Among the animals shown in this nocturnal exhibit are bats; fennecs (desert foxes); and sugar gliders.

The exhibits of more than four hundred kinds of birds from all parts of the world are a delight for bird watchers. The birds are displayed in several areas along the Crowned Crane Trail with its green crane footprints where in the Great Outdoor Flight Cage there are twenty-five or thirty species which remain in this outdoor flight cage all through the year, acclimatized to the Washington summers and winters. In the Bird House tropical birds enjoy free, undisturbed

flight even as visitors move in and out to observe them; and where
miniature exhibits with pictures of these birds not only help identify
them but explain such interesting features as their songs, courtship
displays, and feather colorations. There is a Bird Lab in the Bird House
where visitors learn about birds by examining actual birds' nests,
eggs, diets, feathers, skins, and bones (the Bird Lab is only open at
certain hours—check the Bulletin Boards in the Bird House). Special
yards for cranes, flamingos, and other running birds, and outdoor
enclosures for larger flying birds such as vultures and eagles can
be seen, as well as Chilean flamingos. Abyssinian ground hornbills
and ostriches wander among the hardy-hoofed stock. Ducks, geese,
and swans inhabit the waterfowl ponds.

When live animals were first brought to the Smithsonian's
Mall facilities years ago, they were brought primarily to serve as
study models for the taxidermists who were mounting similar animals
for museum exhibits. At that time many visitors had never had an
opportunity to see wild animals close up and were eager to examine
those found in enclosures or cages at the rear of the original Smithsonian building. Samuel P. Langley, the third Secretary of the
Smithsonian, witnessed this great interest and recognized the need
for a zoo for both educational and conservation purposes. He successfully promoted the establishment of a separate department of living
animals with its home in the one hundred sixty-five acre National
Zoological Park adjacent to Rock Creek Park. In 1890 one hundred
seventy-five animals were transported from the back of the Smithsonian
building to their new quarters in the National Zoo. Since that time,
of course, the number of animals has greatly increased through births,
purchases, expeditions to collect, and gifts.

The National Zoo is following a reconstruction and renovation
program which will ultimately improve quarters for all of the animals
living there and will give the larger animals more pacing space and
the visitors better viewing areas. The enhanced landscaping throughout
the park has helped make the Zoo a delightful place to visit. There
eventually will be heated cages and underground structures for some
of the animal residents, and larger cages and exercise yards for
others. Already there are new and larger yards for the elephants
to which the visitor wishing to see them follows the Elephant Trail
with its brown elephant footprints. The interior renovations of the
Elephant House include improved heating and ventilating systems
and better viewing arrangements for the visitors. Another habitat
the Zoo has improved is the giraffes' new moated yard. The yard
is five times larger than was their previous one. Giraffes, rhinoceros
and hippopatami can also be found along the Elephant Trail with
its brown elephant footprints.

The Mann Memorial Lion and Tiger Building, named in memory
of the Zoo's first director, and found along the Lion Trail with its orange
footprints is the indoor home for lions and tigers, each of whom
has, in addition, about a third of an acre outdoors in which to roam.
Visitors can safely observe the lion and tiger exhibits from a rooftop
walkway, and can watch two films shown continuously indoors in
the audiovisual room of this building. "The Big Cats and How They
Came to Be" is a ten-minute animated color film produced as a joint
venture with the Polish government; "Tiger" is a nine minute film.

Another building along the Lion Trail with its orange footprints is the Reptile and Amphibian House that provides shelter for some four hundred inhabitants representing some ninety species. This is another temperature-controlled building that is attractively decorated. From time to time in the HerpLab keepers and their assistants will explain their work using live amphibians and reptiles to demonstrate as well as to teach broad concepts of biology. The HerpLab hours are posted on Bulletin Boards in the Reptile and Amphibian House. Behind the Reptile and Amphibian House are pools for crocodiles, and near the House are yards for Aldabata tortoises.

Still other interesting exhibits along the Lion Trail with its orange lion footprints show the monkeys and apes. There is a large Monkey Island on which a large group of Barbary macaques enjoy looking out at the public from a twenty-three foot high bluff. The rebuilt, glass-fronted monkey cages, in which the furniture is constructed of plastic drain pipes, provide the tenants in the Monkey House with sixteen times more usable space than they had previously. These include space for exercise and for recreation. The Great Ape House, constructed partly below ground, was designed to meet the needs of gorillas and orangutans who live there. There are privacy areas to which the apes can retire if they wish to get away from the staring eyes of visitors. There are modern innovations such as heating pads built into the floor that are set at different temperatures to allow the apes to choose what is most comfortable for them; there are sculptured fiberglass gunite "trees" for climbing or in which some like to spend time resting; and even television sets provided for the apes' enjoyment (the noisier the programs the better the apes like them). The windows through which the visitors can view the antics of the gorillas and orangutans (while seated on benches in front) are one and one half inches thick.

Finally, two widely separated trails in the park are the Zebra Trail showing black zebra footprints and the Raccoon Trail showing yellow raccoon footprints. Along the Zebra Trail, and part of the Crowned Crane Trail, are located yards for hoofed animals such as antelope, gazelles, deer, kangaroos, zebra, and others. Along the Zebra Trail with its black zebra footprints the visitor will find various kinds of bears of North America as well as sloth bears. There are also kangaroos and giant and lesser pandas. On the Raccoon Trail with gold raccoon footprints are other North American vertebrates like cats (pumas, bobcats, and jaguars), porcupines and kit foxes.

The health, growth, and development of all of the animals is constantly being monitored by the staff of the Zoo. If an animal, as sometimes happens, gets sick, it is taken to the hospital on the grounds of the Zoo where experienced veterinarians carefully examine it to determine what is wrong, prescribe medication or follow other procedures for restoring the sick animal back to health and return it to its place in the Zoo. Ling Ling, one of the giant pandas, was critically ill at one time and the prognosis for her recovery from kidney failure and anemia was poor. Antibiotics, blood transfusions, and dialysis helped cleanse her blood and restore her to good health so that she could once more take her place with Hsing Hsing.

The National Zoo, as well as other zoos in this country, has given technical assistance to people in charge of foreign zoos and wildlife departments, especially nations in underdeveloped countries. The National Zoo is a showplace for millions of visitors who come from all parts of our country as well as from abroad each year. For many of these visitors the Zoo often provides their first glimpse of wild animals. To assure us that the animals will be there for a second glimpse—because of the growing danger of the extinction of some of these animals in the wild and the need to protect them—the National Zoo provides refuge areas, both here at the Zoological Park in Washington and at Front Royal, Virginia (about 75 miles west of Washington) where the 3150 acres allow space for breeding, conservation and research. Both places often provide a haven of last resort which can assure future generations an opportunity to observe animal species that may no longer be roaming or reproducing in their native environments.

In ancient and medieval times animals were kept in private menageries and aviaries for the pleasure of rulers. Later some of these places became centers of animal parks open for public viewing. In comparatively more recent times scientific methods have been applied in many zoos for research, conservation, and breeding. Our National Zoo is committed as one of its principal purposes to saving endangered species faced with extinction such as the Pere David deer (originally natives of China, but now extinct there) and the North American bison which were hunted almost to extinction but which are now gradually being returned to the wild here. It is important to encourage Congress to continue to support our National Zoo and to increase funds for its needs. Its goals are eminently worthwhile.

The following is only a partial list of animals exhibited at the National Zoo. Births, deaths, purchases, and gifts continually add or subtract residents to the Zoo's inventory. The Zoo's population changes, too, as animals are loaned to other zoos for breeding purposes. Animals may also be moved to the Front Royal, Virginia research and conservation area for breeding and research purposes. Visitors can learn the exact locations of particular animals from a free Zoo map available at the Education-Administration Building (near the Connecticut Avenue entrance) or by asking the helpful guards on duty. Zoo hours, entrances, and services are discussed in the QuickGuide (appendix).

AMPHIBIANS

African bullfrog
African clawed frog
African reed frog
Amphiuma
Axolotl
Caecilian
Colorado River toad
Cuban tree frog
Fire-bellied toad
Great Plains toad
Greater siren
Japanese giant salamander

Japanese red-bellied newt
Leopard frog
Lesser siren
Marine toad
Mexican tree frog
Mudpuppy
Red-spotted newt
Smoky jungle frog
South American bullfrog
Surinam toad
Spotted salamander

REPTILES

African helmeted turtle
African house snake
African softshell tortoise
Alligator snapping turtle
American alligator
Banded red snake
Bearded lizard
Beauty snake
Bell's hinged-back tortoise
Big-headed turtle
Black camian
Black racer
Black rat snake
Black tegu lizard
Blood python
Blue-tongued skink
Boa constrictor
Broad-nosed crocodile
Burmese python
Bush lizard
Central American mud turtle
Clark's spiny lizard
Coast garter snake
Common iguana
Common snapping turtle
Cook's tree boa
Corn snake
Cottonmouth
Cuban crocodile
Cunningham's skink
Dumeril's monitor
Eastern milksnake
Eastern painted turtle
European glass lizard
False-map turtle
Fiji Island iguana
Florida cooter
Galapagos tortoise
Giant Aldabra Island tortoise
Giant day gecko
Gila monster
Gliding gecko
Gray racer
Green basilisk lizard
Green tree monitor
Green vine snake
Haitian boa
Helmeted iguana
Home's hinged-back turtle

Indian cobra
Indian python
Indigo snake
Jamaican anole
Jeweled lizard
King cobra
Leopard gecko
Leopard tortoise
Malayasian water monitor
Mexican bearded lizard
Mangrove pit viper
Mata Mata turtle
Mole snake
Nile monitor
Pancake tortoise
Pope's pit viper
Prehensile-tailed skink
Puff adder
Purple-spotted pit viper
Rainbow boa
Red-bellied turtle
Red-eared turtle
Red-footed tortoise
Red-tailed rat snake
Reticulated python
River cooter
Rock iguana
Rufous beaked snake
Salvador's monitor
Slender-snouted crocodile
Smooth-fronted camian
Spiny tree lizard
Spotted turtle
South American plated lizard
South American rattlesnake
Southern copperhead
Starred tortoise
Sungazer lizard
Three-toed box turtle
Tiger salamander
Timber rattlesnake
Tokay gecko
Turnip-tailed gecko
Twist-neck turtle
Water dragon
White-lipped mud turtle
Wood turtle
Yellow anaconda
Yellow-blotched sawback turtle

MAMMALS

African black rhinoceros
African buffalo
African bush elephant
African forest elephant
African palm civet
African porcupine
African pygmy goat
African water mongoose
African white-tailed rat
Allemand's grison
Allen's swamp monkey
American marten
Antelope ground squirrel
Asian elephant
Asiatic palm squirrel
Atlas lion
Austrian fruit bat
Axis deer
Bactrian camel
Badger
Banded palm civet
Barbary ape
Barking deer
Beaver
Bengal tiger
Big-horn sheep
Binturong
Black and red tamarin
Black ape
Black bear
Black footed mongoose
Black gibbon
Black howler monkey
Black-legged mongoose
Black leopard
Black rhinoceros
Blesbok
Blotched genet
Bongo
Brown-headed spider monkey
Brown-headed tamarin
Brown lemur
Brush-tailed possum
Burmese brow-antlered deer
Brush-tailed porcupine
California sea lion
Canada lynx
Caracal
Celebes ape
Ceylon elephant
Chacma baboon

Cheetah
Chickaree
Chimpanzee
Chinese ferret badger
Clouded leopard
Coatimundi
Colobus monkey
Collared anteater
Collared peccary
Common agouti
Common palm civet
Common squirrel monkey
Common wombat
Common zebra
Cotton-headed tamarin
Coyote
Crab-eating fox
Crab-eating macaque
Crested porcupine
Cuban hutia
Dama gazelle
Degu
Diana monkey
Dik-dik
Dingo
Dorcas gazelle
Douglas squirrel
Douroucouli
Duiker
Dusky langur
Eastern flying squirrel
Eastern mouse
Eastern wood rat
Echidna
Elephant shrew
Egyptian spiny mouse
Eurasian badger
European brown bear
Fanaloka
Fennec fox
Fisher
Fishing cat
Formosan masked palm civet
Formosan spotted civet
Formosan tree squirrel
Fossa
Gambia pouched rat
Gelada baboon
Genet
Geoffroy's cat
Geoffroy's marmoset

Geoffroy's tamarin
Giant anteater
Giant panda
Goeldi's marmoset
Golden-bellied ferret badger
Golden-bellied mangabey
Golden cat
Golden lion marmoset
Grant's zebra
Greater dwarf lemur
Great galago
Great Indian rhinoceros
Greater kudu
Grey-checked mangabey
Grey fox
Grey wolf
Grey-headed fruit bat
Grizzly bear
Guiana tayra
Hairy armadillo
Himalayan bear
Hippopotamus
Indian elephant
Indian one-horned rhinoceros
Indian rhinoceros
Jaguar
Jerbel
Jird
Kangaroo rat
Kinkajou
Kit fox
Kodiak bear
Korean bear
Langur
Least pocket mouse
Leopard
Leopard cat
Lesser oriental civet
Lesser panda
Linsang
Lion
Lion-tailed macaque
Llama
Lowland gorilla
Madagascar hedgehog tenrec
Mainland wombat
Malayan sun bear
Malagasy civet
Mantled howler monkey
Markhor
Marsh mongoose
Masai giraffe
Matschie's tree kangaroo

Moustached guenon
Muntjac
Naked-tailed armadillo
New Guinea dasyre
Nile hippopotamus
Nine-banded armadillo
North America striped weasel
North American cacomistle
Northern white rhinoceros
Old World badger
Olingo
Opossum
Orangutan
Owl-faced monkey
Paca
Palawan porcupine
Pallas' cat
Pampas cat
Parma wallaby
Patagonian cavy
Patas monkey
Pere David's deer
Peter's climbing rat
Pig-tailed macaque
Polar bear
Potto
Prairie dog
Prairie vole
Proboscis monkey
Pronghorn antelope
Puma
Purple-faced langur
Pygmy hippopotamus
Raccoon dog
Ratel
Rat kangaroo
Red brocket
Red-faced macaque
Reindeer
Red kangaroo
Red panda
Red uakari
Reeves' muntjac
Ring-tailed lemur
Ring-tailed mongoose
River otter
Roloway monkey
Sable antelope
Scimitar-horned antelope
Senegal bushbaby
Serval
Siamang
Sika deer

Silvered langur
Slender-tailed meerkat
Sloth bear
Slow loris
Small-eared dog
Sooty mangabey
South American squirrel
South American tapir
Southern potoroo
Speckled agouti
Spectacled bear
Spider monkey
Spotted hyena
Squirrel monkey
Sugar glider
Sun bear
Sykes' monkey
Syrian brown bear
Tamandua
Tasmanian devil
Thick-tailed bushbaby

Tickell's slow loris
Timber wolf
Tree shrew
Two-toed sloth
Utah prairie dog
Wanderoo
White-bearded gnu
White-bearded wildebeest
White Bengal tiger
White-cheeked gibbon
White-fronted marmoset
White (or square lipped) rhinoceros
White-fronted wallaby
White-throated capuchin
White-tailed deer
Wildebeest
Wooly monkey
Yellow-backed duiker
Yellow-throated marten
Zorilla

BIRDS

In the Bird House

African black crake
American greater flamingo
Argus pheasant
Black and crimson shrike
Black-headed ibis
Bleeding heart pigeon
Blue-backed grassquit
Blue-backed manikin
Blue-breasted quail
Blue-naped coly (or mouse bird)
Blue-rumped parrotlet
Boat-billed heron
Burrowing owl
Cinnamon-chested bee eater
Common jacana
Common motmot
Crested green wood partridge
Curly-crested toucanet
Cut-throat weaver finch
Elf's owl
Emeral dove
Fairy bluebird
Golden oriole
Gold-fronted chloropsis
Gold song sparrow
Gouldian finch

Grand Canyon white-fronted
  Amazon parrot
Hammer-head stork
Hoopoe
Indian lorikeet
Kikuyu white-eye
Kiwi
Malaysian lesser-grain broad bill
Masked tanager
Nutmeg finch (or spotted munia)
Paradise tanager
Peruvian cock-of-the-rock
Princess (or Alexandra) parrot
Red-backed sandpiper
Red-crested cardinal
Red-billed leiothrix
Red-crested turaco
Red-billed oxpecker
Red-fronted barbette
Red lorry
Red-vented bulbul
Rhinoceros hornbill
Rothschild's mynah
Rufous-thighed falconet
Sacred ibis
Scarlet-breasted parrot

Short-billed dowitcher
Silver-eared mesia
Spur-winged plover
Strawberry finch (or red munia)
Strong-billed woodcreeper
Sun bittern
Turquoise parakeet
Western sandpiper

White eye
White-naped honey eater
Woodcock
Yellow-breasted friot dove
Yellow-legged green pigeon
Yellow rail
Yellow-tufted woodpecker

In the Flight Cage

Collared turtle dove
Golden pheasant
Guanay cormorant
Impyan monal
Inca tern
Purple grackle
Red-crested cardinal

Red-winged starling
Scrub jay
Spotted dove
Superb starling
White-cheeked turaco
Yellow-billed magpie

In the Bird House Yard

Black-necked swan
Black swan
Blue-eared pheasant
Brush turkey
Common crane
Crested seriema
Crown crane
Double-wattled cassowary
Eastern rosella
Eastern wild turkey
Emu
Golden pheasant
Hume's bar-tailed pheasant
Indian peep owl

Kori bustard
Lesser rhea
Raven
Red-shouldered hawk
Roadside hawk
Sarus crane
Savannah hawk
Secretary bird
Stanley (or blue) crane
Stuped owl
Swinhoe's pheasant
White-eared pheasant
White-necked raven

In the Outdoor Bird Enclosure

American white pelican
American widgeon
Bald eagle
Barn owl
Borneo Great Argus pheasant
Cinnamon teal
Collared forest falcon
Crested caracara
Crested serpent eagle
Dalmatian pelican
Demoiselle crane
Egyptian goose
Golden eagle
Griffin vulture
Hawaiian duck

Hawaiian goose
Laysan teal
Lesser kelp goose
Long-crested hawk eagle
Malay fishing owl
Mandarin duck
Nepal brown wood owl
Old World white pelican
Ornate hawk owl
Orinoco goose
Redhead
Ringed teal
Rosy-billed pochard
Silver gull
Snowy owl

Whistling swan
White-bellied sea eagle
White-crested Kalij pheasant

Whooper swan
Woodduck

Among Hardy Hoofed Stock

Abyssinian ground hornbill
Chilean flamingo

Ostrich

In the Waterfowl Ponds

American widgeon
Bar-headed goose
Barrow's golden eye
Black duck
Black brant
Blacked-necked swan
Black swan
Bufflehead
Cackling Canada goose
Canvasback
Cinnamon teal
Common eider
Common golden eye
Common merganser
Common shelduck
Gadwall
Greater scaup
Green-winged teal
Hooded merganser
Indian spotbill

Lesser Magellan goose
Lesser scaup
Mallard
Mandarin duck
North American woodduck
Northern pintail
Pacific white-fronted goose
Philippine duck
Radjah shelduck
Red-crested pochard
Redhead
Ring-necked duck
Ruddy duck
Ruddy shelduck
Ross' goose
Steller's eider
Trumpter swan
Tufted duck
Whistling swan

8

The Kennedy Center for the Performing Arts

On September 8, 1971 the John F. Kennedy Center for the Performing Arts opened its doors with the world premiere of Leonard Bernstein's "Mass" composed especially for the occasion. The opening of the Kennedy Center was accompanied by great fanfare in Washington and received wide publicity in the national press.

Edward Durrell Stone designed the Kennedy Center's six-story structure, a classically proportioned building over six hundred feet long and three hundred feet wide, faced with thousands of tons of Carrara marble, a generous gift from Italy. Under its roof is an Opera House, a Concert Hall, the Eisenhower Theater, the American Film Institute Theater, a Terrace Theater Complex, and other facilities. The Center hosts the finest in dramas, films, and dance programs, symphony concerts, operas, organ and other kinds of recitals, and chamber, choral, as well as popular music concerts. Musical comedies are staged here as well as operettas and lectures. While most of the Center's events feature the premier names in the given fields, the Center is also hospitable to new talent. The Roof Terrace, which can be reached by elevators in the Hall of Nations, offers a lovely view of Washington and the surrounding countryside including a glimpse to the west toward Virginia of an island wildlife sanctuary in the Potomac River established as a memorial to President Theodore Roosevelt. Also on the Roof Terrace is the Terrace Theater and the three restaurants of the Kennedy Center. On weekends the National Park Service offers free talks about the sights of Washington that one can see from the Roof Terrace (check at National Park Service Desk in the lobby for time).

In 1958 the institution, then called the National Cultural Center, was established by an act of Congress and provided with an initial allocation of funds. The center was officially named the John F. Kennedy Center for the Performing Arts shortly after President Kennedy was assassinated as the country's memorial to him in Washington.

The original federal grant for the Kennedy Center was matched by private contributions, including a substantial amount from the Kennedy family. A second federal grant was again matched by private contributions. The balance of the building's final cost was met by a Treasury loan, which revenues from the three-level underground parking garage for 1,450 cars help repay. Like the National

312

Gallery of Art, the Kennedy Center is affiliated with the Smithsonian Institution but it is independently administered.

In addition to the public and private funds that helped erect the building, the Kennedy Center has been the recipient of many wonderful gifts from the states and from foreign governments. On the main level two marble-lined corridors, the Hall of Nations and the Hall of States, are each flanked by appropriate flags. These corridors lead to the vast, red-carpeted Foyer at the rear which runs the entire length of the building parallel to the Potomac River. This Grand Foyer provides access to each of three large theaters (Eisenhower Theater, the Opera House, and the Concert Hall) as well as to the River Terrace. On occasion free performances (such as selections from the Children's Art Series) have been staged in the Grand Foyer. An enormous, rough-hewn bronze head of President John F. Kennedy, sculpted by Robert Berks, dominates this Grand Foyer.

The Grand Foyer's eighteen Orrefors crystal chandeliers and matching sconces on the walls are a gift from the Swedish people; the mirrored wall panels in this Foyer and in the box tier lobby of the Opera House are gifts from Belgium. Other gifts to the Kennedy Center grace not only the Grand Foyer but every area of this modern, classical building. For example, two beautifully woven tapestries are gifts from Yugoslavia; seven tapestries came from Australia with two as gifts from Spain designed after paintings by Goya. The two French tapestries in the box tier lobby of the Opera House are modeled on a Henri Matisse painting. Also from France on display in the box tier lobby of the Opera House are two sculptures done by Henri Laurens.

Twenty specially designed planters of hammered brass and teak are set in the Grand Foyer, the Hall of Nations, and the Hall of States. The planters, a gift from India, are filled with ficus plants, a gift from the people of Florida. The Waterford crystal chandelier and matching sconces that light up the south lounge of the Opera House are gifts to the Kennedy Center from Ireland. A great many other valuable gifts were received from countries throughout the world and are noted in a free brochure available at the Information Desk.

The Kennedy Center for the Performing Arts provides the country with a truly national stage. Its administrators attempt to present the public with the best in all of the performing arts that include drama, dance, opera, concerts (of all kinds), musical comedies, operettas, and others.

Since 1969 selected college, university, and institute theater troupes from across the country have been invited to present the best-performed plays in their repertoires at the American College Festival, presented jointly by the Kennedy Center and the Alliance for Arts Education. The Festival is produced by the American Theatre Association as part of the center's education program. Once held at various other Smithsonian facilities in Washington and under corporate sponsorship, they now are performed in the Kennedy Center at times and places announced in "Two On The Aisle" which can be seen at Information Desks or can be sent for prior to visiting the Kennedy Center (see the QuickGuide).

The Opera House

        In design and luxurious decor, the Kennedy Center's Opera
House has been compared to auditoriums found in both the Paris Opera
House and the Vienna State Opera House. Its magnificent red and
gold silk stage curtain (a gift from Japan), its utterly beautiful
constellation of crystal chandeliers (a gift from Austria), its red walls,
seat covers, and carpeting all combine to create an opulent setting
for its productions. This elegant auditorium seats about twenty-three
hundred and is used for all kinds of performances.
        Bernstein's "Mass" that opened the Kennedy Center was
performed here, as was the premiere of Ginastera's "Beatrix Cenci."
Beverly Sills sang in Handel's "Ariodante," the LaScala Opera Company
performed "Macbeth," "Simon Boccanegra," and "La Boheme," and
the Paris Opera Company presented "Othello" and "Faust" in this
Opera House. The Houston Grand Opera Company, the New York
City Opera Company, and the D'Oyle Carte Company, among many
others, have also staged fine productions here. Audiences heard a
revival (with unmistakeable approval) of Romberg's nostalgic "The
Student Prince" that was beautifully sung and staged.
        Two major dance companies, the American Ballet of New
York and the National Ballet of Washington, show the results of
wonderfully trained and disciplined dancers. These two companies
perform in the Opera House each season, on a regular basis. With
visiting dance companies like the London Festival Ballet, the Stuttgart
Ballet, the Ballet Nacional de Cuba, the National Festive Folk Ballet
of Spain, the Martha Graham Dance Company, and others, the Kennedy
Center's reputation as an important American dance center is assured.
        The Opera House is equipped with infra-red listening equipment
to use with the light-weight loop system (borrowed free) to help the
hearing impaired.

The Concert Hall

        The opening performance in the Kennedy Center's Concert
Hall was given by the National Symphony Orchestra under the direction
of Antal Dorati. Since that performance guests in the twenty-seven
hundred and fifty seat Concert Hall have heard symphonies, chamber
music, and recitals, as well as some popular music concerts, and
occasional lectures. Menuhin, Stern, Perlman, Zukerman, Rostropovich,
Van Cliburn, Ashkenazy, Segovia, Rampal, Dionne Warwick, and Count
Basie are among scores of other artists who have performed here.
The New York Pro Musica, the Beryoazka Dance Company of Moscow,
the Guarneri String Quartet, the New York Philharmonic Orchestra,
and the Mormon Tabernacle Choir are some, among many other groups,
which have given performances in the Concert Hall. The National
Symphony Orchestra has performed here under many well-known
visiting conductors, some of whom were Mehta, Ozawa, Alcantara,
Leinsdorf, Maazel, and Kostelanetz. Many other orchestras and artists
have lighted the stage in the Concert Hall, their music not lost here,

for the acoustics are excellent and bear comparison with Boston's Symphony Hall and other equally fine concert halls.

There are two annual events held here in the fall during Award Week. The first awards are given by the Kennedy Center-Rockefeller Foundation Competition for excellence in the performance of American music. The second awards, called the Friedham Awards, are for meritorius composition in orchestral music one year and alternated with chamber music composition the next.

Band associations throughout the country raised funds to name the auditorium's stage the John Philip Sousa stage, in honor of the great march king. The Filene Organ, with its more than four thousand pipes, forms a dramatic background for the stage. Funds for the organ were donated by members of the Filene family in memory of their parents, Mr. and Mrs. Lincoln Filene.

Eisenhower Theater

On the box tier level of the Eisenhower Theater is Great Britain's gift to the Kennedy Center, "Figure" by sculptor Dame Barbara Hepworth. Another gift, the stage curtain, was given by Canada. Guests in the eleven hundred and fifty seat auditorium, named in honor of President and Mrs. Eisenhower, witnessed a memorable opening performance of Ibsen's "A Doll's House" starring Claire Bloom. Clifford Odets' "The Country Girl" had a run here as did Jerome Lawrence and Robert Lee's "First Monday In October." A new comedy by Donald Driver and Michael Valenti "Oh, Brother!" was presented here; Jane Alexander and Karen Allen appeared here in "Monday After the Miracle;" and Anne Jackson and Eli Wallach who have appeared in the Eisenhower Theater before did "Twice Around the Park" here. Examples of some outstanding Theater Guild Productions that appeared in this theater included Brian Bedford, Len Cariou, and Irene Worth in "The Physicists;" Jean Stapleton in "The Late Christopher Bean;" Judith Anderson and Zoe Caldwell in "Medea;" Alan Arkin in "The Imaginary Invalid;" and Liv Ullmann in "Ghosts." Julie Harris, Jessica Tandy, Hume Cronyn, Zero Mostel, Hal Holbrook, Mary Martin, Jason Robards, Jr., George Gizzard, Maureen Stapleton, Henry Fonda, Peter O'Toole and George F. Scott are among scores of other notable stars who have played the Eisenhower Theater. Cyril Ritchard, Edwin Sherin, and Jose Quintero have directed plays here. This theater has seen many other directors, and many other stars, not only in drama, but in musicals—indeed, one of the musicals which opened here, "Annie," went on to become a Broadway hit. While the theater is intended primarily for drama and live stage performance, it is also equipped to show films and transmit radio and television performances.

The theater is equipped with infra-red listening equipment to aid the hearing-impaired. The light-weight loop system can be borrowed free here.

American Film Institute Theater

Also located on the main level, near the entrance to the Hall of States, is the American Film Institute Theater that seats two hundred and twenty-four. The theater is operated by the American Film Institute which programs silent films as well as avant-garde American and foreign productions from nearly every part of the world. A retrospective series showed classic German films covering the years 1919 through 1945. These showed in chronological sequence over forty feature length films as well as some short films. A retrospective series of French films has also been shown. Some classic American films like "My Fair Lady," "Topper," "Breakfast at Tiffany's," "My Favorite Wife," and films of the Old West are among those that have been screened here. Movies can also vary from old musicals to comedies and dramas. Check the Information Desk at the American Film Institute Desk for names, dates, and times when films will be shown.

Terrace Theater

The Terrace Theater located on the Roof Terrace level seats five hundred and thirteen. It began its life with a three million dollar check presented to the Kennedy Center by the Japanese Prime Minister in honor of the American Bicentennial. The gift was intended for a studio theater that would serve as "a permanent living link" between the two nations and cultures. It is used for chamber music, drama, poetry readings, films, lectures, children's programs, and for experimental works. Its opening presentation was a Kabuki play. Other productions presented here have included Tom Stoppard's "Dogg's Hamlet, Cahoot Macbeth;" "Anos Tiene un Dia?" by the Grupo Ictus Theater Company of Chile; Donizetti's opera "Il Furioso all'Isola di San Domingo" and "An Evening With Rodgers & Hammerstein and Lerner & Lowe" among many others.

The Terrace Theater is also equipped with infra-red listening equipment to use with the light-weight loop system (borrowed free) to help the hearing impaired.

Interest has been centered on public-service programming that includes the development of new works and new talents. The Kennedy Center Corporate Fund has helped bring some of the young performing companies with limited funds to the Terrace Theater. There has also been support for programs for children and youth by corporations, foundations, and private contributions. The Experimental Theater offers diverse and innovative programming for younger companies, among them: The Acting Company (an official touring unit), the Goodman, and the Folger Theater Company. The Theater Lab was the site for presentation of innovative new works and reader's theater productions including Robert Wilson's "Medea;" a musical "Good Sports" and "The Invasion of Addis Ababa" presented under the sponsorship of the Center's National Black Theater and Playwright Project.

Performing Arts Library

This library located adjacent to the Terrace Theater houses

the Kennedy Center's archives and a reference and periodical collection covering all aspects of the performing arts (theater, music, dance, films, and broadcasting). It was opened to the public in March 1979 under the joint sponsorship of the Kennedy Center and the Library of Congress and functions as a resource center for performers, staff, and the public. Its staff has answered requests from all parts of the country on the performing arts. The library has a computer link with reference material at the Library of Congress by way of a video display computer link to its collections.

Free Organ Demonstrations and Recitals at the Kennedy Center

Demonstrations are given on the first Thursday of each month in the Concert Hall, and on the third Thursday of each month in the American Film Institute Theater. Both are given at 1 p.m.

Recitals are held on the first Thursday of each month at 5 p.m. in the Concert Hall.

Quickguide

People planning to visit the Smithsonian can enrich their visit considerably if they will avail themselves of excellent programs, lectures and performances offererd at its facilities throughout the year. Notice of these events are announced in calendars or bulletins giving the names, dates, locations, and if there is a charge, the cost of tickets. Among the offerings are included concerts from classical music to country, gospel and blues to jazz, played by orchestras, artists appearing in ensembles or soloists. The described programs also include films, story telling, illustrated lectures, theater performances (including puppet shows), dance performances, concerts played on restored instruments, and several kinds of dramatic programs. Many splendid programs or performances for which there may be a charge or no charge, as the case might be, are chronologically arranged in the **Smithsonian Calendar** found at Information Desks. Found listed in the **Smithsonian Calendar,** too, are very fine special exhibitions which are different from the permanent exhibits described in this Guide because they are displayed for only a limited time. For anyone planning a visit to the Smithsonian who knows ahead of time the month he will be there, he could write (allowing plenty of time for a reply) to the Office of Public Affairs, Smithsonian Institution, Washington, D.C. 20560, requesting a copy of the **Smithsonian Calendar** for that month. Enclose a stamped, self-addressed business sized envelope for a reply. The **Smithsonian Calendar** can also be found at Information Desks and the events offered are announced on bulletin boards in each facility. A sampling of events that were presented in the past can be found in the pages which follow under the names of the individual facilities.

Additional calendars or bulletins found at Information Desks are issued by the Museum of American Art/Renwick Gallery. "Evenings at Barney Studio House" are limited to 50 people, tickets cost $10 each; for reservations two weeks in advance and information about these "evenings" call 202-357-3111; the Hirshhorn Museum and Sculpture Garden issues bulletins found at its Information Desks; the National Gallery of Art issues its own **Calendar of Events** at Information Desks there. The National Gallery's **Calendar of Events** lists the (often free) lectures, concerts, films, special exhibits, and tours in the East and West Buildings, also listed on bulletin boards in each.

A copy of a **Calendar of Events** issued by the Smithsonian

Performing Arts which describes programs for the entire year can
be obtained on request by writing to Smithsonian Performing Arts,
Washington, D.C. 20560. Some concerts at the Renwick are free as
are occasional events at Baird Auditorium in the Museum of Natural
History and the Carmichael Auditorium in the Museum of American
History, but, generally speaking, there is a charge for most programs
listed in the **Calendar of Events** issued by the Smithsonian Performing
Arts.

To attend one or more of the professional programs offered
at the Kennedy Center one can purchase tickets at the box offices
in the Hall of States or Hall of Nations in the Kennedy Center as
indicated on pages 359-360. Out-of-town visitors may wish to write for
a copy of **Two on the Aisle** which lists chronologically (for each month)
the events and the costs of tickets for the Opera House, Eisenhower
Theater, American Film Institute Theater, Terrace Theater, Grand
Foyer, and Theater Lab. It is important to state the month one expects
to be in Washington when writing for a copy of **Two on the Aisle.**
Mail the request to the Kennedy Center for the Performing Arts,
2700 F Street, N.W., Washington, D.C. 20566 / Request for **Two on
the Aisle.**

Mail the request at least one month in advance of your expected
arrival date. This will allow time to receive the bulletin and, if you
wish to order tickets (very promptly), receive them before leaving
for Washington. For a very quick method one can also order tickets
by calling the box office (phone numbers are listed on page 359) with
your credit card in hand. The box office will give information about
picking up the tickets.

Transportation

On the whole transportation in Washington, except during
peak hours, is quite good. Visitors seeking information about transportation to Smithsonian facilities can call the following numbers:

    Bus and rail transit information: 637-2437
    Handicapped information: 637-1245
    Senior citizen information: 637-1179
    Timetables: 637-1261

Parking

Parking on the Mall is free, but the spaces there are limited
and one can only park for three hours. One can park in the National
Air and Space Museum Garage (400 cars and a charge). There are
a number of parking places on Independence and Pennsylvania Avenues
(charge). Transportation by public conveyance (bus and rail) is quite
rapid and brings one within short walking distance of the museums.
Public transportation to other Smithsonian facilities should be
considered as a feasible alternative to driving one's car.

Food

Cafeterias and a few dining rooms are found in most Smithsonian facilities except for the Castle, Arts and Industries Building, the Freer, the Renwick, and Barney Studio House. Consult the individual facilities in the pages that follow. For card-carrying Smithsonian members and guests a very good dining room is located on the ground floor of the Museum of Natural History.

Information for the Handicapped

Visitors can obtain a free copy of **Smithsonian: A Guide for Disabled People** at all Information Desks. One can also write to the Office of Public Affairs, Smithsonian Institute, Washington, D.C. 20560 requesting a copy. Hearing-impaired visitors can borrow (free) light-weight hearing devices (loop amplification systems) which can enormously increase hearing for the user. Inquire at the Eisenhower Theater, the Opera House, and the Terrace Theater in the Kennedy Center for the Performing Arts; at Information Desks in the Museum of American History for use in the Carmichael Auditorium; and at Information Desks in the Museum of Natural History for use in the center section of the Baird Auditorium for this light-weight listening system. An advanced request can obtain a portable loop system for use anywhere in the Smithsonian.   There are also sign or oral interpreters available on request for certain events. Touch Tours for the visually handicapped can usually be provided if advance arrangements are made. For more information call 202-357-2700 (voice) or 202-357-1729 (TDD-telecommunication device for the deaf). The use of wheelchairs in most facilities is available (free) in checkrooms.

Discovery Theater

This theater is located in the Arts and Industries Building at 1000 Jefferson Drive S.W. Among its varied offerings (for which there is a charge) are puppet shows, radio personalities telling stories, folk tales sometimes told with music and mime, scenes from Shakespeare plays, and a variety of other programs and performances which are announced in the **Smithsonian Calendar** or the **Calendar of Events** issued by the Smithsonian Performing Arts.

Festival of American Folklife

This festival is held each year on the Mall during the summer. In the past it was held for as short a period as a Fourth of July weekend or for as long as a month (as it was during our country's Bicentennial). Its focus each year has generally been on a particular area of our country with exhibitors from that area who can cook the ethnic foods, create the traditional crafts, music, and dancing. One year, for example, it was the traditional music, dances, and crafts of the upper peninsula Ojibway Indians of Michigan who demonstrated their art of canoe making; another year it was Hispanic and native Americans from New Mexico who built an adobe house and oven to illustrate the energy-efficient properties of this building material. In 1983 the Festival was held during June 23-27 and June 30-July 4 from 11 a.m. to 5:30 p.m. The area of our country featured then was New Jersey, but also showed French exhibits from France and from French-American communities. New Jersey seafoods and French-American foods were sold. There were fiddling demonstrations and native dances, too. The events each year attract a large number of people interested in the demonstrations of traditional crafts, preparations of ethnic foods, native dances, and other skills. Generally, there is no charge, except for those buying food or craft items for sale.

Annual Zoo Fest

The annual Zoo Fest is held usually in June for about a week at the Zoo. Interesting events are scheduled for each day. Call 202-673-4717 for details.

Special Discounts at Museum Shops and Bookstores

Smithsonian members presenting membership cards at the time of purchase will, in most cases, be given a 10% discount in every museum shop or bookstore.

Annual Kite Carnival

The annual Kite Carnival is held at the end of March or the beginning of April on the Washington Monument Grounds. Kites must be homemade. Those wishing to enter must register. Call 202-357-3030 or write to the Smithsonian for details about categories and age groups.

Orientation Program

In the original Smithsonian Building—the Castle—slide lectures are given. These help introduce the visitor to its public facilities. Ask at the Information Desk for the location of the room where they are being given. Walk in—they are free. Groups wishing to make arrangements may call 202-357-2700.

Other Current Information

Dial-A-Museum by calling 357-2020
Dial-A-Phenomenon by calling 357-2000

THE ORIGINAL SMITHSONIAN BUILDING - THE CASTLE

Location: 1000 Jefferson Drive S.W. 20560

Entrance: This building on the south side of the Mall,
                    looks like an old castle with many towers, and
                    has a central entrance on the Mall that most
                    visitors use.

Telephone: 357-1300 (ask for the Castle)
                    357-2700 (Visitor Information)

Hours: April 15 – Labor Day   10 am–7:30 pm daily
                    After Labor Day – April 14   10 am–5:30 pm daily

Reception   This is a general visitor reception center for
Center: the Smithsonian. The Reception Desk is very
                    helpful giving information on all of the
                    Smithsonian facilities (except the National
                    Gallery of Art and the Kennedy Center for
                    the Performing Arts which is generally more
                    readily available at Information Desks in their
                    own facilities). One can inquire here about
                    various tours, concerts, films, lectures,
                    demonstrations, and other services at the
                    Smithsonian as well as special exhibitions.
                    Also walk-in slide lecture orientation program
                    about Smithsonian facilities.

                    Smithsonian Associates (members who have
                    joined and receive **Smithsonian**) can obtain
                    a special kit here with a map of Washington
                    and more information about the Smithsonian.
                    They can also obtain this kit to examine before
                    they come to Washington by sending a postcard
                    to:
                        ASSOCIATES RECEPTION CENTER
                        Smithsonian Institution
                        Washington, D.C. 20560
                    Please allow two weeks for delivery. The kits
                    are free.

Special   In a small room, to the left as one enters the
Exhibit: building is the crypt of James Smithson, the
                    donor of the Smithsonian Institution. Exhibited,
                    too, are artifacts associated with Smithson
                    or his family.

Food: There is no food service in this building.

**Woodrow
Wilson
Memorial:**

The Woodrow Wilson International Center for Scholars is housed in this original Smithsonian building. It is the only memorial for President Wilson in Washington. It includes a library and conference rooms for scholars.

**Executive
Offices:**

The offices of higher echelon administrators of the Smithsonian are located on the second floor in this building.

**Other
Changing
Exhibits:**

Examples of exhibits shown in some of the facilities of the Smithsonian; models showing plans for new wings or even new buildings for the Smithsonian; and small special exhibits are shown in this building from time to time.

Transportation:

Metro Subway station: Smithsonian (Mall exit). Call Metro Bus Co. for buses that bring one to the Mall.

NATIONAL MUSEUM OF AMERICAN HISTORY

Location:

Mall—Madison Dr. between 12th and 14th Streets, N.W.
Constitution Avenue—between 12th and 14th Streets, N.W.

Entrances:

The Mall entrance brings one in on the second floor. The Constitution Avenue entrance brings one in on the first floor.

Telephone:

202-357-1300

Hours:

| April 1 - Labor Day | 10 am-7:30 pm |
| After Labor Day - May 31 | 10 am-5:30 pm |

**Information Desks/
Bulletin Boards:**

Located on the first and second floors near the entrances. These are the best sources for current information about programs and performances.

**Floor Plans of
the Museum:**

A leaflet showing floor plans is available free at Information Desks.

Tours (Free):

Walk-in tours including First Ladies' Hall are given. These vary with the season and the availability of volunteer guides. Inquire at Information Desks about when offered.

Tours by appointment: Quilt Collection; First

Ladies' Hall: Needlework; Ceramics; Glass; Tours for the Handicapped; Group Tours. Requests should be made at least two weeks in advance.

Demonstrations (Free):
Spinning and weaving in Textile Hall; in halls where there are machine tools; steam engines; typefounding and eighteenth and nineteenth century printing.

Check Information Desks or Bulletin Boards for days and hours.

Films:
Free films are shown in Carmichael Auditorium on the first floor usually at 12:30 on Wednesdays.

Other free films are generally shown on a continuous basis in the halls of Stamps and the Mail; Photography; Money and Medals; and frequently in other halls.

There is a charge for some films. Example: Historical Films of Rossellini: "Blaise Pascal" (with English subtitles).

Check Information Desks or Bulletin Boards for days and hours of films in Carmichael Aud. (free), or others for which there is a charge.

Concerts:
Free concerts played on restored eighteenth and nineteenth century instruments are given on different days for string, wind or keyboard instruments and are generally performed in the Hall of Musical Instruments. Also twice a month "Saturday Live" free concerts at 2 p.m.

There is a charge for some concerts. Example: Violinist Jaap Schroeder and the Smithsonian Chamber Players performing works in honor of Haydn's 250th birthday.

Check Information Desks or Bulletin Boards for days and hours.

Illustrated Lectures:
Free lectures are given on a variety of topics by scientists and specialists.

There is a charge for some lectures, seminars, or dialogues.

Check Information Desks or Bulletin Boards for days and hours.

Special Exhibits (Free):

There are excellent changing exhibits that remain for a limited period of time. These are shown in addition to the permanent exhibits in halls listed in the Guide.

Example: "Franklin D. Roosevelt: The Intimate Presidency," featured communications and re-creation of White House room where the fireside chats were held.

Check Information Desks or Bulletin Boards for locations.

Special Events:

Some of these are free. Example: Performance. Re-creation of 18th century social dances from George Washington's day. Visitor participation.

For others there is a charge. Example: "Design Evening: The Revolution in Men's Fashions." Six top women designers of menswear discussed their designs. Slide illustrations.

Discovery Corners (Free):

Discussions and Demonstrations
Spirit of '76, Armed Forces Hall, (interesting for little ones) Miniature Theater, Hall of Electricity, Rehabilitation, Hall of Medicine.

Check Information Desks or Bulletin Boards for days and hours.

Food:

Public cafeteria and snack bar open daily on the ground floor.

Smithsonian Associates' Dining Room on the ground floor of the **Museum of Natural History.** Membership card is required.

Check hours at Information Desk.

Other Free Services:

Elevators; escalator; checking; lockers in which to store parcels (ask attendant at checking counter for a free token); a limited number of wheelchairs available at checking counters.

Bookstore:

A Smithsonian bookstore and museum shop is located on the ground floor near the cafeteria. Smithsonian Associates showing a membership card are entitled to a 10% discount.

U.S. Government Post Office (Operational):

This post office is located at the Constitution Avenue entrance. It came from Headsville, West Virginia where at one time it served as both a post office and a country store. Today visitors can buy stamps, postcards, and other philatelic artifacts. Letters or cards sent from here are mailed with a special Smithsonian postmark.

Museum Shops: The largest museum shop in the Smithsonian complex is now on the ground floor of the National Museum of American History, another is located on the second floor near the Mall entrance. They carry, in addition to books, pictures, postcards, slides and related items about the Museum of American History which include American glass, ceramics, pewter, and crafts for sale. Smithsonian Associates showing a membership card are entitled to a 10% discount on their purchases.

Old-Fashioned Ice Cream Parlor: For the foot-weary one can stop to rest here while enjoying a cup of tea or coffee, a soda, sundae or soft drink. There is a charge.

Checkroom/ Lockers (Free): These are available on both the first and second floors. Ask the guard on duty or the checkroom attendant for a free token for the lockers.

Metro Stations: Those closest to the Museum of American History are: Smithsonian (Use Smithsonian exit) and Federal Triangle.

Bus Transportation: Call the Metro Bus Co. to get the numbers of the buses which will bring a visitor closest to the Museum of American History (state your location in Washington).

NATIONAL MUSEUM OF NATURAL HISTORY

Location: Mall—Madison Dr. between 10th and 6th Streets, N.W.
Constitution Avenue—between 10th and 6th Streets, N.W.

Entrances: Mall entrance requires climbing a great number of steps. Constitution Ave. entrance has a ramp for wheelchairs and handicapped. This entrance brings one in on the ground floor where an escalator and elevators are readily available.

Telephone: 202-357-1300 (ask for Museum of Natural History)

Hours:	April 1 – Labor Day	10 am–7:30 pm
	After Labor Day – May 31	10 am–5:30 pm

**Information Desks/
Bulletin Boards:** Located on the first and ground floors near the entrances. These are the best sources for current information about programs and performances; also special exhibits.

**Floor Plans of
the Museum:** A leaflet showing floor plans is available free at Information Desks.

Tours (Free): During the Spring, Fall, and Winter months free tours, depending on the availability of docents (guides), are offered at 10:30, 12 noon, and 1:30. Meet in the Rotunda by the Elephant. These are not given during June and September. During July and August high school students act as guides.

Individuals can rent (at minimal fee) a wand in which is contained taped explanations of many exhibits in some of the exhibition halls recorded by curators of the various departments.

Group tours and tours to particular exhibits or halls must be prearranged at least two weeks in advance.

**Demonstrations
(Free):** Examples of past demonstrations: Japanese Tea Ceremony with Hisashi Yamada of Urasenke Tea Ceremony Society; Traditional Korean embroidery with Madame Suk-soon Seo, noted embroidery designer.

Films: Free films on Natural History subjects are screened (consult bulletin boards or Information Desks). Examples of films shown: "The Asteroid and the Dinosaur" an extinction theory; "Notes of a Biology Watcher: A Film with Lewis Thomas. Events in the lives of sea anemones, blue crabs, tiny worms and plants;" "Lucy in Disguise. Newly-found fossils challenge findings of the Leakeys."

Films for which there is a charge: Example: "There Was Always Sun Shining Someplace. Life in the Negro Baseball Leagues."

Illustrated Lectures: Free lectures are given on a variety of topics by scientists and specialists. Examples of some in the past: "Spring Birds and Wildflowers;" "Newts, Frogs, Snakes in and around Washington, D.C.;" "Fossils for Fuel;" "Ancient Animals of Antarctic Area"; "The Teeth of Man and Other Mammals: Their Differences and What They Reveal;" "The Urban Renewal of Ancient Rome;" "Myth, Symbolism, and Art in Bering Sea Eskimo Culture;" "Billion Years of Earth History."

For some lectures a charge is made. Examples of past lectures: "Wanderings in the Sinai: The Region's Archeology and Culture;" "Skywatchers of Ancient Mexico: Their System of Astronomy;" "American Antique Furniture: Preserving Our Heritage;" "Marine Life on Aldabra Island, the Focus of a Smithsonian Research Expedition."

Special Exhibits (Free): There are excellent changing exhibits that remain for a limited period of time. These are shown in addition to the exhibits in permanent halls listed in the Guide. Examples: "Japanese Ceramics Today: Masterworks from the Kikuchi Collection;" "The Heritage of Islam;" "The Nazca Lines: Ancient Peruvian Desert Art;" "Two Meteorites That Crashed Into Homes in Connecticut in 1971 and 1982, Two Miles from Each Other."

Special Events (Charge): All day seminar: "Ancient Rome: An Archaeological Perspective: From Prehistoric Hut Village to the Grandest Capital of the Ancient World."

International Dance: Suarti and Suarni. Interpreters of Refined Drama/Dance of Bali.

African Dance Concert. "Obade Bii Dancers, Drummers, and Singers from Ghana."

American Musical Theater: "Oh Me, Oh My, Oh Youmans;" A Salute to "Tea for Two Composer."

Draw-Ins (Free): For amateurs and professional artists and illustrators who are twelve years and older. Specimens in the Naturalist Center are used. One must bring own supplies. Science illustrators give assistance.

Other Free Services: Elevators; escalator; checking; lockers (ask attendant at checking counter for a free token); wheelchairs available at checking counters.

Food: Public cafeteria open daily on the first floor.

Smithsonian Associates' Dining Room on the
ground floor. Membership card required.

Museum Shops: Located on ground and first floor. Smithsonian
Associates showing a membership card are
entitled to a 10% discount.

Metro Stations: Those closest to the Museum of Natural History
are: Smithsonian (Use Smithsonian exit) and
Federal Triangle.

Bus Transportation: Call the Metro Bus Co. to get the numbers
of the buses which will bring a visitor closest
to the Museum of Natural History (state your
location in Washington).

Concerts (Charge): "Jazz Weekends" Examples of concerts given:
Art Blakely and the Jazz Messengers; Art
Farmer, fluegelhornist; Joe Williams, Master
of American Jazz.

Folger Concert and Friends. "Music and Theater
from the Middle Ages and Renaissance."

Smithsonian Chamber Orchestra. Performances
of works by Haydn and Mozart.

American Country Music. Slim Whitman and
Thirty Years' Worth of Hit Songs.

Essex Youth Orchestra. Musicians from Great
Britain.

Discovery Room: Located on the first floor, west side. The area
is especially designed for younger children
accompanied by an adult. There are exhibit
areas of touchable objects (not permitted
in other areas of this museum), Discovery
Boxes, film strips, books, stumpers, and
costumes, as well as an aquarium with
interesting tropical fish. Admittance is free,
but visitors should obtain tickets at Information
Desks, especially for weekends to help avoid
long waits in line. Hours opened can be
ascertained at Information Desks.

Naturalist Center: Located on the ground floor. Ask at Information
Desk about days and hours when it is open
and how to reach it. This Center is designed
for the amateur scientist and collector. Children
below 12 years of age not admitted. Admittance
is free. The Center has special resource material
pertaining to: fossils, invertebrates, vertebrates,

insects, plants, rocks and minerals, and anthropology. There is a library, a small audio-visual laboratory, instruments and staff members to assist those serious students in their investigations.

NATIONAL AIR AND SPACE MUSEUM

Location: 6th Street and Independence Ave., S.W. 20560

Entrances: From Independence Avenue; from the Mall.

Telephone: 202-357-1300 (ask for National Air & Space Museum)

Calendar: **Special Presentation Calendar** (issued quarterly). Information about: "Monthly Sky Lectures;" "Briefing Room Lectures;" "Noontime with the Stars;" "Aviation Film Series;" and more.

Available free to the public. Send name and address to:
SPECIAL PRESENTATION CALENDAR
Public Affairs Office
National Air and Space Museum
Washington, D.C. 20560

Hours: April 1 – Labor Day   10 am-9:00 pm daily
                         After Labor Day – May 31   10 am-5:30 pm daily

Information Desks/   Located on the first floor near the entrances.
Bulletin Boards: These are the best sources for current information about special exhibitions, lectures, and other events.

Lectures: Free monthly sky lectures are given by staff members in the Albert Einstein Sky Theater that begin promptly at 9 a.m. on first Saturday of the month. Examples: "Encounter with the Ringed Giant;" "Venus: The Pioneer Perspective;" "Stars: From Stonehenge to the Space Telescope;" "Our Mighty Yellow Dwarf: The Sun." These are followed by a discussion of upcoming celestial events.

Visitors must use the Independence Avenue entrance and must be prompt.

Briefing Room   The lectures are free and given in the Briefing
Lectures: Room at noon on the parking level. Ask at Information Desk for dates.

Aviation Lectures: Free lectures given at 7:30 p.m. in the Langley Theater. Inquire at Information Desk for dates and titles. Examples: "Breaking the Sound Barrier;" "Combat East and West;" "Sheila Scott and Her Pioneering Career."

Films: Free films presented in the Langley Theater at 7:30 p.m. in the fall. Examples: "Battle of Britain;" "The Blue Max;" "Jet Pilot."

Tours: Free tours led by volunteer docents (guides) are available. Inquire at Information Desk about the times. Recorded highlight tours available in five languages at Recorded Tour Desk.

Frisbee Disc Festival: Held in the fall on a site bounded by 3rd and 4th Streets and Independence Avenue and Madison Drive. Sponsored by the National Air and Space Museum, participation is free. In the past workshops have been given for all ages. Inquire at the Information Desk.

Museum Shop: A vast array of kites, astronaut patches, books, postcards, films and much more is available for sale on the first floor.

Food: A public cafeteria located on the third floor has a variety of hot and cold food. What often interests young people are the packages of ice cream that the astronauts carried to the moon.

Parking: A public garage which can accommodate 400 cars is on the lower level. There is a charge. Enter the garage on 7th Street between Independence Avenue and Jefferson Drive, S.W.

Checkroom/Lockers: Free checking. Lockers available in the checkroom. Ask the attendant for a free token. Wheelchairs can be borrowed here. Ask the attendant.

Services for Handicapped: Tours for physically handicapped, visually and mentally impaired can be arranged. Call 202-357-1400.

Transportation: Metra subway line and exit at L'Enfant Plaza station or Smithsonian station.

Call Metro Bus Co. for buses that will bring you close to the National Air and Space Museum.

Special Services: Elevators and escalator.

Samuel Langley   Samuel Langley Theater that has the IMAX
Theater: projector. Examples of films shown: "To Fly;"
                          "Living Planet." Small charge.

Albert Einstein   Albert Einstein Sky Theater on the second
Theater: floor explores the universe with a Zeiss Model
                          VI planetarium instrument. Examples of
                          presentations have included: "New Eyes on
                          the Universe" and "Probe." There is a small
                          charge.

ARTS AND INDUSTRIES BUILDING

Location: Mall—900 Jefferson Drive, S.W.

Entrance: At the above location.

Telephone: 202-357-1300 (ask for the Arts and Industries
                          Building)
                          202-357-1500 for information about the
                          Discovery Theater

Hours: April 1 - Labor Day   10 am-7:30 pm
                          After Labor Day - May 31   10 am-5:30 pm

Information Desk: Here one can get information about locating
                          specific exhibits in the "1876" exhibition. Also
                          current information about programs and
                          performances given in the Discovery Theater,
                          which can also be obtained by calling 357-1500.

Tours: Free group tours can be arranged if one calls
                          357-1300 or writes the Smithsonian Institution
                          at least two weeks in advance.

Discovery Theater   Hours for performances should be confirmed
(charge):   at the Information Desk or by calling 357-1500.

                          Examples of performances given in the past
                          have included:
                          Puppet House Players "The Elves and the
                          Shoemaker;"
                          United Stage of Grand Valley Colleges "The
                          Three Sillies and Other Tales;"
                          Clarion Puppet Theatre "The Witching Hour;"
                          Puppets of Allan Stevens "Pinocchio;"
                          Blackstreet U.S.A. Puppet Theatre "Tick
                          Tock" and "Let's Jam;"

Heather Forest tells folktales with words, music and mime

Jay O'Callahan, radio star, virtuoso storyteller: "Hiro, the Gambler, and other Folktales;"

National Marionette Theatre "Hansel and Gretel;"

"The Golden Axe" Humorous folktale and Japanese-style puppetry

Theatre Beyond Words (1st-5th grades) Cartoon Characters portrayed by Potato People—a troupe from Canada

"1876" Exhibits: Displayed in four large exhibit halls (north, south, east, and west). About 15% of these are originally from the "1876" exhibition of the Philadelphia Centennial and are noted with a gold star. The Philadelphia Centennial was primarily a trade show and when shown there salespeople and promoters were on hand to talk to potential customers, therefore the exhibits for the most part carried no labels. The remaining 85% of the exhibits in the Arts and Industries Building follow that tradition and only carry a few labels for identification. The exhibits are meant to carry the visitor back to another age in an effort to recapture what was going on in this country then in manufacturing and commercial enterprises and to indicate the work going on in some government agencies. The exhibits also indicate the people's interest in ceramics, silver, clothing, musical instruments, photography, pharmaceuticals and in nature.

Tin Type Studio: Located in the Museum Shop, its photographers give customers a choice of "1876" costumes in which they may be photographed if they choose. There is a charge.

Museum Shop: At one time this shop in the Arts and Industries Building was the largest in the Smithsonian complex. It now takes second place in size to the one on the ground floor of the Museum of American History. It still offers a wide selection of items for sale from postcards to kites, books, slides, and many gift items. There is a 10% discount for card-carrying Smithsonian Associates.

Food: There is no food available in this building.

Metro Stations: Those closest to the Arts and Industry Building are: Smithsonian (use Smithsonian exit) and Federal Triangle.

Bus Transportation: Call the Metro Bus Co. to get the numbers of the buses which will bring a visitor closest to the Arts and Industries Building (state your location in Washington).

NATIONAL GALLERY OF ART - EAST & WEST BUILDINGS

Location: West Building—Constitution Ave. between 3rd and 7th Sts., N.W.
East Building—On National Gallery Plaza on 4th St., N.W.

Entrances: West Building—On the Mall; on Constitution Ave. at 6th St.; on 7th St.; and off 4th St.
East Building—On National Gallery Plaza at 4th St.
Underground—Covered connections between the East and West Buildings can be made on a moving walkway.

Ramps for the Handicapped: West Building—Constitution Ave. at 6th St.
East Building—4th St. off National Gallery Plaza

Telephone: 202-737-4215; Education Dept. 202-842-6246

Hours: Open everyday except Christmas and New Years:
April 1 - Labor Day 10 am-9 pm
 Sunday 12 noon to 9 pm
After Labor Day - May 30 10 am-5:30 pm
 Sunday as above

Current Information Information Desks; Bulletin Boards; National Gallery of Arts **Calendar of Events** (at Information Desk)

Floor Plans/ Brief Guides Available free at each building at all Information Desks.

Tours: Free tours are given in each building by art-trained specialists. Consult Information Desks or Bulletin Boards for the exact hours for the following tours: **Introductory Tours** of gallery highlights; **Tour of the Week** that usually will include Special Exhibitions; and **Artwork of the Week** that the visitor usually visits with the art specialist and discusses a selected painting or piece of sculpture.

Free tours in each building for groups of fifteen

or more people are offered by special arrangement. To make these call 202-842-6246 or write to the Education Dept. of the National Gallery at least two weeks in advance.

Taped tours in several languages of many galleries are available at a small rental charge. Inquire at Information Desks.

Illustrated Lectures: Given Sunday at 4 p.m. in the East Building Auditorium. Usually art specialists from this country or abroad, and occasionally staff members of the National Gallery deliver these free lectures.

Films: Free films on art subjects are shown; varied scheduling. Consult the Information Desks, Bulletin Boards, or the National Gallery's **Calendar of Events.**

Concerts: Beginning in October and going through May free concerts are given on Sunday evenings at 7 p.m. in the West Building's East Garden Court. The performers are skilled instrument or vocal artists or the National Gallery of Art Orchestra. Get there early for the limited seats are not reserved.

Special Exhibits: There are especially fine changing exhibits that remain for a limited time. These are free. More and more of these are now shown in the East Building although some are still arranged for the West Building. Consult Information Desks, Bulletin Boards, and the National Gallery's **Calendar of Events.**

Food: Food services available to visitors to the National Gallery of Art include the following:

on the Concourse Level beneath Fourth Street are a Cascade Cafe offering table service, a cafeteria, and a Cascade buffet, with all three having seating arrangements from which all patrons can enjoy a view of the large cascading waterfall in this area;

on the Upper Level of the East Building is a Terrace Cafe that has table service;

on the Ground Floor central lobby around a fountain in the West Building is a Garden Cafe that serves soups, sandwiches, and desserts.

Publication Shops: West Building—located on the Ground Floor near the Constitution Avenue entrance, this shop sells prints of works on exhibition, some of them framed, as well as slides, sculpture reproductions, jewelry, books, catalogues, postcards, and prints with text of the artwork of the week which is sold at a very low price.

East Building—has one shop located in the Concourse next to the Food area where books, prints, cards, and other items are sold; another sales desk is located on the Mezzanine Level.

Other Services: West Building—free checkrooms are available near the entrances. Elevators. The use of free wheelchairs while in the building, as well as strollers for youngsters.

East Building—has free checking service to the right of the entrance. It also has the same arrangement for wheelchairs and strollers. Elevators. Escalator.

Metro Stations: Federal Triangle; Smithsonian

Bus Transportation: Call the Metro Bus Co. to get the numbers of the buses which will bring a visitor closest to the National Gallery of Art (state your location in Washington, D.C.).

HIRSHHORN MUSEUM AND SCULPTURE GARDEN

Location: Independence Avenue at 8th Street, S.W.

Entrances: From Independence Avenue; from the Mall on Jefferson Drive

Telephone: 202-357-1300 (ask for the Hirshhorn Museum)

Hours: Summer Hours   10 am–7:30 pm daily
All other times   10 am–5:30 pm daily

Information Desk/ Bulletin Boards: Located on the first floor near the entrances and the escalator. These are the best sources for current information about special exhibitions, lectures, and other events.

Tours (Free):   Guided tours by docents (volunteer guides) of the permanent collection are given several times daily. (Check with the Information Desk for the exact times.)

Special tours for groups can be arranged about

two weeks in advance. Call or write the Hirshhorn.

Special tours for the handicapped can be arranged as above.

Lectures: Free lectures (illustrated) often accompany the opening of special exhibits. Example: "Early 20th-Century Russian Avant-Garde Art."

Other free lectures are given. Example: "A Medieval Muslim Center for Learning in India," by Anthony Welch, U. of Victoria.

A fee is charged for some lectures. Example: "20th Century Architecture: Diversity/Search for Order," by Tician Papachristou.

Symposiums: From time to time a symposium is held, which generally lasts all day. A fee is charged. Example: "The Eight," in which historians Bernard Perlman and Marc Pachter as well as Mrs. John Sloan participated.

Films (Free):   There are several categories of films shown:
Independent Film Series: Example: "An American Genius: D.W. Griffith," a film biography of this legendary director.
Artists Documentary Films: Example: "Picasso: A Painter's Diary" done by Perry Miller Adato.
Films for Young People: Example: "Journey to the Center of the Earth," an animated film.
Hirshhorn Lunchtime Films: Example: "In Open Air: A Portrait of American Impressionism, French Impressionism Transformed."
Hirshhorn Evening Films: Example: "The Howling," a special Halloween showing of a shocker.

Concerts: A charge is generally made for these. Example: "20th Century Consort Works by Bennett, Shulamit Ran, Adler, Bartok."

Museum Shop: Located on the ground floor the shop sells books, catalogs, prints, postcards, and other items related to the contemporary artworks exhibited in this building.

Checkroom/Lockers: Located on the ground floor. The checking is free. Ask the attendant for a free token for the locker.

Food:
An outdoor cafe on the Museum's Plaza is open throughout the summer. May be open longer, depending on weather.

Metro Stations:
Metro stops nearest the Hirshhorn are Smithsonian Station; and L'Enfant Plaza (on blue line)

Special Services:
Elevator, escalator. Wheelchairs can be borrowed (free) at the checkroom.

FREER GALLERY OF ART

Location:
Jefferson Drive and 12th Street, N.W.; on the south side of the Mall, west of the Castle.

Entrance:
Entrance on the Mall is made at the above location.

Handicapped visitors may enter through the Independence Avenue entrance, but prior arrangements must be made by calling the Freer.

Telephone:
202-357-1300 (ask for the Freer Gallery of Art)

Hours:
10 am to 5:30 pm every day. Closed Christmas.

Information Desk/ Bulletin Boards:
Current information about special exhibits, lectures, and special events can be obtained from these sources or by calling the Freer.

Tours (Free):
Docent led tours are given four times daily except Sunday when there are two given. Each takes about 45 minutes and covers about ten objects from all parts of the exhibits. Tours are generally given Monday through Saturday at 10:30, 11:45, 12:30, and 1:45. Because of changes that do occur, it is best to confirm these hours as well as those for Sunday tours.

Special Exhibits:
Excellent changing exhibits remain for a limited period of time. Examples of past exhibits: "Chinese Art of the Warring States Period: Changes and Continuity" (480-222 B.C.); "Chinese Flower Paintings. Hand and Wall Scrolls, Album Leaves—14th through 19th centuries;" "Japanese and Chinese Lacquer. Containers, Utensils, Furniture from China

and Japan. 10th through 19th centuries;" "Nastaliq Calligraphy," examples by the most celebrated artists of the Islamic world.

Lectures (Free): Lectures by authorities in their field are usually given six or seven times a year. Examples of lectures given: "Late 19th Century Multifaceted Support of Japan: Samuel Bing, Japonisme and Charles Lang Freer."

Museum Shop: Located in the lobby, it sells postcards, books, excellent prints and reproductions, photographs, objects in the round, slides, catalogs, etc.

Food: There are no food services in this building.

Checkroom/Lockers: Free lockers are available; ask the guard for a token. Hangers for coats are available in the locker room.

Library: A library on the ground floor may be visited, but books cannot be withdrawn.

Reserve Collections: Students and scholars with a need to examine material in the reserve collections must first obtain permission.

Authentication Service: Between September and May the Freer offers an authentication service for those who wish to submit objects for examination. Visitors are advised to write the Freer for an appointment.

Metro Stations: Station closest to the Freer is the Smithsonian (use the Mall exit).

Bus Transportation: Call the Metro Bus Co. to get the numbers of the buses which will bring a visitor closest to the Freer (state your location in Washington).

SACKLER GALLERY OF ART

Part of the quadrangle now under construction (1984) on Independence Avenue is the Sackler Gallery of African, Near Eastern and Asian Cultures, a museum and a center for research and study. It will be with the Freer, a center for Asian art. Its purpose is to present objects for examination from a variety of viewpoints: historical, anthropological, as well as art historical.

NATIONAL MUSEUM OF AMERICAN ART

Location: 8th and G Streets, N.W.

Entrances: On G Street between 7th and 8th Streets. From the National Portrait Gallery on the first floor, across the Courtyard; on the second floor from the National Portrait Gallery to the National Museum of American Art on the 7th Street side.

Telephone: 202-357-1300 (ask for the Museum of American Art)
202-357-3176 for information

Hours: 10 am to 5:30 pm daily

Information Desk/ Located near G Street entrance on the first
Bulletin Boards: floor. These are the best sources for <u>current</u> information about special exhibits and <u>special</u> events. A leaflet showing floor plans is available free at the Information Desk.

Tours (Free):   Trained volunteer docents (guides) give walk-in tours, without reservations, at 12:00 noon on weekdays and at 1:45 pm on Sundays.

Prearranged tours are available between 10 am and 2 pm.

Group tours (8-15) can be prearranged by making reservations (about two weeks in advance) by either writing the museum (address above) or calling 202-357-3095.

Films: Admission is free, but because of limited seating tickets (available at Information Desk) must be obtained in advance. Examples of some films shown here:
"Footlight Parade" with James Cagney and Ruby Keeler
"American Madness" with Walter Huston
"Modern Times" with Charlie Chaplin
"The Birth of a Nation" with Lillian Gish and Mae Marsh
"The Life of Emile Zola" with Paul Muni, Joseph Schildkraut
"The Magnificent Ambersons" with Agnes Moorehead, J. Cotten
"All Quiet on the Western Front"
"Sullivan's Travels" directed by Preston Sturges
    Classical musicals: "Maytime," "Top Hat,"

others
French films with English subtitles: "The Little
Match Girl," "Fall of the House of Usher"
"Our Daily Bread" directed by King Vidor
"The Plow That Broke the Plains" a documentary
by Pare Lorent
Avant-garde films in connection with special
exhibits:
"Joseph Cornell: An Explanation of Sources"
"Jose de Creeft;" "Isamu Noguchi;" "Class
Oldenburg: Ice Bag;" "Masters of Modern
Sculpture: The New World"

Storytelling (Free):   Mary Carter Smith, an African storyteller,
told stories in connection with the Christmas
season.

Concerts (Free):   Examples of some heard in the past:
"The Victorian Parlour Ensemble" presented
Victorian era Christmas songs from the
United States and Europe
"St. Columbia Handbell Ringers" presented
festive melodies of the Christmas season
In connection with the special exhibit "Egypt:
Day & Night" Nabila Erian, Egyptian soprano,
gave a concert of contemporary Egyptian
composers
Howard University's Gospel Choir: black sacred
music, early folk songs, spirituals, and gospel
music
John Jackson, blues guitarist, played traditional
country music from the Virginia mountain
region
"The Buck Hill Quartet" presented classic
bebop from the 1950s

Lectures (Free):   Examples of some heard in the past:
"What American Artists Heard" a discussion
with records played of 19th century folk
music of Brittany
In connection with special exhibitions:
"Elizabeth Nourse and Her Context: The
American View of Life in France"
"Mary Cassatt and American Art"
"The Bride of Jesus: The Art of Sister Gertrude
Morgan" in connection with exhibition of
"Black Folk Art in America"
Lectures given by pre and post doctoral
Smithsonian fellows: "The 1839 Washington
Allston Exhibition;" "Thomas Eakins' Gallery
of Eminent Philadelphians;" "The Last Eden:
Albert Bierstadt in California;" "American
Abstract Portraits: A New Face on an Old
Tradition"

QuickGuide

343

Symposiums: Most are free, but ticket required. Examples:
"Creative Women in Paris and New York in the 20s and 30s" in conjunction with Berenice Abbott exhibit. Free
"Looking at Women" images of women portrayed by European and American artists in the late 18th and 19th centuries. Free
"Wonderland: Joseph Cornell's Adventures in the Arts, Humanities, and Sciences"
"Germany in the 20th Century: Floroscence, Destruction, Revival" giving a picture of Germany as seen by Eisenstaedt with a distinguished panel of scholars and artists who assessed Germany's contribution to modern theater, music, film, and the visual arts.

Special Events: Poetry Readings that commemorated Black History Month.
"Children's Day: Faces and Places" an annual arts festival guided by art specialist with free material for the children's use in making their improvisations.

Courtyard Events:
In connection with special exhibition "Americans in Brittany and Normandy: 1860-1910," French music was performed, 19th Century marionettes, and "Le Circus" (included music, juggling, and acrobatics by Wonder Company with performers dressed as 18th and 19th Century French clowns).

Special Exhibits: Examples of some presented in the past:
"Jose De Creeft: Sculpture and Drawings"
"Charles Hawthorne: The Late Watercolors"
"Joseph Cornell: An Explanation of Sources"
"Elihu Vedder's Drawings for the **Rubaiyat of Omar Khayyam**"
"The Prints of Louis Lozowick"
"Familiar But Unique: The Monoprints of Joseph Goldyne"
"Cast and Recast: The Sculpture of Frederic Remington"
"The American Renaissance, 1876-1917"
Exhibit of annual awards in the Visual Arts Exhibition/AVA Competition

Calendar: To receive the free **Calendar of Events** for the month in which you expect to be in Washington, write to:
Calendar of Events
National Museum of American Art
8th and G Streets, N.W.
Washington, D.C. 20560

Be sure to include your name, address, city, state, and zip with your request on a stamped business-sized envelope.

Library: Shared by both the National Museum of American Arts and the National Portrait Gallery contains books, periodicals, audio-visual material and the Archive of American Art with its holdings of documentary material on American art and artists.

Museum Shop: Located on the first floor it sells books, prints, postcards, and other artifacts relating to the Museum of American Art.

Food: A small cafeteria called "Patent Pending" located on the first floor, 7th Street side between the Museum of American Art and the National Portrait Gallery. It is open daily. In fair weather visitors often take their trays out into the courtyard where tables are found.

Transportation: Metro subway exit is called Gallery.

For bus transportation call the Metro Bus. Co. for the numbers of buses to take from your area.

Checkroom/Lockers: Coats, hats, umbrellas and packages can be checked in lockers or hung in the cloakroom. Ask guard or person at Information Desk for a free token for the lockers.

Wheelchairs can be borrowed (free) for use in the building. Ask at Information Desk.

RENWICK GALLERY OF ART

Location: Pennsylvania Avenue at 17th Street, N.W.

Entrances: Front door at Pennsylvania at 17th St., N.W.

Handicapped visitors can use a special elevator at the 17th Street entrance. Call Renwick to arrange for its use and for a wheelchair.

Telephone: 202-357-1300 (ask for the Renwick Gallery)
202-357-2700 for information

Hours: 10 am to 5:30 pm daily

Information Desk: Located at Pennsylvania Avenue entrance.
This is the best place to receive <u>current</u>
information about special exhibits and special
events.

Tours: Prearranged tours are offered between 10
am and 2 pm.

Calendar: The **Calendar of Events** describes events at
the Renwick, Museum of American Art, and
Barney Studio House.

To receive the free **Calendar of Events** for
the month in which you expect to be in
Washington, write to:
Calendar of Events
National Museum of American Art
8th and G Streets, N.W.
Washington, D.C. 20560
Be sure to include your name, address, city,
state, and zip (with your request) on a stamped,
business-sized envelope.

Films (Free):   Many are coordinated with special exhibitions.
Examples:
Films shown in conjunction with "Celebration"
exhibit:
"Getting Married," a collage of events taking
place before, during and after civil and
religious weddings across the U.S.
"The Ainu Bear Festival," illustrated the daily
life of the Ainu in northern Japan
"For Out of Zion" documented the central
role of the Torah (the five books of Moses)
in Jewish life
"La Madonna del Pollino" showed the pilgramage
of Italian people on foot and on mules to
the 6000 foot peak of Monte Pollino
"The Crooked Beak of Heaven" documented
the wood sculptured totem poles and potlatch
ceremonies of Pacific N.W. Indian tribes
"Forms of Light" showed contemporary designs
that included chandeliers and art objects
created by Venini master glass blowers
"Contemporary Australian Ceramica" showed
pottery making by two of Australia's leading
potters

Special Exhibitions   Examples of some presented in the past:
(Free):   "Threads: Seven American Artists and Their
Miniature Textile Pictures" showed quilting,
weaving, knitting, applique, basketmaking,
techniques of knotting crocheting in works

where the principal element in each was
the thread.

"Russel Wright: American Designer"

"Elijah Pierce: Messages in Wood" with some
of his carved panels on religious themes.

"Good as Gold: Alternative Materials in
American Jewelry" showed creative
replacements for precious metals and stones:
wood, steel, bronze, brass, glass, plastic,
and others

"Scandinavian Modern: 1880-1980"

"Venini Glass" with examples of excellent
craftsmanship created by the Venetian firm
founded in 1921

"Celebration: A World of Art and Ritual"
focused in two parts on the universal
phenomenon of celebrations that are shared
among 62 cultural groups on six continents
and islands of the Pacific

Illustrated Lectures: Examples of some lectures presented free
in the past on Wednesday at noon included:

"Artistic Expressions in Glass" with Dan Dailey,
a glass designer for Steuben and Cristallerie
Daum, head of Glass Program at Mass. College
of Arts in Boston

Marc Goldring discussed leather work he has
done

"Danish Applied Art Since 1900" discussed
by Danish architect and designer John
Vedel-Rieper

John Glick discussed his pottery making
techniques

Enamelist-metalsmith Jamie Bennett discussed
his work including cloisonne enamel wall
plaques

Many lectures were often coordinated with
special exhibits:

Ludovico Diaz de Santillano, Director of Venini
International, discussed Venini glass

"Celebration: A World of Art and
Ritual—Rejoicing and Mourning—How People
Celebrate Themselves" was discussed by
Dr. Victor Turner

"Duties of Traditional Music in the Civic and
Religious Celebrations in the City of
Jaisalmar, Rajasthan, India" discussed by
Dr. Nizer Jairazbhoy, ethnomusicologist

Concerts (Free): Examples of some programs given on Sundays
at 3 pm:

"Wolf Trap Opera Company" presented excerpts
from operas

Flutist Michael Parloff played Bach, Donizetti, and others

Members of Folger Consort played music on the viola da gamba and harpsichord

Emerson Quartet in Residence played chamber music

Dancing (Free): Examples of some programs given in the past:

Some Eskimos of an island in the Bering Sea performed dances associated with traditional celebrations

North American Irish step dancing champions demonstrated jig, reel and horn pipe steps; and another group presented informal rural dances with visitors invited to participate

Demonstrations (Free): Some demonstrations held in the past were in connection with the special exhibition "Celebration: A World of Art and Ritual."

Many demonstrations showed ethnic foods:

"Vasilopita," a bread baked with a hidden coin (Greek)

The preparation of Polish Gabka, a yeast bread

The preparation of Tsourek, a Greek yeast bread

The preparation of vegetable dishes and sweets traditionally served each May to honor Buddha in India

Among other ethnic foods prepared were: German stollen, English plum pudding, French buche de Noel, Italian annoli, and Swedish glogg, all for the Christmas season.

Other demonstrations included:

Eskimo residents of island in the Bering Sea who demonstrated Eskimo games, ivory carving, the sewing of skins, and the making of dolls

Craft artists Pedro Linares and his son Daniel of Mexico City created papier-mache objects traditionally made for "El Dia de los Muertos" (the Day of the Dead Celebration)

Food: There is no food sold in this building.

Museum Shop: The shop on the first floor sells books on crafts, design, prints, postcards and items usually coordinated with special exhibitions in the gallery: quilts, jewelry, toys, pottery, those crafted by goldsmiths, baskets, macrame, cornhusk dolls, puzzles, copper plates, and other items.

Special Events: Tea ceremony by members of the Japanese Urasenke Society of Washington area followed by zither music.

Poetry: Ellen Carter and Russell Spicer, Connie Carter and Barbara Angell read some of their own poetry.

Transportation: Metro subway: Exit at Farragut West Station.

Bus transportation: Call Metro Bus Co. to learn the numbers of buses in your area which will bring you closest to the Renwick Gallery of Art.

BARNEY STUDIO HOUSE

Location: 2306 Massachusetts Avenue, N.W. on Sheridan Circle.

Entrance: At the above address.

Telephone: 202-357-3176 (ask for information about Barney Studio House); also 202-357-3111 for reservations.

Hours: Only open for free guided tours for those with reservations: 11 am each Wednesday and Thursday; 1:00 pm the second and fourth Sundays of the month.

Closed from middle of June through August.

Open for "Evenings at Barney Studio House" at 8 pm. Reservations required.

Tours: Free guided tours at hours described above.

Concerts (Charge):   These are part of the "Evenings at Barney Studio House." Reservations (at $10 per person) must be made. 8 pm. Only 50 reservations are accepted. Reception follows.

Those wishing to make reservations:
Make checks payable to Smithsonian Institution.
Enclose a stamped self-addressed envelope with your check.
Mail to:

"Barney Studio House Evenings"
Room 253
National Museum of American Arts
Smithsonian Institution
Washington, D.C. 20560

Examples of concerts presented in the past:
"American Musical Theater: A Retrospective."
Works performed illustrating history of
the American Musical Theater.
"A Varied View of Love: Romantic Songs for
All Occasions." Love songs sung from
operettas by Romberg, Herbert; operatic
arias and some medleys from Broadway
shows.
"Wonderous Machine: Music from the Early
Classical Period." Compositions of Bach,
Boccherini, and Haydn played by a well-known
chamber ensemble.
"Private and Public Patrons of the Arts in
Washington: Alice Pike Barney and Franklin
Delano Roosevelt." Concerts of American
chamber music from the late 19th century
through the 1930s commemorating what
both she and President Roosevelt did to
encourage and support young musicians.
"Cabaret Music by the Folk and Baroque
Players," who performed folk music from
Russia, Greece, Romania, Israel and Poland,
on mandolin, guitar, recorder, clarinet and
double bass. Soloist who sang Yugoslavian,
gypsy, Russian and Polish songs.
"Wing and Song: Music for St. Patrick's Day,"
with noted Irish-born harpist and singer
Barbara Murphy.
"French Cabaret Music," performed by Carmen
Vickers in a one-woman concert.

**Special Programs
(Charge)*:**

Examples of special programs presented in
the past:
"Explorations in American Art," a four part
monthly series of programs tracing America's
artistic and cultural heritage.
"A Cherry Blossom Potpourri," included music,
dance, and poetry of Japan.
Novelist, short story writer, teacher, editor,
and playwright Patricia Browning Griffith
read excerpts from some of her works and
discussed the styles of various forms of
writing.
A Spanish evening that included Renaissance
poetry, flutist and harpist music, and flamenco
dancing.

"Shadows and Sounds of China," in which the Yueh Lung Shadow Theatre of New York performed scenes from traditional Chinese shadow plays accompanied by musical selections on a bowed lute and a zither.

Annual Exhibition:

Alice Pike Barney

Beginning in December of 1982 an annual exhibition has been held of works that illustrate her influence on the cultural life of Washington in the early 1900s. Each focuses on her accomplishments in architecture, painting, dance, theater and her other artistic accomplishments.

*Visitors interested in learning of the offerings at Barney Studio House should consult the **Smithsonian Calendar** at Information Desks or the National Museum of American Art/Renwick **Calendar** in each museum at their Information Desks. Remember that reservations must be made at least two weeks in advance.

NATIONAL PORTRAIT GALLERY

Location:

F Street at 8th Street, N.W.

Entrances:

The main entrance is at the above location. The Museum can also be entered from a courtyard that connects the National Portrait Gallery and the National Museum of American Art.

Handicapped visitors may use the wheelchair entrance (through the garage) at 9th and G Streets, but prior arrangements must be made by calling the National Portrait Gallery.

Telephone:

202-357-1300 (ask for the National Portrait Gallery).

Hours:

Open daily (except Christmas) from 10 am to 5:30 pm.

Information Desk:

On the first floor.

Floor Plan:

A floor plan and brochure about the National Portrait Gallery is available free at the Information Desk.

Tours (Free):

Free guide service available daily from 10 a.m. to

3 pm; weekends and holidays from 12 noon to 3 pm.

Prearranged group tours (at least two weeks in advance) can be made by calling or writing the Portrait Gallery.

Documentary Material: From the Archives of American Art these are exhibited in a special gallery on the first floor, often subjects are tied to Special Exhibits in the gallery.

Films: Free films are presented from time to time usually prepared or presented by the Education Department. Examples of some shown were: John Muir, naturalist; James Weldon Johnson, educator and civil rights leader; Thomas A. Edison, inventor; Elisha Kent Kane, Arctic explorer, and others.

Lectures: Lunchtime lectures (free), examples:
"The Least Trodden Way: Naturalists from Charles Willson Peale to Rachel Carson"
"Remember the Ladies: The Struggles for Women's Suffrage"
"Americans Who Overcame Disabilities"
"Blessed Are the Peacemakers"

Illustrated lectures (charge), example:
"American Portraiture in the Grand Manner"

Readings/Talks: These readings or talks are about persons portrayed in this gallery and are free. Consult Information Desk. Reservations required.
Portraits in Motion, examples:
"'Till Ends My Rope: A Visit With Dorothy Parker," presented by Theresa O'Shea
"Eugene Rawls portrays writers Eudora Welty, Ellen Douglas, Lillian Smith"
"Walt Whitman: Liberal and Lusty As Nature," presented by Will Stutt
"Affectionately, Fanny Kemble," presented by Eugenia Rawls

Drama: Free. Consult Information Desk. Reservations required.
Portraits in Motion, examples:
"The Devil and Daniel Webster," presented by Catholic University Players
"The Legend of Sleepy Hollow"
"John Brown's Body," by University Players
"Clarence Darrow," presented by David Fendrick

Series. Consult Information Desk. Reservations required.

"The Children of Pride." Four plays by Robert Manson Myers drawn from letters of a Georgia family in antebellum Civil War and Reconstruction South. (Charge)

Concerts:

Presented in the Courtyard. There is a charge. Examples:

Courtyard Upbeat Hott Jazz Concert by The Tarnished Six

"Playing the Palace: Salute to American Music Halls"

Latin music performed by Los Hijos del Solo

Special Exhibits:

Changing exhibits that remain for a limited time. Free. Examples:

"Return to Albion: Americans in England, 1760–1940"

"Daniel Webster: The Godlike Black Dan"

"American Portraiture in the Grand Manner: 1720–1920"

"Work of Major Portrait Photographers Since Photography Was Introduced in 1839"

"Portraits of the Civil War"

Research Center:

A study collection for American biography and portraiture to which scholars and students of American history may have access. Permission must be arranged.

Library:

Contains, in addition to bound volumes, a large clipping and pamphlet file, a manuscript collection, and a lending collection of slides. Library shared with the American Museum of Art.

Food:

A small cafeteria called "Patent Pending" located between the National Portrait Gallery and the Museum of American Art. Open daily. Sells salad, soups, sandwiches, and some hot dishes. In fair weather visitors may eat at tables in the courtyard.

Museum Shop:

Sells catalogs, art books, postcards, prints, material related to exhibits.

Checkroom/Lockers:

Available free on the first floor. Ask the guard for a free token for the lockers.

Transportation:

Metro subway exits nearest the National Portrait Gallery are Gallery Place (9th and G Streets on the Red Line) and Metro Center (11th and

G on the Red, Blue, and Orange Line).

Bus transportation: Call the Metro Bus Co. to get the bus number which will bring one closest to the National Portrait Gallery.

MUSEUM OF AFRICAN ARTS

Location:
At present:
318 A Street, N.E.

New building under construction:
Quadrangle on Independence Avenue

Entrances:
Main entrance at 318 A Street, N.E.
Entrance for the handicapped through the courtyard in back.

Telephone:
202-357-1300 (ask for the Museum of African Arts)
202-287-3490

Hours:
Weekdays 10 am to 5 pm
Weekends 12 noon to 5 pm

Information Desk:
Located on the first floor near the entrance. This is the best source for current information about programs, performances, and special exhibits.

Floor Plan:
A brochure showing floor plans is available free at the Information Desk.

Tours (Free):
On Saturday at 3:00 pm an informal talk by a curator is given on an African art gallery tour.

Group tours for children or adults are offered seven days a week by special arrangement. Call 287-3490 or write the Museum of African Arts.

Films (Free):
Following film showings a free tour of the museum is offered. Films are usually shown on Saturdays at 2 pm or Sundays at 3 pm. Some shown in the past included: "Death;" "Dance Rites After the Death of a Nigerian Chief;" "A Great Tree Has Fallen;" "Funeral Ceremony;" "Mourning Dance of the Kenga;" "Women's Death Rites;" "The Baobab—Portrait of a Tree,"

that showed interdependence of animal life in and around this African tree; "No Room for Wilderness;" "Hausa Art in Northern Nigeria and Hausa Village;" "In the Name of Allah: The Pattern of Beauty," that showed basic precepts of Islam applied to daily and cultural life.

Concerts (Free):

Ephant Mujura, Shona musician from Zimbabwe played the mbira or thumb piano.

Illustrated Lectures (Free):

While most often these are given Saturdays or Sundays at 2 pm, some are given Tuesdays at 7 pm. Included in the past have been:
"Explanations of Life/Afterlife in African Oral Literature"
"For the Journey—African Grave Gifts"
"African Memorial Shrines"
"Dance, Music, Art, and Ritual in African Funerary"
"Tribute to Langston Hughes: Hughes Impact on the African Diaspora," music, poetry, readings, film clips, and tributes
"Images of the Stranger in Contemporary Literature"
"The Use of Animals in African Verbal Art"
"Animals in Benin Art"
"Songs in Praise of the Royal and Wealthy"
"Wealth, Status, and Royalty: The Case of the Akan of Ghana"
"The Drama of Color in Senufo Art"
"Art and Status of the Kuba Peoples of Zaire"
"The History of Islam in Africa"
"Bawdiness and Earaka: Oral Poetry of the Muslim Hausa"

Workshops (Free):

Most of these workshops are for children, but there is an occasional one given for adults. Advanced registration is required. Call 202-287-3490 or write.
"Kwanzaa Celebration Workshop," artist Winston Jomes led children 6-12 in making Kwanzaa banners
Family Event. Pre-Kwanzaa Workshop. Slide shows, demonstrations, and workshop
"African Masks for Kids," ages 6-12
"Islamic Art Children's Workshop: Color, Repetition and Design," simple forms and complex patterns in the African Islamic art style
"African Gourds Decorated with Traditional Designs of the African Islamic Peoples"
"Colorful Wall Murals." These were similar

QuickGuide   355

>to those done by the N'Debele people of
South Africa. They were painted on paper
with all materials provided. Children ages
6-12
"Coil, Pinch, and Pummel: African Geometric
Patterning," children ages 6-12

>Workshop for adults. "Islamic Geometric
Patterning," all materials provided.

Storytelling (Free): Some storytelling sessions are given by Nubian
League of Professional Storytellers, others
are given by museum docents. Time varies.
Check Information Desk.
"Afro-American Folktales Retold"
"Tales from Africa," these stories related
to the exhibit "African Emblems of Status"

Library: A special research library for teachers, students,
and scholars is open by appointment from
11 to 5 on Monday through Friday.

Archives: The Eliot Elisofon Archives, which contain
many slides, photographs, and films of African
peoples and their cultures, can be seen Monday
through Friday from 11 am to 5:00 pm only
by appointment.

Special Exhibitions: Some included in the past were:
"Thinking With Animals: Images and
Perceptions," reminders in African art of
man's dependence on the animal world for
physical and emotional well-being
"The Stranger Among Us," figures, masks,
textiles by traditional African artists attest
to strangers encountered by Africans since
the 15th century
"African Emblems of Status," clothing,
adornments, architectural forms, furniture,
sculpture from all levels of society
"From the Earth: African Ceramic Art,"
household and ritual artifacts; photographs
of earth shrines and altars
"African Islam," artifacts of the 19th through
20th centuries reflecting Islamic influence
on the arts of Saharan and sub-Saharan Africa
"African Art in Color," finished artifacts showing
use and symbolism of color

Museum Shop: Located on the first floor, it sells African
sculpture (some original, some copies), other
craft items, jewelry, costumes, musical
instruments, prints, and books.

NATIONAL ZOO

Location:

3001 Connecticut Avenue, N.W., Washington, D.C. 20008

Entrances:

Connecticut Avenue is the west one; Harvard Street at its intersection with Adams Mill Road is the east one; Beach Drive which goes through Rock Creek Park is still another.

Transportation:

Metro Line (ride the Red Line) to Woodley Park stop (three blocks south of the Zoo) or Cleveland Park stop (three blocks north of the Zoo).

Bus Lines use: L-2 and L-4 stop at Connecticut Avenue entrance or H-2 stops at Harvard Street entrance.

Parking:

For those driving cars there are several parking lots (charge). There is a total number of 1000 parking spaces. Vehicular entrances are from Connecticut Avenue, Harvard Street, or Beach Drive.

Telephone:

202-673-4800 Visitor Information
202-357-1300 for general information

Hours:

The Zoo is open seven days a week except for Christmas.
Summer hours: (through Labor Day)
  Zoo Buildings: 10 am to 6 pm
  Zoo Grounds: 8 am to 8 pm
After Labor Day:
  Zoo Buildings: 10 am to 4:30 pm
  Zoo Grounds: 8 am to 6 pm

Information Desks/ Bulletin Boards:

The Information Desk and Bulletin Boards in the Education/Administration Building (just a short walk beyond the Connecticut Avenue pedestrian entrance) can supply all current information about the Zoo's programs, performances, and special exhibits.

Map of the Zoo:

A leaflet showing a map of the Zoo and its six trails and other general information is available free at the Information Desk in the Education Building.

Tours:

Guided tours for organized groups are available. Arrangements should be made at least three weeks in advance by writing or phoning the zoo.

Food:

Open throughout the year is the Mane Restaurant across from the lion/tiger exhibit. Open only seasonally are: the Panda Cafe (on top of the Giant Panda House); the International Cafe (near the Bird House); and the Pop Stop (across from the Small Mammal House). There are kiosks located between the Reptile House and in the Monkey House; behind the Elephant House; and next to the Panda Gift Shop which sells ice cream, snacks, and beverages. Picnic tables are scattered in the park for those who prefer to bring their own food.

Feeding Times for Animals:

Visitors are invited to watch the Zoo's animals receive their daily rations. The schedule is subject to change, so those wishing to be present when the animals are fed should stop in at the Education and Information Building when they arrive and inquire about the feeding times.

Trails:

Six trails each begin and end at Olmsted Walk (with red stripe).

1. The green crane footprints of the Crowned Crane takes the visitor to the Great Flight Cage, the Bird House, and other bird exhibits; past some of the delicate hoofed mammals and to the Giant Panda House.

2. The black zebra footprints take the visitor around and past the hardy hoofed animals and some of the delicate hoofed animals.

3. The brown elephant footprints take the visitor to the elephant territory (and house) as well as to giraffe, rhino, and pygmy hippo areas.

4. The orange lion footprints take the visitor to the Mann Lion-Tiger exhibits (and house), the Monkey House and Monkey Island, Great Ape House, the Small Mammal House, and the Reptile and Amphibian House.

5. The blue polar bear footprints take the visitor to Beaver Valley, 1000 feet long ravine, where he will find aquatic animals (seals, otters, beavers, etc.) and crab-eating foxes, bush dogs, and timber wolves.

6. The yellow raccoon footprints take the visitor to areas exhibiting North American animals like prairie dogs, bears, raccoons, cougars, porcupines, and others.

Services/Programs: In the Education Building (consult Information Desks for time):

Zoo Family Events in the past these have included: Animal training at the Zoo with sea lion and elephant training sessions; psychologist gives tips to chase away fears of animals and insects; Zoo ornithologist teaches how and why birds sing; among others (all free).

Art in the Park (free): Local artists and Zoo staff assist in drawing the animals. Materials provided.

Zoo Summerfest: Demonstrations of animal training and introduction to animals and reptiles; wildlife movies; lectures; workshops; dancing; mime; and storytelling. Program lasts for about a week and varies from year to year.

Labs at the Zoo (Free): **ZooLab** in the Education Building where visitors can learn much general information about Zoo animals. **BirdLab** in the Bird House where visitors can learn much about birds. **HerpLab** in the Reptile and Amphibian House where broad concepts of biology are taught using reptiles and amphibians as subjects.

Shops: In the Education Building; the Mane Gift Shop near the Lion-Tiger exhibit; the Panda Gift Shop near the Giant Panda House; Seal Gift Shop near the seal pool. All sell gift items, books, films, artworks, and other items that are zoo oriented.

Other Services: Strollers can be rented for children and adults at the Lion-Tiger Station and the Panda Station.

All restrooms provide access by wheelchairs for the handicapped.

The Police Station is located near the Mane Restaurant where nearby First Aid is also available.

KENNEDY CENTER FOR THE PERFORMING ARTS

Location: 2700 F Street, N.W., Washington, D.C. 20566

Entrances: Main entrance is from the Plaza where there
                        is a city bus stop, and a taxi stand.

                        The Center also has a parking garage entrance.

                        The handicapped can enter from the main
                        entrance or from parking levels using the
                        elevators. Any needing wheelchairs can reserve
                        them one hour before the performance by
                        calling 202-254-3774.

Telephones: 202-254-3600 General Information
                        202-254-3670 Eisenhower Theater
                        202-254-3770 Opera House
                        202-254-3776 Concert Hall
                        202-254-9895 Terrace Theater
                        202-254-4390 Theater Lab
                        202-785-4600 AFI Theater
                        202-254-3774 Tours
                        800-424-8504 Instant Charge

Bulletins/Brochures: The Kennedy Center issues a bulletin, **Two
                        On The Aisle,** of scheduled monthly events
                        and ticket price information for all of its
                        theaters at the Center; available at Information
                        Desks. Those contemplating a trip to Washington
                        may send for a copy by writing to the Kennedy
                        Center at the address listed above.

                        A free brochure obtained at the Information
                        Desks in the lobby gives a map of the facilities
                        in the Center with a key to their locations.
                        On the back of it there is described a number
                        of valuable services available for visitors and
                        gifts foreign countries made to the Center.

                        A foreign language brochure is also available.

Ticket Information: For those already in the Washington area,
                        tickets can be purchased at the box offices
                        two weeks in advance. Box offices will validate
                        free thirty minute parking tickets for those
                        purchasing tickets for performances.

                        For individuals wishing to purchase tickets
                        using American Express, Visa, MasterCard,
                        Diner's Club, Carte Blanche, or Choice may
                        do so at the box offices or by calling
                        800-424-8504 with card in hand and also ready
                        to show when picking up tickets. The box offices
                        are open Monday through Saturday from 10
                        am to 9 pm and from 12 noon to 9 pm on Sundays
                        and holidays. Tickets for events in the Opera

House and Eisenhower Theater are sold at
the box office in the Hall of States; tickets
for events in the Concert Hall and the Terrace
Theater are sold in the box office in the Hall
of Nations.

Special half-price tickets are available to
most performances for senior citizens (65
or over), full-time students, the handicapped,
limited income people, and enlisted men and
women (E-1 through E-4). Inquire at Friends
of the Kennedy Center at their desk in the
lobby—daily 10 am to 9 pm, or write to them
at the above address, or phone 202-254-3774.

Tours:

The Friends of the Kennedy Center conduct
free, forty minute tours daily from 10 am
to 1 pm. The tours begin every fifteen minutes
at Parking Level A. If sufficient notice is
given by mail or phone, 202-254-3774, the
Friends of the Kennedy Center will arrange
private tours for groups of twenty-five or
more, or for foreign language tours.

Sign language tours for the entire building
are available upon request.

Weather and schedules permitting, the National
Park Service also conducts weekend rooftop
tours, pointing out local landmarks from the
fine vantage point of the Center's roof. Contact
the National Park Service in the lobby for
schedules.

Food:

All restaurants are on the Roof Terrace floor
except the Opera Tier Lounge which is located
between the first and second tier of the Opera
House.

Encore Cafeteria is open daily 11 am to 8
pm.

Curtain Call Cafe (table service) is open Tuesday
through Saturday 11:30 am to 8 pm.

Roof Terrace Restaurant. Reservations,
202-833-8870
    Luncheon Mon-Sat 11:30 am – 3 pm
    Dinner Tues-Sat 5:30 pm – 9:30 pm
    Supper Tues-Sat 9:30 to $\frac{1}{2}$ hour after last
      performance
    Sunday Brunch 11:30 am to 3 pm

Hors D'Oeuvres 5 pm until ½ hour after last
performance. Closed if there is no performance.
Opera Tier Lounge: Open 1 hour before
performance and until last intermission. Bar
and snacks.

Transportation: Get a copy of **Two On The Aisle** for
transportation information or call the Metro
Transportation Services for the route best
from your location in the area.

Index